terra australis 26

Terra Australis reports the results of archaeological and related research within the south and east of Asia, though mainly Australia, New Guinea and island Melanesia — lands that remained *terra australis incognita* to generations of prehistorians. Its subject is the settlement of the diverse environments in this isolated quarter of the globe by peoples who have maintained their discrete and traditional ways of life into the recent recorded or remembered past and at times into the observable present.

Since the beginning of the series, the basic colour on the spine and cover has distinguished the regional distribution of topics as follows: ochre for Australia, green for New Guinea, red for South-East Asia and blue for the Pacific Islands. From 2001, issues with a gold spine will include conference proceedings, edited papers and monographs which in topic or desired format do not fit easily within the original arrangements. All volumes are numbered within the same series.

List of volumes in *Terra Australis*

Volume 1: Burrill Lake and Currarong: Coastal Sites in Southern New South Wales. R.J. Lampert (1971)

Volume 2: Ol Tumbuna: Archaeological Excavations in the Eastern Central Highlands, Papua New Guinea. J.P. White (1972)

Volume 3: New Guinea Stone Age Trade: The Geography and Ecology of Traffic in the Interior. I. Hughes (1977)

Volume 4: Recent Prehistory in Southeast Papua. B. Egloff (1979)

Volume 5: The Great Kartan Mystery. R. Lampert (1981)

Volume 6: Early Man in North Queensland: Art and Archaeology in the Laura Area. A. Rosenfeld, D. Horton and J. Winter (1981)

Volume 7: The Alligator Rivers: Prehistory and Ecology in Western Arnhem Land. C. Schrire (1982)

Volume 8: Hunter Hill, Hunter Island: Archaeological Investigations of a Prehistoric Tasmanian Site. S. Bowdler (1984)

Volume 9: Coastal South-West Tasmania: The Prehistory of Louisa Bay and Maatsuyker Island. R. Vanderwal and D. Horton (1984)

Volume 10: The Emergence of Mailu. G. Irwin (1985)

Volume 11: Archaeology in Eastern Timor, 1966–67. I. Glover (1986)

Volume 12: Early Tongan Prehistory: The Lapita Period on Tongatapu and its Relationships. J. Poulsen (1987)

Volume 13: Coobool Creek. P. Brown (1989)

Volume 14: 30,000 Years of Aboriginal Occupation: Kimberley, North-West Australia. S. O'Connor (1999)

Volume 15: Lapita Interaction. G. Summerhayes (2000)

Volume 16: The Prehistory of Buka: A Stepping Stone Island in the Northern Solomons. S. Wickler (2001)

Volume 17: The Archaeology of Lapita Dispersal in Oceania. G.R. Clark, A.J. Anderson and T. Vunidilo (2001)

Volume 18: An Archaeology of West Polynesian Prehistory. A. Smith (2002)

Volume 19: Phytolith and Starch Research in the Australian-Pacific-Asian Regions: The State of the Art. D. Hart and L. Wallis (2003)

Volume 20: The Sea People: Late-Holocene Maritime Specialisation in the Whitsunday Islands, Central Queensland. B. Barker (2004)

Volume 21: What's Changing: Population Size or Land-Use Patterns? The Archaeology of Upper Mangrove Creek, Sydney Basin. V. Attenbrow (2004)

Volume 22: The Archaeology of the Aru Islands, Eastern Indonesia. S. O'Connor, M. Spriggs and P. Veth (2005)

Volume 23: Pieces of the Vanuatu Puzzle: Archaeology of the North, South and Centre. S. Bedford (2006)

Volume 24: Coastal Themes: An Archaeology of the Southern Curtis Coast, Quuensland. S. Ulm (2006)

Volume 25: Lithics in the Land of the Lightning Brothers: The Archaeology of Wardaman Country, Northern Territory. C. Clarkson (2007)

Volume 26: Oceanic Explorations: Lapita and Western Pacific Settlement. Stuart Bedford, Christophe Sand and Sean P. Connaughton (2007)

terra australis 26

Oceanic Explorations:

Lapita and Western Pacific Settlement

Edited by Stuart Bedford, Christophe Sand and Sean P. Connaughton

© 2007 ANU E Press

Published by ANU E Press
The Australian National University
Canberra ACT 0200 Australia
Email: anuepress@anu.edu.au
Web: http://epress.anu.edu.au

National Library of Australia Cataloguing-in-Publication entry

editors, Stuart Bedford ; Sean P. Connaughton ;
Christophe Sand.
Oceanic explorations [electronic resource] :
lapita and western pacific settlement

Bibliography/Index
ISBN 9781921313325 (pbk.)
ISBN 9781921313332 (web)

1. Lapita culture. 2 Anthropology—Melanesia.
3. Anthropology—Polynesia. 4, Melanesia—Antiquities.
5. Polynesia—Antiquities.

995

Copyright of the text remains with the contributors/authors, 2007. This book is copyright in all countries subscribing to the Berne convention. Apart from any fair dealing for the purpose of private study, research, criticism or review, as permitted under the *Copyright Act*, no part may be reproduced by any process without written permission. Inquiries should be made to the publisher.

Series Editor: Sue O'Connor

Typesetting and design: ANU E Press and Totem Infographie, Noumea

Cover: Vao Island, Malakula, Vanuatu (photo: S. Bedford).
Back cover map: *Hollandia Nova*. Thevenot 1663 by courtesy of the National Library of Australia.
Reprinted with permission of the National Library of Australia.

Terra Australis Editorial Board: Sue O'Connor, Jack Golson, Simon Haberle, Sally Brockwell, Geoff Clarke, Ben Marwick

To the memory of José Garanger (1926-2006)
and Richard Shutler Jr. (1922-2007),
Pacific Pioneers

Preface

This collection of papers evolved from the Oceanic Explorations Conference organised by the Tongan Traditions Committee and Professor David Burley of Simon Fraser University, Burnaby, Canada that was held at Nuku'alofa in the Kingdom of Tonga from August 1st – 7th 2005. A total of 62 papers were presented during the five days of sessions, along with six posters. At the end of the Conference, discussions were held regarding the potential publication of papers and while the all-inclusive nature of the Conference was one of its strong points, the wide range of topics, time periods, disciplines and regions did not easily lend itself to publication. Initially Bedford and David Burley corresponded over the potential of a Lapita focused volume, following in the fine tradition of Spriggs (1990), Galipaud (1992) and Clark *et al.* (2001). After some months of deliberation the form of the volume had been decided and commitments to its publication confirmed. Bedford was joined at that stage by Christophe Sand and Sean Connaughton as the editors. During this time several suitable papers presented in Tonga had been submitted for publication elsewhere (Allen 2006; Clark and Murray 2006; Sheppard and Walter 2006) so a number of those same authors were invited to submit other Lapita-related papers.

Three years can be a very long time in Lapita research and this was the time period between the Kone-Noumea 50th Anniversary Conference (2002) and the Oceanic Explorations Conference in Tonga. It is four years since the proceedings of the Kone-Nouméa Conference were published (Sand 2003) so although it has been a little slow coming this volume does bring together much of the most significant Lapita-related discoveries that have surfaced since 2002. New discoveries often lead to reassessments with new and modified theories. Such is the case in Lapita research as demonstrated by a number of papers included here. Following an introductory paper with an updated inventory of Lapita sites (Bedford and Sand), the 16 papers reflect on a broad range of interrelated themes including Lapita chronology (Burley, Connaughton, Felgate, Nunn, Specht,

Specht and Torrence), site location, geomorphology and settlement patterns (Burley, Connaughton, Dickinson, Felgate, Galipaud and Swete Kelly, Nunn, Specht, Specht and Torrence), migration, interaction and exchange (Galipaud and Swete Kelly, Pawley, Specht, Specht and Torrence, Summerhayes and Allen), sampling strategies (Burley, Sheppard and Green, Specht and Torrence) and ceramic analyses including decorative technique (Ambrose), profiling of specific Lapita regions and sites (Bedford *et al.*, Connaughton, Felgate, Nunn, Sand) and the social significance and meaning of the famously decorated pots (Ambrose, Bedford *et al.*, Chiu, Clark, Summerhayes and Allen).

We would like to thank the contributors who were it must be said widely varied in terms of meeting deadlines but who all eventually produced. A whole host of reviewers from many different countries also played their role in improving the quality of the papers. Particular thanks go to Sue O'Connor, the *Terra Australis* series editor, who welcomed the volume proposal during an uncertain period of infrastructural change in publishing conditions at the Australian National University. Formatting of the volume was undertaken by Aldo Ganter of Totem Infographie, Nouméa and Duncan Beard of ANU E Press designed the cover and has facilitated its final production. The costs for producing the volume came from the Department of Archaeology of New Caledonia and the Centre for Archaeological Research, The Australian National University, Canberra, Australia.

During the gestation of this book, the archaeological community learnt of the sad loss of two of the pioneers of Pacific Archaeology, Professors José Garanger and Richard Shutler Jr. As colleagues and as friends to a great number of the professionals working in the region, and also as mentors to younger generations, these gentlemen had during the last 50 years held a special position in our small community of prehistorians devoted to the past of the peoples of Oceania. They will be sadly missed and it seemed only appropriate to dedicate this volume to their memory. "Au revoir monsieur le professeur" and Richard the "warm-hearted".

The Editors

References

Allen, M.S. 2006. New Ideas about Late Holocene Climate Variability in the Central Pacific. *Current Anthropology* 47:521-536.

Clark, G., A. Anderson and T. Sorovi-Vunidilo (eds) 2001. *The Archaeology of Lapita Dispersal in Oceania*. Canberra: Centre for Archaeological Research and Department of Archaeology and Natural History, Australian National University. Terra Australis 17.

Clark, G. and T. Murray 2006. Decay characteristics of the eastern Lapita design system. *Archaeology in Oceania* 41:107-117.

Galipaud, J-C. (ed.) 1992. *Poterie Lapita et Peuplement*. Nouméa: ORSTOM.

Sand, C. (ed.) 2003. *Pacific Archaeology: assessments and prospects*. Nouméa: Service des Musées. Les Cahiers de l'Archéologie en Nouvelle-Calédonie 15.

Sheppard, P. and R. Walter 2006. A Revised Model of Solomon Islands Culture History. *Journal of the Polynesian Society* 115(1):47-76.

Spriggs, M. (ed.) 1990. *Lapita design, form and composition*. Canberra: Department of Prehistory, Australian National University. Occasional Papers in Prehistory 19.

Content

Introduction

1. Lapita and Western Pacific Settlement: Progress, prospects and persistent problems 1
   Stuart Bedford and Christophe Sand

Lapita Origins

2. The Origins of Early Lapita Culture: The testimony of historical linguistics 17
   Andrew Pawley

3. Small islands in the big picture: the formative period of Lapita in the Bismarck Archipelago 51
   Jim Specht

Lapita Dispersal and Archaeological Signatures

4. Lapita all over: Land-use on the Willaumez Peninsula, Papua New Guinea 71
   Jim Specht and Robin Torrence

5. Lapita Writ Small? Revisiting the Austronesian Colonisation of the Papuan South Coast 97
   Glenn Summerhayes and Jim Allen

6. Leap-frogging or Limping? Recent evidence from the Lapita Littoral Fringe, New Georgia, Solomon Islands 123
   Matthew Felgate

7. Sample Size and the Reef/Santa Cruz Lapita Sequence 141
   Peter Sheppard and Roger C. Green

8. Makué (Aore Island, Santo, Vanuatu): A new Lapita site in the ambit of New Britain obsidian distribution 151
   Jean-Christophe Galipaud and Mary Clare Swete Kelly

9. Echoes from a distance: Research into the Lapita occupation of the Rove Peninsula, Southwest Viti Levu, Fiji — 163
   Patrick Nunn

10. Paleoenvironment of Lapita sites on Fanga 'Uta Lagoon, Tongatapu, Kingdom of Tonga — 177
    William R. Dickinson

11. In Search of Lapita and Polynesian Plainware Settlements in Vava'u, Kingdom of Tonga — 187
    David V. Burley

12. Can We Dig It? Archaeology of Ancestral Polynesian Society in Tonga: A first look from Falevai — 199
    Sean P. Connaughton

Lapita Ceramics

13. The implements of Lapita ceramic stamped ornamentation — 213
    Wallace Ambrose

14. The excavation, conservation and reconstruction of Lapita burial pots from the Teouma site, Efate, Central Vanuatu — 223
    Stuart Bedford, Matthew Spriggs, Ralph Regenvanu, Colin Macgregor, Takaronga Kuautonga and Michael Sietz

15. Detailed analysis of Lapita Face Motifs: Case studies from the Reef/Santa Cruz sites and New Caledonia Lapita Site 13A — 241
    Scarlett Chiu

16. Looking at the big motifs: A typology of the central band decorations of the Lapita ceramic tradition of New Caledonia (Southern Melanesia) and preliminary regional comparisons — 265
    Christophe Sand

17. Specialisation, standardisation and Lapita ceramics — 289
    Geoffrey Clark

1

Lapita and Western Pacific Settlement: Progress, prospects and persistent problems

Stuart Bedford[1] and Christophe Sand[2]

[1] Department of Archaeology and Natural History
Research School of Pacific and Asian Studies
The Australian National University
Canberra, Australia
stuart.bedford@anu.edu.au

[2] Department of Archaeology of New Caledonia
Nouméa
New Caledonia
christophe.sand@gouv.nc

Introduction

Lapita pottery and its associated antiquity and significance first began to be revealed in stratigraphically controlled archaeological excavations some 55 years ago (Gifford and Shutler 1956). Since that time it has remained a central focus for Pacific archaeologists (Clark *et al*. 2001; Kirch 1997; Sand 2003; Spriggs 1990a) and has subsequently led to the definition of a cultural complex that is associated with an archaeological horizon that can be identified from Island New Guinea to Samoa (Golson 1971:75). Reading through earlier general summary articles (Golson 1971; Green 1979; Kirch 1988) one is struck by both the increased progress but also the continuing complications in the understanding of the Lapita phenomenon. The papers published in this volume reflect on a broad range of interrelated themes including Lapita origins, chronology, patterns of settlement, migration, interaction and exchange, sampling strategies and ceramic analyses; all of which relate to aspects highlighting both advances and impediments associated with Lapita research.

Lapita origins

The question of Lapita origins has been debated for decades (see Pawley this volume). As increasing archaeological research results began to emerge from both the Pacific and Island Southeast Asia in the 1970s it was argued that the presence of this intricately decorated ceramic tradition was related primarily to Neolithic Austronesian expansion into the region (Bellwood 1978; Shutler and Marck 1975; Shutler and Shutler 1975).

From the beginning of the 1980s a strongly *indigenist* counter scenario took shape, which advocated that Lapita was equally likely to have been an essentially localised development centred in the Bismarck region and was certainly much more complex than a simple migratory event from the West (Allen 1984; White and Allen 1980; White *et al.* 1988). The multi-institution *Lapita Homeland Project* was specifically designed to test the different hypotheses, but generally failed to achieve a consensus (Allen and Gosden 1991; Gosden *et al.* 1989). The debate on the origins of Lapita culminated or at least has largely remained at a standstill since Green's compromise Triple I model of *intrusion, innovation and integration* (Green 1991). In this short discussion we do not intend to examine in detail the arguments relating to indigenous verses migratory positions, rather we reflect on the nature of ceramic remains and how they might inform us in relation to the wider debate (see also Sand this volume).

Most current views in relation to Lapita tend to coalesce on the subject of the origins of the Lapita ceramic design system and certainly on the location of where that development occurred. The finely decorated Lapita ceramics are generally seen these days as something that developed mainly in the Bismarck Archipelago, following the introduction of the art of pottery making from Southeast Asia (Green 1985; Kirch 1997). Explanations for this, however, have largely been restricted to the idea that the dentate along with the design system may have been a medium used on other surfaces (like tattooing) and that in the Bismarcks it was simply transferred to the ceramics (Green 1985; Kirch 1997:142-143; Torrence and White 2001).

One of the major lines of evidence cited (albeit often with an associated caveat) as supporting its development in the Bismarcks is lack of any similar dentate-stamped ceramics having been identified further to the west. But how confident can we be that this is in fact the actual situation? Although a small number of specifically targeted projects searching for antecedent Lapita sites in the grand expanse of coastal and island West Papua and Southeast Asia have been undertaken (see Spriggs 2007 for the latest summary), the often very large islands of this vast region render the search for first ceramic settlement sites much more difficult than much of the Western Pacific. It must be also added that the majority of excavations that have been carried out in Island Southeast Asia to date have been undertaken in cave and rockshelter sites. If this same strategy had been the primary focus of excavations in the Pacific over the last 50 years of Lapita research, we would have little more than a handful of sherds and sites across the entire Lapita spectrum.

The only site found in the Western Pacific where there has been arguments relating to actual evidence for Lapita antecedents is Mussau. Kirch originally argued that the plainware of Area A at site ECA of Talepakemalai represented "later, 'simplified' Lapitoid ceramics in the first millennium B.C." (Kirch 1987: 172), before later asserting that the concentrations of plainware and decorated sherds found in different parts of the site represented different but contemporaneous activity areas (Kirch 1997:172). He has more recently argued that the plainware ceramics are earlier, have parallels with contemporary plainwares in Southeast Asia and that the dentate-stamping at the site developed later (Kirch 2001:205). While more details regarding the Mussau site assemblage are eagerly awaited, we argue that this scenario along with the idea of simple transference of a design system found on one medium to pottery seems unlikely. The very fact of the "full-blown" nature of the Far Western Lapita ceramics recovered from the earliest sites in the Bismarcks (which are relatively dispersed and chronologically indistinguishable) suggests otherwise to us. At these sites, the earliest thus far identified phase of Lapita ceramics, the pottery is at its most spectacular, with needlepoint dentate, a specific range of vessel forms and often very complex design motifs. There is no hint at any of these sites, or at least none that have been mentioned, that indicate an experimental or developmental phase in the earliest Lapita decoration. These earliest pots and their often elaborate and finely applied decoration required high levels of skill and therefore suggest some degree of familiarity at least with the techniques employed.

Pre-Lapita age dentate-stamped sherds have more recently been reported from northern Luzon (Tsang 2007), indicating the presence of this comb-tool type and its use in the decoration of ceramics prior to its appearance in the Bismarcks. At the same time, however, the tools used in northern Luzon sites appear thus far to have been only straight with no evidence for any use of curved dentate tools. When this decorative technique is employed in the Bismarcks we may possibly be witnessing some level of innovation both in tools and design, although this has yet to be determined. In-depth analysis of the actual combed tools used to make the dentate-stamped Lapita motifs suggests that they were probably made out of turtle scute (Ambrose 1999, and this volume) and for the first time the bent or curved form, which has been demonstrated as being integral in the production of the Lapita motifs, makes its appearance. These data we believe demonstrate that it was unlikely to have been a straight forward transfer of tattooing technique (Kirch 1997:142), but that rather a more complex process was involved (see Sand this volume). Certainly in relation to the emergence of Far Western Lapita, we do not currently have enough accumulated data to fully disentangle and determine the levels of influence that might be ascribed specifically to an intrusive and sudden migratory event or to local innovation.

Whatever the scenario relating to Southeast Asian influences, emerging data associated with pre-Lapita era populations of the Bismarcks are highlighting the essential need to integrate aspects such as the evidence for complex exchange networks and the production of specialized items associated with this period, into the wider debate (Torrence 2007). Other possible regional influences also need to be taken into account including natural events such as the massive W-K2 volcanic eruption in New Britain in reshaping social constrains around 3350 BP, just at the time of the first widespread appearance of Lapita (Specht 2007). A more inclusive debate is also likely to lead to a more balanced picture that avoids the spurious implications or interpretations of supposed greater or lesser levels of social evolution in a particular population, a concern long ago expressed by Golson (1977). The Lapita phenomenon was likely to have involved a myriad of complex contact and interaction situations over the centuries, with varying and changing outcomes depending on the place and the time period, as is the case with all migratory events that arrive on the shores of already occupied beaches.

Lapita boundaries

The number and temporal boundaries of Lapita sites have radically changed since being first tentatively advanced in the 1970s (Golson 1971). While the geographical boundaries or limits of where Lapita pottery has been discovered (Manus to New Caledonia to Samoa) remain fairly much the same (Anderson et al. 2001), the number of recorded Lapita sites has expanded at an exponential rate including in those archipelagos where Lapita was once seen as marginal or non-existent. In 1979 the tally was around 50 sites (Green 1979), up to 79 in 1988 (Kirch and Hunt 1988:9), 182 by the year 2000 (Anderson et al. 2001) and now in 2007 some 229 (see Table 1). They comprise a wide range of site types and activity areas (Burley, Specht, Specht and Torrence this volume) that span an accumulated overall period of around 7-800 years from Northwest to the East. While certainly many sites have only been sampled at the most basic level, the pattern now emerging does point to the widespread nature of the Lapita horizon. In archipelagos where the archaeology has been undertaken in collaboration with geomorphological research or assessment the Lapita "gaps" have either been infilled through the identification of early ceramic sites (e.g. Burley, Connaughton, Felgate this volume) or post-depositional processes have been identified which explain why Lapita sites might be extremely difficult to locate (Dickinson 2006; Felgate 2001; Green 2002a). The more recent discoveries in Fiji (Nunn this volume; Nunn et al. 2007) also highlight that even in regions where there has already been a number of archaeological research programs focusing on the Lapita period it is difficult to confidently state that there will be no further major sites found. The benefits and requirement of long-term research programs committed to specific regions are also being highlighted by the results gleaned over many decades from a number of archipelagos (New Britain [Specht and Torrence this volume; Summerhayes 2000], Solomon Islands [Felgate 2001; this volume], the Reef/Santa Cruz [Chiu this volume; Green 1976], Vanuatu [Bedford et al. this volume; Galipaud and Swete-Kelly this volume], New Caledonia [Sand 2000; this volume] and Tonga [Burley this volume; Burley *et al.* 2002]). We argue that the accumulating evidence is severely weakening arguments postulating "leap-frogging" (Felgate this volume) during initial expansion, a long speculated scenario for some regions of the Lapita distribution and again more recently argued for the central Solomons (Sheppard and Walter 2006). At the same time, our often simple, single directional arrow indicating Lapita expansion into Remote Oceania, being undertaken by one homogeneous cultural group during one narrow time-event, is most likely overshadowing multiple departures of diverse groups in various directions over a couple of centuries, who did not all stop in the same places along their journey (Sand 2007).

Sites like Bourewa (Nunn this volume) or the Teouma Lapita cemetery (Bedford *et al.* 2006), recently discovered on islands with some history of archaeological interest at least, are unlikely to be the last of such discoveries. In fact if current rates of Lapita site discovery in Fiji and Vanuatu continue, then we might expect to easily double the current numbers of sites in these archipelagos. Concomitantly, the previously proposed Lapita preference for small islands appears to be increasingly less supported at least for Remote Oceania, although questions of chronology remain to be integrated into the model. After the numerous examples from Mainland New Caledonia (Sand 2006), a new case in point is Vanuatu, where Lapita sites have now been found at Erueti and Teouma on Efate, the third largest island in the group (915km^2) and at Matantas, Big Bay, northern Santo, the largest island (3900km^2) (Bedford and Spriggs 2007). It may well have been a quite different scenario in Near Oceania where pre-Lapita populations had long been in residence. But the post-Lapita landscape transformations over the last millennia on mountainous islands that are sometimes tens of thousands of square kilometres in area, also renders the finding of the earliest ceramic settlement sites a major challenge (Specht and Torrence this volume). Certainly, particularly in volcanically active regions, surface surveys and excavations in caves and rockshelters alone are not enough to determine Lapita presence. Major post-depositional landscape change and island size are also still likely to be major influencing factors in the current known western boundaries of Lapita, almost certainly on mainland New Guinea but also further west (Kirch 1988:158; Spriggs 1984, 2007). Finally, while Lapita sites remain overwhelmingly coastal there are a growing number of sites that have now been identified some distance from the sea (Anderson *et al.* 2001; Specht and Torrence this volume).

Provinces and chronology

Through the pioneering stylistic analyses of Lapita ceramics along with a limited number of radiocarbon dates, researchers were able to establish that there was a broad clinal west-east pattern of Lapita settlement with accompanying "distance decay" in ceramic decoration. On evidence available in the mid 1970s, Western and Eastern Lapita styles were initially proposed (Green 1978, 1979) with a Far Western being added some years later (Anson 1983). Over time as more and more sites have been excavated across the Lapita spectrum a series of interlinked stylistic "Provinces" have been proposed, namely Far Western (Bismarck Archipelago [cf. Kirch 1997]), Central (Reef/Santa Cruz and north and central Vanuatu [Sand 2001]), Southern (southern Vanuatu and New Caledonia [Sand 2000]) and Eastern (Fiji, Tonga, Samoa [Burley *et al.* 1999; Kirch 1997]).

Summerhayes (2000, 2001) however, has argued that the primary factor in Lapita ceramic variation is chronological and suggested that more appropriate terms for the different phases of the changing Lapita design system should be Early, Middle and Late Lapita. He quite rightly pointed out that geographically-loaded terms such as Western and Eastern can be seen as misleading. He argued in fact, that the data available indicates there was no geographical divide and interaction was sustained, as evidenced for example in the similarities of the late Lapita ceramics from Tonga and the Bismarcks (Summerhayes 2000:235). Best (2002) has argued otherwise, suggesting that perceived similarities have more to do with the simplicity of widespread designs which are seen in the later part of the sequence rather than anything to do with levels of interaction. More recently the proposal of simple temporal divisions has been further questioned, following focused research in relation to gauging chronological variation in Lapita ceramics. Results show that vessel form, decorative finesse, and design structure and content are not always a definitive marker of chronological divergence or levels of interaction (Bedford *et al.* this volume; Clark and Murray 2006; Chiu 2005:27; Sand 2001:70; Sand *et al.* 1998:41).

Far Western or Early Lapita remains geographically restricted to the Bismarck Archipelago as identified some time ago (Anson 1983), with the possible exception of recent evidence from northern Vanuatu (Galipaud and Swete-Kelly this volume; Galipaud pers. comm. 2006). In this northern Melanesian region it has been argued that there was a Lapita "pause" before rapid expansion further east into Remote Oceania (Kirch 1997). This "pause" argument is of course linked to the idea that dentate-stamping was a development that occurred in the Bismarcks and so a time period of some kind is required for this to have happened. Specht (this volume) reviews the time period for this "pause" by reassessing radiocarbon dates for the earliest sites in Near and Remote Oceania and shortens previous estimates of the "pause" to 150-250 years. The emerging overall similarities found amongst the Lapita ceramics in the Reef/Santa Cruz, Vanuatu and New Caledonia as well as the earliest sites in Fiji (Nunn this volume; Nunn *et al.* 2004) and Tongatapu (Burley and Dickinson 2001; Burley pers. comm. 2007), appear to support a scenario of a shorter "pause" before a first phase of very rapid expansion out of Near Oceania. This same scenario is also supported by the linguistic evidence (Pawley this volume).

Whether the primary drivers of ceramic stylistic change across the Lapita spectrum are temporal, geographical, cultural (Best 2002; Clark and Murray 2006; Sand 2001; Summerhayes 2000) or as seems the most likely, a varying combination of all these factors (Green 2003; Sand 2007), it remains an unresolved and on-going debate in Lapita research and one which will remain so until regional Lapita ceramic sequences are further refined and published in detail. One of the few archipelagos which is beginning to produce a more detailed regional Lapita sequence is New Caledonia (Sand 2006). The sequence demonstrates the emergence of some distinctive vessel forms and motif combinations during the 250 years of the local chronology (Sand this volume).

Immediately post-dentate stamped ceramic sequences in different areas are also beginning to shed some light on the regional diversification debate. There is emerging evidence from some archipelagos in Remote Oceania of dentate-stamping dropping out by 2800 BP (e.g. central and southern Vanuatu and New Caledonia) and distinctive regionally diverse ceramic sequences developing (Bedford 2006a; Bedford and Clark 2001; Sand 1999). However, while this is happening dentate-stamping continues a little later in northern Vanuatu (Bedford 2003) and remains present in places like Tonga (Burley 1998) for another one to two centuries, indicating at the very least that there was substantial regional variation and suggesting that at least both geographical and temporal factors have influenced the Lapita design system (Green 2003). As with all things Lapita, we must be wary of assuming that data sets (which can be often outdated or incomplete) restricted to a particular region are representative of the entire Lapita Cultural Complex over space and time (Green and Kirch 1997). Aside from a few possible exceptions (Anson *et al.* 2005; Torrence and Stevenson 2000), we do, however, see it as very unlikely that Lapita dentate-stamping continues anywhere in the Western Pacific beyond c. 2500 BP.

Persistent problems

Lapita archaeology has generally, until relatively recently, been necessarily in a pioneering research mode, establishing boundaries and chronology, settlement patterns, basic artefactual sequences, and the profiling of Lapita ceramic decoration and form. Large-scale areal excavations that would make possible at least partial investigation of villages or even single house sites have been generally lacking and as a consequence there has been limited potential for modelling and discussion of Lapita social dynamics based on archaeological evidence (Green 2002b).

Another major factor that has impaired progress on these topics is the poor state of preservation of many of the Lapita sites excavated to date. As Green noted decades ago "the integrity of deposits in Lapita sites represents a major and continuing problem" (Green 1979:31). The vast majority of the more than 200 Lapita sites that have been recorded to date are generally poorly preserved, as the stratigraphy is often shallow and has been heavily mixed and saturated by tropical rainfall over millennia. Most Lapita sites have been identified through surface survey where collections of sherds and other remains are exposed on the ground surface, indicating post-depositional turbation. The only very recent identification of the potentially widespread nature of painted Lapita is a reflection of this situation (Bedford 2006b). We argue there needs to be a greater assessment of taphonomic process associated with Lapita sites. If patterns of settlement and subsistence are being summarised from the recovered remains they must be assessed against such variables as the site's state of preservation and the percentage of the site that has been sampled (see Sheppard and Green this volume). While an assessment of or comment on the levels of mixing or disturbance at a site is often made, this is rarely translated into the summary conclusions relating to a particular site and the supposed patterns identified from the record (see also Spriggs 1999:17-18).

Another major flaw in Lapita research is the lack of analysis and publication of the Lapita sites that have been excavated (noted amongst others by Clark and Murray 2006; Green 1979; Kirch 1988; Spriggs 1990b; Summerhayes 2001). Often when attempting such a basic exercise as comparing sherds from a number of sites one is forced to revisit the original excavated collections which are inevitably housed in many different institutions.

Chronology has long been a central research aspect in Lapita studies and the results have been used to model such aspects as Lapita migration and cultural and social changes over time. Radiocarbon dating and ceramic seriation have featured prominently although the former tends to hold a somewhat undeserving pre-eminence when conclusions regarding sites are presented. The attraction of "hard science" in the form of radiocarbon dating has long ensnared Pacific archaeologists' but the associated vagaries, of which we have become increasingly aware (see Kirch and Hunt 1988; Spriggs 1990b, 1996; Spriggs and Anderson 1993), have also provided much confusion and uncritical conclusions. There has in the past been a tendency for archaeologists interpretations to be overwhelmingly influenced by radiocarbon dates rather than assessing those dates in relation to the recovered archaeological data. Now long gone are the once widely accepted claims of Lapita appearing soon after 4000 BP, with a succeeding 1500 years or more of a dentate-stamping pottery tradition, to be replaced today by first appearance at around 3400-3300 BP and being present as a decorative technique for 500 to 600 years in Near Oceania and anywhere from 50 to over 400 years in Remote Oceania, depending on individual islands.

However, even though the problems with radiocarbon dating have now long been identified, if we undertake the exercise of compiling radiocarbon dates from a whole number of Lapita sites, especially in Remote Oceania, we repeatedly find that those chosen to date the earliest and latest phases of a Lapita occupation within and across archipelagos will overlap within two standard deviations because of the flatness of the calibration curve around 3000 BP (Anderson and Clark 1999; Pearson 1993: Fig 1b). The flat section of the calibration curve around 2500 BP is also a major obstacle in assessing ceramic change around this crucial period of transition from Lapita to later traditions. Sites that may appear from the archaeological remains to represent a short-lived occupation will return a two sigma date of 2700-2300 BP. Other dating variables which continue to confuse the picture are variability in Delta R values for marine shells of the region (Jones *et al.* 2007), as well as the potential problem of in-built age in unidentified charcoal samples (Kirch and Hunt 1988; Spriggs 1990b) and even in long-lived shell species (Fiona Petchey pers. comm. 2007).

Prospects

With the rapidly accumulating dataset associated with Lapita sites across the Western Pacific, we are beginning to fully realise the complex nature of Lapita and the major challenges in gleaning a deeper understanding from the archaeological record. Increasing awareness of this complexity alone is a major advance and has stimulated a series of critical reassessments (exemplified in a number of papers in this volume) of theories relating to Lapita that were developed decades ago on much sparser evidence than we have at hand today.

Future excavation and sampling strategies need to be modified. Although invariably easier said than done the employment of areal excavations at targeted sites must be a major priority. We might then move beyond collecting and sifting through small samples of very large midden areas and the thus far recorded two house sites for the entire Lapita region (Kirch 1997:171; Sheppard and Green 1991) and into greater intra-site detail which in turn may provide archaeological insights into Lapita social organisation.

As already mentioned the detailed analysis, illustration and publication of excavated sites is essential if we want to go beyond our present-day basic comparative studies. There are many excavated Lapita collections that have languished in boxes for decades or have only reached the preliminary publication stage. A first effort should be a digital record of these collections (which is some cases have deteriorated since excavation) that can ultimately be accessed on the web, as is already the case for part of the Reef/Santa Cruz data (http://magic.lbr.auckland.ac.nz/anthpd/content/archive/).

There needs to be much more fieldwork particularly in those regions which appear to currently represent Lapita gaps or boundaries (West Papua, Central Solomons, Vanua Levu). In particular, further intensive surveys and excavations need to target open coastal sites on a series of islands west of the Bismarcks, with programs taking into account tectonic variability and coastal progradation over the past 4000 years. This remains a major research priority and may provide us with a basic understanding of the cultural specificity of this region during the advent of Lapita (Sand, Liu and Chiu 2007). Recent publications associated with this very research objective show for example the existence of now securely dated pre-Lapita age dentate-stamped pottery in Luzon (see Tsang 2007), a result that has major implications for our discussions relating to the origins of the Lapita design system and the decoration technique in northern Island Melanesia. In parallel with efforts further west, the Bismarcks themselves still require major research input. Although the *Lapita Homeland Project* achieved a number of important results, it is still the case that the overall Lapita chronology of the Bismarcks remains unclear: when does Lapita first appear, is it already fully-blown or are we still missing an earlier step, what are the regional diversification processes like and when do the dentate-stamped decorations finally drop out etc? All these questions pertain directly to our understanding of the Lapita dynamics in the rest of the Western Pacific, which need to be reassessed in tandem with renewed investigations. Without clear answers from the Bismarcks as well as further West, no definitive reconstruction of the first settlement of Remote Oceania can be conclusively proposed.

Finally, it needs to be stressed that some programs should focus on a number of already excavated key Lapita sites which require re-investigation. These are sites which have attracted often heated academic debate over the years, although in some cases it has been an exercise in scrapping over scraps. This sort of initiative appears to be underway at Watom, the earliest Lapita site recorded almost 100 years ago, which has seen a number of contested interpretations. The most recent substantial publication has concluded that the most profitable area of the site in terms of preserved deposits has yet to be excavated (Anson *et al.* 2005) and which may inspire a further archaeological expedition to the site (Richard Walter pers. comm. 2007).

Updated inventory

As part of the overall preparation of this volume, we have compiled an inventory of sites where dentate-stamped pottery has been found since the comprehensive list of Anderson *et al.* (2001). We follow the historical pattern of such inventories (Clark *et al.* 2001; Green 1979; Kirch and Hunt 1988) in that we include sites where a dentate-stamped component of decoration is included in the ceramics recovered. This will no doubt attract the now familiar charge of being "dentate-centric" but dentate decoration is both a chronological and symbolically significant marker. We are well aware that the Lapita ceramic series includes decorative techniques such as appliqué, incision, excising and shell impressing along with an often substantial component of plain pots, but we concur with Summerhayes (2000), amongst many others (e.g., Kirch 1990:128), who notes that where the "fundamental nature of interaction does change is with the end of Lapita. This regionalisation is seen in part with the disappearance of dentate vessels. If dentate vessels were social markers, then their change over time and their disappearance reflects a greater social breakdown" (Summerhayes 2000:235). Dentate decorated vessels were an integral social and cultural component of the populations linked with one of the major Pacific migratory colonising events (Green 2003). Moreover, all non-dentate forms of decorative technique and the plainware vessels are also found after the dentate phase. Additionally, by focusing on the relatively short-lived dentate-stamped phase of Pacific prehistory we are concentrating on fundamental research issues and processes associated with prehistoric migration, interaction and colonisation which have both regional and global significance (Anderson *et al.* 2001:3).

Since the year 2000 there have been eight new sites found in Island New Guinea (six in New Britain; two in New Ireland); two in the Western Province of the Solomons; 14 in Vanuatu; three in New Caledonia; 13 in Fiji and five in Tonga. Jim Specht confirmed the number of newly identified sites from New Britain but also pointed out some modifications required of the 2001 inventory. Sites that were found prior to 2001 but not included in the inventory (Tuam Island, Aitape, Ali Island and Vunailiu, Watom) are included in Table 1 above. Three sites should also be removed (due to an absence of dentate-stamping) from the 2001 inventory, Talasea area FEB, Garua Island FRD, Kandrian area (Apugi Island). As in the case of previous tallies of Lapita sites, reporting of new sites from different archipelagos almost always relates to the levels of research being undertaken in a particular region. The Table follows the format of Anderson *et al.* (2001) and includes national site register codes if available, site name, a general description of locality, site extent, contents, the ceramic series in terms of the localised sequence, age in calendrical years BP (gleaned from relevant radiocarbon dates or design motifs) and key references. We expect that an inventory such as this is bound to include a small number of inaccuracies and we ask that our colleagues simply bear with us.

CODE	LOCATION/ NAME	LOCALITY TYPE	EXTENT (sqm)	CONTENTS	CERAMIC SERIES	AGE	REFERENCE
Mainland New Guinea							
Saudaun Province							
No code	Aitape	unknown	—	surface sherd	?Late	—	Swadling *et al.* 1988
No code	Tubungbale, Ali Island	coastal flat	—	surface sherd	?Late	—	Terrell and Welsch 1997
West New Britain							
Morobe Province							
KLK	Tuam Island, Siassi	coastal flat	2000	pottery	Middle to Late	3150-2750	Lilley 2002
Willaumez Peninsula isthmus							
FACU		hill on divide	—	surface pottery	—	—	Specht and Torrence this volume
FACZ	Mt Krummel	inland foothill	—	surface pottery	—	—	Specht and Torrence this volume
FACR	Whiteman Range	inland foothill	—	surface pottery	Late	2800	Specht and Torrence this volume

Talasea							
FCT	Lagenda Island	beach/intertidal	—	surface pottery	—	—	Specht and Torrence in press
Garua Island							
FYS		beach/intertidal	—	pottery	—	3350-3100	Specht and Torrence in press
FAAL		beach/intertidal	—	surface pottery	—	—	Specht and Torrence in press
East New Britain							
Watom							
SAU	Vunailau	coastal hill/cliff	—	surface pottery	—	—	Specht 1968
New Ireland							
Emira Island							
No code	Erarae	coastal flat	—	full range	Early	—	Summerhayes et al. 2007
Tanga Island							
ETM	Angkitkita	coastal flat	—	pottery and lithics	Late	2750	Garling 2003
Solomons							
New Georgia							
No code	Loloma	intertidal	17500	pottery and lithics	Late	—	Felgate this volume
Kolombangara							
No code	Poitete	intertidal	—	surface sherds	Late	—	Summerhayes and Scales 2005
New Caledonia							
West coast							
V8	Vavouto	coastal flat	10000	full range	Early to Late	2900-2750	Sand 2006
GD 2006-042	Gouaro	coastal flat	no estimate	pottery	?Late	—	Barp 2006
East coast							
No code	Kouaoua	coastal flat	no estimate	pottery	?Late	—	Sand 2006
Vanuatu							
Mota Lava, Banks Islands							
No code	Nerenugman	back beach	3000	full range	Middle to Late	—	Bedford and Spriggs pers. comm.
Santo							
No code	Big Bay/Matantas	back beach	3500	pottery and lithics	Late	2900-2800	Bedford and Spriggs 2007
Aore							
No code	Makué	back beach	—	full range	Early to Late	3150-2950	Galipaud and Swete-Kelly this volume
No code	west coast	back beach	—	surface pottery	—	—	Galipaud 2001
No code	SDA Mission	back beach	—	surface pottery	—	—	Galipaud 2001
Tutuba							
No code	east coast	back beach	—	surface pottery	—	—	Galipaud 2001
No code	southeast coast	back beach	—	surface pottery	—	—	Galipaud 2001
Mavea							
No code	northeast coast	coastal flat	—	pottery	—	—	Galipaud and Vienne 2005
No code	east coast	coastal flat	—	pottery	—	—	Galipaud and Vienne 2005
Malakula							
No code	Uripiv Island	back beach	2000	full range	Late	2800-2600	Bedford 2003; Horrocks and Bedford 2005
No code	Wala Island	back beach	1000	full range	Late	2800-2600	Bedford 2003
No code	Atchin Island	back beach	2000	full range	Late	2800-2600	Bedford 2003
No code	Vao Island	back beach	3000	full range	Early to Late	3000-2600	Bedford 2003, 2006b
Efate							
No code	Teouma	back beach/promontory	2000	full range	Early to Late	3100-2800	Bedford et al. 2004, 2006
Fiji Islands							
Viti Levu and environs							
No code	Bourewa	sandspit/beach	12500	full range	Early to Late	3000-2700	Nunn et al. 2004; Nunn this volume
No code	Rove Beach	coastal flat	—	pottery	Late	—	Kumar et al. 2004
No code	Waikereira Bay	coastal flat	—	surface sherds	Late	—	Nunn this volume
No code	Jugendars Farm Bay	coastal flat	—	surface sherds	Late	—	Nunn this volume

No code	Tomato Patch Bay	coastal flat	—	surface sherds	Late	—	Nunn this volume
No code	Qoqo Island	tombolo	5000	full range	Late	2850-2650	Nunn et al. 2006
No code	Naitabale, Moturiki Island	back beach	300	full range	Early to Late	3000-2700	Nunn et al. 2007
No code	Navutulevu	coastal flat	—	surface sherd	—	—	Kumar et al. 2004
No code	Taviya, Ovalau Island	coastal flat	—	surface sherd	—	—	Nunn et al. 2004
No code	Qaqaruku, NE Viti Levu	rockshelter	—	surface sherd	Late	—	Kumar 2002
Yadua							
No code	Vagariki	coastal flat	—	pottery	Late	2600	Nunn et al. 2005
Lau Group							
Nayau Island							
No code	Na Masimasi	coastal dune	—	full range	Late	—	O'Day et al. 2004
No code	Vulago	coastal dune	5000	full range	Late	—	O'Day et al. 2004
Tonga							
Vava'u							
No code	Vuna, Pangaimotu Island	coastal dune	1500	full range	Late	2850-2750	Burley this volume; Burley and Connaughton 2007
No code	Ofu Island	coastal dune	1500	full range	Late	2900-2750	Burley this volume; Burley and Connaughton 2007
No code	'Otea, Kapa Island	coastal dune	800	full range	Late	2850-2750	Burley this volume; Burley and Connaughton 2007
No code	Falevai, Kapa Island	coastal dune	600	full range	Late	2850-2750	Burley this volume; Burley and Connaughton 2007
No code	Mafana Island	coastal flat	400	pottery	Late	—	Burley this volume

Acknowledgements

Matthew Spriggs read an earlier draft of the paper and provided useful comment.

References

Allen, J. 1984. In search of the Lapita Homeland. *Journal of Pacific History* 19:186-201.

Allen, J and C. Gosden (eds.) 1991. *Report of the Lapita Homeland Project*. Occasional Papers in Prehistory 20. Canberra, Department of Prehistory, Research School of Pacific Studies, Australian National University.

Ambrose, W. 1999. Curves, tines, scutes and Lapita ware. In J-C Galipaud and I. Lilley (eds), *The Western Pacific 5000-2000 BP: Colonisations and transformations*, pp. 119-126. Paris: IRD Éditions.

Anderson, A., S. Bedford, G. Clark, I. Lilley, C. Sand, G. Summerhayes and R. Torrence. 2001. An Inventory of Lapita Sites containing dentate-stamped pottery. In G. Clark, A. Anderson and T. Sorovi-Vunidilo (eds), *The Archaeology of Lapita Dispersal in Oceania: Papers from the Fourth Lapita Conference, June 2000, Canberra, Australia*, pp. 1-14. Canberra: Centre for Archaeological Research and Department of Archaeology and Natural History, Australian National University. Terra Australis 17.

Anderson, A. and G. Clark 1999. The Age of Lapita Settlement in Fiji. *Archaeology in Oceania* 34:31-39.

Anson, D. 1983. Lapita Pottery of the Bismarck Archipelago and its Affinities. Unpublished PhD thesis. University of Sydney, Australia.

Anson, D., R. Walter and R.C. Green 2005. *A revised and redated event phase sequence for the Reber-Rakival Lapita site, Watom Island, East New Britain Province, Papua New Guinea*. Dunedin: University of Otago Studies in Prehistoric Anthropology 20.

Barp, F., D. Baret, S. Domergue and M-K. Haluathr 2006. *Projet Koniambo. Etude archéologique phase 3. Rapport Final d'Opération*. Nouméa : Rapport interne Falconbridge.

Bedford, S. 2003. The timing and nature of Lapita colonisation in Vanuatu: the haze begins to clear. In C. Sand (ed), *Pacific Archaeology: assessments and prospects*, pp. 147-158. Nouméa: Les Cahiers de l'archéologie en Nouvelle-Calédonie 15.

Bedford, S. 2006a. *Pieces of the Vanuatu Puzzle: Archaeology of the North, South and Centre*. Canberra: Pandanus Press, Australian National University. Terra Australis 23.

Bedford, S. 2006b. The Pacific's earliest painted pottery: an added layer of intrigue to the Lapita debate and beyond. *Antiquity* 80:544-557.

Bedford, S. and G. Clark 2001. The Rise and Rise of the Incised and Applied Relief Tradition: a review and reassessment. In G. Clark, A. Anderson and T. Sorovi-Vunidilo (eds), *The Archaeology of Lapita Dispersal in Oceania: Papers from the Fourth Lapita Conference, June 2000, Canberra, Australia*, pp. 61-74. Canberra: Centre for Archaeological Research and Department of Archaeology and Natural History, Australian National University. Terra Australis 17.

Bedford, S and M. Spriggs 2007. Northern Vanuatu as a Pacific Crossroads: the Archaeology of Discovery, Interaction and the Emergence of the 'Ethnographic present'. *Asian Perspectives*.

Bedford, S., A. Hoffman, M. Kaltal, R. Regenvanu and R. Shing. 2004. Dentate-stamped Lapita reappears on Efate, Central Vanuatu: A four decade long drought is broken. *Archaeology in New Zealand* 47:39-49.

Bedford, S., M. Spriggs and R. Regenvanu 2006. The Teouma Lapita site and the early human settlement of the Pacific Islands. *Antiquity* 80:812-828.

Bellwood, P. 1978. *Man's Conquest of the Pacific*. London: Collins.

Best, S. 2002. *Lapita: A View from the East*. Auckland: New Zealand Archaeological Association Monograph No. 24.

Burley, D., 1998. Tongan archaeology and the Tongan Past, 2850-150 BP. *Journal of World Prehistory* 12:337-392.

Burley, D. and S. Connaughton 2007. First Lapita settlement and its chronology in Vava'u, Kingdom of Tonga. *Radiocarbon* 49:131-137.

Burley, D. and W. Dickinson 2001. Origin and significance of a founding settlement in Polynesia. *Proceedings of the National Academy of Sciences* 98(20):11829-11831.

Burley, D., D. E. Nelson and R. Shutler Jr. 1999. A radiocarbon chronology for the Eastern Lapita frontier in Tonga. *Archaeology in Oceania* 34:59-70.

Burley, D., A. Storey and J. Witt 2002. On the Definition and Implications of Eastern Lapita Ceramics in Tonga. In S. Bedford, C. Sand and D. Burley (eds), *Fifty Years in the Field: Essays in Honour and celebration of the archaeological career of Richard Shutler Jr*, pp. 213-226. Auckland: New Zealand Archaeological Association Monograph No.25.

Chiu, S. 2005. Meanings of a Lapita Face: Materialized Social Memory in Ancient House Societies. *Taiwan Journal of Anthropology* 3:1-47.

Clark, G., A. Anderson and T. Sorovi-Vunidilo (eds) 2001. *The Archaeology of Lapita Dispersal in Oceania: Papers from the Fourth Lapita Conference, June 2000, Canberra, Australia*. Terra Australis 17. Canberra: Centre for Archaeological Research and Department of Archaeology and Natural History, Australian National University.

Clark, G. and T. Murray 2006. Decay characteristics of the eastern Lapita design system. *Archaeology in Oceania* 41:107-117.

Dickinson, W. 2006. *Temper Sands in Prehistoric Oceanian Pottery: Geotectonics, Sedimentology, Petrography, Provenance*. Colorado: The Geological Society of America. Special Paper 406.

Felgate, M. 2001. A Roviana ceramic sequence and the prehistory of Near Oceania. In Clark, G., A. Anderson and T. Sorovi-Vunidilo (eds), *The Archaeology of Lapita Dispersal in Oceania: Papers from the Fourth Lapita Conference, June 2000, Canberra, Australia*, pp. 39-60. Terra Australis 17. Canberra: Centre for Archaeological Research and Department of Archaeology and Natural History, Australian National University.

Galipaud, J-C. 2001. Survey of Prehistoric Sites in Aore. Preliminary assessment. Unpublished report to Vanuatu Cultural Centre.

Galipaud, J-C. and B. Vienne 2005. Chronologie du peuplement et réseaux d'échanges dans le nord du Vanuatu. Mission Santo 2005. Rapport préliminaire. Nouméa: IRD.

Garling, S. 2003. Tanga Takes to the Stage: Another model 'Transitional Site'? New Evidence and a contribution to the 'Incised and Applied Relief Tradition' in New Ireland. In C. Sand (ed.), *Pacific Archaeology: assessments and prospects*, pp. 213-233. Nouméa: Les Cahiers de l'archéologie en Nouvelle-Calédonie 15.

Gifford and R. J. Shutler Jr. 1956. *Archaeological Excavations in New Caledonia*. Anthropological Records 18 (1). Berkeley and Los Angeles; University of California Press.

Golson, J. 1971. Lapita ware and its transformations. In R. Green and M. Kelly (eds.) *Studies in Oceanic Culture History*, Vol. 2, pp.67-76. Pacific Anthropological Records No.12. Honolulu: Bishop Museum.

Golson, J. 1977. *The Ladder of Social Evolution: archaeology and the bottom rungs*. Sydney: Sydney University Press for the Academy of the Humanities.

Gosden, C., J. Allen, W. Ambrose, D. Anson, J. Golson, R. Green, P. Kirch, I. Lilley, J. Specht and M. Spriggs 1989. Lapita sites in the Bismarck Archipelago. *Antiquity* 63:561-86.

Green, R.C. 1976. Lapita Sites in the Santa Cruz Group. In Green, R.C. and M.M. Cresswell (eds), *Southeast Solomon Islands Cultural History. A Preliminary Survey*, pp. 245-265. Wellington: The Royal Society of New Zealand, Bulletin 11.

Green, R.C. 1978. New sites with Lapita pottery and their implications for an understanding of the settlement of the Western Pacific. *Working Papers in Anthropology, Archaeology and Maori Studies, No. 51*. Auckland: Department of Anthropology, University of Auckland.

Green, R.C. 1979. Lapita. In J.D. Jennings (ed.) *The Prehistory of Polynesia*, pp. 27-60. Cambridge, Mass.: Harvard University Press.

Green, R. C. 1985. Comment: Sprigg's 'The Lapita Cultural Complex'. *The Journal of Pacific History* 20:220-224.

Green, R.C. 1991. The Lapita Cultural Complex: Current Evidence and Proposed Models. *Bulletin of the Indo-Pacific Prehistory Association* 11(2):295-305.

Green, R.C. 2002a. A Retrospective View of Settlement Pattern Studies in Samoa. In T. Ladefoged and M. Graves (eds) *Pacific Landscapes Archaeological Approaches*, pp. 125-152. The Easter Island Foundation. California: Bearsville Press.

Green, R.C. 2002b. Rediscovering the Social Aspects of Ancestral Oceanic Societies through Archaeology, Linguistics, and Ethnology. In S. Bedford, C. Sand and D. Burley (eds), *Fifty Years in the Field. Essays in Honour and Celebration of Richard Shutler Jr's Archaeological Career*, pp. 21-36. Auckland: NZ Archaeological Association Monograph 25.

Green, R.C. 2003. The Lapita horizon and traditions – Signature for one set of oceanic migrations. In C. Sand (ed.), *Pacific Archaeology: assessments and prospects (Proceedings of the Conference for the 50th anniversary of the first Lapita excavation. Koné-Nouméa 2002)*, pp. 95-120. Nouméa: Les Cahiers de l'archéologie en Nouvelle-Calédonie 15.

Green, R. C. and P. V. Kirch 1997. Lapita exchange systems and their Polynesian transformations: seeking explanatory models. In M. Weisler (ed.), *Prehistoric long-distance interaction in Oceania: an interdisciplinary approach*, pp. 19-37. Auckland: New Zealand Archaeological Association Monograph 21.

Horrocks, M, and S. Bedford 2005. Microfossil analysis of Lapita deposits in Vanuatu reveals introduced Araceae (aroids). *Archaeology in Oceania* 39:67-74.

Jones, M., F. Petchey, R.C. Green, P. Sheppard and M. Phelan 2007. The Marine ΔR for Nenumbo (Solomon Islands): A case study in calculating reservoir offsets from paired sample data. *Radiocarbon* 49:95-102.

Kirch, P.V. 1987. Lapita and Oceanic cultural origins: Excavations in the Mussau Islands, Bismarck Archipelago, 1985. *Journal of Field Archaeology* 14:163-180.

Kirch, P.V. 1988. Problems and Issues in Lapita Archaeology. In P.V. Kirch and T. Hunt (eds), *Archaeology of the Lapita Cultural Complex: A Critical Review*, pp. 158-165. Seattle: Thomas Burke Memorial Washington State Museum Research Report No.5.

Kirch, P.V. 1990. Specialization and exchange in the Lapita complex of Oceania (1600-500 B.C.). *Asian Perspectives* 29:117-133.

Kirch, P.V. 1997. *The Lapita Peoples. Ancestors of the Oceanic World.* Oxford: Blackwell.

Kirch, P.V. (ed.) 2001. *Lapita and its Transformations in Near Oceania.* Contribution No. 59, Archaeological Research Facility. Berkeley: University of California.

Kirch, P.V. and T. Hunt 1988. The Spatial and Temporal Boundaries of Lapita. In P.V. Kirch and T. Hunt (eds), *Archaeology of the Lapita Cultural Complex: A Critical Review*, pp. 9-32. Thomas Burke Memorial Washington State Museum Research Report No.5. Seattle: The Burke Museum.

Kumar, R. 2002. Discovery of a Lapita sherd inland of the northeast coast of Viti Levu Island, Fiji: insights and implications. *The University of the South Pacific, Institute of Applied Sciences Technical Report 2002/6.*

Kumar, R., P.D. Nunn and W.R. Dickinson 2004. The emerging pattern of earliest human settlement in Fiji: four new Lapita sites on Viti Levu Island. *Archaeology in New Zealand* 47:108-117.

Lilley, I. 2002. Lapita and Type Y pottery in the KLK site, Siassi, Papua New Guinea. In S. Bedford, C. Sand and D. Burley (eds), *Fifty Years in the Field. Essays in Honour and Celebration of Richard Shutler Jr's Archaeological Career*, pp. 79-90. Auckland: New Zealand Archaeological Association Monograph 25.

Nunn, P.D., R. Kumar, S. Matararaba, T. Ishimura, J. Seeto, S. Rayawa, S. Kuruyawa, A. Nasila, B. Oloni, A. Rati Ram, P. Saunivalu, P. Singh and E. Tegu 2004. Early Lapita settlement site at Bourewa, southwest Viti Levu Island, Fiji. *Archaeology in Oceania* 39:139-143.

Nunn, P.D., T. Ishimura, W. Dickinson, K. Katayama, F. Thomas, R. Kumar, S. Matararaba, J. Davidson and T. Worthy 2007. The Lapita occupation of Naitabala, Moturiki Island, Central Fiji. *Asian Perspectives* 46:96-132.

Nunn, P.D., S. Matararaba, T. Ishimura, R. Kumar and E. Nakoro 2005. Reconstructing the Lapita-era geography of northern Fiji: a newly-discovered Lapita site on Yadua Island and its implications. *New Zealand Journal of Archaeology* 26 (2004):41-55.

Nunn, P.D., S. Matararaba, R. Kumar, C. Pene, L. Yuen and M.R. Pastorizo 2006. Lapita on an island in the mangroves? The earliest human occupation at Qoqo Island, southwest Viti Levu, Fiji. *Archaeology in New Zealand* 49:205-212.

O'Day, S.J., P. O'Day and D. Steadman 2004. Defining the Lau Context: Recent findings on Nayau, Lau Islands, Fiji. *New Zealand Journal of Archaeology* 25 (2003): 31-56.

Pearson, G.W. 1993. High Precision Bidecadal Calibration of the radiocarbon time scale 500-2500 BC. *Radiocarbon* 35:25-33.

Sand, C. 1999. Lapita and non-Lapita ware during New Caledonia's first millennium of Austronesian settlement. In J-C Galipaud and I. Lilley (eds), *The Western Pacific from 5000 to 2000 BP. Colonisation and transformations*, pp. 139-159. Paris: IRD Éditions.

Sand, C. 2000. The specificities of the 'Southern Lapita Province': the New Caledonian case. *Archaeology in Oceania* 35:20-33.

Sand, C. 2001. Evolutions in the Lapita Cultural Complex: a view from the Southern Lapita Province. *Archaeology in Oceania* 36:65-76.

Sand, C. (ed.) 2003. *Pacific Archaeology: assessments and prospects (Proceedings of the Conference for the 50th anniversary of the first Lapita excavation. Koné-Nouméa 2002).* Nouméa: Les Cahiers de l'archéologie en Nouvelle-Calédonie 15.

Sand, C. 2006. Le Lapita Calédonien. Archéologie d'un premier peuplement insulaire océanien. Unpublished "Habilitation à diriger les recherches", EHESS Paris.

Sand, C. 2007. "Strings of Pearls" and Provinces: modelling the divergent ceramic chronologies of the Western Pacific during the Lapita period. Presentation at the "Lapita antecedents and successors" Conference, Honiara, Solomon Islands, July 2007.

Sand, C., K. Coote, J. Bole and A. Ouetcho 1998. A pottery pit at locality WKO013A, Lapita (New Caledonia). *Archaeology in Oceania* 33:37-43.

Sand, C., Y-C. Liu and S. Chiu 2007. What next? Pressing archaeological questions in Austronesian studies in Island Southeast Asia. In S. Chiu and C. Sand (eds), *From Southeast Asia to the Pacific. Archaeological Perspectives on the Austronesian Expansion and the Lapita Cultural Complex*, pp. 269-291. Taipei: Center for Archaeological Studies. Research Center for Humanities and Social Sciences, Academia Sinica.

Sheppard, P. and R.C. Green 1991. Spatial analysis of the Nenumbo (SE-RF-2) Lapita site, Solomon Islands. *Archaeology in Oceania* 26:89-101.

Sheppard, P. and R. Walter 2006. A Revised Model of Solomon Islands Culture History. *Journal of the Polynesian Society* 115(1):47-76.

Shutler, R. Jr. and J. Marck 1975. On the dispersal of the Austronesian Horticulturalists. *Archaeology and Physical Anthropology in Oceania* 13 (2&3):215-28.

Shutler, R. Jr. and M.E. Shutler 1975. *Oceanic Prehistory*. California: Cummings Publishing.

Specht, J. 1968. Preliminary Report of Excavations on Watom Island. *Journal of the Polynesian Society* 77(2): 117-34.

Specht, J. 2007. Lapita antecedents: the Bismarck Archipelago as homeland or transit lounge? Presentation at the "Lapita antecedents and successors" Conference, Honiara, Solomon Islands, July 2007.

Specht, J. and R. Torrence in press. *Pottery of the Talasea area, West New Britain Province, Papua New Guinea*. Technical Reports of the Australian Museum.

Spriggs, M. 1984. The Lapita Cultural Complex: origins, distribution, contemporaries and successors. *Journal of Pacific History* 19 (4):202-23.

Spriggs, M. (ed.) 1990a. *Lapita design, form and composition: proceedings of the Lapita design workshop, Canberra, Australia, December 1988*. Occasional Papers in Prehistory 18. Canberra: Department of Prehistory, Australian National University.

Spriggs, M.J.T. 1990b. Dating Lapita: Another View. In M.J.T. Spriggs (ed.), *Lapita design, form and composition: proceedings of the Lapita design workshop, Canberra, Australia, December 1988*, pp.6-27. Occasional Papers in Prehistory 18. Canberra: Department of Prehistory, Research School of Pacific and Asian Studies, Australian National University.

Spriggs, M.J.T. 1996. Chronology and colonisation in Island Southeast Asia and the Pacific: New data and an evaluation. In J. Davidson, G. Irwin, F. Leach, A Pawley and D. Brown (eds.), *Oceanic Culture History. Essays in Honour of Roger Green*, pp. 33-50. New Zealand Journal of Archaeology Special Publication.

Spriggs, M. 1999. Archaeological dates and linguistic sub-groups in the settlement of the Island Southeast Asian-Pacific Region. In P. Bellwood, D. Bowdery, D. Bulbeck, M. Kiskesjo, R. Green, I. Lilley and B. Maloney (eds), *Indo-Pacific Prehistory: The Melaka Papers*, pp. 17-24. Bulletin of the Indo-Pacific Prehistory Association 18. Canberra: Australian National University.

Spriggs, M. 2007. The Neolithic and Austronesian expansion within Island Southeast Asia and into the Pacific. In S. Chiu and C. Sand (eds), *From Southeast Asia to the Pacific. Archaeological Perspectives on the Austronesian Expansion and the Lapita Cultural Complex*, pp. 104-140. Taipei: Center for Archaeological Studies. Research Center for Humanities and Social Sciences, Academia Sinica.

Spriggs, M. and A. Anderson 1993. Late Colonisation of East Polynesia. *Antiquity* 67: 200-17.

Summerhayes, G. 2000. *Lapita Interaction*. Terra Australis 15. Canberra: Department of Archaeology and Natural History and the Centre for Archaeological Research, Australian National University.

Summerhayes, G. 2001. Far Western, Western and Eastern Lapita: A re-evaluation. *Asian Perspectives* 39:109-138.

Summerhayes, G., L. Matisoo-Smith, J. Specht and H. Mandui 2007. Observations of a Lapita site on Emira. Presentation at the "Lapita antecedents and successors" Conference, Honiara, Solomon Islands, July 2007.

Summerhayes, G. and I. Scales 2005. New Lapita Pottery Finds from Kolombangara, Western Solomon Islands. *Archaeology in Oceania* 40:14-20.

Swadling, P., B. Hauser Schäublin, P. Gorecki and F. Tiesler 1988. *The Sepik-Ramu: an introduction.* Boroko: A PNG National Museum Publication.

Terrell, J. and R. Welsch 1997. Lapita and the temporal geography of prehistory. *Antiquity* 71:548-572.

Torrence, R. 2007. Holocene interaction spheres: implications of Melanesian antecedents to Lapita. Presentation at the "Lapita antecedents and successors" Conference, Honiara, Solomon Islands, July 2007.

Torrence, R. and C. Stevenson 2000. Beyond the beach: changing Lapita landscapes on Garua Island, Papua New Guinea. In A. Anderson and T. Murray (eds), *Australian Archaeologist. Collected Papers in honour of Jim Allen*, pp. 324-347. Centre for Archaeological Research and Department of Archaeology and Natural History. Canberra: Australian National University.

Torrence R. and J.P. White. 2001. Tattooed faces from Boduna Island, Papua New Guinea. In G.A. Clark, A. Anderson and T. Sorovi-Vunidilo (eds.) *The Archaeology of Lapita Dispersal in Oceania: Papers from the Fourth Lapita Conference, June 2000, Canberra, Australia*, pp. 135-140. Terra Australis 17. Canberra: Centre for Archaeological Research and Department of Archaeology and Natural History, Australian National University.

Tsang, C.H. 2007. Recent archaeological discoveries in Taiwan and Northern Luzon. Implications for Austronesian expansion. In S. Chiu and C. Sand (eds), *From Southeast Asia to the Pacific. Archaeological perspectives on the Austronesian Expansion and the Lapita Cultural Complex*, pp. 47-74. Taipei: Centre for Archaeological Studies.

White, J.P. and J. Allen 1980. Melanesian Prehistory: Some recent advances. *Science* 207:728-734.

White, J.P., J. Allen and J. Specht 1988. Peopling the Pacific: the Lapita Homeland Project. *Australian Natural History* 22:410-416.

2

The origins of Early Lapita culture: the testimony of historical linguistics

Andrew Pawley

Department of Linguistics
Research School of Pacific and Asian Studies
The Australian National University
Canberra, ACT, 0200, Australia
andrew.pawley@anu.edu.au

Introduction

Debate on the nature and origins of the culture known as Early (Western) Lapita has been clouded by the limited range of the available archaeological evidence defining this culture[1]. Although 50 years of archaeological research in the southwest Pacific have yielded more than 200 sites distributed from the Bismarck Archipelago to western Polynesia where Lapita pottery has been found (see Bedford and Sand this volume), and archaeologists have gained a detailed understanding of regional and temporal variations in decorative styles and vessel forms, sampling problems have prevented them from recovering anything like the full range of material culture associated with Lapita communities.

One kind of sampling problem has to do with the scale of excavations. Few Lapita habitation sites have been excavated on the large scale needed to recover a fully representative range of materials - artefacts, settlement patterns, faunal remains, etc. This sort of sampling deficiency is likely to be ameliorated by further research. But there is a second kind of shortfall that cannot be remedied because it is in the nature of archaeological assemblages. In Neolithic societies a very high proportion of artefacts are made of perishable materials. This means that even the most artefact-rich assemblages will contain only a small fraction of the total range of artefact types. Kirch and Green (2001:164ff) examined ethnographic records of artefacts for a sample of five traditional Polynesian material cultures and found that, on average, only around 18 percent of artefact types were durable (the range was 14-23 %). And when it comes to drawing inferences from non-material culture, archaeologists generally have even less material to work with. These sampling problems, of course, apply not only to Lapita sites but to the cultural traditions that preceded Lapita in the archaeological record for the Bismarck Archipelago and Island Southeast Asia.

This paper will focus on two questions:[2]

1. What can lexical evidence from historical linguistics add to the accounts of Early Lapita culture provided by archaeology?
2. What can lexical evidence tell us about the antecedents of Early Lapita culture in the Neolithic cultures of Island South Asia?

A third question will also be briefly addressed:

3. Can comparative linguistics tell us anything about the interaction between speakers of Austronesian and non-Austronesian languages in the Lapita period?

Historical linguistics can, under certain circumstances, provide evidence that supplements the archaeological record. The lexicon of a language (its store of words and fixed multiword expressions) is a body of intangible artefacts that tells much about the way of life of the speech community. By tracing the histories of words, but more especially tight-knit terminologies, sets of words representing particular semantic fields, we can learn a great deal about continuities and changes in the way of life of the people who used these words.

However, anyone seeking to marry a (reconstructed) linguistic prehistory with a (reconstructed) archaeological prehistory faces a number of methodological challenges. The most fundamental one is to match particular archaeological assemblages with particular languages. In many regions of the world, this sort of matching has proved impossible to achieve with any degree of confidence. It happens that in Pacific prehistory we have a rare piece of good fortune: there is a well-attested archaeological horizon, namely Lapita, that can be securely correlated with a well-established linguistic dispersal, namely, that of the Oceanic languages. In particular, the bearers of the Early Lapita culture who occupied parts of the Bismarck Archipelago around 3300 BP can be equated with the speech community that spoke Proto Oceanic, the Austronesian interstage that was the immediate ancestor of all the Oceanic languages.

The argument will be that if it can be shown that Proto Oceanic speakers retained a named concept from an earlier stage, Proto Malayo-Polynesian, generally regarded as having been spoken in the Philippines (see below), then (by definition) that concept was part of the cultural apparatus they brought with them into the Bismarcks. I will present evidence from terminologies belonging to 11 cultural domains, most of which concern material culture. The domains are 1. canoes and sailing, 2. houses and settlement patterns, 3. fishing methods and technology, 4. agriculture and arboriculture, 5. domestic animals, 6. pottery, 7. cooking, 8. cutting implements, 9. clothing, weaving, ornaments and decoration, 10. kinship, and 11. leadership and other social categories.

How Southeast Asian is Lapita? The debate about Lapita origins

In the 1970s a case was built up that Lapita pottery forms were simply the most visible part of a culture complex whose distinctive elements were fairly homogeneous throughout the geographic range of Lapita habitation sites (Bellwood 1978; Golson 1971; Green 1979). A number of scholars argued that the spread of the Oceanic branch of Austronesian languages across the southwest Pacific was associated with Lapita and with other Neolithic cultures of Island Melanesia which were roughly contemporaneous with, or in some cases, possibly even earlier than Lapita, and that all were ultimately derived from Island Southeast Asia (Bellwood 1978; Pawley and Green 1973; Shutler and Marck 1975).

Lapita was seen as being a culture quite different from any which preceded it in the record for Melanesia. Its most prominent markers are earthenware vessels with red-slipped surfaces, made in a characteristic variety of shapes, including large carinated jars and bowls, globular and spherical pots, flat-bottomed dishes and pedestal stands. A minority of vessels were decorated with precise and elaborate geometric motifs, done by dentate stamping, i.e. with repeated applications of a set of toothed implements.

In Lapita sites representing permanent settlements the pottery is part of a cluster of elements - artefact types, architecture, settlement patterns and items representing long distance trade. Settlements are in the hamlet to village range and are nearly always situated on small islands or on the coast of large islands and close to beaches that would provide good launching sites and reef passage for canoes. Lapita assemblages contain ground and polished stone and shell adzes; obsidian and chert flake tools, often imported from remote sources; one-piece shell fishhooks; pearlshell knives and scrapers; various kinds of conus shell disks and pendants. Houses were typically rectangular. In some settlements houses were built on stilts over the reef flat. Middens are typically full of lagoon fish and turtle bones, attesting to the importance of fishing and to a variety of fishing techniques. The bones of chicken and pig are sometimes present, indicating that these animals (neither of which was native to Near Oceania) were kept as domesticates.

By 3300-3200 BP Early Lapita communities were established over a wide area of the Bismarcks, including north New Britain, south New Britain, Mussau in the St Matthias group, the Anir group off the southeast coast of New Ireland and (though less well attested in the archaeological record) almost certainly also in the Admiralty Islands. There are several signs that the dispersed communities formed a network of societies, probably related by kinship and marriage, that kept in regular contact at least for two or three centuries. The clearest indicator is the long distance movement between these communities of obsidian from one or both of the only two sources in the region (the Talasea region, on New Britain's Willaumez Peninsula and the Manus group), and also the movement of chert, oven stones and adzes. Another indicator is the parallel changes in pottery styles over the New Britain-Mussau-Anir region over the period 3300-3000 BP (Summerhayes 2000a,b, 2001). By around 3000 BP the intensity of contacts had diminished markedly. In the meantime, by 3200-3100 BP, people carrying Early Lapita had moved beyond the Bismarcks and settled parts of Remote Oceania.

During the 1980s and 1990s, as the archaeological record improved and the history of regional archaeological sequences was clarified, it became evident that the carriers of Lapita were, in fact, the foundation settlers of all those parts of Melanesia that lie in Remote Oceania, as well as of western Polynesia, and that the Lapita dispersal took no more than three or four centuries to reach the Tonga-Samoa area (Burley and Connaughton 2007; Burley *et al.* 2001; Irwin 1981, 1992; Green 1991a, 1999, 2003; Kirch 1997; Spriggs 1997).

A contrary case for Lapita origins was developed in the latter half of the 1980s and 1990s by a number of scholars associated with the Lapita Homeland Project (Allen and Gosden 1991). This project, beginning in 1985, added greatly to knowledge of the Upper Pleistocene and Early and Mid Holocene archaeological record for the Bismarck Archipelago. Having demonstrated that the Bismarck archipelago has a continuous history of human occupation going back some 30-40,000 years these scholars proposed a predominantly local origin of the Lapita cultures of the Bismarck archipelago (Allen and Gosden 1996; Allen and White 1989; White *et al.* 1988). They pointed out that the pre-Lapita materials contain precedents for up to 10 elements of Lapita technology and trade patterns, including lagoon fishing, trochus shell armrings, one piece shell fishhooks, earth ovens, and trade in obsidian.

Green (1991a, 1997, 2003) argued against a single source for Lapita. He proposed a "Triple I model", in which some elements of Early Lapita were *intrusive*, i.e. brought from South East Asia into northwest Melanesia, some were local *innovations*, developed by Lapita people in Melanesia, and some were of local (Melanesian, presumably non-AN speaking peoples of Melanesia) origin that were *integrated* into (adopted by) Early Lapita communities.

In broad terms, the Triple I model seems now to be accepted by most specialists. However, "broad" is the operative term. The debate continues over which Early Lapita cultural elements are intrusions, innovations, or borrowings, in the above senses. Kirch (1995, 1997, 2000) emphasises continuity, observing that "the early

Lapita assemblages ... fit comfortably within the range of varieties ... for cultural complexes dating to the second and third millennia B.C. in island southeast Asia (1995:2832). Having asked 'How South-East Asian is Lapita?', Spriggs concludes (with Green) that it "is basically of South-East Asian Austronesian origin, with added elements innovated in the Bismarcks, and some integration of pre-Lapita Melanesian elements" (Spriggs 1997:102). As to the balance between these three components, he comments as follows:

> Lapita elements of South-East Asian origin would appear to be pottery (or at least particular kinds of pottery), domestic animals, quadrangular adzes, polished stone chisels, various shell ornament types, rectangular houses (some on stilts), large villages, language, and probably aspects of boat technology, tattoo chisels, pearlshell knives, trolling hooks and various stone-artefact classes (Spriggs 1997:101-102). Unique to Melanesia on current evidence were very few elements: some crops, obsidian-stemmed tools and possibly, dorsal-region Tridacna adzes (Spriggs 1997:102).

Spriggs points to a third class of artefacts that are indeterminate between intrusion and integration: items that were present in Melanesia in pre-Lapita times but were also present in early Neolithic assemblages in Island South East Asia. These include "grindstones, hinge-region *Tridacna* adzes, pierced shell pendants, shell beads, *Trochus* armbands, one-piece fishhooks, bone points or awls, vegetation clearance by fire, most of the Oceanic domesticated crop complex, shellfishing and reef fishing, earth ovens (at least in Maluku), and some level of long-distance exchange" (Spriggs 1997:102). (He also includes oval/lenticular polished adzes, but there are no pre-Lapita polished stone adzes in Island Melanesia and oval as well as quadrangular adzes are known from Island Southeast Asia (R. Green pers.comm.)).

I turn now to the linguistic evidence bearing on these issues.

The subgrouping and dispersal of Austronesian languages

Although the outlines of the Austronesian family were discovered in the eighteenth century, it was only in the 1930s that Otto Dempwolff established conclusively that most of the Austronesian languages of the Pacific Islands belong to a single branch of the family. Building on a series of papers he wrote in the 1920s, and on the work of earlier scholars, Dempwolff published a three volume work which provided by far the most systematic reconstruction of the Proto-Austronesian (PAn) sound system (phonology) to date along with more than 2000 reconstructed roots (Dempwolff 1934-38). (Because his sample, crucially, did not include the then little-known Formosan languages Dempwolff's "Proto Austronesian" reconstructions are nowadays equated with "Proto Malayo-Polynesian" (PMP), the largest first-order branch of Austronesian, to be discussed below.)

Dempwolff's sample of some 30 languages from Melanesia showed largely regular correspondences with PMP consonants and vowels. They also showed something even more striking. In vocabulary inherited from PMP, the Austronesian languages of Melanesia shared a sizeable set of common changes to the PMP sound system, changes not present in Austronesian languages west of New Guinea. Furthermore, he observed that the Polynesian languages have undergone the same innovations. This body of shared innovations thus defines a subgroup, nowadays called "Oceanic". Subsequent work has confirmed and extended Dempwolff's main findings in this respect. The innovations of the Oceanic group are shared by all the Austronesian languages of Melanesia east of 138 degrees (from the Sarmi coast of Irian Jaya) but excluding those of Cenderawasih Bay and the Bird's Head of New Guinea, and they are also shared by all the languages of Micronesian except Chamorro and Palauan.

The main phonological innovations attributable to Proto Oceanic (POc) are as follows. (For convenience I refer here to contemporary reconstructions, which make various modifications to Dempwolff's reconstructed sound system and orthography.) In the consonants, there were several mergers (where contrasts between certain pairs of PMP consonants were lost) in POc. PMP *p and *b merged, as did *k and *g, *d and *r, and *s and *Z.

PMP *h was lost. Several new consonants were added: the labiovelars *bw, *pw, and *mw. In the vowels, PMP *e and *aw merged as *o and *i and *uy merged as *i. The sequence *-ay, which occurred only word-finally, simplified to *-e. There were some other rather complicated developments in the sound system that need not detain us here (for a fuller account see Lynch et al. 2002:63-67). There are also a number of morphological and lexical innovations defining Oceanic.

The proofs of an Oceanic group, now known to contain some 450-500 of the 1000-1200 languages in the Austronesian family, was the first important breakthrough in the high-order subgrouping of Austronesian languages. Subsequent work has shown that Oceanic is no higher than a fourth-order division of Austronesian. The sequence of branchings in the topmost parts of the Austronesian family tree have only become reasonably clear over the past 30 years, mainly due to the work of Robert Blust. Blust has pointed to evidence that supports an initial division of Austronesian into a number of branches represented only in Taiwan and a branch that contains all members of the family spoken outside of Taiwan. This large branch, labelled Malayo-Polynesian (MP), is defined by a number of phonological and morphological innovations (Blust 1977, 1982, 1995b, 1999; Ross 1992, 2005). Blust (1999) now thinks that the Taiwan languages fall into as many as nine different primary subgroups, reinforcing an already strong argument that Taiwan was the Austronesian homeland.

Malayo-Polynesian is in turn classified into (a) a Greater Philippines group (Blust 1991) and an indeterminate number of groups represented in Sulawesi and the Austronesian-speaking areas west of Sulawesi, including Madagascar (Blust and others tend to refer to these groups plus Greater Philippines, collectively, as "Western Malayo-Polynesian"), and (b) a Central-Eastern Malayo-Polynesian (CEMP) branch that contains some 650 languages (Blust 1983-84a, 1993). The dispersal centre of Proto MP was almost certainly the northern Philippines - the Batanes Islands and Luzon - an area settled at around 4000 BP by bearers of a Neolithic culture with close affinities to cultures of south and eastern Taiwan (Bellwood and Dizon 2005).

Proto CEMP was evidently a dialect complex, centred in the Moluccas, that soon broke up into a Central Malayo-Polynesian (CMP) dialect complex and an Eastern Malayo-Polynesian (EMP) branch. CMP comprises chiefly the languages of the Moluccas, the Lesser Sundas east of Sumbawa, and the Austronesian languages of the south side of the Birds Head of New Guinea. EMP divides into the large Oceanic group and a smaller South Halmahera-West New Guinea (SHWNG) group (Blust 1978a). Proto EMP was probably spoken around Cenderawasih Bay, at the neck of the Bird's Head, where the greatest diversity of daughter languages is found.

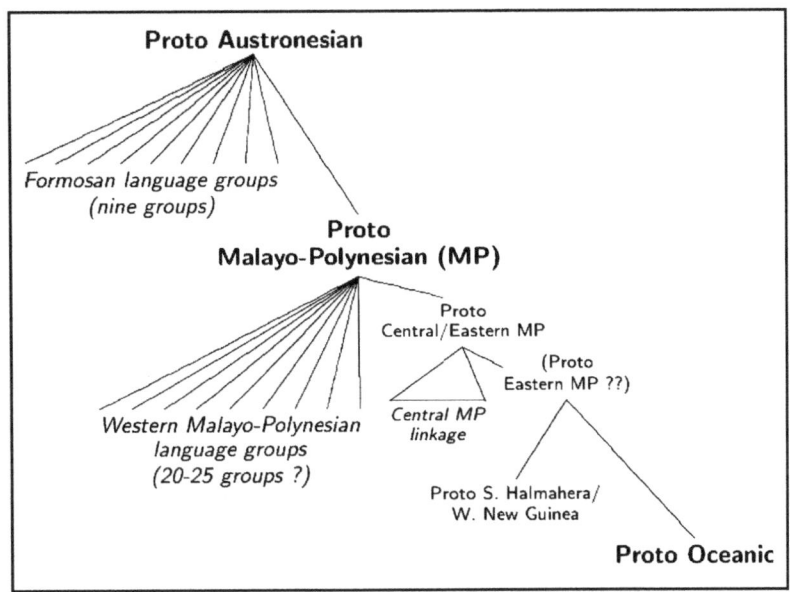

Figure 1. Austronesian family tree: higher order branches.

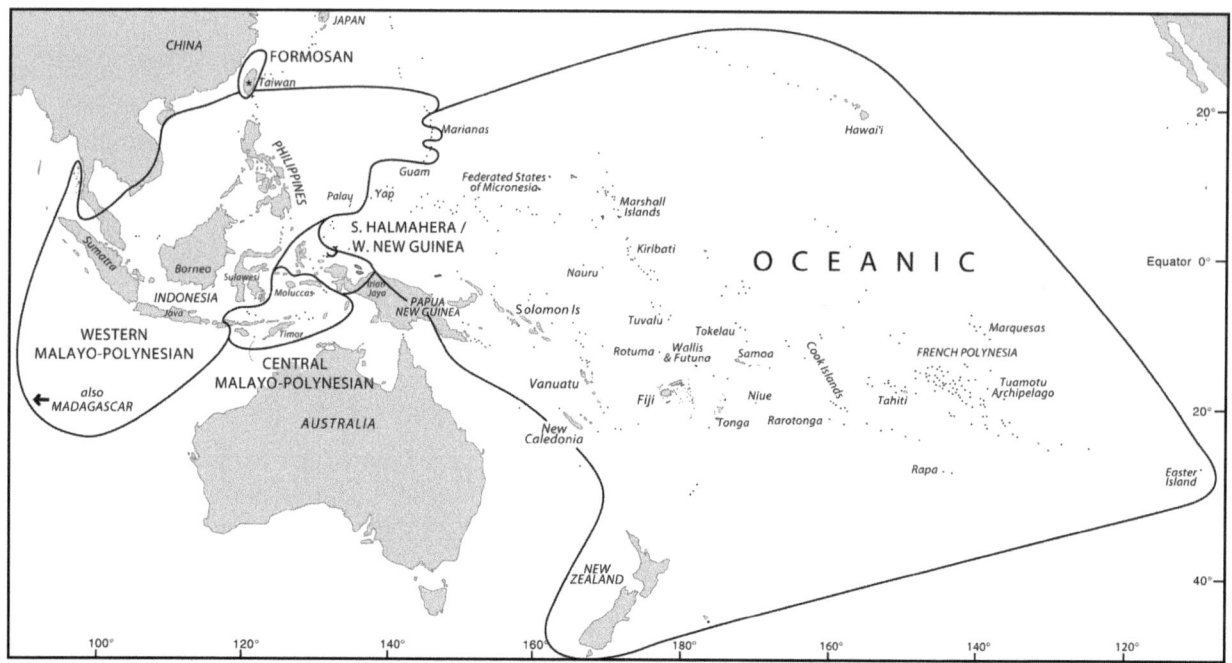

Figure 2. Distribution of the major subgroups of Austronesian.

The Oceanic branch stems from a movement of EMP speakers from the Cenderawasih Bay area of western New Guinea east to the Bismarck Archipelago. The considerable number of innovations defining Oceanic suggests that a significant period of time, probably a few centuries, elapsed between (a) the separation of this branch from the SHWNG subgroup and (b) the breakup of Proto Oceanic (POc).

Given that the closest relatives of Oceanic lie around the neck of the Birds' Head, one might reasonably expect that speakers of pre Oceanic (the phase between Proto SHWNG and Proto Oceanic) at one time lived along the coast of north New Guinea or its offshore islands west of the Bismarcks. But there are no linguistic survivors of such settlements, only tantalising traces in the form of loanwords to Papuan languages of Madang Province (Ross 1988:21). All the Oceanic languages of the north coast of New Guinea are relatively recent "backwash" from the Bismarcks.

The centre of genetic diversity within Oceanic, and the most likely primary dispersal centre for the surviving Oceanic languages, is in the Bismarck Archipelago, where three groups are found that have claims to be first-order subgroups: Admiralties (Blust 1978b, 1996; Ross 1988), Western Oceanic (Ross 1988) and St Matthias (Mussau) (Blust 1984; Ross 1988).

Proto Western Oceanic appears to have been a network of dialects spoken over parts of New Britain, the French Island (Bali-Vitu) and New Ireland (or its offshore eastern islands). It broke up into (a) a Meso-Melanesian dialect complex, initially occupying much the same area as Proto Western Oceanic but later spreading into the northwest Solomons, (b) a North New Guinea dialect complex, extending from the Huon Gulf to Jayapura, and including parts of New Britain, and (c) a Papuan Tip branch, consisting of the Oceanic languages of the Northern Milne Bay and Central Provinces of Papua (Ross 1988).

There is less agreement about the high-order relationships of the Oceanic languages spoken in the eastern half of the main Solomons group and in Remote Oceania. A conservative view is that the following groups may be first-order branches: Southeast Solomonic (Guadalcanal, Gela, Malaita and Makira) (Pawley 1972), Te Motu (the non-Polynesian languages of Te Motu Province, in the eastern Solomons) (Ross and Naess 2007), Yapese (Ross 1996a), Micronesian (Bender 1971; Bender and Wang 1985; Jackson 1983, 1986), North-Central Vanuatu, Southern Vanuatu (Lynch 2001), New Caledonia-Loyalties (Haurdricourt 1971), and Central

Pacific (Fijian, Rotuman and Polynesian) (Geraghty 1983, 1996; Grace 1959; Pawley 1972). However, there is some evidence for linking certain of these groups (reflected in the groupings outlined in Lynch *et al.* 2002). Figure 3 gives a conservative view of the more important high-order subgroups of Oceanic.

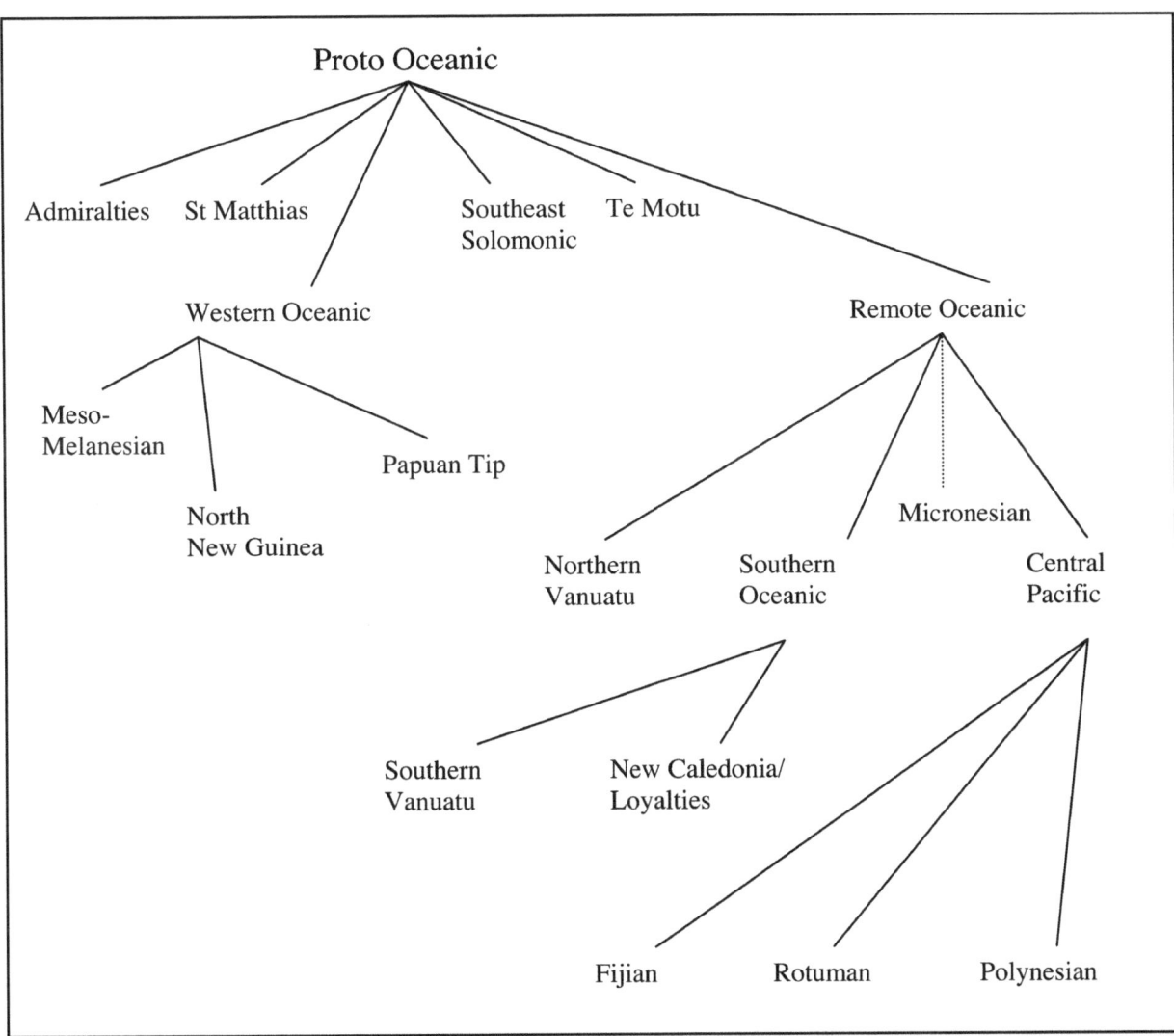

Figure 3. Internal classification of the Oceanic languages.

Equating particular Austronesian stages with archaeological entities

It seems reasonable to make the following equations between particular Austronesian stages and particular archaeological traditions (Bellwood 1997; Green 2003; Kirch and Green 2001).

Proto Austronesian	Neolithic cultures of Taiwan 5000-4,000 BP
Proto Malayo-Polynesian	Neolithic of the Batanes Is. and N. Luzon c. 4000-3600 BP
Proto Oceanic	Early Lapita of the Bismarcks 3400-3100 BP
Proto Central Pacific	Lapita of Fiji-Tonga 3000-2900 BP
Proto Polynesian	Post-Lapita cultures of the Tonga-Samoa region c. 2000-1500 BP

As a consensus about the subgrouping of Austronesian has emerged, it has become ever more apparent that the initial spread of the Lapita culture and the initial dispersal of the Oceanic languages were part of one and the same event. The spread of Early Lapita across the Bismarck Archipelago around 3400-3300 BP can be equated with the first stage in the diversification of Oceanic into its surviving branches. When Lapita was carried into Remote Oceania, reaching Reefs/Santa Cruz, Vanuatu, New Caledonia, Fiji and Tonga, in the period 3200-2900 BP, all the indications are that the carriers spoke still mutually intelligible dialects of early Oceanic. There is no linguistic evidence for a lengthy pause at any point along the way, between the Bismarcks and West Polynesia, in the first few centuries after the breakup of POc. Such evidence would take the form of a sizeable body of innovations linking some languages located say, in the main Solomons group, to languages spoken further east, or linking languages of Vanuatu to the Fijian and Polynesian languages, or linking the Fijian languages to Polynesian. Insofar as any subgroups have been proposed along these lines, they rest on very few innovations - nothing that would require a pause of more than a century or two.

By contrast, there is ample evidence for some significant pauses in the expansion of Oceanic languages over Polynesia and Micronesia. The Polynesian subgroup is defined by a massive set of shared innovations, consistent with a period of common development of 1000 years or more in the West Polynesia area (Clark 1979; Pawley 1996a). The innovations defining Micronesian are not nearly so extensive but nonetheless point to a significant period of unity.

By contrast, evidence for a unified Proto Central Pacific (PCP) stage (ancestral to the Fijian and Polynesian languages and Rotuman) is slender. There is one phonological innovation, loss of *R (e.g. POc *baRa 'fence > Standard Fijian *baa*, PPn *paa, POc *tiRo 'oyster' > S. Fijian *tio*, PPn *tio, POC *paqoRu 'new' > S. Fijian *vou*, PPn *foʔou. There are a few lexical innovations, e.g. POC *matuluR 'sleep' is replaced in PCP by a non-cognate word, *moðe, giving S. Fijian *moðe*, Rotuman *mose*, Tongan *mohe*, Maori *moe*, and a very few grammatical innovations, e.g. Fijian and PPn developed a preposition *ki 'to towards' and came to use the locative preposition *i to mark cause as well as location. The distribution of innovations indicates that PCP took the form of a chain of dialects centred in Fiji, possibly extending to Tonga, that the Polynesian branch diverged from the eastern part of this chain (Geraghty 1983) and that Rotuman diverged from the western part of this chain (Pawley 1996b).

Reconstructing the lexicons of different stages of Austronesian

The recoverable part of the lexicon of a prehistoric proto-language is that which has left residues, in the form of cognate vocabulary, detectable in daughter languages. How large that detectable residue will be depends on a number of different factors:

(1) The number of languages in the group. The more languages, the more witnesses there are to attest features of the proto-language.
(2) The quality of the descriptive data available for contemporary languages.
(3) The subgrouping or family tree structure. Agreement between a pair of closely related witnesses has a different value from agreement between a pair of distantly related languages.
(4) The time depth of the language group. The greater the time depth the more languages change and the smaller the residue of elements retained from the proto-language.
(5) How conservative the languages have been. The nature and rate of linguistic change will be shaped by the demographic and geographic history of speech communities, e.g. whether they were isolated or in close contact with other communities, how large the communities were, and whether they moved from one kind of environment to another, and so on.

The Austronesian family has proved to be something of a historical lexicographer's paradise. Several factors have combined to make it easy to reconstruct a relatively high proportion of the lexicon of various stages. Austronesian is a very large family, with more than 1,000 member languages, and it has a highly structured family tree. Many of the subgroups are widely separated geographically, thereby reducing the problem of sorting out borrowings from shared inheritances. Some of the interstages (intermediate proto-languages) have many daughter languages, providing many independent witnesses when it comes to making decisions about reconstructions. The time depth of the family (the interval since the breakup of PAn) is not very great, probably on the order of 4000-5000 years.

The following is a brief account of works which give reconstructions with supporting cognate sets for particular stages of Austronesian that are relevant to the present discussion.

Proto Austronesian, Proto Malayo-Polynesian, Proto Central-Eastern Malayo-Polynesian, Proto Eastern Malayo-Polynesian

For lexical items attributed to these early stages by far the largest database is Blust's (1995a) *Austronesian Comparative Dictionary* (ACD), a computer file equivalent to several thousand pages of printout, based in the Department of Linguistics at the University of Hawaii. Blust's cognate sets in many cases also include Oceanic material and reconstructions attributed to POc. Other important sources for early Austronesian reconstructions with cognate sets are various articles by Blust (esp. 1970, 1972a, 1980a,b, 1982, 1983–84b, 1986, 1989, 1991, 1993, 1994).

Proto Oceanic[3]

An important source is the *Lexicon of Proto Oceanic* project based in the Department of Linguistics, Research School of Pacific and Asian Studies, The Australian National University. This aims to produce a six volume series that examines various semantic domains and critically evaluates cognate sets and reconstructions in each domain. Although the main body of reconstructions is at the level of POc, particular cognate sets allow reconstructions to be attributed to particular lower-order proto-languages, as well, as is the case with Blust's ACD. The first two volumes, dealing with material culture and with the physical environment, respectively, have been published (Ross *et al.* 1998, 2003). The third and fourth volumes, on plants and animals, respectively, are almost complete (most chapters have either been published separately or are available in electronic form). The fifth, dealing with people and society, is partly drafted, and the sixth is still in the planning stage. Other sources for POc cognate sets include Chowning (1991), Osmond (1998b, 2000), Ross (1988, 1996b), Pawley (1982, 1985, 2005), and a number of papers in Pawley and Ross (1994).

Proto Central Pacific

There is no general compilation other than a problematic early attempt by Hockett (1976). But see Biggs (1965), Geraghty (1983, 1986, 1990, 1996), Ross *et al.* (1998, 2003, in prep.).

Proto Polynesian

The major source is Biggs and Clark (2006), which also contains many reconstructions for proto-languages of lower-level subgroups, such as Tongic, Nuclear Polynesian and Eastern Polynesian. See also Ross *et al.* (1998, 2003, in prep.).

Proto Admiralties.

No general compilation but see Blust (1978b, 1996), Ross *et al.* (1998, 2003, in prep.).

Proto Western Oceanic, Proto Meso-Melanesian, Proto North New Guinea, Proto Papuan Tip

No general compilations but see Ross (1988), 1994, Ross *et al.* 1998, 2003, in prep.).

Proto Micronesian
The main source is Bender *et al.* (2003a, b).

Proto Central and North Vanuatu
The main source is Clark (2007).

Proto South Vanuatu
The main source is Lynch (2001).

Proto New Caledonia/Loyalties
There is no general compilation but see Haudricourt (1971), Ozanne-Rivierre (1992, 1995), Ozanne-Rivierre and Rivierre (1989), Rivierre (1991).

Proto Southeast Solomonic
No general compilation but see Cashmore (1969), Levy (1980, Ross *et al.* (1998, 2003, in prep.).

A very rough indication of the number of lexical reconstructions made to date for certain stages of Austronesian is given below. The variations in the totals for different stages have to do both with the factors listed above and with the amount of work that has been done.[4]

> Proto Austronesian 1,000
> Proto Malayo-Polynesian............. 4,000
> Proto Oceanic 1500-2,000
> Proto Central Pacific............. 1000-1500
> Proto Polynesian...................... 3000

The total lexicon of an average Austronesian language spoken by a Neolithic community was probably in excess of 30,000 lexical units, counting each distinct sense of a word and each derived word and compound as a distinct lexical unit. By this measure 4,000 lexical units is just a small part of the total lexicon (though 4,000 roots would be a high proportion of the total number of roots). Even a set of 1000 reconstructions will typically include extensive terminologies for many fundamental domains of material and non-material culture and gives us a large body of material to work with.

Lexical evidence for selected cultural domains

This section gives reconstructed terminologies for 11 semantic fields in five Austronesian interstages: Proto Austronesian (PAn), Malayo-Polynesian (PMP), Proto Oceanic (POc), Proto Central Pacific (PCP) and Proto Polynesian (PPn). We are chiefly interested in the comparison between PMP and POc. PCP and PPn reflexes of POc reconstructions are included as well, to exemplify patterns of lexical retention and loss in languages associated with Lapita and post-Lapita archaeological traditions in the Fiji-West Polynesia area. Because of the large number of reconstructions treated the supporting cognate sets cannot be included and the discussion will necessarily be very sketchy. The reader is referred to the primary sources for supporting cognate sets and more detailed commentary.

Canoes and sailing
More than 20 terms for canoe parts and associated items are attributable to POc (Pawley and Pawley 1994). These includes names for parts of a five piece built up hull, end pieces, projecting parts of the outrigger complex, platform, sail, boom of sail, steering oar, paddles, bailers, rollers for beaching and launching canoes, and anchor, indicating that POc speakers built substantial ocean-going outrigger canoes.

Thirteen of the POc terms continue PMP words (Blust 1995c). Several terms for parts of the canoe complex are missing from the PMP list, but in some cases we can infer that names for these items were present in PMP because their existence is logically implied by the presence of other terms, e.g. although there is no PMP etymon for 'outrigger float' the presence of PMP *(c,s)a(R)man 'outrigger boom' indicates that it must have been present.

No term for double canoe is attributable to POc. PPn *faʔurua 'double canoe' (from *faʔu 'lashed, constructed (of house, canoe)', *rua 'two', i.e. two hulls lashed together) is well supported, e.g. by Rennellese *haʔugua*, Maori *hourua*, Tuvalu *foulua* 'double canoe'. Compare also Samoan *fou-lua-lua* 'bind together, as 2 canoes', Tongan *foʔu-vaka* 'build a canoe'. Forms outside of Polynesian that resemble PPn *faʔurua, e.g. Kiribati *baurua*, Lau (Malaita) *foorua*, are very probably loans from Polynesian sources. Fijian *drua* 'twin, double canoe' is likely a separate development. Terms for double canoes in South East Papua and New Caledonia are not related to the Polynesian cognate set.

Table 1: Terms for canoes and sailing

1. *Terms continued from PMP*

	PAn	PMP	POc	PCP	PPn
prop, post, mast	*tuku	*tuku	*tuku	*tuku[1]	*tuku
boat rollers		*laŋen	*laŋon	*laŋo	*laŋo
outrigger canoe or hull[2]		*katiR	*kati(R)		
outrigger float		*(c,s)a(R)man	*saman	*ðama	*hama
sail	*layaR	*layaR	*layaR	*laða	*laa
steering oar, steer		*quli(n, ŋ)	*quliŋ	*quli	*quli
canoe paddle		*be(R)(c,s)ay	*pose	*voðe	*fohe
to paddle		*pa-luja	*paluca		
punting pole		*teken	*tokon	*(i)toko	*toko
bailer		*limas	*(l,n)ima(s)	*(i)nima	
anchor		*sauq	*jau(q)	*jau	*tau
channel in reef		*sawa(ŋ,q)	*sawaŋ	*sawa	*awa
make a sea voyage		*pa-lahud	*palau(r)	*volau	*folau
load a vessel; cargo		*lujan	*lujan	*uja	*uta
embark, ride on a vessel		*saŋkay	*sake	*ðake	
raft		*dakit	*raki(t)		

2. *Terms continued from POc, without known antecedents in PMP*

	POc	PCP	PPn
canoe, sailing canoe	*waga	*waga	*waka
topstrake	*(q)oRa	*(q)oa	*(q)oa
outrigger boom	*kiajo	*kiajo	*kiato
sticks attaching float	*patoto	*vatoto	*fatoto
side opposite outrigger	*katae	*katae	*katea
boom/yard of sail	*jila	*sila	*tila
bow of boat	*muqa	*muqa	*muqa
prow, end-piece of prow	*(i,u)cuŋ	*isu	*isu
stern	*muri	*muri	*muri
landing place	*mata-sawaŋ	*mata-sawa	
boat owner	*tau (ni) waga	*tau (ni) waga	*tau waka

3. *PAn/PMP terms without known reflexes in Oceanic*

	PAn	PMP
boat, canoe	*qabaŋ	*qabaŋ

Notes: 1. PCP and PPn *tuku* 'running stay supporting sail'. 2. In various Western MP languages reflexes mean 'outrigger float', 'provide a boat with outrigger'.

Architecture and settlement patterns

Seventeen PMP terms have been reconstructed for types of house and parts of the house (Green and Pawley 1999). POc retains 11 of these and has another six that have no known cognates in PMP. The POc house terms point to solidly built rectangular houses, sometimes raised on stilts, with thatched gable roofs. The existence of a term for 'village' or 'nucleated settlement' in POc is uncertain. *panua and *pera are candidates. *panua is a polysemous word whose senses included 'land', 'inhabited place' and probably 'people of a community', and it has reflexes that mean 'village' in various languages (Pawley 2005).

Table 2: Terms for house and settlement patterns

1. *POc terms continued from PAn and PMP*

	PAn	PMP	POc
house	*Rumaq	*Rumaq	*Rumaq
post	*SadiRi	*hadiRi	*aRiRi

2. *Terms continued from PMP*

	PMP	POc	PCP	PPn
open-sided building	*balay	*pale	*vale[1]	*fale
men's house	*kamaliR	*kamali(R)		
hut, temporary shelter	*uduŋ	*uru(ŋ)		*uru[2]
ridgepole	*bubuŋ	*pupuŋ-an	*vuvu	*(taqu)fufu
sago thatch	*qatep	*qatop	*qato	*qato
thatch	*daSun	*rau(n)	*rau	*rau
rafter	*kasaw	*kaso	*kaso	*kaso
prepare thatch for roofing	*sasa(h,q)	*saja(q)		
secure thatch with battens	*kapit	*kapit		
post	*turus	*turu(s)	*(t,d)uru	
crossbeam	*seŋkar	*soka(r)	*ðoka	*soka
platform, shelf	*pa(n)tar	*patar	*vata	*fata
storage rack	*pa(l,R)a	*pa(r,R)a	*vara	
ladder, bridge, notched log	*titey	*tete		
board, plank	*papan	*baban	*baba	*papa
wooden peg	*pak(o,u)	*pako	*(i)vako	*faqo
fireplace	*dapuR	*rapu(R)	*dravu	*refu
fence	*ba(l,r,R)a	*baRa	*baa	*paa
land, inhabited place, etc.	*banua	*panua	*vanua	*fanua

3. *Terms continued from POc, but without known antecedents in PMP*

	POc	PCP	PPn
area under house on stilts	*gabwari		
doorway	*kataman		
main bearer	*bou	*bou	*pou
partition	*logi	*logi	*loki
stone oven³	*qumun	*qumu	*qumu
boundary marker	*bayat	*bai	*pae
cleared area, ? village centre	*mwalala	*ŋwalala	
? public space, village green	*malaqi	*mala?(e,i)	*mala?e
? settlement, village	*pera		

4. *PAn and/or PMP terms without known reflexes in POc*

	PAn	PMP
shed, shelter	*sapaw	*sapaw
hamlet	*kuan	*kuan
bamboo split, flattened	*saqsaq	*saqsaq
peel rattan, bamboo	*rauC	*raut
mat	*Sikam	*hikam
mat		*lamak
notched log, ladder		*haRezan
room		*bilik
roof, ridge		*ubuŋ
crossbeam		*ataŋ

Notes: *1. PCP *vale 'house, dwelling'. 2. Tongan uu 'sheltered'. 3. POc *qumun 'stone oven' has a cognate in at least one non-Oceanic language of Maluku.*

Fishing technology and methods

Fishing and collecting sea invertebrates were clearly very important parts of the economy of PMP and POc speakers. Table 3 lists 28 POc terms for fishing technology and methods (Osmond 1998b). Continued from POc are names for one kind of fish net, fishnet float, basketry fish trap, fishing line and pole, spear, corral, fish drive, fish poison continued from PMP (Blust 1995c). Several other POc terms having to do with fishing have no known etyma in PMP, including two for kinds of net, one for netting needle and one for dragline.

About 140 POc terms for kinds of fish have been reconstructed (Osmond in prep.) and another 50 or so terms for kinds of molluscs, crustaceans and echinoderms (Pawley 1996c) - too many to be listed here. The totals for PMP are not much smaller. As ethnographic observations show (Dye 1983; Kirch and Dye 1979) different kinds of fish require different capture methods. Thus, indirect evidence for several fishing techniques can be found in the archaeological record, in the range of fish species caught (Walter 1989).

Table 3: Terms for fishing methods and technology

1. *POc terms continued from PAn and/or PMP*

	PAn	PMP	POc	PCP	PPn
fishing line		*hapen	*apon	*avo	*afo
fishhook	*kawil	*kawil	*kawil	*kau	*kau
bait, trolling lure	*paen	*paen	*bayan	*baya	*paa
bait		*baŋi	*baŋi	*baŋi	*paŋi
basketry fish trap	*bubu	*bubu	*pupu	*vuvu	
seine net		*puket	*pukot		
fish net, ? dip net		*lawa(n,q)	*lawa(n,q)	*lawa	*lawa[1]
cowrie shell sinker		*buliq	*buli(q)	*buli	*pule
fishnet float		*apuŋ	*apu-apuŋ		
fish drive		*kebuR	*kopu(R)	*kovu[2]	*kofu
derris fish poison		*tuba	*tupa	*tuva	
torch, fish with torch		*damaR	*(d)ramaR	*rama	*rama
spear		*saet	*sao(t)	*jao	*tao
fish corral		*belat	*polat	*vola	

2. *POc terms without known antecedents in PMP*

	POc	PCP	PPn
fish hook	*ta(g,k)o	*ta(a,o)ko	*t(a,o)ko
fish net	*reke	*dreke[3]	*reke
fish net, ? with handle or frame	*kup(w)ena	*kube (n, ŋ)a	*kupeŋa
float of fishnet	*utoŋ	*uto	*uto
mesh of fishnet	*mata	*mata	*mata
netting needle	*sika	*sika	*sika
dragline	*rau(n)	*rau	*rau
stone fish weir	*baRa	*baa	*paa
fish spear	*kuj(i,u)r		
spear with prong	*tara	*tara	*tala[4]
spear retained in hand	*sua	*sua(k)	*sua
gather seafood on reef	*paŋoda	*vaŋoda	*faŋota
seafood gathered on reef	*p-in-aŋoda	*vinaŋoda	*finaŋota
torch, fish at night with torches	*(d)rama(R)	*rama	*rama

Notes: 1. PPn *lawa 'wrap in sennet'. 2. PCP *kovu 'wrap up fish, etc. 3. PCP *dreke 'pocket in a net'. 4. Tongan *tala* 'spike, barb', Samoan *tala* 'spike, prong'

Agriculture and aboriculture

Some 20 terms for agricultural activities and artefacts are attributable to POc (French-Wright 1983; Osmond 1998a). A dozen or so of these are continued from PMP (Blust 1995c, ACD), including terms for garden or swidden, cleared land, fallow land, weed gardens, plant in holes and sow seed. POc has another eight or so terms that lack known PMP antecedents.

Table 4: Terms relating to gardening activities

1. *POc terms continued from PAn/PMP*

	PAn	PMP	POc	PCP	PPn
garden, swidden	*qumah	*quma	*quma	*uma	
bushland, hinterland	*quCaŋ	*qutan	*qutan	*quta[1]	*quta
land cleared for garden	*tebaS	*teba	*topa	*tova	*tofa[2]
fence	*qa(l,R)ad	*qalad	*qaRa(r)	*qaa	*qaa
fallow land		*talun	*talu(n)	*talu	*talu-talu
burn fields		*zeket	*soko(t)		
pull weeds	*buCbuC	*butbut	*pupu(t)[3]	*vuvu	*fufu[4]
weed garden		*babaw	*papo	*vovo	
plant in holes		*hasek	*asok		
sow seed		*kambuR	*kabu(R)	*kabu	*kapu[5]

2. *POc terms without known antecedents in PMP*

	POc	PCP	PPn
hoe, adze	*salu	*saru	*salu
strip vegetation	*sani	*sani	*sani
clear rubbish	*sara	*ðara	
digging stick	*waso		
bury, plant tuber	*tanum	*tanum	*tanu
make yam mound	*(p,b)uk(i,e)	*buke	*puke
break up ground	*suar	*sua	*sua
garden fence	*kaRi		
fence, boundary marker	*bayat	*bai	*pae

Notes: 1. PCP *quta 'land, as from the sea; inland, as from the coast'. 2. PPn *tofa 'open up something new'. 3. POc *pupu(t) 'pluck fruit'. 4 PPn *fufu 'strip off, as leaves, fibre'. 5. PPn *kapu 'spread over, surround, envelop'.

A major change in POc was the loss of the PMP rice and millet terminology, including terms for granary, pestle and mortar. This is consistent with the widely accepted view that the Austronesian speakers who entered Northwest Melanesia in the second half of the 2nd millennium BC had completely abandoned the cultivation of grain crops.

Table 5: PAn/PMP terms relating to grain crops, which lack known reflexes in POc

	PAn	PMP
rice plant	*pajay	*pajay
seed rice for planting	*bineSiq	*binehiq
husked rice	*beRas	*beRas
cooked rice	*Semay	*hemay
foxtail millet	*beCeŋ	*beteŋ
chase (birds etc.) from field	*buRaw	*buRaw
harvest	*qanih	*qanih
thresh by trampling	*(e,i)Rik	*eRik

thresh by beating	*paspas	*paspas
winnow	*tapeS	*tapeh
rice straw	*zaRami	*zaRami
pestle	*qaSelu	*qahelu
mortar	*lesuŋ	*lesuŋ
hut, granary	*lepaw	*lepaw
canal, ditch	*kali	*kali
pull out weeds	*SebuC	*hebut

POc retained PMP terms for three root crops (taro, *Alocasia* taro and the greater yam), *Musa* bananas and sugar cane. It also retained PMP terms for a good many useful trees and other plants. A very large set of POc terms is reconstructable for useful trees (Ross 1996b, Ross *et al* in prep.; Tryon 1994) pointing to the importance of tree culture in the economy. Table 6 includes a selection of these.

Table 6: Terms for root and fruit crops and other useful plants

1. *POc terms continued from PAn/PMP*

	PAn	PMP	POc	PCP	PPn
giant taro, *Alocasia indica*	*biRaq	*biRaq	*piRaq	*via[1]	
sugar cane	*CebuS	*tebu	*topu	*dovu	*too
yam, *Dioscorea alata*		*qubi	*qupi	*quvi	*qufi
taro, *Colocasia*		*tales	*talo(s)	*talo	*talo
banana, *Musa* hybrids		*punti	*pudi	*vudi	*futi
breadfruit, *Artocarpis atilis*		*kuluR	*kuluR	*kulu	*kulu
sago, *Metroxylon* sp.		*Rambia	*Rabia	*abia[1]	
cordyline		*siRi	*jiRi	*jii	*sii
coconut		*niuR	*niuR	*niu	*niu
pandanus		*paŋdan	*padran	*vadra	*fara
coastal pandanus		*kiRay[2]	*kiRe	*kie-kie	*kie-kie
Barringtonia		*butun	*putun	*vutu	
mango, prob. *Mangifera indica*		*pahuq	*pau(q)		
mango, generic		*wai	*wai		
Indian almond, *Terminalia* sp.		*talisay	*talise	*taliðe	*talie
chestnut, *Inocarpus* sp.		*(q)ipi	*qipi	*ivi	*ifi
Canarium almond, *Canarium indicum*[3]		*kanaRi	*kaŋaRi		*makari[3]
Burckella obovata		*natu	*(n,ñ)atu		
citrus spp.		*limaw	*molis	*moli	*moli
ginger, *Zingiber* sp.		*laqia	*laqia	*laya	
curcurbit		*[ka]timun	*[ka]timun	*timo	*timo
chew on sugar cane		*ququs	*ququ(s)		

2. *POc terms without known antecedents in PMP*

potato yam, *Dioscorea bulbifera*	*pwatik		
taro, Colocasia	*mwapo(q)	*mavu	*mafu
taro seedling	*upea		
prepare yam for planting	*sopu		
cut seed yams for planting	*paji	*vaði	
banana (*Australimusa* group)	*joRaga	*soaga	*soaka
k.o. cooking banana	*sakup		
breadfruit	*baReko		
core of breadfruit	*malo	*malo	*malo
Abelmoschus manihot	*was(i,a)		
Paper mulberry, *Broussonetia papyrifera*	*m(w)ase	*masi	
Malay apple, *Syzygium malaccense*	*kapika	*kavika	*kafika
Polynesian plum, *Pometia pinnata*[4]	*tawan	*tawa	*tawa
Indian mulberry, *Morinda citrifolia*	*ñoñum	*ñoñu	*nonu
Indian mulberry, *Morinda citrifolia*	*kurat	*kura	
Vi apple, *Spondias dulcis*	*quRis	*uRi	*wii
Canarium almond, *Canarium indicum*	*qalip		
turmeric	*yaŋo	*yaŋo	*aŋo
large pandanus	*p(w)asa	*vasa	*fasa
edible wild cane	*pijo	*viðo	*fiso

Notes: 1. Bauan Fijian *abia*, arrowroot. 2. PCEMP *kanaRi. 3. PPn *makari '*Canarium samoensis*'. 4. PEMP *tawan.

Domestic animals

Two terms for 'pig' are reconstructable in PMP. Blust (1995c) argues that one term (*beRek) referred solely to domestic pigs and the other (*babuy) was a generic name for pigs, and was used in compounds to denote categories of pig and pig-like animals. At any rate, only *beRek was retained in POc. There is some evidence for a second POc term for 'pig, (?) sow', *bukas, which had no PMP etymon.

No POc term for 'domestic fowl, chicken' is well supported, although chicken bones occur in Early Lapita sites. The PMP name for the domestic fowl, *manuk, appears in POc as the generic for 'bird' (Clark 1994).

PMP had a generic term for 'dog' but this was not preserved in POc. There are several candidates for a POc term for 'dog' but all are problematic to some extent (Hudson 1989). This is consistent with the absence of dog remains from early Lapita sites. Its earliest appearance is in Reefs/Santa Cruz plainware assemblages dating to about 2600 BP, after which it disappears (R. Green pers. comm.).

Table 7: Terms for domestic animals

1. *PAn/PMP terms without known reflexes in POc*

	PAn	PMP
pig	*babuy	*babuy
dog	*asu, wasu	*asu
rooster		*laluŋ

2. *POc terms continued from PAN/PMP*

	PAn	PMP	POc	PCP	PPn
pig	*beRek	*beRek	*boRok	*bwoo	
fowl		*manuk	*manuk (bird)	*manu	*manu

3. *POc terms without known antecedents in PMP*

	PAn	PMP	POc	PCP	PPn
pig			*(b,p)ukas	*vuaka	*puaka

Pottery, wooden vessels

Names for four distinct kinds of ceramic vessel can be reconstructed for PMP (Blust 1995c). (It is curious that none have known PAn etyma, although the archaeological record for Taiwan makes it clear that pottery was made by PAn speakers.) At least three of the PMP terms were continued in POc (Osmond and Ross 1998). A number of other terms for food and water containers are reconstructable for POc, most of which lack PMP antecedents.

Table 8: Terms for pottery and other vessels used for holding food and liquid

1. *POc terms continued from PMP*

	PMP	POc	PCP	PPn
1. cooking pot 2. generic for pots	*kuDen	*kuron	*kuro	*kuro
shallow pot	*balaŋa	*palaŋa		
large pot	*baŋaq	*bwaŋa		
narrow-necked jar	*kalalaŋ	*kalala (?)		
trivet	*dalikan			
drinking vessel		*ibu/ubi	*ibu	*ipu
ladle, dipper	*kaŋbuq	*kabu	*kabu	*kapu

2. *POc terms which lack known antecedents in PMP*

	POc	PCP
wooden bowl	*tabiR(a,i)	*tabili
coconut shell container	*b(w)ilo	*bilo
coconut shell half cup	*lasa	
cup, ladle	*kulopi	
water-bottle	*wai(p)	

Cooking

A small set of cooking terms can be reconstructed (Lichtenberk and Osmond 1998)

Table 9. Terms relating to cooking

1. *POc terms continued from PMP*

	PAn	PMP	POc	PCP	PPn
roast on fire	*Cunuh	*tunu	*tunu	*tunu	*tunu
cook by boiling	*nasuq	*nasuq	*nasu(q)		
preserve by smoking	*Capa	*tapa	*tapa		
eat raw (meat)	*qetaq	*qetaq	*(k,q)oda	*qoda	*ʔota

2. *POc terms which lack known antecedents in PMP*

earth oven[1]	*qumun	*qumu	*qumu
steam-bake in stone oven	*papi	*vavi	
steam-bake in stone oven	*taqo	*ta?o	ta?o
cooked, burnt, lit	*mwaRi		

Note: 1. A cognate occurs in a SHWNG language, supporting the reconstruction of PEMP *qumun.

Cutting and piercing instruments

POc retained PMP *kiRam, which was almost certainly the generic term for axe/adze, along with the term for axe/adze handle. POc had a second term for axe/adze but there are no clues to how it differed in reference from *kiRam. Two terms for cutting tools are continued from PMP, one made of turtle shell (named after the Hawksbill turtle), the other, probably, of bamboo. POc continues PMP *saRum '(bone) needle'. Oceanic reflexes commonly apply to bat-wing needles used for tattooing.

POc *nad(r)i appears to have been a general term for any kind of stone whose flakes have a very sharp edge, such as obsidian, chert and flint. There is, however, a PWOc reconstruction for obsidian, *qa(r,R)iŋ, that may continue a POC etymon that has been lost elsewhere.

Table 10: Terms for cutting implements and processes

1. *POc terms continued from PMP*

	PMP	POc	PCP	PPn
axe or adze	*kiRam	*kiRam	*kia	
cutting implement of turtle shell	*ta(ŋ)kub	*taku(p)	*taku	*taku
bone needle, awl[1]	*zaRum	*saRum	*sau	*sau
adze/axe handle	*paRada	*paRara	*vara	
to hew, plane	*taRaq	*taRaq	*taa	
bamboo knife	*pisaw	*piso		
cutting edge, sharp point	*mata	*mata	*mata	*mata
grind, grate, sharpen like this	*asaq	*asaq-i	*asa	*asa
file, rasp	*kir-kir	*kiri		

2. *POc terms which lack known antecedents in PMP*

	POc	PCP	PPn
axe, adze	*matau	*matau	*matau
stone with sharp cutting edge: obsidian, chert, flint	*nad(r)i		
pierce, bore a hole	*puruk-i		

Note: 1. Reflexes often refer to tattooing needle, typically made of wing bone of fruit bat (Osmond and Ross 1998:87).

Clothing, weaving, ornaments and decoration

Blust (1995c:493-494) argues that weaving and bark cloth manufacture were both practised by PAn, PMP and POc societies, though with different emphases. PMP clothing was probably chiefly made from woven cloth, as indicated by the considerable number of terms relating to weaving of garments that can be reconstructed. None of these terms have known reflexes in POc, which may point to a greater use of bark cloth. No reflexes of PMP *qatip 'backstrap loom' are known from Oceanic languages. Although Blust observes that the backstrap loom occurs in several Oceanic societies (in the Banks Is., the Carolines and Santa Cruz) and that this distribution suggests that it was known to POc speakers, the ethnographic record indicates that the loom spread to Melanesia more recently through Micronesia and Polynesian Outliers. Several POc words for items of clothing and ornamentation (Osmond and Ross 1998) have no known antecedents in PMP.

PMP terms for a *Trochus* armband (same term as for the shell itself) and comb persisted in POc.

Table 11: Terms for clothing, weaving, ornaments and decoration

1. *PAn/PMP terms without known reflexes in POc*

	PAn	PMP
to weave	*tenun	*tenun
to weave	*tinequn	*tinequn
batten of the loom	*baRija	*balija
part of loom	*qatip-an	*qatip
weaving spindle	*qaNi	*qani
woven skirt	*tapis	*tapis
beads	*Siŋuq	*hinuq
waistband, belt	*bakes	*bakes
wrap-around cloth worn by women	*Seban	*heban
head cover		*tuduŋ
to sew	*taqiS	*taqih

2. *POc terms continued from PMP*

	PMP	POc	PCP	PPn
to sew	*zaqit	*saqi(t)		
to plait, woven, braided	*añ(a,e)m	*aña(m)		
to plait/weave (mats, baskets)	*batuR	*patuR-i	*vatu²	fatu²
comb	*saRu	*saRu	*seru	*selu
trochus armband	*lalak	*lalak		
barkcloth mallet	*ikay¹	*ike		

3. *POc terms without known antecedents in PAn/PMP*

	POc	PCP	PPn
pearlshell ornament	*japi	*jiva	*tifa
shell disk used as ear-ring	*(sabi-)sabi⁴		
barkcloth garment	*malo	*malo	*malo
man's clothing, esp. loincloth	*tipi		
to weave, plait s.th.	*paus-i		
to weave	*pai		
to (?finish off) plaiting a mat	*tiki		
woman's grass skirt³	*nai		
oil or paint the body	*pani	*(p,v)ani	*pani
decorate	*noŋo⁵		
herringbone pattern	*mwati		
plaited cane armlet	*bara		

Note: 1. A single non-Oceanic cognate in a MP language has been noted. 2. More generally, also to assemble, construct. 3. Reflexes only in Admiralties and North New Guinea, so possibly borrowed into one or the other group. 4. Possibly not distinct from *japi. 5. Weakly supported.

Kinship

A fairly extensive set of kinship terms has been reconstructed for POc (Blust 1980b; Chowning 1991; Marck in prep. a; Milke 1958), including distinct sets of terms of reference and address. Table 11 shows only terms of reference for the relevant proto-languages. About half of the POc reference terms continue PMP etyma, including those for 'grandparent', 'father', 'mother', 'mother's brother', 'younger sibling of same sex', 'grandchild', 'spouse', 'parent-in-law' and 'sibling-in-law'. The presence of terms for siblings of opposite sex implies the existence of descent groups (Blust 1980b, 1994; Hage 1998, 1999a,b).

Table 12: Kinship terms of reference

	PAn	PMP	POc	PCP	PPn
A. Consanguineous kin					
1. *2nd generation up*					
grandparent, ancestor	*apu	*apu			
grandparent, ancestor		*t-impu	*tubu	*tubu	*tupu-na[1]
2. *1st generation up*					
father, FaBro	*ama	*t-ama	*tama	*tama	*tama-na
mother, mosis	*ina	*t-ina	*tina	*tina	*tina-na
mother's brother	*ma(n)tuqaS	*ma(n)tuqa	*matuqa		
father's sister			*aya[2]		*mahakitanga
3. *Ego's generation*					
older sibling same sex		*tata			
older sibling same sex			*tuaka	*tuaka	*tuaka-na
younger sibling same sex		*ta-huaji	*tasi	*taði	*tahi-na
brother (w. speaking)			*mwaqane[3]	*mwaqane	*tua-ŋaqane
sister (m. speaking)			*papine		*tua-fafine
sister (m. speaking)		*betaw			
4. *1st generation down*					
child	*aNak	*anak			
child, Bro ch, sis ch.			*natu		
sister's child (man speaking)			*qalawa		
sister's son/daughter's husband		*(d,D)awa	*rawa[4]		
5. *2nd generation down*					
grandchild	*umpu	*t-umbu	*tubu		
grandchild			*makubu	*makubu	*makupu-na
B. Affinal kin					
1. *1st generation up*					
parent-in-law			*puŋao-	*vuŋao	*fuŋao-na
2. *Ego's generation*					
spouse		*qasawa	*qasawa	*ʔaðawa	*ʔahawa-na
sibling-in-law, wife's brother, possibly also husband's father		*hipaR	*qipaR	*ʔiva	

Note: 1. Many PPn kin terms contain a petrified suffix *-na, which reflects PCP -*ña '3rd person singular possessor, his/her'. 2. Blust (1980b) reconstructs *aya. Others have suggested the evidence as insufficient but Marck (in prep., a) gives reflexes from five different high-order subgroups. 3. Blust reconstructs *maRuaqane. There is support for both forms but *mwaqane is more widely reflected within Oceanic. 4. Blust (1980b:213) appears to favour 'affine not of Ego's generation, parent-in-law, child-in-law' as a gloss for POc *rawa.

Leadership and other social categories

A number of terms for social categories (other than kin) are attributable to POc. Only a few of these are known to come from PAn and/or PMP etyma. There has been some debate over whether POc society had descent groups and hereditary chieftainship. Hage (1998, 1999a) and Marck (in prep., b) propose, on a variety of grounds, that POc society had unilineal, probably matrilineal descent groups, and unilocal, underpinned by matrilocal or matri-avunculocal residence rules. Green (1994, 2002:25-6) proposes that the POc reflex of PMP term *Rumaq 'house' was also used to designate a descent group of some sort, as it is in any societies of eastern Indonesia but there is little support for this second sense among Oceanic witnesses.

Pawley (1982) proposed a pair of POc reconstructions *qalap(s) 'hereditary leader of a lineage, chief' and *qadiki 'son or heir of chief'. He also proposed two further reconstructions: POc *tau mwala, 'commoner, person of low rank' and (to an early Oceanic stage, ancestral to Micronesian and Polynesian) *kainaŋa 'lineage, higher descent group'. Lichtenberk (1986) revised the form of the first reconstruction to *ta-la(m)pat (a compound of *ta- 'man', *la(m)pat 'big, great') and argued that its meaning is indeterminate between 'chief' and 'big-man'. He also proposed that the reconstructed meaning of *tau mwala is indeterminate between 'commoner' and 'worthless person'. Hage (1999a,b) and Blust (1995c) give other reasons for thinking that POc society had hereditary rank. Archaeologists point to features of Lapita pottery, especially the highly decorated vessels with stands, which suggest differential rank in Lapita society. Lichtenberk (1986) also revised the gloss for POc *adiki to 'eldest child' (we now write this form as *ariki), and argued that it was preceded by the personal article *qa to mark it as a kin term.

Table 13: Terms for social categories

1. *POc terms continued from PMP*

	PAn	PMP	POc	PCP	PPn
spirit of the dead	*qaNiCu	*qanitu	*qanitu	*ʔanitu	*ʔaitu
powerful spirit		*(qa)tuan	*qatua(n)	*ʔatua	*ʔatua
human being, person	*Cau	*tau	*tau	*tau[1]	*tau[1]
outsiders, aliens	*qa(R)(CtT)a	*qa(R)ata	*qata[2]		
woman	*binaHi	*ba-binay	*papine	*vavine	*fafine
person of marriageable age		*paqoRu	*(tau-)paqoRu	*taupoʔou	*taupoʔou

2. *POc terms without known antecedents in PMP*

	POc	PCP	PPn
lineage, descent group (?)	*kainaŋa[3]	*kainaŋa	*kainaŋa
leader, prob. hereditary chief	*ta-la(m)pat[4]		
first-born child	*qa-ariki	*ʔariki	*ʔariki
person of low status	*(tau)-mwala		
mariner, fisherman/sailor	*tau-tasi	*tau-taði	*tau-tai
canoe owner/captain	*tau-ni-waga	*tau ni waga[5]	*tau-waka
person of the place	*kai + Place	*kai [+ Place]	
stranger, foreigner	*tau-kese	*tau-keðe	*tau-kehe
human being (living)	*tamwata	*taŋwata	*taŋata
dead person, ghost	*tau-mate		
man, male	*(ta)mwaqane	*taŋwaqane	*taqane
girl	*keni		

Note: 1. POc *tau 'person' is reflected only in compound nouns in PPn (often in the shortened form *ta-). This was probably the case in PCP, too. 2. In POc the meaning may have been 'people, person' (Blust 1972b). 3. Reflexes only in Micronesian and Polynesian, so attribution to POc is questionable. 4. Literally *ta- 'person', *la(m)pat 'great'. 5. Reflected in PPn (as *tau-waka) but lost in Fijian. But unlike PPn, PCP compounds of this type generally contained the genitive linker *ni.

Summary

Almost all historical linguists would agree with the view, advocated in numerous works by Peter Bellwood, that the rapid spread of a language family strongly indicates migration of segments of the parent speech community. The initial dispersal of the Malayo-Polynesian languages appears to be a classic case of this type of rapid spread. In the space of 1000 years, between about 4000 and 3000 BP, people speaking the descendants of a single ancestral language-culture system spread from the Philippines into the Indo-Malaysian archipelago and Northwest Melanesia and then on into Remote Oceania. We can only date this sequence of movements by correlating it with archaeological events. Such a large demographic and cultural event should have left archaeological footprints and clearly this is so.

Lexical reconstructions greatly extend the archaeological record for the Austronesian-linked Neolithic cultures of the Philippines c. 4000-3600 BP (equated with PMP), the Bismarck Archipelago c. 3300-3100 BP (POc), Fiji ca 3000 BP (PCP) and the Tonga-Samoa region c. 2000-1500 BP (PPn). The extensions apply particularly to non-material culture but also to material culture. For example, the outrigger canoe complex is missing from the relevant archaeological records, as is most of the house complex and almost all traces of the fishing net complex but these are all well attested in the linguistic record.

It can be seen that in most of the 11 lexical fields considered here there is very considerable continuity between PMP and POc, strongly supporting the conclusion that the Early Lapita cultural complex in large part continues a Southeast Asian tradition, and that there is considerable continuity in PCP and PPn. Many elements of this tradition were continued in PCP and PPn society. The powerful linguistic evidence for an Austronesian dispersal of the outrigger canoe complex, fishing techniques, house types and settlement patterns, agriculture and so on, does not preclude the possibility that some of the same cultural elements already existed in northwest Melanesia in pre-Lapita times. All it shows is that Austronesian speakers already had these elements when they entered northwest Melanesia.

What of those artefacts in the archaeological record considered to be indeterminate between "intrusion" and "integration", i.e. between an Austronesian-linked Southeast Asian origin and a pre-Austronesian origin in Near Oceania? Recall that Spriggs' list for this indeterminate category includes oval/lenticular polished adzes, grindstones, hinge-region *Tridacna* adzes, pierced shell pendants, shell beads, *Trochus* armbands, one-piece fishhooks, bone points or awls, vegetation clearance by fire, shellfishing and reef fishing, earth ovens and most of the Oceanic domesticated crop complex.

There is continuity in the general terms for axe/adze and handle but these give no indication as to the material or shape of the axe/adze itself or manner of hafting. The absence of a PMP term for stone oven or earth oven suggests that this method of cooking may have been borrowed by Austronesian speakers when they entered the Moluccas or Melanesia. There is continuity between PMP and POc in terms for angling (words for fishhook, line, and trolling lure) and in the term for the *Trochus* shell and armbands made from this.

PMP terms for the root crop complex and for some of the tree crops persist in POc, along with a number of words for agricultural practices. The fact that POc speakers carried their tradition of root and tree crop cultivation with them with them does not preclude the possibility that some of the plants were first domesticated in the New Guinea area, and that they moved westwards into Island Southeast Asia in the millennia before the Austronesian dispersal. A number of domesticated plants of New Guinea origin are candidates for this status (Kennedy 2007; Kennedy and Clarke 2004; Yen 1991). However, that is another story, separate from the question of the immediate origins of the Lapita culture.

On interaction between Austronesian and non-Austronesian communities in the early Lapita period

Finally, let us turn to the third question: Can linguistics say anything about the interaction between speakers of Austronesian and non-Austronesian languages in the early Lapita period? Some bold speculations recently put forward by Spriggs can serve as a point of departure:

> My current view is that ... Lapita represents a new ethnic identity in the western Pacific, forged around a new prestige language (now labelled Proto-Oceanic Austronesian), which was spoken by people of originally disparate geographical and genetic origins. The new language was used to encode powerful origin myths to unite this disparate population, and Lapita pottery designs had an originally important role in the ritual performance of this group's identity ... This new iconography in the material culture, often representing an anthropomorphic face - perhaps the putative ancestor figure? - was an important mobilising and legitimating force as the Lapita culture was spread from the Bismarcks out into the Pacific ... (Spriggs 2003:205)

I read Spriggs as implying, in the first part of this passage, that while the Proto Oceanic language and its original speakers were intruders to the Bismarcks this language was soon learnt by diverse communities in the Bismarck Archipelago who were originally speakers of non-Austronesian languages and who were biologically distinct from the immigrant Austronesians. Learning the Lapita language was essential for these outsiders to gain entry into Lapita society. A further implication is that these originally non-Austronesian speaking communities also adopted much of the immigrants' material culture and social organisation while also retaining elements of their own.

What evidence can be found to test these speculations? I will leave aside the matter of biology and concentrate on language. On the linguistic front we have to look for evidence that might distinguish between acquisition of POc by communities of second language speakers and continuous transmission by successive generations of native speakers.[5] Unfortunately, it is virtually impossible to find direct evidence of specific lexical borrowings from non-Austronesian languages into Oceanic that may have occurred in the Bismarcks some 3000 years ago – for one thing, the donor languages are unlikely to have left descendants. However, statistical evidence of borrowing may be sought by examining the number and nature of replacements in the lexicon of POc itself, compared with earlier stages, or in that of the immediate descendants of POc, namely proto-languages ancestral to high order subgroups of Oceanic, compared to POc.

Blust (1993) reconstructed PMP, PCEMP, PCMP and POc forms for the Swadesh 200 item basic vocabulary list and calculated the number of retentions and losses in each of the daughter proto-languages below PMP, with results as shown in Table 14.

Table 14: Percentages of PMP basic vocabulary (Swadesh 200 word list) retained in PCEMP, PCMP and POc

Proto Central-Eastern MP	98
Proto Central MP	94
Proto Oceanic	88

POc replaced 12 % of PMP items on the PMP list. If we assume a 600 year gap between PMP and POc (a rough estimate based on the archaeological dates for the arrival of an Austronesian-associated Neolithic in the northern Philippines and Bismarcks, respectively) this gives a replacement rate of 2 percent per century, or 20 percent per millennium, which is almost exactly the mean rate of loss recorded for the sample of Indo-European languages used by Swadesh in his pioneering studies of rates of lexical replacement in the 1950s.

There is no evidence here that extensive borrowing from non-Austronesian sources took place in the line of descent leading from PMP to POc.

The next place to look for signs of major perturbations in basic lexicon is in the proto-languages of the better-documented high-order subgroups of Oceanic. If language contact in the Bismarcks in the immediate post-POc period led to many lexical replacements these should show up in reconstructions of the proto-languages.

A recent study (Pawley 2007) compares retention rates for a sample of basic vocabulary in two subgroups of Oceanic, Northwest Solomonic and Southeast Solomonic, that are believed to have had very different histories of contact. In the area occupied by the Northwest Solomonic subgroup (Buka-Bougainvillle, Choiseul, the New Georgia Group and Santa Isabel) some 10 non-Austronesian languages still survive in two locations; Bougainville and the New Georgia Group. Two more non-Austronesian languages are spoken on Savo and Russell, small islands close to Guadalcanal on the eastern margin of the Northwest Solomonic group and the western margin of Southeast Solomonic. These 12 or so languages fall into several apparently unrelated families and are thought to be the relics of a much larger number of non-Austronesian languages that occupied the region when Oceanic speakers arrived. By contrast, there is reason to think that the region occupied by Southeast Solomonic languages had very few occupants when Oceanic speakers arrived. No non-Austronesian languages survive there (although two are spoken immediately to the west, on Savo and Russell).

The baseline in this study consisted of reconstructions of the 60 POc words with the highest high retention rates. A retention rate for each word was established by comparing basic vocabulary in 40 different contemporary Oceanic languages. Some 3000 years after the breakup of POc the more conservative Oceanic languages, such as those of Fiji and Polynesia, generally retain around 80 percent of these 60 words without significant change of meaning.

The study found a very large difference between the two subgroups. All Northwest Solomonic languages in the sample have replaced many more of the POc words than any of the Southeast Solomonic languages. Among Southeast Solomonic languages the average percentage of retentions is 73. The highest single percentage is 86 and the lowest is 65. Within Northwest Solomonic the average percentage of retentions is 49. The highest is 59 and the lowest is 40. The explanation given for this striking and consistent difference was that Northwest Solomonic languages have borrowed heavily from non-Austronesian languages while Southeast Solomonic languages have not. There seems to be no other reasonable explanation.

When did the large scale replacements take place in Northwest Solomonic? It can be shown that the replacements take different forms in different branches of Northwest Solomonic. The proto-language of the Northwest Solomonic group was lexically quite conservative: it had replaced only about four of the 60 POc words, giving a retention rate of 93 percent. (The figure for Proto Southeast Solomonic is similar.) That it to say, most of the large scale lexical change in Northwest Solomonic languages occurred after Northwest Solomonic speakers had dispersed across the region and, presumably, after they had established stable contacts with non-Austronesian speech communities, leading to long-term bilingualism and language shift.

The same study found that Proto Central Pacific (ancestral to Fijian, Rotuman and Polynesian) retained all of the 60 POc lexical items and Proto Polynesian kept 55 of the 60. By this measure, PCP was a very conservative Oceanic language and PPn also very conservative, considering that it belongs to a time 1000 years or more after the breakup of POc. No precise figures are available for other high-order subgroups, such as Proto Admiralties, Proto Western Oceanic, Proto Meso-Melanesian, Proto North & Central Vanuatu and Proto Micronesian but my impression is that all will be found to retain 55 or more of the 60 items.

I read the lexical evidence as indicating that when Oceanic speakers first moved into Remote Oceania at about 3200-3100 BP they spoke a language little changed from POc. This in turn suggests that in the first few generations after Oceanic speakers arrived in the Bismarck Archipelago contact with non-Austronesian speakers was seldom of the kind that led Oceanic speakers to borrow basic vocabulary or for non-Austronesian speech communities to shift to Oceanic languages. Events of that kind were to become commonplace in various parts of Northwest Melanesia but not until somewhat later (see various papers in Dutton and Tryon 1994 and also Bradshaw 1995, Pawley 2006, Ross 1996c for a consideration of social and linguistic mechanisms associated with large scale borrowing and language shift in Melanesia). These conclusions are not inconsistent with archaeologists' findings about the preferred site locations of Early Lapita sites in the Bismarcks and the maintenance of intensive contacts between dispersed Lapita communities for the first few generations. The DNA record indicates that outsiders who entered Lapita communities as spouses were chiefly males. This is consistent with POc society as being matrilocal, with children growing up speaking the language of their mother and mother's sisters (Marck in prep., a).

Notes

1. I am grateful to Roger Green, Jeff Marck, Malcolm Ross and Matthew Spriggs for helpful comments on drafts of this paper.

2. I draw on a considerable literature on Austronesian culture history viewed from the standpoint of lexical reconstructions and subgrouping and, in particular, on a masterly overview by Blust (1995c). Other relevant works include, for the early stages of Austronesian, Blust (1976, 1980a,b, 1985) and Zorc (1994) and some of the contributions to Pawley and Ross (1994), for Proto Oceanic, Chowning (1991), Green (1994), Pawley and Green (1973, 1984), Pawley and Ross (1995) and Ross et al. (1998, 2003, in prep.), for Proto Polynesian, Kirch and Green (2001) and Marck (2000), as well as more general inter-disciplinary syntheses by Bellwood (1978, 1997), Kirch (1997, 2000), Shutler and Marck (1975), Pawley (2002) and Spriggs (1997). See also the references in the section on Austronesian lexical reconstructions. However, none of these works explicitly examines the lexical evidence pertaining to questions (1)-(3).

3. For a fuller bibliography of comparative historical works on Oceanic see Lynch et al. (2002).

4. Of course the words reconstructed for each stage are not all retentions from earlier stages. In every language there is constant lexical change: over time some words are completely lost and others undergo shifts of meaning. For example, about 140 fish names have been reconstructed for POc (Ross et al. in prep.). Of these, 85 have reflexes in PCP and about 57 in PPn (Ross et al. in prep.). That is to say, according to these data, PCP lost about 40 % of the fish names reconstructed for POc and PPn lost about 60 %. The interval between POc and PPn was probably on the order of 1500 years - plenty of time to accumulate many changes.

5. Spriggs (pers.comm.) suggests that, given that the Lapita language became a badge of membership in the new prestige society in the Bismarck Archipelago, non-Austronesian speakers had to acquire it 'properly', without lots of foreignisms, and that this would explain why we don't find traces of extensive borrowing in POc or its immediate descendants. Unfortunately this claim, which assumes nativelike transmission in all cases, is not falsifiable linguistically. Indirect evidence for it must be sought in the genetic makeup of populations of Oceanic speakers.

References

Allen, J. and C. Gosden (eds) 1991. *Report of the Lapita Homeland Project*. Canberra: Department of Prehistory, Research School of Pacific Studies, The Australian National University. Occasional Papers in Prehistory 20.

Allen, J. and C. Gosden 1996. Spheres of Interaction and Integration: Modeling the Culture History of the Bismarck Archipelago. In J. Davidson, F. Leach, G. Irwin, A. Pawley and D. Brown (eds), *Oceanic Culture History: Essays in Honour of Roger Green*, pp. 183-197. Wellington: New Zealand Journal of Archaeology Special Publication.

Allen, J. and P. White 1989. The Lapita Homeland: Some New Data and an Interpretation. *Journal of the Polynesian Society* 98(2):129-146.

Bellwood, P. 1978. *Man's Conquest of the Pacific*. London: Collins.

Bellwood, P. 1995. Austronesian Prehistory in Southeast Asia: Homeland, Expansion and Transformation. In P. Bellwood, J. Fox and D. Tryon (eds), *The Austronesians*, pp. 96-111. Canberra: Department of Anthropology, Research School of Pacific Studies, The Australian National University.

Bellwood, P. 1997. *The Prehistory of the Indo-Malaysian Archipelago*. (2nd edition). Honolulu: University of Hawaii Press.

Bellwood, P. and E. Dizon 2005. The Batanes Archaeological Project and the "Out of Taiwan" Hypothesis for Austronesian Dispersal. *Journal of Austronesian Studies* 1(1):1-33.

Bender, B. 1971. Micronesian Languages. In T.E. Sebeok (ed.), *Current Trends in Linguistics*, pp. 426–465. Vol. 8. Oceania. The Hague: Mouton.

Bender, B. and J. Wang 1985. The Status of Proto-Micronesian. In A. Pawley and L. Carrington (eds), *Austronesian Linguistics at the 15th Pacific Science Congress*, pp. 53-92. Canberra: Pacific Linguistics.

Bender, B., F. Jackson, J.C. Marck, K. Regh, H-M. Sohn, S. Trussel and J. Wang 2003. Proto-Micronesian Reconstructions - I. *Oceanic Linguistics* 42(1):1-110. Proto-Micronesian Reconstructions - II. *Oceanic Linguistics* 42(2):271-358.

Biggs, B. 1965. Direct and Indirect Inheritance in Rotuman. *Lingua* 15:383-415.

Biggs, B. and R. Clark 2006. POLLEX. Proto Polynesian Lexicon. Computer files. School of Languages and Linguistics, University of Auckland.

Blust, R. 1970. Proto-Austronesian Addenda. *Working papers in Linguistics, University of Hawaii* 3(1):1-107 and Proto-Oceanic Addenda with Cognates in non-Oceanic Languages. *Working Papers in Linguistics, University of Hawaii* 4(1):1-43, 4(8):1-17.

Blust, R. 1972a. Proto-Oceanic Addenda with Cognates in Non-Oceanic Languages. *Working Papers in Linguistics, University of Hawaii* 1(10):27-62.

Blust, R. 1972b. A Note on PAN *qa(R)(CtT)a 'outsiders, alien people'. *Oceanic Linguistics* 11(2):166-171.

Blust, R. 1976. Austronesian Culture History: Some Linguistic Inferences and their Relation to the Archaeological Record. *World Archaeology* 8(1):19-43.

Blust, R. 1977. The Proto-Austronesian pronouns and Austronesian Subgrouping: A Preliminary Report. *University of Hawaii Working Papers in Linguistics*, 9.2:1-15.

Blust, R. 1978a. Eastern Malayo-Polynesian: A Subgrouping Argument. In S.A. Wurm and L. Carrington (eds), *Second International Conference on Austronesian Linguistics: Proceedings*, pp. 181-234. Canberra: Pacific Linguistics.

Blust, R. 1978b. *The Proto-Oceanic Palatals*. Auckland: Polynesian Society.

Blust, R. 1980a. Austronesian Etymologies - I. *Oceanic Linguistics* 19:1-181.

Blust, R. 1980b. Early Austronesian Social Organization. *Current Anthropology* 21(2):205-247.

Blust, R. 1981. Variation in Retention Rates among Austronesian Languages. Paper presented to Third International Conference on Austronesian Linguistics, Bali, August 1981.

Blust, R. 1982. The Linguistic Value of the Wallace Line. *Bijd. Taal, Land, Volkenkund*, 138(2-3):231-250.

Blust, R. 1983–84a. More on the Position of the Languages of Eastern Indonesia. *Oceanic Linguistics*, 22-23:1-28.

Blust, R. 1983-84b. Austronesian Etymologies - II. *Oceanic Linguistics* 22-23:29-149.

Blust, R. 1984. A Mussau Vocabulary, with Phonological Notes. In *Papers in New Guinea Linguistics* No. 23, pp. 159-208. Canberra: Pacific Linguistics.

Blust, R. 1985. The Austronesian Homeland: a Linguistic Perspective. *Asian Perspectives* 26:45-67.

Blust, R. 1986. Austronesian Etymologies - III. *Oceanic Linguistics* 25:1-123.

Blust, R. 1989. Austronesian Etymologies - IV. *Oceanic Linguistics* 28:111-180.

Blust, R. 1991. The Greater Central Philippines hypothesis. *Oceanic Linguistics*, 30:73-129.

Blust, R. 1993. Central and Central Eastern Malayo-Polynesian. *Oceanic Linguistics*, 32.2:241-293.

Blust, R. 1994. Austronesian Sibling Terms and Culture History. In A. Pawley and M. Ross (eds), *Austronesian Terminologies: Continuity and Change*, pp. 31-72. Canberra: Pacific Linguistics.

Blust, R. 1995a. Austronesian Comparative Dictionary. Computer files, Department of Linguistics, University of Hawaii.

Blust, R. 1995b. The Prehistory of the Austronesian-speaking Peoples. *Journal of World Archaeology* 9(4):453-510.

Blust, R. 1995c. The Position of the Formosan languages: Method and Theory in Austronesian Comparative Linguistics. In P. Li, C. Tsang, Y. Huang, D. Ho and C. Tseng (eds), *Austronesian Studies Relating to Taiwan*, pp. 585-650. Taipei: Academia Sinica.

Blust, R. 1996. The Linguistic Position of the Western Islands, Papua New Guinea. In J. Lynch and F. Pat (eds), *Oceanic Studies: Proceedings of the First International Conference on Oceanic Linguistics*, pp. 1-46. Canberra: Pacific Linguistics.

Blust, R. 1998. A Note on Higher-order Subgroups in Oceanic. *Oceanic Linguistics* 37(1):182-188.

Blust, R. 1999. Subgrouping, Circularity and Extinction: Some Issues in Austronesian Comparative Linguistics. In E. Zeitoun and P. J-K Li (eds), *Selected Papers from the 8th International Conference on Austronesian Linguistics*, pp 31-94. Taipei: Academia Sinica.

Bradshaw, J. 1995. How and Why Do People Change Their Languages? *Oceanic Linguistics* 34(1):191-202.

Burley, D. and S.P. Connaughton 2007. First Lapita Settlement and its Chronology in Vava'u, Kingdom of Tonga. *Radiocarbon* 49(1):131-137.

Burley, D., W.R. Dickinson, A. Barton and R. Shutler Jr. 2001. Lapita on the Periphery: New Data on Old Problems in the Kingdom of Tonga. *Archaeology in Oceania* 36(2):89-104.

Cashmore, C. 1969. Some Proto-Eastern Oceanic Reconstructions with Reflexes in Southeast Solomon Islands Languages. *Oceanic Linguistics* 8(1):1-25.

Chowning, A. 1991. Proto Oceanic Culture: the Evidence from Melanesia. In R. Blust (ed.), *Currents in Pacific Linguistics. Papers on Austronesian Languages in Honour of George W. Grace*, pp. 43–75. Canberra: Pacific Linguistics.

Clark, R. 1979. Language. In J.D. Jennings (ed.), *The Prehistory of Polynesia*, pp. 249-270. Canberra: The Australian National University Press.

Clark, R. 1994. Evolution, Migration and Extinction of Oceanic Bird Names. In A. Pawley and M. Ross (eds), *Austronesian Terminologies: Continuity and Change*, pp. 73-86. Canberra: Pacific Linguistics.

Clark, R. 2007. Proto North and Central Vanuatu Reconstructions. Computer Files. Dept of Applied Language Studies and Linguistics, University of Auckland.

Dempwolff, O. 1934-38. *Vergleichende Lautlehre des Austronesischen Wörtschaftzes*: 1. *Induktiver Aufbau einer indonesischen Ursprache* (1934). 2. *Deduktiver Anwendung des Urindonesichen auf austronesische Einzelsprachen* (1937). 3. *Austronesiches Wörterverzeichnis* (1938). Zeitschrift für Eingeborenen-Sprachen supplements 15, 17, 19. Berlin: Dietrich Reimer.

Dutton, T.E. and D.T. Tryon (eds) 1994. *Language Contact and Change in the Austronesian World*. Berlin: Mouton de Gruyter.Berlin.

Dye, T. 1983. Fish and Fishing on Niuatoputapu. *Oceania* 53:241-271.

French-Wright, R. 1983. Proto Oceanic Horticultural Practices. Unpublished MA thesis, Department of Anthropology, University of Auckland.

Geraghty, P. 1983. *The History of the Fijian Languages*. Oceanic Linguistics Special Publication 19. Honolulu: University of Hawaii Press.

Geraghty, P. 1986. The Sound System of Proto-Central-Pacific. In P. Geraghty, L. Carrington and S.A. Wurm (eds), *Focal II: Papers from the Fourth International Conference on Austronesian Linguistics*, pp. 289-312. Canberra: Pacific Linguistics.

Geraghty, P. 1989. The Reconstruction of Southern Oceanic. In R. Harlow and R. Hooper (eds), *VICAL 1: Oceanic Languages. Papers from the Fifth International Conference on Austronesian Linguistics*, pp. 141-156. Auckland: Linguistic Society of New Zealand

Geraghty, P. 1990. Proto Oceanic *R and its Reflexes. In J.H.C.S. Davidson (ed.), *Essays in Honour of G.B. Milner*, pp. 51-93. London: School of Oriental and African Studies/ University of Hawaii Press.

Geraghty, P. 1996. Problems with Proto Central Pacific. In J. Lynch and F. Pat (eds), *Oceanic Studies: Proceedings of the First International Conference on Oceanic Linguistics*, pp. 83-91. Canberra: Pacific Linguistics.

Golson, J. 1971. Lapita ware and its transformations. In R.C. Green and M. Kelly (eds), *Studies in Oceanic Culture History*, Vol. 2, pp. 67-76. Pacific Anthropological Records 12. Honolulu: Bernice P. Museum.

Grace, G.W. 1959. *The Position of the Polynesian Languages within the Austronesian (Malayo-Polynesian) Language Family*. Bloomington: International Journal of American Linguistics.

Green, R.C. 1979. Lapita. In J.D. Jennings (ed.), *The Prehistory of Polynesia*, pp. 7-60. Canberra: The Australian National University Press.

Green, R.C. 1991a. The Lapita Cultural Complex: Current Evidence and Proposed Models. In P. Bellwood (ed.), *Indo-Pacific Prehistory* Vol. 2, pp. 295-305. Canberra: Bulletin of the Indo-Pacific History Association.

Green, R.C. 1991b. Near and Remote Oceania - Disestablishing "Melanesia" in Culture History. In A. Pawley (ed.), *Man and a Half: Essays in Pacific Anthropology and Enthnobiology in Honour of Ralph Bulmer*, pp. 491-502. Auckland: The Polynesian Society.

Green, R.C. 1994. Archaeological Problems with the Use of Linguistic Evidence in the Reconstruction of Rank, Status and Social organization in Ancestral Polynesian Society. In A. Pawley and M. Ross (eds), *Austronesian Terminologies: Continuity and Change*, pp.171-184. Canberra: Pacific Linguistics.

Green, R.C. 1999. Integrating Historical Linguistics with Archaeology: Insights from Research in Remote Oceania. *Bulletin of the Indo-Pacific Prehistory Association*, 18:3-15.

Green, R. C. 2000. Lapita and the Cultural Model for Intrusion, Integration and Innovation. In A. Anderson and T. Murray (eds), *Australian Archaeologist: Collected Papers in Honour of Jim Allen*, pp. 372-392. Canberra: Coombs Academic Publishing.

Green, R.C. 2002. Rediscovering the Social Aspects of Ancestral Oceanic Societies through Archaeology, Linguistics, and Ethnology. In S. Bedford, C. Sand and D. Burley (eds), *Fifty Years in the Field. Essays in Honour and Celebration of Richard Shutler Jr's Archaeological Career*, pp. 21-36. Auckland: NZ Archaeological Association Monograph 25.

Green, R.C. 2003. The Lapita Horizon and Traditions: Signature for One Set of Oceanic Migrations. In C. Sand (ed.), *Pacific Archaeology: Assessments and Prospects. Proceedings of the International Conference for the 50th Anniversary of the First Lapita Conference (July 1952)*, pp. 95-129. Nouméa: Les Cahiers de l'Archéologie en Nouvelle-Calédonie, Vol. 15.

Hage, P. 1998. Was Proto-Oceanic Society Matrilineal? *Journal of the Polynesian Society* 107(4):365-379.

Hage, P. 1999a. Linguistic Evidence for Primogeniture and Ranking in Proto-Oceanic Society. *Oceanic Linguistics* 38:366-375.

Hage, P. 1999b. Reconstructing Ancestral Oceanic Society. *Asian Perspectives* 38:200-228.

Haudricourt, A. 1971. New Caledonia and the Loyalty Islands. In T.E. Sebeok (ed.), *Current Trends in Linguistics*, pp. 359–96. Vol. 8. *Oceania*. The Hague: Mouton.

Hockett, C.F. 1976. The Reconstruction of Proto Central Pacific. *Anthropological Linguistics* 18:187-228.

Hudson, E. 1989. All *Nggaun*. Oceanic Terms for 'Dog' In R. Harlow and R. Hooper (eds), *VICAL 1: Oceanic Languages. Papers from the Fifth International Conference on Austronesian Linguistics*, pp. 283-304. Auckland: Linguistic Society of New Zealand.

Irwin, G. 1981. How Lapita lost its pots: the question of continuity in the colonisation of Oceania. *Journal of the Polynesian Society* 90:481-494.

Irwin, G. 1992. *The Prehistoric Exploration and Colonization of the Pacific*. Cambridge: Cambridge University Press.

Jackson, F.H. 1983. The Internal and External Relationships of the Trukic Languages of Micronesia. PhD dissertation, Department of Linguistics, University of Hawaii.

Jackson, F.H. 1986. On Determining the External Relationships of the Micronesian Languages. In P. Geraghty, L. Carrington and S.A. Wurm (eds), *Focal II: Papers from the Fourth International Conference on Austronesian Linguistics*, pp. 201-238. Canberra: Pacific Linguistics.

Kennedy, J. 2007. Pacific Bananas: Complex Origins, Multiple Dispersals? *Asian Perspectives.*

Kennedy, J. and W. Clarke 2004. *Cultivated Landscapes of the Southwest Pacific.* RMAP Working Paper No. 50. Canberra: Resource Management in Asia-Pacific, Research School of Pacific and Asian Studies, Australian National University.

Kirch, P.V. 1995. The Lapita Culture of Western Melanesia in the Context of Austronesian Origins and Dispersal. In P. Li, C. Tsang, Y. Huang, D. Ho and C. Tseng (eds), *Austronesian Studies Relating to Taiwan*, pp. 255-294. Taipei: Academia Sinica.

Kirch, P.V. 1997. *The Lapita Peoples: Ancestors of the Oceanic World.* Oxford: Blackwell.

Kirch, P.V. 2000. *On the Road of the Winds: an Archaeological History of the Pacific Islands before European Contact.* Berkeley: University of California Press.

Kirch, P.V. and T. Dye 1979. Enthnoarchaeology and the development of Polynesian fishing strategies. *Journal of the Polynesian Society* 88:53-76.

Kirch, P.V. and R.C. Green 2001. *Hawaiki, Ancestral Polynesia: an Essay in Historical Reconstruction.* Cambridge: Cambridge University Press.

Levy, R. 1980. Languages of the Southeast Solomon and the reconstruction of proto-Oceanic. In P.B. Naylor (ed.) *Austronesian Studies: Papers from the Second Eastern Conference on Austronesian Languages*, pp. 213-222. Ann Arbor: University of Michigan Center for South and South-East Asian Studies.

Lichtenberk, F. 1986. Leadership in Proto Oceanic Society: Linguistic Evidence. *Journal of the Polynesian Society* 95(3):341-356.

Lichtenberk, F. and M. Osmond 1998. Food Preparation. In M. Ross, A. Pawley and M. Osmond (eds), *The Lexicon of Proto Oceanic.* Vol. 1. *Material Culture*, pp.143-172. Canberra: Pacific Linguistics.

Lynch, J. 1991. Pigs and Dogs in Island Melanesia. In A. Pawley (ed.), *Man and a Half: Essays in Pacific Anthropology and Enthnobiology in Honour of Ralph Bulmer*, pp. 421-432. Auckland: The Polynesian Society.

Lynch, J. 2001. *The Linguistic History of Southern Vanuatu.* Canberra: Pacific Linguistics.

Lynch, J., M. Ross and T. Crowley 2002. *The Oceanic Languages.* Richmond, Surrey: Curzon.

Marck, J.C. 2000. *Topics in Polynesian Language and Culture History.* Canberra: Pacific Linguistics.

Marck, J.C. in prep. a. Proto Oceanic kin terms. In M. Ross, A. Pawley and M. Osmond (eds), *The Lexicon of Proto Oceanic. The Culture and Environment of Ancestral Oceanic Society*: Vol. 5, *People and Society*. Canberra: Pacific Linguistics.

Marck, J.C. in prep. b. Proto Polynesian *kainanga 'Matrilineal Clan or Lineage; Populace'.

Milke, W. 1958. Ozeanische Verwandtschaftsnamen. *Zeitschrift für Ethnologie* 83:226-229.

Osmond, M. 1998a. Horticultural Practices. In M. Ross, A. Pawley and M. Osmond (eds), *The Lexicon of Proto Oceanic.* Vol. 1. *Material Culture*, pp. 115-142. Canberra: Pacific Linguistics.

Osmond, M. 1998b. Fishing and Hunting Implements. In M. Ross, M., A. Pawley and M. Osmond (eds), *The Lexicon of Proto Oceanic.* Vol. 1. *Material Culture.* pp. 201-232. Canberra: Pacific Linguistics.

Osmond, M. 2000. Proto Oceanic Insects: the Supernatural Association. In S.R. Fischer and W. Sperlich (eds), *Leo Pasifika: Proceedings of the Fourth International Conference on Oceanic Linguistics*, pp. 383-302. Auckland: Institute of Polynesian Languages and Literatures.

Osmond, M. in prep. Proto Oceanic Fish Names. In M. Ross, A. Pawley and M. Osmond (eds), *The Lexicon of Proto Oceanic. The Culture and Environment of Ancestral Oceanic Society*: Vol. 4 *Animals*. Canberra: Pacific Linguistics.

Osmond, M. and M. Ross 1998. Household Artefacts. In Ross, M., A. Pawley and M. Osmond (eds), *The Lexicon of Proto Oceanic.* Vol. 1. *Material Culture*, pp. 67-114. Canberra: Pacific Linguistics.

Ozanne-Rivierre, F. 1982. Langues de Hienghène et proto-oceanic: phonologie comparée. In A-G. Haudricourt and F. Ozanne-Rivierre (eds), *Dictionnaire thématique des languages de la region de Hienghène* (Nouvelle-Calédonie), pp. 9-61. Paris: SELAF.

Ozanne-Rivierre, F. 1992. The Proto Oceanic Consonantal System and the Languages of New Caledonia. *Oceanic Linguistics* 31(2):191-207.

Ozanne-Rivierre, F. 1995. Structural Changes in the Languages of Northern New Caledonia. *Oceanic Linguistics* 34(1):44-72.

Ozanne-Rivierre, F. and J-C. Rivierre 1989. Nasalization/oralization: Nasal Vowel Development and Consonant Shifts in New Caledonian Languages. In R. Harlow and R. Hooper (eds), *VICAL 1: Oceanic Languages. Papers from the Fifth International Conference on Austronesian Linguistics*, pp. 413-432. Auckland: Linguistic Society of New Zealand

Pavlides, C. and C. Gosden 1994. 35000 Year-old Sites in the Rainforests of West New Britain, Papua New Guinea. *Antiquity* 68:604-610.

Pawley, A. 1972. On the Internal Relationships of Eastern Oceanic Languages. In R.C. Green and M. Kelly (eds), *Studies in Oceanic Culture History*, vol. 3, pp. 1-142. Pacific Anthropological Records No. 13. Honolulu: Bishop Museum.

Pawley, A. 1982. Rubbishman, Commoner, Big-man, Chief? Linguistic Evidence for Hereditary Leadership in Proto-Oceanic Society. In J. Siikala (ed.), *Oceanic Studies. Essays in Honour of Aarne A. Koskinen*, pp. 33-52. Helsinki: The Finnish Anthropological Society.

Pawley, A. 1985. Proto-Oceanic Terms for 'Person': A Problem in Semantic Reconstruction. In V. Acson and R. Leed (eds), *For Gordon Fairbanks*, pp. 92-105. Honolulu: Oceanic Linguistics (Special Publication No. 20).

Pawley, A. 1996a. The Polynesian Subgroup as a Problem for Irwin's Continuous Settlement Hypothesis. In J. Davidson, F. Leach, G. Irwin, A. Pawley and D. Brown (eds), *Oceanic Culture History: Essays in Honour of Roger Green*, pp. pp. 387–410. Wellington: New Zealand Journal of Archaeology Special Publication.

Pawley, A. 1996b. On the Position of Rotuman. In B. Nothofer (ed.), *Reconstruction, Classification, Description- Festschrift in Honor of Isidore Dyen*, pp. 85–119. Hamburg: Abera-Verlag.

Pawley, A. 1996c. Proto Oceanic Terms for Reef and Shoreline Invertebrates. In J. Lynch and F. Pat (eds), *Oceanic Studies: Proceedings of the First International Conference on Oceanic Linguistics*, pp. 133-162. Canberra: Pacific Linguistics.

Pawley, A. 2002. The Austronesian Dispersal: Languages, Technologies, Peoples. In P. Bellwood and C. Renfrew (eds), *Examining the Farming/Language Dispersals Hypothesis*, pp. 251-273. Cambridge: McDonald Institute of Archaeological Research, Cambridge University.

Pawley, A. 2003. Locating Proto Oceanic. In M. Ross, A. Pawley and M. Osmond (eds), *The Lexicon of Proto Oceanic*, Vol. 2, pp.17-34. Canberra: Pacific Linguistics.

Pawley, A. 2005 The Meaning(s) of Proto Oceanic *panua. In C. Gross, H.D. Lyons and D.A. Counts (eds), *A Polymath Anthropologist: Essays in Honour of Ann Chowning*, pp. 133-145. Research in Anthropology and Linguistics Monograph 6. Auckland: Department of Anthropology, University of Auckland.

Pawley, A. 2006. Explaining the Aberrant Languages of Southeast Melanesia: 150 years of Debate. *Journal of the Polynesian Society* 115(3):215-258.

Pawley, A. 2007. Was There Early Lapita Settlement of the Solomon Islands? Bringing Linguistic Evidence to an Archaeological Debate. Paper presented at 7th International Conference on Oceanic Linguistics, Nouméa, July 2-6 2007.

Pawley, A. in prep. Patterns of Stability and Change in Oceanic Fish Names. In M. Ross, A. Pawley and M. Osmond (eds), *The Lexicon of Proto Oceanic. The Culture and Environment of Ancestral Oceanic Society*: Vol. 4 *Animals*. Canberra: Pacific Linguistics.

Pawley, A. and R.C. Green 1973. Dating the Dispersal of the Oceanic Languages. *Oceanic Linguistics* 12:1-67.

Pawley, A. and R.C. Green 1984. The Proto-Oceanic Language Community. *Journal of the Pacific History* 19(3):161-184.

Pawley, A. and M. Pawley 1994. Early Austronesian Terms for Canoe Parts and Seafaring. In A. Pawley and M. Ross (eds), *Austronesian Terminologies: Continuity and Change*, pp. 329-361. Canberra: Pacific Linguistics.

Pawley, A. and M. Ross 1995. The Prehistory of Oceanic Languages: a Current View. In P. Bellwood, J. Fox and D. Tryon (eds), *The Austronesians*, pp. 39-74. Canberra: Department of Anthropology, Research School of Pacific Studies, The Australian National University.

Rivierre, J-C. 1991. Loss of Final Consonants in the North of New Caledonia. In R. A. Blust (ed.), *Papers on Austronesian Languages and Ethnolinguistics in Honor of George Grace,* pp. 415-432. Canberra: Pacific Linguistics.

Ross, M. 1988. *Proto Oceanic and the Austronesian Languages of Western Melanesia.* Canberra: Pacific Linguistics.

Ross, M. 1992. The Sound System of Proto Austronesian: an Outsider's View of the Formosan Evidence. *Oceanic Linguistics* 31(1):23-64.

Ross, M. 1994. Central Papuan Culture History: Some Lexical Evidence. In A. Pawley and M. Ross (eds), *Austronesian Terminologies: Continuity and Change,* pp. 389-479. Canberra: Pacific Linguistics.

Ross, M. 1996a. Is Yapese Oceanic? In B. Nothofer (ed.), *Reconstruction, Classification, Description-Festschrift in Honor of Isidore Dyen,* pp. 121-166. Hamburg: Abera-Verlag.

Ross, M. 1996b. Reconstructing Food Plant Terms and Associated Terminologies in Proto Oceanic. In J. Lynch and F. Pat (eds), *Oceanic Studies: Proceedings of the First International Conference on Oceanic Linguistics,* pp. 163-221. Canberra: Pacific Linguistics.

Ross, M. 1996c. Contact-induced Change and the Comparative Method. In M. Durie and M. Ross (eds), *The Comparative Method Reviewed: Regularity and Irregularity in Language Change,* pp. 180-217. New York: Oxford University Press.

Ross, M. 2005. The Batanic Languages in Relation to the Early History of the Malayo-Polynesian Family. *Austronesian Studies* 1(2):1-24.

Ross, M. in press. The integrity of the Austronesian language family: from Taiwan to Oceania. In A. Sanchez-Mazas, R. Blench, M. Ross, I. Peiros and M. Lin (eds), *Past Human Migrations in East Asia: Matching Archaeology, Linguistics and Genetics.* London: Routledge Curzon.

Ross, M. and A. Naess 2007. An Oceanic Origin for Aiwoo, a Language of the Reef Islands? Paper read at 7th International Conference on Oceanic Linguistics, Nouméa, July 2007.

Ross, M., A. Pawley and M. Osmond (eds) 1998. *The Lexicon of Proto Oceanic.* Vol. 1. *Material Culture.* Canberra: Pacific Linguistics.

Ross, M., A. Pawley and M. Osmond (eds) 2003. *The Lexicon of Proto Oceanic. The Culture and Environment of Ancestral Oceanic Society*: Vol. 2 *The Physical Environment.* Canberra: Pacific Linguistics.

Ross, M., A. Pawley and M. Osmond (eds) in prep. *The Lexicon of Proto Oceanic. The Culture and Environment of Ancestral Oceanic Society*: Vol. 3 *Plants;* Vol. 4 *Animals;* Vol. 5 *People and Society.* Canberra: Pacific Linguistics.

Shutler, R. and J. Marck 1975. On the Dispersal of the Austronesian Horticulturalists. *Archaeology and Physical Anthropology in Oceania* 10:81-113.

Spriggs, M. 1996. What is Southeast Asian about Lapita? In T. Akazawa and E. Szathmary (eds), *Prehistoric Mongoloid Dispersals,* pp. 324-348. Oxford: Oxford University Press.

Spriggs, M. 1997. *The Island Melanesians.* Blackwell: Oxford.

Spriggs, M. 2003. Post-Lapita Evolutions in Island Melanesia. In C. Sand (ed.), *Pacific Archaeology: Assessments and Prospects. Proceedings of the International Conference for the 50th Anniversary of the First Lapita Conference (July 1952),* pp. 205-212. Les Cahiers de l'Archéologie en Nouvelle-Calédonie, Vol. 15. Nouméa: New Caledonia Museum.

Summerhayes, G. 2000a. *Lapita Interaction.* Terra Australis 15. Canberra: Archaeology and Natural History and the Centre for Archaeological Research, The Australian National University.

Summerhayes, G. 2000b. Recent Archaeological Investigations in the Bismarck Archipelago, Anir-New Ireland Province, Papua New Guinea. *Indo-Pacific Prehistory Bulletin* 19:167-174.

Summerhayes, G. 2001. Lapita in the Far West: Recent Developments. *Archaeology in Oceania* 36:53-63.

Tryon, D. 1994. Oceanic Plant Names. In A. Pawley and M. Ross (eds), *Austronesian Terminologies: Continuity and Change,* pp. 481-509. Canberra: Pacific Linguistics.

Walter, R. 1989. Lapita Fishing Strategies: a Review of the Archaeological and Linguistic Evidence. *Pacific Studies* 13(1):127-149.

White, P., J. Allen and J. Specht 1988. Peopling the Pacific: the Lapita Homeland Project. *Australian Natural History* 22:410-416.

Yen, D.E. 1991. Domestication: the Lessons from New Guinea. In A. Pawley (ed.), *Man and a Half: Essays in Pacific Anthropology and Enthnobiology in Honour of Ralph Bulmer*, pp. 558-569. Auckland: The Polynesian Society.

Zorc, D. 1994. Austronesian Culture History through Reconstructed Vocabulary (an Overview). In A. Pawley and M. Ross (eds), *Austronesian Terminologies: Continuity and Change*, pp. 595-624. Canberra: Pacific Linguistics.

3

Small islands in the big picture: the formative period of Lapita in the Bismarck Archipelago

Jim Specht

Anthropology Unit
Australian Museum Sydney
NSW 2010, Australia
jspecht@bigpond.com

Locations with dentate-stamped Lapita pottery are widely viewed as expressions of activities associated with 'settlements,' 'hamlets' or 'villages.' Such terms run the danger of concealing spatial diversity of function and differentiation of activities, with the obvious exception of burial grounds such as Teouma in Vanuatu (Bedford *et al*. 2006). Often this situation is the inevitable outcome of the small scale examination of sites, as commonly such small areas are sampled that it is impossible to discuss issues of site structure and spatial differentiation. The few exceptions to this approach include the RF-2 site in the SE Solomons (Green 1976; Green and Pawley 1998; Sheppard and Green 1991), the ECA complex on Eloaua Island (Kirch 1988a, 2001a), the Makekur site in the Arawe Islands (Gosden and Webb 1994), and SAC on Watom Island (Anson *et al*. 2005; Green and Anson 2000). In each case sampling programs and/or areal excavations allowed significant insights into the sedimentary history and internal organisation of human use of the areas. People do not conduct their lives in one spot, but distribute their activities across the landscape and, in coastal locations, the sea (e.g., Gosden 1989). No one locality is sufficient for gardening, fishing, hunting, raw material extraction, canoe building and other industrial production, food preparation and consumption, dying, trading and ceremonial or religious activities. While some activities leave distinctive or unique archaeological 'signatures,' others do not. The result is that a group of people generates a range of archaeological 'signatures' over time and space that may reflect these different activities, and the interpretation of these activities should be argued from the evidence, rather than by assumption. This applies particularly to Lapita period use of offshore islands. I propose in this paper that some very small islands in the Bismarck Archipelago might have been used for purposes other than day-to-day living, perhaps as places for the conduct of ritual or ceremonial activities. This invites consideration of a possible analogous relationship with the construction of stilt buildings over inter-tidal reefs, which seems characteristic of many Lapita pottery sites in Near Oceania (Felgate 2003; Gosden and Webb 1994; Kirch 1988a; Specht 1991; Wickler 2001).

Interpretations of dentate-stamped Lapita pottery sites in non-secular, religious or ceremonial terms have come to the fore over the last decade. Terrell and Welsh (1997:568) suggested that in the Bismarck Archipelago 'Lapita pots were culture elements in the material paraphernalia ...of some kind of cult, dance complex or social ritual.' Less specifically, Kirch (1997:147) noted possible differences in the functions of dentate-stamped decorated vessels and those with no decoration at the ECA site in the Mussau Islands, and Summerhayes (2000a:62) extended this possibility in utilitarian and non-utilitarian terms to the entire Bismarck Archipelago. Kirch (2001a: 103) also proposed that the 'special objects and ceramics' associated with the stilt structure of ECA/B could indicate that the building had a 'special-function.' The striking nature of the ECA/B finds led him to introduce the idea of 'house societies' as a potential organising principle for societies within the Lapita cultural complex (Kirch 1997:188-191), and Chiu (2003, 2005) explicitly used this concept in her study of New Caledonian Lapita pottery. Best (2002:98-100) speculated on the ideological basis of the Lapita design system and the rapid dispersal of Lapita potters, and invoked the possibility of 'a charismatic individual able to manipulate and enlarge an established hierarchical and religious system.' Spriggs (2002, 2003a) applied some of Best's ideas to the 'post-Lapita' period, suggesting that its beginning was not marked by the end of the dentate-stamped technique, but by the breakdown of the design system to the point where it became 'faceless' and presumably lost much of its meaning, even though dentate-stamped designs persisted (Spriggs 2002:55). Finally, Noury (2005) combined aspects of these authors' ideas, particularly 'house societies' and respect for the ancestors, in the context of funerary ritual.

This brief review of recent interpretations only scratches the surface, but illustrates that the non-secular role of some Lapita vessels and locations is firmly established in the literature. The comments of Terrell and Welsch, Summerhayes and Kirch relate directly to the Bismarck Archipelago, which for a long time has been regarded as the 'homeland' of the Lapita cultural complex (Allen 1984; Green 1979). The rest of this paper focuses on that region, but is not concerned with debates on ultimate origins or the introduction of Austronesian languages from insular Southeast Asia (e.g., Green 2003; Kirch 1996, 1997; Spriggs 1996, 1997; Terrell 1998). I accept that some aspects of the Lapita cultural complex had their origins outside the Bismarck Archipelago, but am not concerned with how they came into the Archipelago. The paper occasionally extends to Nissan Island in the north Solomons on account of that island's position between the Archipelago and more southerly expressions of Lapita (Spriggs 1991, 2000)[1].

This paper does not present new data, but reviews aspects of existing data and interpretations. It first looks at matters of dating. Once pottery production was established in the Bismarck Archipelago there was a 'pause' before dispersal into Remote Oceania. When did this 'Bismarck pause' occur and how long did it last? Next it reviews briefly various schemes used to describe the period of dentate-stamped pottery development in the Bismarck Archipelago and introduces the idea of a 'formative' period. The third part discusses the location of sites in the Archipelago and possible reasons for their selection, particularly those on offshore islands. Finally, it considers the pottery from various sites and suggests a possible interpretation of some locations on tiny islands and their possible humanly constructed equivalents in the form of structures over inter-tidal reefs.

How long was the 'Bismarck pause'?

The length of the pause in the Bismarck Archipelago is critical for understanding the developments that led to the formation of the Lapita phenomenon before its southerly dispersal into Remote Oceania. The temporal limits of this pause are set by the earliest dates for Lapita pottery in the Archipelago and for its presence to the south. Here I review briefly the evidence and offer a revised date of 3450-3350 cal. BP for the appearance of Lapita pottery that replaces the 3300-3200 cal. BP date that I once supported (Specht and Gosden 1997).

Kirch and Hunt (1988a:164) concluded that 'the Lapita horizon in Melanesia spans the period from ca 1600-500 BC,' and that there was no evidence for a substantial pause in the Bismarck Archipelago as required by Anson's (1986) proposal for a 'Far Western' stage. Additional evidence has led to a modified view and the pause is now variously estimated at between 200 to 400 years (e.g., Kirch 1997:58-62; Spriggs 2002:52). The initial date for the appearance of Lapita pottery in the Bismarck Archipelago, however, has remained an issue. Specht and Gosden (1997:188) questioned the 3550 cal. BP date preferred by Kirch and Hunt, and proposed 3300-3200 cal. BP in an attempt to resolve a discrepancy between the Mussau and New Britain dates, while allowing the possibility that pottery began in the Mussau group slightly before its appearance in New Britain. Green (2003: Fig. 3) and Summerhayes (2001a; 2004:Table 1) have opted for ca 3500 cal. BP. Kirch (2001b:219) now entertains an initial date possibly as late as 3350-3250 cal. BP, while noting that older results from ECA/A and ECB 'hint at settlement one or even two centuries earlier' than this, around 3550-3450 cal. BP.

All of these estimates were based on results from plant and marine shell samples. Marine shell samples are now recognised as being extremely problematic in the Bismarck Archipelago, as they require locality-specific ΔR values rather than the default value of 0±0 years or some generalised regional value (Kirch 2001b; Petchey et al. 2004, 2005:37). Unfortunately, few locality-specific values are available for the Archipelago, and those that are available display considerable variability (Kirch 2001b; Petchey et al. 2004, 2005; Summerhayes in press). On the other hand, the number of dates on plant-derived materials is now sufficient to discuss the initial date of Lapita pottery without reference to marine shell samples. In choosing this approach I assume that the oldest levels of the sites have been dated by plant-derived samples, though this may not always be so.

Table 1 presents 26 radiocarbon dates on charcoal, carbonised nutshells or wood from 11 sites in the Bismarck Archipelago and on Nissan Island. It includes 12 dates published after the Specht and Gosden (1997) review. The results have been calibrated with the atmospheric dataset of the CALIB 5.0.1 program (Reimer et al. 2004; Stuiver and Reimer 1993 [version 5]), expressed as 2σ ranges, with short-lived nutshell samples assigned a one-year growth span, and wood and charcoal samples a nominal ten-year growth span. The Table includes only samples excavated from stratigraphic units directly associated with plain or dentate-stamped Lapita pottery, and with the upper end of their 2σ age range exceeding 3000 years cal. BP for the highest probability distribution (HPD, p=1 or >0.9). The Table omits results with calibrated ranges that are clearly too old and/or with standard deviations exceeding 120 years that produce very large age spans. This cut-off point is arbitrary[2].

The calibrated ranges are ordered from oldest to youngest according to the upper end of their ranges. As with previous reviews the oldest dates with upper limits exceeding 3500 cal. BP (Beta-20453: 3573-3262 cal. BP; Beta-30864: 3563-2996 cal. BP) are from ECA and ECB, and have ranges exceeding the next oldest sample by over 150 years (Beta-20452: 3404-3060 cal. BP, from ECA/B). Beta-30864 has a large standard deviation that yields the widest age span (567 years) on Table 1. This span embraces the ranges of all but two of the next seven oldest dates, suggesting that we should not place too much reliance on this sample. Kirch (2001b:231) has reservations about Beta-20453 and raises the possibility of the sample including 'old wood' with in-built age. The next seven oldest dates, which have upper limits between 3300 and 3400 cal. BP, extend the geographical range of sites to the Anir group and to Nissan and Garua Islands. Three of these dates (Beta-72144, Wk-7563 and NZA-3734) are essentially the same as Beta-20452, though Kirch (2001b:214, 231) suggests that Beta-20452 could be from old wood, as its associated pottery seems to conflict with that found with Beta-30684 in another part of ECA.

The two oldest dates at ECA and ECB (Beta-20453, Beta-30864) thus contrast strongly with the main series of dates for the Bismarck Archipelago, which indicate that Lapita pottery was widespread throughout the Archipelago and on Nissan by or soon after 3400-3350 cal. BP. Leaving the two 'outlier' dates to one side for the moment, I suggest that the upper limit for Lapita pottery is likely to be about 3450-3400 cal. BP in the

Table 1. Radiocarbon dates on plant-derived materials for Lapita pottery deposits in the Bismarck Archipelago and on Nissan Island, arranged from oldest to youngest by their highest probability distribution (HPD) ranges. See text and endnote 2 for details of sample selection and calibration. 'WP isthmus' refers to the base of Willaumez Peninsula on New Britain. Sources: Eloaua – Kirch 2001b; Garua – Torrence and Stevenson 2000; Adwe and Anir – Summerhayes 2001a; Willaumez Peninsula isthmus – Specht and Torrence, this volume; Watom – Petchey et al. 2005; Nissan – Spriggs 2003b; Makada – White and Harris 1997.

Island or region	Site code	Excavation context	Material	Lab. code	CRA	Cal. range at 2σ	Cal. range at HPD	HPD prob.	HPD span
Eloaua	ECB	Unit 9, level 5	charcoal	Beta-20453	3200±70	3573-3261	3573-3261	1,000	312
Eloaua	ECA	W250N170 level 3	wood	Beta-30684	3100±110	3563-2996	3563-2996	1,000	567
Eloaua	ECA/B	W198N145, C3, post B30	wood	Beta-20452	3050±70	3438-3007	3404-3060	0,987	344
Garua	FYS	II, layer 5 spit 3	nutshell	Beta-72144	3060±60	3390-3078	3390-3078	1,000	312
Anir	ERA	TP1, spit 9	charcoal	Wk-7563	3075±45	3386-3162	3386-3201	0,964	185
Garua	FYS	II, layer 5 spit 4	nutshell	NZA-3734	3030±69	3381-3005	3381-3058	0,965	323
Anir	ERA	TP1, spit 6	charcoal	Wk-7561	3035±45	3361-3080	3361-3139	0,951	222
Nissan	DGD/2	Layer 4 (110-120cm)	charcoal	ANU-6809	2990±60	3347-2997	3347-2997	1,000	350
Eloaua	ECA/B	W200N150, post B1	wood	ANU-5790	2950±80	3400-2887	3340-2921	0,983	419
Eloaua	ECA/A	W200N120, III level 9	coconut shell	Beta-20451	2950±70	3335-2926	3335-2926	1,000	409
Eloaua	ECA/B	W199N151, post B2	wood	ANU-5791	2930±80	3329-2872	3271-2872	0,955	399
Eloaua	ECA	W250N140, level 6, post	wood	Beta-30682	2970±50	3327-2988	3270-2988	0,946	282
WP isthmus	FADC	LVI, layer 9 spit 3	nutshell	Wk-12845	2963±47	3320-2976	3265-2976	0,966	289
Eloaua	ECA/B	W200N150, levels 12-13	charcoal	ANU-5079	2840±115	3318-2751	3264-2751	0,992	513
Adwe	FOH	E2 spit 9	charcoal	ANU-11186	2800±110	3241-2740	3241-2740	1,000	501
Garua	FYS	II, layer 5 spit 1	nutshell	NZA-3733	2883±64	3216-2851	3216-2851	1,000	365
Adwe	FOH	TP21B, spit 13	charcoal	Beta-54165	2850±80	3209-2784	3172-2784	0,965	388
WP isthmus	FAAH	XVII, layer 9 spit 1	nutshell	Wk-10463	2880±59	3209-2859	3170-2859	0,960	311
Eloaua	ECA	W250N120, level 9, post	wood	Beta-30681	2860±60	3206-2808	3166-2844	0,976	322
Watom	SAC	G13, spit 2	coconut shell	Wk-7370	2860±60	3207-2844	3165-2844	0,975	321
Eloaua	ECA/C	W250N188, post C3	wood	Beta-30686	2850±70	3204-2791	3164-2791	0,983	373
Adwe	FOH	D3, spit 9	charcoal	ANU-11187	2730±100	3159-2542	3159-2700	0,977	459
Nissan	DGD/2	Layer 4 (100-110cm)	charcoal	ANU-8301	2820±70	3144-2771	3082-2771	0,948	311
WP isthmus	FAAH	XVII, layer 9 spit 3	nutshell	Wk-19190	2847±34	3067-2868	3067-2868	1,000	199
Garua	FSZ	13/92, layer 1/2	nutshell	NZA-6099	2781±68	3063-2758	3063-2758	1,000	305
Makada	SEP	TP2, layer 1	charcoal	SUA-3062	2730±80	3062-2729	3039-2729	0,991	310

Mussau group, and 3400-3350 cal. BP or slightly earlier in New Britain and New Ireland. For New Britain, this range falls squarely within the revised range of 3480-3200 cal. BP for the W-K2 volcanic event that devastated the central part of the island, and this suggests quite rapid re-colonisation of the area after the eruption (Petrie and Torrence in prep; Specht and Torrence, this volume). The difference of 50-100 years between the Mussau sites and those of New Britain-New Ireland may be more apparent than real, given the nature of radiocarbon dates and issues surrounding their calibration (Kirch 2001b:220). A slightly earlier date for Mussau, however, would be consistent with Kirch's claim for a red-slipped plain ware phase preceding the main dentate-stamped phase at ECA, an issue to which I return later. For this paper I use 3450-3350 cal. BP for the appearance of Lapita pottery in the Bismarck Archipelago.

The dispersal out of the Bismarck Archipelago is indicated by the oldest dates in more southerly sites. Pottery imported from New Britain and the New Ireland region (Dickinson 2006:Table 25D9, 113, 139) reached Nissan soon after its appearance in the Bismarck Archipelago (ANU-6809 on Table 1). This could represent the first stages of the dispersal, though we do not know whether the transfer of pottery to Nissan also involved the relocation of people. Further south, the next oldest dates are in the Reef Islands of the SE Solomons, where four charcoal dates for the RF-2 site are usually cited as a pooled mean of 3137-2826 cal. BP (Green 1991a:201, Table 3). Three of these dates have calibrated ranges older than the pooled mean (I-5747: 3357-2877 cal. BP; ANU-6476: 3275-2750 cal. BP; ANU-6477: 3210-2678 cal. BP). Three charcoal samples at the

Atanoasao site on Malo in Vanuatu have similar ranges: 3237-2754 cal. BP (Beta-110143), 3209-2885 cal. BP (Beta-110144) and 3141-2785 cal. BP (Beta-110146) (Galipaud 2000:49; Pineda and Galipaud 1998). In Fiji, the Bourewa site has two charcoal dates of 3205-2889 cal. BP (Wk-14237) and 3141-2868 cal. BP (Wk-14236) (Nunn et al. 2004). Considered together, these results suggest that the southerly dispersal of Lapita pottery began around 3250-3200 cal. BP, within 100-200 years of its appearance in the Bismarck Archipelago. The pause was thus probably slightly shorter than is currently accepted.

The 'formative' period

The initial scheme for dividing the Lapita phenomenon in time and space established Western and Eastern Lapita regions (Green 1979). Although these terms were geographical, the Eastern group of sites was acknowledged as younger than the Western ones. Anson (1986) introduced a 'Far Western Bismarck' stage preceding Western Lapita in the Bismarck Archipelago, adding a further temporal dimension to the geographical term. Spriggs (1995:116; 1997:70) made this more explicit by re-naming Anson's stage 'Early Western.' An alternative approach is based on temporal units (Early, Middle and Late Lapita), on the grounds that changes in Lapita pottery across its distribution were more correlated with time than with distance (Summerhayes 2000b, 2001b, 2001c). Green (2003:Fig. 3) later combined aspects of both time and space in his scheme of local Lapita traditions that had their own geographical and temporal dimensions.

Green's local traditions incorporated Kirch's (1996:65, 2001a:85, 2001b:219) suggestion of a red-slipped plain ware phase at ECA preceding the florescence of dentate-stamped decoration on Eloaua Island in the Mussau area, consistent with the proposed derivation of Lapita pottery from comparable wares in island Southeast Asia (Bellwood 1992; Kirch 1996:65, 1997:141). The dating of the putative ECA phase, however, relies heavily on the choice of ΔR value for calibrating marine shell dates and, as Kirch (2001b: 213-214, 219) acknowledged, the choice can affect results by several hundred years. The phase has not been identified in other parts of the Bismarck Archipelago, though red-slipped plain sherds and dentate-stamped sherds co-occur in the oldest levels of FYS and FEA in the Talasea area and at FAAH on the Willaumez Peninsula isthmus (Specht and Summerhayes in press; Specht and Torrence in press, this volume). While this absence could reflect the slightly younger dates for other Bismarck sites, I suggest below another interpretation.

Given the uncertainty about the earliest stages of Lapita pottery development in the Bismarck Archipelago, I suggest that it would be useful to adopt a more general term for the period under discussion, and refer to it as the 'formative period.' For adherents of the Lapita-as-new-people model, the formative period encompasses the time required for the 'integration' and 'innovation' aspects of the Triple-I model (Green 1991b, 2000, 2003). The period witnessed developments in the pottery and arguably other elements of material and social culture that laid the foundation for the later dispersal into Remote Oceania. It embraced the entire Bismarck region, as pottery comparable to that of ECA/B occurs in the Arawe Islands (Summerhayes 2000a, 2000b), the Duke of York Islands (White in press), the Talasea area (Specht and Summerhayes in press; Specht and Torrence in press), the Anir group (Summerhayes 2001a, 2001b), and on Nissan (Spriggs 1991:239, 1997:126)[3].

The location of Lapita sites

The most detailed studies of Lapita site locations remain those of Frimigacci (1980), who dealt in general terms with major landscape and seascape features, and Lepofsky (1988), who employed a site catchment analysis approach. Here I extend Lepofsky's (1988:Table 3.3) use of island size to look more closely at the islands on which Lapita sites occur. Lepofsky (1988:42) found that 'Lapita sites are more densely packed on small islands than on large ones,' but noted that 'it is difficult to evaluate what these results actually tell us about Lapita settlement patterns.' A particular problem facing her was the 'comparability of the surveys conducted on large islands with those on smaller ones.' Since her innovative paper, much new data has become available.

The regular occurrence of dentate-stamped Lapita pottery sites on small offshore islands or in coastal locations on large islands has long been acknowledged (Frimigacci 1980; Green 1979; Groube 1971; Spriggs 1984), though recent studies in New Britain and Fiji have revealed dentate-stamped pottery at inland and upland situations (Anderson et al. 2000, 2001:Table 1; Kumar 2002; Kumar and Nunn 2003; Specht and Torrence, this volume; Torrence and Stevenson 2000). The distribution of the earliest sites in the Bismarck Archipelago nevertheless remains heavily weighted towards coastal and offshore island situations, even after allowing for bias in site discovery strategies and post-Lapita geomorphic changes, especially on larger islands (Spriggs 1984, 1997:118; Torrence and Stevenson 2000).

Marked differences in the size of dentate-stamped pottery sites have also been acknowledged for a long time. Some of the smallest sites occur in caves and rock shelters, which naturally impose physical constraints on site size. Open sites, on the other hand, range from small (500-5000 m^2) to very large (>80,000 m^2) (Anderson et al. 2001:Table 1; Kirch 1997:167; Sheppard and Green 1991:100, Fig.18). These have been interpreted as settlements of different scales such as 'hamlets' or 'villages' (Green 1979:31; Kirch 1997:166-167; Kirch and Hunt 1988a:Table 2.1). Site size, however, reflects not only the number of people using a location, but also the activities undertaken and the length of use of a particular space, during which the locales of activities might have been periodically relocated. Examples of this are expressed at ECA and ECB on Eloaua and FOH on Adwe in the Bismarck Archipelago, where relocation of activities over time was possible as lowering of sea level and prograding shorelines created new land (Gosden and Webb 1994:Fig.8; Kirch 1988a, 2001a:Figs. 4.45, 4.47). This progressive relocation of activities resulted in a horizontal stratigraphy covering several centuries. In such situations it is inappropriate to assume that the total area now covered by cultural refuse of the Lapita period was occupied or used at any one time.

The kinds of landscape changes identified on Eloaua and Adwe increased the land area of the islands, though the islands remained small. But how big is a 'small' island? Many authors use 'small' without reference to a scale by which the reader can assess what they mean. Boduna Island (~1 ha.), for example, is small relative to Garua Island (~9 km^2), but Garua in turn is small relative to New Britain (~41,000 km^2) (Table 2). The same applies to Adwe, Pililo and Kumbun Islands relative to New Britain, Eloaua and Emananus relative to Mussau, Makada relative to Duke of York Island and both relative to New Britain and New Ireland, and Babase relative to Ambitle. Unspecific terms such as 'large' and 'small' obscures these differences.

The capacity to locate and occupy successfully remote small landmasses has been one of the defining features of Pacific peoples throughout their history (Kirch 2000), though the degree of isolation and size of an island can set severe constraints on the ability of a population to survive and expand. This is particularly true of atolls that have limited land area and even more limited natural resources (Pisarik 1975; Weisler 2001a, 2001b). This is not the case in the Bismarck Archipelago, where Lapita sites on islands are always close to a larger landmass and inter-island visibility is the norm. Occupants of offshore islands were not dependent solely on the resources immediately available to them, but could exploit those of larger nearby islands either directly or through exchange.

On Table 2 the islands in the Bismarck Archipelago with dentate-stamped pottery are arranged in four arbitrary groups that represent current size and not that at the time of Lapita use: those 1 km^2 or less in area, those between 1 km^2 and 10 km^2, those between 10 km^2 and 50 km^2, and those above 50 km^2. New Ireland and New Britain are included for contrasts of scale, and the numbers of sites are approximate only, as it is not always clear whether adjacent locations with dentate-stamped sherds should be treated as one or more sites. The Table suggests a slight preference for islands less than 10 km^2 in area (49 sites out of 91), though sample

Table 2. Sizes of islands in the Bismarck Archipelago where pottery of the Lapita ceramic series has been recovered. The data are drawn from literature statements and topographic maps, and are approximate only. Numbers in brackets with each entry indicate the number of locations where pottery has been recovered.

	Less than 1 km²	1 to 10 km²	10 to 50 km²	>50 km²
Siassi Is.		Tuam 2 km² (1)		
New Britain				41,000 km² (~20)
Arawe Is.	Adwe 8 ha. (1)	Agussak 1.25 km² (1)		
		Pililo 2.5 km² (1-2)		
		Maklo 3 km² (1)		
		Kumbun 5 km² (2)		
Kandrian		Apugi ~2 km² (2)		
Kove Islands	Kautaga <1km² (1)			
	Poi <1 km² (2)			
	Talagone <1 km² (1)			
	Kalapiai <1 km² (2)			
	Kou <1 km² (1)			
Willaumez Pen.	Boduna 1 ha. (1)	Garua 9 km² (~7)		
	Depa 1 ha. (1)			
	Valahia 1 ha. (1)			
	Lagenda ~1.5 ha. (1)			
	Langu ~2.5 ha. (1)			
	Numundo ~5 ha. (1)			
	Garala ~6 ha. (1)			
Watom			Watom 14 km² (3+?)	
Duke of York Is.	Utuan 0.5 km² (1)	Mioko 1.5 km² (4)	Duke of York 50 km² (8)	
	Kabakon <1 km² (1)	Kerawara 1.5 km² (2)		
		Makada 3 km² (3)		
		Ulu 5 km² (2)		
New Ireland				9,600 km² (~3)
Mussau Is.	Boliu ~1 km² (1)	Emananus 4 km² (1)		Mussau 350 km² (1)
		Eloaua 5-7.5 km² (2)		
Tanga Is.		Lif 2 km² (1)		
Anir Is.			Babase 30 km² (2)	Ambitle 107 km² (3)
Manus Is.	Mouk ~20 ha. (1)		Baluan 25 km² (1)	Manus 2,500 km² (1)
Totals	~18	~31	~14	~28

bias is almost certainly a factor (Lepofsky 1988:42; Spriggs 1984). The Table also suggests that if dentate-stamped pottery occurs on an offshore island, it is also likely to occur on a nearby larger one. The Talasea area of New Britain is a good example of this. The area has been intensively surveyed over 30 years, and has records of 18 locations with dentate-stamped pottery and 13 others with pottery but not dentate-stamped sherds (Specht and Torrence in press:Tables 1, 2). Five of the seven islands in Garua Harbour have dentate-stamped pottery (Boduna, Lagenda, Langu, Garala and Garua). Of these, only Garua (9 km²) is larger than 6 ha. The nearby mainland of Willaumez Peninsula has seven dentate-stamped pottery locations (under New Britain on Table 2), which include at least one early site (FCR/FCS; Specht 1974, in press) that Anson (1986) placed in his 'Far Western' group. The location of dentate-stamped sites, then, is not necessarily a function of time. From the earliest presence of dentate-stamped Lapita pottery in this area, people did not confine their activities to offshore islands but were using, if not occupying, the adjacent mainland.

This raises the question why people making and using Lapita dentate-stamped pottery chose to use offshore islands, especially those less than 1 km² in area. Several possible answers can be considered. The first is suggested by the reconstructed coastal histories in the Arawe and Mussau Islands (Gosden and Webb 1994:Fig. 8;

Kirch 1988a, 2001a:Fig. 4.45). In many areas prior to and during the early stages of Lapita pottery sea level was 1-1.5 m higher than at present and there were no beaches above high tide level suitable for occupation (Kirch 1997:163-165; Spriggs 1997:119-120). Settlement at sea level, therefore, was only possible by the construction of stilt settlements over the reef flat, as still occurs in parts of Near Oceania. The availability of a small island of only a few hectares in area, yet close to a larger and more resource-rich island, could have been an attractive alternative.

A second answer assumes that the makers of Lapita pottery were immigrants to the Bismarck Archipelago and suggests that existing populations prevented or discouraged Lapita settlement on larger landmasses (e.g., Bellwood 1978:55; Kirch 1997:166; Irwin [1981:483] expresses a contrary view). Offshore islands not claimed or used by the existing populations were available for the immigrants as living space, and provided a degree of security from potential aggression by those on the mainland who might have objected to their presence. Spriggs (1997:88) describes this as 'a defensive posture.' While this view has some appeal, it fails as a blanket answer because there is clear evidence of pre-Lapita use of Pililo and Kumbun Islands in the Arawe group (Gosden and Webb 1994; Gosden et al. 1994; cf. Specht and Gosden 1997:189), and on Nissan (Spriggs 1991). In the Mussau group, Kirch (2001a:60) specifically sought evidence for a pre-Lapita presence but was unsuccessful. While the lack of rail bones in excavated avifaunal assemblages could indicate pre-Lapita activity in the area (Steadman and Kirch 1998), other explanations are possible (Steadman 2006:128). The absence of evidence for pre-Lapita use of other offshore islands is arguably a reflection of the lack of targeted investigation. Furthermore, the 'defensive posture' line of reasoning does not apply to the Willaumez Peninsula and its adjacent islands, as this region was devastated around 3480-3200 cal. BP by deep tephra deposits from the W-K2 eruption that would have caused depopulation of the area. There is no evidence for re-settlement of the Peninsula and the adjacent islands before the appearance of people with Lapita pottery (Specht and Torrence this volume). This could explain why the FCR/FCS site was established on the mainland: in human terms, it was 'empty' space. It does not explain, however, why some people found it necessary or desirable to place themselves on the tiny islands of Garua Harbour, unless environmental conditions on the mainland made the coastline an unsuitable or unhealthy living environment. Emplacement of the W-K2 tephra and its subsequent erosion caused landscape changes in the isthmus area by infilling a shallow embayment and creating coastal swamps (Boyd et al. 2005). Comparable landscape changes could have occurred locally in parts of the Talasea area.

This takes us to the final reason for Lapita use of offshore islands: the avoidance of disease or discomfort caused by mosquitoes (and sandflies), as people on islands would 'catch more of the cooling breezes' that discourage mosquitoes, particularly Anopheline mosquitoes that are malaria vectors and which have limited ability to disperse across water (Kirch 1997:110-113; Spriggs 1997:120)[4]. The use of islands in Garua Harbour could have begun as a result of people at mainland locations seeking to avoid mosquito and malaria problems caused by conversion of the coastal zone into swamps after the W-K2 eruption. Occupation of offshore islands and construction of 'artificial islands' has long been seen as a strategy for avoidance of malaria-carrying mosquitoes and sandflies, as well of enemies (Groves 1934:47; Ivens 1930:54; Parsonson 1965, 1968), though Chowning (1968) warns against over-emphasising the impact of malaria on human populations in Near Oceania. My personal experience is that mosquitoes and malaria can be as troublesome on offshore islands as at coastal mainland locations, particularly as many present-day villages on offshore islands in the New Britain region are on the leeward side facing the mainland, and do not necessarily catch night breezes. It is precisely in these sheltered, leeward sides of islands that Lapita pottery sites occur in the Arawes, around Kandrian and in Garua Harbour. Indeed, the distribution of pottery sites in the Talasea area generally suggests that shelter from bad weather was probably a major consideration in site selection (Specht and Torrence in press). This is reinforced by the fact that people today do not use tiny islands in Garua Harbour for permanent settlements, though some have useful functions for occasional small gardens or short-term fishing camps. Perhaps tiny offshore islands with Lapita pottery sites also had non-residential functions. I explore this possibility in the next section.

The use of offshore islands in the formative period

Kirch's (1988a, 2001a:136, Fig. 4.47) reconstruction of the geomorphological history of the Mussau Lapita sites suggests that ECB was a stilt village in the inter-tidal zone of a small islet across a reef flat from a similar village at ECA on the main part of Eloaua[5]. During or after the Lapita period the islet and Eloaua were united by a slight fall in sea level and silting of the channel between them. Kirch (2001b:214) places the earliest level of ECB at about the same age as Zone C1 (*sic*) at ECA/B, somewhat later than the ECA/A palaeobeach. This is based on the nature of the pottery from these areas, rather than radiocarbon dates, and allows time for the proposed red-slipped plain ware phase. While there are some difficulties with Beta-20453 from ECB and Beta-30684 from W250N170 at ECA, as discussed above, their ranges overlap that of Beta-20451 at ECA/A (Table 1), and this perhaps indicates that the three areas were used more or less at the same time. This, however, would seem to conflict with the nature of their pottery.

ECA/A is dominated by red-slipped plain ware, with only two dentate-stamped sherds, and W250N170 has only 'small quantities of plain ware ceramics' (Kirch 2001a:85, 2001b:229). The more extensive excavations at ECA/B yielded over 2400 decorated sherds, and ECB is described as having 'significant quantities of fine dentate-stamped pottery' (Kirch 2001a: Tables 4.1 and 4.3, 85; 2001b:214)[6]. While the difference in pottery could be a function of time or sample bias, Best (2002:97) suggests that it could reflect contemporary but different activities. The assemblage of ECA/A comprises mostly plain large jars with restricted orifices and everted rims, whereas that associated with the stilt structure of Zone C at ECA/B displays a diverse range of forms and decoration, including the now-famous cylinder stand (Kirch 2001a:85, 102-103). Zone C also produced a range of shell ornaments and an anthropomorphic figure carved from bone (Kirch 1988b, 2001a:103). This richness of finds led Kirch to suggest that this stilt structure might have been a 'special-function structure' (Kirch 2001a:103), and he further observed that

> we must not ignore the fact that the Zone C deposits also contain heavy concentrations of shell and bone midden, oven stones, and food preparation equipment (scrapers and peeling knives). Thus food preparation (and consumption) was also a major activity at this structure.

This 'major activity' need not have been part of the daily round of survival, as food preparation and consumption have long been, and continue to be, essential elements of ceremonial and religious events in many cultural contexts within the Pacific Islands and beyond. We have, then, the possibility that the restricted range of forms among the ECA/A pottery is the result of domestic activities, whereas the remarkable ECA/B finds represent spatially differentiated 'major' activities of some religious or other ceremonial nature (cf. Kirch 1997:172-175). This could also apply to the pottery of ECB and perhaps EHB, where the pottery is a 'fine-dentate stamped assemblage with a high percentage of pedestalled bowls' (Kirch 2001b:219).

Separation of activities could also be reflected in the Talasea area of New Britain. Pottery from the lagoon floor and inter-tidal zone of FEA at Boduna Island differs in terms of vessel forms, aspects of decoration and sherd thickness from that excavated in 1989 (Specht and Summerhayes in press; White *et al.* 2002). Whereas the excavated assemblage has much in common with surface collections from the FCR/FCS site on the mainland (Specht in press), the FEA surface sherds are thick and come from large vessels of complex forms, including a cylinder stand and bowl-on-stand (Kirch's 'pedestalled bowl') (Specht and Summerhayes in press)[7]. With one exception, complex forms have been recorded in the Talasea area only on Boduna, Garala and Langu, each 6 hectares or less in area. The exception is a complex rim sherd from the mainland beach location of FDK (Specht and Torrence in press)[8]. The pottery sample from the early FYS site on Garua Island is too small for meaningful comparisons, but its few distinctive features seem consistent with FCR/FCS and the FEA excavated material. Further south in the isthmus area of Willaumez Peninsula, the only sherd from a complex form (probably a cylinder stand) came from Numundo Island (about 5-10 ha). There are none in the

1300-plus sherds excavated at the adjacent hilltop site of FAAH. A similar spatial separation might apply in the Duke of York Islands between New Britain and New Ireland. In his review of Lapita pottery sites in this island group, White (in press) observes that

> Among the sites there are two pairs, obvious in terms of their location on opposite sides of narrow sea channels. In each case, one site seems satellite to the other – SEF to SEE and SFF to SDQ – in the sense of having fewer sherds distributed over a smaller area.

This 'satellite' relationship recalls the positions of ECA and ECB prior to the silting of the channel between them, and could be repeated at ERA and ERG in the Anir Islands (Summerhayes 2001c:Fig. 3). It also recalls the distinction between the excavated and surface collections of FEA. Is it possible that during the formative period there were two kinds of contemporary Lapita pottery locations with different roles that are reflected in their associated pottery, one with a ritual or ceremonial function, the other a more mundane, domestic role (cf. Kirch 1997:172)?

I turn now to evidence for the function of the pottery. Residue analyses of plain sherds from ERA in the Anir group and Uripiv Island in Vanuatu suggest that some vessels were used in association with cooking or consumption of aroids, possibly taro (Crowther 2005; Horrocks and Bedford 2005; Bedford, personal communication). In both cases the sherds could represent the use of undecorated vessels for domestic food preparation and consumption. Bearing in mind Kirch's (2001a:103) observations on food preparation and consumption at ECA/B, perhaps highly decorated vessels were used in relation to food in non-domestic contexts, though not necessarily for cooking or storage (Kirch 1997:140; cf. Chiu 2003:242 and Summerhayes 2001c). Here the cylinder stands, pedestal stands and flat-based bowls are relevant. These occur widely, though in small numbers, in the Bismarck Archipelago and the nearer archipelagos of Remote Oceania: ECA in the Mussau group (Kirch 1997:Plate 1.1, Fig. 5.5; 2001a: Fig. 4.26); FEA on Boduna Island and Numundo Island of New Britain (Specht and Summerhayes in press; Specht and Torrence this volume); possibly SAC on Watom Island (Best 2002:82); EAQ in the Anir group (Best 2002:82); RF-2 in the Reef Islands (Best 2002:82, Fig. 25); and among the burials at Teouma in Vanuatu (Bedford *et al.* 2006:819). There is a possibly related form in the Arawe Islands (Summerhayes 2000b:Fig. 6.2), though Bedford *et al.* (2006:821) appear to discount this example. Cylinder stands seem absent from New Caledonia, though 'descendants' may occur there (Best 2002:82, citing C. Sand personal communication). More recently, Bedford *et al.* (2006:821) have confirmed their presence.

Kirch (1997:139-140, 294 footnote 16) interprets cylinder stands as possible supports for open bowls. This seems feasible, as circular grooves on the bases of some flat-based open bowls at Teouma (Bedford *et al.* 2006:819) and WKO013A in New Caledonia (Chiu 2003:174) are about the same diameter as the cylinder stand tops. In the Arawe Islands a flat base sherd has a circular ridge that could have served the same function as a groove (Summerhayes 2000b:Fig. 5.33). Chiu (2003:242) suggests that dishes or bowls attached to pedestal stands might have been used for the display or serving of food. Bowls supported on cylinder stands could have served a similar purpose.

An alterative interpretation of cylinder stands is possible. The form recalls that of recent hourglass-shaped hand drums of wood found throughout the New Guinea-Bismarck Archipelago region (Kunst 1967: Endmap; McClean 1994:Figs 2a, 2b). These drums often have relief ribs around the narrow central part reminiscent of the relief bands on the ECA/B cylinder stand (Fischer 1983:Plates IX to XIII). The heads of these drums are plain and take a reptile or possum skin membrane (McClean 1994:4). The cylinder stands in the Mussau Islands also have plain tops (Kirch 1997:294 footnote 16) that seem well suited for the attachment of a membrane. In his landmark paper on face designs Spriggs (1990:119) suggested they could represent 'deities, chiefs, clan ancestors, and so on.' Kirch (1997:143-144) extended this to the pots themselves, which 'may conceivably have been regarded as representations of human beings, particularly ancestors' and related this to Lapita communities as 'house societies' (also Chiu 2005). Were cylinder stands some kind of sound-producing instrument, through which the ancestors or deities 'spoke'[9]? Such a function could be consistent with the recovery of cylinder stand fragments in association with the 'special-function structure' at ECA/B and in the Teouma burial ground.

This speculative suggestion is not necessarily extreme, as the Austronesian-speaking Adzera people of the upper Markham Valley of Papua New Guinea make pottery hand drums (Holzknecht 1957; May and Tuckson 1982:Fig. 6.18) [10]. Food-related and sound-producing uses, moreover, were clearly not the sole functions of decorated Lapita pots. At the Teouma site in Vanuatu some large, elaborately decorated vessels were used as ossuaries for secondary burials (Bedford *et al.* 2006). Were these vessels made explicitly for this use, or did they once have other functions but were re-purposed into funerary contexts [11]?

Discussion

There is wide acceptance of a period of development in Lapita pottery and presumably other elements of material and social culture in the Bismarck Archipelago. This I term the formative period of the Lapita cultural complex. On the basis of dates from plant-derived samples the period began about 3450-3350 cal. BP, and probably lasted no more than 100-200 years. Two dates for ECA and ECB in the Mussau group are still slightly older than those of southern New Ireland and New Britain, though whether the gap of 50-100 years between is real or a function of dating materials or techniques remains to be tested. Certainly by 3400-3350 cal. BP Lapita pottery sites were established throughout the Archipelago, and obsidian and finished pots or clays and tempers were being moved both locally and over considerable distances. The dispersal phase through southern Near Oceania into Remote Oceania began around 3250-3200 cal. BP.

Dentate-stamped Lapita sites occur on islands of all sizes in the Archipelago. Where they are on offshore islands, other Lapita pottery sites are almost always present on the adjacent 'mainland.' As early sites are in leeward locations, away from open sea or the prevailing bad weather direction, selection of their position may have had more to do with shelter than with avoidance of malaria or hostile neighbours. Of course, several factors could have come into play in the decision-making process, and not all of these were necessarily relevant to every context. Pililo, Kumbun and Nissan Islands were occupied or used long before the appearance of Lapita pottery and raise an intriguing question: if we accept the orthodox view that the introduction of pottery was the result of immigrants settling in the region, did these immigrants choose to live alongside pre-existing peoples on these islands in some kind of symbiotic relationship? This was not the case on the Willaumez Peninsula and its adjacent islands, where Lapita-using people were the first to re-colonise the area after the W-K2 eruption. In both situations, if we reject the orthodox view of immigrants, other scenarios come into play that have yet to be explored, but lie beyond the scope of this paper.

The suitability of offshore islands for the production of pottery is rarely addressed in considerations of Lapita pottery in the Bismarck Archipelago. In his prospectus for the Lapita Homeland project Allen (1984:188) observed that it is improbable that pottery was made on islands formed by elevated coral reef platforms, as they lack suitable clays. It is unlikely that the development of Lapita pottery took place solely on such islands in the Bismarck Archipelago, but must have also involved people living on geologically more complex islands. Allen's position can be questioned, as in recent times in Papua New Guinea potters on islands that lack suitable raw materials imported them from neighbouring islands or the New Guinea mainland (e.g., Bilbil, Yabob and Hus: May and Tuckson 1982:166, 330). The potters of the Amphlett Islands of SE Papua undertake a day's voyage to Fergusson Island to obtain clay (Lauer 1973:45), and on one such voyage 400 kg of clay was obtained (Lauer 1970:389). Furthermore, even when suitable clays do occur on offshore islands, potters sometimes seek better quality raw materials from elsewhere (e.g., Tumleo and M'buke: May and Tuckson 1982:310, 337). Similar situations probably existed in the time of Lapita pottery in the Bismarck Archipelago.

Compositional studies of Lapita pottery in the New Britain region have demonstrated widespread local movement of finished pots or raw materials between the mainland and adjacent offshore islands in the Arawes (Summerhayes 2000b:225-229), Duke of Yorks (Thomson and White 2000), on Boduna (Specht and Summerhayes in press), and on Watom (Dickinson 2000). There is also evidence for transport of pots or raw materials over longer distances throughout the Archipelago during the formative period. Summerhayes (2000b: Fig. 11.36) identified movement between the Arawes and Garua Harbour and vice-versa. All of the Lapita pottery on Nissan was imported from Buka and the New Britain-New Ireland region (Spriggs 1991:239, 1997:126; Dickinson 2006:Table 25D9, Appendix Table A1). At the Lapita sites in the Mussau Islands, Hunt (1989:213, 215; cf. Kirch *et al.* 1991:159) concluded that between 88 % and 100 % of the pottery was of non-local origin, with some probably originating from the Manus area. Dickinson (2006:76, Table 25E5-7, Appendix Table A1) extended this to include the Tabar-Lihir-Tanga-Feni Islands off the east coast of New Ireland, with Tanga also contributing to the Anir group to the south. Dickinson (2000:177, 2006: Table 25C2) has further suggested a possible Manus and New Ireland-New Hanover origin for some Watom pottery.

This widespread transport of pottery across the entire Archipelago emphasises the connectedness of Lapita pottery-using communities that is also indicated by the distribution of obsidian from the New Britain and Manus sources (Kirch 1997:242-246; Summerhayes 2001b, 2003, 2004). We do not know whether this connectedness, which lasted for several hundred years, involved only finished pots or the raw materials, with or without the potters themselves (Summerhayes 2001a, 2001c). The high proportion of exotic pottery in the Mussau sites and the importation of all pottery to Nissan raise several questions. For example, what did the inhabitants of the islands receiving the pottery contribute to its development in the formative period? Were only completed pots transferred between the islands, or did potters and their raw materials move together? Can we assume that the transfer of pots or raw materials was between culturally, if not socially related communities? This invites reconsideration of the 'Lapita without pots' scenario (Spriggs 1991:237, 1997:111; cf. Green 1992). Were there production centres that supplied pottery to a local region, and over longer distances to Mussau and Nissan, in return for other commodities, materials or perhaps spouses? We can reasonably assume that if Lapita activity on tiny islands less than 10 hectares in area involved residential use, this must have been sustained by reliance on neighbouring larger landmasses for essential resources of food and materials, either by direct access or through exchange relationships with those resident on the larger landmasses. Were exchange relationships with members of the same or a different ethnolinguistic group? These and other questions have yet to be explored, especially in terms of how we might address them through the archaeological record (Specht and Torrence this volume).

The association of 'special objects and ceramics' with the stilt structure at ECA/B, and the contrast in the finds from this area and those from ECA/A and W250N170 might be repeated at other locations, such as Boduna and the Duke of York Islands. Perhaps the construction of buildings in the inter-tidal zone was an alternative to using tiny offshore islands. The linking of face designs and some vessel forms with deities or ancestors, and the possible use of cylinder stands as sound-producing instruments open opportunities for viewing at least some Lapita spaces as focal points of ceremonial or religious activity that required close association with the sea and comparative isolation from land.

Conclusions

The complex human history of the Bismarck Archipelago matches its complex geological history. The local environments of many Lapita sites in the Archipelago have undergone substantial post-depositional alteration as a result of natural processes and events, as well as sediment accumulation and disturbance due to human activities. Today's landscapes often bear little resemblance to those of the formative period, and there is clearly need for focused environmental histories such as those constructed for the Mussau Islands and the Arawes.

Improved chronologies are also essential for understanding the formative period, and could include re-dating of key locations to take advantage of the greater precision offered by the AMS technique. We need to understand better the internal structure of individual sites as a product of a complex range of human activities, and to disentangle the temporal relationships of sites in the same and different island groups. These are essential steps for testing suggestions about contemporary use of areas for different activities and the possibility of 'satellite' relationships between adjacent sites. Improved chronologies, however, will not be the complete answer. The degree of discrimination we need to address some questions may be beyond the capacity of radiocarbon dating to deliver, particularly if the duration of the formative period is encompassed by the age spans of calibrated results (cf. Kirch 2001b:220). Bayesian analysis of dates may assist, but this must be informed by detailed stratigraphic, stylistic and spatial studies of pottery and other categories of the archaeological record.

This paper has dealt with questions and speculations without resolving specific issues, but hopefully it has raised some potentially useful lines for further examination of the formative period of Lapita cultural complex in the Bismarck Archipelago. Pursuit of these, however, will require us to suspend orthodox views about the history and nature of the complex across its vast distribution, so we can focus on the increasingly complex record in the area of its initial expression. This hopefully will open new perspectives that are more nuanced than current models permit, and perhaps result in 'an unfamiliar Lapita' (Spriggs 2002:55) that also illuminates the wider picture.

Endnotes

1. I use 'Bismarck Archipelago' in the German-period sense to refer to the islands that today form the Manus, New Ireland and East and West New Britain Provinces of Papua New Guinea. Nissan was part of the 'deutsche Salomo-Inseln' ('the German Solomon Islands'), which I refer to here as the 'north Solomons' in a geographical sense. 'Solomon Islands' refers to the entire Solomon Islands chain without geo-political reference.
2. The potential number of plant-derived samples was more than the 26 included in Table 1. Samples with standard deviations greater than 115 years are excluded as they yield large calibrated age ranges (600-1360 years at 2σ) of limited value for defining the chronology of Lapita sites. Most samples selected have age spans of less than 400 years at the HPD; the four samples with standard deviations of 100-115 years have the largest age spans (459-567 years). The text does not take into account the effect of plateaux in the calibration curve around 3500-2500 cal. BP (Blackwell *et al.* 2006:411).
3. There is, of course, a terminological issue here. The vessel forms and designs and other cultural elements that were transported southwards during the initial dispersal would have been the same as in the Bismarck Archipelago and could therefore logically be seen as part of the 'formative' period. These close similarities applied only to the earliest stage of dispersal; each area subsequently diverged from the ancestral forms and took on distinctive local characteristics.
4. Parsonson (1965:14-15, 1968:571) included relative humidity, temperature and wind speed as factors in deterring mosquito activity, and observed a mosquito '600 yards out to sea,' though '50-60 yards of salt-water is sufficient to throw the mosquito "off the scent."' Groube (1993), Spriggs (1997:39-40, 103-104) and Kirch (1997:110-113, 292 footnote 45) discuss mosquitoes and malaria, including the impact of malaria on life expectancy, levels of immunity and possible genetic advantages in some populations.
5. The term 'village' is used explicitly in the title of the chapter describing research at ECA, ECB and EHB (Kirch 2001a).
6. The 6 m^3 excavated at ECA/A produced about 1500 sherds (~250 sherds/m^3), of which only two were decorated (Kirch 2001a:Table 4.1, 85). In contrast, the 17.6 m^3 excavated at ECA/B yielded nearly 24,000 sherds (~1350 sherds/m^3), about 10 % of which were decorated (Kirch 2001a:Table 4.3). Comparable data are not available for ECB.

7. The base of FEA is dated on marine shells to about 3340-3000 cal. BP, with ΔR=0±0 (Specht and Summerhayes in press). Ambrose and Gosden (1991:187) described the pottery recovered in 1985 as 'Western Lapita.' White *et al.* (2002) extended this to include 'Far Western Lapita.' The weathered nature of the Ambrose-Gosden sherds limits what can be said about them, but they are generally closer to the 1989 excavated sample than to the inter-tidal zone and lagoon floor collections. The expression 'complex forms' used in this paragraph refers to vessels with elaborated rims and/or markedly angular carinated shoulders, bowl-on-stand, pot stand and cylinder stand.
8. FDK is an inter-tidal location at the foot of a 40 m-high ridge running from Mt Kutau. The narrow 'coastal plain' here is primarily the result of landfill in the colonial period to construct a road between Talasea and settlements on the western side of Willaumez Peninsula. In Lapita times FDK was probably a locale over the inter-tidal reef flat.
9. Matthew Spriggs (personal communication) tells me he has discussed with several others the idea of cylinder stands as sound-producing instruments.
10. Garanger (1971:65, Fig. 2) compared the animal figurines of his 'Early Mangaasi' pottery with those on modern Adzera meat-cooking pots, where the animals represent a flying fox, bat, amphibians and birds (May and Tuckson 1982:142-143, Figs 6.16, 6.17). Bird figures have also been found on a dentate-stamped vessel at Teouma (Bedford *et al.* 2006:819), as well as 'human' heads at several other Lapita sites (Torrence and White 2001).
11. The Teouma cemetery provides the only evidence for the use of Lapita vessels as ossuaries. No vessels, complete or otherwise, were associated with the burials at SAC on Watom Island (Green *et al.* 1989) or at other locations where human remains of the dentate-stamped Lapita period have been recovered. A large bowl with paddle-impressed decoration of the 'Podtanean tradition' covered the skull of a burial at WKO013C (Valentin 2003:285). The 'pottery pit' at WKO013A in New Caledonia did not contain bones, but both main pots had part of their bases removed prior to insertion into the pits (Sand *et al.* 1998:37). Bedford (2006) has described a dentate-stamped pot from Vao in Vanuatu where the design was deliberately obscured by a white pigment. Perhaps the WKO013A and Vao vessels also played a role in mortuary or related rites?

References

Allen, J. 1984. In search of the Lapita homeland: reconstructing the prehistory of the Bismarck Archipelago. *Journal of Pacific History* 19(4): 186-201.

Ambrose, W.R. and C. Gosden 1991. Investigations on Boduna Island. In J. Allen and C. Gosden (eds), *Report of the Lapita Homeland Project*, pp.182-188. Canberra: Department of Prehistory, Australian National University. Occasional Papers in Prehistory 20.

Anderson, A., G. Clark and T. Worthy 2000. An inland Lapita site in Fiji. *Journal of the Polynesian Society* 109: 311-316.

Anderson, A., S. Bedford, G. Clark, I. Lilley, C. Sand, G. Summerhayes and R. Torrence 2001. An inventory of Lapita sites containing dentate-stamped pottery. In G.R. Clark, A.J. Anderson and T. Vunidilo (eds), *The Archaeology of Lapita Dispersal in Oceania*, pp. 1-13. Canberra: Pandanus Books, Research School of Pacific and Asian Studies, Australian National University. Terra Australis 17.

Anson, D. 1986. Lapita pottery of the Bismarck Archipelago and its affinities. *Archaeology in Oceania* 21(3): 157-165.

Anson, D, R. Walter and R.C. Green 2005. *A Revised and Redated Event Phase Sequence for the Reber-Rakival Lapita Site, Watom Island, East New Britain Province, Papua New Guinea.* Dunedin: Department of Anthropology, University of Otago. University of Otago Studies in Prehistoric Archaeology 20.

Bedford, S. 2006. The Pacific's earliest painted pottery: an added layer of intrigue to the Lapita debate and beyond. *Antiquity* 80: 544-557.

Bedford, S., M. Spriggs and R. Regenvanu 2006. The Teouma Lapita site and the early settlement of the Pacific Islands. *Antiquity* 80: 812-828.

Bellwood, P. 1978. *Man's Conquest of the Pacific. The prehistory of Southeast Asia and Oceania.* Auckland: Collins.

Bellwood, P. 1992. New discoveries in Southeast Asia relevant for Melanesian (especially Lapita) prehistory. In J-C. Galipaud (ed.), *Poterie Lapita et Peuplement*, pp. 49-66. Nouméa: ORSTOM.

Blackwell, R.R., C.E. Buck and P.J. Reimer 2006. Important features of the new radiocarbon calibration curves. *Quaternary Science Reviews* 25: 408-413.

Best, S. 2002. *Lapita: A view from the East*. Auckland: New Zealand Archaeological Association. Monograph 24.

Boyd, W.E., C.J. Lentfer and J. Parr 2005. Interactions between human activity, volcanic eruptions and vegetation during the Holocene at Garua and Numundo, West New Britain. *Quaternary Research* 64: 384-398.

Chiu, S. 2003. *The Socio-economic Functions of Lapita Ceramic Production and Exchange: A Case Study from Site WKO013A, Koné, New Caledonia*. Unpublished PhD thesis, University of California, Berkeley.

Chiu, S. 2005. Meanings of a Lapita face: materialized social memory in ancient house societies. *Taiwan Journal of Anthropology* 3(1): 1-47.

Chowning, A. 1968. The real Melanesia: a critique of Parsonson's theories. *Mankind* 6(12): 641-652.

Crowther, A. 2005. Starch residues on undecorated Lapita pottery from Anir, New Ireland. *Archaeology in Oceania* 40(2): 62-66.

Dickinson, W.R. 2000. Petrography of sand tempers in prehistoric Watom sherds and comparison with temper suites of the Bismarck Archipelago. *New Zealand Journal of Archaeology* 20 (1998): 161-182.

Dickinson, W.R. 2006. *Temper Sands in Prehistoric Oceanian Pottery: Geotectonics, Sedimentology, Petrography, Provenance*. Boulder: The Geological Society of America. Special Paper 406.

Felgate, M.W. 2003. *Reading Lapita in Near Oceania: Intertidal and Shallow Water Pottery Scatters, Roviana Lagoon, New Georgia, Solomon Islands*. Unpublished PhD thesis, University of Auckland, Auckland.

Fischer, H. 1983. *Sound-producing Instruments in Oceania*. Translated by P.W. Holzknecht and edited by D. Niles. Boroko (PNG): Institute of Papua New Guinea Studies.

Frimigacci, D. 1980. Localisation éco-géographique et utilisation de l'espace de quelques sites Lapita de Nouvelle-Calédonie. *Journal de la Société des Océanistes* 66-67 (36): 5-11.

Galipaud, J-C. 2000. The Lapita site at Atanoasao, Malo, Vanuatu. *World Archaeological Bulletin* 12: 41-55.

Garanger, J. 1971. Incised and applied-relief pottery, its chronology and development in Southeastern Melanesia, and extra-areal comparisons. In R.C. Green and M. Kelly (eds), *Studies in Oceanic Culture History vol. 2*, pp. 53-66. Honolulu: B.P. Bishop Museum. Pacific Anthropological Records 12.

Gosden, C. 1989. Prehistoric social landscapes of the Arawe Islands, West New Britain Province, Papua New Guinea. *Archaeology in Oceania* 24(2): 45-58.

Gosden, C. and J. Webb 1994. The creation of a Papua New Guinean landscape: archaeological and geomorphological evidence. *Journal of Field Archaeology* 21(1): 29-51.

Gosden, C., J. Webb, B. Marshall and G.R. Summerhayes 1994. Lolmo Cave: a mid- to late Holocene site, the Arawe Islands, West New Britain Province, Papua New Guinea. *Asian Perspectives* 33(1): 97-119.

Green, R.C. 1976. Lapita sites in the Santa Cruz group. In R.C. Green and M.M. Creswell (eds), *Southeast Solomon Islands Cultural History*, pp. 245-265. Wellington: Royal Society of New Zealand. Bulletin 11.

Green, R.C. 1979. Lapita. In J.D. Jennings (ed.), *The Prehistory of Polynesia*, pp. 27-60. Cambridge (Mass.): Harvard University Press.

Green, R.C. 1991a. A reappraisal of the dating of some Lapita sites in the Reef/Santa Cruz Group of the southeast Solomons. *Journal of the Polynesian Society* 100(2): 197-207.

Green, R.C. 1991b. The Lapita Cultural Complex: current evidence and proposed models. *Indo-Pacific Prehistory Association Bulletin* 11: 295-305.

Green, R.C. 1992. Definitions of the Lapita Cultural Complex and its non-ceramic component. In J-C. Galipaud (ed.), *Poterie Lapita et Peuplement*, pp. 7-20. Nouméa: ORSTOM.

Green, R.C. 2000. Lapita and the cultural models for intrusion, integration and innovation. In A. Anderson and T. Murray (eds), *Australian Archaeologist: collected papers in honour of Jim Allen*, pp. 372-392. Canberra: Coombs Academic Publishing, Australian National University.

Green, R.C. 2003. The Lapita horizon and traditions – signature for one set of Oceanic migrations. In C. Sand (ed.), *Pacific Archaeology: Assessments and prospects*, pp. 95-120. Nouméa: Département d'Archéologie, Service des Musées et du Patrimoine de Nouvelle-Calédonie. Les Cahiers de l'Archéologie en Nouvelle-Calédonie 15.

Green, R.C. and D. Anson 2000. Excavations at Kainapirina (SAC), Watom Island, Papua New Guinea. *New Zealand Journal of Archaeology* 20 (1998): 29-94.

Green, R.C., D. Anson and J. Specht 1989. The SAC burial ground, Watom Island, Papua New Guinea. *Records of the Australian Museum* 41(3): 215-221.

Green, R.C. and A. Pawley 1998. Architectural forms and settlement patterns. In M. Ross, A. Pawley and M. Osmond (eds), *The Lexicon of Proto Oceanic: The culture and environment of ancestral Oceanic society. Vol. 1. Material culture*, pp. 37-65. Canberra: Pacific Linguistics. Pacific Linguistics C152.

Groube, L.M. 1971. Tonga, Lapita pottery and Polynesian origins. *Journal of the Polynesian Society* 86: 7-36.

Groube, L.M. 1993. Contradictions and malaria in Melanesian and Australian prehistory. In M. Spriggs, D.E. Yen, W. Ambrose, R. Jones, A. Thorne and A. Andrews (eds), *A Community of Culture: The people and prehistory of the Pacific*, pp. 164-186. Canberra: Department of Prehistory, Research School of Pacific Studies, Australian National University. Occasional Papers in Prehistory 21.

Groves, W.C. 1934. The natives of Sio Island, south-eastern New Guinea: a study in culture contact. *Oceania* 5(1): 43-63.

Holzknecht, K. 1957. Über Töpferei und Tontrommeln der Azera in Ost-Neuguinea. *Zeitschrift für Ethnologie* 82: 97-111.

Horrocks, M. and S. Bedford 2005. Microfossil analysis of Lapita deposits in Vanuatu reveals introduced Araceae (aroids). *Archaeology in Oceania* 40(2): 67-74.

Hunt, T.L. 1989. *Lapita Ceramic Exchange in the Mussau Islands, Papua New Guinea*. Unpublished PhD thesis, University of Washington, Seattle.

Irwin, G. 1981. How Lapita lost its pots: the question of continuity in the colonisation of Polynesia. *Journal of the Polynesian Society* 90(4): 481-494.

Ivens, W.G. 1930. *The Island Builders of the Pacific*. London: Seeley, Service and Co.

Kirch, P.V. 1988a. The Talepakemalai Lapita site and Oceanic prehistory. *National Geographic Research* 4(3): 328-342.

Kirch, P.V. 1988b. Long-distance exchange and island colonisation: the Lapita case. *Norwegian Archaeological Review* 21(2): 103-117.

Kirch, P.V. 1996. Lapita and its aftermath: the Austronesian settlement of Oceania. In W.H. Goodenough (ed.), *Prehistoric Settlement of the Pacific*, pp. 57-70. Philadelphia: American Philosophical Society. Transactions of the American Philosophical Society 86(5).

Kirch, P.V. 1997. *The Lapita Peoples: Ancestors of the Oceanic world*. Oxford: Blackwell.

Kirch, P.V. 2000. *On the Road of the Winds: An archaeological history of the Pacific Islands before European contact*. Berkeley: University of California Press.

Kirch, P.V. 2001a. Three Lapita villages: excavations at Talepakemalai (ECA), Etakosarai (ECB), and Etapakengaroasa (EHB), Eloaua and Emananus Islands. In P.V. Kirch (ed.), *Lapita and its Transformations in Near Oceania*, pp. 68-145. Berkeley: Archaeological Research Facility, University of California at Berkeley. Contribution 59.

Kirch, P.V. 2001b. A radiocarbon chronology for the Mussau Islands. In P.V. Kirch (ed.), *Lapita and its Transformations in Near Oceania*, pp. 196-222. Berkeley: Archaeological Research Facility, University of California at Berkeley. Contribution 59.

Kirch, P.V. and T.L. Hunt. 1988a. The spatial and temporal boundaries of Lapita. In P.V. Kirch and T.L. Hunt (eds), *Archaeology of the Lapita Cultural Complex: A critical review*, pp. 9-31. Seattle: Thomas Burke Memorial Washington State Museum. Report 5.

Kirch, P.V. and T.L. Hunt 1988b. Radiocarbon dates from the Mussau Islands and the Lapita colonization of the Southwest Pacific. *Radiocarbon* 30(2):161-169.

Kirch, P.V., T.L. Hunt, M. Weisler, V. Butler, and M.S. Allen 1991. Mussau Islands prehistory: results of the 1985-86 excavations. In J. Allen and C. Gosden (eds), *Report of the Lapita Homeland Project*, pp. 144-163. Canberra: Department of Prehistory, Research School of Pacific Studies, Australian National University. Occasional Papers in Prehistory 20.

Kumar, R. 2002. Discovery of a Lapita sherd inland of the Northeast coast of Viti Levu Island, Fiji: insights and implications. *IAS Technical Report* 2002/5. Suva: Institute of Applied Sciences, University of the South Pacific.

Kumar, R. and P.D. Nunn 2003. Inland and coastal Lapita settlement on Vitilevu Island, Fiji: new data. *Domodomo* 16(1): 15-20.

Kunst, J. 1967. *Music in New Guinea. Three studies*. Verhandelingen van het Koninklijk Instituut voor Taal-, Land- en Volkenkunde 53.

Lauer, P.K. 1970. Sailing with the Amphlett Islanders. *Journal of the Polynesian Society* 79(4): 381-398.

Lauer, P.K. 1973. The technology of pottery manufacture on Goodenough Island and in the Amphlett Group, S.E. Papua. *Ocasional Papers of the Anthropology Museum, University of Queensland* 2: 25-60.

Lepofsky, D. 1988. The environmental context of Lapita settlement locations. In P.V. Kirch and T.L. Hunt (eds), *Archaeology of the Lapita Cultural Complex: A critical review*, pp. 33-47. Seattle: Thomas Burke Memorial Washington State Museum Report 5.

May, P. and M. Tuckson 1982. *The Traditional Pottery of Papua New Guinea*. Sydney: Bay Books.

McClean, M. 1994. *Diffusion of Musical Instruments and their Relationship to Language Migrations in New Guinea*. Port Moresby: National Research Institute. Kulele: Occasional Papers in Pacific Music and Dance 1.

Noury, A. 2005. *Le Reflet de l'Âme Lapita*. Versailles: A. Noury, privately published.

Nunn, P.D., R. Kumar, S. Matararaba, T. Ishimura, J. Seeto, S. Rayawa, S. Kuruyawa, A. Nasila, B. Oloni, A.R. Ram, P. Saunivalu, P. Singh and E. Tegu 2004. Early Lapita settlement at Bourewa, southwest Viti Levu Island, Fiji. *Archaeology in Oceania* 39(3): 139-148.

Parsonson, G.S. 1965. Artificial islands in Melanesia: the role of malaria in the settlement of the Southwest Pacific. *New Zealand Geographer* 22(1): 1-21.

Parsonson, G.S. 1968. The problem of Melanesia. *Mankind* 6(11): 571-584.

Petrie, C., and R. Torrence in prep. The chronology of eruption, abandonment and reoccupation, West New Britain c.7500 BC – AD 1880.

Petchey, F., M. Phelan and P. White 2004. New ΔR values for the southwest Pacific Ocean. *Radiocarbon* 46(2): 1005-1014.

Petchey, F., R.C. Green, M. Jones and M. Phelan 2005. A local marine reservoir correction value (ΔR) for Watom Island, Papua New Guinea. *New Zealand Journal of Archaeology* 26(2004): 29-40.

Pineda, R. and J-C. Galipaud 1998. Evidences archéologiques d'une surrection différentielle de l'île Malo (archipel du Vanuatu) au cours de l'Holocène recent. *Comptes-rendus de l'Académie des Sciences de Paris. Sciences de la Terre et des Planètes* 327: 777-779.

Pisarik, S. 1975. *Micronesian Atoll Populations: A Path Analysis*. Unpublished MA thesis, University of Iowa, Iowa City.

Reimer, P.J., M.G.L. Baillie, E. Bard, A. Bayliss, J.W. Beek, C.J.H. Bertrand, R.G. Blackwell, C.E. Buck, G.S. Burr, K.B. Cutler, P.E. Damon, R.L. Edwards, R.G. Fairbanks, M. Friedrich, T.P. Guilderson, A.G. Hogg, K.A. Hughen, B. Kromer, F.G. McCormac, S.W. Manning, C.B. Ramsey, R.W. Reimer, S. Remmele, J.R. Southon, M. Stuiver, S. Talamo, F.W. Taylor, J. van der Plicht and C.E. Weyhenmeyer 2004. IntCal04 terrestrial radiocarbon age calibration, 26-0 ka BP. *Radiocarbon* 46: 1029-1058.

Sand, C., K. Coote, J. Bolé and A. Ouetcho 1998. A pottery pit at locality WKO013A, Lapita (New Caledonia). *Archaeology in Oceania* 33(1): 37-43.

Sheppard, P.J. and R.C. Green 1991. Spatial analysis of the Nenumbo (SE-RF-2) Lapita site, Solomon Islands. *Archaeology in Oceania* 26(3): 89-101.

Specht, J. 1974. Lapita pottery at Talasea, West New Britain, Papua New Guinea. *Antiquity* 48: 302-306.

Specht, J. 1991. Kreslo: a Lapita site in southwest New Britain, Papua New Guinea. In J. Allen and C. Gosden (eds), *Report of the Lapita Homeland Project*, pp. 189-204. Canberra: Department of Prehistory, Research School of Pacific Studies, Australian National University. Occasional Papers in Prehistory 20.

Specht, J. in press. The Lagenda Lapita site (FCR/FCS), Talasea area, Papua New Guinea. *Technical Reports of the Australian Museum*.

Specht, J. and C. Gosden 1997. Dating Lapita pottery in the Bismarck Archipelago. *Asian Perspectives* 36(2): 175-199.

Specht, J. and G. Summerhayes in press. The Boduna Island (FEA) Lapita site, Papua New Guinea. *Technical Reports of the Australian Museum*.

Specht, J. and R. Torrence in press. Pottery sites of the Talasea area, Papua New Guinea. *Technical Reports of the Australian Museum*.

Spriggs, M. 1984. The Lapita cultural complex: origins, distribution, contemporaries and successors. *Journal of Pacific History* 19(4): 202-223.

Spriggs, M. 1990. The changing face of Lapita: transformations of a design. In M. Spriggs (ed.), *Lapita Design, Form and Composition*, pp. 83-122. Canberra: Department of Prehistory, Research School of Pacific Studies, Australian National University. Occasional Papers in Prehistory 19.

Spriggs, M. 1991. Nissan: The island in the middle. In J. Allen and C. Gosden (eds), *Report of the Lapita Homeland Project*, pp. 222-243. Canberra: Department of Prehistory, Research School of Pacific Studies, Australian National University. Occasional Papers in Prehistory 20.

Spriggs, M. 1995. The Lapita culture and Austronesian prehistory in Oceania. In P. Bellwood, J.J. Fox and D. Tryon (eds), *The Austronesians: Historical and Comparative Perspectives*, pp. 112-133. Canberra: Department of Anthropology, Research School of Pacific and Asian Studies, Australian National University.

Spriggs, M. 1996. What is Southeast Asian about Lapita? In T. Azakawa and E. Szathmary (eds), *Prehistoric Mongoloid Dispersals*, pp. 324-348. Oxford: Oxford University Press.

Spriggs, M. 1997. *The Island Melanesians*. Oxford: Blackwell.

Spriggs, M. 2000. The Solomon Islands as bridge and barrier in the settlement of the Pacific. In A. Anderson and T. Murray (eds), *Australian Archaeologist: Collected Papers in Honour of Jim Allen*, pp. 348-364. Canberra: Coombs Academic Publishing, Australian National University.

Spriggs, M. 2002. They've grown accustomed to your face. In S. Bedford, C. Sand and D. Burley (eds), *Fifty Years in the Field. Essays in honour and celebration of Richard Shutler Jr's archaeological career*, pp. 51-57. Auckland: New Zealand Archaeological Association Monograph 25.

Spriggs, M. 2003a. Post-Lapita evolutions in Melanesia. In C. Sand (ed.), *Pacific Archaeology: Assessments and prospects*, pp. 205-212. Noumea: Département d'Archéologie, Service des Musées et du Patrimoine de Nouvelle-Calédonie. Les Cahiers de l'Archéologie en Nouvelle-Calédonie 15.

Spriggs, M. 2003b. Chronology of the Neolithic transition in Island Southeast Asia and the Western Pacific: a view from 2003. *The Review of Archaeology* 24(2): 57-80.

Steadman, D.W. 2006. *Extinction and Biogeography of Tropical Pacific Birds*. Chicago: University of Chicago Press.

Steadman, D.W. and P.V. Kirch 1998. Biogeography and prehistoric exploitation of birds in the Mussau Islands, Bismarck Archipelago, Papua New Guinea. *Emu* 98: 13-22.

Stuiver, M. and P.J. Reimer 1993. Extended 14C database and revised CALIB radiocarbon calibration program. *Radiocarbon* 35: 215-30.

Summerhayes, G. 2000a. What's in a pot? In A. Anderson and T. Murray (eds), *Australian Archaeologist. Collected papers in honour of Jim Allen*, pp. 291-307. Canberra: Coombs Academic Publishing, Australian National University.

Summerhayes, G. 2000b. *Lapita Interaction*. Canberra: Department of Archaeology and Natural History, and Centre for Archaeology, Australian National University. Terra Australis 15.

Summerhayes, G.R. 2001a. Defining the chronology of Lapita in the Bismarck Archipelago. In G.R. Clark, A.J. Anderson and T. Vunidilo (eds), *The Archaeology of Lapita Dispersal in Oceania*, pp. 25-38. Canberra: Pandanus Books, Research School of Pacific and Asian Studies, Australian National University. Terra Australis 17.

Summerhayes, G.R. 2001b. Far Western, Western, and Eastern Lapita: a re-evaluation. *Asian Perspectives* 39(1-2): 109-118.

Summerhayes, G.R. 2001c. Lapita in the Far West: recent developments. *Archaeology in Oceania* 36(2): 53-64.

Summerhayes, G.R. 2003. Modelling differences between Lapita obsidian and pottery distribution patterns in the Bismarck Archipelago, Papua New Guinea. In C. Sand (ed.), *Pacific Archaeology: Assessments and prospects*, pp. 135-145. Noumea: Département d'Archéologie, Service des Musées et du Patrimoine de Nouvelle-Calédonie. Les Cahiers de l'Archéologie en Nouvelle-Calédonie 15.

Summerhayes, G. 2004. The nature of prehistoric obsidian importation to Anir and the development of a 3,000 year old regional picture of obsidian exchange within the Bismarck Archipelago, Papua New Guinea. *Records of the Australian Museum, Supplement* 29: 145-156.

Summerhayes, G.R. in press. The rise and transformation of Lapita in the Bismarck Archipelago. In S. Chiu and C. Sand (eds), *From Southeast Asia to the Pacific: Archaeological perspectives on the Austronesian expansion and the Lapita Cultural Complex*. Taipei: Center for Archaeological Studies Research and Center for Humanities and Social Sciences, Academia Sinica.

Terrell, J.E. 1998. 30,000 years of culture contact in the southwest Pacific. In J.G. Cusick (ed.), *Studies in Culture Contact: Interaction, culture change, and archaeology*, pp. 191-219. Carbondale: Centre for Archaeological Investigations, Southern Illinois University. Occasional Paper 25.

Terrell, J.E. 2004. Introduction: 'Austronesia' and the great Austronesian migration. *World Archaeology* 36(4): 586-590.

Terrell, J.E. and R.L. Welsch 1997. Lapita and the temporal geography of prehistory. *Antiquity* 71: 548-572.

Thomson, J-A.R. and J.P. White 2000. Localism of Lapita pottery in the Bismarck Archipelago. In A. Anderson and T. Murray (eds), *Australian Archaeologist: Collected papers in honour of Jim Allen*, pp.308-323. Canberra: Coombs Academic Publishing, Australian National University.

Torrence, R. and C.M. Stevenson 2000. Beyond the beach: changing Lapita landscapes on Garua Island, Papua New Guinea. In A. Anderson and T. Murray (eds), *Australian Archaeologist: Collected Papers in Honour of Jim Allen*, pp. 324-345. Canberra: Coombs Academic Publishing, Australian National University.

Torrence, R. and J.P. White 2001. Tattooed faces from Boduna Island, Papua New Guinea. In G.R. Clark, A.J. Anderson and T. Vunidilo (eds), *The Archaeology of Lapita Dispersal in Oceania*, pp. 135-140. Canberra: Pandanus Books, Australian National University. Terra Australis 17.

Valentin, F. 2003. Human skeletal remains from the site of Lapita at Koné (New Caledonia): Mortuary and biological factors. In C. Sand (ed.), *Pacific Archaeology: Assessments and prospects*, pp. 285-293. Noumea: Départment Archéologie, Service des Musées et du Patrimoine de Nouvelle-Calédonie. Les Cahiers de l'Archéologie en Nouvelle-Calédonie 15.

Weisler, M. 2001a. Life on the edge: prehistoric settlement and economy on Utrok Atoll, northern Marshall Islands. *Archaeology in Oceania* 36: 109-133.

Weisler, M. 2001b. *On the Margins of Sustainability: Prehistoric Settlement of Utrok Atoll, Northern Marshall Islands*. Oxford: Archaeopress. British Archaeological Reports, International Series 967.

White, J.P. in press. Ceramic sites on the Duke of York Islands. *Technical Reports of the Australian Museum*.

White, J.P., C. Coroneos, V. Neall, W. Boyd and R. Torrence 2002. FEA site, Boduna Island: further investigations. In S. Bedford, C. Sand and D. Burley (eds), *Fifty Years in the Field. Essays in honour and celebration of Richard Shutler Jr's archaeological career*, pp. 101-107. Auckland: New Zealand Archaeological Association. Monograph 25.

White, J.P. and M-N. Harris 1997. Changing sources: early Lapita period obsidian in the Bismarck Archipelago. *Archaeology in Oceania* 32(1): 97-107.

Wickler, S. 2001. *The Prehistory of Buka: A stepping stone island in the Northern Solomons*. Canberra: Department of Archaeology and Natural History, and Centre for Archaeological Research, Australian National University. *Terra Australis* 16.

4

Lapita all over: Land-use on the Willaumez Peninsula, Papua New Guinea

Jim Specht and Robin Torrence

Anthropology Unit
Australian Museum
Sydney NSW 2010, Australia
jspecht@bigpond.com; robint@austmus.gov.au

Introduction

The remarkable achievements of the first colonisers of the Remote Pacific have long captured the interest of archaeologists and the wider public alike. Perhaps for this reason the character of the archaeological evidence in that particular region has been implicitly used as the exemplar for all areas where Lapita pottery is found (cf. Green 1992:16). For example, one of the long held tenets of Lapita archaeology is that settlement was mainly restricted to small, offshore islands or, where it occurred on larger islands, it was almost exclusively limited to the coastal margins and to beaches in particular (e.g., Frimigacci 1980; Kirch 1997:162-167; Lepofsky 1988; Spriggs 1997:88, 122). Recently, this view was challenged by a study of cultural landscapes on Garua Island, Papua New Guinea in the western area of Lapita pottery distribution (Figure 1), where intentional searching of zones usually overlooked by Pacific archaeologists has revealed an intriguing shift in land-use patterns during the dentate-stamped phase of the Lapita ceramic series (Torrence 2002a; Torrence and Stevenson 2000). The earliest sites with dentate-stamping were located on beaches or in the inter-tidal zone of Garua and adjacent small islands, but from about 3050-2750 cal. BP the focus of activity shifted to elevated inland locations, possibly to take advantage of defensive capabilities provided by steep-sided hills and ridges (Torrence and Stevenson 2000).

The Garua Island study raises important questions about the homogeneity of behaviour across the huge expanse where Lapita pottery has been found, particularly in terms of the use of inland hills and forests. A recent gazetteer of 184 Lapita sites with dentate-stamped pottery (Anderson *et al.* 2001: Table 1) highlights the contrast between the islands of the Bismarck Archipelago that had been settled

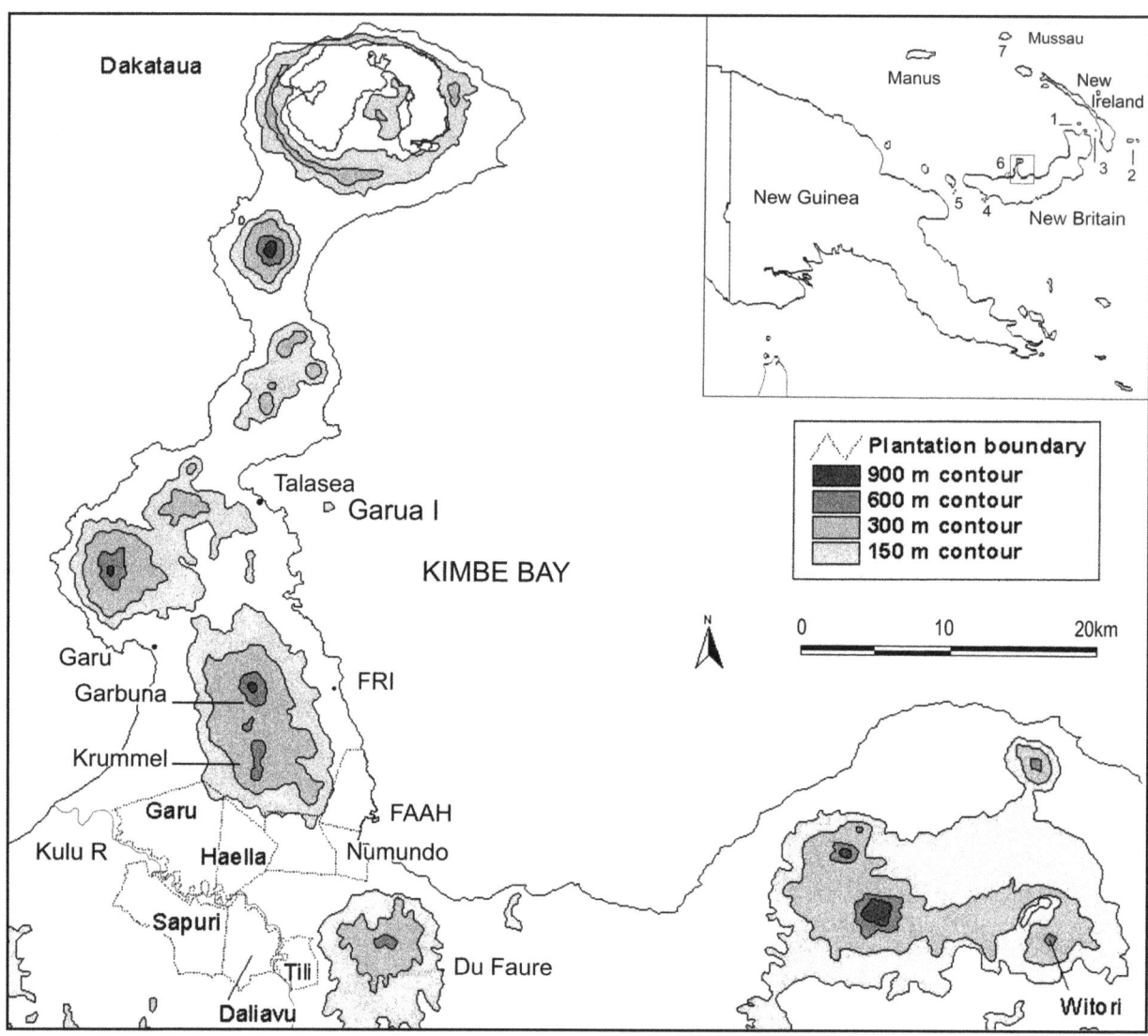

Figure 1. Map of the Willaumez Peninsula showing major volcanic centres, the boundaries of the plantations that formed the isthmus study region and other localities mentioned in the text. The inset shows the location of other Lapita pottery sites in the Bismarck Archipelago mentioned in the paper: 1 – Watom Island; 2 – Anir; 3 – Duke of York Islands; 4 – Arawe Islands; 5 – Siassi Islands; 6 – Kove Islands; 7 – Mussau Islands.

for at least 40,000 years and the more isolated islands to the east where Lapita dentate-stamped pottery marks initial human colonisation. Only five sites other than those on Garua are not at sea level or on small islands, and only two of these are not located on the Willaumez Peninsula mainland [1].

Is Garua Island representative of a wider trend or is it a local anomaly, perhaps generated by the presence of obsidian on the island and/or its proximity to the major Kutau obsidian outcrops? In this paper we address this question with data derived from a new

Table 1. Distribution of test pits in the isthmus region of Willaumez Peninsula by landform and occurrence of pottery. The Table includes only those test pits where the 'W-K2 soil' and/or pottery occur.

Landform	Pottery and obsidian	Obsidian only	Totals
Coastal plain	3	1	4
Coastal hill	5	4	9
Coastal foothill	0	4	4
Divide	3	1	4
Inland foothill	0	17	17
Floodplain foothill	1	8	9
Totals	12	35	47

landscape study in the isthmus region of the Willaumez Peninsula mainland. Our focus is on the nature and distribution of the ceramic finds. These new data substantiate the Garua findings and demonstrate that the widely held model of settlements concentrated on beaches and small offshore islands is likely to be a product of taphonomic factors and biased research practices. Consequently, the model is seriously flawed. Moving beyond the beach, however, we still find the pattern is not uniform. Explaining the differences in the timing and distribution of pottery on Garua Island and the mainland of Willaumez Peninsula will lead landscape research in new directions. We conclude that if archaeologists explicitly search for variation, there is much to learn about the nature of settlement and land-use throughout the region where Lapita pottery has been found.

Volcanic landscapes

Important changes in theory and method underpin the findings from Garua Island and the more recent mainland Willaumez Peninsula project. In the first place, the shift of focus from specific places to the whole landscape forces the research to move beyond individual sites and consider the entire area that was part of people's lives: i.e., where they travelled, exploited resources, conducted rituals, etc. To understand human behaviour during the time of Lapita pottery, it is important to study this wide range of activities. Even if settlements were concentrated in specific places, and this assumption needs to be tested, most subsistence tasks would have occurred elsewhere. A comprehensive analysis, therefore, must include the 'off-site' components of prehistoric lifeways.

This focus on landscapes requires new methodologies to search for a broad range of evidence of past human activities. The most important innovation is to look for archaeological evidence across a range of environmental zones, including those where settlement would not be expected. Following on from this shift in approach, a broader class of archaeological evidence becomes relevant (e.g., small lithic scatters, so-called 'stray finds,' and rock art).

The Pacific region poses many obstacles to landscape archaeology, the most difficult being the dense vegetation cover typical even of areas under cultivation. Another problem is the instability of the coastal zone, which creates taphonomic problems and difficulties with interpreting the source and date of surface scatters (e.g., Felgate 2003; Gosden and Webb 1994; Kirch 1988; Spriggs 1984; Wickler 2001). The Willaumez Peninsula and its offshore islands provide an excellent place to undertake landscape archaeology because some of these problems can be overcome. Firstly, the recent large-scale development of oil palm plantations has opened up a vast area for archaeological investigation on a scale and level of accessibility that were previously impossible (Boyd *et al.* 2005; Torrence 2002b; Torrence and Doelman in press). Archaeological reconnaissance began late in the development scheme, but was nevertheless able to monitor some freshly cleared areas, new road cuts, and deep trenches. Material disturbed by development activities has lost its stratigraphic integrity but still indicates an ancient human presence. Targeted excavations near these surface scatters occasionally helped place the finds into their original chronological setting.

Secondly, the volcanic history of the region has created a series of tephras, each of which has sealed and preserved a relatively short-lived landscape. The tephras are physically and chemically distinctive and can be easily identified in the field. Recent work has provided reasonably secure dates for the volcanic events that created these chronostratigraphic units (Petrie and Torrence in prep.). The resulting tephrostratigraphy provides a method of relative dating that can be used consistently over a significant portion of West New Britain (Torrence *et al.* 2000; Pavlides 2006). Research on Garua Island has already benefited from the use of tephras as chronologically secure marker horizons (Torrence 2002a;

Torrence and Stevenson 2000). On the southern Willaumez Peninsula mainland additional Holocene tephras are preserved, thereby reducing the time elapsed between the discard of cultural materials and the burial of the land surface by the next tephra deposit (Torrence and Doelman in press).

The isthmus region

The Willaumez Peninsula of West New Britain province is characterised by an exceptionally high number of pottery localities attributable to the Lapita ceramic series (Anderson *et al.* 2001:Table 1; Specht and Torrence in press). Although most sites are situated on offshore islands, prior work indicated the potential for dentate-stamped pottery to occur on the mainland away from the shoreline. The FRI site at Walindi Plantation is distinguished by its elevated inland position, extending over several ridges up to 95 m above sea level at about 1 km inland from the present coastline (Figure 1; Specht *et al.* 1991). The date of around 2300-1850 cal. BP for plain sherds excavated here is much later than the inland shift recorded on Garua Island, though surface finds of dentate-stamped sherds at FRI suggest an earlier phase of activity there (Specht and Torrence in press; Torrence *et al.* 1990). The site thus indicated that further exploration in the southern region of Willaumez Peninsula might prove fruitful.

The transect across the base of Willaumez Peninsula, termed the 'isthmus,' was selected because it enables a study of human land-use across a wide range of environmental zones, including beach, coastal plain, coastal and inland foothills, river floodplain, and coastal swamp. The study area

Figure 2. Aerial view from the west of Numundo Plantation and the divide separating the Kulu River floodplain and the Numundo coastal plain. Five localities with pottery are indicated: Numundo Island in the foreground, FAAH and FAAY on coastal hills, FABI on an inland foothill, and FABD on the divide. The peak of Mt Krummel at the extreme top right is partly concealed by cloud. The Whiteman Range is faintly visible on the horizon. Photo: courtesy of W.E. Boyd.

Figure 3. The divide between the Numundo coastal plain and the Kulu River floodplain showing the extent of landscape modification for plantation development in 1999, with the slopes of Mt Du Fauré on the horizon. Photo: J. Specht.

comprises the six oil palm plantations of Numundo, Haella, Tili, Garu, Daliavu and Sapuri developed by New Britain Palm Oil Ltd. These plantations, covering about 150 km^2, lie between two Quaternary volcanoes, Mt Krummel (854 m) to the north and Mt Du Fauré (752 m) to the south (Figure 1). The two volcanoes are part of a series of more than a dozen Quaternary eruptive centres of the Kimbe Volcanics geological unit that forms the central spine of Willaumez Peninsula (Johnson and Blake 1972; McKee et al. 2005; Ryburn 1975). The base of the isthmus along the southwestern edge of our study area links with the northern foothills of the Whiteman Range of central New Britain that is partly formed by much older volcanic formations of Tertiary age (Ryburn 1975). Ridges of lava flows from Du Fauré, Krummel and Mt Garbuna (810 m, located to the north of Krummel) coalesce on the isthmus to form a narrow divide less than 40 m high that separates the coastal plain of Numundo on the eastern side from the extensive floodplain of the Kulu River and its tributaries on the western side (Figures 2, 3).

The Kulu floodplain was swampy and difficult to access until it was cleared and drained for plantation development (Figures 4, 5). In contrast, the Numundo coastal plain is drier and has several perennial streams dissecting it, though prior to plantation development much of its seawards margin consisted of mangrove swamps (Boyd et al. 2005; Torrence 2002b). Several small hills rise to about 20 m above the coastal plain and one of these, Numundo Hill, stands on the western shore of Kimbe Bay facing Numundo Island (Figure 2). Several smaller hillocks (< 10 m) on the coastal plain are remnants of late Pleistocene landscapes; at least one of these hillocks contains evidence for human activity prior to the Last Glacial Maximum (Torrence et al. 2004a).

The isthmus region today offers a diverse though dispersed range of habitats and resources for human utilisation, most of which were probably available during the period when Lapita pottery was used (Boyd et al. 2005). The Numundo coastal plain is relatively level and today provides easily accessible arable land, with swampy shorelines and nearby coral reefs. In contrast, the coast fronting the Kulu floodplain lacks reefs but is an important source of swamp resources for the people of Garu village at the northern

Figure 4. Aerial view from the east of Garu Plantation at the northern end of the Kulu River floodplain, with Boku Hill (FABN) in the centre. Dentate-stamped pottery was found in the bulldozed area around the pair of houses on the western edge of Boku Hill. Photo: courtesy of W.E. Boyd.

Figure 5. Looking south from the top of Boku Hill across Garu Plantation and the Kulu River floodplain towards Sapuri and Daliavu Plantations. The Whiteman Range in the distance is partly covered by clouds. Photo: R. Torrence.

end of the floodplain. In the foothills of Mt Krummel and Mt Garbuna to the east of Garu village there are geothermal areas with megapode colonies, and additional geothermal areas occur within the crater of Garbuna (Johnson and Blake 1972). Mt Krummel and Mt Du Fauré are composed of highly porphyritic, low-silica andesites and dacites, whereas Garbuna has higher-silica bearing rocks. In the past all three volcanoes could have provided rock suitable for ground stone axe blades and other artefacts, though no quarries or production sites have yet been recorded. There are no obsidian outcrops in the isthmus region, but the Willaumez sources are only 25 km to the north, within one day's walking distance along the eastern coastal plain that extends almost to Talasea. The Mopir source at about the same distance to the southeast is accessible by land across rugged, steep hills and ridges of several volcanic complexes, whereas travel by sea or rivers would require a longer journey. Other rock resources are available in the more complex lithology of the Whiteman Range to the southwest of the isthmus.

Tephrostratigraphy

A key to the success of landscape archaeology in the isthmus region is the tephrostratigraphy composed of distinctive Holocene tephras from the Witori and Dakataua volcanic centres (Machida *et al.* 1996). For Lapita pottery the most important tephras are W-K2 (3480-3200 cal. BP) and W-K3 (1750-1550 cal. BP) (Petrie and Torrence in prep.). Dentate-stamped pottery is only found stratified between these two layers. The large W-K2 event was a major disaster that caused human populations to abandon the region for as much as 100 years or so. The landscape that was colonised by people making Lapita pottery was considerably altered by this event. The emplacement and subsequent erosion of the deep layer of W-K2 tephra extended the isthmus coastlines towards their present position. On the eastern side the tephra contributed to the conversion of coastal swamps and reef flats into the Numundo coastal plain. Similarly, on the western side of the isthmus the tephra infilled an earlier sea embayment and began the formation of the Kulu River floodplain (Boyd *et al.* 2005; Torrence and Doelman in press).

Landscape sampling

Archaeological research in the isthmus combined foot and vehicle surveys with a programme of test pitting to sample all environmental zones, although emphasis was placed on the older and well-preserved landscapes where the full stratigraphic record was preserved. Sixty-two 1-m^2 test pits were excavated, each identified by a Roman numeral (Figure 6). This strategy was supplemented by inspection of numerous exposures resulting from works associated with the development of the plantations, including drainage-channels, the terracing of slopes, and the construction of roads, housing and processing plants.

Palaeosols formed on the W-K2 tephra (hereafter 'the W-K2 soil') were present in 58 test pits, although artefacts were absent in 11 of these. Of the other 47 pits, 12 (25 %) contained pottery and obsidian artefacts whereas only obsidian was recovered from the other 35 (Table 1). Pottery was also recovered in surface collections at 12 localities. For analytical convenience, and with the exception of Numundo Island, these find spots are grouped into 14 wider areas that are allocated Papua New Guinea National Museum and Art Gallery four-letter site codes.

The sequence of tephras makes it possible to recognise situations where artefacts have been redeposited. These include test pits on the slopes and at the base of Numundo Hill (and, by implication, surface collections in the same areas), where most finds are almost certainly derived from the hilltop component of FAAH. The surface finds at FACR and FACQ were in areas disturbed by road construction and probably came from deposits that were completely removed by bulldozers, as no sherds were found in test pits excavated in adjacent undisturbed locations.

The distribution of test pits within different physiographic zones presented in Table 1 shows the broad spatial spread of material dating to the period between the W-K2 and W-K3 tephras. It is also interesting to note the large variation in the distance of the locations with pottery from the current coastline and their approximate elevation above present-day sea level (Table 2; elevations not adjusted for the 1 m or so of post-W-K2 tephra deposits). Numundo Island is the only beachside find spot, though pottery was recovered in trenches on the coastal plain below FAAH at depths close to or within the water table. Table 2 illustrates that pottery find spots occur on every major landform at elevations up to 80 m above sea level and up to 18 km inland from the current coastline; indeed, eight of the 14 locations are 2 km or more inland. FACZ is exceptional, as the 15 sherds found there were in a spring that waters a small taro garden at about 80 m above sea level on a foothill of Mt Krummel. Several test pits were excavated in the area surrounding the spring but none contained pottery. Three localities (FACQ, FACR, FADC) are on low spurs of the Whiteman Range foothills to the south of the Kulu River. These spurs are 17-18 km inland, and 17-20 m above sea level. Although the precise position of the coastline at the time of pottery use is unknown, these locations would have looked out across extensive swamps and tidal creeks and were not perched above ocean beaches. Significantly, perhaps, no pottery was recorded on the floodplain itself, although this landform was not intensively sampled as it was gradually built up after the W-K2 event and the water table is still high.

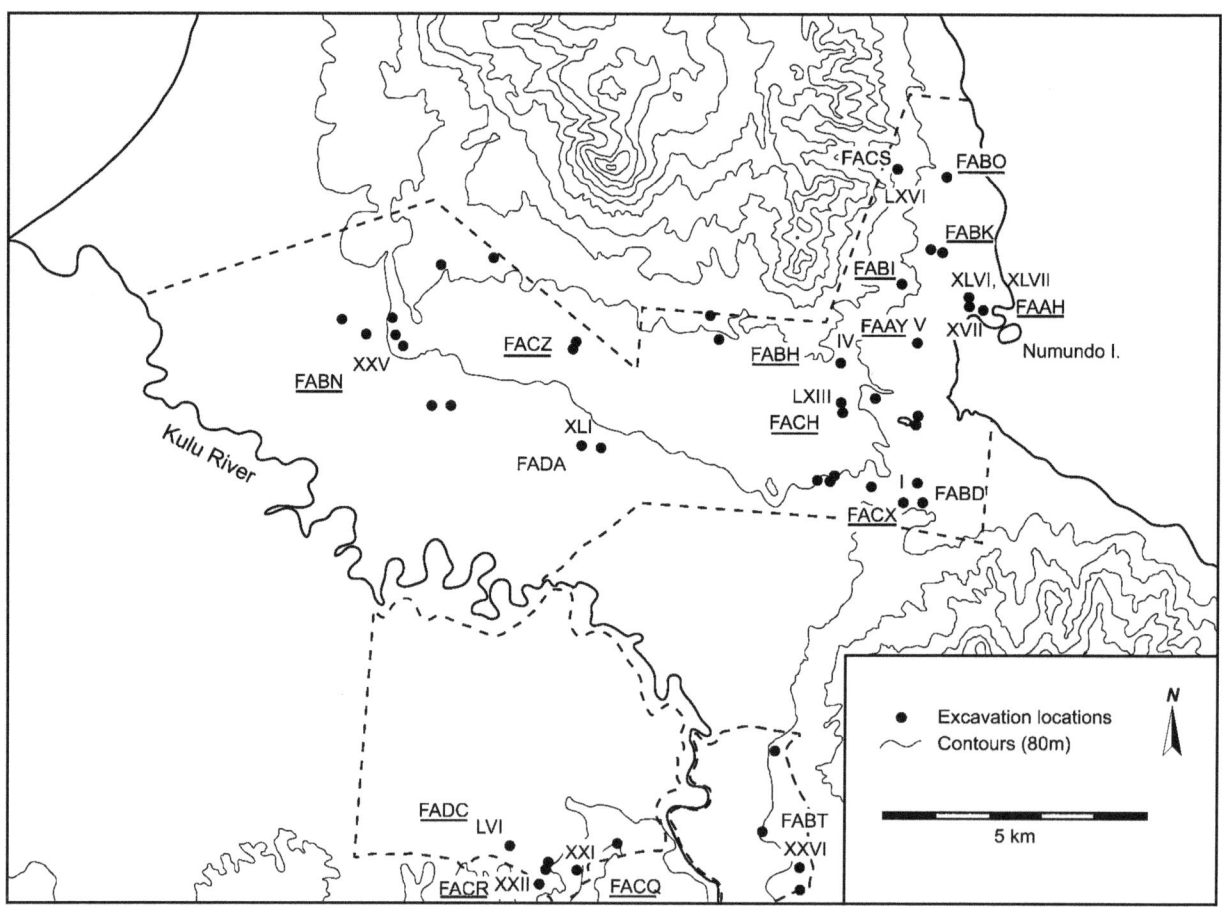

Figure 6. Distribution of test pits and locality codes in the isthmus region where the W-K2 soil was preserved. Roman numerals indicate test pit number; localities with pottery underlined.

Table 2. Distribution of localities on the Willaumez Peninsula isthmus where pottery was recovered in excavated or surface contexts. The entries under '?' indicate sherds with heavily weathered surfaces that might be decorated but the technique is not identifiable. Italicised entries for FAAH and FACU indicate totals for each locality.

Locality	Landform	Distance to sea	Elevation	Area or trench	Sherds count	Sherds wgt	Sherds mean wgt	Dentate stamp	Plain stamp	Incised	Circle imp.	Small arcs	Nail imp.	?	Notch lip	Scallop lip
Excavated																
FAAH	*Coastal hill/plain*	*0.5-1 km*	*20-40 m*	*all strat.*	*681*	*4075,6*	*6,0*	*21(?23)*	*15(?16)*	*10*	*3*	*0*	*1*	*6*	*24*	*6*
	Coastal plain	~0.25 km	~1 m	VIII	42	266,1	6,3	1(?2)	0	0	1	0	0	2	0	0
	Coastal hill	~0.25 km	12 m	XVII	575	3436,1	6,0	15	9(?10)	10	1	0	1	3	21	6
	Coastal hill	~0.5 km	~15 m	XXVIII	15	225,7	15,1	4(?5)	3	0	1	0	0	0	1	0
	Coastal hill	~1 km	21 m	XLVI	47	133,4	2,8	1(?2)	3	0	0	0	0	1	2	0
	Coastal hill	~1 km	21 m	XLVII	2	14,3	7,2	0	0	0	0	0	0	0	0	0
FAAY	Coastal hill	~1.5 km	16 m	V	8	41,9	7,0	0	0	0	0	0	0	0	0	0
FABO	Coastal hill	~1.5 km	20-40 m	XIV	5	32,3	6,5	0	0	2	0	0	0	0	0	0
FABK	Coastal plain	~1.5 km	19 m	VII	1	51,4	[51.4]	0	0	1	0	0	0	0	0	0
FACX	Hill on divide	~2 km	<40 m	XXXIII	4	10,4	2,6	0	0	0	0	0	0	0	0	0
FACU	*Hill on divide*	*~2.5 km*	*40-80 m*	*all strat.*	*13*	*82,4*	*6,3*	*0*	*0*	*0*	*0*	*0*	*0*	*0*	*3*	*0*
	Hill on divide	~2.5 km	40-80 m	XXXI	9	49,5	5,5	0	0	0	0	0	0	0	3	0
	Hill on divide	~2.5 km	40-80 m	LXIII	4	32,9	8,2	0	0	0	0	0	0	0	0	0
FADC	Floodplain hill	~17 km	17-18 m	LVI	3	4,3	1,4	0	0	0	0	0	0	0	0	0
Surface																
Numundo Is.	Beach	0 km	0 m	n/a	1	38,2	[38.2]	0	(?1)	1	0	0	0	0	0	0
FAAH	Coastal plain	0.25 km	1-5 m	Locs 5, 6	163	1503,8	9,2	2(?3)	(?1)	0	1	0	0	0	1	0
	Coastal hill	0.25-0.5 km	10-15 m	Locs 1, 2	19	380,6	20,0	2	1(?2)	2	0	0	0	0	0	1
FABI	Coastal hill	~1 km	~40 m	Area G	2	2,7	1,4	0	0	1	0	0	0	0	0	0
FACU	Hill on divide	~2.5 km	40-80 m	02/01C	1	6,1	[6.1]	1	0	0	0	0	0	0	0	0
FABH	Hill on divide	~2.5 km	40-80 m	Area E	7	30,6	4,4	0	0	0	0	0	0	0	0	0
FABN	Inland foothill	~6 km	40-80 m	Loc. 1	8	40,3	5,0	1	0	0	0	0	0	0	2	0
FACZ	Inland foothill	~7 km	~80 m	spring	15	371,1	24,7	5	0	0	3	0	0	0	0	0
FACR	Floodplain hill	~17.5 km	19-20 m	017/01	11	40,3	3,7	2	0	0	0	0	0	0	0	0
FACQ	Floodplain hill	~18 km	19-20 m	01/12	8	60,9	7,6	0	0	0	0	0	0	0	1	0
Totals					950	6772,9		34(?38)	16(?20)	17	4	3	1	6	31	7

It is clear from the spatial distribution of obsidian and ceramics across the isthmus that land-use during the period between the W-K2 and W-K3 volcanic events was not limited to the coastal zone, thereby confirming the overall finding of the Garua study. To understand how this wide scale patterning compares to Garua Island and what it might represent in terms of the nature of human activities, we begin with an analysis of the pottery focusing on dating and potential types of activities represented at the locations where ceramics have been recovered. We then incorporate these findings into a broader analysis of settlement history in the isthmus region.

Radiocarbon dates

Seventeen radiocarbon dates from test pits at 12 localities are presented in Table 3 (Figure 7). They are arranged in four groups according to whether sherds were (a) present in the dated levels, (b) present only in adjacent surface collections, (c) absent from the level dated but present below that, or (d) not present in either test pits or surface collections. A 'modern' result from FABO is omitted. All samples were fragments of charred nutshells (probably *Canarium* spp.) with growth spans not exceeding one year. Most of the age ranges were calibrated by Cameron Petrie (University of Cambridge) using the OxCal program as part of a larger Bayesian analysis of ^{14}C dates relating to Holocene volcanic eruptions and human activity on Willaumez Peninsula (details of this analysis will be reported elsewhere by Petrie and Torrence in prep.). The calibrated ranges marked by an asterisk are as supplied by the University of Waikato Radiocarbon Dating Laboratory. The age ranges are listed at 2σ and represent the highest probability distribution at 95.4 %.

Three dates relate directly to dentate-stamped sherds. Those for FAAH/XVII (Wk-10463: 3210-2850 cal. BP; Wk-19190: 3070-2860 cal. BP) conform well to dates for this technique elsewhere in Near Oceania. Several conjoins of sherds in layer 9 of FAAH/XVII suggest minimum post-discard disturbance of this soil unit, though different degrees of weathering of sherds could indicate two phases of discard (compare Figures 8A-C with 8D-F). If this were so, the two dates indicate that the interval between the two phases was very short. For the present purpose the pottery from this layer is treated as belonging to

Table 3. Radiocarbon dates for archaeological materials recovered from the 'W-K2 soil' in the test pits on the Willaumez Peninsula isthmus. All samples consisted of charred nutshell fragments. The calibrated age ranges are at 2σ for the highest probability distribution (95.4 %) using the OxCal program. The entry in square brackets for dentate-stamped pottery at FACU indicates that plain sherds were present in the test pit, but dentate-stamped sherds were present only in the surface collection.

Localities with or without pottery	Landform	Distance from sea	Elevation a.s.l.	Trench	Layer	Dentate present	Lab code	Reported age	2σ calibrated range (95.4 %)
In dated level									
FADC	Floodplain hill	~17 km	17-18 m	LVI	9 spit 3	no	Wk-12845	2963±47	3240-2960
FAAH	Coastal hill	0.25 km	12 m	XVII	9 spit 1	yes	Wk-10463	2880±59	3210-2850
*FAAH	Coastal hill	0.25 km	12 m	XVII	9 spit 3	yes	Wk-19190*	2847±34	3070-2860
FACU	Hill on divide	~2.5 km	40-80 m	LXIII	7 spit 1	[yes]	Wk-12834	2473±48	2720-2360
FAAY	Coastal hill	~1.5 km	16 m	V	7 spit 1	no	Wk-9026	2472±57	2720-2360
FAAH	Coastal hill	~0.25 km	21 m	XLVI	3 spit 1	yes	Wk-12824	2055±56	2300-1900
On surface only									
FACQ	Floodplain hill	~18 km	19-20 m	XXI	4 spit 1	no	Wk-10478	2883±63	3210-2850
FACR	Floodplain hill	~17.5 km	19-20 m	XXII	8 spit 1	yes	Wk-10459	2831±57	3110-2780
FABN	Inland foothill	6 km	40-80 m	XXV	6 spit 1	yes	ANSTO OZF-110	2280±30	2360-2160
FABH	Hill on divide	~2.5 km	40-80 m	IV	3 spit 2	no	Wk-10471	2182±61	2340-2040
Not in dated level but present below									
*FAAH	Coastal hill	0.25 km	21 m	XLVII	4 spit 1	n/a	Wk-19189*	2301±33	2360-2160
*FADC	Floodplain hill	~17 km	17-18 m	LVI	9 spit 1	n/a	Wk-19188*	2199±34	2330-2130
No pottery at all									
FADA	Floodplain hill	~7 km	~80 m	XLIV	5 spit 1	n/a	Wk-12840	2965±46	3240-2970
FACS	Coastal foothill	~2 km	40-80 m	LXVI	5 spit 2	n/a	Wk-12831	2535±45	2760-2460
FABT	Inland foothill	~24 km	~40 m	XXVI	7 spit 2	n/a	Wk-10470	2272±70	2470-2110
*FABD	Coastal foothill	~2 km	~40 m	I	8 spit 2	n/a	Wk-19191*	2251±39	2350-2150
FABD	Coastal foothill	~2 km	~40 m	I	8 spit 3	n/a	ANSTO OZF-109	2250±40	2350-2150

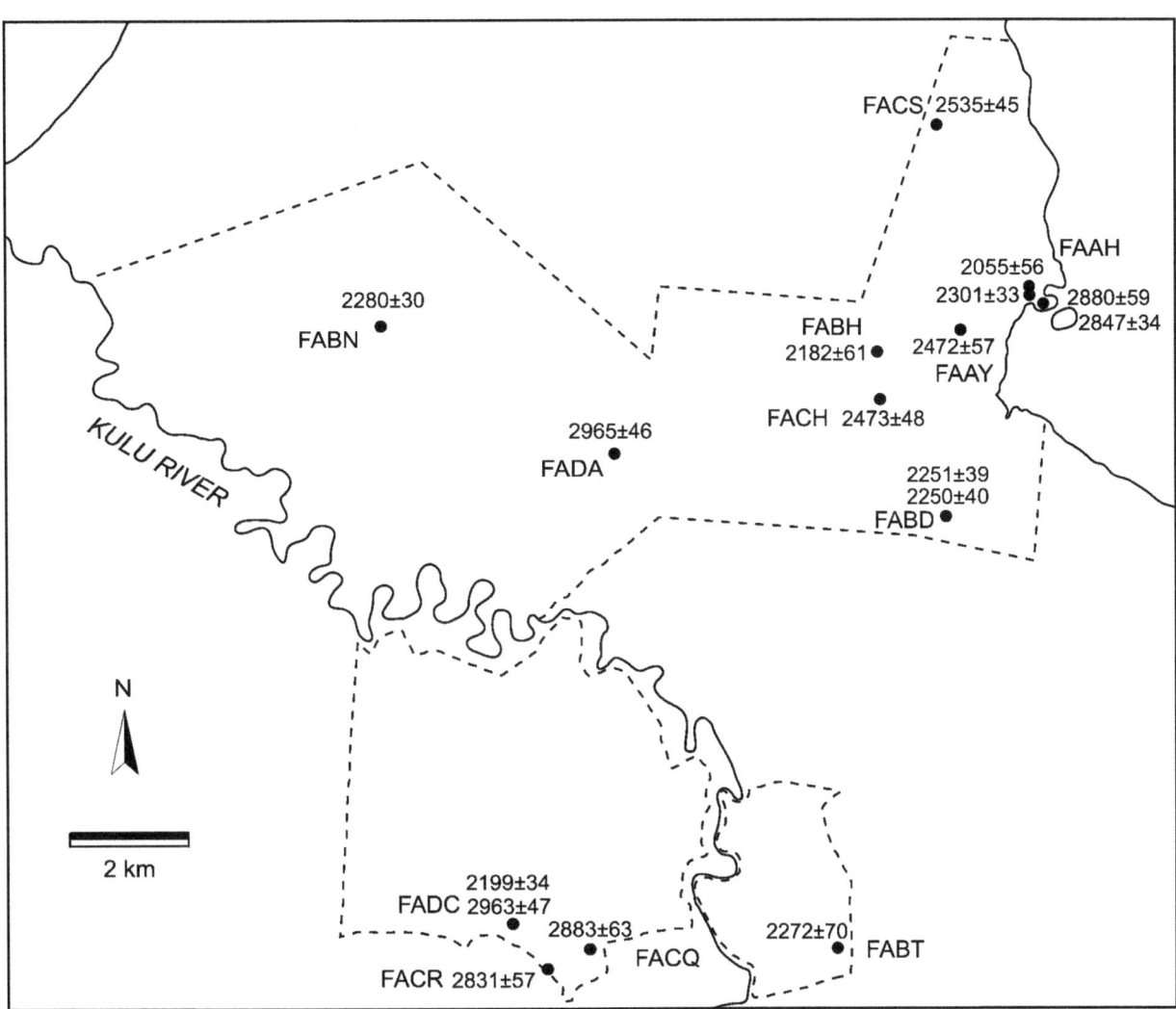

Figure 7. Distribution of radiocarbon dates for cultural materials recovered from the W-K2 soil on the Willaumez Peninsula isthmus.

a single depositional phase. The other sample (Wk-12824: 2300-1900 cal. BP) relates to a dentate-stamped sherd in the top of the W-K2 soil at FAAH/XLVI. This sherd is contemporary with aceramic levels at FABN and FABH, where sherds (including one with dentate-stamping at FABN) were recovered in surface collections. All the sherds in FAAH/XLVI are moderately to heavily weathered and small, with a low mean weight (2.9 g). While not ruling out the possibility of a lag deposit or some degree of post-depositional disturbance, we tentatively accept the dating result at this stage. It is important to note that the sherds were stratified between the W-K2 and W-K3 tephras, so any post-depositional disturbance must have occurred during this limited time period. We note, furthermore, that the date matches six others for non-pottery contexts. The implications for the end of the Lapita ceramic series raised by sample Wk-12824 will be discussed further in the final report on the isthmus pottery (Specht and Spry in prep.).

Figure 8. Sherds from FAAH and Numundo Island on Willaumez Peninsula isthmus. Scale bars equal to 20 mm. A: FAAH/35, XVII layer 9 spit 2; carinated shoulder, dentate-stamped. B: FAAH/27, XVII layer 9 spit 2; form I? rim, dentate-stamped. C: FAAH/46, XVII layer 9 spit 2; carinated shoulder, fingernail impressed. D: FAAH/36, XVII layer 9 spit 2; body, dentate- and plain arc stamped. E: FAAH/28, XVII layer 9 spit 2; body, dentate-stamped and plain circle impressed. F: FAAH/38, XVII layer 9 spit 2; body, plain arc stamped and carved surface. G: FAAH/62, XVII layer 9 spit 2; body, dentate-stamped. H: Numundo Island, surface; cylinder stand fragment, incised, plain arc or straight-line stamped on flange, deeply incised and carved body.

The pottery

Although our focus in this paper is on the Lapita ceramic series, it is worth noting four sherds of unusual style or dating to more recent periods. Two incised sherds in Layer 9 at FABO/XIV are of uncertain affiliation and age, but could be part of the late incised component of the Lapita ceramic series (Figures 9A, 9B). An incised Type X sherd (Figure 9C; Lilley 1988) found on the surface of FABI indicates pottery use around 1000-500 cal.

Figure 9. Sherds from pottery localities on the Willaumez Peninsula isthmus. Scale bars equal to 20 mm. A: FABO/1, XIV layer 9 spit 1; rim/neck (form uncertain), incised. B: FABO/2, XIV layer 9 spit 2; body, incised. C: FABI/1, surface; body, incised, Type X; 10R 3/6 dark red. D: FABK/1, VII W-K2 soil; body, incised. E: FACZ/3, surface; body, dentate-stamped; 10R 4/6 red. F: FACZ/1, surface; body, dentate-stamped, and plain arc and circle impressed; 2.5R 4/4 reddish brown. G: FACZ/4, surface; body, dentate- and plain arc stamped, circle impressed. H: FACZ/2, surface; body, dentate- and plain arc stamped, circle impressed; 10R 4/6 red.

BP (Lilley and Specht in press), and therefore after the W-K3 event. This is the first documentation of Type X in the Willaumez Peninsula area. Another incised sherd with an unusual design in the W-K2 soil at FABK/VII (Figure 9D) is of unknown age and affiliation.

The remaining 947 excavated and surface sherds that are likely to belong to the Lapita ceramic series are summarised in Tables 2 and 4 in terms of decoration and form. Sample sizes are generally small. With the exception of FAAH, the largest number of sherds at any locality is 15 at FACZ and most localities yielded fewer than ten. In contrast, there were dense concentrations of sherds at FAAH, representing over 90 % (862) of all sherds recovered on the isthmus. Most of these (575) came from Layer 9 of test pit XVII. The sample is thus heavily biased towards FAAH, but the smaller collections from other localities contribute significant information about past land-use.

No detailed fabric analysis has yet been carried out, but preliminary inspection suggests that most sherds have volcanic sand and lithic fragments up to 1-3 mm in length, and a few may have calcareous inclusions. The eight surface sherds from FACQ, from a single pot, appear to lack volcanic sand or lithic fragments. These sherds are thin and hard, and include a notched rim with an unusual brownish-yellow surface colour (Munsell 10YR 6/6) that is probably the result of the fabric composition or firing conditions rather than the application of pigment (Figure 10F).

Vessel forms include seven of the eight forms proposed by Summerhayes (2000) for the Arawe Islands, plus a probable cylinder stand (Table 4). The most common and widespread forms are round-bodied jars with everted rims (V and VI), jars with incurving upper body and vertical rims (VII), and open bowls (I) (Figure 10). Not surprisingly, FAAH has the widest range of forms (7). Two angular sherds at FAAH are from flat-based open bowls. Carinated shoulders (7 examples) occur only at FAAH, where round shoulders are more common (15); there is also one round shoulder at FACU. At FAAH the carinated shoulders are statistically significantly thicker than round shoulders, though there is no statistical difference in thickness between plain shoulders and those with dentate – or plain-stamped decoration (Student's-t test, two-tail, p=0.4251). The Numundo Island sherd has a prominent rounded flange, and we identify this as part of a cylinder stand (Figures 8H, 10G; cf. Best 2002:82, Fig. 25). No pot stands (Summerhayes Form VIII) have been identified in the samples.

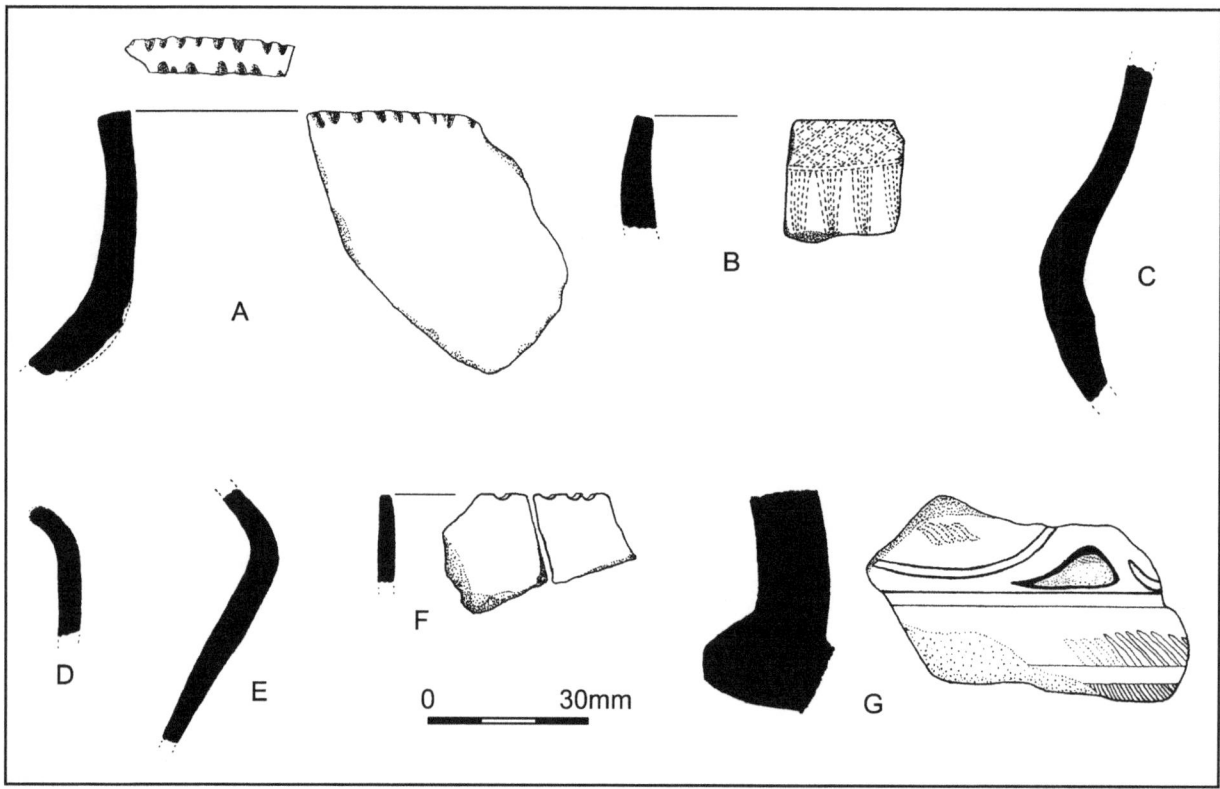

Figure 10. Sherds from pottery localities on the Willaumez Peninsula isthmus. A: FABN/1, surface; form VII double-notched rim. B: FABN/2, surface; form I rim, dentate-stamped. C: FACU/9, XXXI layer 6 spit 2; form V? rounded shoulder/neck, plain. D: FABO/1, XIV layer 9 spit 1, rim (form uncertain), incised (Plate 5A). E: FAAY/1, V layer 7 spit 2 (below Wk-9026: 2472±57); form V neck, plain. F: FACQ/1, surface; form V or VI rim, plain, 10R 6/6 brownish yellow. G: Numundo Island, surface; cylinder stand fragment, incised, plain arc stamped and carved.

Table 4. Distribution of vessel forms at the Willaumez Peninsula isthmus pottery localities. The FAAH forms include sherds from the base of the hill.

Locality	Landform	I	I flat base	II	III	IV	V	VI	VII	VIII	Cylinder stand	Total sherds	Total forms
Numundo Island	Beach	0	0	0	0	0	0	0	0	0	1	1	1
FAAH	Coastal hill	4	2	1	1	1	2	0	5	0	0	16	7
FAAY	Coastal hill	0	0	0	0	0	2	0	0	0	0	2	1
FABI	Coastal hill	0	0	0	0	0	0	0	0	0	0	0	0
FABK	Coastal hill	0	0	0	0	0	0	0	0	0	0	0	0
FABO	Coastal hill	0	0	0	0	0	1	0	0	0	0	1	1
FACX	Coastal hill	0	0	0	0	0	0	0	0	0	0	0	0
FABH	Hill on divide	0	0	0	0	0	0	0	0	0	0	0	0
FACU	Hill on divide	0	0	0	0	0	0	0	0	0	0	0	0
FABN	Inland foothill	1	0	0	0	0	0	0	1	0	0	2	2
FACQ	Inland foothill	0	0	0	0	0	2	0	0	0	0	2	1
FACR	Inland foothill	0	0	0	0	0	0	1	0	0	0	1	1
FACZ	Inland foothill	0	0	0	0	0	0	0	0	0	0	0	0
FADC	Inland foothill	0	0	0	0	0	0	0	0	0	0	0	0
Totals		5	2	1	1	1	7	1	6	0	1	25	8(9)

Surface modifications include pigments or slips that mostly (14 of 15) fall within the red ranges (Munsell 7.5R 4/8; 10R 4-5/6-8). A reddish-brown (2.5R 4/4) body sherd at FACZ may reflect post-depositional surface alteration, as it appears to come from the same vessel as the red sherds. Whereas some red-pigmented sherds have a matte finish, others (including dentate-stamped sherds) appear to have been burnished. There is no evidence for the application of a white infill or coating on dentate-stamped sherds as noted elsewhere (Bedford 2006; Green and Anson 2000:Fig. 14I).

Decoration is confined to the rim-upper body-shoulder areas, with few rims decorated on their interior surface (Figure 11D). The main technique, dentate-stamping, is twice as common as plain-stamping and linear incision. The dentate impressions are generally medium to large in size, though one surface sherd at FAAH has much finer impressions (Figure 11G). Impressed circles (4 examples) occur only at FAAH (Figures 8E, 11A). Small plain-impressed arcs are present only at FACZ, where they close the ends of groups of short dentate-stamped lines (Figures 9E, 9G, 9H). The category 'incised' includes several sherds at FAAH and that from Numundo Island where the incision forms a broad, shallow groove with rounded cross-section. A body sherd at FAAH and the possible cylinder stand fragment from Numundo Island have part of the surface carved away, putting the decorated surface into bas-relief (Figures 8F, 8H, 10G). The only example of fingernail impressions is on a carinated shoulder in Layer 9 at FAAH/XVII (Figure 8C).

Lip modifications consist primarily of notching or wavy scalloped impressions, usually on flat lips, with scalloped lips present only at FAAH (6 excavated, 1 surface). Single-notched lips (25) outnumber double-notched lips (6). Both occur at FAAH (20 single, 5 double) and FABN (1 each), but only single notching is present at FACQ (1) and FACU (3) (Figures 10A, 10F). There are two definite and two possible examples of dentate-stamped lips at FAAH, where the designs consist of triangles and arcs, and alternating groups of diagonal lines and plain-stamped arcs (Figure 11D). There are no applied plain or notched relief bands (other than the flange on the Numundo Island sherd), applied relief knobs, excised triangles, cut-outs, punctations or shell-edge impressions.

Figure 11. Selected sherds from FAAH on Willaumez Peninsula isthmus. Scale bars equal to 20 mm. A: FAAH/91, XXVIII W-K2 soil; carinated shoulder, incised, plain arc stamped, impressed circles. B: FAAH/98, XXVIII W-K2 soil; body, dentate-stamped. C: FAAH/92, XXVIII W-K2 soil; body, dentate-stamped. D: FAAH/4, XXVIII W-K2 soil; form IV rim (exterior, interior, rim/lip), dentate- and plain arc stamped. E: FAAH/1, surface; form I? rim, dentate-stamped and incised/plain arc stamped. F: FAAH/2, surface; probable flat-based bowl, dentate-stamped. G: FAAH/102, surface; body, dentate-stamped; 7.5R 4/8 red.

The designs are primarily rectilinear, but many decorated sherds are too small to identify their motifs with certainty. Dentate – and plain-stamped motifs include narrow bands of overlapping arcs forming zone markers that often separate groups of other repeated elements including rows of arcs and rectilinear compositions (e.g., Figures 8A, 8D, 11D, 11F) and two examples of triangles formed by dentate-stamped lines (Figures 10B, 11D). There are no obvious faces or 'earplugs', though one sherd at FAAH (Figure 8E) could have a section of the 'labyrinth' design (Siorat 1990:62) that occasionally appears as a 'space-filler' between faces (Spriggs 1990). The incised sherds at FAAH indicate groups of parallel straight and curved lines that commonly occur with dentate-stamped designs at other Lapita sites (see refs in Specht and Summerhayes in press; Specht and Torrence in press).

Comparison with the Talasea area

The isthmus sherds show both similarities and contrasts with those of the Talasea area (Table 5). The differences may be due partly to the small sample sizes for the isthmus, but could also reflect temporal and behavioural variations. Around Talasea, the earliest dentate-stamped pottery at FYS (Torrence and Stevenson 2000: Table 1) and FEA (White *et al.* 2002) are located at beach level. On the isthmus, only the cylinder stand sherd from Numundo Island comes from a similar location. At ECA/B in the Mussau Islands a cylinder stand is dated to about the same time or slightly later than FYS while overlapping substantially with Wk-10463 for FAAH/XVII (Kirch 2001a). On the other hand, Wk-10463 (3210-2850 cal. BP) and Wk-19190 (3070-2860 cal. BP) are slightly younger than the oldest date of 3390-3080 cal. BP at FYS (Beta-72144; Specht and Torrence in press: Table 5). We suggest, then, that there could be a small but important difference in age between FAAH/XVII and the Numundo Island beach find, and this might explain the scarcity of fine, needlepoint dentate-stamping at the

Table 5. Comparison between FAAH and the Talasea area in terms of selected pottery attributes. For the age ranges '(P)' indicates plant samples, '(S)' indicates shell sample.

	FCR/FCS	FEA	FEA	FAAH	FSZ	FAO
Location	Garua Harbour	Garua Harbour	Garua Harbour	Isthmus	Garua Harbour	Garua Harbour
Landform	Beach/intertidal	Beach level	Beach/intertidal	Coastal hill	Coastal hill	Coastal hill
Number of sherds	~750	>8,000	>600	863	>4550	676
Oldest date	n/a	3340-3000 (S)	n/a	3210-2850 (P)	3060-2760 (P)	2715-2350 (P)
Form I bowl	x	x	x	x	x	x
Form I flat-based bowl	x	x	x	x	x	-
Form II	(x)	x	-	x	x	-
Form III	x	x	x	x	-	-
Form IV	x	x	x	x	-	-
Form V	x	x	x	x	(x)	-
Form VI	x	x	x	x	-	x
Form VII	(x)	x	(x)	x	x	x
Form VIIIA stand	-	-	x	-	-	-
Form VIIIB stand	x	x	x	-	x	-
Bowl-on-stand	x	-	x	-	-	-
Cylinder stand	-	x	x	-	-	-
Notched lip	x	x	x	x	x	x
Scalloped lip	x	x	x	x	x	x
Dentate-stamped	x	x	x	x	x	x
Incised/plain stamped	x	x	x	x	x	x
Circle impressed	x	x	x	x	x	x
Excised triangles	x	x	x	-	-	-
Cut-outs	-	-	x	-	-	-
Fingernail impressed	x	-	-	x	x	x
Shell impressed	-	-	-	-	x	x
Punctation	-	-	x	-	x	x
Applied relief	-	x	x	-	x	x
Modelled heads	-	-	x	-	-	-
Face motifs	x	x	x	-	-	-
N=25	16(18)	18	21(22)	14	14(15)	12

isthmus sites, the exception being sherd FAAH/102 (Figure 11G). Alternatively, activity at the two areas could be essentially of the same age but reflecting different kinds of activities, as the oldest isthmus dates for pottery at FADC (Wk-12845: 3240-2960 cal. BP) and FAAH (Wk-10463 (3210-2850 cal. BP) overlap substantially with Beta-72144 (3390-3080 cal. BP) for FYS.

In terms of the presence or absence of certain stylistic attributes, Table 5 shows that the FAAH site is closer to the early Talasea area sites of FEA and FCR/FCS than it is to the younger FAO and FSZ sites, as would be expected from the date for FAAH/XVII. The FAAH collection shares all 14 of its pottery attributes with FEA and FCR/FCS, but only 11 with the younger sites. At this stage FAAH and the isthmus sites in general lack several early forms (e.g., pot stands, bowl-on-stand and thick channelled rims), several decorative techniques (e.g., cut-outs, excised triangles) and design elements (e.g., faces and curvilinear forms in general) that characterise early Lapita contexts in the Talasea area. The undated FACZ sherds could be as old as FAAH/XVII as they share with the earliest Talasea area groups of straight dentate-stamped lines with the ends closed by small plain arc impressions (cf. also the Arawe Islands: Summerhayes 2000).

The red surface treatments on the isthmus sherds match the values recorded for sherds in the Talasea area and in the Mussau Islands (Kirch 2001b:85; Specht and Torrence in press;). The technique of carving the sherd surface to form bas-relief at FAAH is currently not represented in the Talasea area, but is present in the Arawe Islands (Summerhayes 2000: Figs 5.31, 5.32), Duke of York Islands (White in press), on Ambitle Island off SE New Ireland (White and Specht 1971:Fig. 3), and on Eloaua Island in the Mussau group, where it occurs with broad grooved incision (e.g., Kirch 1997: Plate 5.1). The notched rim with an unusual surface colour at FACQ (Figure 10F) is similar to undated sherds on Garua Island that are also very thin and hard, though with dark grey surfaces (Specht and Torrence in press).

The isthmus assemblages have only one fingernail-impressed sherd. This sherd from FAAH has parallels on Garua Island (Specht and Torrence in press: Figs 5r, 5s), where the oldest fingernail impressions are dated to 2715-2350 cal. BP (NZA-3729) at FAO, somewhat later than the FAAH example (Specht and Torrence in press:Table 5). The isthmus lacks several decorative techniques that characterise the later pottery of the Talasea area, such as applied notched relief bands, applied angular knobs, punctate and shell-impressed designs. Sample bias is an obvious explanation, but as the techniques occur in the Talasea area in small samples comparable in size to those of the isthmus (Specht and Torrence in press:Tables 1, 2), this may not be the only reason. An alternative explanation may lie in their radiocarbon dates for the two areas. The six youngest isthmus dates bracket ca 2360 to 1900 cal. BP, well before the W-K3 event (1750-1550 cal. BP), and only one of these came from an excavation level with pottery (Wk-12824, at FAAH/XLVI). The isthmus, then, might have been abandoned prior to the W-K3 event, whereas in the Garua Harbour area activity appears to have continued up to the W-K3 event, but with changes in the pottery assemblages.

In summary, the ceramic analysis provides important information about the potential history of site use in the isthmus region. Based on stylistic criteria and comparisons with the Talasea area, the oldest pottery was probably deposited at FAAH and on Numundo Island. As at Talasea, there might have been a dichotomy between the coastal location of the small island of Numundo that was used for special purposes and mainland locations such as FAAH. On the other hand, the presence of what may be an early design element on the FACZ sherds, high on an inland foothill of Mt Krummel, and the early date (3240-2960 cal. BP) for plain pottery at FADC indicate that use of locations away from the coast occurred during an early phase of settlement in the isthmus region. This pattern contrasts with Garua Island, where the earliest dates come from a coastal location (FYS). Since we are monitoring human activities across a wide range of mainland environments rather than on a small island, the different pattern is perhaps not surprising. We can now incorporate the ceramic analyses into a broader discussion of land-use within the isthmus region.

Rapid re-colonisation

Not surprisingly, the isthmus region was abandoned following the W-K2 volcanic disaster around 3480-3200 cal. BP. The depth of tephra deposited would have totally devastated settlements, cultivated plots, forests and reefs (Torrence and Doelman in press). Combined with the massive erosion and re-deposition that followed the eruption, the lack of resources would have made the area uninhabitable for some time (Torrence 2002b; Torrence and Doelman in press). Just how long the area was unoccupied is uncertain, but the dates show that the region was re-colonised by 3240-2960 cal. BP. These people introduced the knowledge of how to make and use pottery. But were they descendants of those who had previously lived in the area, or did they represent a new population? One way to approach this question is to examine the timing and nature of how the region was re-colonised.

Ceramic analysis has provided important indications that some sites in the isthmus region are likely to be as early as those in the Talasea area and therefore to be contemporary with the earliest re-colonisation of Willaumez Peninsula. This conclusion is supported by the radiocarbon results from the isthmus test pits with pottery, which suggest that the appearance of pottery there was at the same time as or shortly after its appearance in the Talasea area.

Six of the 17 radiocarbon dates (Table 3) relate to pottery found in excavated contexts, two come from excavated levels without pottery but above sherds in lower levels, four are from test pits where pottery was found only in surface contexts, and five are from localities without any pottery. The oldest dates in each group in Table 3 are the same across the groups. This absence of difference suggests that pottery was present from the start of the re-colonisation phase; there was not an aceramic re-colonisation phase prior to the introduction of pottery.

The dates fall into two chronological groups: an older one of six dates where the age ranges exceed 3200-3000 years, and a younger one where they do not exceed 2760 years. This apparent pattern might be a function of the small number of dates, but could also indicate two phases of human activity in the region. Localities with pottery and those without are represented in each period. Secondly, the dates from different physiographic zones and elevations in the older group are similar to each other. The six oldest dates come from a range of elevations up to 40-80 m above sea level and up to 17-18 km from the current coastline.

We interpret this pattern as indicating that from the earliest arrival of people after W-K2 and until the W-K3 event, all areas of the landscape were used for a wide range of activities, some of which included the use of ceramics. Since aceramic and ceramic localities are contemporary, there is no evidence to support the hypothesis that pottery was introduced from outside to people already in residence. Both types of sites occur in all landscape zones and are not segregated into different parts of the region. The most parsimonious interpretation of the data is that the same people created the artefact scatters at the ceramic and aceramic sites in the course of the many different kinds of activities that were necessary to sustain their livelihood. Pottery was probably used in only a small number of activities. Groups are unlikely to have always carried fragile pottery vessels wherever they went, particularly while engaged in hunting or foraging for bush foods and other useful products.

The widespread distribution of early dates shows that unlike on Garua Island, people moved into the inland zones of the isthmus very rapidly after the appearance of pottery in the Talasea area, possibly spreading inland from both east and west coasts. The speed of the re-colonisation suggests a number of possible models of behaviour. Firstly, people may have returned to places that were known to them because they were used prior to W-K2. The finding of three stemmed tools at FABN may indicate that this area was a particularly important place (Torrence 2004a), and there are dense scatters of obsidian artefacts and fire-cracked stone at locations on the spurs of the inland foothills, such as FACR and FACQ, suggesting repeated and/or heavy use of these locations prior to W-K2. Although the infilling of the tidal basin markedly changed the availability of local resources, these elevated positions would have been ideal for settlement and within range of the prime resources of the newly created river valley and swamp.

This point relates to a second possible explanation. The rapid movement of people into elevated settings both on the coast and inland may relate to landscape change following the W-K2 event. At the time when Lapita pottery was introduced, the low-lying areas on each side of the isthmus divide were swampy, locally saline and unsuitable for cultivation. Consequently, the selection of elevated locations on hills and ridges would have been a more practical and appropriate solution than the construction of stilt-houses over water or in swamps. Elevated situations such as the floodplain foothills of FADC, FACQ and FACR or the coastal hill of FAAH would have been more attractive locales for domestic activities.

Thirdly, the rapid spread of people could represent an extensive use of landscape based on the intensive use of wild resources, and/or cultivation with short fallow periods. Palaeo-environmental studies on the isthmus indicate widespread vegetation disturbance during the pottery period and this was probably associated with gardening (Boyd *et al.* 2005), but much more research is necessary to determine the precise system of cultivation.

A final possibility is that the region was heavily utilised from an early stage of re-colonisation, as the founding population was so large that people were forced to disperse quickly into the hinterland. An influx of people returning to a familiar environment following a natural disaster could certainly have created the observed pattern.

Activity differentiation

Following initial re-colonisation, activities were probably focused in particular locations, with others used less intensively or for specialised functions. The density of sherds at FAAH (especially in test pit XVII) suggests the use of the area as a settlement on a permanent or recurrent basis. In contrast, the smaller quantity of sherds recovered at the inland locations could indicate that the nature of activities expressed by the presence of pottery differed from those at FAAH. It is important to note that sherds did not occur in substantial numbers at the inland locations; Table 2 lists all sherds visible on the ground surface. In addition, a serious effort was made to test as many ridges as possible in the area where pottery had been exposed by road construction. The small areas available for settlement on these narrow, steep-sided ridges may have been as significant as their inland location near the swamps of the Kulu River floodplain. These small ridge locations could represent residential hamlets that were only occupied for a short time, whereas FAAH was a more permanent settlement or a focal point for some sort of special purpose activities, such as particular ceremonies, that involved the discard of relatively large amounts of pottery.

Several other places could have been used for special activities in which pottery played a role. During the early period of pottery use Numundo Island might have been used for activities that required a degree of isolation and/or proximity to the sea, as has been suggested for Boduna Island (site FEA) in the Talasea area (Specht and Summerhayes in press) and for other small islands (Specht this volume). The presence of dentate-stamped sherds that probably came from a single pot in the spring at FACZ could signify another type of special activity involving a relationship between water and pottery, although whether this was for ritual purposes or simply for collecting water for domestic consumption is open to speculation.

The remainder of the places where small samples of sherds were found are harder to interpret because they do not fit the typical model of a Lapita pottery village. At these locations only small amounts of pottery were used either because of the restricted nature of activities that took place, a low rate of breakage (and, by implication, the nature of ceramic use), or short-term occupation perhaps associated with the preparation and maintenance of cultivation plots. If these were settlements, then the limited quantities raise questions about the place and/or nature of pottery manufacture in daily life. Combining the small scatters into a single use category may be misleading, however, since they occur in a range of settings, including the seemingly different environments of inland and coastal hills and the strategic position of the divide between the eastern coastal plain and the Kulu floodplain. The widespread distribution of these locations with small amounts of pottery, as well as those with only obsidian artefacts, demonstrates that there is still much to learn about land-use practices during this period. Clearly both new methodologies and fresh perspectives are required to develop appropriate models for the cultural landscapes created by the users of Lapita pottery.

The overall picture obtained from the distribution of ceramics across the isthmus region is of an extensive system of land-use with a spatially differentiated pattern of various activities. The use of ceramics was not confined to permanent settlements. Finding out exactly how long places were utilised and for what reasons are obviously difficult tasks that will require larger excavations combined with rigorous analyses of the ceramic and non-ceramic assemblages. What is most important at this stage of research, however, is the range of new questions about land-use raised by the results of landscape archaeology in the isthmus region.

Conclusions

The adoption of a landscape perspective has enabled archaeology on Willaumez Peninsula to capitalise on the secure tephra sequence of the region and the increased access to inland zones made possible by plantation development. The results constitute a strong confirmation of the land-use strategies identified on Garua Island during the dentate-stamped phase of Lapita pottery, although the isthmus dates suggest that the inland component was established on the mainland earlier than on the offshore island. Just how long after the arrival of the pottery-makers the extensive land-use strategy was developed or whether an old pattern was re-established by the colonisers remains to be determined, but the available dates indicate that it could have occurred within a generation or two of arrival. Further survey and excavation work is clearly needed to address this issue and to determine the nature of the activities at the different kinds of locations, including off-shore islands (especially Numundo Island), high density ceramic discard at coastal settings (FAAH), small scatters on the coast (FAAY, FABO), inland (FACQ, FACR) and divide (FABH, FACU), and perhaps special-purpose cache-like contexts (FACZ).

The common presence of dentate-stamped Lapita pottery in the Garua Harbour area might reflect a location strategy designed to facilitate – and perhaps monopolise – exploitation of the Kutau obsidian source, the products of which dominate early Lapita obsidian assemblages in Near Oceania and the SE Solomon Islands (Green 1987; Sheppard 1993; Specht 2002; Summerhayes 2004) as well as the isthmus itself (Torrence 2004b). No such explanation can be applied to the isthmus area. The number of dentate-stamped pottery sites currently on record in this area is much fewer than around Garua Harbour, but localities with pottery occur on both sides of the divide and some, on the eastern side at least, have direct access to the sea. Perhaps they formed part of a network of nodes for the distribution of obsidian and other products of the Peninsula, with the 'western' sites servicing Lapita settlements on the Kove and Siassi Islands (Lilley 1991, 2002, 2004), and the 'eastern' sites supplying areas such as Watom Island (Green and Anson 2000), the Duke of York Islands (White and Harris 1997) and locations further to the east and south.

The apparent gap between the youngest W-K2 soil dates on the isthmus and those in the Garua Harbour area suggests the possibility that the isthmus was abandoned before the W-K3 event. As is evident in the range of dates on Table 3, an effort was made to test the apparent difference between the two areas by dating aceramic levels stratified directly under the W-K3 tephra. The seeming abandonment might explain the absence from the isthmus of certain pottery traits that characterise the later pottery of Garua Harbour. The proposal by Torrence and Stevenson (2000:339-339) that the archaeological expression of shifting cultivation combined with relatively low population densities can simulate patterns of abandonment at small spatial scales might be appropriate here, but further research is clearly needed to find an explanation why there is a significant temporal break in the discard of cultural material in the isthmus region before the W-K3 event.

The changing use of landscape on Willaumez Peninsula has profound implications for the interpretation of Lapita archaeology in other areas of its distribution. The oldest isthmus dates fall into the 'formative' period of the Lapita cultural complex in the Bismarck Archipelago (Specht this volume), arguably just before its dispersal southwards into Remote Oceania at about 3200-3000 years ago (Bedford 2003; Galipaud and Swete Kelly this volume; Pineda and Galipaud 1998; cf. Green 2003). The presence of early dates at elevated inland locations and the putatively early-stage dentate-stamped sherds at FACZ demonstrate that Lapita pottery-users on New Britain were already adept at exploiting non-marine zones by the time the cultural complex was carried southwards. These early Lapita communities were not tethered to coastal resources, but where opportunity allowed, they exploited inland resource zones. This has implications for modelling survival strategies and mobility potential within Near Oceania south of the Bismarck Archipelago and in at least some archipelagos of large islands in western Remote Oceania, such as Vanuatu and New Caledonia (cf. Anderson 2001).

In conclusion, the isthmus research has confirmed the inland component of land-use indicated by the Garua Island and FRI sites. It has revealed variations in land-use on Willaumez Peninsula that open new sets of questions and issues that will require new conceptual approaches and methods, as well as more intensive analyses of this rich new data set. More broadly, the results reinforce the view that Pacific archaeology would benefit from the extension of research throughout the Lapita pottery distribution into a wider range of environmental zones, including the inland sectors of islands (Anderson *et al.* 2000:315; Torrence and Stevenson 2000).

Acknowledgments

We acknowledge with appreciation funding and support provided by the Australian Research Council, Australia and Pacific Foundation, Pacific Biological Foundation, Australian Museum, Australian Institute of Nuclear Science and Engineering, and New Britain Palm Oil Ltd. We thank the following organisations for research permits, logistical and other support: National Research Institute (PNG); National Museum and Art Gallery (PNG); University of Papua New Guinea; West New Britain Provincial Cultural Centre; Mahonia Na Dari Research Station; Walindi Plantation Resort; Kimbe Bay Shipping Agencies, and especially the staff and management of New Britain Palm Oil Ltd. The isthmus project would have been impossible without the dedicated efforts of many volunteers whose hard work is much appreciated. We also thank Peter White for elevations of test pits; Richelle Spry for assistance with the ceramic analysis; Trudy Doelman for GIS analysis; Ghada Daher for pottery drawings; Fiona Roberts for the maps and figure lay-outs; and Cameron Petrie for radiocarbon age calibrations.

Endnote

1. Anderson *et al.* (2001: Table 1) list five sites on Garua Island (FRD, FAAQ) and Willaumez Peninsula (FRI, FABH and FABN) that are not on or close to present-day shorelines. FRD should be deleted, as this site has not produced dentate-stamped pottery. The inland site of Vunailau (SAU) on Watom Island should be added (Specht 1968:120). The only other inland sites listed are Vaturekuka (Parke 2000) and Qara-I-Oso II (Anderson *et al.* 2000) in Fiji. Since the gazetteer was published, another inland dentate-stamped pottery site has been reported from Fiji (Kumar 2002; Kumar and Nunn 2003). Two of these Fijian sites were recorded during non-archaeological field studies.

References

Anderson, A. 2001. Mobility models of Lapita migration. In G.R. Clark, A.J. Anderson and T. Vunidilo (eds), *The Archaeology of Lapita Dispersal in Oceania*, pp. 15-23. Canberra: Pandanus Books, Australian National University. Terra Australis 17.

Anderson, A., G. Clark and T. Worthy 2000. An inland Lapita site in Fiji. *Journal of the Polynesian Society* 109: 311-316.

Anderson, A., S. Bedford, G. Clark, I. Lilley, C. Sand, G. Summerhayes and R. Torrence 2001. An inventory of Lapita sites containing dentate-stamped pottery. In G.R. Clark, A.J. Anderson and T. Vunidilo (eds), *The Archaeology of Lapita Dispersal in Oceania*, pp. 1-13. Canberra: Pandanus Books, Australian National University. Terra Australis 17.

Bedford, S. 2003. The timing and nature of Lapita colonisation in Vanuatu: the haze begins to clear. In C. Sand (ed.), *Pacific Archaeology: Assessments and prospects*, pp. 147-158. Noumea: Département d'Archéologie, Service des Musées et du Patrimoine de Nouvelle-Calédonie. Les Cahiers de l'Archéologie en Nouvelle-Calédonie 15.

Bedford, S. 2006. The Pacific's earliest painted pottery: an added layer of intrigue to the Lapita debate and beyond. *Antiquity* 80: 544-557.

Best, S. 2002. *Lapita: A View from the East*. Auckland: New Zealand Archaeological Association. Monograph 24.

Boyd, W.E., C.J. Lentfer and J. Parr 2005. Interactions between human activity, volcanic eruptions and vegetation during the Holocene at Garua and Numundo, West New Britain. *Quaternary Research* 64: 384-398.

Felgate, M.W. 2003. *Reading Lapita in Near Oceania: Intertidal and shallow-water pottery scatters, Roviana Lagoon, New Georgia, Solomon Islands*. Unpublished PhD thesis, University of Auckland.

Frimigacci, D. 1980. Localisation éco-géographique et utilisation de l'espace de quelques sites Lapita de Nouvelle-Calédonie. *Journal de la Société des Océanistes* 66-67 (36): 5-11.

Gosden, C. and J. Webb 1994. The creation of a Papua New Guinean landscape: Archaeological and geomorphological evidence. *Journal of Field Archaeology* 21(1): 29-51.

Green, R. C. 1987. Obsidian results from the Lapita sites of the Reef/Santa Cruz Islands. In W.R. Ambrose and J.M.J. Mummery (eds), *Archaeometry: Further Australasian Studies*, pp.239-249. Canberra: Australian National University.

Green, R.C. 1992. Definitions of the Lapita Cultural Complex and its non-ceramic component. In J-C. Galipaud (ed.), *Poterie Lapita et Peuplement*, pp. 7-20. Noumea: ORSTOM.

Green, R.C. 2003. The Lapita horizon and traditions – signature for one set of Oceanic migrations. In C. Sand (ed.), *Pacific Archaeology: Assessments and prospects*, pp. 95-120. Noumea: Département d'Archéologie, Service des Musées et du Patrimoine de Nouvelle-Calédonie. Les Cahiers de l'Archéologie en Nouvelle-Calédonie 15.

Green, R.C. and D. Anson 2000. Excavations at Kainapirina (SAC), Watom Island, Papua New Guinea. *New Zealand Journal of Archaeology* 20 (1998): 29-94.

Johnson, R.W. and D.H. Blake 1972. *The Cape Hoskins area, southern Willaumez Peninsula, the Witu Islands, and associated volcanic centres, New Britain: volcanic geology and petrology*. Canberra: Bureau of Mineral Resources, Geology and Geophysics. Record 1972/133.

Kirch, P.V. 1988. The Talepakemalai Lapita Site and Oceanic Prehistory. *National Geographic Research* 4(3): 328-342.

Kirch, P.V. 1997. *The Lapita Peoples: Ancestors of the Oceanic World*. Oxford: Blackwell.

Kirch, P.V. 2001a. A radiocarbon chronology for the Mussau Islands. In P.V. Kirch (ed.), *Lapita and its Transformations in Near Oceania*, pp. 196-222. Berkeley: Archaeological Research Facility, University of California at Berkeley. Contribution 59.

Kirch, P.V. 2001b. Three Lapita villages: Excavations at Talepakemalai (ECA), Etakosarai (ECB), and Etapakengaroasa (EHB), Eloaua and Emananus Islands. In P.V. Kirch (ed.), *Lapita and its Transformations in Near Oceania*, pp. 68-145. Berkeley: Archaeological Research Facility, University of California at Berkeley. Contribution 59.

Kumar, R. 2002. Discovery of a Lapita sherd inland of the Northeast coast of Viti Levu Island, Fiji: insights and implications. Suva: Institute of Applied Sciences, University of the South Pacific. IAS Technical Report 2002/5.

Kumar, R. and P.D. Nunn 2003. Inland and coastal Lapita settlement on Vitilevu Island, Fiji: New data. *Domodomo* 16(1): 15-20.

Lepofsky, D. 1988. The environmental context of Lapita settlement locations. In P.V. Kirch and T.L. Hunt (eds), *Archaeology of the Lapita Cultural Complex: A critical review*, pp. 33-47. Seattle: Thomas Burke Memorial Washington State Museum. Report 5.

Lilley, I. 1988. Type X: description and discussion of a prehistoric ceramic ware from northeastern Papua New Guinea. *Bulletin of the Indo-Pacific Prehistory Association* 8: 90-100.

Lilley, I. 1991. Lapita and post-Lapita developments in the Vitiaz Strait-West New Britain area. *Bulletin of the Indo-Pacific Prehistory Association* 11: 313-322.

Lilley, I. 2002. Lapita and Type Y in the KLK site, Siassi, Papua New Guinea. In S. Bedford, C. Sand and D. Burley (eds), *Fifty Years in the Field. Essays in honour and celebration of Richard Shutler Jr's archaeological career*, pp. 79-90. Auckland: New Zealand Archaeological Association. Monograph 25.

Lilley, I. 2004. Trade and culture history across the Vitiaz Strait, Papua New Guinea: the emerging post-Lapita coastal sequence. *Records of the Australian Museum, Supplement* 29: 89-96.

Lilley, I. and J. Specht in press. Revised dating of Type X pottery, Morobe Province, Papua New Guinea. *Technical Reports of the Australian Museum*.

Machida, H., R. Blong, J. Specht, H. Moriwaki, R. Torrence, Y. Hayakawa, B. Talai, D. Lolok and C.F. Pain 1996. Holocene explosive eruptions of Witori and Dakataua caldera volcanoes in West New Britain, Papua New Guinea. *Quaternary International* 34-36: 65-78.

McKee, C.O., H. Patia, J. Kuduon and R. Torrence 2005. *Volcanic Hazard Assessment of the Krummel-Garbuna-Welcker Volcanic Complex, Southern Willaumez Peninsula, W.N.B., Papua New Guinea*. Port Moresby: Geological Survey of Papua New Guinea. Report 2005/4.

Parke, A.L. 2000. Coastal and inland Lapita sites in Vanua Levu, Fiji. *Archaeology in Oceania* 35(3): 116-119.

Pavlides, C. 2006. Life before Lapita: new developments in Melanesia's long-term history. In I. Lilley (ed.), *Archaeology of Oceania: Australia and the Pacific Islands*, pp. 205-227. Oxford: Blackwell.

Petrie, C. and R. Torrence in prep. The chronology of eruption, abandonment and reoccupation, West New Britain c.7500 BC – AD 1880.

Pineda, R. and J-C. Galipaud 1998. Evidences archéologiques d'une surrection différentielle de l'île Malo (archipel du Vanuatu) au cours de l'Holocène récent. *Comptes-rendus de l'Académie des Sciences de Paris. Sciences de la Terre et des Planètes* 327: 777-779.

Ryburn, R. J. 1975. *Talasea-Gasmata, New Britain. Sheet SB/56-5 & SB/56-9. 1:250,000 Geological Series – Explanatory Notes*. Canberra: Australian Government Publishing Service.

Sheppard, P.J. 1993. Lapita lithics: trade/exchange and technology. A view from the Reefs/Santa Cruz. *Archaeology in Oceania* 28(3): 121-137.

Siorat, J.P. 1990. A technological analysis of Lapita pottery decoration. In M. Spriggs (ed.), *Lapita Design, Form and Composition*, pp. 59-82. Canberra: Department of Prehistory Australian National University. Occasional Papers in Prehistory 19.

Specht, J. 1968. Preliminary report of excavations on Watom Island. *Journal of the Polynesian Society* 77(2): 117–134.

Specht, J. 2002. Obsidian, colonising and exchange. In S. Bedford, C. Sand and D. Burley (eds), *Fifty Years in the Field. Essays in honour and celebration of Richard Shutler Jr's archaeological career*, pp. 37-49. Auckland: New Zealand Archaeological Association. Monograph 25.

Specht, J., R. Fullagar and R. Torrence 1991. What was the significance of Lapita pottery at Talasea? *Bulletin of the Indo-Pacific Prehistory Association* 11: 281-294.

Specht, J. and R. Spry in prep. Pottery from the isthmus sites, Willaumez Peninsula, West New Britain, Papua New Guinea.

Specht, J. and G. Summerhayes in press. The Boduna Island (FEA) Lapita site, Papua New Guinea. *Technical Reports of the Australian Museum*.

Specht, J. and R. Torrence in prep. Pottery of the Talasea area, West New Britain Province, Papua New Guinea. *Technical Reports of the Australian Museum*.

Spriggs, M. 1984. The Lapita cultural complex: origins, distribution, contemporaries and successors. *Journal of Pacific History* 19(4): 202-223.

Spriggs, M. 1990. The changing face of Lapita: transformations of a design. In M. Spriggs (ed.), *Lapita Design, Form and Composition*, pp. 83-122. Canberra: Department of Prehistory, Australian National University. Occasional Papers in Prehistory 19.

Spriggs, M. 1997. *The Island Melanesians*. Blackwell: Oxford.

Summerhayes, G. 2000. *Lapita Interaction*. Canberra: Department of Archaeology and Natural History and Centre for Archaeological Research, Australian National University. Terra Australis 15.

Summerhayes, G. 2004. The nature of prehistoric obsidian importation to Anir and the development of a 3,000 year old regional picture of obsidian exchange within the Bismarck Archipelago, Papua New Guinea. *Records of the Australian Museum, Supplement* 29: 145-156.

Torrence, R. 2002a. Cultural landscapes on Garua Island, Papua New Guinea. *Antiquity* 76: 766-776.

Torrence, R. 2002b. What makes a disaster? A long-term view of volcanic eruptions and human responses in Papua New Guinea. In R. Torrence and J. Grattan (eds), *Natural Disasters and Cultural Change*, pp. 292-302. London: Routledge.

Torrence, R. 2004a. Pre-Lapita valuables in island Melanesia. *Records of the Australian Museum, Supplement* 29: 163-172.

Torrence, R. 2004b. Now you see it. Now you don't. Changing obsidian source use in the Willaumez Peninsula, Papua New Guinea. In J. Cherry, C. Scarre and S. Shennan (eds), *Explaining social change: studies in honour of Colin Renfrew*, pp. 115-126. Cambridge: McDonald Institute for Archaeological Research.

Torrence, R. and T. Doelman in press. Chaos and selection in catastrophic environments. In J. Grattan and R. Torrence (eds), *Living Under the Shadow: The Archaeological, Cultural and Environmental Impact of Volcanic Eruptions*. Walnut Creek, California: Left Coast Press.

Torrence, R., C. Pavlides, P. Jackson and J. Webb 2000. Volcanic disasters and cultural discontinuities in Holocene time, in West New Britain, Papua New Guinea. In W.G. McGuire, D.R. Griffiths, P.L. Hancock and I.S. Stewart (eds), *The Archaeology of Geological Catastrophes*, pp. 225-244. London: The Geological Society of London. Special Publication 171.

Torrence, R., J. Specht and R. Fullagar 1990. Pompeiis in the Pacific. *Australian Natural History* 23(6): 456-463.

Torrence, R. and C.M. Stevenson 2000. Beyond the beach: changing Lapita landscapes on Garua Island, Papua New Guinea. In A. Anderson and T. Murray (eds), *Australian Archaeologist: Collected Papers in Honour of Jim Allen*, pp. 324-345. Canberra: Coombs Academic Publishing, Australian National University

Torrence, R., V. Neall, T. Doelman, E. Rhodes, C. McKee, H. Davies, R. Bonetti, A. Guglielmetti, A. Manzoni, M. Oddone, J. Parr and C. Wallace 2004. Pleistocene colonisation of the Bismarck Archipelago: new evidence from West New Britain. *Archaeology in Oceania* 39(3): 101-130.

White, J.P. in press. Ceramic sites on the Duke of York Islands, Papua New Guinea. *Technical Reports of the Australian Museum*.

White, J.P., C. Coroneos, V. Neall, W. Boyd and R. Torrence 2002. FEA site, Boduna Island: further investigations. In S. Bedford, C. Sand and D. Burley (eds), *Fifty Years in the Field. Essays in honour and celebration of Richard Shutler Jr's archaeological career*, pp. 101-107. Auckland: New Zealand Archaeological Association. Monograph 25.

White, J.P. and M-N. Harris 1997. Changing sources: early Lapita period obsidian in the Bismarck Archipelago. *Archaeology in Oceania* 32(1): 97-107.

White, J.P. and J. Specht 1971. Prehistoric pottery from Ambitle Island, Bismarck Archipelago. *Asian Perspectives* 14: 88-94.

Wickler, S. 2001. *The Prehistory of Buka: A Stepping Stone Island in the Northern Solomons*. Canberra: Department of Archaeology and Natural History and Centre for Archaeological Research, Australian National University. Terra Australis 16.

5

Lapita Writ Small? Revisiting the Austronesian Colonisation of the Papuan South Coast

Glenn R. Summerhayes[1] and Jim Allen[2]

[1] Department of Anthropology
University of Otago, Dunedin
New Zealand
glenn.summerhayes@stonebow.otago.ac.nz
[2] Department of Archaeology
La Trobe University
Bundoora, Australia
jjallen8@bigpond.net.au

There may be something to be gained by comparing different episodes of colonisation with one another to see what they have in common as processes (Irwin 1991:506).

Introduction

By the late 1970s the prehistoric sequence of the Papuan coast was perhaps the best known in Melanesia. This was a product of the establishment in 1969 of archaeology at the University of Papua New Guinea and a succession of doctoral theses from the Australian National University (ANU). By this time data informing this sequence were known from excavations right along the south Papuan coast and Massim area (see Figure 1 and Table 1).

A subsequent shift of interest at the ANU to island Melanesia and the parallel growth of Lapita studies has seen the archaeology of mainland Papua languish, with only a couple of research investigations resulting in one major published study (Frankel and Rhoads 1994) and associated articles on Papuan Gulf research (Frankel and Vanderwal 1982a, 1982b, 1985; Rhoads 1982; Rhoads and MacKenzie 1991) together with some lesser enquiries around Port Moresby (Bickler 1997, 1999a). However, in the Massim more recent research by Irwin (1983, 1991), Bickler (1999b, 2006; Bickler *et al.* 1997), Burenhult (2002) and Kewibu (pers comm.) has extended what might loosely be called the South Papuan Province into these islands.

Much of the significance of these early pieces of research is now diminished because they were written, if not in ignorance of Lapita, certainly in the absence of our vastly improved knowledge of Lapita and

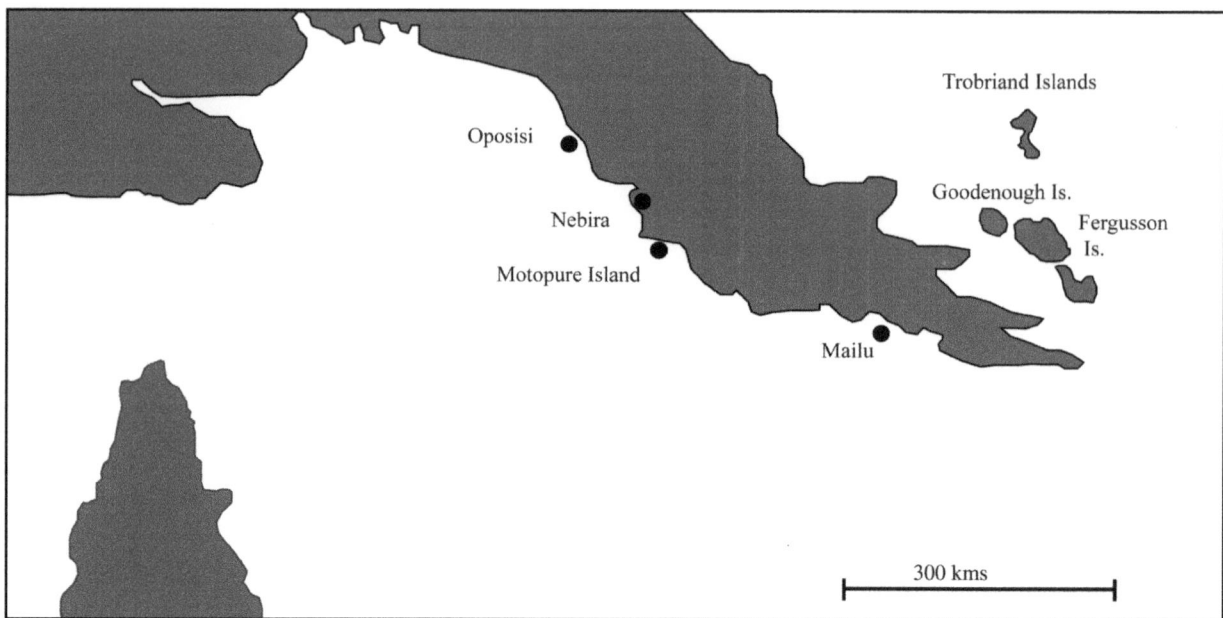

Figure 1. Map of the South Papuan Coast with sites.

post-Lapita archaeology in the Bismarcks and nearer Melanesian islands, and the specific research questions that now occupy researchers in those areas (for an update see Summerhayes in press a). Research into the Lapita assemblages from the Bismarck Archipelago has had a fundamental impact on the way the region's past is now modelled.

For example, early research into Lapita sites suggested that similarities in pottery were due to trade or exchange from a single or small number of production centres. Yet, research using chemical and petrographic techniques has now shown that pottery was mostly made locally. At the same time, we now recognise temporal changes to the production techniques for this pottery. Production during the Early Lapita period used many combinations clays and types of filler, while later Lapita assemblages indicated local production using only one clay associated with one filler in any particular area. Summerhayes (2000a, 2000b, 2003) used this analysis of pot production to argue for a change from a mobile society to a more sedentary one, with the long distance exchange of pottery in the Bismarck Archipelago occurring after Lapita pottery had disappeared. Models of this sophistication were not available to inform early syntheses of south coast Papuan prehistory, although Irwin's (1977) doctorate on the emergence of Mailu as a specialised pottery manufacturing village was seminal in offering moves away from earlier culture history approaches.

We consider it worthwhile to revisit the south coast data for two reasons. The first is to examine the degree to which the colonisation of the Papuan coast is similar to or different from the Lapita colonisation, despite differences of scale. Although the Papuan diaspora involved pot-making Austronesian speakers, themselves ultimately Lapita descendants, an important difference between the two colonisations is that in Papua, people colonised a continental size landmass, something that Lapita itself seems not to have achieved, whether or not it was attempted. The only suggestions of Lapita-like connections with mainland Papua New Guinea are based on tenuous links. There is a Lapita sherd reputedly collected by Leask from the Aitape area of the New Guinea north coast, that has yet to be chemically provenanced; a weathered sherd from Ali Island thought to be dentate stamped (Terrell and Welsch 1997); and from the Wanigela area of Collingwood Bay, cut-out pedestaled bowls reported by Egloff (1971a, 1979) in undated situations are seen by Kirch (2000:122) to possess a "striking Lapita affinity". These finds, together with the single piece of Fergusson Island obsidian recovered from a Lapita site in the Solomons' Reef-Santa Cruz Islands (Green and Bird 1989), does not rule out the future discovery of

Lapita on the Papuan mainland and in the Massim. On the other hand, given the now extensive work in the Massim, it seems improbable that Lapita sites have been missed, given their high visibility elsewhere.

The second reason is that in many Pacific areas it is difficult to choose between two models of post-Lapita change, one being localisation and adaptation and the other being cultural replacement. The occupation of the south coast by pottery users is considered by all researchers there to represent cultural replacement. Thus the question emerges, can the Papuan example inform post-Lapita studies elsewhere in Melanesia?

Following Irwin's directive, this paper draws attention to the similarities between the Lapita colonisation and the colonisation of the Papuan coast by pottery-using communities. Irwin (1991) himself pointed to this comparison without emphasising it and also listed most of the colonising characteristics we also discuss here. This paper is designed to continue that dialogue.

Table 1. Excavations along the south Papuan Coast and Massim Area prior to the 1980s.

Site	Reference
Gulf	
Rupo	Rhoads 1980
Kulupuari	Rhoads 1980
Samoa	Bowdler's work not published
Samoa	Rhoads 1980
Kairuku Region	
Kukubu Cave	White, J.P. 1965
Kukubu Cave	Vanderwal 1973
Oposisi	Vanderwal 1973
Ape Venuna	Vanderwal 1973
Urourina	Vanderwal 1973
Port Moresby	
Nebira 2	Bulmer 1971, 1978, 1979
Taurama	Bulmer 1971, 1978, 1979
Eriama	Bulmer 1971, 1978, 1979
Motupore	
Nebira 4	Allen 1972
Ava Garau (near Boera)	Swadling 1980, 1981
Papa Salt Pan	Swadling and Kaiku 1980
Amazon Bay	
Mailu Is. 01 and 03	Irwin 1974, 1977, 1978a and b
Selai	
Collingwood Bay	
Wanigela Area	Egloff 1971a and b, 1978, 1979
Goodenough Island	
Nuamata	Egloff 1978
Surface Goodenough, Amphletts	Lauer 1970, 1971, 1974
Trobriands	
Kiriwina, Kaileuna, Kitava, Vakuta - surface collections	Egloff 1978, 1979

The South Coast sequence

Sites older than 2,000 years are few along the south Papuan and Papuan Gulf coasts. Two examples from the Gulf are Ouloubomoto and Rupo from the Kikori region (Rhoads 1980). To the east of these it is remarkable that only a single pre-ceramic site has so far been recognised, at Kukuba Cave (ADL) near Yule Island, where a flaked stone assemblage yielded a mid-Holocene date (Vanderwal 1973:44-47, 51). This dearth of evidence is less likely to reflect a landscape empty of humans and more the difficulties of finding these earlier sites. But for the moment we have no idea

Table 2. The South Coast Sequence.

1.	Pre-ceramic ? -2,000 BP
2.	Colonisation 2,000 – 1,600 BP
3.	Regional Isolation 1,600 – 1,000 BP
4.	Pottery Transformation 1200 – 800 BP
5.	Interaction, Specialisation and Exchange 800 – 200 BP

what sort of cultural landscape the earliest pottery-bearing colonists encountered. The remainder of the regional sequence (Table 2) presented above was proposed by Irwin in 1991 and is used here to overcome the earlier confusion of local geographical and decorative style names given by various researchers to their own sites and regions.

Before reviewing Irwin's regional sequence we note that almost universally, early researchers divided the ceramic sequences into a more recent phase, where pots although prehistoric, have generic associations with local ethnographic wares, and an earlier phase where different generic relationships were observed archaeologically between regions. As a radiocarbon chronology was developed, local sequence disruptions were recognised at various sites along the coast somewhere between 800 and 1200 years ago that separated these earlier and later phases. This general disruption, dubbed the "ceramic hiccup" by Irwin (1991), appears to have carried beyond ceramic style changes, invoking socio-economic system changes along the entire coast.

Within this gross Early/Late dichotomy, pottery associated with the earlier phase has been given many labels. At first widely known as Red Slip pottery, this term was rejected because much of the pottery in this tradition is not slipped (Allen 1972). It has also been called the Laloki style (Bulmer 1999), the Initial Ceramic Phase (Vanderwal 1973:232, 1978:426), Early Period (Allen 1977a and b; Bickler 1997), Early Papuan Ware (Irwin 1991:503), and, jokingly, SPECHT ware (South Papuan Early Ceramic Horizon or Tradition). We now prefer and use the term Early Papuan pottery (EPP). While early researchers analysed pot shapes and rim forms of EPP and found changes through time (Allen 1972), decorative techniques and motif analyses have been most informative and these are what we concentrate on here.

Irwin's Regional Sequence (Irwin 1991)

Period 1 represents the sketchy pre-ceramic occupation down to c.2000 BP. Around this time or a little later, a number of sites, spread over 500 km of the south Papuan coast, were occupied for the first time by people using an identical style of pottery (Bulmer 1999:543). Period 2, representing this colonisation phase, is primarily defined from three major locations: Mailu Island's O1 and O3, and the site of Selai (Layer D) on the opposing mainland (Irwin 1977, 1985), Nebira 4 (Horizon III) near Port Moresby (Allen 1972), and Oposisi on Yule Island (Vandewal 1973, 1978) (see Figure 1). Early pottery was also found at Taurama (AJA) (Bulmer 1978), but the site may be disturbed (White with O'Connell 1982:201-2).

At all locations where the stratigraphy is intact, the earliest decorative form is elaborate shell impression (see Allen 1972: Fig. 7; Vanderwal 1978:420), lime infilled, mostly on bowls and found in all zones of the exterior surface. This is consistent from the Massim to the Gulf of Papua. The bowls without shell impression are either plain or have a single groove round the outside of the rim. Other vessel forms include small orifice vessels which Vanderwal (1978:418) called water jars, some with red paint, and the cooking pot which is larger with a wide flat rim. These forms are also found at Nebira 4 (Allen 1972), Taurama (Bulmer 1999) and Mailu (Irwin 1977) at least for cooking pots. As this implies there was some variation, such as the lack of rim grooving at Nebira that was dominant at Oposisi, and the absence of globular water pots at Mailu (see Bulmer 1999 for a review of the pottery). Multiple body grooving below the rim was also found on shell impressed bowls at Nebira 4 and in the Mailu assemblages. (Such grooving is also found in the Lapita assemblages of the Arawes (Summerhayes 2000a)). As discussed below this period was also associated with a wide range of non-ceramic material culture, particularly at Oposisi.

Periods 2 and 3 are separated by Irwin to accommodate a division between a period of initial colonisation where the same ceramics are found from the Massim to the Gulf and the first indication of regional variation in pottery styles. Examples of the latter are seen at Mailu where some local motifs develop and other more widely distributed motifs like multiple grooving and painting continue, and at Port Moresby and Yule Island, where a similar series of parallel styles continue in both places down to about 1200 BP.

Contact between Mailu and localities further west is difficult to judge because Irwin did not report in detail any temporal sequencing of styles within the EPP tradition at Mailu, however this parallel sequence of styles at Nebira 4 in Port Moresby and Oposisi on Yule Island was quickly recognised. Shell impression in both regions in turn gave way to finely incised wares, again frequently lime-infilled (see Allen 1972: Figure 7 nos. 1-17), then multiple grooving (Allen 1972: Figure 6 nos. 9, 12) and finally etched decoration (Allen 1972: Figure 6 nos. 1-7) where the slip is scraped off prior to firing. Painted wares, present in the Port Moresby and Mailu sites and occurring throughout the Nebira 4 sequence, are absent in the Yule Island area. Conversely, etching, the most recent EPP style in the Port Moresby and Yule Island sites does not occur at Mailu. For a full description of the decoration see the original reports (Allen 1972; Irwin 1977, 1985; Vanderwal 1973, 1978).

Period 4 occupies the period between 1200 BP and 800 BP in which socio-economic systems and accompanying ceramic styles "transformed" in Irwin's terms from the earlier period to the later period as described above. Whereas the sudden appearance of pottery making communities a thousand years earlier is seen universally as a migration/colonisation, this transformation, initially argued by some to represent another migration event, is now seen to be a set of separate local reorganisations that were different from each other but likely to be causally related because of their contemporaneity. We return to this point in the discussion. In each region the record differs; in Mailu Irwin noted continuity in settlement patterns and other non-ceramic data; in Port Moresby Bulmer (1971) thought new pottery styles indicated external introductions from the Massim, a view she later retracted (Bulmer 1978). In the Port Moresby and Yule Island regions settlement patterns changed. At the peripheries changes occurred that were different again. In the Gulf pottery sites disappeared for a time, while in the Louisiade Archipelago "antique" EPP continued to be made for several more centuries (Irwin 1991:507-508).

As stated, all researchers accept that EPP, whatever the local sub-style forms, was abruptly replaced between 1200 BP and 800 BP. Taking a line through several western Port Moresby sites dug by Pam Swadling and colleagues (1977, n.d.; Swadling and Kaiku 1980) we now put the start of this disruption very close to 1200 BP, at least for the Port Moresby area. Elsewhere the dating is less precise and the sequences at the major sites now warrant re-dating. Change and reorganisation over the next 400 years led to the subsequent emergence of the immediate antecedent systems of specialised exchange seen in the ethnographically described Kula, Mailu and the Port Moresby Hiri systems. These occupy Period 5 in the Irwin scheme.

The rest of this paper concentrates on the Period 2 phase of colonisation and structural similarities with the Lapita colonisation of the Bismarck Archipelago and the Western Pacific.

Period 2 Phase - Colonisation of the south coast - the Argument

Any similarity between the dynamics of the original Lapita colonisation and the subsequent colonisation of the south Papuan coast by pottery-users could reflect some of the shared processes of colonisation that Irwin urges us to seek. Here we look at six of these: speed of colonisation, site location, economy, obsidian, other material culture, and pottery, with the latter two being indicators of connectedness. The first five will be looked at briefly, the last in more detail.

Speed of colonisation

No one working in the region doubts that the appearance of pottery-users along the south coast reflects a sea-borne migration of deliberate colonists, which is also the dominant model for Lapita. While some researchers (Kirch 2000) have argued for a west-to-east temporal cline in Lapita colonisation of the Bismarck Archipelago the distinctions may reflect the vagaries of radiometric dating as much as reality. Summerhayes has recently argued that the Lapita colonisation of the Bismarck Archipelago was instantaneous, with differences in dating due to the different calculation of oceanic reservoir effects used on shell samples (Summerhayes in press a). Available dates in Papua (Table 3) show this event also to be archaeologically instantaneous, likely occurring somewhere short of 2,000 years ago. Allen's (1972:109) Horizon III at Nebira correlates with Vanderwal's (1973) Style IIb and IIc, and Irwin's Early Papuan ware (Irwin 1977). Re-dating all these sites using more modern techniques might pinpoint the colonising period more accurately, especially given the presence of "red slip" pottery in Torres Strait argued to be 2,500 years old (McNiven et al. 2006). However, despite earlier opinions such as Pawley (1969:3), who suggested on linguistic grounds that Austronesians might have been present on this coast 3,000 years ago, the existing radiocarbon ages are sufficiently similar to put the age of the pottery in Torres Strait in doubt if it reached Torres Strait via Papua, rather than from somewhere to the west.

The ease with which both the Lapita and the Papuan colonisations were achieved has tended to render prior occupants archaeologically invisible. In the case of Lapita in the Bismarcks, sheer persistence by a few workers has forced some recognition of this problem (Specht 2005; Torrence et al. 2004). Equally, on the south coast it would be foolish to believe these colonists encountered empty landscapes. Within the Bismarck Archipelago, Summerhayes (in press a) has argued that the population levels for the existing mobile hunting and gathering communities was low and the absence of evidence for earlier hunters on the Papuan coast suggests that the same is true there. In neither case has much attention been paid to the probable interactions between incumbents and new arrivals in these situations (e.g. Kirch 2000:93).

Table 3. Radiocarbon dates from earliest pottery occupation levels of the south Papuan Coast.

Site	Radiocarbon date	Reference
Mailu Area		
Mailu 01	1900±70 BP (ANU-1229)	Irwin 1988:66
Selai	1790±70 BP (ANU-1316)	Irwin 1977:82
Port Moresby Area		
Nebira 4	1760±90 BP (I-5796)	Allen 1972:99
Eriama	1930±230 (GaK-2670)	Bulmer 1978:213
Yule Island		
Oposisi	1890±305 BP (ANU-425)	Vanderwal 1973:48
	1530±160 BP (ANU-729)	
	1600±210 BP (ANU-728)	
Gulf		
Samoa	1850±95 BP (I-6153)	Rhoads 1980:250
	2430±370 BP (ANU-2061A)	

Site Locations

Lapita site locations are predominantly coastal, with most being beach locations (Anderson et al. 2001). The EPP sites are also mostly coastal. Oposisi is located on Yule Island on the highest part of the island at 125 metres a.s.l. (Vanderwal 1973, 1978:417) (Figure 2). Mailu is a small island, while Selai is a beach location (Figure 3; Irwin 1977). In the Port Moresby region EPP sites occur on beaches and headlands such as Taurama beach and headland and on islands, such as Daugo Island. Nebira on the other hand is 15 kilometres inland from the present coast. Nebira 4 is located at the northern base of Nebira Hill, a twin peaked hill rising c. 180 m from the flat Waigani plain (Figure 4). Nebira 2, excavated by Bulmer (1978), was located in the saddle of the two hills. Allen (1972) pointed out that although the areas is now savannah woodland, it need not have been in the past, since the sea may have been much closer than it is today. The higher sea stand of 1.5 metres at 3300 BP would have covered nearby low lying areas, likely locating Nebira Hill much closer to the sea than it is now. The subsequent infilling of this area is also to be expected, given that Swadling *et al.* (1976:56) point out that the Papuan Coast has prograded with the Angabanga plains being produced by Holocene age alluvial and littoral deposits. Roro traditions note that the Hall Sound area once had islands and Redscar Head, which is today joined to the mainland by a mangrove swamp, was recorded by the Spaniard Don Diego de Prado in 1606 as being an island (Swadling *et al.* 1976:56). More detailed geomorphological work in the region is needed.

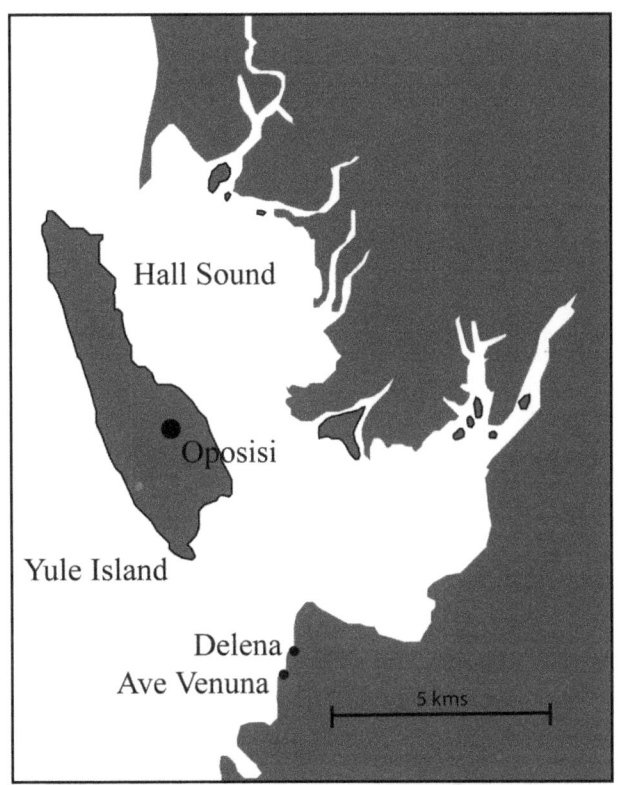

Figure 2. Location of Oposisi and surrounding sites (from Vanderwal 1978).

In summary, site locations reflect the sea-borne nature of the Papuan colonisation, with village sites occurring on larger and smaller offshore islands, beaches and headlands, but with inroads into coastal hills and river valleys occurring quickly. While these last locations probably reflect the utilisation of better gardening land, pottery is also found in caves and rockshelters (e.g. Eriama, Kukubu Cave). Is this reflecting

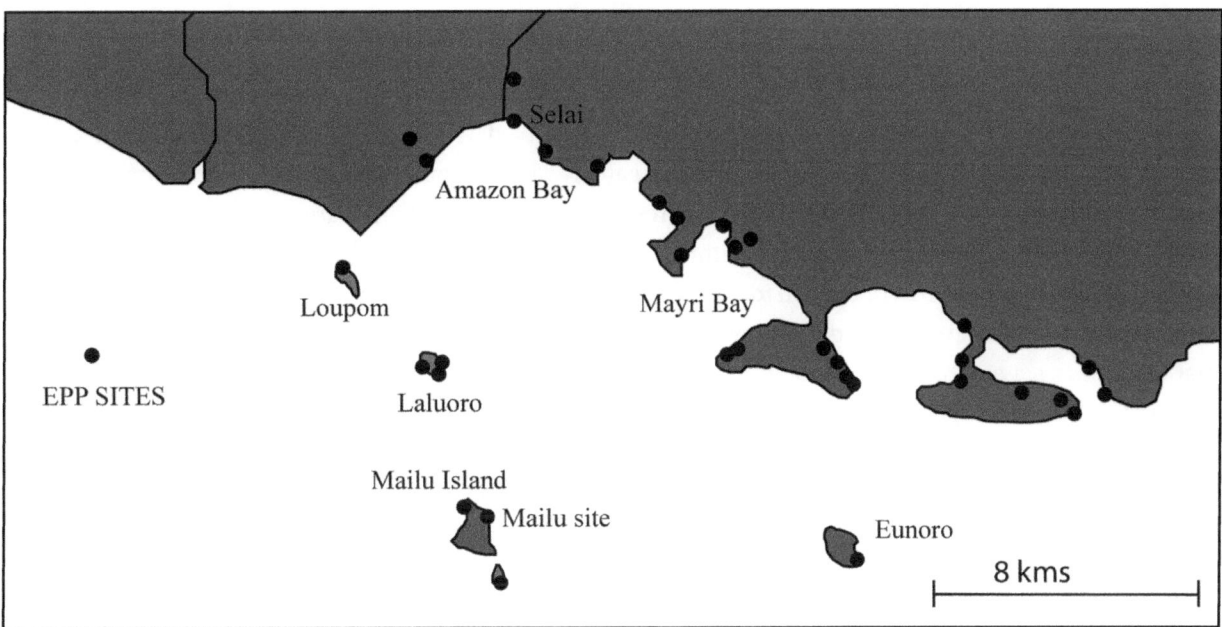

Figure 3. Location of EPP sites and findspots recorded by Irwin on Mailu Island and surrounding areas (Irwin 1985 Table 17).

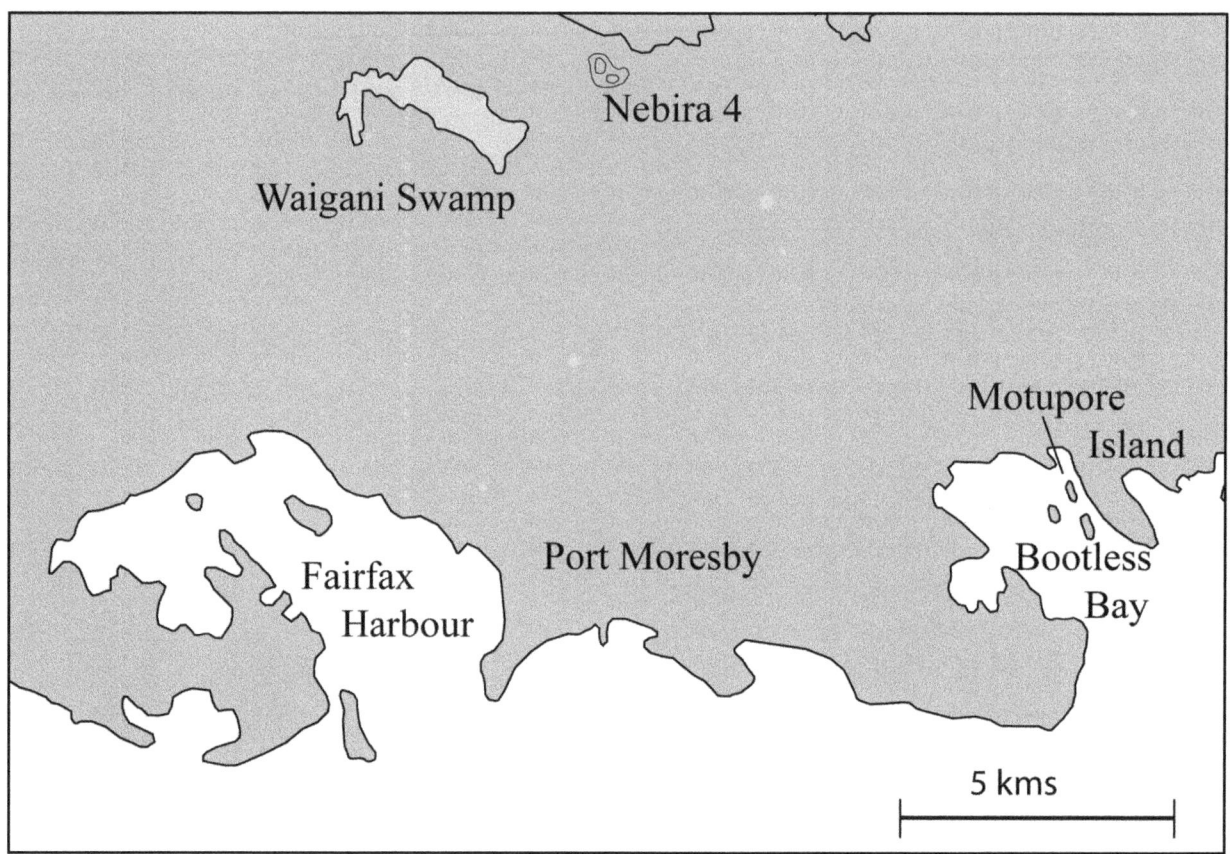

Figure 4. Location of Nebira (from Allen 1972).

the broad spectrum subsistence activities of the colonists or the transfer of pottery to prior occupants through exchange? Certainly in some Lapita situations where there are no prior occupants, it represents the former. On the Papuan coast we simply need more data to investigate this question.

Economy

The economies of both Lapita and Papuan sites appear to be mixed, with strong emphasis on marine resources (fishing and collecting) supplemented by hunted and gathered land resources and with the continuing inference of horticulture. Nebira's inland location is of interest in this respect since the faunal material from the early phase at Nebira 4 reflects a strong marine imput that diminished over time (Allen 1972:116). Apart from catfish (*Tachysuridae*), the rest of the fish found at Nebira 4 were coastal reef dwellers (*Aluteridae* or *Balistidae*, *Scaridae* and *Labridae*). Turtle and dugong were also found in the earliest levels, as were thirty-six species of marine molluscs. Less than 1 % of molluscs were fresh water species (*Melania* sp and *Velesuni* sp). The most common marine shell species among the 36 species identified were *Chama* sp., and various strombus species (*S. labiatus, S. luhuanus, S. gibberulus gibbosus* and *S. canarium*). Of importance is the presence of *Chama* sp. At Nebira Allen mused over its presence, as the shell has a high shell/meat ratio (Allen 1972:119). Why carry it so far inland? The answer may well lay in the geomorphological changes that have occurred over the last 2,000 years, and may provide support for Nebira being closer to the sea at its initial occupation. Evidence for local hunting was seen in the presence of wallaby (*M. agilis*) and horticulture in the presence of pig.

The economy of the earliest layers at Oposisi was similar, providing evidence that both land and sea were exploited for subsistence. Shellfish remains were found in large quantities, along with wallaby, fish, turtle, dugong, crocodile, cassowary and pig (Vanderwal 1973:178, Table VII-23)

The economy of Mailu in the early pottery period was coastal (see Irwin 1985: Chapter X). Midden material was mostly shell fish, with species of shell reflecting the ecological differences between Mailu and mainland sites. Turtle, dugong, fish, crabs and sea urchins are also found. Shellfish, however, was found in great volume. Vertebrate remains were in Irwin's terms meagre (1985:241). Pig and dog were found, along with two types of wallaby (*M. agilis, Dorcopsis* sp.) which must have derived from the mainland (Irwin 1985:237).

Like the Papuan assemblages, the coastal location of Lapita settlement was reflected in the economy. From the Early Lapita site of Kamgot (on Anir) for instance, fish bone dominates the faunal assemblage. The most popular fish were inshore varieties such as *Scaridae* and *Diontidae*. Most of the fishing was inshore or from the reef, although shark, tuna, dolphin, turtle and barracuda were also present. As expected with some of these species a number of fishhooks were recovered from Anir (Szabo and Summerhayes 2002). A similar exploitation of fish occurs at another Early Lapita site, Mussau, as well as the later Lapita site of Watom (Butler 1988; Green and Anson 2000:52; Kirch *et al.* 1991). Fishhooks are also found at these sites. From Kamgot, the midden remains also have a high land mammal content, including phalanger, *Thylogale browni*, pig, chicken, dog, and *Rattus exulans*. Found in association with house structures, pig, chicken and dog are domesticated, and as such, are also good indicators of horticulture. There is also evidence for arboriculture from the Early Lapita assemblages at Mussau and the Arawe Islands (Kirch 1989; Matthews and Gosden 1997).

From later Lapita assemblages the diet was mostly terrestrial. At Watom for instance it was argued on the basis of stable isotope analysis on human bone that 64 % of the diet was land based, the rest made up of shellfish (8.7 %), coral reef fish (9 %) and non-reef fish (21.3 %) (Green and Anson 2000:51). Plant foods made up most of the food energy (Leach *et al.* 2000:158). Large numbers of pig bones were also found at Watom enabling a detailed study on age distribution that suggests animal husbandry (Smith 2000:145). Green and Anson argue that this is indirect evidence for agriculture necessitating "domesticated plant foods in sufficient abundance to feed both pigs and people" (Green and Anson 2000:50).

Independent evidence for Lapita agriculture using either starch residue analysis on pottery and/ or phytolith analysis on sediments is now provided from the following Lapita sites: Kamgot (Crowther 2005); Uripiv Island, Vanuatu (Horrocks and Bedford 2005) and Bourewa, Fiji (Horrocks and Nunn 2007) where *Colocasia esculenta* has been identified. Palms and banana (Eumusa) have also been identified from Watom (Lentfer and Green 2004). Unfortunately, these newer scientific techniques have not yet been applied to the pottery and deposits from the south coast.

It is hardly legitimate to list a mixed economy of fishing, collecting, horticulture and hunting as a distinctive marker, since these may well have occurred before the colonisations and certainly after. But for the first time in both the Bismarcks and the Papuan coast an increased intensity of subsistence acquisition in the archaeological record is sufficient to equate it with the first appearance of open village sites (although these may have already been present in the Bismarcks (Allen 2000:156-163)). While it is acknowledged that the high visibility of sherds in tropical landscapes might explain an increase in recognised sites, it is not sufficient to explain this sudden increased visibility. Sites are occupied by more people for longer periods.

Obsidian

All or most models of Lapita emphasise connections between sites and sometimes back to homeland regions. These linkages continue through time but are most visible and elaborate in the early phases of the colonising process (Kirch 1988; Summerhayes 2000a). Archaeologically this connectedness is marked by similar pottery styles and the distribution of obsidian and these are clearly parallelled in the Papuan case.

Obsidian, all sourced from Kukuia and Fagalulu, west Fergusson Island, has been reported from a number of EPP sites as far west as Yule Island but not in the Gulf (Ambrose 1976; Bird *et al.* 1981; Green and Bird 1989; Irwin 1991:Fig. 3). The amount of Fergusson obsidian reaching these sites reflects the distance from the source (Irwin 1991: Fig. 3; White *et al.* 2006). In the Oposisi assemblage, two Kukuia flakes were found, more than 650 km from the source area (Vanderwal 1973:214). Two others came from nearby Apere Venuua (Vanderwal 1973:214). From Nebira, which is 550 km from the source, small quantities of flakes were found from the earliest levels to the most recent. From Mailu, which is 350 kilometres from the source, obsidian was found in larger quantities (146 for the early period), however, this decreases over time to only a handful after 1600 BP, with numbers rising again in the second millennium AD (Irwin and Holdaway 1996). However while obsidian again reaches Mailu in significant numbers at the beginning of the post-EPP phase, it does not get as far west as Port Moresby. Obsidian was still traded to Mailu up to the beginning of the twentieth century (Green and Bird 1989).

As modelled by Irwin (1991), the distribution of obsidian is what might be expected by down-the-line exchange, with much more appearing in Mailu sites, nearer to the source. While we believe the two pieces of obsidian reported at Oposisi are an underestimate resulting from the sieve mesh sizes used there (1/2 inch or 1/4 inch used variably in the excavation (Vanderwal 1973:29), these general distinctions of volume between regions remain accurate. Sue Bulmer interpreted the small number of pieces in the Port Moresby sites as reflecting the unimportance of the trade in obsidian to Port Moresby (Bulmer 1979:23). Certainly the ready local availability of good quality chert reduced any utilitarian need for obsidian, and thus we see its small but continuing presence there as an important indicator of the maintenance of eastward linkages throughout the EPP phase, and not merely a reflection of the initial pulse of first colonisation. Yet, was the distribution of obsidian "down the line exchange"?

Changes in the nature of obsidian reaching Mailu inform us about the nature of interaction among these communities. The obsidian found in these early sites is technologically different from later assemblages suggesting different distribution processes. Technological studies on the obsidian assemblages from the Mailu region showed that the earlier "colonising phase" in Mailu had heavier obsidian than later periods, which is "incidental to the high frequency of communication among related communities undergoing a phase of expansion" (Irwin and Holdaway 1996:228). This is different to obsidian reaching Mailu during later periods in what Irwin called a later "trader mode" (Irwin 1991:506).

Similar processes are seen in the distribution of obsidian in the early Lapita assemblages. Earlier Lapita assemblages show an expedient technology not seen in the earlier pre-Lapita or later assemblages away from the source regions (Summerhayes 2004, in press b). Hanslip (2001:196) for instance argues that the earliest assemblages from the Reef Islands and Santa Cruz, RF-2 and SZ-8, which are also part of the colonising phase, not only had the largest pieces of obsidian and lacked bipolar flaking, but also showed no signs of on-site production. That is, the material was imported as is, not as blocks. Such an expedient technology is not expected from a down the line exchange network. Specht (2002:42) also shows that the earlier Lapita assemblages had heavier pieces of obsidian (mean weights) and from the one site where data is available (Adwe) there is a decline in this mean weight over time in the Middle Lapita period. Taken together the reduction in the size and weight of obsidian indicates an "economising" behaviour associated with later down the line exchange.

Yet, like the assemblages from Moresby, obsidian continues to be distributed after the initial colonisation pulse is over. Obsidian continues to be imported into Lapita assemblages in the Reef Islands and Santa Cruz well after it was initially colonised (Green 1987). East of the southeast Solomons obsidian is rare (although see Galipaud and Swete Kelly this volume) although still found in post colonisation contexts, such as in Naigini, Fiji (Best 1987), and Tikopia where it was found in Middle to Late Lapita contexts (Kirch and Yen 1982). Communication between these far-flung communities still existed after the colonisation phase in western Melanesia was over.

Non-ceramic material culture of the EPP phase

The EPP phase contained a suite of artefacts beyond obsidian and pottery that is more reminiscent of the insular Pacific and Lapita sites than the post-EPP phase that eventually replaced it along the Papuan south coast. The best examples come from the Yule Island sites. Oposisi in particular produced an elaborate range of bone and shell artefacts, among them awls, scrapers and gouges, spatulas with handles, tubular bone beads, including some from human bone, human cranial tablets, pierced animal teeth and pendants, shell beads and conus and trochus bracelets. Vanderwal (1973:129-32) also described 26 adzes of which 16 were trapezoidal in form, different from the more common lenticular Papuan forms. These trapezoidal forms occurred mainly in the earliest stratigraphic unit of Oposisi (IIC) and at the nearby site of Apere Venuna, which Vanderwal equated with Oposisi IIC on ceramic grounds (Vanderwal 1973:131). Two similar adzes occurred in the surface collections from Nebira, but no other parallels are known within the EPP phase or subsequent to it along the Papuan coast. There are, however, 127 similar adzes in the Australian Museum in Sydney collected in 1934 by R. V. Oldham, and catalogued as coming from Delena, an existing town adjacent to Apere Venuna. This collection is thus considered to be a part of the Apere Venuna assemblage described by Vanderwal.

Most (but not all) of these artefact types occur only in the early part of the Oposisi sequence and are not seen in this abundance at other EPP sites, although aspects of this assemblage do occur at these other sites. Alone among Papuan researchers, Vanderwal considered that the more elaborately decorated shell impressed pottery and the associated rich bone and shell assemblages of the initial colonisers, when compared to the simpler material culture of later inhabitants at Oposisi, were sufficiently different to argue cultural replacement of the former by the latter. Today this view no longer holds, but the simplification of material culture that accompanied settling into the landscape raises other issues that we will return to in the conclusion.

Pottery

We have already touched upon connectedness reflected in similar sequencing of decoration styles between regions. Here we identify and compare pottery production patterns and changes over time between the south coast and Lapita assemblages in order to identify a pot production signature for colonising societies. This will be done by first outlining Lapita pottery production and its change over time; secondly by reviewing past attempts at identifying pottery production on the south coast using physical/chemical analyses; thirdly, presenting the results of our pottery production analyses using the electron microprobe; and lastly by comparing and contrasting the results of our analysis with Lapita pottery production patterns.

Lapita Pottery Production

Despite the amount of attention that has been given to Lapita pottery, relatively little has been done on identifying production and distribution patterns. With rare exceptions, most of the physical/chemical analyses of pottery have been limited to assessing whether pots have been locally made or imported. However, a study by one of us (GS) has attempted to tie production patterns to mobility/settlement models in Lapita settlements within the Bismarck Archipelago (Summerhayes 2000a, 2000b, 2003). Two patterns of production were identified.

The first suggests that production of Early Lapita pottery was mostly local. Technologically these potters were not conservative, using a number of combinations of tempers/fillers from different river systems and beaches and different clays to produce an identical variety of vessel forms and decorations (Figure 5).

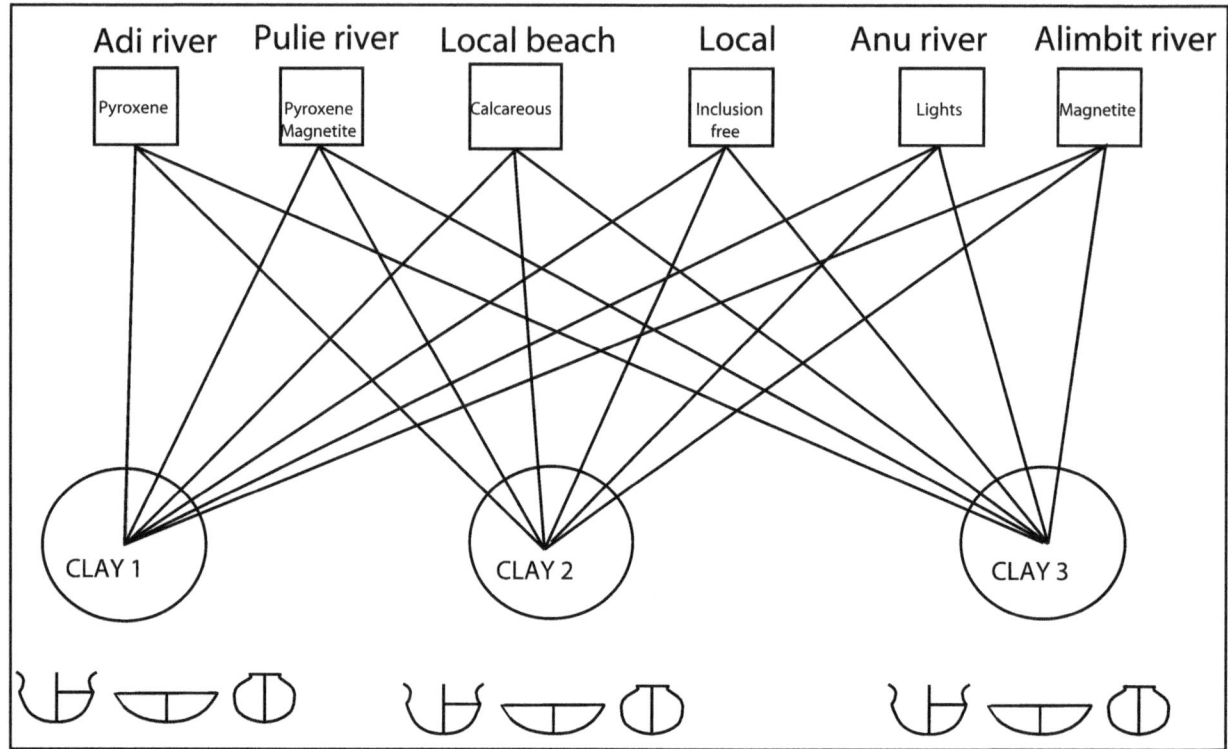

Figure 5. Early Lapita Production Pattern.

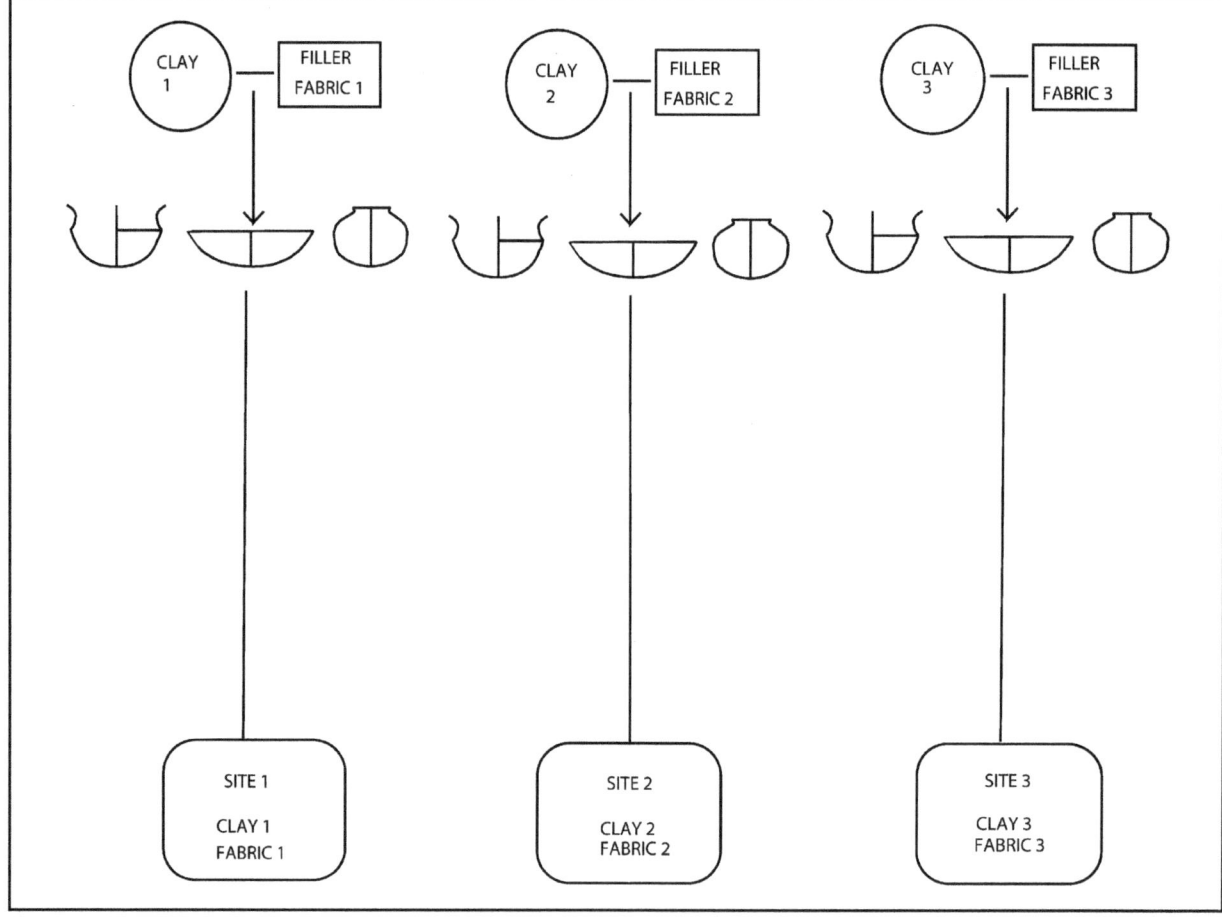

Figure 6. Late Lapita Production Pattern.

A different pattern of production occurred for later Lapita styles. While production continued to be locally based, production became more conservative and standardised with only one temper/filler found with associated clays (Figure 6).

This change in production was interpreted as reflecting a change in settlement patterns, with the early production pattern resulting from higher mobility associated with the initial colonisation period and the later pattern reflecting more sedentary communities.

Neither pattern is like specialist pottery production for exchange seen in the ethnographic past from a number of areas in Papua New Guinea. These differences are represented graphically by comparing Figures 5 and 6 with the representation of specialist production in Figures 7 and 8.

Previous attempts at identifying pot production along the south coast

This characterisation of Lapita ceramic production allows comparison with south coast EPP production for the first time, but several previous attempts to characterise this latter set are instructive and are briefly reviewed here.

Previous attempts have mainly used physical characterisation analyses. Bill Dickinson, for example, undertook thin section petrographic analysis on selected pot sherds from Nebira 4 sent by Allen (1972:121).

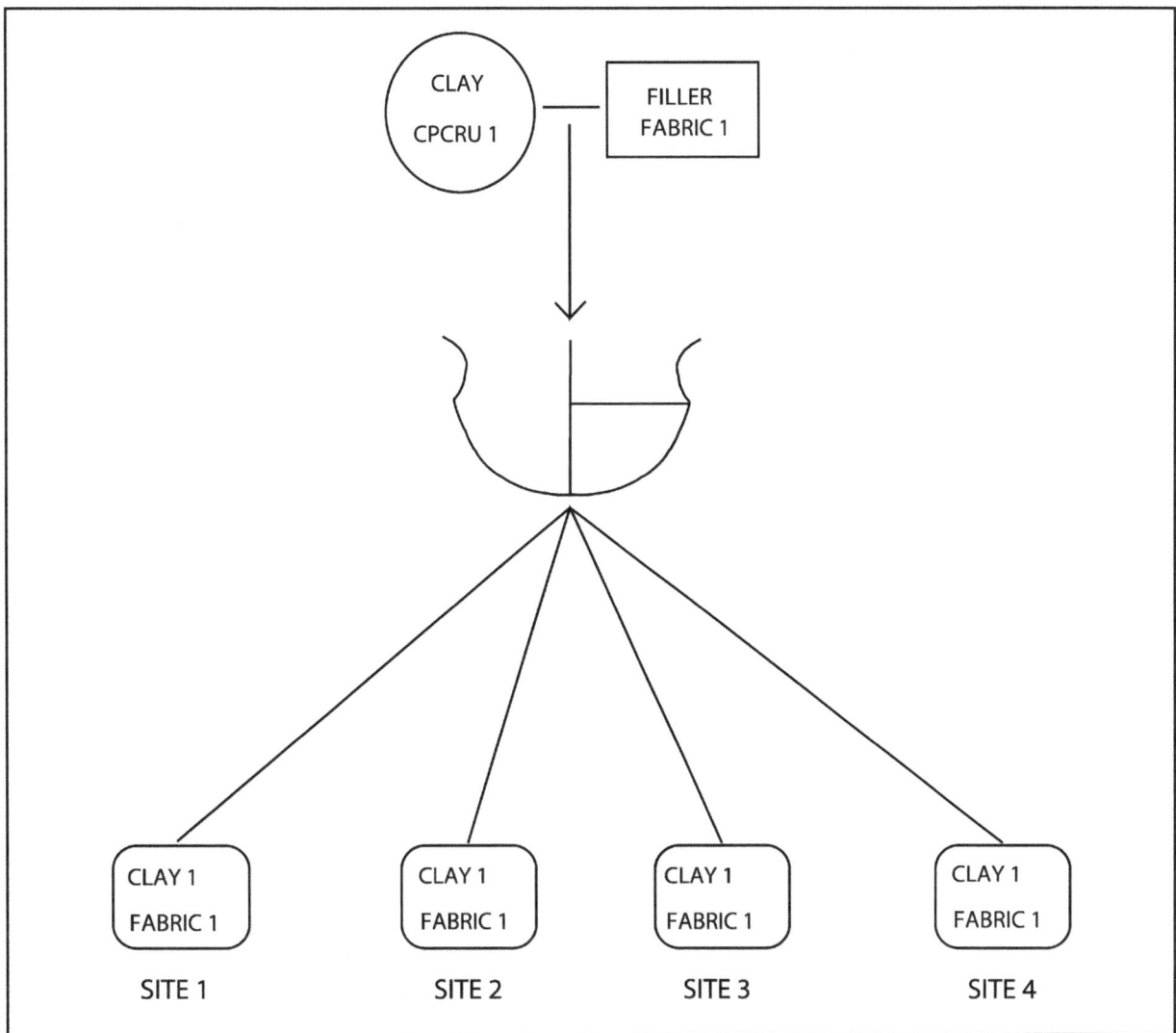

Figure 7. Selection of fabrics from later specialist production, e.g. Motu.

Oceanic Explorations: Lapita and Western Pacific Settlement

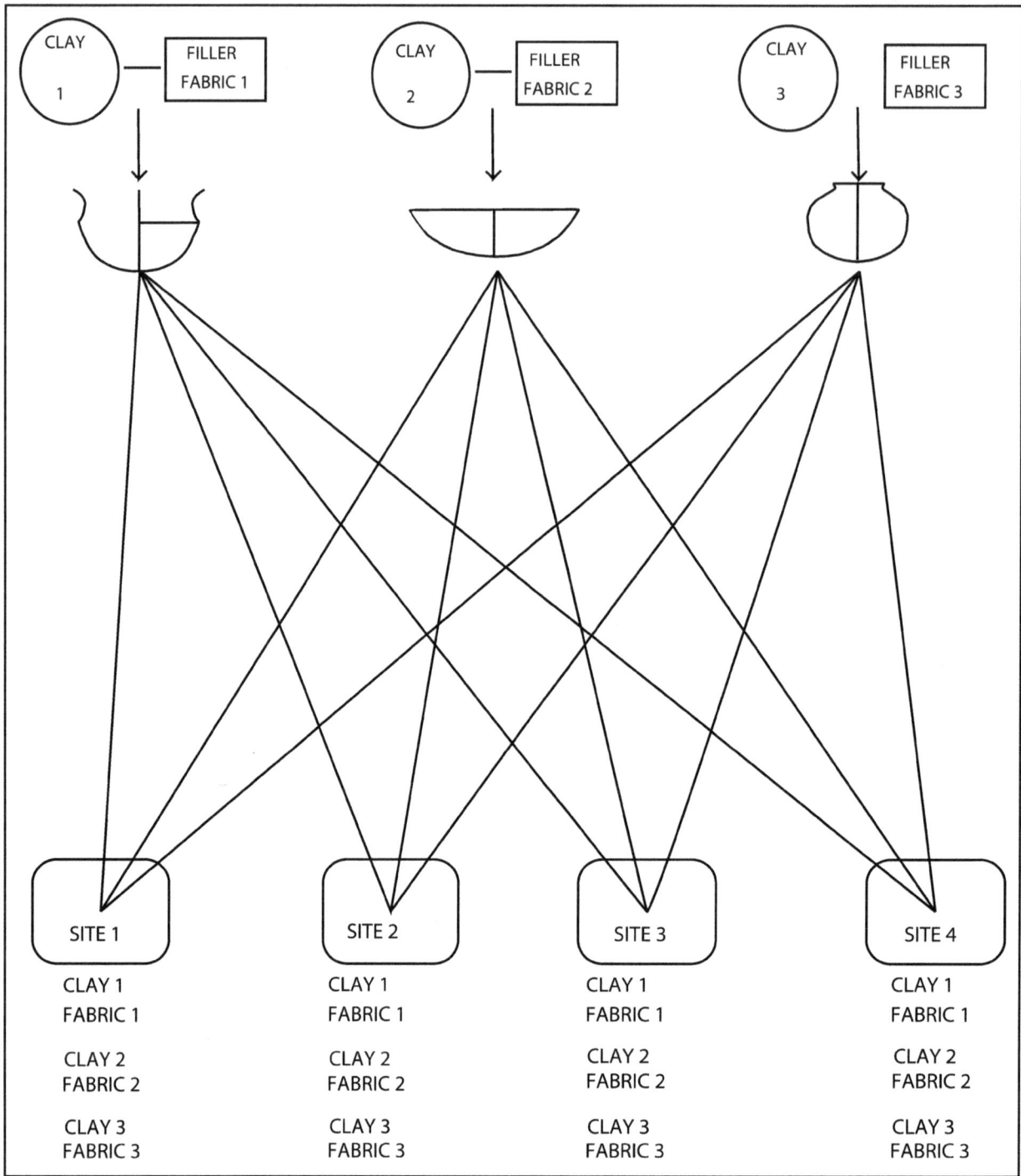

Figure 8. Selection of fabrics expected from a number of operating specialist production centres.

His results led Allen to argue that identically decorated pottery from Oposisi and Nebira 4 was in each case locally made, rather than made in one area and traded out. Allen also noted the presence of misfired pot sherds at both sites, suggesting local production. Allen noting that both sites, although 120 km apart, shared a similar sequence and must have maintained good communication for over 1,000 years: "cultural contact between sites must have been very close" (Allen 1972:121).

Geoff Irwin, as part of his doctoral research into Mailu, argued that there was more than one pot manufacturing area during the early period. He based this on the petrographic analysis of 25 samples, and XRF analysis of 139 samples.

Mike Worthing (1980), a geologist at UPNG, attempted to identify production sites by comparing sands collected from selected beaches from the south coast (Boera, Bootless Bay, Moresby Harbour, Papa, Lealea) to sands in pot sherds from Motupore using petrographic analysis. On the basis of Worthing's work, Swadling (1980) argued that very few late EPP pots from Moresby came from the Kairuku area. Swadling, based on Worthing's identification of quartz with mica from his beach sands, also argued that late EPP in the Gulf came from Lealea-Boki area.

Unfortunately Worthing's analysis is limited since, as Bickler (1997) points out, there is little chronological control on the samples such that we cannot determine which samples are early or late. Further, mica and quartz are common to many beaches along the south Papuan Coast and need not be a marker for the Lealea-Boki area alone.

Jim Rhoads as part of his doctoral research had the geologist D. MacKenzie undertake petrographic analysis on EPP potsherds from Kulupuari in the Papuan Gulf. MacKenzie claimed to have sourced the clays (or minerals in them) used to make the pottery to the coastal plain around the Angabunga and Lakekamu rivers, Hall Sound and Motu Motu respectively (Rhoads and Mackenzie 1991:41).

The most recent attempt was by Simon Bickler, then an MA student at the University of Auckland. Pottery from the National Museum and Art Gallery of Papua New Guinea, Port Moresby, was analysed using both petrographic techniques (69 samples) and XRF (128 samples) from 42 EPP sites. Again, Bickler argued that production was mostly local, but with Yule Island area pottery moving to the Gulf during the EPP, and subsequently with Port Moresby pottery taking over at c.1200 BP. The implication here is that Moresby EPP was made locally and not exported.

Other attempts at pottery analysis from the south coast include Thompson (1980), Allen and Rye (1982), Allen and Duerden (1982), Rye (1976,1981), Rye and Allen (1976, 1980), and Rye and Duerden (1982) using different techniques. However these studies were on post-EPP wares and are passed over here.

There are problems with these attempts at identifying production. XRF is not appropriate for analysing coarse pottery, since the technique requires the sample being crushed into a powder. Thus the chemical analysis is a fingerprint of *both* the ceramic matrix and the inclusions within the fabric. Attempts to characterise production localities is made difficult because of the mineral noise. Thus groupings of production areas based on the chemistry of this analysis may indicate both the variability of the mineral inclusions and combinations of minerals with clays (see Summerhayes 1997 for further explanation). It follows that any comparisons with Lapita pottery production and distribution patterns determined by these studies would be based on faulty data. To redress this problem, we decided to re-analyse new EPP samples.

Detecting production patterns of EPP using the electron microscope

We employed electron microscopy to provide characterisation data allowing the modelling of production patterns. For this study a sample of 40 sherds were provided by the National Museum and Art Gallery of Papua New Guinea, Port Moresby, from the EPP assemblages of Oposisi, Nebira and Mailu, and analysed using electron microscopy. The electron microscope provides separate chemical analyses of the clay matrix and minerals, rather than the blend of both which most other techniques provide. The reason for this is that the samples are not crushed and a smoothly prepared sample can be moved under the electron beam for spot analysis. The chemical results allow the characterisation of production by grouping sherds on the basis of their chemical similarity into groups called "Chemical Paste Compositional Reference Units" (CPCRU) – see Summerhayes (2000a:Chapter 4) for a detailed description. The samples for chemical analysis consisted of early and later styles of EPP from Oposisi (15 samples), Nebira 4 (15 samples) and Mailu (10 samples).

Every sherd from the earliest levels of each site was examined using a low powered (x15) microscope, and a relative sample was selected to cover all fabrics and major styles. The fabrics were described using the macro-categories: ferro/magnesium (hornblende, pyroxene), lights (either quartz, feldspars or glass), or shell (calcareous). The selection of samples was not exhaustive, yet was adequate to cover the basic questions of production. Of this sample, two sherds from a late EPP Oposisi level (sample A5 and A6) were included to compare with the earlier EPP material. Table 4 presents a description of the sample, decoration, CPCRU, and fabric from each site.

Pottery was analysed using a scanning electron microscope (JEOL JSM-6700F) with an EDS (Energy Dispersive Spectrometer) attachment. Machine conditions used a negative potential of 15 KeV accelerating voltage. Analyses were undertaken at x20,000 while photos were taken at x100. Sherd samples were impregnated in epoxy resin pellets. Preparation of sample pellets is identical to those outlined in Summerhayes (2000a), with the exception that slides were not made. Elements analysed were Na, Mg, Al, Si, K, Ca, Ti, Mn and Fe. Multivariate statistics (Principal Components Analysis and Correspondence Analysis) were used to identify clusters in the chemical analysis and define CPCRUs. A primary aim in the quantitative elemental characterisation of pottery was to define groupings. The groupings were expected to not only make chemical sense, but also archaeological sense.

The macroscopic fabric analysis showed that both Nebira and Oposisi had three fabric groups (Fe/Mg, shell and lights), while Mailu only had two (Fe/Mg and shell). The chemical analysis on all samples produced four CPCRUs. One consists of all the Mailu samples (CPCRU I). Two CPCRUs comprise only Nebira 4 samples (CPCRU II and III) but these do not contain all the samples from Nebira 4. The last consists of all Oposisi samples and seven Nebira 4 samples, including all the shell impressed samples and the two grooved lip samples from

Table 4. List of samples for chemical analysis with CPCRU's

Sample No.	Notes on decoration	CPCRU	Fabric
OPOSISI			
A1	shell impressed	I	Light
A2	incised	I	Light
A3	shell impressed	I	Light
A4	shell impressed	I	Light
A5	incised	I	Shell
A6	incised? (thru red slip)	I	Light
A7	plain rim	I	Fe/mg
A8	cut dec lip, incision inside	I	Shell
A9	incised? (thru red slip)	I	Light
A10	plain rim	I	Light
A11	plain rim	I	Fe/mg
A12	plain rim, incised inside?	I	Fe/mg
A13	None	I	Light
A14	grooved & incised	I	Light
A15	incised lines	I	Light
MAILU			
M1	shell impressed, notched lip	IV	Fe/mg
M2	shell impressed?/incised	IV	Fe/mg
M3	incised	IV	Fe/mg
M4	impressed?	IV	Fe/mg
M5	impressed?	IV	Shell
M6	incised	IV	Shell
M7	plain rim	IV	Fe/mg
M8	plain	IV	Fe/mg
M9	plain	IV	Fe/mg
M10	?notched	IV	Fe/mg
NEBIRA 4			
N1	linear incised	III	Fe/mg
N2	linear incised	I	Fe/mg
N3	plain rim	III	Light
N4	plain rim	III	Light
N5	plain rim	II	Light
N6	incised rim - grooved lip	I	Light
N7	rim	II	Light
N8	rim	III	Light
N9	rim	I	Light
N10	incised lines rim	III	Fe/mg
N11	shell impressed	I	Fe/mg
N12	incised?	II	Shell
N13	incised and grooved	I	Fe/mg
N14	shell impressed	I	Shell
N15	shell impressed	I	Light

there (see Table 5 and Figure 9). As previously discussed these sherds comprise the earliest styles at Nebira 4 (Allen 1972:102-8).

In short, most pottery was locally produced at each site, with the important exception of seven samples from Nebira which reflect a similar production to Oposisi and for which the most parsimonious explanation is that the raw materials or much more likely the finished pots came from the Oposisi area. Figure 10 represents the use of fabric (defined macroscopically) with the CPCRUs (defined chemically).

Table 5. CPCRU's of the South Coast pottery assemblages.

	Site CPCRU	Site CPCRU
I.	OPSISI	NEBIRA SHELL IMPRESSED
II.	NEBIRA	
III.	NEBIRA	
IV.	MAILU	

Results of this analysis compared with Lapita patterns

The results from this limited analysis clearly suggests that pottery production is local during the early part of the EPP and at the same time a number of fabrics are being manufactured with different local clay sources. As with early Lapita, potters are not "conservative" in that they produced similar vessels using different clays and fabrics. Yet, unlike Lapita, there is an indication that some of the earliest EPP wares

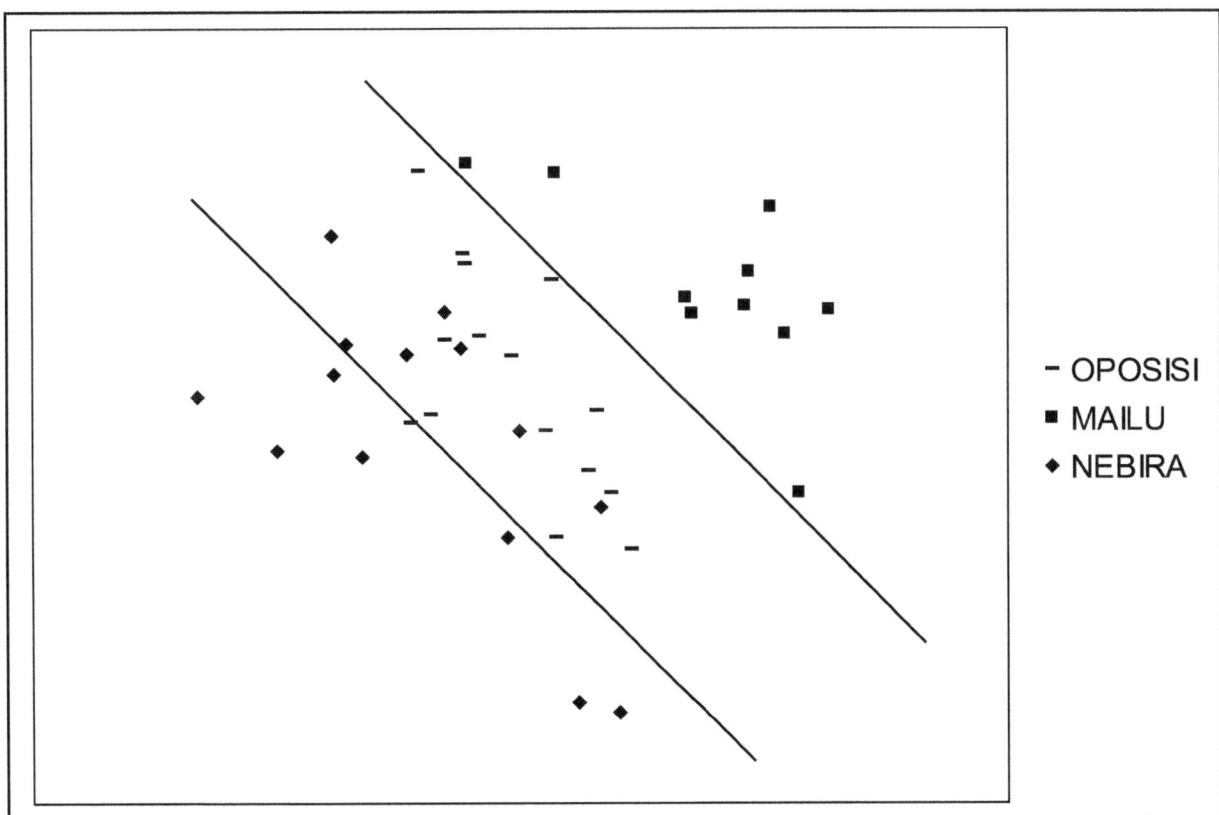

Figure 9. PCA of the pottery analysis.

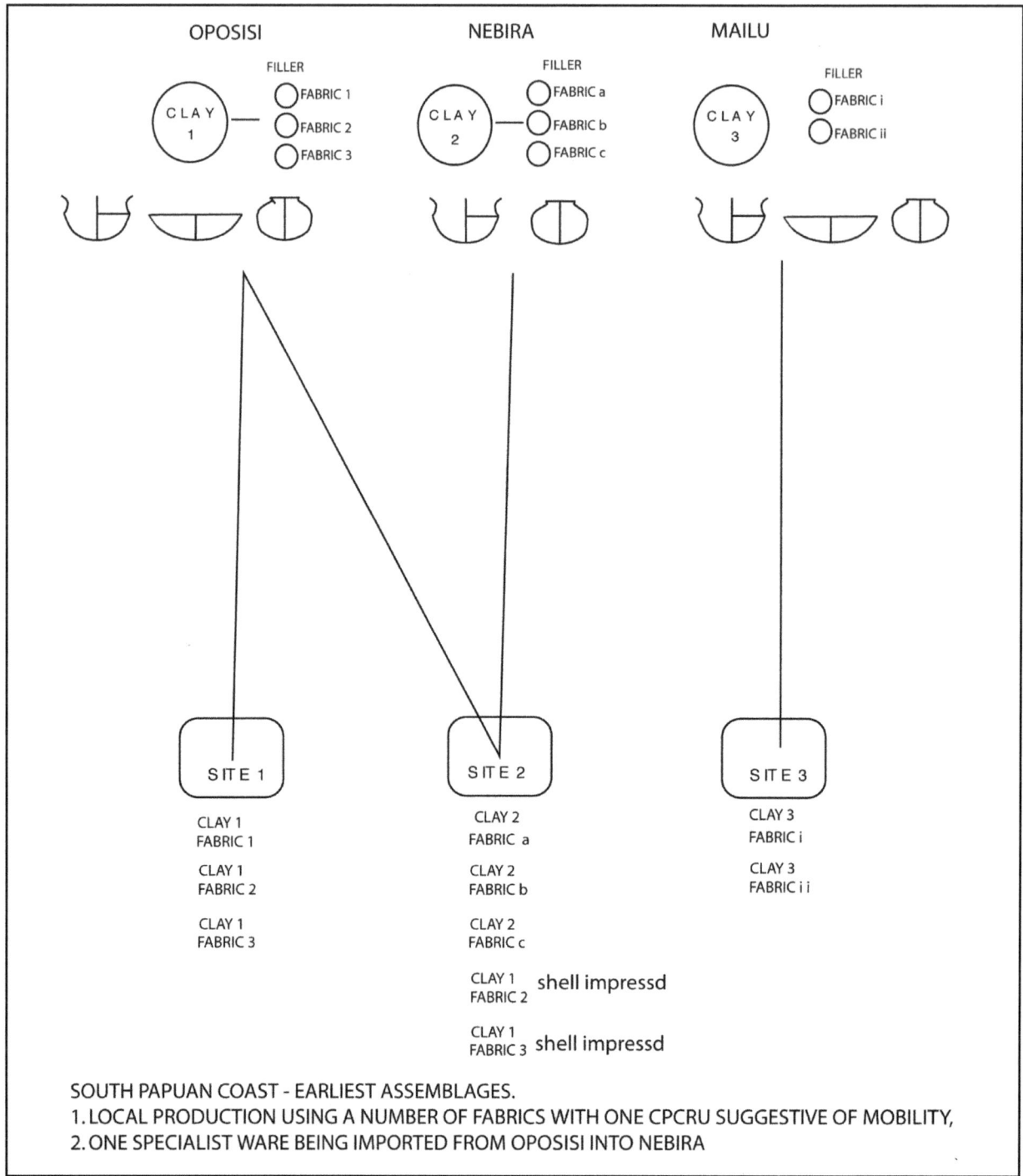

Figure 10. South Coast Pottery Production Pattern.

from Nebira 4 were made in the Oposisi area and taken to Nebira 4. We address this matter further in the discussion.

We would expect this production pattern to change over time as communities become more sedentary. While continuing close connections between EPP groups have been argued on the basis of continuing similarities in general material culture and especially in ceramic forms and decoration, we would still predict that the production patterns of pottery changed, evolving towards the conservative and simple patterns exemplified in later Lapita pottery. This is an eminently testable hypothesis that we hope to approach with further analysis of later EPP styles and post-EPP wares from these same areas.

The final point to make is that while these similarities in production between EPP and Lapita are evident in the data, both these signatures remain fundamentally different to the pottery production systems witnessed in Papua New Guinea by Europeans in the nineteenth and early twentieth centuries (Figures 7 and 8).

Discussion

Comparing the EPP and Lapita colonisations

It might be legitimately argued that the general similarities between EEP and Lapita in respect of site locations, economies, movements of obsidian, associated non-ceramic materials, and the elaboration of pottery decoration styles, put forward here as similarities in the two colonisations, could equally reflect anticipated similarities between marine communities anywhere in Near Oceania practising a mixed hunter/collector, fishing and horticultural economy. Our argument is rather to suggest that two different rapid colonisations, separated in time and space, both occupying new large territories, did not differ in these general characteristics. These provide the background for more specific characterisations that do relate more directly to the similarities of these colonisations.

Pottery production systems and their implications

Our data show that the pottery production systems associated with these colonisations were not conservative and probably differed from pottery production systems in the homelands of the colonising groups. They reveal local experimentation using different combinations of clays and fillers to make culturally similar pots, in terms of forms and decoration styles, across wide distances. In the case of later Lapita ceramics we know that production techniques simplified towards a single clay and single filler in any local area, and although we are yet to demonstrate it we would hypothesise the same is true for EPP. At the same time these early production techniques in both cases are different from those associated with later specialised trading communities in Melanesia.

As an observation, technological experimentation amongst colonising potting communities is not unexpected to the point of being predictable. However it signals in the archaeological record the expectation that a range of other technologies not preserved in that record, from canoes and fishing technologies to terrestrial subsistence patterns must also have undergone experimentation and adaptation. This in turn focusses on risk and risk minimisation in the colonising process, exemplified in those archaeological indicators that reflect connectedness between colonies and back to putative homelands, such as obsidian and ceramic decorative styles.

Modelling colonisation

In another context one of us (JA) together with Jim O'Connell (University of Utah) is currently modelling the initial colonisation of Australia and New Guinea some 45,000 years ago. In considering continents devoid of previous humans we favour the Ideal Free Distribution (IFD) model developed by Fretwell (1972:83 and ff.). This model suggests that the way individuals occupy new territories is set up via habitat selection. The model suggests that in an empty landscape the "best" habitats, that is, those that optimise evolutionary success, will be occupied first. These "best" habitats we call sweet spots. As well as offering the best avenues to subsistence, sweet spots will have other advantages ranging from good defences against predators (human or non-human), to the availability of required raw materials, to open lines of communication with other related groups of colonists in order to ensure longer term biological success, a difficult task for small groups of isolated colonists. Sweet spots diminish in suitability as populations within them increase, at which time new sweet spots further afield may be sought or less sweet spots behind the line of colonisation, by-passed in the first onwards movement, may be subsequently occupied. If the colonists are fishing/hunting horticulturalists, a variation on this model might see initial "beach head" colonies expanding locally to occupy other valuable niches.

Although we would not push the case too far we see that Nebira 4, an outlier in a locational sense among EPP sites, might have been particularly dependent on a parent colony in the Oposisi area, thus making sense of the Oposisi fabrics identified in the early EPP wares at Nebira 4.

How this model applies in occupied landscapes (as is the case with EPP and Lapita in Near Oceania), is less certain. While some locations such as small offshore islands may have been little used by non-pottery using hunter-gatherers, other parts of the coastline and inland are assumed to have been occupied before these colonisations, and valuable resources such as New Britain obsidian would likely have been controlled by incumbent groups. The IFD model assumes that new arrivals are free to settle where they want and the model loses coherence when this assumption is not met. A possible archaeological signature reflecting the colonising of occupied lands is discussed in the next section.

The elaboration of material culture by colonising groups

A striking feature of both colonisations is an initial elaborate material culture that becomes less elaborated through time. This decline is particularly rapid in the case of EPP. It has sometimes been argued that the early elaborate material is a reflection of the homeland culture, and at some level it must be – no group can invent a new and elaborate material culture instantaneously and *in vacuo*. But the fact that these 'homeland cultures' remain elusive demonstrates that this explanation is at best only a partial one. In the case of Lapita there has been a long and fruitless search for immediate antecedents for highly elaborate dentate stamped pottery west of the Bismarcks, nor can we point to antecedents of the initial highly decorated shell impressed wares of the EPP beyond the Massim.

The evident conclusion in both instances is that pottery decoration is elaborated internally as part of the colonising process.

In seeking an explanation for this we have been drawn to "costly signalling", a theory of behavioural ecology applied to human and non-human organisms that has developed from Veblen (1994[1899]) and Mauss (1969[1925]) and has had a recent resurgence as an explanatory tool in anthropology (Bliege Bird and Smith 2005 plus comments and references). For present purposes we can define costly signalling as expensive displays designed to show the signaller's worth to observing predators and competitors. In two papers on turtle hunting in Torres Strait, Smith and Bliege Bird (2000) and Smith *et al.* (2003) propose that costly signalling must be observable by others, be beneficial to others, be truthful, must demonstrate some strength or fitness of the signaller and must be costly to the signaller in ways that cannot be directly reciprocated. Thus, altruistic acts, while costly, establish reputation that encourages others to engage in reciprocal altruism.

We see two immediate applications of this theory to the colonisations described here. The elaboration of pottery decoration and the bone and shell components of the earliest phases of both the EPP and Lapita can be seen to have two roles within the framework of costly signalling as just described.

The first is in relationships between colonisers and incumbent groups. Although they may have superior technology it is in the best long term interests of colonists to avoid conflict with incumbent groups when, by the very nature of the colonising act, the newcomers will inevitably compete for land and resources with existing groups. By elaborating their material culture the colonists signal their own strength or fitness and provide objects that by exchange will confer prestige or other more utilitarian values on the recipients. Exchanges of colonisers' artefacts for hunted food and raw materials would facilitate the success of a new settlement both directly and by promoting peaceful relationships. Alternatively if colonists could access wives from local incumbent groups they could improve their likelihood of biological success and again promote peaceful relationships. As the colonisers became established the levels of costly signalling would become less immediately necessary and would predictably diminish, but should never completely disappear.

The second use of costly signalling should be between different colonising villages to maintain access to resources not available locally and also to marriage partners. If women were potters, well-made, elaborately decorated pots could signal the fitness of marriage partners. This model makes sense of movement of pots (and their contents) between villages that all most likely made pottery. We have already seen in our sourcing results this process on the Papuan coast, in respect of Oposisi area pots appearing in the early levels of Nebira 4, even though pots were also being made at this latter site; for Lapita, Kirch (2000:113) notes that during its earliest phase the Mussau site of Talepakemalai received a significant range of outside materials, including obsidian, basalt and andesite rocks, chert, metavolcanic adzes and pottery, "especially decorated vessels", from at least 12 different localities/clay sources thought to include Manus, New Ireland and New Ireland's offshore islands. While these were likely traded against a range of locally made shell valuables, under the model we would anticipate that decorated pots might also move out of Mussau.

On the central Papuan coast this internal reciprocity continues throughout the EPP phase at least between sites in the Port Moresby and Yule Island areas. Although the most elaborate shell impressed decoration disappears quickly the subsequent EPP bowls in particular are still well-decorated, especially when compared to the most recent millennium. It may be telling that the percentage of decorated bowls at Nebira 4 rarely falls below 50 % until the end of the sequence.

In conclusion this proposal offers an alternative explanation for the initial phase of elaborate dentate stamping in the early period of Lapita (see also Clark this volume). It is an idea that has sprung directly from a comparison of two different but similar colonisations as we have been urged to do by Irwin. Its explanatory power seems difficult but perhaps not impossible to test in the EPP case, but seems to have a straightforward test that might be applied in the case of Lapita, since that colonisation occurred firstly in the previously occupied lands of Near Oceania and very soon after in the unoccupied islands of Remote Oceania. A detailed review of highly decorated wares in the early sites of each main island group on either side of this divide, in terms of their nature, the lengths of time they endured and their frequency within the wider Lapita ceramic repertoire, could illuminate this question. If this model has any usefulness we would predict that the frequency of elaborate decoration would be lower and its loss quicker in Remote Oceania compared with Near Oceania.

Acknowledgements

We would like to thank the National Museum and Art Gallery of Papua New Guinea for the loan of and permission to analyse the pottery from Oposisi, Nebira and Mailu. In particular thanks to Mr Herman Mandui for facilitating the loan. We acknowledge and thank the support of the National Research Institute of Papua New Guinea, and the help of Mr Jim Robins. Special thanks to Amy Findlater, Otago University, for help with the electron microprobe analysis of the pottery. Thanks also to Lorraine Patterson and the Department of Geology, Otago University, for their support in this work.

References

Allen, J. 1972. Nebira 4: An early Austronesian site in Central Papua. *Archaeology and Physical Anthropology in Oceania* 7:92-124.

Allen, J. 1977a. Fishing for wallabies: trade as a mechanism for social interaction, integration and elaboration on the Central Papuan coast. In J. Friedman and M. Rowlands (eds), *The Evolution of Social Systems*, pp. 419-455. London: Duckworth.

Allen, J. 1977b. Management of resources in prehistoric coastal Papua. In J.H. Winslow (ed.), *The Melanesian Environment*, pp. 35-44. Canberra: ANU Press.

Allen, J. 2000. From beach to beach: the development of maritime economies in prehistoric Melanesia. In S. O'Connor and P. Veth (eds), *East of Wallace's Line; Studies of Past and Present Maritime Cultures of the Indo-Pacific Region*, pp. 139-177. Published as *Modern Quaternary Research in SE Asia* 16. Rotterdam: A. A. Balkema.

Allen, J. and P. Duerden 1982. Progressive results from the PIXE program for sourcing prehistoric Papuan pottery. In W. Ambrose and P. Duerden (eds), *Archaeometry: An Australasian Perspective*, pp.45-49. Canberra: Department of Prehistory, RSPAS, Australian National University, Occasional Papers in Prehistory 12.

Allen, J. and O. Rye 1982. The importance of being earnest in archaeological investigations of prehistoric trade in Papua. In T. Dutton (ed.), *The Hiri in History*, pp.99-116. Canberra: Australian National University, Pacific Research Monograph 8.

Ambrose, W. 1976. Obsidian and its prehistoric distribution in Melanesia. In N. Barnard (ed.), *Ancient Chinese Bronzes and Southeast Asian Metal and other Archaeological Artefacts*, pp. 351-78. Melbourne: National Gallery of Victoria.

Ambrose, W. 1978. The loneliness of the long distance trader in Melanesia. *Mankind* 11:326-333.

Anderson, A., S. Bedford, G. Clark, I. Lilley, C. Sand, G. Summerhayes and R. Torrence 2001. An inventory of Lapita sites containing dentate-stamped pottery. In G.R. Clark, A.J. Anderson and T. Vunidilo (eds), *The archaeology of Lapita dispersal in Oceania*, pp. 1-14. Canberra: Pandanus Books, Terra Australis 17.

Best, S. 1987. Long distance obsidian travel and possible implications for the settlement of Fiji. *Archaeology in Oceania* 22:31-32.

Bickler, S. H. 1997. Early pottery exchange along the south coast of Papua New Guinea. *Archaeology in Oceania* 32:151-162.

Bickler, S. 1999a. Characterisation without sources: Early Prehistoric pottery from the South Coast of New Guinea. In J-C Galipaud and I. Lilley (eds), *The Western Pacific from 5000 to 2000 BP. Colonisation and transformations*, pp.461-475. Paris: IRD editions.

Bickler, S.H. 1999b. Secondary Burial Practices in the Northern Kula Ring. In M. Boyd, J.C. Erwin and M. Hendrickson (eds), *The Entangled Past: Integrating History and Archaeology*, pp.98-107. Calgary: University of Calgary.

Bickler. S.H. 2006. Prehistoric stone monuments in the northern region of the Kula ring. *Antiquity* 80:38-51.

Bickler, S.H., B. Ivuyo and V. Kewibu 1997. Archaeology at the Suloga Stone Tool Manufacturing Sites, Woodlark Island, Milne Bay Province, PNG. *Archaeology in New Zealand* 40: 204-219.

Bird, J.R., W.R. Ambrose, L.H. Russell and M.D. Scott 1981. *The characterisation of Melanesian obsidian sources and artefacts using proton induced gamma-ray (PIGME) emission technique.* AAEC/E510. Lucas Heights: Australian Atomic Energy Commission.

Bliege Bird, R. and E.A. Smith 2005. Signalling theory, strategic interaction, and symbolic capital. *Current Anthropology* 46:221-248.

Bulmer, S. 1971. Prehistoric settlement patterns and pottery in the Port Moresby area. *Journal of Papua New Guinea Society* 5:28-91.

Bulmer, S. 1978. Prehistoric change in the Port Moresby Region. Unpublished PhD thesis. University of Papua New Guinea.

Bulmer, S. 1979. Prehistoric ecology and economy in the Port Moresby region. *New Zealand Journal of Archaeology* 1:5-27.

Bulmer, S. 1999. Revisiting red slip: the Laloki style pottery of Southern Papua and its possible relationship to Lapita. In J-C. Galipaud and I. Lilley (eds), *The Western Pacific from 5000 to 2000 BP. Colonisation and transformations*, pp. 543-577. Paris: IRD editions.

Burenhult, G. (ed.) 2002. *The Archaeology of the Trobriand Islands, Milne Bay Province, Papua New Guinea. Excavation Season 1999*. Oxford: BAR International Series 1080.

Butler, V.L. 1988. Lapita fishing strategies. In P.V. Kirch and T.L. Hunt (eds), *Archaeology of the Lapita Cultural Complex: A Critical Review*, pp. 9-31. Seattle: Burke Museum. Thomas Burke Memorial Washington State Museum Research Report No. 5.

Crowther, A. 2005. Starch residues on undecorated Lapita pottery from Anir, New Ireland. *Archaeology in Oceania* 40: 62-66.

Egloff, B. 1971a. Collingwood Bay and the Trobriand Islands in recent prehistory: Settlement and interaction in coastal and Island Papua. Unpublished PhD thesis, Australian National University, Canberra.

Egloff, B. 1971b. Archaeological research in the Collingwood Bay area of Papua. *Asian Perspectives* 14:60-64.

Egloff, B. 1978. The Kula before Malinowski: A changing configuration. *Mankind* 11(3) 429-35.

Egloff, B. 1979. *Recent Prehistory in Southeast Papua*. Canberra: Department of Prehistory, Australian National University, Terra Australis 4.

Frankel, D. and J.W. Rhoads 1994. *Archaeology of a coastal exchange system: Sites and Ceramics of the Papuan Gulf*. Canberra: Australian National University, Research Papers in Archaeology and Natural History No. 25.

Frankel, D. and R. Vanderwal 1982a. Archaeological investigations near Kerema, Gulf Province, Papua New Guinea 1980-81: Preliminary field report. *Research in Melanesia* 6:20-32.

Frankel, D. and R. Vanderwal, R. 1982b. Prehistoric research at Kinomere Village, Papua New Guinea, 1981: Preliminary field report. *Australian Archaeology* 14:86-95.

Frankel, D. and Vanderwal, R. 1985. Prehistoric research in Papua New Guinea. *Antiquity* 59:113-15.

Fretwell, S. D. 1972. *Populations in a Seasonal Environment*. Princeton New Jersey: Princeton University Press.

Green, R.C. 1987. Obsidian results from the Lapita sites of the Reef/Santa Cruz Islands. In W.R. Ambrose and J.M. Mummery (eds), *Archaeometry: Further Australasian Studies*, pp.239-249. Canberra: RSPAS, Australian National University. Occasional Papers in Prehistory 14.

Green, R.C. and D. Anson 2000. Excavations at Kainapirina (SAC), Watom Island, Papua New Guinea. *New Zealand Journal of Archaeology* 20 (1998): 29-94.

Green, R.C. and J.R Bird 1989. Fergusson Island obsidian from the D'Entrecasteauz Group in a Lapita site of the Reef Santa Cruz Group. *New Zealand Journal of Archaeology* 11: 87-99.

Hanslip, M. 2001. Expedient technologies? Obsidian artefacts in Island Melanesia. Canberra. Unpublished PhD thesis, Australian National University.

Horrocks, M. and S. Bedford 2005. Microfossil analysis of Lapita deposits in Vanuatu reveals introduced Araceae (aroids). *Archaeology in Oceania* 40:67-74.

Horrocks, M. and Nunn, P.D. 2007. Evidence for introduced taro (Colocasia esculenta) and lesser yam (Dioscorea esculenta) in Lapita-era (c.3050-2500 cal. Yr BP) deposits from Bourewa, southwest Viti Levu Island, Fiji. *Journal of Archaeological Science* 34:739-748.

Irwin, G. 1977. The emergence of Mailu as a central place in the prehistory of coastal Papua. Unpublished PhD thesis, Australian National University.

Irwin, G. 1978a. Pots and entrepots. *World Archaeology* 9:299-319.

Irwin, G. 1978b. The development of Mailu as a specialised trading and manufacturing centre in Papuan prehistory: The causes and implications. *Mankind* 11:406-415.

Irwin, G. 1983. Chieftainship, kula, and trade in Massim Prehistory. In J.W. Leach and E. Leach (eds), *The Kula: New Perspectives on Massim Exchange*, pp. 29-72. Cambridge: Cambridge University Press.

Irwin, G. 1985. *The Emergence of Mailu*. Canberra: Department of Prehistory, Australian National University. Terra Australis 10.

Irwin, G. 1991. Themes in the prehistory of Coastal Papua and the Massim. In A. Pawley (ed.) *Man and a Half: Essays in Pacific anthropology and ethnobiology in honour of Ralph Bulmer*, pp.503-510. Auckland: Polynesian Society.

Irwin, G. and S. Holdaway 1996. Colonisation, trade and exchange: From Papua to Lapita. In J. Davidson, G. Irwin, F. Leach, A.Pawley and D. Brown (eds), *Oceanic Culture History: Essays in Honour of Roger Green*, pp. 225-35. Dunedin: New Zealand Journal of Archaeology Special Publication.

Kirch, P.V. 1988. Long-distance exchange and island colonization: the Lapita case. *Norwegian Archaeological Review* 21:103-117.

Kirch, P.V. 1989. Second millennium B.C. arboriculture in Melanesia: Archaeological evidence from the Mussau Islands. *Economic Botany* 43: 225-40.

Kirch, P.V. 2000. *On the Road of the Winds: An Archaeological History of the Pacific Islands before European Contact*. Berkeley: University of California Press.

Kirch, P.V. and D.E.Yen 1982. *Tikopia: The Prehistory and Ecology of a Polynesian outlier*. Honolulu: Bishop Museum Press, Bishop Museum Bulletin 238.

Kirch, P.V., Hunt, T.L, Weisler, M., Butler, V. and Allen, M.S. 1991. Mussau Islands prehistory: results of the 1985-86 excavations, in Allen, J. and Gosden, C. (eds), *Report of the Lapita Homeland Project,* pp.144-163. Canberra: Department of Prehistory, Australian National University, Occasional Papers in Prehistory 20.

Kewibu, V. pers. comm. PhD candidate, Department of Archaeology and Natural History, Australian National University.

Lauer, P. 1970. Amphlett Islands pottery trade to the Trobriand Islands. *Mankind* 7:165-76.

Lauer, P. 1971. Changing patterns of pottery trade to the Trobriand Islands. *World Archaeology* 3:197-209.

Lauer, P. 1974. *Pottery traditions in the d'Entrecasteaux Islands of Papua*. Brisbane: University of Queensland Press. Occasional Papers in Anthropology 3.

Leach, B.F., C.J. Quinn, G.L. Lyon, A. Haystead and D.B. Myers 2000. Evidence of Prehistoric Lapita Diet at Watom Island, Papua New Guinea, using Stable Isotopes. *Journal of New Zealand Archaeology* (1998) 20:149-159.

Lentfer, C.J. and R. Green 2004. Phytoliths and the evidence for banana cultivation at the Lapita Reber-Rakival Site on Watom Island, Papua New Guinea. *Records of the Australian Museum Supplement* 29: 75-88.

Mauss, M. 1969(1925). *The Gift. Forms and Functions of Exchange in Archaic Societies*. London: Cohen and West Ltd.

Mc Niven, I., W.R. Dickinson, B. David, M. Weisler, F. von Gnielinski, M. Carter and U. Zoppi 2006. Mask cave: Red-slipped pottery and the Australian-Papuan settlement of Zenadh Kes (Torres Strait). *Archaeology in Oceania* 41: 49-81.

Matthews, P. J. and C. Gosden 1997. Plant remains from waterlogged sites in the Arawe Islands, West New Britain Province, Papua New Guinea: Implications for the history of plant use and domestication. *Economic Botany* 51:121-133.

Pawley, A. 1969. Notes on the Austronesian Languages of Central Papua. Mimeo., Department of Anthropology and Sociology, U.P.N.G.

Rhoads, J. 1980. Through a Glass Darkly: Present and past land-use systems of Papuan Sagopalm users. Unpublished PhD thesis, Australian National University.

Rhoads, J. 1982. Prehistoric Papuan Exchange Systems: The Hiri and its Antecedents. In T. Dutton, (ed.), *The Hiri in History. Further Aspects of Long Distance Motu Trade in Central Papua*, pp.131-150. Pacific Resource Monograph 8. Canberra: Australian National University.

Rhoads, J. and D. Mackenzie 1991. Stone axe trade in prehistoric Papua: The travels of the Python. *Proceedings of the Prehistoric Society* 57:35-49.

Rye, O. 1976. Keeping your temper under control. *Archaeology and Physical Anthropology in Oceania* 11:106-137.

Rye, O. 1981. *Pottery Technology: Principles and Reconstruction*. Washington: Taraxacum.

Rye, O. and J. Allen 1976. New approaches to Papuan pottery analysis. In J. Garanger (ed.), *Colloque XXII, La Préhistoire Océanienne, Prétirage*, pp.198-222. Nice: IXe Congrés, Union Internationale des Sciences Préhistoriques et Protohistoriques.

Rye, O. and J. Allen 1980. New approaches to Papuan pottery analysis. *Journal de la Société des Océanistes* 69:305-314.

Rye, O. and P. Duerden 1982. Papuan pottery sourcing by PIXE: Preliminary studies. *Archaeometry* 24:59-64.

Smith, I. 2000. Terrestrial fauna from excavations at the Kainapirina (SAC) locality, Watom Island, Papua New Guinea. *New Zealand Journal of Archaeology* 20:137-147.

Smith, E. A. and R. Bliege Bird 2000. Turtle hunting and tombstone opening. Public generosity as costly signalling. *Evolution and Human Behaviour* 21:245-261.

Smith, E. A., R. Bliege Bird and D.W. Bird 2003. The benefits of costly signalling: Meriam turtle hunters. *Behavioural Ecology* 14:116-26

Specht, J. 2002. Obsidian, colonising and exchange. In S. Bedford, C. Sand and D. Burley (eds), *Fifty years in the field. Essays in Honour and celebration of Richard Shutler Jr's Archaeological Career*, pp.37-49. Auckland: New Zealand Archaeological Association Monograph 25.

Specht, J. 2005. Revisiting the Bismarcks: some alternative views. In A. Pawley, R. Attenborough, J. Golson and R. Hide (eds), *Papuan Pasts: cultural, linguistic and biological histories of Papuan-speaking peoples*, pp.235-288. Canberra: Pacific Linguistics 572, Australian National University.

Summerhayes, G.R. 1997. Losing your temper: the effect of mineral inclusion on pottery analysis. *Archaeology in Oceania* 32:108-118

Summerhayes, G.R. 2000a. *Lapita Interaction*. Canberra: Centre of Archaeological Research, Australian National University. Terra Australis No.15

Summerhayes, G.R. 2000b. Far Western, Western and Eastern Lapita – A re-evaluation. *Asian Perspectives* 39:109-138.

Summerhayes, G.R. 2003. Modelling differences between Lapita obsidian and pottery distribution patterns in the Bismarck Archipelago. In C. Sand (ed.), *Pacific Archaeology: assessments and prospects. Proceedings of the International Conference for the 50th anniversary of the first Lapita excavation (July 1952), Koné-Nouméa*, pp. 139-149. Nouméa: Les Cahiers de l'Archéologie en Nouvelle-Calédonie 15.

Summerhayes, G.R. 2004. The nature of prehistoric obsidian importation to Anir and the development of a 3,000 year old regional picture of obsidian exchange within the Bismarck Archipelago, Papua New Guinea. In V.J. Attenbrow and R. Fullagar (eds), *Archaeologist and Anthropologist in the Western Pacific: Essays in Honour of Jim Specht*, pp. 245-156. Sydney: Records of the Australian Museum Supplement 29.

Summerhayes, G.R. In press (a). The rise and transformation of Lapita in the Bismarck Archipelago. In S. Chui and C. Sand (eds), *From southeast Asia to the Pacific: Archaeological perspectives on the Austronesian expansion and the Lapita Cultural Complex*. Taipei: Academia Sinica.

Summerhayes, G.R. In press (b). Melanesian Obsidian – Its Sources, Characterisation and Distribution. In M. Suzuki, W. Ambrose and G.R. Summerhayes (eds), *Proceedings of the International Obsidian Summit, Tokyo 2004*. Tokyo: Rikkyo University.

Swadling, P. 1977. A review of the traditional and archaeological evidence for early Motu, Koita and Koiari settlement along the Central South Papuan Coast. *Oral History* V: 37-57.

Swadling, P. 1980. Decorative features and sources of selected potsherds from archaeological sites in the Gulf and Central Province. *Oral History* VIII:101-123.

Swadling, P. 1981. The settlement history of the Motu and Koita speaking people of the Central Province, Papua New Guinea. In D. Denoon, D. and R. Lacey (eds), *Oral Tradition in Melanesia*, pp. 241-251. Port Moresby: University of PNG and the Institute of Papua New Guinea Studies.

Swadling, P. (n.d.). Was there a hiatus in human settlement 1,000 years ago in the Port Moresby Area? Unpublished manuscript.

Swadling, P. and O. Kaiku 1980. Radiocarbon date from a fireplace in the clay surface of an eroded village site in the Papa salt pans, Central Province. *Oral History* VIII P. 86.

Swadling, P., L. Aitsi, G. Trompf and M. Kari 1976. Beyond the early oral traditions of the Austronesian speaking people of the Gulf and Western Central Provinces: a speculative appraisal of early settlement in the Kairuku District. *Oral History* V:50-80.

Szabo, K. and Summerhayes, G. 2002. Worked Shell Artefacts – New Data from Early Lapita. In S. Bedford, C. Sand and D. Burley (eds), *Fifty Years in the Field. Essays in Honour and Celebration of Richard Shutler's Archaeological Career*, pp. 91-100. Auckland: New Zealand Archaeological Association Monograph 25.

Terrell, J.E. and R.L. Welsch 1997. Lapita and the temporal geography of prehistory. *Antiquity* 71:548-572.

Thompson, K. 1982. Beyond Description: A compilation and explanation of pottery from six archaeological sites in the Gulf Province, Papua New Guinea. Unpublished BA (Hons) thesis. La Trobe University, Melbourne.

Torrence, R., V. Neall, T. Doelman, E. Rhodes, C. McKee, H. Davies, R. Bonetti, A. Gugliemetti, A. Manzoni, M. Oddone, J. Parr, and C. Wallace 2004. Pleistocene colonisation of the Bismarck Archipelago: new evidence from West New Britain. *Archaeology in Oceania* 39: 101-130.

Vanderwal, R. L. 1973. Prehistoric Studies in the Central Coast Papua. Unpublished PhD Thesis. Australian National University, Canberra.

Vanderwal, R. 1978. Exchange in Prehistoric Coastal Papua. *Mankind* 11:416-28.

Veblen, T. 1994(1899). *The Theory of the Leisure Class*. Dover, New York.

White, J.P. 1965. An archaeological survey in Papua New Guinea. *Current Anthropology* 6:334-335.

White, J.P. with O'Connell, F. 1982. *A Prehistory of Australia, New Guinea and Sahul*. Sydney: Academic Press.

White, J.P., H. Jacobsen, V. Kewibu and T. Doelman 2006. Obsidian traffic in the southeast Papuan Islands. *Journal of Island and Coastal Archaeology* 1: 101-108.

Worthing, M.A. 1980. South Papuan Coastal sources of potsherds from the Gulf area of PNG. *Oral History* VIII: 87-100.

6

Leap-frogging or Limping? Recent Evidence from the Lapita Littoral Fringe, New Georgia, Solomon Islands

Matthew Felgate

Felgate and Associates
P.O. Box 3155,
Shortland Street Mail Centre,
Auckland, New Zealand.
felgate@xtra.co.nz

Introduction

Lapita pottery is a component of an archaeological horizon-style found from the Bismarck Archipelago to Samoa, dating to approximately 3300-2700 BP. Lapita pottery marks the first human colonisation of Remote Oceania (Figure 1), that part of the Pacific that cannot be reached other than by making lengthy ocean crossings (Green 1991b) indicating that this pottery style was correlated in Remote Oceania with a maritime colonising cultural adaptation and a period of rapid expansion (Green 1991a). Near Oceania has by contrast been occupied for about 30000 years, at least as far to the southeast as Buka, to the north of Bougainville (Allen *et al.* 1989; Wickler 1995, 2001; Wickler and Spriggs 1988), thus requiring a more complex model of local formation of the maritime colonising adaptation, incorporating intrusive Island-Southeast-Asian Neolithic elements, local innovations, and integration with pre-existing indigenous populations (Green 1991a).

Lapita and Solomon Islands: The Lapita Gap

Establishing the distribution of the Lapita Pottery horizon has been a major goal of Pacific archaeology since the 1950s. The Near Oceanic Solomon Islands (the Solomon Islands including Bougainville and excluding Ontong Java, Te Motu Province and Rennell-Bellona) comprise a major gap in the recorded distribution of early-Lapita pottery sites (Green 1978; Kirch 1997:53; Kirch and Hunt 1988; Roe 1992, 1993; Spriggs 1997:128). More recently the argument has been made extensively, with supporting data, that this gap in the record is explicable as an artefact of predominantly stilt-village early-Lapita settlement pattern in Near Oceania, with consequent poor detectability of early sites by the usual terrestrial targeted survey methodology (Felgate 2001, 2003; Felgate

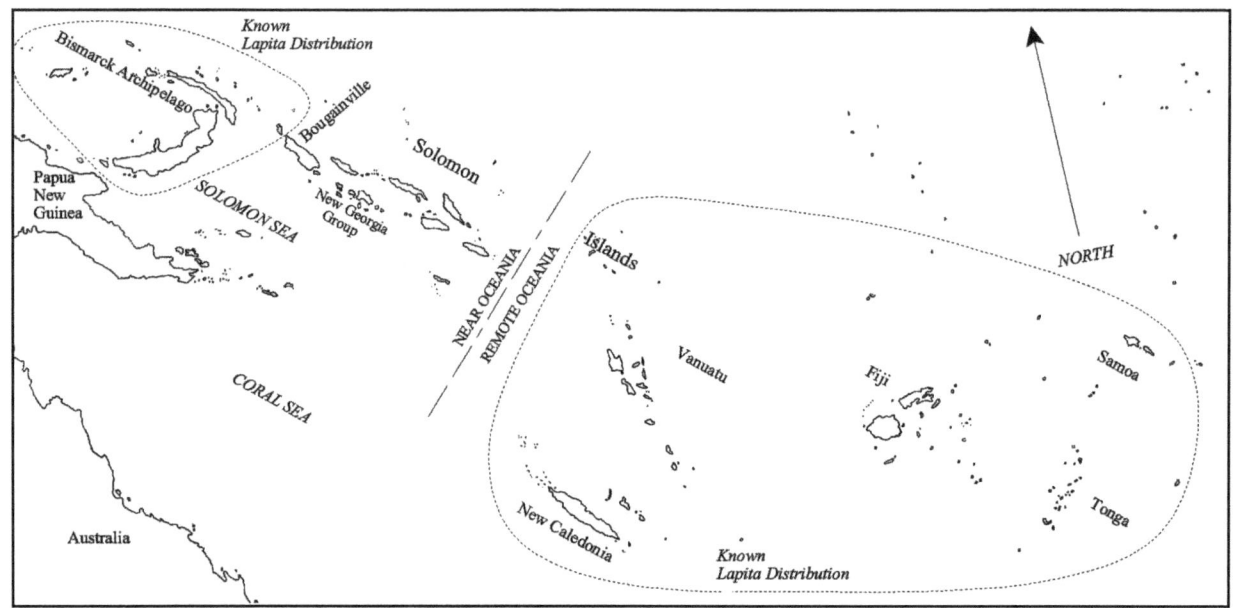

Figure 1. Map of Near/Remote Oceania showing the recorded distribution of Lapita pottery prior to the New Georgia Archaeological Survey.

and Bickler n.d). The view persists, however, that early-Lapita period colonisers avoided the near-Oceanic Solomon Islands, although a late-Lapita presence is now acknowledged (Sheppard and Walter 2006).

Whether the distribution of early-Lapita pottery was continuous or discontinuous in Near Oceania is a primary issue, as it has significant implications for our ideas about what Lapita represents. A continuous distribution of early-Lapita pottery across this region would favour a model of the largely indigenous development of Lapita pottery, or at least raise the probability of integration into local populations of any migrants from Island Southeast Asia at an early stage in the development of the Lapita cultural complex. A discontinuous distribution would favour an avoidance model of Lapita colonisation (e.g. Sergeantson and Gao 1995:169), where Lapita represents "foreign" intrusion, by an expansionist society living at the fringes of an already occupied hostile and/or malarious Near-Oceanic Solomon Islands. In this sort of model Lapita expansion "colonies" are seen as confined initially mostly to offshore islands in the Bismarck Archipelago, and remain culturally and genetically relatively distinct from earlier occupants of Near Oceania for an extended period; generally bypassing the bulk of the Near Oceanic Solomon Islands in favour of a previously unoccupied and/or otherwise healthier Remote Oceania.

Opinion amongst archaeologists with an interest in Lapita is divided as to the reasons for the gap in the distribution of early Lapita sites. Two possible explanations commonly discussed previously are (a) that the gap is purely an artefact of insufficient survey in this region (Green 1978; Spriggs 1997:128) and (b) that the gap directly reflects a discontinuous distribution of Lapita in this region or even complete avoidance of this region by Lapita peoples in the past (Gorecki 1992; Roe 1992, 1993:185; Sheppard and Walter 2006; Sheppard et al. 1999). Some take an equivocal position in relation to these possibilities (e.g. Kirch 1997:53). An additional possibility less often considered is (c), that tectonic instability has reduced coastal site visibility/preservation in the Near-Oceanic Solomon Islands (Kirch and Hunt 1988:18).

Discussion has been conditioned until recently by the complete lack of Near-Oceanic Solomon Islands Lapita pottery discoveries. This allowed considerable scope for theories explaining the lack of Lapita pottery sites as avoidance of the area by Lapita-using people. For example, at the 1996 Port Vila Lapita conference, the first two field seasons of the Roviana Archaeological survey were summarised, concluding, among other things, that,

> "The Roviana survey, like all previous work by archaeologists - including the considerable fieldwork by the Solomon Islands National Museum and Ministry of Culture, Western Province, has failed to recover any Classic Lapita dentate-stamped ceramics in the Western Solomons. I would add this data to that from the central Solomons and extend Roe's (1993) hypothesis of no Lapita occupation in the central Solomons to include the Western Solomons. If this hypothesis is correct it adds an interesting wrinkle to the Lapita expansion story and forces us to consider the effect of interaction of Lapita with established populations....It seems possible that the colonisation of the Reefs/Santa Cruz (Green 1979) may mark a very big first step, leap-frogging previously established populations and cultural networks" (Sheppard et al. 1999).

Subsequent to that paper I continued to focus my efforts under the umbrella of the same project on the intertidal and shallow water pottery scatters initially investigated in the 1980s (Reeve 1989), and re-examined in the course of the first seasons of the Roviana survey, when a number of additional similar sites were found by the team (Felgate 2002, 2003, Felgate and Bickler n.d; Felgate and Dickinson 2001; Sheppard et al. 1999). A small number of dentate sherds were recovered from various sites in the course of that work by various members of the team, and one shallow-water site, at Honiavasa in Roviana Lagoon, yielded more substantial evidence for Lapita occupation. At about the same time Ian Scales of the Australian National University was undertaking a roving extended four-fields study of the Western Solomons, and discovered two early pottery sites in the sea at Kolombangara, in the Western Solomons (Figure 2), one of which (Poitete), Summerhayes and Scales suggest, and I agree, has affinities to the Honiavasa site (Summerhayes and Scales 2005).

These finds have had little effect on the leap-frogging theory, most recently stated as:

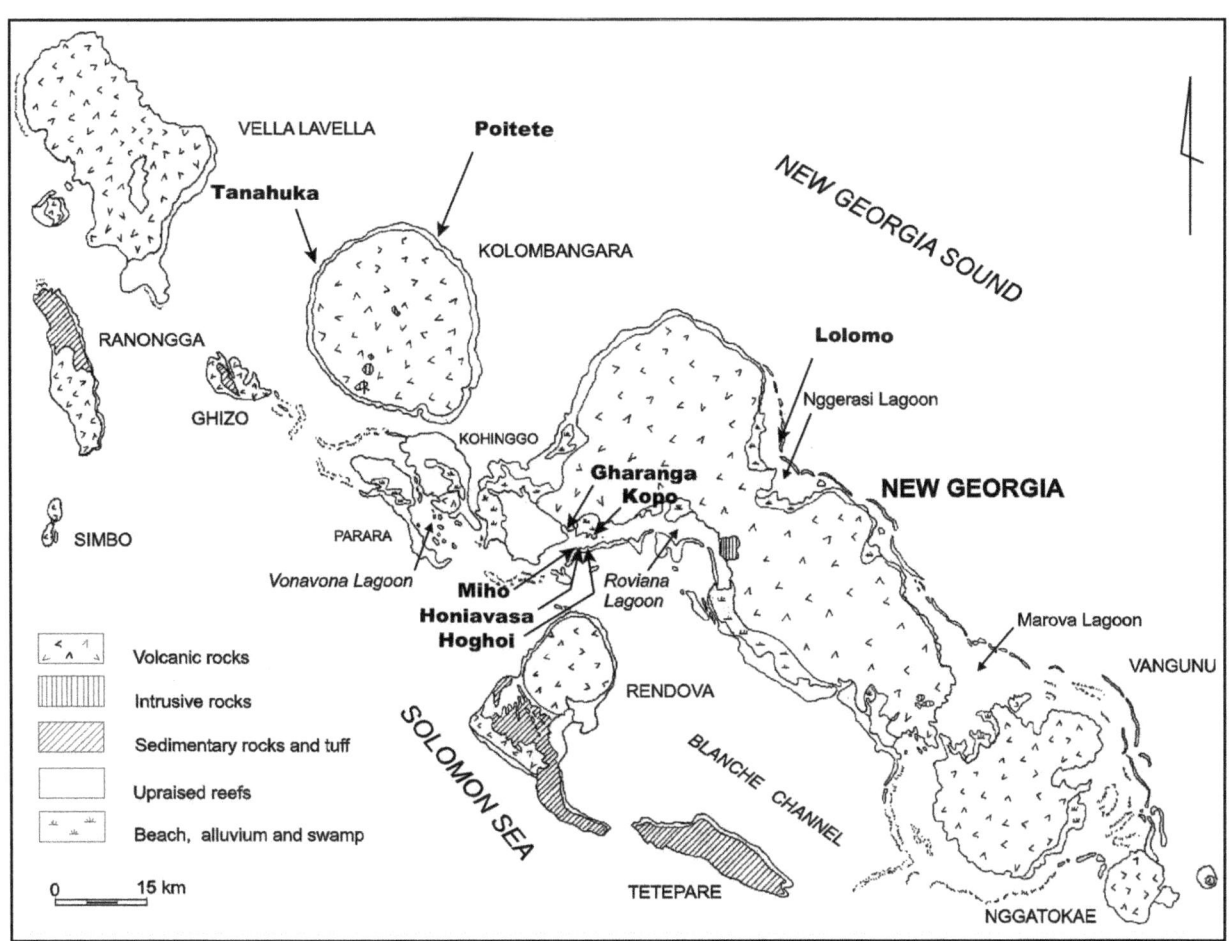

Figure 2. Geology of New Georgia, showing locations of Roviana Lagoon and Nggerasi Lagoon.

> *"The Lapita occupation of the Reef/Santa Cruz Islands in the early Lapita period leapfrogged the main Solomons, giving it some unique characteristics of significance for colonization of Remote Oceania"* (Sheppard and Walter 2006)

The principal revision is the use of the word "Early" instead of "Classic". The prospect of spectacular future early-Lapita finds from the sea in the Near-Oceanic Solomon Islands is not predicted by this model.

We have no evidence yet that early Lapita was absent from the Western Solomons. Sheppard and Walter stress the differences between the Buka reef sites and RF-2 in the Reef Islands, and while pointing out that DJQ on Buka has a high ratio of dentate-to-incised decoration, approaching that of the early Reef/Santa Cruz sample, argue that this site (undated in terms of any absolute technique) is much later than RF-2. I have gone over the similarities between Buka, Honiavasa, Tongan and New Caledonian Lapita vessel forms elsewhere (Felgate 2003:500), and the evidence for regionalisation across time in Wickler's data (Felgate 2003:128). I feel the difference between RF2 and the Near-Oceanic Solomons Lapita sites is overstated given that the Lapita sites of the Western Solomons are undated by any absolute technique. Only two sites in the Western Solomons of the many intertidal sites recorded can be ascribed confidently to the Lapita period on the basis of form or decoration (Honiavasa and Poitete) as opposed to being later sites with the occasional Lapita sherd present, so I would regard our current sample from the area of the Lapita period as unsaturated in Kintigh's sense (Kintigh 1984).

The linguistic scenario as constructed by Tryon and Hackman is for a higher-order subgrouping of the Austronesian languages of Bougainville, the Western Solomons and New Ireland (Tryon and Hackman 1983:54), later all included under the wider subgroup "Meso-Melanesian" as its "South New Ireland/ North-West Solomonic Network" (Ross 1988:259). The languages of the Southeast Solomons by contrast are classified separately, sometimes together with the languages of northern and central Vanuatu, Fijian and the languages of Polynesia (Tryon and Hackman 1983:53-54). Northern Ysabel languages just to the north of the Tryon/Hackman linguistic boundary constitute the late front of Meso-Melanesian language expansion.

Sheppard and Walter see a correlation between the Tryon-Hackman linguistic boundary and the absence of ceramics in the known archaeological record of the Near-Oceanic Solomon Islands to the south of this line, together with the presence of ubiquitous late (post 550 BP) terrestrial ceramic deposits north of the line. They suggest a revision of Tryon's and Hackman's linguistic interpretation of a late Meso-Melanesian southward expansion largely obliterating a previous SE Solomonic substrate north of the Tryon-Hackman line, preferring to see the linguistic boundary as a meeting of eastwards expansion of Late Lapita with westwards aceramic back-migration of Southeast Solomonic speakers whose ancestors lost pottery very early, after leap-frogging the Near-Oceanic Solomons and settling Remote Oceania via the Reef-Santa Cruz Islands. They suggest the reason for this ceramic and linguistic distribution is a lack of early Lapita settlement in the entire Near-Oceanic Solomons area, with settlement north of the line by Lapita people late in the series. They imply that the reason for the presence of late terrestrial ceramics north of the Tryon-Hackman linguistic boundary is a cultural hangover from late-Lapita settlement in that area alone. As supporting evidence they note the widespread use of the word "Raro" (pot) in the Meso-Melanesian languages of the west and Bougainville, and the absence of pottery terms in SE Solomonic languages.

I prefer the theory that the late terrestrial pottery ubiquitous in the west is a feature of a late Meso-Melanesian-speaking cultural expansion, (beginning sometime post-Lapita), and having strikingly similar archaeological expression in the megalithic architecture of South Bougainville as documented in John Terrell's PhD thesis (Terrell 1976). Sheppard and Walter are arguing for cultural continuity between the early ceramics in the sea and the late ceramics on land, but what is the explanation for abandonment of this intertidal pattern and development of megalithic *Tambu* places and terrestrial ceramic deposition in the West Solomons and Bougainville? I think there is a fundamental question here concerning cultural continuity rather than current data providing an answer.

One possible environmental or human biogeographic *explanation* for a theory of late expansion of the Meso-Melanesian linguistic grouping can be constructed by turning to the ethnological distribution of canoe types. Nissan, an atoll between Bougainville and the Bismarcks, is an outlier in the distribution of twin-outrigger trimaran-style of canoes as used in ethnohistoric times around the margins of the Arafura sea, north to the Philippines and west to Madagascar/east Africa (Doran 1973:40). In addition to this possibly intrusive type, the Near-Oceanic Solomon Islands had, at contact, monohull plank-built canoes rather than dugouts (on both sides of the Tryon-Hackman Line (Haddon and Hornell 1937:332). The smaller plank-built fishing canoes in this distribution (the *Mola* in Roviana language) have a pan-Solomonic similarity in being based on a flat-bottomed keel plank, with a deadrise plank and a topside plank added on either side, with additional raised planks at bow and stern. The Roviana *Hore*, or dugout, similarly has a pan-Solomonic distribution in recent times. The antiquity of these distributions is presently unknown.

The *Tomoko* is a large war canoe carrying about thirty paddlers (Waterhouse 1949). It is, in its general structure and design, a complete contrast to the *Mola* and *Hore*. It can be classified as a keel-ship (Doran 1973), being of very complex sewn-plank construction on a vertically oriented central keel. These war-canoes are similar in a functional sense, although the similarity is analogous rather than homologous, to the New Zealand Maori *Waka Taua*. Like the *Waka Taua*, they have their origins outside the tradewind belt, and can maintain high speeds in calm or windless conditions, giving their users a strategic advantage and greater raiding range in calm conditions over users of outrigger canoe types.

Tomoko have not been recorded south of the Tryon-Hackman line, but are distributed throughout the Western Solomons north of the line, and provide a mechanism for the expansion of the Meso-Melanesian Languages, as a late-prehistoric torrid-zone war vessel. I find the idea tempting that the spread of the *Tomoko*, the Meso-Melanesian Languages, and the megalithic *Tambu* places in Bougainville and the Western Solomons may have happened at about the same time. These *Tomoko* may have a homologous relationship to Indic construction techniques of Island Southeast Asia, and may have been introduced to the area long after the spread of single-outrigger technology into Remote Oceania circa 3000 BP. Hornell drew attention to the similarities with ancient craft of Scandinavia regarding the general classification of the construction techniques, and suggested a close (homologous?) similarity of this advanced type of construction to canoes recorded from the island of Botel Tobago near Taiwan and also the Moluccan *Orembai* (Hornell 1936).

The theory of a later expansion of the Meso-Melanesian languages, during which NAN languages survived in pockets, begs the question of why no SE Solomonic survivals north of the Tryon Hackman Line. The saltwater/bush dichotomy may have made any SE-Solomonic speaking communities north of the Tryon-Hackman line more vulnerable to language-loss than NAN bush-dwellers. Some of the NAN languages (Kazukuru, for example) are regarded today as languages of inland-dwellers, with an uneasy relationship to coastal Meso-Melanesian speakers in the ethnohistoric period. Kenneth Roga and I interviewed a very elderly man in 1996, reputed to be the last survivor in Roviana of inland people who moved to the coast after pacification of the area. He told how inland women and lagoon women exchanged resources in an uneasy truce while the respective male warriors stood back on each side ready for any sign of conflict. The coastal people had limited access to bush resources and the bush people to marine resources even in the early mission period as a result of this uneasy relationship, and bush people were clearly distinct and not to be trifled with in the early 20th century. It is possible that such relationships extended back into the distant past, and that the Meso-Melanesian expansion was primarily coastal, at the expense of earlier more vulnerably-located coastal languages of the SE Solomonic subgroup. This very point is in fact made on linguistic grounds by Ross (1988:384-385).

The absence of terrestrial and ethnohistoric ceramic traditions south of the Tryon Hackman line is consistent with the record from the Reef/Santa Cruz area of pottery being lost relatively rapidly after the Lapita period, **if** it is accepted that Lapita and post-Lapita settlement south of the Tryon/Hackman line in the Near-Oceanic Solomon Islands was predominantly over the water, and did not create a terrestrial ceramic record (there seems to be accumulating evidence for this now from the Western Solomons). The question now is whether relative sea-level studies of the last 3000 years in the area will offer support to such a model. Such studies have not yet been carried out, and existing information (Mann *et al.* 1998) is not specifically directed at this period and provides sparse and contradictory results for late sea level changes, of limited relevance to this archaeological question. Detailed sea-level studies and appropriately targeted intertidal/underwater surveys from south of the line are needed to test such a sweeping revision of the Solomons linguistic sequence.

Dating the Honiavasa site

Elsewhere I have referred to the Honiavasa site, situated at the main entrance passage to Roviana Lagoon, as a late Lapita site, as have Summerhayes and Scales, but it is worth noting that chronological assignment is based principally on seriation chronologies of ceramic attributes. A radiocarbon date was obtained from surface soot on a plain sherd from the Hoghoi site at Roviana lagoon (NZA12353: 2619 ± 45 BP) which calibrates to 2900 BP (86.7%) 2780 BP; 2690 BP (3.5%) 2660 BP; 2640 BP (3.6%) 2590 BP; 2580 BP (1.6%) 2550 BP using atmospheric data from Stuiver *et al.* (1998), OxCal version 3.10 (Bronk Ramsey 2005). This determination is thought to post-date the Honiavasa site on the basis of a seriation chronology, used in conjunction with a relative chronology obtained from thermoluminescence dates of quartz-calcite hybrid tempered sherds (Felgate 2003:451-481).

While this data is reassuring in that it reinforces the notion that no gross chronological error has been made in assigning Honiavasa to the Lapita period, it does not inform as to the age of the site in relation to other Lapita sites, leaving artefact and stylistic studies as the principal method for chronological comparisons (although there is some potential for thermoluminescence relative chronologies for granitic-tempered sherds, and for calibrated calendrical dates if an adequate model of fading can be developed for this specific temper type, especially the potassium feldspar grains).

Examples of Miho, Gharanga and Kopo styles are shown in Figures 3-5. The

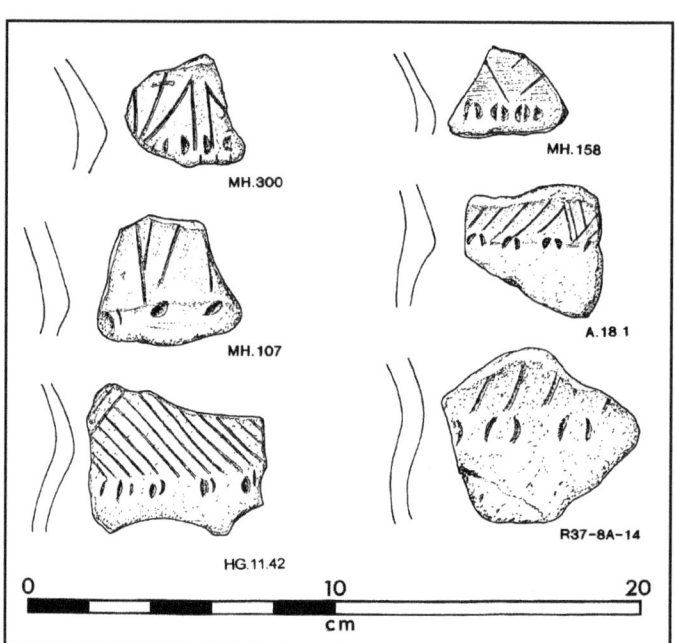

Figure 3. Miho-style sherds from Roviana Lagoon.

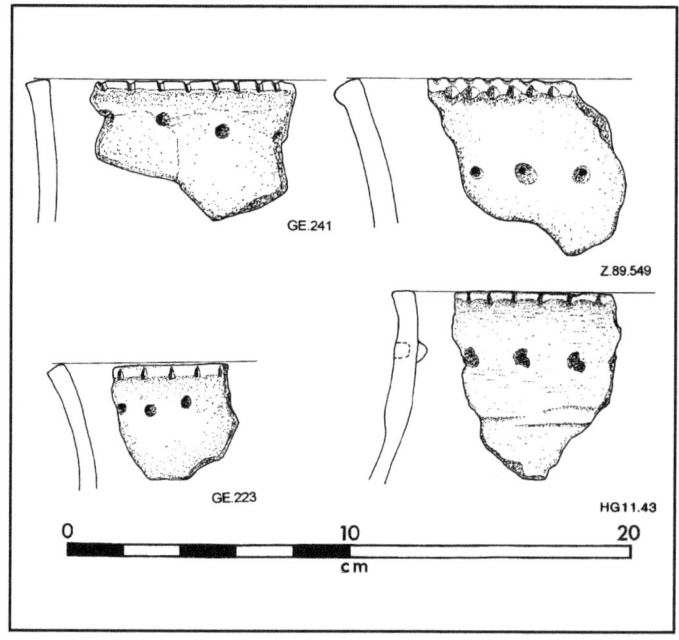

Figure 4. Kopo-style sherds from Roviana Lagoon.

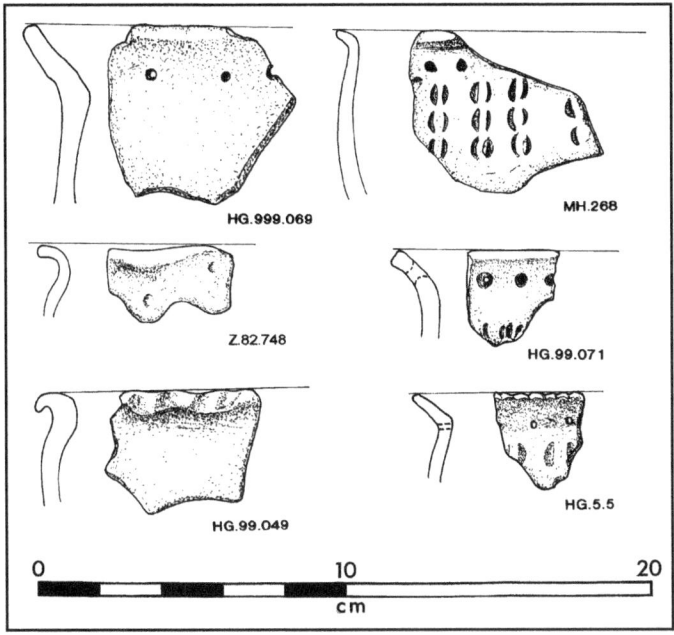

Figure 5. Gharanga-style sherds from Roviana Lagoon.

sequence in which Gharanga and Kopo occur is uncertain, but a phyletic series from Honiavasa Lapita bounded decoration to Miho, followed by Gharanga/Kopo seems to be the most economical arrangement. The positioning of these other styles later than Honiavasa in the series is well supported by thermoluminescence data. Miho-phase decoration may be homologous/contemporaneous with Wickler's unbounded incised decoration at DAF on Buka (Wickler 2001:112-113) while Gharanga-Kopo punctate necks may relate to two sherds found at DES (Wickler 2001:120). Wickler noted the similarity between these sherds and some from Lapita sites in the Bismarck Archipelago.

New vessel-form evidence presented in this paper from the Lolomo underwater site at North New Georgia (an annotated aerial view of the site is shown in Figure 6) suggests that the dated sherd from Hoghoi is intermediate between the Miho and Gharanga phases of the Roviana sequence (for a fuller discussion of the chronological issues see Felgate 2003: Chapters 12 and 13) and thus post-dates the Lapita pottery at Honiavasa by a substantial margin. The Hoghoi vessel which was dated is illustrated in Figure 7b together with some other Roviana neck and rim sherds having similar characteristics. None of the other Roviana sherds provide a robust match to the dated sherd, which combines the thin body, neck and rim of the Gharanga style with the tall fragile rim form of the Miho style, but has, like the Gharanga style, a pronounced vertical curve at the neck, rather than the gentler curve of the Miho style, and lacks the local thickening of the neck profile so characteristic of the Miho style (rendering neck sherds weaker and thus biasing assemblages against this neck type).

Figure 7a shows a sherd from Paniavile at Roviana lagoon with a fairly thin neck and fairly tight vertical curve at the neck which bears comparison with the dated Hoghoi sherd (Figure 7b). Figure 7c shows a flat-lipped sherd from the Honiavasa Lapita site, which has the pronounced neck with thin and excurvate tall rim of the dated Hoghoi sherd, but is virtually unique among the Roviana ceramics by virtue of its lip form, and which is made using an exotic sand temper of the anomalous Quartz-Calcite hybrid class (Felgate and Dickinson 2001). Figure 7d from Honiavasa is of the right general neck form, but has a very small orifice diameter and is much thicker than the dated Hoghoi sherd. Figure 7e is the most complete cooking pot recovered from the Honiavasa site, and illustrates a tendency towards very gentle vertical curvature of the neck which can make neck sheds from the site difficult to identify. Figure 7f from the Zangana site is a large and particularly thin sherd with a sharp, although slightly thickened inflection in the neck profile, and is broadly comparable to the dated Hoghoi sherd. Figure 7g is a particularly thin-rimmed and thin-bodied sherd from the Miho site which differs from the dated Hoghoi sherd in having typical Miho-phase thickening of the neck interior in the profile, thus providing a poor match. Figure 7h, from Miho, is better, being a tall thin rim without thickening of the neck, but as is the case with many thin-profiled neck sherds, is broken at the neck and thus provides a poor basis for comparison. The same holds for Figure 7i, from Zangana. Figure 7j shows a sherd from Miho which is suitably thin and sharply inflected at the neck, emphasizing the links between Miho phase and the dated Hoghoi sherd. Figures 4k, l, m and n are the sort of rims that potentially could be from the dated Hoghoi

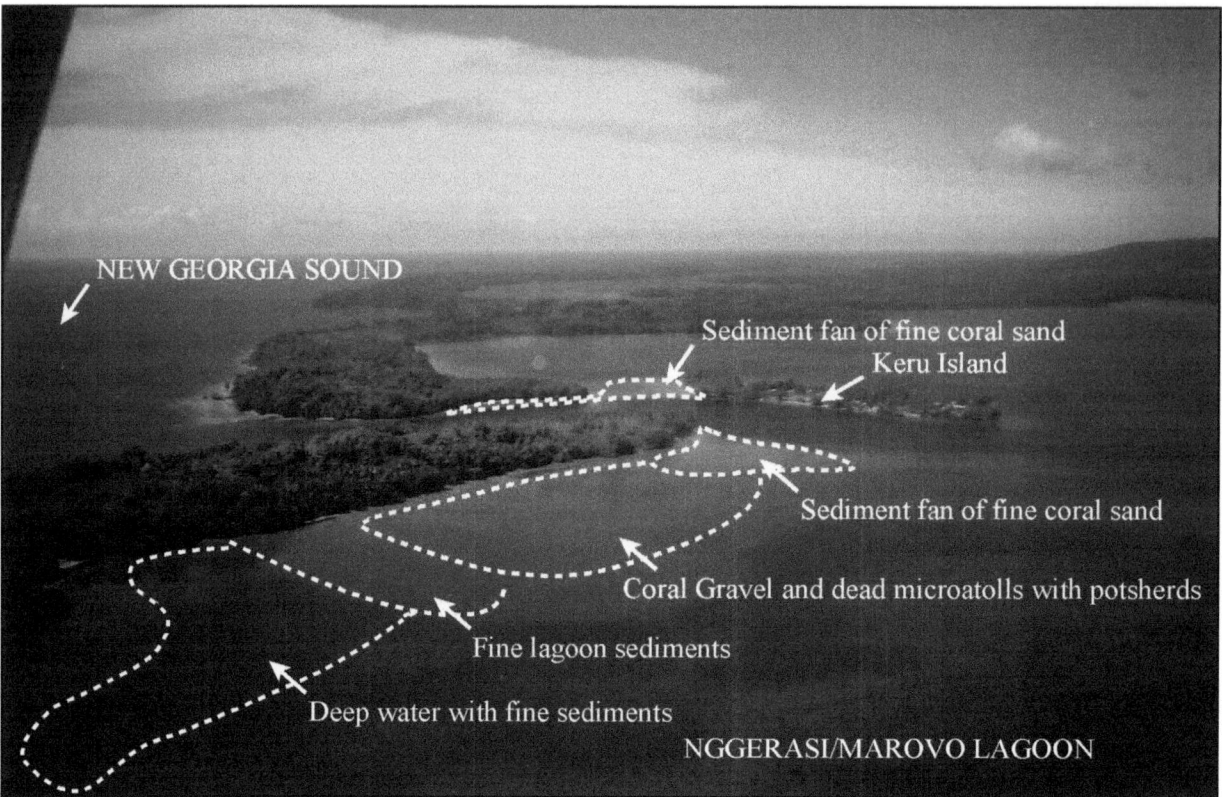

Figure 6. The Lolomo site, situated just to the north of the Keru passage into Ngerrasi Lagoon, showing sediment zonation.

sherd, being everted, thin and tall, but the necks are incomplete or missing, illustrating the difficulties of extrapolating from the Hoghoi radiocarbon date using ceramic style/form.

New Data From Lolomo

As part of a Wenner-Gren funded research project, underwater survey was conducted in the Nggerasi and Marovo lagoons (Figure 2). An underwater ceramic distribution measuring 250 metres by 70 metres was located at Lolomo (Figure 6). The Lolomo site was much more deeply immersed than other scatters on the mainland shore, and several weeks spent diving resulted in the recovery, recording and sampling of 413 sherds, many of them large and well-preserved, in one case being approximately one-third of a whole vessel. Collection zones of approximately 1-metre radius were marked by long stakes of a heavy wood that was not buoyant, and locations of these were surveyed by theodolite, along with shoreline profiles. These locations provide approximate spatial provenance for the sherds (the distribution of found sample locations is shown approximately in Figure 8). All sherds were desalinated in rainwater, dried, drawn and photographed. Temper samples were taken for analysis, and the sherds were returned to their found locations in the sea. A steel datum point for the theodolite survey was cemented into the coral beach and its location recorded by handheld GPS. This data has not yet been written up in detail for publication. Analysis of ceramic variability and spatial analysis is underway. The new data will only be briefly introduced here, insofar as it is relevant to Sheppard and Walter's interpretation of the Hoghoi radiocarbon date.

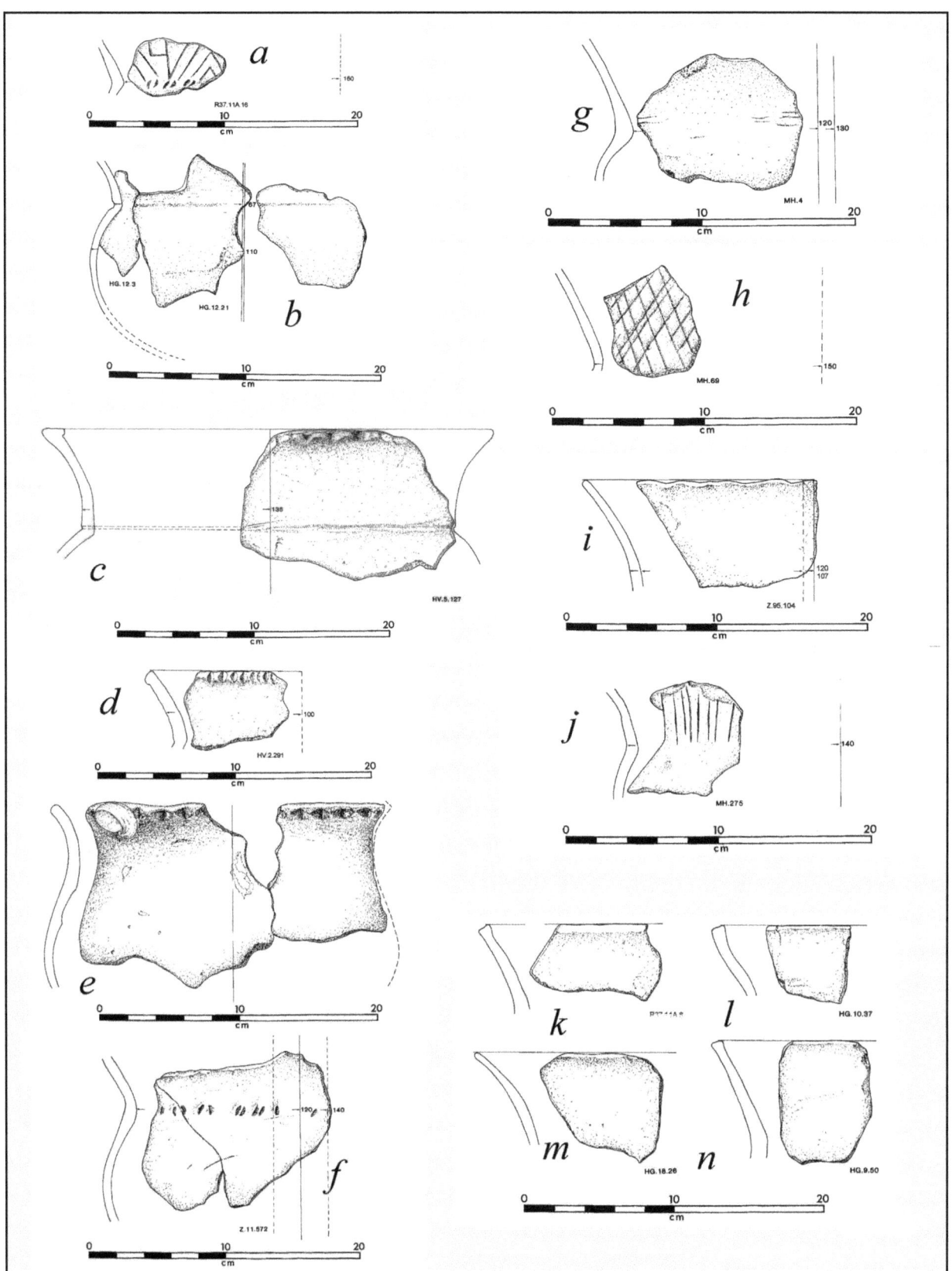

Figure 7. Significant sherds from the Roviana series in relation to the radiocarbon date from Hoghoi.

Lolomo Site Physiography

The barrier islands of the New Georgia lagoon system are composed of Plio-Pleistocene reefs with a complex tectonic history, resulting in multiple reef formations approximately concentric with the New Georgia volcanic cones. These barrier islands have fringing reefs of Holocene age, uplifted to varying extents (Dunkley 1986; Mann *et al.* 1998). In general the Roviana lagoon barrier islands and mainland shore are notable for a shoreline flat covered in relatively fresh fragmented *acropora* corals, except where mainland rivers provide a sediment supply and create fine-sediment fans and swampy deltas, while the Nggerasi Lagoon barrier islands lack this evidence for very recent uplift, tending to have a shore platform covered in terra rossa weathered reefal soils. Data on this has not been collected, this is a very preliminary observation only, requiring more detailed examination. One characteristic common to all the barrier islands around New Georgia is a low sediment supply with consequent high archaeological visibility in the sea. There are no rivers on any of these islets, and sediment from mainland rivers is deposited as deltaic fans forming muddy shorelines, with consequent low archaeological visibility in their vicinity.

The Lolomo site is situated along the lagoon shore of the barrier island forming the northern shore of the Keru Reef Passage (Ramata Island), on which there is an airstrip (out of action at the time of fieldwork, due to a lawnmower breakdown, necessitating an 80km canoe trip from Munda). Sediment zonation along the Ramata Island lagoon-side shoreline is shown in Figure 6. If a Lapita site was present and is preserved at the Keru Reef passage, it will be under the fine coral sands either side of the lagoon end of the reef passage. The sediment supply for these fans is most likely the abrasion of Plio-Pleistocene coral boulder shorelines along the reef passage, where wave exposure is considerable at times in some weathers. This is a major contrast to the inner end of the Honiavasa reef passage of Roviana Lagoon, where both the Honiavasa and Miho sites are located, which have very little build-up of sand.

Significance of the Lolomo Ceramics

In analysing sherds recovered from the sea at Roviana Lagoon, it was hypothesised that a tall, thin, weak rim form was likely to be characteristic of the Miho ceramic style, the latter thought to postdate Roviana Lapita ceramics from Honiavasa (Felgate 2003:385-386). The dated Hoghoi sherd had a neck form unlike the typical Miho thickened neck profile, however, but had a thin everted rim, too tall to fit comfortably into the Gharanga style of short, heavily-everted rim. The deeper water in which the Lolomo site is located has resulted in better preservation of fragile tall thin rim forms, of which there are numerous examples in the Lolomo sample.

Some of the tall thin rims recorded from Lolomo correspond to the hypothesised Miho-phase form, but differ from the dated Hoghoi sherd in having a thickened neck profile and gentle external vertical curvature at the neck restriction (these are characteristics of the Miho Phase, and some plain sherds of this general form were present in the Honiavasa site also). A sherd recovered from Lolomo illustrates this (see Figure 9c). Thin-necked everted-rim sherds consistent with the dated Hoghoi sherd were also found at Lolomo (Figures 9f, 6g and 6h). The sherds lie in the dense deposit of ceramics at the north-western edge of the site Figure 8), in water of about 2.5m depth at the time of collection and well buried in sand and gravels, hence the good state of preservation of these fragile neck forms.

While there is considerable form variability between these three vessels, they are all even thinner than the dated Hoghoi sherd but provide the closest match so far to the unusual Hoghoi neck, illustrating the biasing effect of differential preservation on our available information concerning vessel form.

It must be stressed that neither Hoghoi nor Lolomo are Lapita sites, although both are very clearly Lapita derived, permitting phyletic seriation. This is apparent for example, in the twinned vertical decorative elements used as design zone markers for Miho-phase ceramics, examples of which occur at Lolomo (Figure 9c). Where this differs from the Honiavasa carinated jars, in terms of the design system, is the absence of twinned horizontal decorative elements. This twinned or sometimes tripled horizontal design zone marker is very much a feature of most geometric Lapita design, and it looks to have partially broken down in the Lolomo

Figure 8. An approximate overlay of survey data from Lolomo on an oblique aerial photograph. The white crosses are surveyed stakes marking underwater collection provenance zones from which pottery was recorded.

decoration, which tends more towards the Miho-style unbounded designs (there are examples of Gharanga and Kopo style decoration and corresponding forms also at Lolomo).

There are no examples of the strongly-carinated Honiavasa slab-built Lapita jars at Lolomo. These are clearly a feature of Lapita almost everywhere, all the way to Tonga, including Honiavasa and Poitete, and other occasional find spots at Roviana lagoon. A jar of this sort recently recovered from Honiavasa during a second collection of the site is illustrated in Figure 9e, providing a good decorative match to a Poitete vessel illustrated by Summerhayes and Scales (Summerhayes and Scales 2005:Figure 3e).

At Lolomo there are none of the compound rims characteristic of the Honiavasa Lapita site, and characteristic of Lapita at Buka, especially at DJQ, DES and on the outer reef edge at DAF (Wickler 2001:79-81 and see Wickler's Figure 4.2) and also found as far east as Tonga (Poulsen 1987). A second collection at Honiavasa recovered three more of these (one is illustrated in Figure 9j).

The absence of characteristic Lapita forms from both Lolomo and Hoghoi, and the presence of the fragile neck form in both sites provides additional support for assignment of the Hoghoi date to the Miho-Gharanga phase of the series. A number of Gharanga-style rims are present in the Lolomo site (not illustrated), which supports this conclusion. There was one sherd with a single line of dentate stamping at Lolomo (Figure 9a), as well as two open bowls with slight carination/restriction (Figure 9b and 6d) as well as one incised (?Lapita) small everted excurvate form that is unlike anything found in the Western Solomons so far (Figure 9i).

The dated Hoghoi sherd seems to me to be intermediate in form between Miho-phase and Gharanga phase, and, to make a just-so-story out of it, made at a time when pottery is becoming so thin and finely made that the tall Miho-Style rim form with thickened neck is gradually giving way to the Gharanga style of short, heavily-everted rim, as a way of retaining the strength of the vessel neck. Reduction in thickness (and concurrent reduction in thickness variability) would confer better thermal properties for cooking, and possibly better firing survival rates and shorter drying times prior to firing, as well as less thermal stress during firing and use.

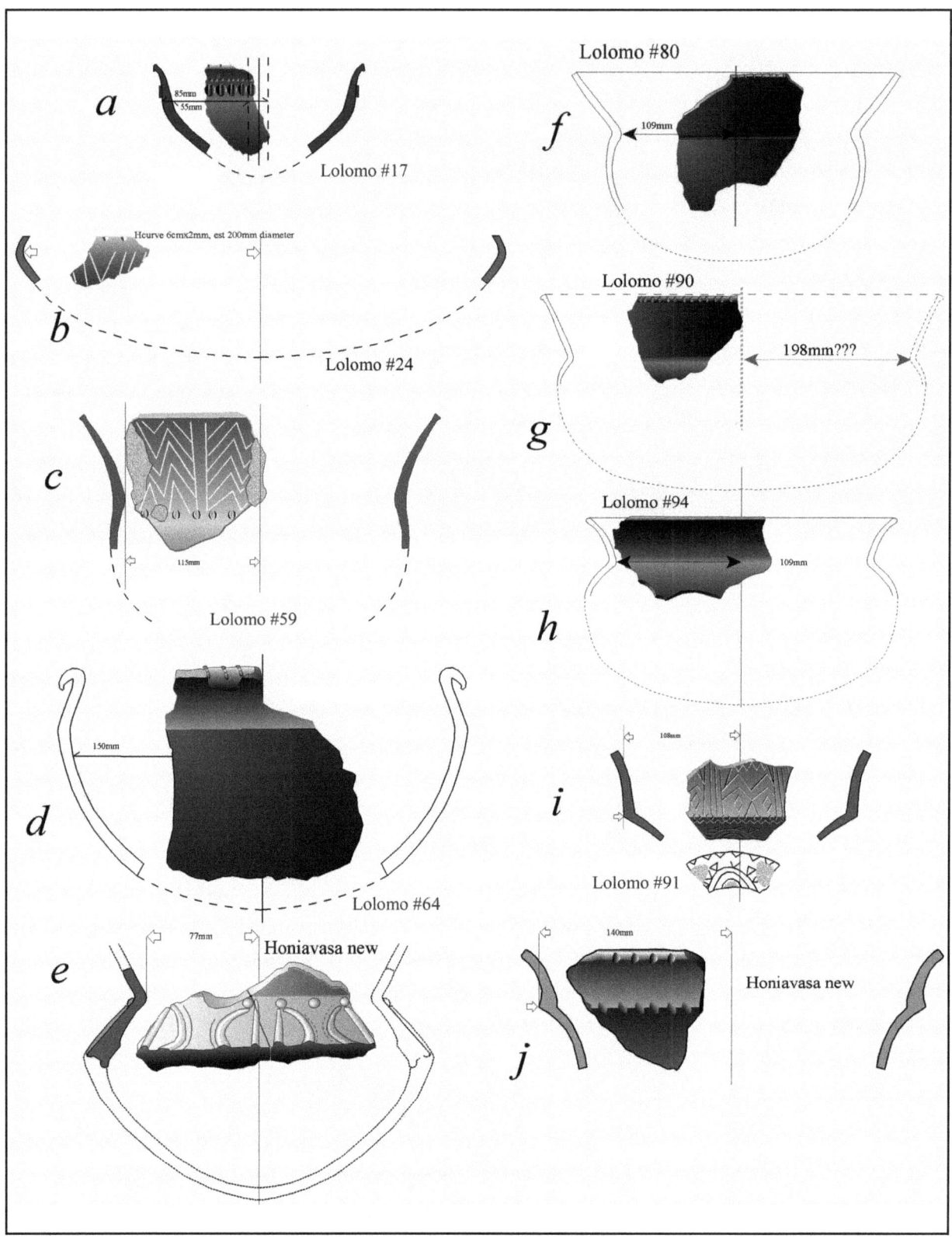

Figure 9. A selection of pottery finds from Lolomo and Honiavasa.

New Pottery finds from Honiavasa: Strengthening the link to Poitete

Honiavasa, at Roviana Lagoon (Figure 2) was revisited in the course of the North New Georgia Lapita Pottery Project, during the season of daytime low tides (initial collection had been in midsummer in difficult rough-weather rising-tide conditions) and an additional deeper part of the site was discovered adjacent to the main Honiavasa reef passage. New pottery finds from Honiavasa strengthen the link between the small Poitete sample and Honiavasa (compare Figure 3e of Summerhayes and Scales (2005) with Figures 6e in this paper). The greater incidence of dentate decoration in the Poitete sample than at Honiavasa provides an even clearer link to the Buka reef sites than that noted after the initial collection from Honiavasa, although overlapping rather than identical occupation spans may be a factor in the differences between the Poitete sample and that from Honiavasa.

Conclusion: the age of the Honiavasa site

I estimate the age of the Honiavasa carinated jars with horizontally bounded decoration to be somewhere in the period 3000 to 2800 BP. I personally don't see sufficient difference between the Reef/Santa Cruz assemblages from RF2, early New Caledonian and Vanuatu Lapita pottery, the Poitete pottery, and Wickler's Buka reef pottery to conclude that the people responsible for the RF-2 pots were anything but closely related in terms of cultural phylogeny to those at Honiavasa. The similarities are more marked in terms of vessel form than in terms of decorative technique in the case of Honiavasa (but decorative structure is another thing- we should avoid dentate-centrism). The principal difference in terms of form is the absence of RF-2 broad everted-rim serving-dish forms, with stands, (although one possible stand was recovered from the Zangana site in Roviana Lagoon). These differences could easily be taphonomic, as the sherds recovered from the Honiavasa site were mostly robust and well-fired, being either heavily carinated slab-built vessels (interpreted as fluid transport forms- most probably water-carrying jars with a high use and breakage rate) or globular cooking pots, similarly with a high breakage rate according to ethnoarchaeological theory.

Interpreting the Evidence: Lapita Limping rather than Leapfrogging

Sheppard and Walter review the pollen-core evidence from the Solomons, in support of late-Lapita influx rather than early. They note that Haberle's Laukutu swamp core (Haberle 1996) shows fluctuation in the level of charcoal after 3200BP, but that a dramatic rise occurs later in that core, and that similar dramatic and sustained rises are happening about 2600 BP in the Roviana cores under analysis by Grimes (unpublished). They note the correlation of this rise with the date from the Hoghoi sherd from Roviana lagoon, although it is worth pointing out that the Hoghoi sherd could date as early as 2900 BP at 95% confidence limits.

Early Lapita colonists must have trod lightly in the Near-Oceanic Solomons. If the Hoghoi sherd substantially postdates the Lapita sites of Poitete and Honiavasa (which is supported by both ceramic seriation and thermoluminescence relative chronology), more thought needs to be given to the possibility that the early fluctuations in charcoal influx are consistent with the presence of a *low-density* Lapita settlement pattern of intertidal sites in the Western Solomons beginning somewhere around 3200 BP. I cannot see that there are four to five centuries between the early well-dated Reef/Santa Cruz Lapita sites and the Buka/West Solomons reef Lapita sites, but certainly could accept this for the later Buka/West Solomons reef sites, where characteristic Lapita vessel forms and design structure have been largely lost, and unbounded decoration is the norm. The dramatic and sustained rise in charcoal influx about 2600 BP (Sheppard and Walter 2006) under this scenario correlates with the dramatic infill of the intertidal/subtidal ceramic distribution, in the form of the many sites with Miho and Gharanga/Kopo styles at Roviana, North New Georgia, Marovo, Gizo and Tanahuka on Kolombangara.

Taphonomy

The Roviana pottery from the sea has had a hammering, and only a tiny proportion of the discarded sherdage remains to be found as a general rule, and this in localities extraordinarily well sheltered from the effects of cyclone and tsunami (Felgate 2003:247-286). This means that taphonomic biases are highly likely - sherds need to have been strong and lucky to have survived millennia of relatively sheltered water processes. This has implications for ceramic seriation in the Near-Oceanic Solomon Islands, and comparison of like-with-like, in a taphonomic sense, is important in such circumstances (Felgate and Bickler n.d). This means that at present the principal sites with which to compare the recent finds of Lapita and post-Lapita in the Western Solomons are the Buka reef sites (Wickler 1995, 2001) and the Poitete material from Kolombangara. Wickler collected 60 000 sherds from Buka, the Roviana sample was around 3,000 (initial sherd count at Honiavasa was 442, while a second collection in the course of the North New Georgia Lapita Pottery Project yielded an additional 93 Honiavasa sherds, generally fairly large). There were 28 sherds collected from Poitete, 15 of them decorated.

Long distance exchange

Sheppard and Walter are thus far correct in characterising Reef/Santa Cruz long-distance exchange as unique in terms of the evidence for long-distance large-scale sourcing of Talasea obsidian from New Britain (but see Galipaud and Swete-Kelly this volume for new data from northern Vanuatu). There are tantalising hints that very-long-distance links were maintained by Lapita people at Honiavasa too, and into the post-Lapita period also at nearby sites. While none of the lithic materials have yet been unequivocally sourced, these sites do contain a great diversity of imported lithic resources, including stone tools and abraders, and of course the anomalous granitic-hybrid pottery temper, thought to be indicative of tropical continental margin geological origin (Felgate and Dickinson 2001). Expert opinion has shifted slightly recently to the granite islands of the Queensland coast as the most attractive source for this sand on geoarchaeological grounds (Dickinson 2006:115). It should also be noted that one sherd matching the Roviana volcanic placer temper was recovered from Bellona in Remote Oceania (Dickinson 2006:115). A conclusion that the Reef /Santa-Cruz obsidian shows that Reef/ Santa Cruz Lapita people were the only Lapita settlements to maintain such long-distance contacts, and that they were not receiving obsidian from intermediate early-Lapita settlements elsewhere in the Solomons (as yet undiscovered) may turn out to be premature.

The possibility of some sort of down-the-line exchange should not be ruled out until we have satisfactorily excluded the possibility of undiscovered (submerged ?) early Lapita sites around Malaita, for example (preferably supported by detailed sea-level studies). The absence of obsidian in inland sites such as Vatuluma Posovi on Guadalcanal doesn't demonstrate a lack of down-the-line exchange until the absence of coastal Lapita sites with Talasea obsidian is demonstrated. Avoidance theorists cannot have their cake and eat it too: if people are avoiding the main Solomons to some extent because of hostile NAN prior inhabitants, they would hardly be fraternising with NAN speakers in Vatuluma Posovi cave on Guadalcanal over a good chunk of obsidian, which would explain the absence of Talasea obsidian in Lapita-age deposit from that excavation, but certainly might have done so with hitherto-undiscovered Lapita coastal colonists in the general area. Cherts were moving out from the Solomons (Sheppard 1993), so it is not as though the Reefs/Santa Cruz were not in contact with anyone but Talasea. There is recent evidence for links to central north Vanuatu also (Bedford pers. comm.). It does seem clear that Reef/Santa Cruz Lapita people were highly desirous of Talasea obsidian, to have acquired it in such quantity, suggesting a strong cultural link to Talasea.

Survey methods and evidence of absence

Sheppard and Walter open a review of Lapita in the Solomons with the question "Are there any Lapita sites in the Solomons?" The central thesis emerging from my eight-year study of Lapita and its derivatives in the Western Solomons (Felgate 2003) is that we cannot read the Lapita archaeological record in that region without concerted programs of littoral geo-archaeology, including sea-level studies. My conclusion on examining existing evidence in 2003 was that the Lapita gap, if it hadn't already been filled, would completely disappear if appropriate surveys were targeted at places where Lapita stilt-settlements were: a) likely to have been located; b) likely to have been preserved; and c) are reasonably accessible to the archaeologist (which might involve underwater archaeology gear). Sheppard and Walter concede that the absence of evidence for stilt house villages from the Central Solomons cannot be said to be a change in settlement pattern without "some targeted surveys of intertidal sheltered areas in Remote Oceania". Some targeted surveys in Near Oceania may be **more** appropriate, as clearly there is a voluminous terrestrial Lapita record in Remote Oceania, suggesting either a founder effect or environmental factor that made terrestrial settlement more feasible. Regarding the latter possibility, it should be remembered that the Near/Remote Oceanic boundary is a biogeographic one, involving some dangerous and discomfiting fauna that might encourage living off the ground, and over water, in Near-Oceania.

Sheppard and Walter argue for absence of Lapita in the New Georgia group. They consider that, for the sites with dentate-stamp pottery currently known, that

> "...the remainder of the decorated assemblage is composed of ceramics that seem identical in all respects to the incised and applied relief tradition of the Bismarck Archipelago" (Sheppard and Walter 2006).

I have argued in detail elsewhere that the temporal conflation of various admixtures of various periods is a major problem in the archaeology of Lapita and its derivatives throughout Near Oceania, and see the definition of Post-Lapita sequences as a subject still in its infancy.

Lapita Limping

The leap-froggers may be partly right in that Lapita is far less common in the intertidal/subtidal record from the Western Solomons than later derivatives. I concluded in my thesis that we have every reason from the data at hand to consider our Lapita sample from the Near-Oceanic Solomons to be "unsaturated" in Kintigh's sense (Kintigh 1984). I believe this to be true even of the ubiquitous Post-Lapita pottery from the sea, which is much more easily found. The Lolomo post-Lapita pottery under analysis provides ample new information, as will each new site in the foreseeable future.

The current data indicate **very** clearly that Lapita is far less common and more difficult to find in New Georgia than Post-Lapita pottery. By extension, our Lapita sample from New Georgia is **less** saturated than our post-Lapita sample. This goes beyond differential preservation, as the robust Honiavasa and Poitete jars are clearly able to withstand the rigours of deposition in the sea in some cases. This suggests that Lapita demographic increase in this region was slow rather than explosive, unlike Remote Oceania, where the early Lapita signal is far stronger. It should be borne in mind also that the overall quantities of Lapita tend to be large in Remote Oceania and the Bismarcks due to vastly greater sediment supply in the form of tephras, hence good preservation, in combination in the case of Remote Oceania with numerous examples of terrestrial primary deposition.

Groube (ironically in the course of noting the contradiction of the lack of a community of culture between Australia and Island Melanesia) suggested that the "predators within" profoundly affected patterns of prehistoric social development (Groube 1993). Malaria or complications arising from malarial illness are the biggest killers of children today in Near Oceania, and otherwise healthy adults are ravaged by the disease and its complications such as pneumonia and brain damage.

The predators without may have been a factor also in Lapita limping in the Solomons and elsewhere where it should be but has not been found. Present in Near-Oceania were pre-Lapita populations who may also have taken their toll initially on small-scale intrusions of culturally distinct people 3000 years ago (the same holds for any putative Lapita colonists of Australia). In addition, predation by crocodiles would have been a far more significant factor in Near Oceania 3000 years ago than we see today. Crocodile populations are relatively young today in Near/Oceanic Island Melanesia due to heavy hunting until about thirty years ago, and are only becoming more obstreperous towards humans in recent years.

Compounding the complications posed by deposition in the sea, we should expect therefore that early Lapita settlement would limp demographically in Near Oceania in comparison to Remote Oceania. And this is consistent with the record from the Solomons. Moore's (2001:396, 406) "string of pearls" model cited by Green (2003:113) in relation to Lapita migration can be expected to have been more thinly strung in Near Oceania, and be a more discreet adornment beyond its successful start in the Bismarck Archipelago. Perhaps limping might be a better characterisation than leapfrogging.

As I write it is getting late, and I must wake in the small hours to catch an aeroplane in which to pursue sand samples pointing to Lapita colonists in North Queensland. The deadline for this paper has expired. I present it in unfinished form.

Postscript

This paper was revised on return from Queensland, but I like the ending, and leave it in its abrupt form, as it expresses both the constraints of being an unpaid researcher who must fit academic publication in between the business of attempting to make a living by other means, and also expresses the confident anticipation that one's theory is on track and is successfully predicting the physical evidence, which I suspect is the satisfaction that drives many of us to spend our lives doing this.

Acknowledgements

The research at Lolomo was made possible by a postdoctoral fieldwork grant from the Wenner-Gren Foundation. I gratefully acknowledge a grant from the Green Foundation. Without such support and recognition this paper would have been so much more difficult to write. The research at Lolomo was carried out with institutional support from the University of Auckland Anthropology Department, especially Peter Sheppard. I wish to acknowledge the research permission granted by the Solomon Islands Ministry of Education, and locally by the Christian Fellowship Church. Support from Lawrence Foanaota, Kenneth Roga, Solomon Roni, James Agolo and the Reverend Opportunity Kuku is gratefully acknowledged in that regard. Fieldwork was carried out by a team of four divers from Roviana and Keru, and the hospitality of the Pule family is remembered with gratitude. Stuart Bedford read the first draft and improved the paper as did Matthew Spriggs with a later version.

References

Allen, J., C. Gosden and J.P. White 1989. Human Pleistocene Adaptations in the Tropical Island Pacific: Recent Evidence from New Ireland, a Greater Australian Outlier. *Antiquity* 63: 548-561.

Bronk Ramsey, C., 2005. OxCal version 3.10 Radiocarbon Calibration software. < http://c14.arch.ox.ac.uk/embed.php?File=oxcal.html >

Dickinson, W. R. 2006. *Temper Sands in Prehistoric Oceanian Pottery: Geotectonics, Sedimentology, Petrography, Provenance*. The Geological Society of America Special Paper 406.

Doran, E., 1973. *Nao, Junk and Vaka: Boats and Culture History*. Texas A&M University: University Lecture Series.

Dunkley, P. N. 1986. *The Geology of the New Georgia Group, Western Solomon Islands*. British Technical Cooperation Report, Western Solomon Islands Geological Mapping Project.

Felgate, M. W. 2001. A Roviana Ceramic Sequence and the Prehistory of Near Oceania: Work in Progress. In G. R. Clark, A. J. Anderson and T. Vunidilo (eds), *The Archaeology of the Lapita Dispersal in Oceania*, pp.39-60. Canberra: Pandanus Press, Terra Australis 17.

Felgate, M.W. 2003. Reading Lapita in Near-Oceania: Intertidal and Shallow-Water Pottery Scatters, Roviana Lagoon, New Georgia, Solomon Islands. PhD thesis, University of Auckland.

Felgate, M. W. and S. H. Bickler n.d. Pots as Species: Estimating a Parent Population of Vessels from a Sherd Sample. Unpublished manuscript in the possession of the authors.

Felgate, M. W. and W. R. Dickinson 2001. Late-Lapita and Post-Lapita Pottery Transfers: Evidence from Intertidal-Zone Sites of Roviana Lagoon, Western Province, Solomon Islands. In M. Jones and P. J. Sheppard (eds), *Proceedings of the 2001 Australasian Archaeometry Conference*, pp.105-122. Auckland: Research Papers in Anthropology and Linguistics, Number 5.

Gorecki, P. 1992. A Lapita Smoke Screen ? In J-C. Galipaud (ed.), *Poterie Lapita et Peuplement*, pp.27-47. Nouméa: ORSTOM.

Green, R. C. 1978. *New Sites with Lapita Pottery and Their Implications for an Understanding of the Settlement of the Western Pacific*. Auckland: University of Auckland, Working Papers in Anthropology, Archaeology, Linguistics and Maori Studies 51.

Green, R.C. 1991a. The Lapita Cultural Complex: Current Evidence and Proposed Models. *Bulletin of the Indo-Pacific Prehistory Association* 11: 295-305.

Green, R.C. 1991b. Near and Remote Oceania: Disestablishing "Melanesia" in Culture History. In A. Pawley (ed.) *Man and a Half: Essays in Pacific Anthropology and Ethnobiology in Honour of Ralph Bulmer*, pp.491-502. Auckland: The Polynesian Society.

Green, R.C. 2003. The Lapita horizon and traditions – Signature for one set of oceanic migrations. In C. Sand (ed.), *Pacific Archaeology: assessments and prospects Proceedings of the Conference for the 50th anniversary of the first Lapita excavation. Kone-Noumea 2002*, pp. 95-120. Noumea: Les Cahiers de l'archeologie en Nouvelle-Calédonie 15.

Groube, L. 1993. Contradictions and Malaria in Melanesian and Australian Prehistory. In M. Spriggs, D. Yen, W. Ambrose, R. Jones, A. Thorne and A. Andrews (eds), *A Community of Culture: The People and Prehistory of the Pacific*, pp.164-186. Canberra: Department of Prehistory, Australian National University. Occasional papers in Prehistory 21.

Haberle, S. G., 1996. Explanations for Paleoecological Changes on the Northern Plains of Guadalcanal, Solomon Islands: The Last 3200 Years. *The Holocene* 6: 333-338.

Haddon, A. C. and J. Hornell 1937. *Canoes of Oceania Volume II: The Canoes of Melanesia, Queensland and New Guinea*. Honolulu: Bishop Museum Press, BP Bishop Museum Special Publication 28.

Hornell, J. 1936. Boat Construction in Scandinavia and Oceania: Another Parallel in Botel Tobago. *MAN* XXXVI:200-232.

Kintigh, K. W. 1984. Measuring Archaeological Diversity by Comparison with Simulated Assemblages. *American Antiquity* 49 (1):44-54.

Kirch, P. V. 1997. *The Lapita Peoples: Ancestors of the Oceanic World*. Oxford: Blackwell.

Kirch, P. V. and T.L. Hunt 1988. The Spatial and Temporal Boundaries of Lapita. In P. V. Kirch and T. L. Hunt (eds), *Archaeology of the Lapita Cultural Complex: A Critical Review*, pp.9-31. Seattle: Thomas Burke Memorial Washington State Museum Research Report No. 5.

Mann, P., F.W. Taylor, M.B. Lagoe, A. Quarles and G. Burr 1998. Accelerating Late Quaternary Uplift of the New Georgia Island Group (Solomon Island Arc) in Response to Subduction of the Recently Active Woodlark Spreading Centre and Coleman Seamount. *Tectonophysics* 295: 259-306.

Moore, J.H. 2001. Evaluating five models of human colonization. *American Anthropologist* 103:395-408.

Poulsen, J. 1987. *Early Tongan Prehistory*. Canberra: Department of Prehistory, Australian National University, Terra Australis 12.

Reeve, R. 1989. Recent Work on the Prehistory of the Western Solomons, Melanesia. *Bulletin of the Indo-Pacific Prehistory Association* 9: 44-67.

Roe, D. 1992. Investigations into the Prehistory of the Central Solomons: Some Old and Some New Data from Northwest Guadalcanal. In J-C. Galipaud (ed), *Poterie Lapita et Peuplement*, pp.91-101. Nouméa: ORSTOM.

Roe, D. 1993. Prehistory without Pots: Prehistoric Settlement and Economy of Northwest Guadalcanal, Solomon Islands. PhD thesis, Australian National University.

Ross, M. 1988. *Proto-Oceanic and the Austronesian Languages of Western Melanesia*. Canberra: Department of Linguistics, Australian National University. Pacific Linguistics, Series C – No. 98.

Sergeantson, S. W. and X. Gao 1995. Homo Sapiens Is an Evolving Species: Origins of the Austronesians. In P. Bellwood, J. J. Fox and D. Tryon (eds), *The Austronesians: Historical and Comparative Perspectives*, pp.165-180. Canberra: Australian National University.

Sheppard, P. J. 1993. Lapita Lithics: Trade/Exchange and Technology. A View from the Reefs/Santa Cruz. *Archaeology in Oceania* 28:121-137.

Sheppard, P. J., M.W. Felgate, K. Roga, J. Keopo and R. Walter 1999. A Ceramic Sequence from Roviana Lagoon (New Georgia, Solomon Islands). In J-C. Galipaud and I. Lilley (eds), *The Pacific from 5000 to 2000 BP: Colonization and Transformations*, pp.313-322. Paris: Editions de IRD.

Sheppard, P. and R. Walter 2006. A Revised Model of Solomon Islands Culture History. *Journal of the Polynesian Society* 115 (1): 47-76.

Spriggs, M., 1997. *The Island Melanesians*. Oxford: Blackwell.

Stuiver, M., P.J. Reimer, E. Bard, J.W. Beck, G.S. Burr, K.A. Hughen, B. Kromer, G. McCormac, J. van der Plicht and M. Spurk 1998. INTCAL98 radiocarbon age calibration: 24000-0 BP. *Radiocarbon* 40:1041-1083.

Summerhayes, G. and I. Scales 2005. New Lapita Pottery Finds from Kolombangara, Western Solomon Islands. *Archaeology in Oceania* 40:14-20.

Terrell, J. E. 1976. Perspectives on the Prehistory of Bougainville Island, Papua New Guinea: A Study in the Human Biogeography of the Southwestern Pacific. PhD thesis, Harvard University.

Tryon, D. T. and B.D. Hackman 1983. *Solomons Islands Languages: An Internal Classification*. Canberra: Department of Linguistics, RSPacS, Australian National University, Pacific Linguistics Series C. 72

Waterhouse, J. H. L. 1949. *A Roviana and English Dictionary: With English-Roviana Index, List of Natural History Objects and Appendix of Old Customs*. Sydney: Epworth Publishing and Printing House.

Wickler, S. 1995. Twenty-Nine Thousand Years on Buka: Long-Term Cultural Change in the Northern Solomon Islands. PhD thesis, University of Hawaii.

Wickler, S. 2001. *The Prehistory of Buka: A Stepping Stone Island in the North Solomons*. Canberra: Department of Archaeology and Natural History and Centre for Archaeological Research, Australian National University, Terra Australis 16.

Wickler, S. and M. Spriggs 1988. Pleistocene Human Occupation of the Solomon Islands, Melanesia. *Antiquity* 62: 703-706.

7

Sample Size and the Reef/Santa Cruz Lapita Sequence

Peter Sheppard and Roger Green

Department of Anthropology,
The University of Auckland,
Private Bag 92019, Auckland, New Zealand.
p.sheppard@auckland.ac.nz; pounamu@ihug.co.nz

A fundamental problem in archaeology is the nature of our samples and sampling (Orton 2000). Although this encompasses issues ranging from the transformation of dynamic behavioural systems into static archaeological records, to the subsequent taphonomic effects which over time alter that record, at the most basic level we can ask the question: All else being equal, what is the effect of where and how much we dig in a site? Ultimately this reflects the specific question we wish to ask of the site and the structure of the particular data type under investigation. If we are interested in a behaviour which is only represented by very rare data associated with specific contexts of unknown distribution in the site then we might need to excavate very large samples and hopefully find ways to identify and target the specific context. Alternatively, if we are looking for abundant data which are randomly distributed across the site, then a small sample employing a stratified systematic unaligned strategy or some similar approach might suffice. Pottery sherds have, of course, always been popular as they preserve well and are usually found in large quantities. We generally assume that the original population of pots was fragmented and preserved in a similar fashion. Of course this is problematic as it stands to reason that large pots will generate more fragments than small pots, thick sherds will preserve better than thin sherds, rim sherds better than body sherds, etc. Such variation may be of little importance for many studies. However, if the question relates to the study of pottery decoration which is to be used for chronological seriation, then we should consider the full range of factors which might influence the variation of decorative classes within sites, assemblages, and samples.

At the most basic level a very small sherd sample of a large target assemblage might provide a very poor sample; however if there was no variation in the assemblage, then 1 sherd is as informative as 1000, and would provide the same answer in a seriation. If on the other hand there were a large number of motifs in the large target assemblage, then a small sample could seriously under-estimate both the total number of motifs present and the motif proportions in the assemblage – a very poor piece of data in a seriation. This is the familiar sample size – richness problem. If knowing how many motifs are actually present in a target assemblage is critical to the analysis, then we need to be confident that our sample is large enough to reasonably estimate the number of motifs, *all else being equal*. Of course all else is often not equal. Ceramic deposition throughout a site is not uniform. Almost by definition sites have low densities of ceramics on the edge and varying densities throughout the site area. Even if the entire site was occupied over one short time period or comprised a series of samples each derived from separate layers within any given site (an absolutely necessary assumption in seriation), then there may be unknown structure in the distribution of sherds. For example, cooking pots may have a different spatial distribution than serving ware. Therefore, beyond simple sample size we need to consider how our sample relates to total site area and consider if unknown structure in the site might have been poorly sampled. This problem might also correlate with the issue of differential preservation or representation of motifs. As noted above, variation in pot form which could correlate with motif, might result in some motifs being under-represented e.g. motifs associated with thin pots may be under-represented as the sherds are too small for the motif to be recorded. Finally the analyst needs to consider what effect under-representation of motif numbers might have on the results of the analysis. If, for example, rare motifs have very little influence on the outcome of the seriation method, then their under-estimation will not be a problem. In this paper we will further discuss ceramic sampling issues relating to the Reef/Santa Cruz Lapita sites in the Outer Eastern Islands of the Solomons excavated in the early 1970s as part of the Southeast Solomons Culture History Project (Green 1976) . These were among the first and largest well excavated Lapita sites and their analysis and position on the western edge of Remote Oceania has made them central to discussions of the definition of the Lapita Complex and its movement into the Pacific (Green 1979, 1987, 1991a, 1991b, 1992, 2003; Sheppard and Green 1991; Sheppard and Walter 2006).

In the Pacific we often have small poorly preserved ceramic samples which have very poorly understood relationships to the target population (site, context) from which they are derived. This subject has most recently been critically reviewed by Felgate (2003), although other authors have attempted to address issues of ceramic sample size and comparability in Lapita assemblages (Anson 1987; Chiu 2003:250-254; Kirch *et al.* 1987) . Felgate dealt specifically with our ability to generate chronological seriations using available Lapita ceramic data sets and concluded that our ability to work with the data was very limited. Although Felgate (2003:85) noted the Reef/Santa Cruz dataset was among the best available, he felt it too needed to be used with caution, especially when making comparisons beyond the Reef/Santa Cruz region. A more pointed critique has come from Best (2002) who has argued that the seriation and more generally the chronological sequence proposed for the Lapita sites (SE-SZ-8, SE-RF-2, SE-RF-6) excavated by Green is in fact wrong.

Simon Best (2002:91) has legitimately raised issues that should be addressed with respect to the initial databases for motifs from Lapita sites SE-SZ-8, SE-RF-2 and SE-RF-6. They apply to both presence/absence and to frequency counts. His claims reduce essentially to two concerns:

(a) Best avers the samples recovered through excavation are in fact non-representative when sampling the results of human behaviour, given the enormous disparity in percentage terms of the area of each site and the at times fairly small areas *actually* subjected to excavation. More generally this is a question of sampling, through excavation, of unknown but potentially complex spatial structure within ceramic data variation across the site.

(b) Best also deduces that the number of motifs recorded for each site during their recording by Donovan in 1972-73 is directly proportional to the actual areas excavated at that time, and that it is this factor in large part which controls their frequency. Thus any changes in motif frequencies between sites do not reflect chronological differences in their age as was claimed by (Donovan 1973) and subsequent analysts building on her records. More generally then this is a question of sample size, motif richness and sample comparability.

The conclusion drawn from these contentions by Best is that it is simply not possible to demonstrate any ordering of sites SE-SZ-8, RF-2 and RF-6 on the basis of their motif content. All attempts to do so, whether based on presence/absence as with Green (1978), or on frequency (Anson 1986, 1987), are flawed and these or other analyses employing such data for temporal or similarity purposes have limited potential for revealing outcomes of significance when carrying out comparative analyses.

In the following we provide the early 1970s motif database under consideration, published here in full for the first time. We then discuss issues of site sampling and structure [1] and conclude with evaluation of the sample size effect on motif richness.

The Dataset and Site Sampling

In the late 1960s and early 70s sampling issues were becoming very important in archaeology (Asch and Mueller 1975; Redman 1974) and the Reef/Santa Cruz sites were excavated with these problems in mind. As a result the sampling strategies were state of the art and must still rate amongst the better site samples available for the Lapita period, given the logistic and preservation issues which continue to make sampling of these sites difficult.

It is perhaps ironic that given the explicit sampling strategies employed in the excavation of the Reef/Santa Cruz sites and the comparatively large absolute numbers of sherds recovered, that these datasets should now be considered problematic. In particular the fact that a very large portion of the small RF-2 site (Table 1) was eventually excavated in two separate investigations would now almost appear to be a handicap as it might make comparison with the samples from the other two very much larger sites questionable. Excavation of RF-2 was conducted after a systematic surface collection of ceramics from over 676 m² or 61 % of the site's area. Following this in February 1971 the central portion of the site was targeted for excavation which consisted of an irregular central area of 64 m² and a few outlying 4 m sized squares for a total of 72 m². This actually sub-sampled a range of the central squares with different densities of surface sherds (21 m² where the frequency was greater than 20, 18 m² where the frequency was less than 10 surface sherds per m², and 33 m² where the

Table 1. Comparisons of survey and excavation strategies on three Lapita sites in 1971 (with revisions from Green 1976 Table 18).

A. Survey and Excavation Details

Site Number	SE-RF-6	SE-RF-2	SE-SZ-8
Nearest Modern Village	Ngamanie	Nenumbo	Nanggu
Approx. Dimensions of Site (m)	40 x an estimated 60	25 x 25	100 x 250
Total Estimated Area in 1971 (m²)	c.2400+.[i]	1105	c.14,000
Sampling Area (m²)	180	106	459
Excavated Area in 1971 (m²)	20	72[ii]	51

B. Sampling Methods

Site Number	Sample Type	Method	Shape of Sample Area Excavated
SE-RF-2	Near total, or systematic aligned	Screening and analysis of content of top 3 cm followed by [targeted] excavation	Guided by the surface distribution of sherds a rectangular area with extensions into centre of site comprising 64 m² plus some outlying squares in the north of the site
SE-RF-6	Stratified, systematic unaligned	Random sampling of a target area through a 1 m in 9 interval of excavated squares	Cross section (9 m ≥ 24 m) at what has proved to be one end of a larger site
SE-SZ-8	Stratified, systematic unaligned	Random sampling of a target area through a 1 m in 9 interval of excavated squares	T-shape intersecting main intersecting main axis of site

i. In 1976 a new investigation of the surface evidence increased its length and thus the estimated size to a total of 8,400 m².
ii. Another 81.5 m² was excavated in 1976, making the total area finally investigated being 153.5 m².

frequency was fairly typical, lying between 10 and 20 sherds). The main 1971 excavation unit was bounded by squares W-P 39-40 and B-V 21-22. In 1976 an additional 81.5 m² was excavated making the total area finally investigated 153.5 m², or 13.9 percent of the total site area.

The resulting area has been shown to encompass both the end of a large house and an adjacent cooking area which appear to be the remains of a small hamlet or house-hold unit (Green and Pawley 1999; Sheppard and Green 1991) such as is common throughout the Pacific. It would seem most probable that this is the fundamental unit making up larger Lapita living sites (Kirch 1997:167) and the one with the greatest potential to structure ceramic variation within sites beyond simple fall-off in activity density, such as one sees at the margins of sites. The other potential source of variation within sites is of course temporal variation with large sites representing long-term occupations or horizontal palimpsest of serial or new occupations. Our study of RF-2 has indicated that within this house-hold unit there is some patterning in the form of pots, with globular cooking pots more commonly associated with the cooking area and flat bottomed bowls more commonly associated with the house area (Sheppard and Green 1991:78-79). If there is motif variation associated with this variation in form, and that remains to be determined for RF-2, then our work suggests that small test units or trenches into Lapita sites might conceivably recover a biased sample if they recover samples from only house or cooking areas. The long 1971 excavation unit which provided the ceramic sample discussed by Best and Felgate covered , though only in part, both the household and cooking area and therefore would appear to have sampled the potential range of ceramic variation in the central southern half of the site. The age of the site is well established with six statistically contemporaneous dates (Jones *et al.* in press) and they, together with the structural coherence of the site and the absence of any stratigraphic evidence of multiple occupations (Sheppard 1993; Sheppard and Green 1991), suggest a very limited occupation span perhaps of no more than 25 years. Thus, in the most recent paper by Jones *et al.* (2007) examining a probable dating for RF-2, a prior of 50 years at most was employed in the Bayesian calculations. It had been thought that perhaps the northern portion of the site might represent a somewhat later stage in the site's occupation (Felgate 2003; Green 1976:255) though that unsupported supposition has now been replaced by another rather more convincing interpretation based on the different character of its probable function as a men's house, zones which were in ethnography proscribed to women (Green and Pawley 1999:78-79 & Fig 1.9; Green ms.). Moreover, that has no bearing on the integrity of the central excavated sample of the south portion as representative of a narrow time-slice in Reef Islands Lapita prehistory. Taken together, all of these facts confirm that the RF-2 sample is very good and among the best Lapita ceramic samples available.

The SE-SZ-8 Nanggu site on the island of Santa Cruz is the largest of the three Lapita sites excavated in March 1971 by Green and at *circa* 14,000 m², at the larger end of Lapita site sizes. The excavated area is located toward the centre of the southern end of this long oblong-shaped site (Green *et al.* nd). It should be made clear that a total area of 459 m² was sampled with each 9 m block being randomly sampled and a 1 m square excavated. This is a systematic stratified unaligned sampling strategy which was very popular in the early 70s (Plog 1976) and has yet to be improved upon as a compromise between a purely random sampling approach and a purposive sample which takes into consideration archaeological knowledge (e.g. site boundaries, density of surface material etc.) although adaptive sampling as reviewed by Orton (2000:133) might be usefully considered today. Therefore we have a sample of motifs for an area twice the size of the total area excavated at RF-2 and, given our information on structures in RF-2, it seems probable that we have intercepted one or more household units. Further, because the sampling protocol is randomized, the motif ratios should be unbiased. It seems highly probable then that this sample is comparable, in terms of the representation of ceramic variation *within the area sampled*, with the RF-2 sample. This site is very large. It is likely that there are older or younger deposits elsewhere on the site, but again that is not the issue as we are simply interested in comparing areas tested in the various sites. The maximum depth of deposit in the site was 60 cm and although it was gardened there was no evidence of multiple occupations in the Lapita period. There was however, evidence of much later pits dug into the deposit. The dating of the Lapita deposits has produced statistically identical dates, providing no basis for thinking there is much time depth to the sample (Green, *et al.* nd).

The SE-RF-6 sherd sample is the smallest from the three sites and is the site with the smallest absolute area excavated at 20 m². But as in SZ-8 these squares were randomly selected from 9 m² units using a random 1 m in 9 interval in a rectangular strip of 9 by 24 m creating a stratified randomly sampled area of 180 m². The sampled area was a cross-section across what was originally thought to be a small (40 m wide by an estimated 60 m long) site consisting of a band of deposit lying parallel to and back of the modern shore. After a brief excavation in February 1971, it became apparent on further investigation in 1976 that this was just one end of a site extending for *circa* 180 m along the shore. Therefore it is quite possible that earlier portions of the site exist, however whether or not the area sampled is representative of other areas of the site is not under question. The question is whether it adequately represents motif variation in the deposits created during the occupation[2] of the area sampled. The area sampled is significantly larger than the area excavated in RF-2, however it is rather narrow at 9 m. A 9 m wide strip dropped at random across the long axis of RF-2 could easily miss the house area and intersect the cooking area, however if it intersected a house, the area would exceed by a considerable margin even the largest dimension of the RF-2 house. Therefore the motif sample would come both from a house and the surrounding area. Clearly if there is structured motif variation within RF-6 this smaller area has a greater potential to be non-representative, however the area is large enough to ensure that the bias is less than would be the case if only a house was sampled. Moreover, the probability of a random sample at an interval of 1 in 9 from a 180 m² strip across one end of the site seriously biasing the dominate motif ratios would seem to us to be rather low.

It is rather difficult to assess how well any sampling strategy would have sampled the sites in question given the fact that we know very little about the structure of motif variation across these or any large Lapita sites. Using the household cluster seen at RF-2 as a model of activity, which may have structured motif variation, we have considered how large an area would need to be sampled to adequately sample such a unit. If we assume that these household clusters would have produced the highest density of sherds, as seen in RF-2, then Green's strategy of targeting areas of high sherd density would likely have sampled such units. All of the areas sampled are large enough to have sampled a large percentage of such a household cluster. The shape and orientation of the RF-6 site might have generated a somewhat biased sample because it intersected one end of such a unit. At present we have no way of knowing whether this is true, although consideration of pot form might be one way to investigate this possibility.

Bootstrap Analysis of Sample Size

Although evaluating the effect of the unknown structure in attribute variation across unexcavated archaeological sites is rather difficult and generally limited to assessing the scale of sampling required, there has been considerable research (Cochrane 2003; Grayson 1978; Jones *et al.* 1983; Kintigh 1989; Meltzer *et al.* 1992) into simple sample size effects. Many studies have simply looked at the correlation between sample size and number of classes recovered; more recently analysts have made increasing use of sample simulations or boot-strapping to assess the probability of the number of classes in a sample being simply the result of sample size. Put another way, these methods allow us to examine how large a sample we need to take before the increase in classes from a particular sampling distribution levels off. In the case of seriation, the point at which the distribution levels off would be the point at which the ratios of the dominant motifs, upon which the seriation would be founded, would stabilize. In the following we use such an approach to evaluate the Reef/Santa Cruz motif sample sizes.

Bootstrapping requires us to randomly sample a large number of times an empirical probability distribution based on known data and from that create a probability distribution for a parameter of interest, in this

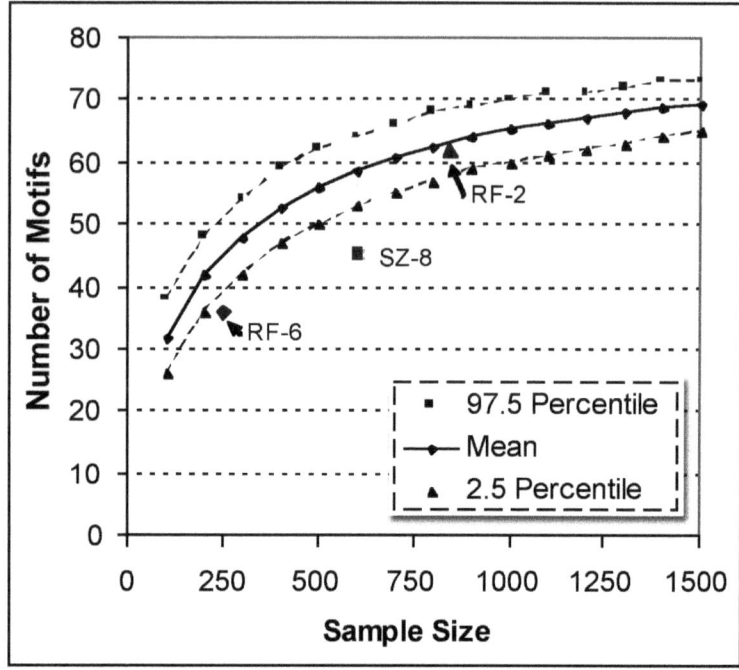

Figure 1. Results of bootstrapping simulation.

case sample size. For the Reef/Santa Cruz data (Table 2) the sum of all motifs combined from the three sites was used to make an empirical probability distribution (e.g. the probability of any motif appearing in a site is proportional to the motif abundance in the combined samples from all three sites). All sites are then assumed to be equally likely to have any motif as a null hypothesis. This distribution was then randomly sampled with replacement (bootstrap) for different sample sizes (100 to 1500 motifs incremented by 100) with 10,000 samples generated for each data point[3]. The average of the number of motifs was calculated for each sample size and a 95 % confidence interval selected (97.5 and 2.5 percentile) and plotted as shown in Figure 1.

If the number of motifs in each sample was simply a function of sample size then one would expect the samples to fall (Figure 1) near the mean number of motifs for that sample size. Both RF-6 and SZ-8 have considerably fewer motifs than would be expected under the null hypothesis, while RF-2 has an expected number of motifs based on sample size. Therefore the variation in the number of motifs between sites cannot be explained simply by sample size, given the assumption that the samples are derived and representative of a population of motifs equivalent to those found in the combined assemblages.

Conclusions

Although all of our archaeological samples could stand to be improved, as we have seen above it is rather difficult to devise the ideal sampling strategy given our need to understand site structure before we sample or excavate. All of the sites discussed here seem to have sampled adequate site areas if we use our knowledge of site RF-2 as a guide, although the RF-6 transect has the greatest potential to be non-representative of the entire site now that its true size is better appreciated. Both SZ-8 and RF-6 have considerably fewer motifs than one would expect if variation was accounted for by sample size alone. If we look at Figure 1 as providing a guide to the sample size required to adequately sample most of the motif variation in these sites, then a sample size of 500 sherds would cover 85 % of the variation. If our object was to conduct a seriation, then it seems a sample of 500 sherds would have been more than adequate to sample the common motifs which would provide the basis of any seriation. Rare motifs will have contributed very little to such a seriation (Anson 1987). Although the sample size, in the analysis reported here represented by only 247 sherds would appear to be on the small side, that analysis does suggest a very real decrease in the number of motifs in the area sampled at RF-6. This result can be considered to lend support to the alternate original model of decreasing numbers of motifs in the late period of highly dentate-decorated pots consistent with a widespread pattern to be observed within the Lapita horizon; although we must now also consider the anomalously low number of motifs in SZ-8 site which based on radiocarbon dating appears to be older than RF-2.

Table 2. A previously unpublished database listing the total frequency counts for each of the formally described Lapita motifs in the Mead/Donovan analytical system used for the percentage calculations. (NOTE: all alloforms of a motif are bundled under the general number assigned to any one motif as employed in most comparative exercises).

Motif	SZ-8 (607)	RF-2 (840)	RF-6 (247)	Motif	SZ-8 (607)	RF-2 (840)	RF-6 (247)
M1	19 (3.13 %)	21 (2.50 %)	31 (12.55 %)	M51	3 (0.49 %)	-	-
M2	18 (2.97 %)	50 (5.95 %)	18 (7.29 %)	M52	-	2 (0.24 %)	-
M3	2 (0.33 %)	3 (0.36 %)	-	M53	3 (0.49 %)	3 (0.36 %)	3 (1.21 %)
M4	-	1 (0.12 %)	-	M54	-	1 (0.12 %)	-
M5	45 (7.41 %)	72 (8.57 %)	31 (12.55 %)	M55	-	9 (1.07 %)	-
M6	39 (6.43 %)	33 (3.93 %)	21 (8.50 %)	M56	11 (1.81 %)	13 (1.55 %)	-
M7	-	-	-	M57	-	7 (0.83 %)	-
M8	4 (0.66 %)	56 (6.67 %)	10 (4.05 %)	M58	-	2 (0.24 %)	-
M9	1 (0.16 %)	16 (1.90 %)	-	M59	7 (1.15 %)	4 (0.48 %)	-
M10	2 (0.33 %)	12 (1.43 %)	2 (0.81 %)	M60	1 (0.16 %)	12 (1.43 %)	-
M11	-	-	-	M61	-	2 (0.24 %)	-
M12	-	-	-	M62	4 (0.66 %)	8 (0.95 %)	2 (0.81 %)
M13	-	4 (0.48 %)	-	M63	-	1 (0.12 %)	-
M14	3 (0.49 %)	29 (3.45 %)	5 (2.02 %)	M64	4 (0.66 %)	7 (0.83 %)	-
M15	-	-	-	M65	-	10 (1.19 %)	-
M16	5 (0.82 %)	6 (0.71 %)	-	M66	-	5 (0.60 %)	-
M17	-	2 (0.24 %)	-	M67	21 (3.46 %)	50 (5.95 %)	31 (12.55 %)
M18	28 (4.61 %)	53 (6.31 %)	8 (3.24 %)	M68	-	4 (0.48 %)	1 (0.40 %)
M19	61 (10.05 %)	46 (5.48 %)	5 (2.02 %)	M69	161 (26.52 %)	56 (6.67 %)	19 (7.69 %)
M20	-	-	-	M70	1 (0.16 %)	1 (0.12 %)	1 (0.40 %)
M21	-	-	-	M71	-	1 (0.12 %)	-
M22	-	-	-	M72	-	3 (0.36 %)	2 (0.81 %)
M23	-	-	-	M73	-	3 (0.36 %)	-
M24	26 (4.28 %)	21 (2.50 %)	4 (1.62 %)	M74	-	6 (0.71 %)	-
M25	-	1 (0.12 %)	-	M75	-	4 (0.48 %)	-
M26	-	-	-	M76	3 (0.49 %)	5 (0.60 %)	-
M27	-	5 (0.60 %)	-	M77	33 (5.44 %)	29 (3.45 %)	6 (2.43 %)
M28	9 (1.48 %)	35 (4.17 %)	4 (1.62 %)	M78	3 (0.49 %)	-	2 (0.81 %)
M29	11 (1.81 %)	3 (0.36 %)	3 (1.21 %)	M79	4 (0.66 %)	35 (4.17 %)	2 (0.81 %)
M30	1 (0.16 %)	20 (2.38 %)	1 (0.40 %)	M80	4 (0.66 %)	3 (0.36 %)	2 (0.81 %)
M31	-	-	-	M81	-	4 (0.48 %)	-
M32	-	-	-	M82	-	3 (0.36 %)	-
M33	-	-	-	M83	1 (0.16 %)	2 (0.24 %)	2 (0.81 %)
M34	-	-	1 (0.40 %)	M84	-	4 (0.48 %)	-
M35	-	-	-	M85	-	6 (0.71 %)	1 (0.40 %)
M36	-	-	-	M86	-	-	2 (0.81 %)
M37	-	-	-	M87	1 (0.16 %)	-	1 (0.40 %)
M38	-	-	-	M88	-	-	-
M39	23 (3.79 %)	8 (0.95 %)	2 (0.81 %)	M89	3 (0.49 %)	-	2 (0.81 %)
M40	-	-	-	M90	2 (0.33 %)	-	1 (0.40 %)
M41	-	-	-	M91	2 (0.33 %)	-	-
M42	-	-	-	M92	1 (0.16 %)	-	-
M43	-	-	-	M93	3 (0.49 %)	-	-
M44	-	-	-	M94	2 (0.33 %)	-	-
M45	-	11 (1.31 %)	-	M95	1 (0.16 %)	-	-
M46	-	-	-	M96	1 (0.16 %)	-	-
M47	-	2 (0.24 %)	-	M97	-	-	-
M48	7 (1.15 %)	8 (0.95 %)	1 (0.40 %)	M98	-	1 (0.12 %)	-
M49	4 (0.66 %)	14 (1.67 %)	1 (0.40 %)	M99	19 (3.13 %)	1 (0.12 %)	15 (6.07 %)
M50	-	1 (0.12 %)	-	M100	-	-	4 (1.62 %)

Although we have explored the issue of sample size in this paper further development of our sampling model would require trying to model the structure of motif variation within Lapita sites. Questions to ask include: are motifs randomly distributed across sites?; to what extent do motifs correlate with potential taphanomic factors (e.g. pot thickness etc)? and does purposive sampling based on sherd density bias our motif sample? Some of these issues may be investigated using sampling experiments on current datasets. However, additional data on Lapita site structure, resulting from large areal excavation is needed before we can confidently assess how well our samples reflect the target population. As Felgate (2003) concluded most of our Lapita samples are very small and it is hard to know how well they usefully represent target populations.

Endnotes

1. This is extracted in part from a much longer treatment of motif variation and sampling at these sites (Green ms.) currently available as a manuscript , though destined for eventual issuance in the newly instituted University of Auckland *Research in Archaeology and Linguistics* e-journal for easier permanent access by those who may wish such data and its interpretation. This long article is a highly detailed evaluation of adequacy exhibited by the motif analyses of decorated ceramic collections from three Reef/Santa Cruz Lapita sites in the Outer Eastern Islands of the Solomons which treats each motif listed in Table 2 of this paper separately. This makes it possible not only to identify the set of motifs which prove highly indicative in placing the three sites in their expected chronological order, but also a smaller set of motifs over-represented due to far greater size of the RF-2 assemblage.
2. The population under investigation in each of these cases might be a notional assemblage of ceramic motifs produced during an occupation.
3. Re-sampling was conducted using the re-sampling add-on for Excel by Resampling Stats Inc 2006.

References

Anson, D. 1986. Lapita Pottery of the Bismarck Archipelago and its affinities. *Archaeology in Oceania* 21:157-165.

Anson, D. 1987. Reply to Kirch *et al. Archaeology in Oceania* 22:127-128.

Asch, D. L. and J. W. Mueller 1975. *Sampling in archaeology*. Tucson: University of Arizona Press.

Best, S. 2002. *Lapita: A View from the East*. Auckland: New Zealand Archaeological Association Monograph 24.

Chiu, S. 2003. *The Socio-Economic Function of Lapita Ceramic Production and Exchange: A Case Study from Site WKO013A, Koné, New Caledonia*. Unpublished PhD, University of California Berkeley.

Cochrane, G. W. G. 2003. Artefact attribute richness and sample size adequacy. *Journal of Archaeological Science* 30(7):837-838.

Donovan, L. J. 1973. *A Study of the Decorative System of Potters in the Reefs and Santa Cruz islands*. Unpublished Research Essay, University of Auckland.

Felgate, M. 2003. *Reading Lapita in Near Oceania: Intertidal Shallow-water Pottery Scatters, Roviana Lagoon, New Georgia, Solomon Islands*. Unpublished PhD, University of Auckland.

Grayson, D. K. 1978. Minimum numbers and sample size in vertebrate faunal analysis. *American Antiquity* 43(1):53-65.

Green, R. C. 1976. Lapita sites in the Santa Cruz Group. In R.C. Green and M.M. Cresswell (eds), *Southeast Solomon Islands Cultural History. A Preliminary Survey*, pp. 245-265. Wellington: The Royal Society of New Zealand, Bulletin 11.

Green, R. C. 1978. *New sites with Lapita Pottery and their Implications for an Understanding of the Settlement of the Western Pacific*. Working Papers in Anthropology, Archaeology and Maori Studies, No. 51. Auckland: Department of Anthropology, University of Auckland.

Green, R. C. 1979. Lapita. In J. Jennings (ed.), *Prehistory of Polynesia*, pp. 27-60. Cambridge, Mass.: Harvard University Press.

Green, R. C. 1987. Obsidian Results from the Lapita Sites of the Reef/Santa Cruz Islands. In W. Ambrose and J. Mummery (eds), *Archaeometry: Further Australasian Studies*, pp. 239-249. Canberra: Australian National University.

Green, R. C. 1991a. The Lapita Cultural Complex: Current Evidence and Proposed Models. In P.S. Bellwood (ed.) *Indo-Pacific Prehistory 1990*, vol. 2, pp. 295-305. Canberra: Indo-Pacific Prehistory Association Bulletin 11.

Green, R. C. 1991b. A reappraisal of the dating from some Lapita sites in the Reef/Santa Cruz Group of the Southeast Solomon Islands. *Journal of the Polynesian Society* 100:197-207.

Green, R. C. 1992. Definitions of the Lapita Cultural Complex and its Non-Ceramic Component. In J-C. Galipaud (ed.), *Poterie Lapita and Peuplement: Actes du Colloque Lapita, Nouméa, Nouvelle Calédonie, Janvier 1992*, pp. 7-20. Nouméa: ORSTOM.

Green, R. C. 2003. The Lapita horizon and traditions – Signature for one set of oceanic migrations. In C. Sand (ed.), *Pacific Archaeology: assessments and prospects*, pp. 95-120. Nouméa: Service des Musées et du Patrimoine de Nouvelle-Calédonie Volume 15.

Green, R.C. ms. An evaluation of adequacy for motif analyses of decorated ceramic collections from three Reef/Santa Cruz Lapita sites in the Outer Eastern Islands of the Solomons. [Prepared in November 2006 for submission to an electronic journal]

Green, R. C., M. D. Jones and P. J. Sheppard n.d. The absolute dating and reconstructed environmental context of the SZ-8 (Nanggu) dentate-decorated Lapita site of the Reef Santa Cruz region of the Outer Eastern Islands of the Solomon Islands.

Green, R. C. and A. K. Pawley 1999. Early Oceanic architectural forms and settlement patterns: Linguistic, archaeological and ethnological perspectives. In R. Blench and M. Spriggs (eds), *Archaeology and Language III: Artefacts, Languages and Texts*, pp. 31-39. London: Routledge.

Jones, G. T., D. K. Grayson and C. Beck 1983. Artifact class richness and sample size in archaeological surface assemblages. *Anthropological papers-Museum of Anthropology, University of Michigan* (72):55-74.

Jones, M. D., F. J. Petchey, R. C. Green, P. J. Sheppard and M. Phelan 2007. The Marine ΔR for Nenumbo (Solomon Islands): a case study in calculating reservoir offsets from paired sample data. *Radiocarbon* 49(1).

Kintigh, K. W. 1989. Sample size, significance, and measures of diversity. *Quantifying Diversity in Archaeology*, pp. 25-36. Cambridge, Eng.: Cambridge University Press.

Kirch, P. V. 1997. *The Lapita Peoples: Ancestors of the Oceanic World*. Cambridge: Blackwell.

Kirch, P. V. M. Allen, V. Butler and T. Hunt 1987. Is there an early Far Western Lapita province? Sample size effects and new evidence from Eloaua Island. *Archaeology in Oceania* 22:123-128.

Meltzer, D. J., R. D. Leonard and S. K. Stratton 1992. The relationship between sample size and diversity in archaeological assemblages. *Journal of Archaeological Science* 19(4):375-387.

Orton, C. 2000. *Sampling in archaeology* Cambridge: Cambridge University Press.

Plog, S., 1976. Measurement of prehistoric interaction between communities. In K.V. Flannery (ed.), *The Early Mesoamerican Village*, pp. 136-158. New York: Academic Press.

Redman, C. L. 1974. *Archeological sampling strategies*. New York: Addison-Wesley.

Sheppard, P. J. 1993. Lapita lithics: trade/exchange and technology. A view from the Reefs/Santa Cruz. *Archaeology in Oceania* 28(3):121-137.

Sheppard, P. J. and R. C. Green 1991. Spatial analysis of the Nenumbo (SE-RF-2) Lapita site, Solomon Islands. *Archaeology in Oceania* 26:89-101.

Sheppard, P.J. and R. Walter 2006. A revised model of Solomon Islands Cultural History. *Journal of the Polynesian Society* 115:47-76.

8

Makué (Aore Island, Santo, Vanuatu): A new Lapita site in the ambit of New Britain obsidian distribution

Jean-Christophe Galipaud[1] and Mary Clare Swete Kelly[2]

[1] Research Institute for Development (IRD),
PO Box A5 98848 Nouméa,
New Caledonia.
galipaud@noumea.ird.nc
[2] Archaeology and Natural History,
Research School of Pacific and Asian Studies,
Australian National University,
Canberra, ACT 0200, Australia.
maryclare.swetekelly@anu.edu.au

Obsidian and Lapita

The emergence of Lapita in the New Britain area is closely associated with the use of flaked obsidian artefacts. Sources of raw material include, among others, the Willaumez Peninsula in New Britain and later the Lou and Pam Islands, both of which are situated in the Bismarck Archipelago (Ambrose 1976). Obsidian is particularly important for the interpretation of long-distance movement of artefacts because it is possible to determine its source with a high level of accuracy. Obsidian from both of the aforementioned sources found in Lapita sites has also been used to infer the chronology of occupation as well as the patterns of movement and exchange (Green 1987; Specht 2002; Summerhayes 2003).

Obsidian is relatively rare in most Lapita sites in Remote Oceania which can be attributed to the lack of suitable sources of volcanic glass beyond the Bismarck archipelago. In a few sites from Fiji, New Caledonia and north Vanuatu a limited amount of small obsidian flakes sourced to the Bismarck have been considered to attest to long distance exchange systems in the Lapita sphere. However, up until now, relatively large amounts of obsidian from sites in Remote Oceania have only been identified in the Reef Islands, particularly Nenumbo (Green 1976, 1979; Sheppard 1993; Sheppard and Green 1991).

Herein the discovery and source data concerning obsidian artefacts found on the recently discovered site of Makué on Aore Island (south Santo, Vanuatu) are presented. The large amount of obsidian flakes found there, the early dates from the site as well as the pottery style suggest that Makué represents an early, if not founding, Lapita settlement in Vanuatu. A comprehensive description of the site will be published shortly.

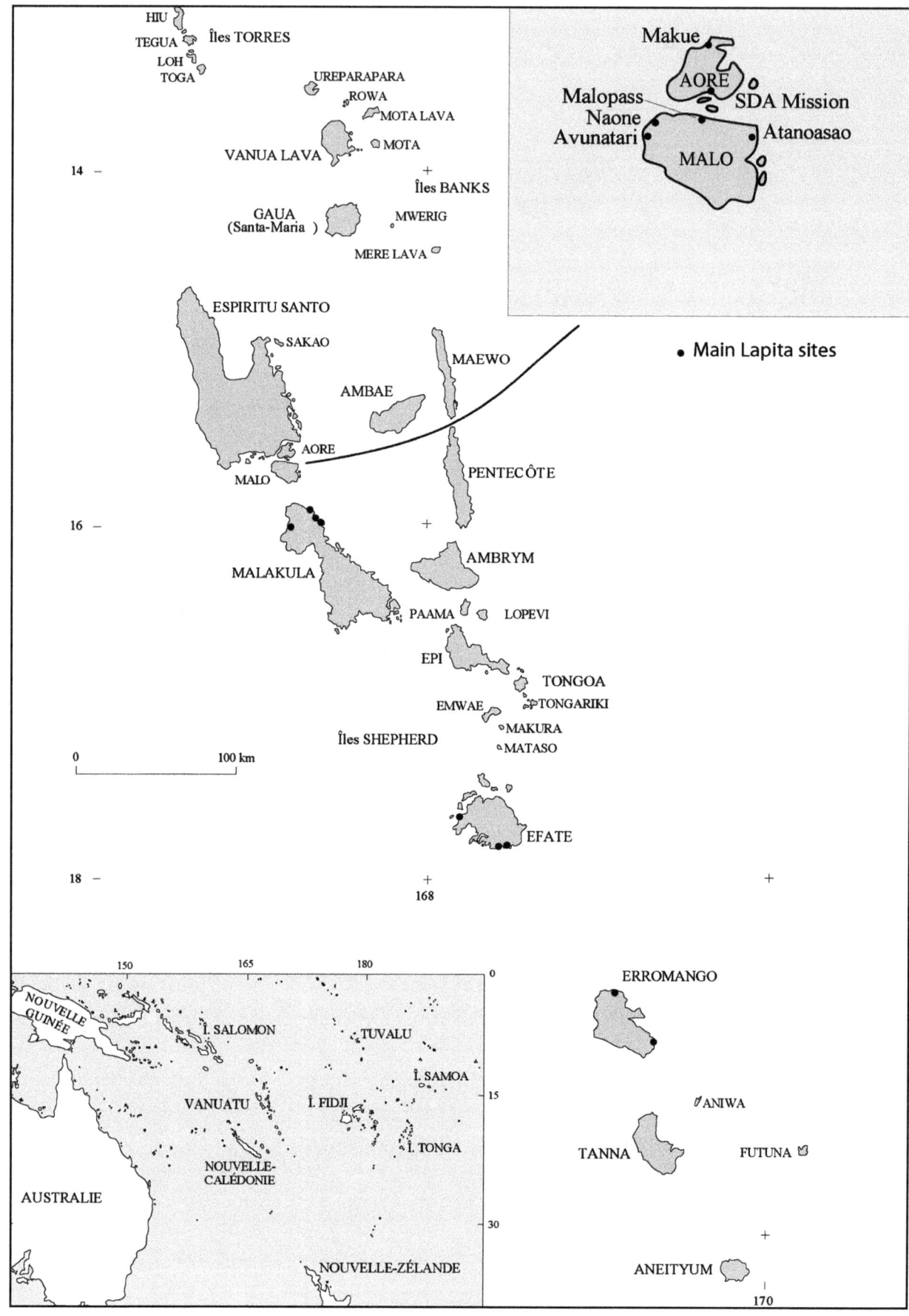

Figure 1. A map of Vanuatu indicating the positions of the main Lapita sites currently identified.

Lapita in Vanuatu

Until relatively recently few Lapita sites had been identified in Vanuatu (Figure 1). Apart from several very disturbed Lapita sites on Malo Island in the north (Hedrick 1971), the only other sites that had been located prior to the year 1997 were the site of Erueti on the central island of Efate (Garanger 1972; Hébert 1965), Ifo on Erromango in the south (Bedford 2006; Spriggs and Wickler 1989) and Malakula (Malua Bay) in the north (Bedford 2006). Limited excavations were undertaken at Erueti where the site proved to be very disturbed (Garanger 1972). While the site of Ifo was less disturbed the some 1.5m of cultural stratigraphy in places, covering a 1000 year period, restricted the potential of large area excavations. At both sites the sum total of dentate-stamped Lapita sherds was small. A single dentate-stamped sherd only was recovered from the predominantly plainware site of Malua Bay (Bedford 2006). The paucity of Lapita sites in the Vanuatu islands could hardly, however, be explained by a lack of interest in these islands during the initial period of exploration and settlement, rather the invisibility of these early sites is due largely to the tectonically and volcanically active nature of the archipelago (Bedford 2003, 2006; Pineda and Galipaud 1998).

From 1997 onwards, intensive research in the Santo area (Galipaud 2000) led to the discovery of many Lapita sites, some in a good state of preservation. These sites are generally covered by a metre or more of sandy humic soil and located on uplifted terraces behind the present shore. They were discovered after a thorough study of environmental changes and uplift history in the region (Pineda and Galipaud 1998). Lapita sites were also identified on the islands of north-east Malekula in 2001 and 2002 (Bedford 2003) and in 2003, a well preserved Lapita site with a cemetery was fortuitously found on Efate (Bedford et al 2006). More sites are likely to be discovered in similar environments in the future.

Among the many sites found in the Santo-Malo area, Makué, in the northern part of Aore, is outstanding for its general preservation, its early dates and evidence of at least two subsequent short Lapita occupations with large amounts of obsidian flakes, among other cultural remains. A short description of the site and its excavation history follows.

The Makué Lapita site

A survey in 2000 on Aore Island was focused on areas where ancient beach deposits could be located. The two areas chosen for survey were the north point around the Aore Beach Resort and the south-western coast near the Seven-Day Adventists' mission (Figures 1 and 2).

In the north of Aore, decorated Lapita sherds were found in several instances just below the surface, demonstrating that this area had been settled some 3000 years ago. The patterns

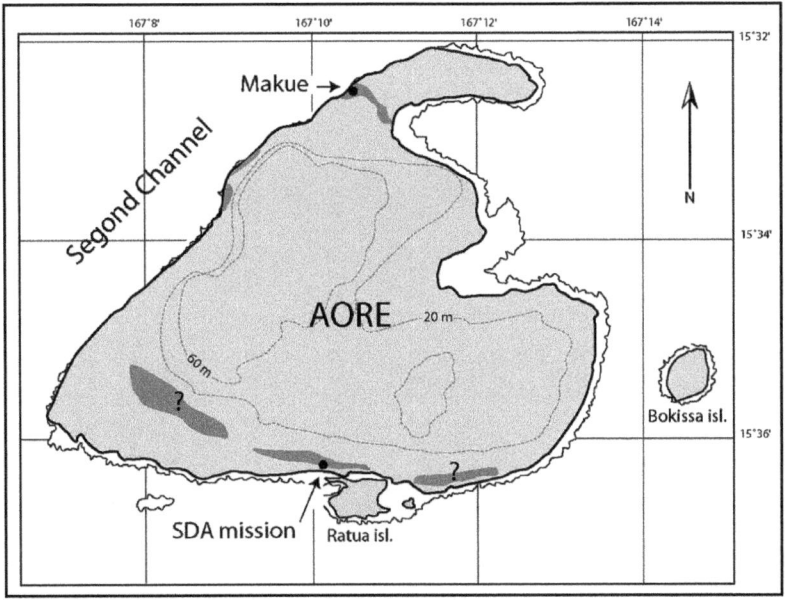

Figure 2. A map of Aore Island indicating the main Lapita sites (in dark grey) and potential Lapita sites (dark grey with question mark).

of deposition suggest that remains from this early period are scattered along several hundred metres on the north-west coastline around the Aore Resort, and might extend as much as 100 meters to the east along what used to be the north point of Aore.

Along the west coast, several surface scatters with decorated Lapita were also located near Baracira but have not yet been excavated. Another Lapita occupation was located at Port Latour, in the south of Aore. This site, opposite the Batuni Urunga Lapita site on Malo Island (also known as Malo Pass) (Hedrick 1971) was tested in 2003. Two other potential Lapita occupations on the south-west and south-east coast await further investigation.

Like Malo, most sites on Aore Island are in a poor state of preservation, reflecting their proximity to the sea and their shallow nature. Most sites are now largely destroyed and scattered sherds are the only indicators of early human activity. In contrast, the Makué site is exceptionally well preserved and the excavations so far have given valuable insights into the early Lapita occupation in the area.

Excavation History

The Makué site (or Aore Resort Lapita site, as it was called in 2002) is located on the north western coast of Aore, facing the South Santo coast. It is separated from the island of Santo by the narrow Segond Channel (Figure 2). The north coast of Aore is formed by an elongated sand strip, stabilised by dense secondary vegetation. Several low terraces (1 to 3 metres high) attest to the uplift of ancient shorelines. The site is in a coconut plantation, six to eight meters above current sea-level, on the upper terrace and close by the Aore Resort.

In contrast to the many Lapita sites found on Malo Island in a similar environment, the archaeological deposits here are extensive and do not seem to have been greatly affected by either their initial proximity to the sea, or the subsequent uplift processes. Parts of the site, however, were probably disturbed by the construction of an American base camp during the Second World War.

The Makué site was discovered in 2001 through extensive drilling work, in the north Aore area. In 2002, a series of test pits behind the Aore Resort (Area A, see Figure 3) uncovered a substantial quantity of remains, but revealed no structures. Only a possible pit, containing some human bones, was found just beneath the surface. It cannot yet be confidently associated with the Lapita occupation. Among the other remains recovered in 2002 was a relatively large number of obsidian flakes.

In 2003, a 12m² area was excavated beside the Aore Resort, close to the sea (Area B). An *in situ* Lapita layer was identified, containing several fireplaces, large pottery sherds (including the pedestal of an open bowl), shell artifacts, faunal remains as well as some additional obsidian flakes. In November 2005, the Area B excavation was extended and this provided further

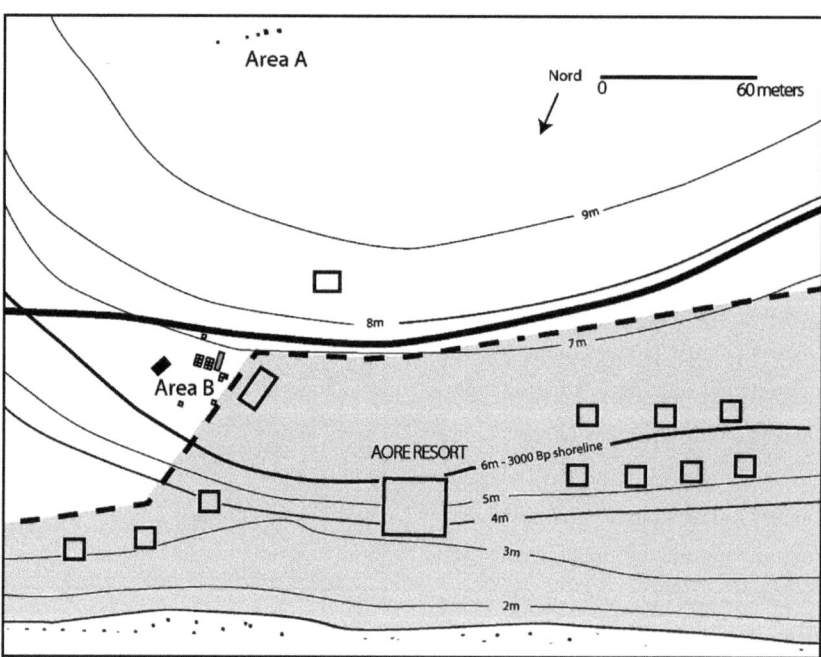

Figure 3. Location of excavated area on the northern coast of Aore Island.

clarification of the stratigraphy at the site. This excavation also recovered another *in situ* archaeological deposit below the first one containing large fragments of pottery vessels.

Stratigraphy

The stratigraphy in Area A differs slightly from that in Area B. In Area A (Figure 4), a dark, humic, sandy layer varying between 15 and 40 centimetres in depth (1) overlays a fine, sandy, grey sediment (2). An indurated layer (3) appears in all test pits between 60 and 80 centimetres. The irregularity of the thickness of the first layer suggests some recent surface disturbance, possibly during the Second World War. Remains of glass bottles, as well as other modern artefacts, attest to some disturbance. Lapita sherds found in Area A are small and fragmented. They occur mostly in the lower layers but are also present in the top-most, disturbed layer. Some features have been observed in the sections and at the bottom of some of the trenches. The most obvious is the base of a small pit filled with humic sediment and containing fragments of one or several human skeletons.

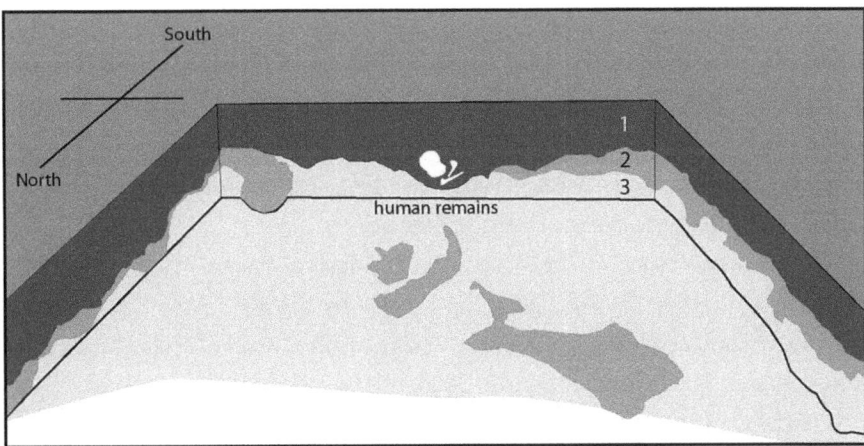

Figure 4. Profile diagram, Area A, Makué 2002.

Figure 5. Photo of Area B profile, Makué 2005.

The stratigraphy of Area B is similar to that in Area A but the cultural levels are deeper and better preserved (Figure 5). The top 50 cm is a dark, humic, sandy sediment becoming lighter with depth (Zone 1). This contains shells and fragmented pottery. Below is a grey, ashy compacted layer with evidence of burning, and accumulation of large pieces of *in situ* cultural material, especially turtle bone (Zone 2). A sterile fine, sandy layer separates this level from a deeper fine, sandy deposit containing cultural remains (Zone 3). This contains fewer bones but more common large fragments of pottery. Culturally sterile sand, mixed with coral cobbles, lies below this layer.

The overall stratigraphy suggests that the Lapita occupations occurred very close to the shore in a sandy environment without vegetation. Later disturbances by the sea is evident in some parts of the excavated area but the general condition of the site is excellent with few disturbances having been observed in Zones 2 and 3, which appear to be *in situ*.

Dating Makué

Absolute dating of Vanuatu sites is often difficult due to the lack of good quality dating material. Makué, however, has in some instances delivered good amounts of charcoal especially in the lower levels. Dating of shell has not been favoured because the Delta R value for marine shells in the region has not been precisely established. Relative dating was also possible with some level of confidence due to the fact that a large amount of obsidian flakes sourced to the Bismarck Archipelago had been recovered (see below). The only other sites in Remote Oceania with similar quantities of obsidian from the Bismarck Archipelago are sites in the Reef and Santa-Cruz Islands, which have been tentatively dated to around 3200-2900 BP (Green 1991). A similar antiquity was expected for Makué.

Three AMS dates were obtained for this site in 2003 and four more in 2005. The first one [WK-11447] is from the bottom cultural layer in the 2002 B1 test pit (close by the 2003 Area B excavation), the other two come respectively from a fireplace [WK-13722] on the *in situ* cultural level (Zone 2) and from below this same level [WK-13721] in the Area B 2003 excavation. In 2005, the two cultural levels were dated again in Area B [Wk-19704] [Wk-19705] as well as in a test pit closer to the sea (F16) where the stratigraphy was not so obvious but nevertheless produced evidence of several occupations partly disturbed by the sea [Wk-19706] [Wk-19707]. Results of the dating are presented in the table below:

Table 1. Radiocarbon dates obtained from the Makué site. Calibration was performed using OxCal v4.4 Bronk Ramsey (2007) and SHCal04 Southern Hemisphere calibration (McCormac *et al.* 2004).

14C Lab.Code	CRA	Cal 1σ (68.2 % probability)	Cal 2σ (95.4 % probability)	Context
Wk-19704	2891±32BP	3070BP (68.2 %) 2966BP	3158BP (95.4 %) 2925BP	2005 / Area B, Zone 2
Wk-19705	2962±32BP	3207BP (59.4 %) 3078BP	3245BP (95.4 %) 3004BP	2005 / Area B, Zone 3
Wk-19706	2800±34BP	2947BP (68.2 %) 2863BP	2992BP (95.4 %) 2795BP	2005 / Area B, F16 layer 2-9
Wk-19707	2886±32BP	3065BP (68.2 %) 2965BP	3156BP (95.4 %) 2890BP	2005 / Area B, F16, layer 2-13
Wk-13721	2957±51BP	3215BP (68.2 %) 3007BP	3320BP (95.4 %) 2964BP	2003 / Area B, Zone 3
Wk-13722	2982±50BP	3245BP (68.2 %) 3078BP	3334BP (95.4 %) 3000BP	2003 / Area B, Zone 2
Wk-11447	2935±41BP	3161BP (68.2 %) 3005BP	3238BP (95.4 %) 2959BP	2002 / Area B, B1, layer 10-2

In Area A in 2002, little charcoal was found and the area could not be dated. All samples from Area B are in secure stratigraphic units and in clear association with other cultural remains. Unfortunately, the small size of the samples did not allow for a prior determination of the wood species, and therefore the discussion of the results is limited due to the potential problem of in-built age in unidentified charcoal samples.

Nonetheless, these results are very consistent and suggest that the first Lapita occupation of the site occurred sometime around 3200 BP. This occupation (Zone 3) is in all excavated levels characterised by very fine dentate stamped decorations on pottery, a characteristic generally attributed to Far Western Lapita, as well as plain and incised pottery and obsidian flakes. A second Lapita occupation (Zone 2) occurred a short time afterwards, possibly around 3000 BP and perhaps earlier. It is associated with large amounts of burnt turtle bone and ash as well as dentate-stamped pottery of a different style from Zone 3. The dating of test pit F16 in 2005 suggests the same two occupations with possible evidence for a third, later occupation period, around 3000-2900 BP (Wk19706).

These results indicate that Makué was first settled around 3200 BP and that the Lapita occupation at this site had ended by around 2800 BP. These early dates are consistent with the associated cultural remains, obsidian and fine dentate pottery, and conform with the proposed chronology for the Santa Cruz Islands (Green 1991) reinforcing at the same time the evidence of a very rapid spread from the Bismarck Archipelago into Remote Oceania. Makué represents the earliest well dated evidence of human occupation of the Vanuatu islands discovered to date. A comparison of the pottery assemblage of the site with the one from Teouma on the island of Efate will probably help confirm the date of occupation of this later site. Obsidian is present throughout and there is no obvious difference in the distribution pattern observable at this stage between that found in Zone 3 and that in Zone 2.

Obsidian analysis

As mentioned previously, the Makué Lapita excavation uncovered a relatively large amount of obsidian – in comparison to most other Lapita sites in Remote Oceania including those in Vanuatu. Preliminary attempts to allocate the obsidian to a particular source were completed using density analysis.

Ambrose (1976) first demonstrated that the relative density of obsidian could be used to differentiate between the sources in the Pacific. This method has since been refined several times (Ambrose and Duerden 1982; Harris 1994; Torrence and Victor 1995). In this instance, artefacts were weighed in air, and then weighed again while immersed in PFMD (perfluoro-1-methyl-decalin) solution. A Mettler (AT261 DeltaRange) analytical balance with a density attachment was used for determining the weights. These weights and the temperature of the PFMD at the time of the analysis were incorporated into the following equation that applies Archimede's Theory of Water Displacement (Ambrose and Stevenson 2004 give an up-to-date explanation of this method to determine density):

$$d = \frac{m_a((T-965.99)/(-480.88))}{(m_a - m_l)}$$

where d = relative density, m_a = weight in air, m_l = weight in PFMD,
T = temperature in degrees Celsius

Previous studies have shown that artefacts from New Britain have densities close to 2.35, while those from the Admiralty Islands have densities close to 2.38 (Ambrose 1976; Green and Anson 2000). The Banks Island sources, in Vanuatu, have a density around 2.44 (Ambrose 1976).

Density analysis is a fast and efficient analytical technique for the preliminary sourcing of an obsidian assemblage. Although the accuracy of measuring single artefacts can be adversely affected by a number of different variables, including high porosity or the presence of inclusions of different materials, the results at an assemblage level can be informative. This has been demonstrated by comparisons between obsidian artefacts analysed using both density and PIXE-PIGME (a chemical characterisation method) techniques (White and Harris 1997; Swete Kelly 2001).

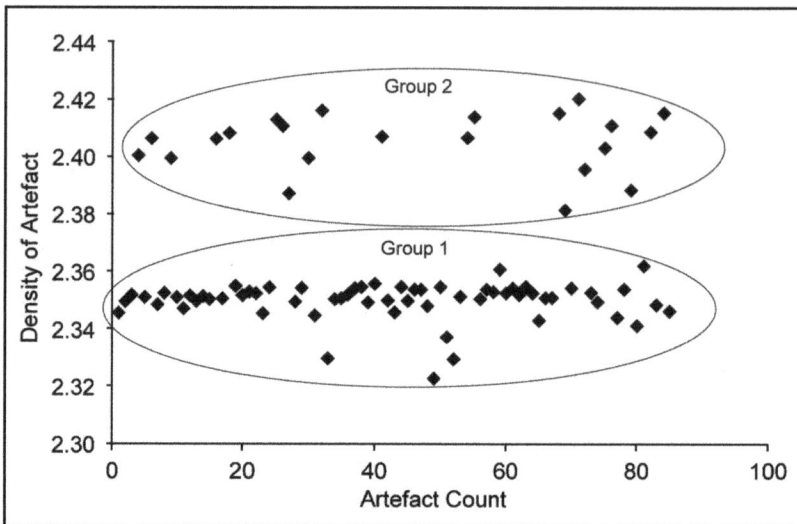

Figure 6. Density of obsidian finds from the 2002 and 2003 field seasons at Makué.

Results of Sourcing Study

All the obsidian artefacts collected from the site of Makué (in the 2002 and 2003 field seasons) have been included in this analysis. In the 2002 field season, 62 pieces of obsidian were excavated. A further 25 pieces of obsidian were excavated in the 2003 field season. One artefact was left out of the final results, as it gave a very low density reading which was attributed to its coarse, friable nature.

A large proportion of the obsidian found at Makué is coming from the island of New Britain in Papua New Guinea, most likely the Willaumez Peninsula sources (Group 1, Figure 6). As mentioned above Willaumez Peninsula sources have a density close to 2.35. The source location of Group 2 is not as easy to determine. The Banks Island obsidian sources have a density of around 2.44, however none of the artefacts match this value. Nor do the obsidian artefacts in Group 2 clearly come from the source on Lou Island in the Admiralty group. While the range of obsidian densities from Lou Island vary between 2.38 and 2.404 this would still only encompass approximately half of the obsidian pieces tested (Group 2, Figure 6). These issues will be addressed by chemical analyses in the future, for now the clusters will be referred to as Group 1 and Group 2.

Results of Comparative Measurements

Basic measurements of maximum length, thickness and weight were made for the obsidian from the site of Makué. A broader technological analysis was also completed which will be included in a later article. The aim of these basic measurements was to provide a simple comparison to the sites excavated by Roger Green in the Reef and Santa Cruz Islands (Table 2). These assemblages were examined by Sheppard (1993) and the methods of analysis used herein are consistent with those used in his analyses. Although the sample sizes vary greatly, it can be seen that the average sizes and weights are quite similar. However, it is interesting to note that the Makué specimens lie at the lower end of the size and weight range of the Reef and Santa Cruz Islands.

Table 2. Average measurements (mm) of obsidian from Makué, Aore Island compared to those of obsidian from the Reef and Santa Cruz Islands (from Sheppard 1993).

	Max. Length	Thickness	Weight
Aore Island, Makué			
All artefacts (n=84)	17.45	4.00	1.17
Group 1 (n=61)	16.59	3.65	0.89
Group 2 (n=20)	20.23	5.06	1.83
Reef/Santa Cruz Islands			
SZ-8 (n=329)	19.6	5.63	2.39
RF-2 (n=625)	18.6	5.24	1.86
RF-6 (n=27)	13.7	3.78	1.06

Discussion

An examination of the palaeo-coastlines on the island of Aore has revealed a new site of early human occupation in northern Vanuatu. This site, Makué contains a large amount of obsidian, when compared to other sites in the region of similar antiquity.

Occupation and uplift

Uplift has been a major cause of coastal change in Vanuatu which has important implications for the early archaeology of the islands (Pineda and Galipaud 1998; Bedford 2006; Bedford *et al.* 2006). The first settlements on Makué were probably located on a well protected, large, sandy shore, near a probable small freshwater stream on what used to be the north coast of Aore. It was also only a short sailing distance from the large Sarakata River on the Santo mainland. Over two centuries, the site was used several times as a seasonal camp rather than a long-term occupation. Evidence of abandonment is visible especially on the lower level (Zone 3) where some artefacts have been partly eroded before being covered by a sandy, sterile layer. The second occupation of the site probably occurred in the same sandy coastal environment. It is at this stage unclear whether the scattered shells and fragmented pottery found on the upper layer (Zone 1) attest to a further occupation of the site or are a disturbed component of the underlying level (Zone 2). It is also unclear yet how the undated Area A excavation relates to the well stratified Area B. On the basis of evidence provided by a comparison of the pottery and obsidian found in each of the areas, Area A could be of similar antiquity to Zone 3 in Area B. This will be investigated further in 2007.

The occupation of this site became unattractive as uplifting gradually affected the coastal environment. Dating this event is difficult and will require more research. The end of the Lapita occupation in Makué is possibly related to this event and therefore we cannot assume at this stage of the research that the latest date in Makué represents the latest occurrence of Lapita on Aore Island. No other human occupation is attested in this area prior to European arrival.

Obsidian sources

Makué is the first Lapita site with a large amount of obsidian south of the Santa Cruz Islands. A few pieces of obsidian (8 flakes, analysed by Ambrose and sourced to the Talasea and Lou area) had already been found in Malo (Hedrick 1971) but no site with large quantities of obsidian had been found so far south of the Santa Cruz area. There is, however, recent evidence from Teouma that this boundary may be extended south to Efate (Bedford *et al.* 2006). The preliminary density results suggest that most obsidian from Makué, as is the case in the Reef and Santa Cruz Islands, originated from Talasea, on the Willaumez

Peninsula (New Britain) with some additional material from a yet unknown source, possibly Lou Island or the Banks Islands. Chemical analysis will be performed to verify the origin of these artefacts.

The density method of obsidian sourcing reveals large scale patterns in obsidian sourcing. However, obsidian from the Banks Islands overlaps in density with that from the Lou Islands sources and it is therefore difficult to establish with precision the respective proportion of each source with the density method. The problems associated with the density methods have been addressed by a number of researchers (Ambrose 1976; Ambrose and Stevenson 2004; Torrence and Victor 1995) and this aspect will be addressed with further analyses. Despite the limitations of the density method, upon initial observation the results presented herein appear to be similar to those obsidian sources identified for the sites on the Reefs-Santa Cruz Islands.

Obsidian from the Banks Islands is a low quality volcanic glass which has been widely used over the last millennium or so across a vast area, from Tikopia (Kirch and Yen 1982) in the west to Fiji in the east (Best 1984) and as far south as Santo (Galipaud 1998). The noted presence of a few flakes of Banks obsidian in some Malo Lapita sites could be interpreted as an admixture from more recent levels. However, in Makué, where the only occupation is Lapita, the presence of Banks obsidian, if it is confirmed, will indicate that Lapita sailors knew of the Banks and utilised its resources despite the fact that no Lapita sites have yet been located in the Banks group.

Obsidian finds in Makué were comparatively more abundant in the area excavated in 2002. It was first thought that this would demonstrate a chronological difference in the settlement, with an initial occupation further away from the sea (or at a time of higher sea level). So far dating of Area A has not been possible and future excavations will focus on obtaining an accurate chronology for this area.

Comparisons with other sites

The artefacts from Makué and those in the sites from the Reef and Santa Cruz Islands are similar in both size and weight. Sheppard (1993) examined the latter assemblages within a resource maximisation framework. He concluded that the use and discard of the obsidian was not consistent with a resource maximisation model. He concluded that social influences were affecting the use of the material and that the obsidian was 'socially maximised' upon acquisition but later utilised in an expedient manner. Specht's (2002) review of Lapita era obsidian finds was consistent Sheppard's conclusion, at least for the early Lapita sites. Since the evidence so far suggests that the Makué site is associated with the earliest Lapita occupation of Vanuatu and since the obsidian from Makué is similar in size to that from the Reef and Santa Cruz Islands, a similar commodity history may be present in northern Vanuatu. In future, a broader review of the Makué obsidian, taking into account a comprehensive technological analysis and comparisons with other Lapita assemblages, will address these issues further.

Conclusions

It is now clear that occupation at Makué was an important part of the original settlement of Vanuatu. The similarity of the assemblage of Makué with that from the Reef-Santa Cruz Islands, especially at Nenumbo suggest that the Reef-Santa Cruz area and northern Vanuatu have been an important stepping stone for the Lapita sailors on their voyage of discovery towards the south and east. The very early dates of the several layers of occupation at Makué support the hypothesis of an equally early settlement of Fiji and perhaps New Caledonia and are compatible with the tentative chronology for the Teouma site further to the south. The large amounts of flaked obsidian found at Makué are a good indicator of this antiquity but are probably also a distinctive trait of the function of this site, which needs to be further assessed following future excavations.

Acknowledgments

The work in Malo and Aore was supported by a grant from IRD and later financial support from the French Embassy and the New Zealand High Commission in Port-Vila, as well as from the Department of Archaeology and Natural History, Australian National University. The Vanuatu Cultural Centre and Vanuatu Historic and Cultural Site Survey (VCHSS) staff helped at every stage to promote and implement the project. Many Vanuatu Cultural Centre fieldworkers and staff of the VCHSS took part in the research. Yoko Nojima and François Wadra played an important part during the initial phase of the project. The owner and manager of the Aore Resort and Aore Plantation supported us while in the field and gave us access to the archaeologically important areas. Our thanks extend to all who took part in the excavations, especially Stephan, and Rufino for their help in the field. Thanks also to Wal Ambrose who agreed to review this paper. We are particularly indebted to Chief Takau Mwele, traditional owner of the place and Chief Vira Joseph from Malo for the interest they have always shared and the kindness of their welcome.

References

Ambrose, W.R. 1976. Obsidian and its Prehistoric Distribution in Melanesia. In N. Barnard (ed.), *Ancient Chinese Bronzes, Southeast Asian Metal and other Archaeological Artefacts*, pp. 351-378. Melbourne: National Gallery of Victoria.

Ambrose, W.R. and P. Duerden 1982. PIXE Analysis in the Distribution and Chronology of Obsidian Use in the Admiralty Islands. In W.R. Ambrose and P. Duerden (eds), *Archaeometry: an Australasian Perspective*: 83-90. Canberra: Department of Prehistory, RSPacS, Australian National University.

Ambrose, W.R. and C.M. Stevenson 2004. Obsidian density, connate water, and hydration dating. *Mediterranean Archaeology and Archaeometry* 4(2):17-31.

Bedford, S. 2003. The Timing and Nature of Lapita Colonisation in Vanuatu: The Haze Begins to Clear. In C. Sand (ed.), *Pacific Archaeology: Assessment and Proposals. Proceedings of the International Conference for the 50th Anniversary of the First Lapita Excavation Koné-Nouméa 2002*, pp. 147-158. Nouméa: Les Cahiers de l'Archéologie en Nouvelle Calédonie 15.

Bedford, S. 2006. *Pieces of the Vanuatu Puzzle: Archaeology of the North, South and Centre*. Canberra: Pandanus Press, Australian National University. Terra Australis 23.

Bedford S., M. Spriggs and R. Regenvanu 2006. The Teouma Lapita Site and the early Human Settlement of the Pacific Islands. *Antiquity* 80:812-828.

Best, S. 1984. Lakeba: the prehistory of a Fijian Island. Unpublished PhD thesis, University of Auckland.

Bronk Ramsey, C. 2007. Deposition models for chronological records. *Quaternary Science Reviews* (INTIMATE special issue) in press.

Galipaud, J-C. 1998. Recherches archéologiques aux îles Torres. *Journal de la Société des Océanistes* 107:159-168.

Galipaud, J-C. 2000. The Lapita Site of Atanoasao, Malo, Vanuatu. *World Archaeological Bulletin* 12:41-55.

Garanger, J. 1972. *Archéologie des Nouvelles Hébrides*. Paris: Publication de la Société des Océanistes 30.

Green, R.C. 1976. Lapita Sites in the Santa Cruz Group. In R.C. Green and M.M. Cresswell (eds), *Southeast Solomon Islands Culture History: A Preliminary Survey*, pp. 245-65. Wellington: The Royal Society of New Zealand Bulletin 11.

Green, R.C. 1979. Lapita. In J.D. Jennings (ed.), *The Prehistory of Polynesia*, pp. 27-60. Cambridge, Mass.: Harvard University Press.

Green, R.C. 1987. Obsidian results from the Lapita sites in the Reef/Santa Cruz Islands. In W.R. Ambrose and J.M.J Mummery (eds), *Archaeometry: Further Australasian Studies*, pp. 239-249. Canberra: Department of Prehistory, Australian National University.

Green, R.C. 1991. A reappraisal of the dating for some Lapita sites in the Reef/Santa Cruz group of the southeast Solomons. *Journal of the Polynesian Society* 100:197-207.

Green, R.C. and D. Anson 2000. Excavations at Kainapirina (SAC), Watom Island. *New Zealand Journal of Archaeology* 20 (1998):29-94.

Harris, M-N. 1994. Relative Density Source Characterisation of Obsidian from the Bismarck Archipelago. Honours thesis. University of Sydney.

Hébert, B. 1965. Nouvelles Hébrides. Contribution à l'Étude Archeologique de l'Île Éfaté et des Îles Avoisantes. *Études Mélanésiennes* 18-20:71-98.

Hedrick, J.D. 1971. Lapita Style Pottery from Malo Island. *Journal of the Polynesian Society* 80(1):5-19.

Kirch, P.V. and D.E. Yen 1982. Tikopia: *The Prehistory and Ecology of a Polynesian Outlier*. Honolulu: BP Museum Bulletin 238.

McCormac F.G., A.G. Hogg, P.G. Blackwell, C.E. Buck, T.F.G. Higham and P.J. Reimer 2004. SHCal04 Southern Hemisphere Calibration 0 - 1000 cal BP *Radiocarbon* 46:1087-1092.

Pineda, R. and J-C. Galipaud 1998. Evidences archéologiques d'une surrection différentielle de l'île de Malo (Archipel du Vanuatu) au cours de l'holocène récent. *Comptes-Rendus de l'Académie des Sciences* 327:777-779.

Sheppard, P.J. 1993. Lapita Lithics: Trade/Exchange and Technology. A View from the Reefs/Santa Cruz. *Archaeology in Oceania* 28:121-137.

Sheppard, P.J. and R.C. Green 1991. Spatial analysis of the Nenumbo (SE-RF-2) Lapita Site, Solomon Islands. *Archaeology in Oceania* 26:89-101.

Specht, J. 2002. Obsidian, Colonising and Exchange. In S. Bedford, C. Sand and D. Burley (eds), *Fifty Years in the Field : Essays in honour and celebration of Richard Shutler Jr's Archaeological career*, pp. 37-49. Auckland: New Zealand Archaeological Association Monograph 25.

Spriggs, M. and S. Wickler 1989. Archaeological Research on Erromango: Recent Data on Southern Melanesian Prehistory. *Bulletin of the Indo-Pacific Prehistory Association* 9:68-91.

Summerhayes, G. 2003. Modeling differences between Lapita obsidian and pottery distribution patterns in the Bismarck Archipelago, Papua New Guinea. In C. Sand (ed.), *Pacific Archaeology: Assessments and Prospects*, pp. 135-145. Nouméa: Les Cahiers de l'Archéologie en Nouvelle Calédonie 15.

Swete Kelly, M C. 2001. Lapita Lithics: an analysis of obsidian acquistion, utilisation and discard on the Anir Islands. Honours thesis, Australian National University.

Torrence, R. and K.L. Victor 1995. The Relativity of Density. *Archaeology in Oceania* 30:121-131.

White, J.P. and M-N. Harris 1997. Changing Sources: Early Lapita Obsidian in the Bismarck Archipelago. *Archaeology in Oceania* 32:97-107.

9

Echoes from a distance: research into the Lapita occupation of the Rove Peninsula, southwest Viti Levu, Fiji

Patrick D. Nunn

Department of Geography
The University of the South Pacific
Suva, Fiji
nunn_p@usp.ac.fj

Introduction

There is much remaining to be discovered about the first people in the western tropical Pacific Islands, particularly where and when they settled particular island groups, how they lived and interacted. The period of interest, constrained by the manufacture of distinctively decorated Lapita ceramics, is approximately 3050-2500 BP in Fiji. The Fiji Islands are a mixed group of islands, dominated by the two largest – Viti Levu and Vanua Levu – which are surrounded by subgroups of volcanic islands in the west (Yasawa), centre (Lomaiviti), and south (Kadavu and Yasayasamoala). The scattered Lau group of eastern Fiji comprises mostly smaller limestone islands (Figure 1).

Until the Bourewa site on the Rove Peninsula was first discovered in December 2003, the earliest human settlements in the Fiji Islands appeared to be on Naigani and Moturiki Islands in the central part of the group, both perhaps established around 2900-2850 BP (Best 2002; Nunn et al. 2007). Other Lapita sites in the group, particularly that at Natunuku, have been shown to have been dated unsatisfactorily but probably postdated those in the central group (Anderson and Clark 1999). The possible corollary – that the central group was colonised first via the reef-free Bligh Water – appears to have been challenged by the late date for the Lapita occupation of Yadua Island (Nunn et al. 2005a). The pattern of dates and other chronological indicators suggests that the Lapita colonisation of the Fiji group was broadly from west to east (Clark and Anderson 2001), although there is a possibility that the Tongan archipelago to the east of Fiji was colonised before the Lau group of eastern Fiji (Burley and Clark 2003).

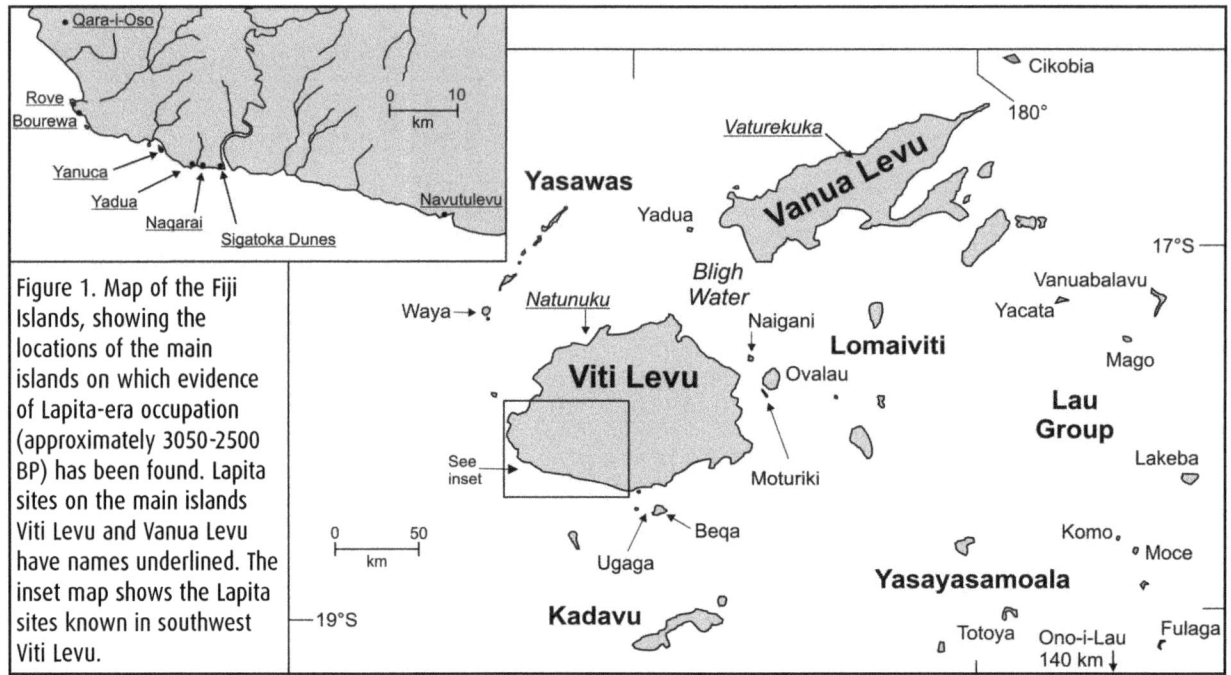

Figure 1. Map of the Fiji Islands, showing the locations of the main islands on which evidence of Lapita-era occupation (approximately 3050-2500 BP) has been found. Lapita sites on the main islands Viti Levu and Vanua Levu have names underlined. The inset map shows the Lapita sites known in southwest Viti Levu.

Lapita occupation of southwest Viti Levu Island was demonstrated before the Rove Peninsula sites were discovered. In particular, the presence of Lapita people on the Sigatoka Sand Dunes has been known for more than 50 years (Burley 2003; Anderson et al. 2006) while sites have been reported on Yanuca Island and Qara-i-Oso (cave), and Yadua (not the island) (Anderson et al. 2000; Clark and Anderson 2000; Kumar et al. 2004). The earliest indication that that Rove Peninsula might have been the site of Lapita settlement was the report by Palmer (1965) of a dentate-stamped sherd discovered "near Natadola". The location of this sherd was subsequently traced using unpublished records at the Fiji Museum to the Waikereira coast flat adjoining Bourewa (see Figure 2) and in 2002 dentate-stamped sherds were found during surface collection at Rove Beach (Kumar et al. 2004). Since those surface finds a team from the University of the South Pacific and the Fiji Museum has undertaken three phases of fieldwork in the area.

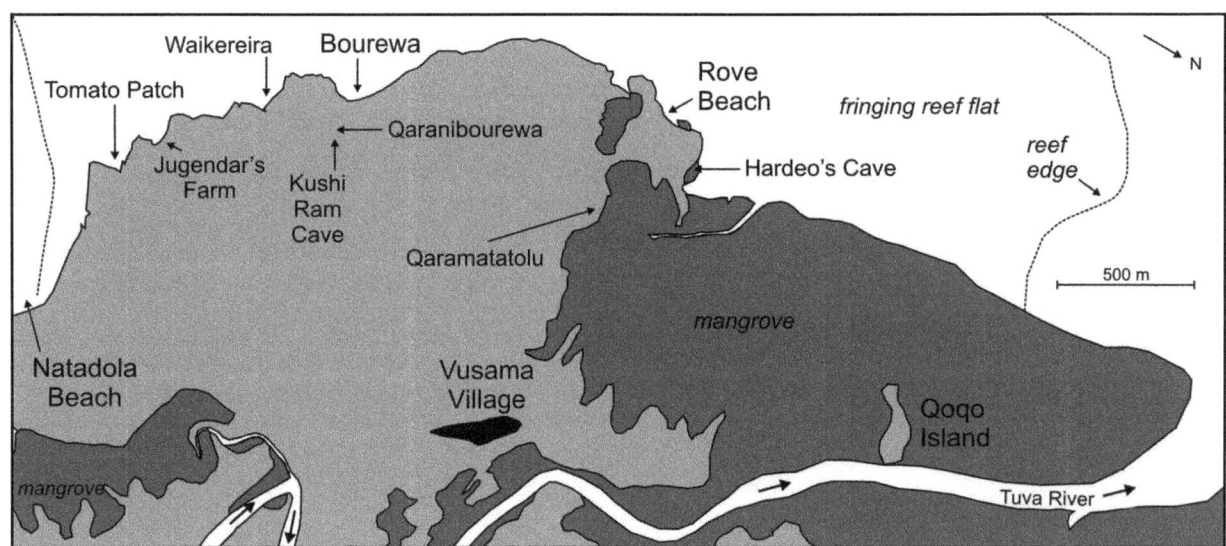

Figure 2. The Rove Peninsula showing the locations of Tomato Patch, Jugendar's Farm, Waikereira, Bourewa, Rove Beach and Qoqo Island where evidence for Lapita-era occupation has been discovered. Locations are also shown of four caves (Kushi Ram Cave, Qaranibourewa, Qaramatatolu, Hardeo's Cave) where evidence for early occupation was sought but not found.

The Rove Peninsula

The Rove Peninsula is a limestone promontory rising to about 35 m above sea level, bordered on its north side by the mangrove forest at the mouth of the Tuva River, and fringed in the south and west by one of the broadest reefs in the Fiji group, reaching almost 3 km in places (Figure 2). The first phase (Phase 1) of geoarchaeological investigations on the Rove Peninsula took place in December 2003 and focused on Rove Beach. This proved, despite the earlier discovery of dentate-stamped sherds on the shoreflat, to be a late or post-Lapita site in which Lapita-associated pottery comprised almost exclusively of notched rims which are associated with the end of the dentate-stamped period about 2500 BP. It is assumed that much of the Lapita site at this location has been eroded. Mapping of the topography of this area revealed that the Rove settlement would have been on an island (at least 1 km² in area) at the time of its Lapita occupation (Nunn 2005).

During Phase 1, surface collections were made of ceramics from other coastal flats and beaches, and it was in this way that the site at Bourewa (Beach) was discovered. Large quantities of dentate-stamped pottery were found along the beach at this location, and in the cane fields behind. Four test pits were dug in the coastal flat at the rear of the beach during Phase 1. The cultural sequence was as much as 1.8 m thick (below a disturbed 40 cm layer) and contained an uncommonly high proportion of dentate-stamped sherds with Western rather than Eastern motifs (Nunn *et al.* 2004).

Phase 2 of the fieldwork was undertaken on the Rove Peninsula in December 2004, targeting the area's caves, surveying and delimiting the Bourewa site by test excavations and surface collections, and excavating the Lapita settlement on nearby Qoqo Island. Excavations within the area's caves revealed little evidence of human occupation, most of which was recent (Nunn *et al.* 2005b). Survey of the Bourewa area revealed an elongate settlement stretched along a sand spit (or barrier island) partly enclosing a tidal inlet. Test pits at Qoqo revealed a Lapita occupation on a tombolo connecting two bedrock islands (Nunn *et al.* 2006).

The principal aim of the Phase 3 research at Bourewa was to excavate the centre of the site, where the earliest cultural deposits were assumed to exist. A team of 32 people spent four weeks in the field in June-July 2005 and excavated a total of 27 pits (each 2 m²) that, with extensions, involved excavation of an area of 127 m² (Figure 3) with a total volume of material of 103 m³ sieved, sampled and sorted.

Most of the research effort to date has focused on Bourewa, so it is this site that is discussed in most detail below. There follows an account of the five other Lapita sites known from the Rove Peninsula and nearby, then a separate account of the radiocarbon chronology of the peninsula's early occupation. This is a progress report and as such does not provide comprehensive detail on the sites and recovered materials; rather it is intended to communicate key findings to date.

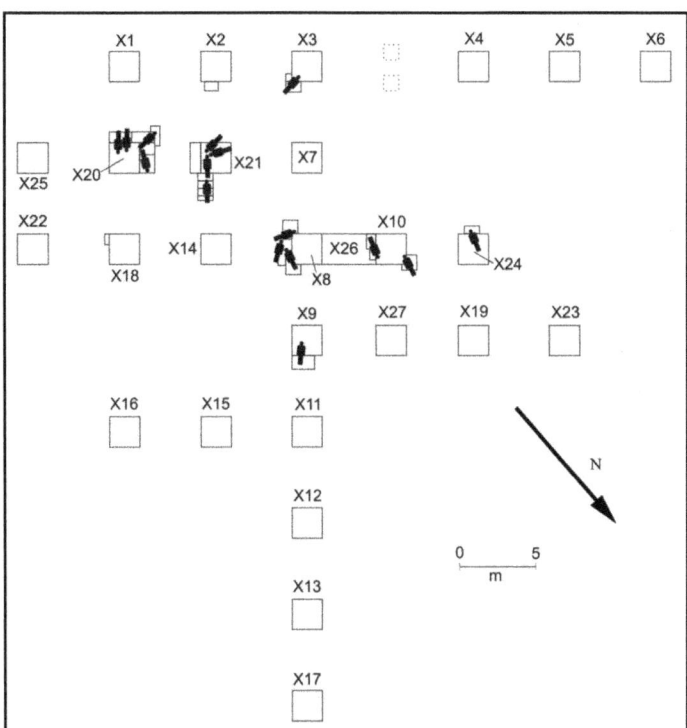

Figure 3. Map of the pits (each 2 m²) that were excavated during Phase 3 of research at Bourewa in June-July 2005. Locations and orientations of the 16 burials are also shown.

The earliest site at Bourewa

The largest and earliest Lapita settlement on the Rove Peninsula appears to have been at Bourewa. The site is currently being eroded, so its minimum extent as determined by the scatter of dentate-stamped pottery, is approximately 12,500 m^2 (Figure 4). The central part of the site – an elongate area between TP2 and TP3 – has yielded the earliest occupation ages and the highest proportion of ceramics with Western motif associations. The peripheral areas of the site – to the northwest and southeast of the centre – have yielded the youngest ages and ceramics displaying more Eastern motifs (see below).

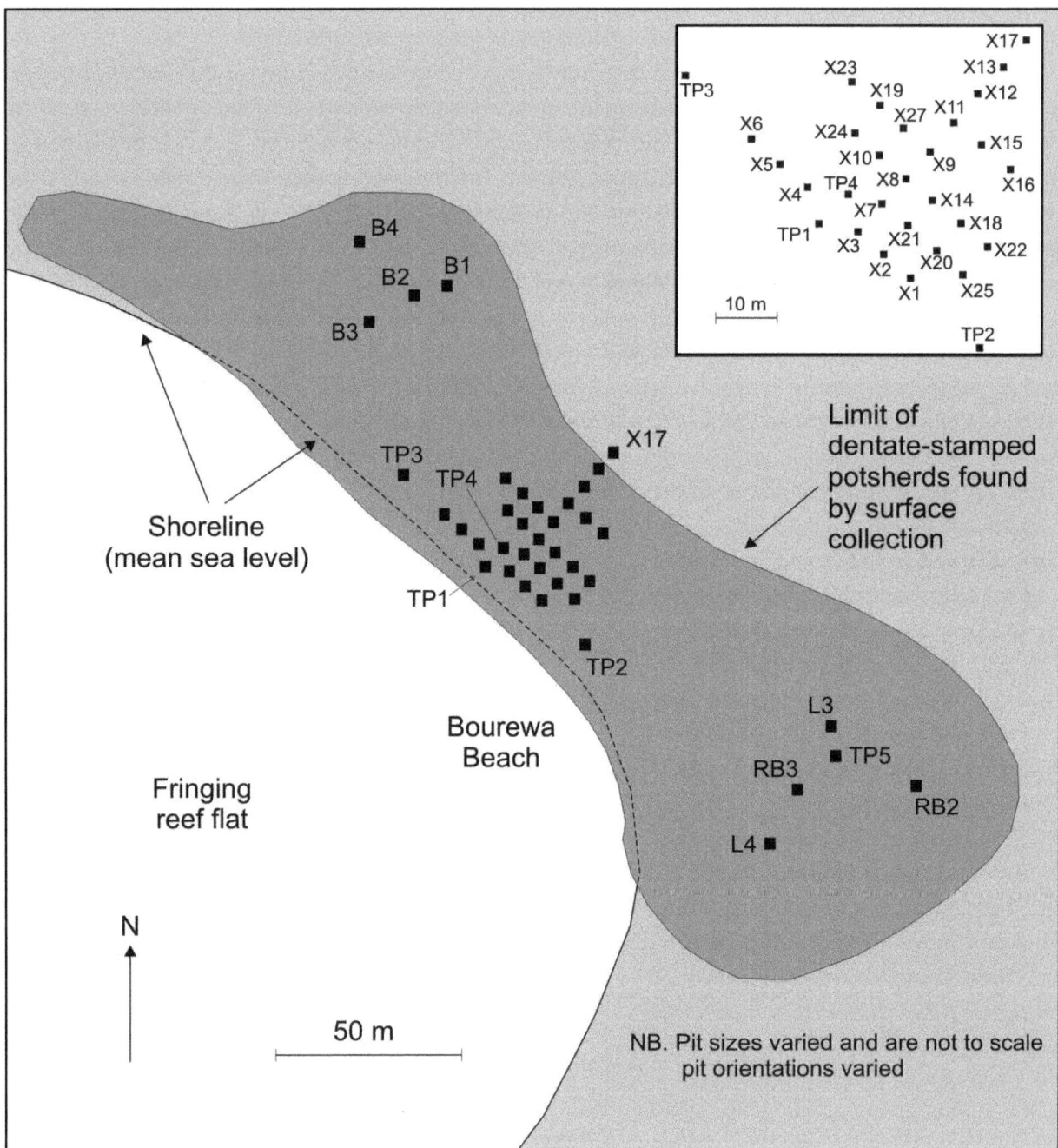

Figure 4. Map showing the extent of the Bourewa Lapita site, as delimited by dentate-stamped potsherds on the ground surface and excavation. Note that some Lapita sherds were found below mean sea level. Locations of all pits excavated in Phases 1-3 at Bourewa are also shown; the inset map names all the pits in the central part of the site.

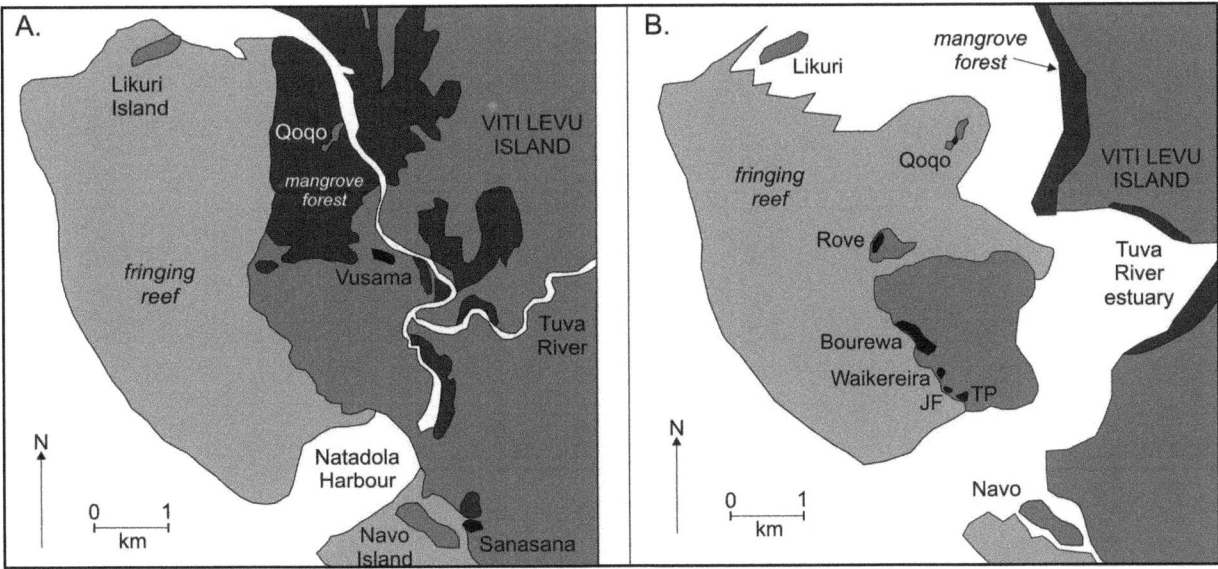

Figure 5. Changes in the geography of the Rove Peninsula and adjoining areas. A. Modern geography of the area. B. Geography of the area about 2950 BP showing the locations of the Lapita settlements.

Palaeogeography

At the time of the Lapita colonisation of the Rove Peninsula, about 3050 BP (see below), the sea level in Fiji was around 1.5 m higher than today. By the end of the Lapita occupation of this area, about 2500 BP, the sea level had fallen to 0.95 m (figures derived from Nunn and Peltier 2001). The higher sea level rendered the environment of the Rove Peninsula quite different to the modern environment.

The principal difference was that throughout the Lapita period the entire peninsula was an offshore island within the estuary of the Tuva River, with coral reef developed along its southern windward side, which the island shielded from the freshwater of the Tuva River (Figure 5). The overall sea-level fall since Lapita times has resulted in the shoaling of the Tuva estuary and the connecting of the island to the Viti Levu mainland (Nunn 2005).

The Bourewa site itself was also quite different, as the results of the GPS survey directed by Gennady Gienko show. The Bourewa site – at least its earliest part – was located on a sandspit extending 70-80 m southeastwards parallel to the present coast from a mainland promontory. It may be that the earliest settlement at Bourewa was on beach-barrier islands that transformed into a sand spit as sea level fell during the early part of the site's occupation. There is some evidence for post-holes within the spit deposits (Figure 6) suggesting possible stilt-style houses, similar to those found elsewhere in the Lapita realm (Kirch 1997). The spit partly enclosed a tidal inlet, the form of which is shown in Figure 7.

Figure 6. Possible postholes exposed in the northwest wall of Pit X9. Photo Patrick Nunn.

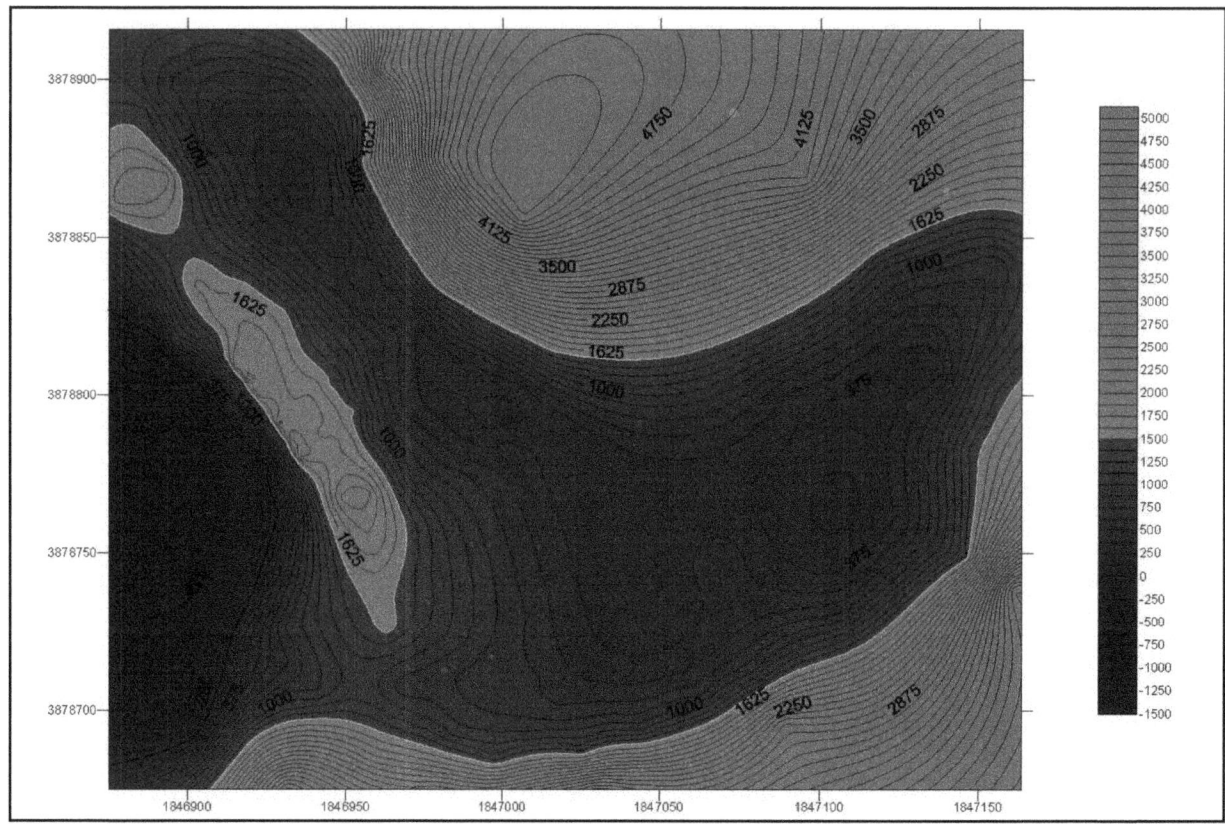

Figure 7. Palaeogeographic map of the Bourewa area at about 3050 BP when sea level was about 1.5 m higher than present. Contours are in mm above present mean sea level. The white line marks the +1.5 m shoreline. In this reconstruction the Lapita settlement appears to have been located on an elongate barrier island at the entrance to a tidal embayment.

Ceramics

Detailed examination and illustration of the recovered sherds is on-going. However, the preliminary analysis of the decorated pottery from Phases 1 and 2 at Bourewa has identified 235 pottery motifs and it is clear from this and a cursory examination of the decorated sherds obtained during Phase 3 that the site contains a comparatively high proportion of sherds with motifs that are Western Lapita in style (Figure 8). Amongst the sherds illustrated all (apart from 11 and 14) are decorated with concentrated and fine dentate designs with frequent use of zone markers. Significantly a number of face motifs are also in evidence which confirms the site's antiquity as they are on the whole relatively rare in Fijian sites (Best 2002; Spriggs 1990). The Long-nose and associated 'earlugs' infilled with a zigzag motif (8.2 and 8.3) are very reminiscent of face motifs found in New Caledonia (Sand 1999:53) and Teouma in Vanuatu (Bedford and Spriggs 2007). Other sherds may also be variants of face motifs (Figures 8.1 [top left] and 8.12). Although it is difficult to tell from the small size of the sherds these face motif sherds also show some parallels to sherds from Naitabale (Nunn et al. 2007) and Naigani (Best 1981, 2002:43; Carpenter 2002:108). Another design motif recovered from the site that is generally associated with Western Lapita is a version of the labyrinth motif (Figure 8.7). Several of the sherds including a dentate sherd also appear to have remnants of 'paint' on their exterior surface (cf. Bedford 2006).

Lapita sherds from Bourewa (27) and Qoqo (3) were analysed petrographically by William Dickinson (2005) who found that all tempers were indigenous to southwest Viti Levu. He distinguished non-hybrid tempers derived from stream sands from hybrid varieties containing both terrigenous (stream) sands and calcareous material derived from beaches, suggesting that groups of Lapita potters at Bourewa had contrasting temper-gathering strategies. The non-hybrid tempers probably derive from stream sediments in the immediate hinterland of Bourewa and cannot be distinguished from other ceramic tempers associated with the dissected

Figure 8. Selected potsherds from Phase 1 at Bourewa showing a majority of motifs characteristic of Western Lapita. Photo montage Tomo Ishimura.

orogen of southern Viti Levu. The lack of quartz, which figures prominently in other orogen tempers, can be explained by the absence of exposure of plutonic rocks in southwest Viti Levu. The hybrid tempers contain beach sands mixed with other sand sources. They can be classified as (i) beach reworked sands from Bourewa containing varying amounts of clinopyroxene, (ii) well-sorted clinopyroxene-dominant sands from Bourewa, and (iii) Tomato Patch sands that contain a contrasting selection of minerals to those from Bourewa.

Shell and shell artefacts

Shells from the various excavations at Bourewa are currently being analysed and no preliminary results are available. Analysis of 74 shell-derived artefacts and pieces of worked shell has been undertaken by Katherine Szabó (2006) (Table 1) who found a focus on ring production and reworking (73 %) and double-perforated long units in *Tridacna* shell (8 %). One of the most interesting finds was a piece of a composite fishhook made from *Trochus niloticus* suggesting that the Lapita occupants of Bourewa were also engaged in pelagic fishing, something that may yet be confirmed once the analysis of the faunal material has been completed. The degree to which shell artefacts were reworked at Bourewa is surprising, 12 % of the shell rings exhibiting 3 or more curation episodes perhaps implying that these were not being manufactured at Bourewa itself. The shell artefact assemblage from Bourewa is typical in many respects to Lapita sites in general apart from the presence of a composite fishhook perhaps signifying new fish-catching strategies.

Table 1. Numbers of different shell artefact types recovered from Bourewa (Szabó 2005).

Broad ring	21
Narrow ring	27
Bead	3
Narrow ring preform	3
Ring blank	2
Fishhook	1
Long unit	6
Utilised edge	1
Ground/perforated spire	3
Adze	1
Modified piece	6
TOTAL	**74**

Lithics

A total of 260 stone artifacts from three of the 2005 pits at Bourewa have been analysed by Valerie Campbell. Most of the stone artifacts as opposed to the stones used for earth ovens (*lovo* in Fijian) are made from dacite, a fine-grained, commonly green-coloured rock that outcrops in the hinterland of the Rove Peninsula, and is found in gravel bars in the Tuva and other river channels. These dacites fracture cleanly to create sharp edges. Dacites do not appear to have been imported as *lovo* stones. The most recognisable stone tools are scrapers, some of which exhibit step-flaking along their working margins implying wood-working. Eighteen adzes, either ovoid or rectangular in cross section, were found throughout the Lapita layers. Scattered around the Bourewa site, but not necessarily contemporary with the Lapita layers, are limestone net sinkers and fragments of abraded stone used for polishing.

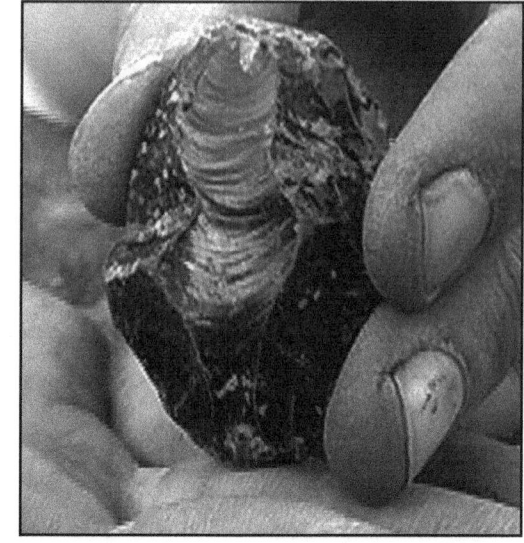

Figure 9. The piece of obsidian recovered during Phase 3 excavations at Bourewa. Photo Sangeeta Singh.

A single piece of worked obsidian was found in the Lapita layers (ca. 2850 BP) in the central part of the site (Figure 9). Density analysis undertaken by Wallace Ambrose showed that this obsidian has the same density as those samples from the Kutau-Bao sources on the Talasea Peninsula on New Britain Island in Papua New Guinea, a distance of some 3250 km from Bourewa.

Human skeletons

During the 2005 excavations, a total of 16 human skeletons were discovered at Bourewa (Figure 3). They were located at the same level as the Lapita bearing layers but preliminary dating results suggest that all skeletons are in fact post-Lapita in age although this may be subject to revision. There were no clear signs of graves having been dug into the surrounding sediments but the identification of such cuts may have been made more difficult by the fact that

Figure 10. Examples of burials discovered at Bourewa during Phase 3. Locations shown in Figure 3. Photos Patrick Nunn. A. Burial located in east side of Pit X10. B. Pair of burials in southern part of Pit X20.

the top 40 cm of the site had been ploughed and the fill of the graves may have largely composed of the same, only slightly mixed lower matrix, which had been initially dug out.

The burials were all intact, except for minor damage associated with the ploughing. Most individuals appear to have been buried on their sides with arms and legs bent and drawn up close to the body. There appeared to be no preferential burial orientation, although some individuals were buried head to foot or head to head, and others side by side (Figures 3 and 10).

The individuals were robust in build, probably of slightly above average dimensions compared to modern populations in the area. No children were among these burials, suggesting that they may have been buried in a separate area. There were no indications of artefacts being intentionally placed with the burials. One of the first observations of these skeletons made by Kazumichi Katayama was that yaws appeared to be prevalent in the population.

Evidence for horticulture

Samples from Lapita cultural layers (ca. 2850 BP) in the central part of the Bourewa site were analysed by Mark Horrocks for starch residues, pollen and phytoliths. Using a process of elimination of other possible taxa by cross-correlation of microfossil types, starch grains, calcium oxalate crystals and xylem cells of introduced taro (*Colocasia esculenta*) and lesser yam (*Dioscorea esculenta*) were identified (Horrocks and Nunn 2007). This is the first time that evidence of Lapita-era horticulture has been identified east of Vanuatu.

Other Lapita settlements on the Rove Peninsula and nearby

To date, the only other Lapita settlement to have been excavated along the side of the Rove Peninsula is at Rove Beach (Figure 2), where a Late and Post-Lapita site was uncovered. It is likely that the earliest part of the Lapita site at this location has all been eroded, which is why the occasional dentate-stamped sherd is found on the shoreflat (Kumar et al. 2004) but not in the four test pits landwards of the modern beach.

A Lapita presence at Waikereira (or Covularo) Bay, the first to the southeast of Bourewa, was suggested by the record of Palmer (1965) and confirmed by the surface collection of dentate-stamped pottery from the cane fields on the slope at the back of the bay 2-4 m above present mean sea level.

Dentate-stamped pottery was also found in the two bays immediately southeast of Waikereira – Jugendar's Farm and Tomato Patch – both on slopes at

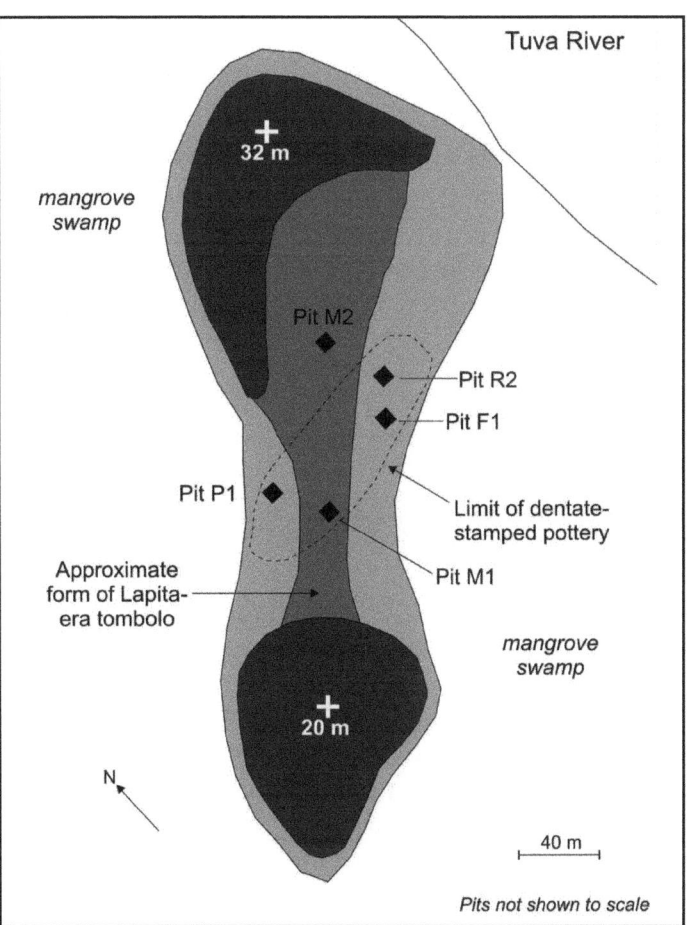

Figure 11. Map of Qoqo Island showing the two bedrock hills (dark shading) that were connected by a tombolo in Lapita times. Map also shows the locations of the five pits excavated in Phase 2 of this project.

elevations of 2-5 m above present mean sea level. Like Waikereira, these two bays are far smaller than Bourewa, and were probably occupied late in the Lapita history of the area. The elevation at which the dentate-stamped potsherds were found is intriguing – despite extensive searching, no such potsherds were found at this elevation on the fringes of the Bourewa site. The Lapita occupations at Waikereira, Jugendar's Farm and Tomato Patch may therefore represent overflow from a crowded Bourewa site. No Lapita potsherds have been found in the next bay to the northwest of Bourewa.

Qoqo Island presently lies surrounded by mangrove forest at the mouth of the Tuva River, but during the Lapita period, as inferred from palaeoenvironmental reconstruction and the character of the Lapita shell midden there, it was in an open-water location, fringed by coral reef. Mangrove spread across this reef flat probably only within the last 600-700 years (Nunn 2005; Nunn et al. 2006). The Lapita occupation of Qoqo probably postdated the initial settlement at Bourewa and involved the occupation of a narrow tombolo connecting two bedrock islands (Figure 11). Dentate-stamped sherds made up as much as 5 % of those collected (in Pit R2). Shell analysis undertaken by Linda Yuen shows that the dominant bivalves utilised during the Lapita occupation of Qoqo were *Gafrarium pectinatum* (44 % of all bivalves by weight) and *Anadara antiquata* (30 %). The dominant gastropod was *Trochus niloticus* (46 % of all gastropods by weight) (Nunn et al. 2006: Table 2).

Radiocarbon chronology of the Rove Peninsula sites

Radiocarbon dates have been obtained from Bourewa (25) and Qoqo (3) (Table 2). The Bourewa dates, shown graphically in Figure 12, suggest occupation of the site went through a number of distinct stages, almost certainly associated with population increase either locally-induced or perhaps involving influxes of people from elsewhere. A single date on a fragment of *Conus* sp. from the base of the shell midden is improbably early (WK-17544 3450-3250 cal. BP) and it seems likely to have been introduced naturally to this location. The earliest occupation (Period A) saw the centre of the sand spit occupied around 3139-2795 BP, with subsequent extensions along its length (Period B) and into peripheral areas to the northwest (Period C) and probably southeast. The earliest settlement of Qoqo probably occurred during Period B, around 2850 BP.

The radiocarbon dates are consistent with a pioneering group settling Bourewa in Period A, increasing population numbers occurring during Period B, which saw the wider occupation of the Bourewa spit but also offshore Qoqo Island, and probably also other sites in the area. Period B may have been the time during which taro and yam cultivation became more intensified, and when Eastern Lapita style motifs began to dominate. Within the Bourewa site, further expansion occurred during Period C, a time at which overflow into the bays to the southeast (Waikereira, Jugendar's Farm, Tomato Patch) may have occurred.

Conclusion

Despite the fact that Lapita was identified in Fiji more than 50 years ago and in relative terms the archipelago has been the focus of a considerable number of archaeological investigative programs, there is still much to be learnt. This is highlighted by the more recent discoveries at Bourewa and Naitabale of Lapita sites that indicate Fiji was colonised at an earlier period than once thought. There are clearly strong parallels with sites to the immediate west (Vanuatu and New Caledonia). This might seem logical and was a scenario that was put forward many years ago (Anson 1983, 1986; Green 1978) but the similarity in the ceramics and radiocarbon dates have implications for Lapita settlement pattern and chronology generally. If ceramic style is anything to go by the push out from the west across to Fiji appears to have been very rapid and it is something that cannot be differentiated with conventional radiocarbon dating (Anderson and Clark 1999).

The research on the southwest coast of Viti Levu has also highlighted the essential need for the integration of geomorphology and archaeology if comprehensive and systematic surveys and excavations are to be successful in the identification and further elucidation of this initial colonising phase of Fijian history.

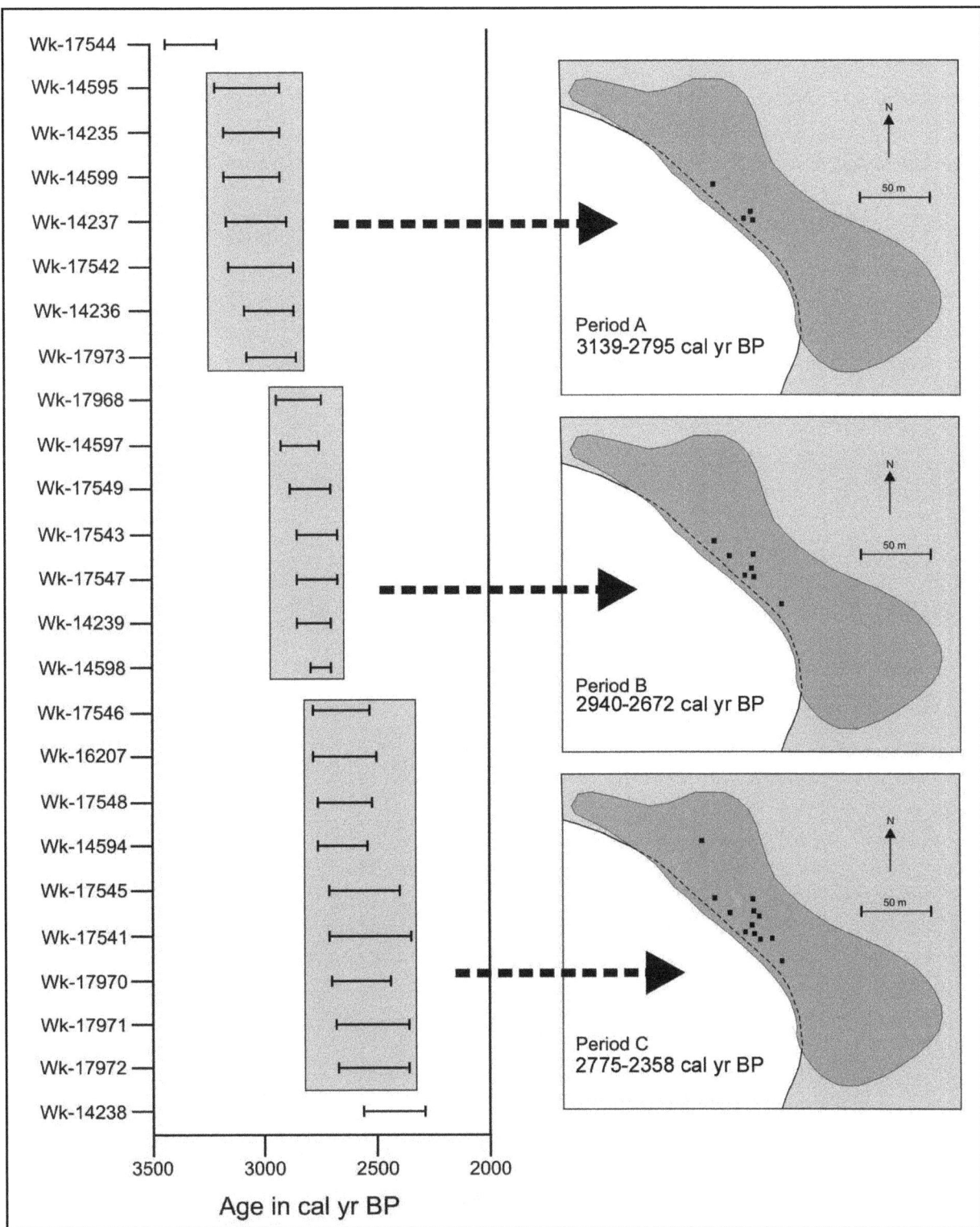

Figure 12. Summary of radiocarbon ages for the Bourewa site. The ages tend to fall into three groups. The maps on the right show the locations of the pits from which dates within particular groups were obtained. The result shows the likely earliest settlement (Period A) of Bourewa in the central part, gradually spreading to the periphery (Period C).

Table 2. Radiocarbon dates for the early human settlement of Bourewa. Dates are in order obtained; those from Pits 1-4 are from Phase 1, those from Pits B3, B4 and L4 from Phase 2, and those from Pits with an X prefix from Phase 3. All dates provided by the University of Waikato Radiocarbon Dating Laboratory calibrated using OxCal 4.0 (Bronk Ramsey 2007) using southern hemisphere atmospheric data from McCormac et al. (2004) and a Delta-R of 38±16 yrs for marine samples (Toggweiler et al. 1991).

Pit	Sample	Lab No.	sample	Depth (cm)	d13C	CRA	Cal 1 σ	Cal 2 σ
1	Bourewa 33	Wk-14598	charcoal	54	-23.1	2612±41	2750-2517	2760-2487
1	Bourewa 31	Wk-14239	marine shell (Trochus niloticus)	71	3.5±0.2	3027±42	2807-2716	2867-2686
1	Bourewa 34	Wk-14599	charcoal	85	-24.7	2894±42	3003-2869	3138-2799
2	Bourewa 23	Wk-14238	Marine shell (Fimbria fimbriata and Codakia punctata)	55	2.5±0.2	2740±43	2459-2330	2594-2297
2	Bourewa 26	Wk-14597	charcoal	57	-23.6	2717±40	2841-2744	2859-2729
3	Bourewa 17	Wk-14594	Marine shell (Codakia punctata)	105	2.9±0.2	2944±38	2743-2618	2767-2528
3	Bourewa 15	Wk-14236	charcoal	109	-25	2867±40	2966-2853	3061-2791
3	Bourewa 13	Wk-14235	charcoal	123	-27.4	2896±40	3002-2872	3139-2805
4	Bourewa 22	Wk-14237	Marine shell (Tellinidae)	52	-12.8	3259±42	3111-2956	3190-2892
4	Bourewa 20	Wk-14595	charcoal	54	-23.5	2915±42	3063-2890	3156-2855
B3	Bourewa 48	Wk-16207	Marine shell (Anadara sp. and Codakia sp.)	90	2.9±0.2	2940±41	2740-2613	2765-2510
X1	Bourewa 105	Wk-17541	charcoal	105	-26.1	2506±32	2694-2364	2705-2358
X2	Bourewa 20	Wk-20282	Marine shell (Trochus niloticus)	20	3.6±0.2	3014±39	2694-2364	2705-2358
X2	Bourewa 90	Wk-20281	Marine shell (Trochus niloticus)	90	3.6±0.2	3038±40	2816-2727	2817-2696
X2	Bourewa 120	Wk-17548	Marine shell (Anadara sp.)	120	1.6±0.2	2938±36	2738-2615	2758-2526
X3	Bourewa 30	Wk-20284	Marine shell (Trochus niloticus)	30	3.6±0.2	3044±40	2822-2732	2877-2700
X3	Bourewa 70	Wk-20283	Marine shell (Trochus niloticus)	70	4.3±0.2	2976±39	2757-2683	2826-2605
X3	Bourewa 104	Wk-17549	Marine shell (Trochus niloticus)	104	4.4±0.2	3046±39	2821-2734	2878-2702
X3	Bourewa 121	Wk-17973	charcoal	121	-25.8	2870±30	2958-2867	3059-2795
X3	Bourewa 124	Wk-17546	Marine shell (Codakia punctata, Gafrarium tumidum, Turbo sp.)	124	2.4±0.2	2951±38	2745-2659	2775-2536
X3	Bourewa 135	Wk-17542	charcoal	135	-24.4	2920±31	3063-2928	3140-2867
X6	Bourewa 68	Wk-17968	Marine shell (Atactodea striata)	68	2.4±0.2	3107±35	2880-2772	2940-2745
X6	Bourewa 94	Wk-17547	Marine shell (Trochus niloticus)	94	4.5±0.2	3006±39	2780-2703	2845-2672
X10	Bourewa 78	Wk-17970	Marine shell (Tridacna squamosa)	78	2.3±0.2	2866±31	2675-2530	2705-2452
X20	Bourewa 60	Wk-17971	marine shell (Turbo chrysostomus)	60	3.8±0.2	2831±39	2650-2461	2683-2372
X20	Bourewa 69	Wk-17972	Marine shell (Turbo sp.)	69	3.0±0.2	2824±36	2643-2450	2673-2370
X23	Bourewa 98	Wk-17545	Marine shell (Codakia punctata)	98	2.9±0.2	2851±38	2698-2559	2721-2476
X24E	Bourewa 52	Wk-17543	Marine shell (Trochus niloticus)	52	4.1±0.2	3006±39	2816-2733	2868-2705
X25	Bourewa 140	Wk-17544	Marine shell (Conus sp.)	140	3.2±0.2	3474±39	3410-3312	3450-3250

Acknowledgements

Given that this is a progress report on an ongoing research project, the author has taken the liberty to include current results from various collaborators. These include Gennady Gienko (University of the South Pacific) who compiled the palaeogeographic maps, Tomo Ishimura (National Research Institute for Cultural Properties, Nara, Japan) who undertook ceramic motif analysis, William Dickinson (University of Arizona) for ceramic temper analysis, Linda Yuen (SOPAC, Fiji) for shell analysis from Qoqo, Katherine Szabó (Australian National University) for shell artefact analysis, Valerie Campbell for stone-tool analysis, Wallace Ambrose (Australian National University) for obsidian density analysis, Kazumichi Katayama (Kyoto University) for human skeletal analysis.

Field research was made possible with the courtesy of the landowners: Kushi Ram and Ram Lal at Bourewa, Hardeo at Rove Beach, Peter Jones on Qoqo, and the *Turaga na Tui Gusunituva* and the people of Vusama Village. Funds for field research were received from the University of the South Pacific (Grants 6546, 64005, 64010) and the Government of France. Roselyn Kumar and Sepeti Matararaba helped direct fieldwork on all three occasions on the Rove Peninsula between 2003 and 2005. An anonymous reviewer supplied critical comment.

References

Anson, D. 1983. Lapita Pottery of the Bismarck Archipelago and its Affinities. Unpublished PhD thesis, University of Sydney.

Anson, D. 1986. Lapita pottery of the Bismarck Archipelago and its affinities. *Archaeology in Oceania* 21(3):157-165.

Anderson, A. and G. Clark 1999. The age of Lapita settlement in Fiji. *Archaeology in Oceania* 34:31-39.

Anderson, A., G. Clark and T. Worthy 2000. An inland Lapita site in Fiji. *Journal of the Polynesian Society* 109:311-316.

Anderson, A., R. Roberts, W.R. Dickinson, G. Clark, D. Burley, A. de Biran, G. Hope and P.D. Nunn 2006. Times of sand: sedimentary history and archaeology at the Sigatoka Dunes, Fiji. *Geoarchaeology* 21:131-154.

Bedford, S. 2006. The Pacific's earliest painted pottery: an added layer of intrigue to the Lapita debate and beyond. *Antiquity* 80:544-557.

Bedford, S. and M. Spriggs 2007. Birds on the rim: a unique Lapita carinated vessel in its wider context. *Archaeology in Oceania* 42:12-21.

Best, S. 1981. Excavations at Site VL 21/5, Naigani Island, Fiji. A preliminary report. Unpublished report. Department of Anthropology, University of Auckland.

Best, S. 2002. *Lapita: a view from the east*. Auckland: New Zealand Archaeological Association Monograph 24.

Bronk Ramsey, C. 2007. OxCal version 4.0 Radiocarbon Calibration software. http://c14.arch.ox.ac.uk/embed.php?File=oxcal.html

Burley, D.V. 2003. Dynamic landscapes and episodic occupations: archaeological interpretation and implications in the prehistory of the Sigatoka Sand Dunes. In C. Sand (ed.), *Pacific Archaeology: Assessments and Prospects*, pp. 307-315. Nouméa: Les Cahiers de l'archéologie en Nouvelle-Calédonie 15.

Burley, D.V. and J.T. Clark 2003. The archaeology of Fiji/West Polynesia in the Post-Lapita era. In C. Sand (ed.), *Pacific Archaeology: Assessments and Prospects*, pp. 235-254. Nouméa: Les Cahiers de l'archéologie en Nouvelle-Calédonie 15.

Carpenter, J.P. 2002. Fragments of Fiji. A prehistoric ceramic assemblage from Naigani Island. MA thesis, Anthropology Department, University of Auckland.

Clark, G. and A. Anderson 2000. The age of the Yanuca Lapita site, Viti Levu, Fiji. *New Zealand Journal of Archaeology* 22 (1998):15-30.

Clark, G. and A. Anderson 2001. The pattern of Lapita settlement in Fiji. *Archaeology in Oceania* 36:77-88.

Dickinson, W.R. 2005. Petrography of sand tempers in Lapita potsherds from Bourewa, southwest Viti Levu, Fiji. Unpublished petrographic report WRD-250.

Green, R.C. 1978. New sites with Lapita pottery and their implications for an understanding of the settlement of the Western Pacific. *Working Papers in Anthropology, Archaeology and Maori Studies, No. 51*. Auckland: Department of Anthropology, University of Auckland.

Horrocks, M. and P.D. Nunn 2007. Evidence for introduced taro (*Colocasia esculenta*) and lesser yam (*Dioscorea esculenta*) in Lapita-era (ca. 3050-2500 cal. yr BP) deposits from Bourewa, southwest Viti Levu Island, Fiji. *Journal of Archaeological Science* 34:739-748.

Kirch, P.V. 1997. *The Lapita Peoples*. Oxford: Blackwell.

Kumar, R., P.D. Nunn and W.R. Dickinson 2004. The emerging pattern of earliest human settlement in Fiji: four new Lapita sites on Viti Levu Island. *Archaeology in New Zealand* 47:108-117.

Nunn, P.D. 2005. Reconstructing tropical paleoshorelines using archaeological data: examples from the Fiji Archipelago, southwest Pacific. *Journal of Coastal Research, Special Issue* 42:15-25.

Nunn, P.D. and W.R. Peltier 2001. Far-field test of the ICE-4G (VM2) model of global isostatic response to deglaciation: empirical and theoretical Holocene sea-level reconstructions for the Fiji Islands, Southwest Pacific. *Quaternary Research* 55: 203-214.

Nunn, P.D., T. Ishimura, W.R. Dickinson, K. Katayama, F. Thomas, R. Kumar, S. Matararaba, J. Davidson and T. Worthy 2007. The Lapita occupation at Naitabale, Moturiki Island, central Fiji. *Asian Perspectives* 46:96-132.

Nunn, P.D., R. Kumar, S. Matararaba, T. Ishimura, J. Seeto, S. Rayawa, S. Kuruyawa, A. Nasila, B. Oloni, A. Rati Ram, P. Saunivalu, P. Singh and E. Tegu 2004. Early Lapita settlement site at Bourewa, southwest Viti Levu Island, Fiji. *Archaeology in Oceania* 39:139-143.

Nunn, P.D., S. Matararaba, T. Ishimura, R. Kumar and E. Nakoro 2005a. Reconstructing the Lapita-era geography of northern Fiji: a newly-discovered Lapita site on Yadua Island and its implications. *New Zealand Journal of Archaeology* (2003) 26:41-55.

Nunn, P.D., C. Pene, S. Matararaba, R. Kumar, P. Singh, I. Dredregasa, M. Gwilliam, T. Heorake, L. Kuilanisautabu, E. Nakoro, L. Narayan, M.R. Pastorizo, S. Robinson, P. Saunivalu and F. Tamani 2005b. Human occupations of caves of the Rove Peninsula, southwest Viti Levu Island, Fiji. *South Pacific Journal of Natural Science* 23:16-23.

Nunn, P.D., S. Matararaba, R. Kumar, C. Pene, L. Yuen and M.R. Pastorizo 2006. Lapita on an island in the mangroves? The earliest human occupation at Qoqo Island, southwest Viti Levu, Fiji. *Archaeology in New Zealand* 49:205-212.

McCormac, F.G., A.G. Hogg, P.G. Blackwell, C.E. Buck, T.F.G. Higham and P.J. Reimer 2004. SHCal04 Southern Hemisphere calibration, 0-11.0 cal kyr BP. *Radiocarbon* 46 (3):1087-1092.

Palmer, B. 1965. Lapita style potsherds from Fiji. *Journal of the Polynesian Society* 75:373-377.

Sand, C. 1999. *Lapita. The pottery collection from the site at Foué, New Caledonia*. Noumea: Les cahiers de l'archéologie en Nouvelle-Calédonie, Volume 7.

Spriggs, M. 1990. The Changing face of Lapita: the transformation of a design. In M. Spriggs (ed.), *Lapita design, form and composition: proceedings of the Lapita design workshop, Canberra, Australia, December 1988*, pp.83-122. Canberra: Department of Prehistory, Australian National University. Occasional Papers in Prehistory 18.

Szabó, K. 2005. Shell artefacts from the Lapita site of Bourewa, Viti Levu, Fiji. Unpublished report, RSPAS, The Australian National University.

Toggweiler, J.R., K. Dixon and W.S. Broecker 1991 The Peru upwelling and the ventilation of the South Pacific thermocline. *Journal of Geophysical Research* 96:20467- 20497.

10

Paleoenvironment of Lapita sites on Fanga 'Uta Lagoon, Tongatapu, Kingdom of Tonga

William R. Dickinson

Department of Geosciences,
University of Arizona,
Tucson, Arizona 85721, USA
wrdickin@dakotacom.net

Introduction

The density of Lapita archaeological sites surrounding Fanga 'Uta Lagoon indenting the north coast of Tongatapu is the greatest in Tonga. On average, at least one site is known per 2.5 km of reconstructed curvilinear paleoshoreline and many additional sites probably remain to be discovered. All the sites give the archaeological impression of having been coastal habitations, but most lie now at the seaward edge of the flat tephra-covered surface of interior Tongatapu along a slope declivity marking the position of an emergent mid-Holocene paleoshoreline that stands varying distances inland from beaches and mangrove thickets along the present lagoonal shoreline. To understand the original paleoenvironmental setting of the Lapita sites, the mid-Holocene paleoshoreline of Fanga 'Uta Lagoon associated with a hydro-isostatic highstand in tropical Pacific sea level was traced in as much detail as recent urban and agricultural modification of the Tongatapu landscape allows.

Lapita sites in the varied island groups of the southwest Pacific were occupied thousands of years ago when nearly all local coastal environments were different than today. Paleoenvironmental change at archaeological sites on Pacific island coasts has been affected by multiple influences including tectonic uplift or subsidence of individual islands or island clusters (Dickinson 2001; Dickinson and Green 1998), the spread of lava flows or blankets of volcanic ash over islands near eruptive centers (Green 2002; Green and Anson 2000; Torrence *et al.* 2000), enhanced sedimentation that was triggered by accelerated erosion of slopes in island interiors in response to deforestation that accompanied expanding human impact on inland vegetation (Anderson *et al.* 2006; Clark and Michlovic 1996; Dickinson *et al.* 1998), the accretion of beach ridges to form enlarged coastal strands (Dickinson and Burley 2007; Kirch 1998, 1993; Kirch *et al.* 1990), and drawdown in local sea level following the regional mid-Holocene hydro-isostatic highstand in tropical Pacific sea level (Dickinson 2001).

Drawdown in sea level from the mid-Holocene highstand has had the most general and ubiquitous impact on coastal Lapita sites, and has been the dominant impact where other influences on relative sea level are absent or minimal. The Lapita sites surrounding Fanga 'Uta Lagoon illustrate especially well the effect of hydro-isostatic change in sea level on coastal Lapita sites because neither uplift nor subsidence has affected Tongatapu since Lapita occupation, post-Lapita tephra falls have not been detected, surface streams transporting sediment are virtually non-existent on Tongatapu, and surf action required to expand coastal beaches and spits is restricted to passages near the mouths of the lagoon. In effect, the setting of Fanga 'Uta Lagoon isolates hydro-isostatic effects to the near exclusion of other effects on coastal environments.

Highstand-Lapita relations

Isotopic dating of emergent mid-Holocene reef flats on Tongatapu by combined uranium-series and radiocarbon methods suggest that the mid-Holocene hydro-isostatic highstand of regional sea level in Tonga peaked at some time during the interval 4800-3600 BCE with appropriate analytical uncertainties taken into account (Dickinson *et al.* 1999; Taylor 1978; Taylor and Bloom 1977; Spenneman 1997). Supportive radiocarbon ages in the calibrated range of 4000-3400 BCE have been obtained from calcarenitic sands that directly overlie emergent mid-Holocene reef limestone in seacliffs near Kolonga on northeast Tongatapu (Nunn and Finau 1995), and from the base of marine mid-Holocene bay deposits sandwiched between mangrove peat layers beneath the west arm of Fanga 'Uta Lagoon southwest of Folaha (Ellison 1989). Theoretical global calculations of post-glacial hydro-isostatic effects in the tropical Pacific Ocean imply a peak highstand between 2000 BCE (Mitrovica and Peltier 1991) and 3000 BCE (Mitrovica and Milne 2002). Provisional reconciliation of the empirical and theoretical estimates for highstand timing indicates an approximate date of 3000 BCE for the end of the peak mid-Holocene highstand in Tonga.

Excavated Lapita horizons within Tonga date generally to the interval 850-650 BCE (Burley 1998; Burley *et al.* 1999, 2001), distinctly later than the peak of the mid-Holocene highstand. Slightly older dates (900-875 BCE) for the basal cultural horizon at Nukuleka (Figure 1), thought to be the founding Lapita settlement in Tonga (Burley and Dickinson 2001), are not significantly older. As the rate of post-mid-Holocene drawdown in regional sea level is uncertain, the exact position of local relative sea level on Tongatapu at the time of initial Lapita occupation cannot be retrodicted with full confidence. Analysis of shoreline evolution in Australia suggests, however, that the post-highstand decline in Pacific hydro-isostatic sea level was gradual, monotonic, and linear (Chappell 1983; Harvey *et al.* 1999; Woodroffe *et al.* 2000). With that assumption, relative sea level on Tongatapu at Lapita time can be hindcast closely.

Elevations of emergent mid-Holocene paleoreef flats on the leeward coast and of coeval paleoshoreline notches on the windward coast jointly document post-mid-Holocene hydro-isostatic emergence of Tongatapu (Dickinson and Burley 2007; Dickinson *et al.* 1999). Remnants of emergent paleoreef-flat limestone in downtown Nuku'alofa stand 2.2 above modern reef flats rising to low-tide level, and paleoshoreline notches stand 2.3±0.4 m (n=8 sites, range 1.8-2.8 m) above modern shoreline notches incised at high-tide level. More voluminous data of Nunn and Finau (1995) measured from the same assemblage of paleoshoreline notches provides an independent coordinate estimate of 2.2±0.4 m (n=16 sites, range 1.6-2.9 m) for island emergence.

The indicated emergence is in close accord with the theoretical estimate (2.1-2.6 m) of the magnitude of the mid-Holocene hydro-isostatic highstand in tropical Pacific sea level in Tonga derived from global calculations (Mitrovica and Peltier 1991: Fig. 8i-k).

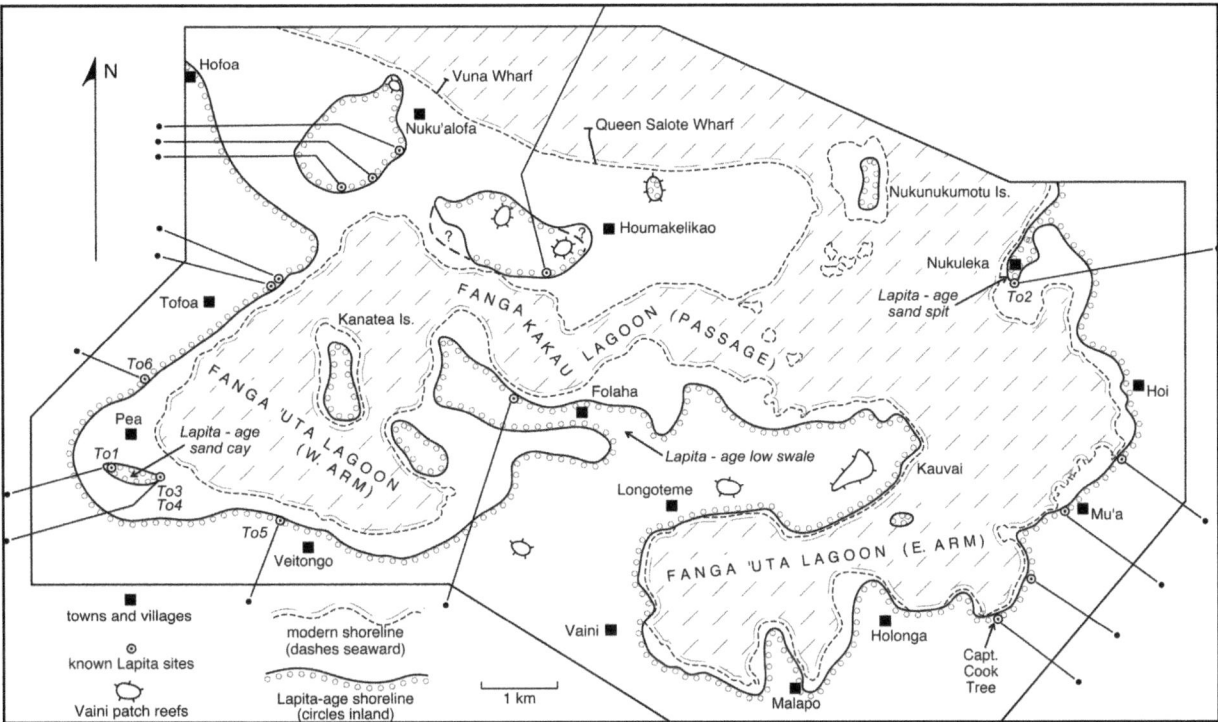

Figure 1. Modern shoreline and Lapita paleoshoreline of Fanga 'Uta Lagoon, Tongatapu, Tonga. *To1-To6* Lapita sites are designations of Poulsen (1987).

Interpretations of paleoshoreline features that postulate significant Holocene tectonic deformation of Tongatapu (Ellison 1989; Nunn and Finau 1995) are discounted here because last-interglacial (~125 ka) paleoshoreline features stand at an elevation of 6.7 m above modern counterparts (Dickinson and Burley 2007; Dickinson *et al* 1999; Taylor 1978; Taylor and Bloom 1977; Spenneman 1997; Woodroffe 1988). This observed elevation is coordinate, without tectonic uplift, with the inferred magnitude of 6±1 m (Dickinson 2001; Israelson and Wohlfarth 1999) for the last-interglacial eustatic highstand in global sea level. As noted below, the consistent elevation of the mid-Holocene paleoshoreline surrounding Fang 'Uta Lagoon, which penetrates deep into Tongatapu, precludes significant late Holocene tilt of the island.

In the cove west of Keleti Beach on the windward coast 3 km from the head of the west arm of Fanga 'Uta Lagoon, the difference in elevation between a well preserved mid-Holocene paleonotch and the active shoreline notch, developed at modern high-tide level, was scaled directly as 2.6 m. Combining this observation with data on the emergence of mid-Holocene coral heads in Nuku'alofa on the north flank of Fanga 'Uta Lagoon, post-mid-Holocene emergence of the lagoon by 2.2-2.6 m is inferred. From highstand-Lapita age relations, post-Lapita emergence can be calculated as 1.2-1.4 m. Given the tidal range of 1.0-1.2 m for Tongatapu, this estimate of post-Lapita emergence implies that high-tide level during Lapita time had not dropped below the level of paleoreef flats constructed upward to low-tide level during the mid-Holocene highstand. At high tide during Lapita time, seawater swept as far inland, in relation to modern geography, as the older pre-Lapita paleoshoreline. In effect, the edge of dry land had not shifted seaward from the mid-Holocene paleoshoreline at Lapita time, except where buildup of sand cays or spits above gradually shoaling mid-Holocene paleoreef flats had created patches of dry land at sites that had previously been fully submerged.

Fanga 'Uta Geomorphology

The present island of Tongatapu was formed by Pleistocene (>250 ka) uplift of the Vaini paleoreef complex developed along the crest of the forearc Tonga platform (Dickinson and Burley 2007; Dickinson et al. 1999; Roy 1990, 1997). A Vaini paleoisland, now forming the highest topography at the southeast tip of Tongatapu, was flanked by barrier reefs that have been uplifted to form the high ridges extending parallel to the eastern and southern coasts of Tongatapu. The interior lowlands of Tongatapu represent the emergent floor of the Vaini paleolagoon, which was tilted gently northward at 0.05°-0.15° during uplift (Roy 1990, 1997; Taylor 1978). Multiple isolated hills (many now being quarried for limestone) which rise from the lowlying paleolagoon floor represent ancestral patch reefs of the Vaini paleoreef complex (Dickinson and Burley 2007; Dickinson et al. 1999; Lewis et al. 1997). In a broad context, the modern Fanga 'Uta Lagoon is an undrained remnant of the Vaini paleolagoon.

In detail, however, the shoreline of Fanga 'Uta Lagoon has been modified by post-uplift and post-tilt coastal processes during late Pleistocene (<125 ka) and Holocene time: (1) post-uplift and post-tilt erosion, largely by coastal corrosion of exposed limestone, has incised low seacliffs into pre-Holocene limestone; (2) fringing reefs of last-interglacial (~125 ka) and mid-Holocene (~5 ka) age have been accreted to the older limestone core of Tongatapu in patterns not yet elucidated in full detail, although dated mid-Holocene coral was collected from an emergent paleoreef flat exposed by excavations in downtown Nuku'alofa only a kilometer from Fanga'Uta Lagoon (Taylor 1978); and (3) wave action has locally built beach ridges and spits along Holocene shorelines favorably situated to receive calcareous sand from sources of detritus on expanding offshore reef flats to the north of the island (Roy 1990, 1997). Longshore drift of calcareous sand is dominantly westward along the northern coast of Tongatapu under the influence of surf driven by the prevailing trade winds.

Modification of last-interglacial paleoshoreline features has been too extensive to allow pre-Holocene positions of the Fanga 'Uta lagoonal shoreline to be specified closely, but the morphology of the mid-Holocene paleoshoreline is well preserved in many areas. Its position is marked for long reaches of its course by a distinct slope declivity, rising 2-4 m from coastal flats within a horizontal distance of 10-25 m. The slope forms an abrupt break in local topography, with much flatter ground both above and below. Tephra cover over the interior of Tongatapu is characteristic of the surface behind the paleoshoreline, but is absent below the paleoshoreline declivity. Lapita sites are irregularly distributed with respect to modern geography, some near the coast and some well inland, but all lie close to the paleoshoreline trend. The shell middens and sherd scatters of a number of sites are perched atop or along the lip of the paleoshoreline declivity (Figure 1). The persistent occurrence of mid-Holocene paleoshoreline features encircling Fanga 'Uta Lagoon at the consistent elevation expected without tectonic deformation supports the inference of no significant Holocene uplift, subsidence, or tilting of Tongatapu.

The surface of Lapita-age "paleo-Tongatapu" lying inland from the mid-Holocene paleoshoreline is composed of undulating topography mantled by a cover of weathered tephra, which thickens from east to west toward volcanic sources along the active Tongan island arc. The net tephra thickness varies from 5.5 m to 1.5 m on Tongatapu as a whole (Spenneman 1997), with the youngest tephra layer thinning eastward from 1.0 to 0.5 m on uplands surrounding Fanga 'Uta Lagoon (Cowie 1980).

Post-Lapita coastal flats are nestled along the present Fanga 'Uta lagoonal shoreline, extending inland to the base of the declivity marking the mid-Holocene paleoshoreline trend. This late Holocene "new ground", generally devoid of tephra cover, typically stands only a meter or less above the water level in mangrove swamps fringing Fanga 'Uta Lagoon, and is subject to widespread ponding of surface water during rainy periods.

Paleoshoreline trace

The position of the mid-Holocene paleoshoreline (Figure 1) generally mimics but differs slightly from the location inferred by Spenneman (1988, 1997:Figs. 2e, 13 bottom), who positioned the paleoshoreline at the 2-m contour on available topographic maps. The paleoshoreline was plotted during this study by tracing on the ground the slope declivity marking its trend. The position of the paleoshoreline was established within narrow lateral limits wherever the slope declivity is transected by streets and roads (approximately 60 localities), or lies along accessible village waterfronts, with its position between those intersections and shorefronts sketched by eye in the field.

In a few areas, the mapped paleoshoreline departs significantly from positions anticipated from contours shown on available topographic maps. These departures from expectation seemingly imply topographic discordances along the paleoshoreline trend. In my judgment, however, the apparent discordances do not record any tectonic deformation of the paleoshoreline, but instead reflect minor inaccuracies in the placement of contour lines drawn by photogrammetric methods across a landscape of low relief and variable tree height.

Westward from Nuku'alofa, the restriction of pottery finds to the topographic crest of a feature interpreted as a paleobeach ridge (Groube 1971:291-292) suggests that the Lapita-age paleoshoreline could be traced successfully near the north shore of Tongatapu well beyond the limits of the mapping undertaken around Fanga 'Uta Lagoon. In the Kolovai district of westernmost Tongatapu, however, an emergent last-interglacial paleobeach ridge forms a prominent component of the island landscape (Lewis *et al.* 1997; Roy 1997), and might be misinterpreted as a mid-Holocene paleoshoreline feature.

Paleoenvironmental relations

The present-day Fanga 'Uta Lagoon, and especially its innermost arm west of the Fanga Kakau passage south of Nuku'alofa (Figure 1), is a severely restricted body of partly brackish water with a muddy bottom, limited shellfish fauna, and extensive fringing mangrove swamps. Even its eastern arm, leading directly to the landing place of Captain Cook near Mu'a in 1777, is screened by shoals that bridge the lagoon entrance, only 1.5 km wide between the lowlying island of Nukunukumotu and the Tongatapu mainland at Nukuleka (Figure 1).

In mid-Holocene time, extending at least until the initial Lapita occupation, the paleogeography of Fanga 'Uta Lagoon was qualitatively different. At present (Figure 2A), the Nuku'alofa peninsula forms a nearly continuous barrier across the mouths of both arms of Fanga 'Uta Lagoon. An additional screen of offshore reef islets further separates the modern Fanga 'Uta environment from open sea to the north. In Lapita time (Figure 2B), multiple passes between paleoislands then occupying the area of the present-day Nuku'alofa peninsula gave much more direct and extensive tidal access for ocean water into twin but separate Fanga 'Uta embayments (eastern and western). Both embayments were deeper and less landlocked than the two derivative arms of the present-day Fanga 'Uta Lagoon, into which the twin embayments evolved through post-mid-Holocene time. Shellfish middens at Lapita sites flanking Fanga 'Uta Lagoon are rich in marine genera that are sparse or absent in the modern Fanga 'Uta Lagoon, and point to a marked change in lagoonal ecology over time (Burley *et al.* 2001).

The trend of the principal island shoreline in Lapita time (Figure 2B) followed an arcuate course, slightly concave to the north, extending from Hofoa to the west of Nuku'alofa along a path near the southern shoreline of the present-day Fanga Kakau passage to the south of the present-day Nuku'alofa peninsula. This segment of the paleoshoreline lay directly along the northern edge of the Folaha peninsula between the two ancestral Fanga 'Uta embayments, and extended eastward beyond the mouth of the eastern embayment past

Oceanic Explorations: Lapita and Western Pacific Settlement

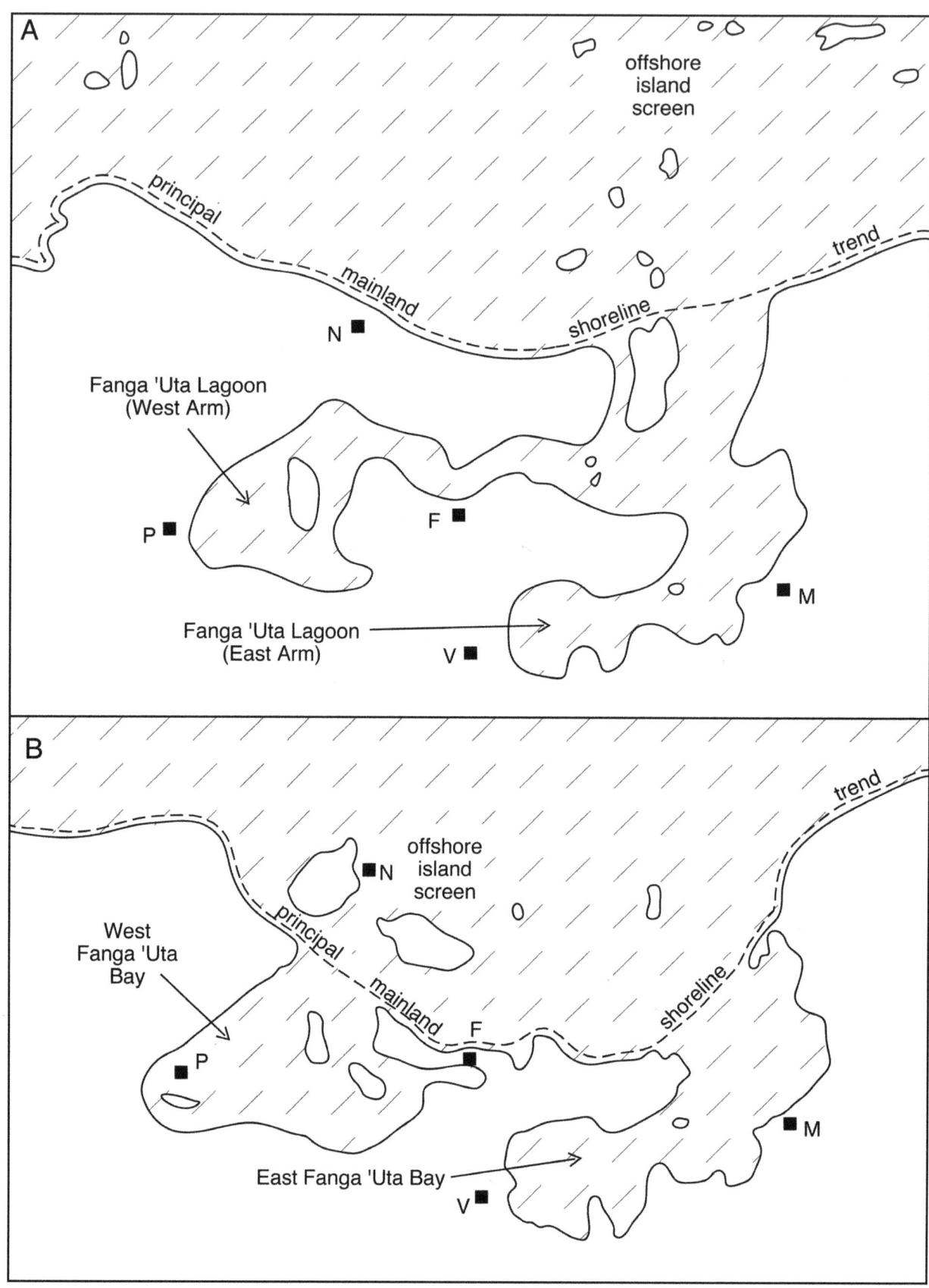

Figure 2. Modern (A) and Lapita (B) configurations (same scale) of the north coast of Tongatapu at Fanga 'Uta Lagoon (twin embayments at Lapita time) derived from Figure 1: F, Folaha; M, Mu'a; N, Nuku'alofa; P, Pea; V, Vaini.

a prominent spit built at Nukuleka by longshore drift of beach sand. The beach sand was transported toward the southwest under the influence of the prevailing tradewinds from the coastline adjacent to more elevated tracts of northeastern Tongatapu. The heads of both the eastern and western Fanga 'Uta embayments lay no more than 5 km inland from comparatively open water north of the paleoshoreline trend.

In Lapita time, the site of modern Nuku'alofa was occupied in part by two small paleoislands nucleated around remnant Vaini patch reefs (Figure 1) that still form prominent hills on the urban landscape (including Brush Hill just west of the Royal Palace), but was otherwise drowned reef flat. The continuous barrier formed by the present-day Nuku'alofa peninsula did not yet exist. Sea water could pass from the open sea to the north directly across the site of modern Nuku'alofa into the western Fanga 'Uta embayment. Access from the eastern Fanga 'Uta embayment to the open sea was also closer and easier than today across a baymouth that was approximately 2 km wide between the Folaha peninsula and Nukuleka, and was located only 2 km offshore from Mu'a (Figure 2B). High ground near the northwestern tip of the Folaha peninsula, which separates the eastern and western arms of the present-day Fanga 'Uta Lagoon, was almost a separate island, linked to the main part of the peninsula to the southeast by a low swale rising only slightly above the mid-Holocene intertidal zone (Figure 1).

Lapita Sites

As indicated on the accompanying geoarchaeological map (Figure 1), a number of Lapita sites are distributed along the edge of Lapita-age "paleo-Tongatapu" at or just above the lip of the slope declivity marking the mid-Holocene paleoshoreline. Several sites lie southward from Nuku'alofa along the paleoshoreline trend west of Fanga 'Uta Lagoon and several others lie along the paleoshoreline trend within and near Mu'a east of Fanga 'Uta Lagoon. Two comparatively isolated sites occur along the paleoshoreline trend south of the west arm of Fanga 'Uta Lagoon and on the north side of the Folaha peninsula between the two arms of the lagoon, but their apparent isolation may be a function of limited archaeological surveying in areas distant from Nuku'alofa or Mu'a. Additional unsurveyed Lapita sites may well be present at intervals along the whole paleoshoreline trend.

Four known Lapita sites within the area of the present-day Nuku'alofa urban complex lay near the coasts of offshore paleoislands (Figure 1) that partially screened the western Fanga 'Uta embayment from the open sea (Figure 2B). Elsewhere within the Lapita region, Lapita settlements were commonly located on small islets offshore from larger landmasses (Lepofsky 1988). In two localities, known Lapita settlements stand at somewhat lower elevations with respect to modern sea level than the crest of the slope declivity along the mid-Holocene paleoshoreline, but their elevations are compatible with post-Lapita emergence of Tongatapu by 1.2-1.4 m (as inferred above):

(1) At Nukuleka north of Mu'a, an excavated Lapita horizon near the southern limit of the modern village lies only 1.2-1.5 m above modern high-tide level. This Lapita settlement apparently occupied the extreme southern tip of a sandy spit (Figures 1-2) built part way across the mouth of the eastern of the twin Lapita-age Fanga 'Uta embayments as hydro-isostatic sea-level began to recede from the mid-Holocene highstand. As the oldest known Lapita site in Tonga (Burley and Dickinson 2001), Nukuleka may have been founded at the first dry land encountered at the entrance from the sea to the eastern and most open of the twin Lapita-age Fanga 'Uta embayments (Figure 2B). The Nukuleka spit is one of only two prominent Holocene spits built along the north shore of Tongatapu by westward longshore drift of reef-derived calcareous sand under the influence of the prevailing tradewinds. The other spit, initiated in post-Lapita time, extends westward from Nuku'alofa where its crest is marked by the course of the western segment of Vuna Road (Roy 1997).

(2) Within a lowlying modern village complex near Pea at the southwestern corner of Fanga 'Uta Lagoon, two known Lapita horizons stand only 1.2-1.5 m above present water level in the adjacent lagoon. Both lie along the subdued crest of a low rise interpreted as the remnant of a paleoisland that formed as a slightly emergent sand cay constructed near the head of the western of the twin Lapita-age Fanga 'Uta embayments as hydro-isostatic sea level began to recede from the mid-Holocene highstand. The paleocay stood well into the mid-Holocene embayment from well defined paleoshoreline declivities (to the west and south) that converge toward a poorly defined mid-Holocene bayhead southwest of the paleocay (Figure 1). Examination of the sediment beneath the paleocay suggests deposition within a shallow tidal lagoon (Crook 1987), implying formation of the paleocay by tidal currents within the shoaling bayhead environment.

The comparatively lowlying Lapita sites at Nukuleka and near Pea may not have provided as much protection from incursions by the sea during stormy periods as the Lapita sites at slightly higher elevations along the mid-Holocene paleoshoreline declivity, but were located on sandy paleobeaches where canoe landing may have been easier than anywhere else along the paleoshoreline of Fanga 'Uta Lagoon. The Lapita sites on small paleoislands now incorporated into the Nuku'alofa peninsula lie along inner paleocoasts at locales that would have been shielded to some extent from wave activity in the open sea to the north.

Overall conclusions

Lapita paleoenvironments near Fanga 'Uta Lagoon cannot be understood with the modern landscape as a reference guide. Paleoshoreline analysis of Fanga 'Uta Lagoon and its environs reveals a mid-Holocene paleogeography different in significant respects from the present-day environment. Not only did the Lapita-age shoreline lie well inland from the modern shoreline, but the two arms of Fanga 'Uta Lagoon were embayments harboring deeper water, with less restricted access to the open sea north of Tongatapu. Lapita sites now set back at varying distances from the shoreline of the modern muddy lagoon fringed by mangrove swamps stood at the time of occupation atop the beaches of embayments or associated islets with ready access to abundant marine resources. From paleogeographic analysis, it seems likely that rich shellfish resources of the ancestral Lapita-age Fanga 'Uta embayments, coupled with attractive sheltered paleoshorelines lying along the fringes of the embayments and on associated offshore islets, may have attracted to Tongatapu one of the densest Lapita populations in the ancient Pacific world. The geoarchaeology and paleogeography of Fanga 'Uta Lagoon underscores the value of coordinated archaeological and geological investigations in Pacific Oceania.

Acknowledgements

The base map for Figure 1 was compiled from Sheets 21-22 of the 1975 topographic map (scale 1:25,000) of the Tongatapu Group prepared by the British Directorate of Overseas Surveys, and published for the Kingdom of Tonga by the British Ministry of Overseas Development. All locations of Lapita archaeological sites were plotted in company with David V. Burley (Archaeology Department, Simon Fraser University), who also pointed out to me the distinctive break in slope along the mid-Holocene paleoshoreline trend from Vaiola Hospital to Tufu Mahina (located between Nuku'alofa and Pea). Drivers Aki and Vaha of Tokomololo village provided expert and cheerful guidance among the streets and lanes of Nuku'alofa, and along the byways of multiple villages and intervening countryside flanking the various shores of Fanga 'Uta Lagoon. Patient directions and advice on road conditions from numerous Tongans met during the course of field work, together with gracious permission to enter selected off-road properties, were essential for completion of the mapping project. My investigations were part of the research project of David V. Burley approved by the Office of the Prime Minister of the Kingdom of Tonga, and pursued by gracious permission of His Majesty King Taufa'ahau IV. Funds provided by the Social Sciences and Humanities Research Council of Canada supported my field work in 1999.

References

Anderson, A., R. Roberts, W. Dickinson, G. Clark, D. Burley, A. de Biran, G. Hope and P. Nunn 2006. Times of sand: Sedimentary history and archaeology at the Sigatoka dunes, Fiji. *Geoarchaeology* 21:131-154.

Burley, D.V. 1998. Tongan archaeology and the Tongan past, 2850-150 B.P. *Journal of World Prehistory* 12:337-392.

Burley, D.V. and W.R. Dickinson 2001. Origin and significance of a founding settlement in Polynesia. *National Academy of Sciences Proceedings* 98:11829-11831.

Burley, D.V. D.E. Nelson and R. Shutler, Jr. 1999. A radiocarbon chronology for the Eastern Lapita frontier in Tonga. *Archaeology in Oceania* 34:59-70.

Burley, D.V., W.R. Dickinson, A. Barton and R. Shutler, Jr. 2001. Lapita on the periphery: New data on old problems in the Kingdom of Tonga. *Archaeology in Oceania* 36:89-104.

Chappell, J. 1983. Evidence for smoothly falling sea levels relative to north Queensland, Australia during the past 6,000 years. *Nature* 302:406-408.

Clark, J.T. and M.G. Michlovic 1996. An early settlement in the Polynesian homeland: Excavations at 'Aoa Valley, Tutuila Island, American Samoa. *Journal of Field Archaeology* 23:151-167.

Cowie, J.D. 1980. Soils from andesitic tephra and their variability, Tongatapu, Kingdom of Tonga. *Australian Journal of Soil Research* 18:273-284.

Crook, K.A.W. 1987. Analysis of soil samples from To.1. In J. Poulsen, *Early Tongan Prehistory (Vol. I)*, p. 268. Canberra: Department of Prehistory, Australian National University, Terra Australis 12.

Dickinson, W.R. 2001. Paleoshoreline record of relative Holocene sea levels on Pacific islands. *Earth-Science Reviews* 55:191-234.

Dickinson, W.R. and R.C. Green 1998. Geoarchaeological context of Holocene subsidence at the ferry berth Lapita site, Mulifanua, Upolu, Samoa. *Geoarchaeology* 13:239-263.

Dickinson, W.R. and D.V. Burley 2007. Geoarchaeology of Tonga: Geotectonic and geomorphic controls. *Geoarchaeology* 22:231-261.

Dickinson, W.R., D.V. Burley, P.D. Nunn, A. Anderson, G. Hope, A. de biran, C. Burke and S. Matararaba 1998. Geomorphic and archaeological landscapes of the Sigatoka dune site, Viti Levu, Fiji: Interdisciplinary investigations. *Asian Perspectives* 37:1-31.

Dickinson, W.R., D.V. Burley and R. Shutler, Jr. 1999. Holocene paleoshoreline record in Tonga: Geomorphic features and archaeological implications. *Journal of Coastal Research* 15:682-700.

Ellison, J.C. 1989. Pollen analysis of mangrove sediments as a sea-level indicator: Assessment from Tongatapu, Tonga. *Palaeogeography, Palaeoclimatology, Palaeoecology* 74:327-341.

Green, R.C. 2002. A retrospective view of settlement pattern studies in Samoa. In T.N. Ladefoged and M.W. Graves (eds), *Pacific Landscapes: Archaeological Approaches*, pp. 125-152. Los Osos, California: Easter Island Foundation.

Green, R.C. and D. Anson 2000. Archaeological investigations on Watom Island: Early work, outcomes of recent investigations, and future prospects. *New Zealand Journal of Archaeology* 20(1998): 183-197.

Groube, L.M. 1971. Tonga, Lapita pottery, and Polynesian origins. *Journal of the Polynesian Society* 80:278-316.

Harvey, N., E.J. Barnett, R.P. Bourman and A.P. Belperio 1999. Holocene sea-level change at Port Pirie, South Australia: A contribution to global sea-level rise estimates from tide gauges. *Journal of Coastal Research* 15:607-615.

Israelson, C. and B. Wohlfarth 1999. Timing of the last-interglacial high sea level on the Seychelles Islands, Indian Ocean. *Quaternary Research* 51:306-316.

Kirch, P.V. 1988. *Niuatoputapu, the Prehistory of a Polynesian Chiefdom*. Seattle: Thomas Burke Memorial Washington State Museum Monograph 5.

Kirch, P.V. 1993. The To'aga site: Modelling the morphodynamics of the land-sea interface. In P.V. Kirch and T.L. Hunt (eds), *The To'aga Site: Three Millenia of Polynesian Occupation in the Manu'a Islands, American Samoa*, pp. 31-42. Berkeley: Univerity of California Archaeological Research Facility Contribution No. 51.

Kirch, P.V., T.L. Hunt, L. Nagaoka and J. Tyler 1990. An ancestral Polynesian occupation site at To'aga, Ofu Island, American Samoa. *Archaeology in Oceania* 15:1-15.

Lepofsky, D. 1988. The environmental context of Lapita settlement locations. In P.V. Kirch and T.L. Hunt (eds), *Archaeology of the Lapita Cultural Complex: A Critical Review*, pp. 33-47. Seattle: Thomas Burke Memorial Washington State Museum Research Report No. 5.

Lewis, K.B., R.B. Smith and J.S. Pow 1997. Future sand supplies for Tongatapu, Kingdom of Tonga. In R. Howorth and P. Rodda (eds), *Coastal and Environmental Geoscience Studies of the Southwest Pacific Islands*, pp. 175-191. Suva: South Pacific Applied Geoscience Commission (SOPAC) Technical Bulletin 9.

Mitrovica, J.X. and G.A. Milne 2002. On the origin of late Holocene sea-level highstands within equatorial ocean basins. *Quaternary Science Reviews* 21: 2179-2190.

Mitrovica, J.X. and W.R. Peltier 1991. On postglacial geoid subsidence over the equatorial oceans: *Journal of Geophysical Research* 96:20052-20071.

Nunn, P.D. and F.T. Finau 1995. Holocene emergence of Tongatapu island, south Pacific. *Zeitschrift für Geomorphologie* 39:69-95.

Poulsen, J. 1987. *Early Tongan Prehistory (Vol. I)*. Canberra: Department of Prehistory, Australian National University, Terra Australis 12.

Roy, P.S. 1990. The morphology and surface geology of Tongatapu and Vava'u, Kingdom of Tonga. Suva: South Pacific Applied Geoscience Commission (SOPAC) Technical Report 62.

Roy, P.S. 1997. The morphology and surface geology of the islands of Tongatapu and Vava'u, Kingdom of Tonga. In R. Howorth and P. Rodda (eds.), *Coastal and Environmental Geoscience Studies of the Southwest Pacific Islands*, pp. 153-173. Suva: South Pacific Applied Geoscience Commission (SOPAC) Technical Bulletin 9.

Spenneman, D.H. 1988. *Pathways to the Tongan past*. Nuku'alofa: Tonga Government Printer.

Spenneman, D.H. 1997. A Holocene sea-level history for Tongatapu, Kingdom of Tonga. In R. Howorth and P. Rodda (eds.), *Coastal and Environmental Geoscience Studies of the Southwest Pacific Islands*, pp. 115-151. Suva: South Pacific Applied Geoscience Commission (SOPAC) Technical Bulletin 9.

Taylor, F.W., Jr. 1978. *Quaternary Tectonic and Sea-Level History, Tonga and Fiji, Southwest Pacific*. PhD dissertation, Cornell University.

Taylor, F.W., Jr. and A.L. Bloom 1977. Coral reefs on tectonic blocks, Tonga island arc. *Third International Coral Reef Symposium Proceedings (Miami)* 2:275-281.

Torrence, R., C. Pavlides, P. Jackson and J. Webb 2000. Volcanic disasters and cultural discontinuities in Holocene time in West New Britain, Papua New Guinea. In W.G. McGuire, D.R. Griffiths, P.L. Hancock and I.S. Stewart (eds), *The Archaeology of Geological Catastrophes*, pp. 225-244. London: Geological Society Special Publication 171.

Woodroffe, C.D. 1988. Vertical movements of isolated oceanic islands at plate margins: Evidence from emergent reefs in Tonga (Pacific Ocean), Cayman Islands (Caribbean Sea), and Christmas Island (Indian Ocean). *Zeitschrift für Geomorphologie Supplement-Band* 69:17-37.

Woodroffe, C.D., D.M. Kennedy, D. Hopley, C.E. Rasmussen and S.G. Smithers 2001. Holocene reef growth in Torres Strait. *Marine Geology* 170:331-346.

11

In Search of Lapita and Polynesian Plainware Settlements in Vava'u, Kingdom of Tonga

David V. Burley

Department of Archaeology
Simon Fraser University
Burnaby, B.C. V5A 1S6, Canada
burley@sfu.ca

Introduction

The Vava'u group in the Kingdom of Tonga includes 71 islands with a total land area of 143 km² (Crane 1992:86) (Figure 1). These consist of a mixture of raised coral limestone formations and sand cays, with the largest and most dominating being 'Uta Vava'u (89 km²). 'Uta Vava'u is a hilly and relatively high-island formation rising to cliffed shorelines on the north and west with respective heights of 179 m and 213 m. A friable tephra-based clay loam dominates Vava'u soils and supports a productive agricultural base. The majority of reefs and shoals with substantive biogenic productivity occur to the south and east as also do most of the sand cays. Respectively to the southwest and northwest of the coral limestone islands are Late and Fonualei. These are islands of the Tofua volcanic arc with active volcanism occurring within the past two centuries. The contemporary population of Vava'u is centred on the coral limestone islands.

The islands of Vava'u are positioned along the southwest to northeast chain of forearc islands atop the Tongan platform. Seasonal southeast trade winds facilitate maritime travel along this chain from Tongatapu in the south, to Ha'apai in central Tonga, to Vava'u, and subsequently on to Niuatoputapu and Samoa (Figure 1). The presence of this sailing corridor, the richness of agricultural soils throughout Vava'u, and the sizeable area of land available for settlement lead to an expectation of both early settlement and a sizeable population in prehistory. Previous archaeological surveys however (Burley 1996; Davidson 1971), failed to find more than a marginal presence of peoples in the initial Lapita settlement period and later Polynesian Plainware phase. This scarcity of ceramic period sites seemed not only anomalous but in direct contrast to the high density of such sites in the Ha'apai and Tongatapu island groups, particularly in the Polynesian Plainware phase (Burley 1998; Burley et al. 1999, 2001).

Archaeological studies were carried out in Vava'u between 2003 and 2005 to resolve the question of ceramic period occupation, to document first settlement by Lapita peoples and to record subsequent transformations in the Polynesian Plainware phase. Initial survey in 2003 included a systematic survey of habitable raised coral limestone islands, a brief reconnaissance of the volcanic island of Late, and test excavations

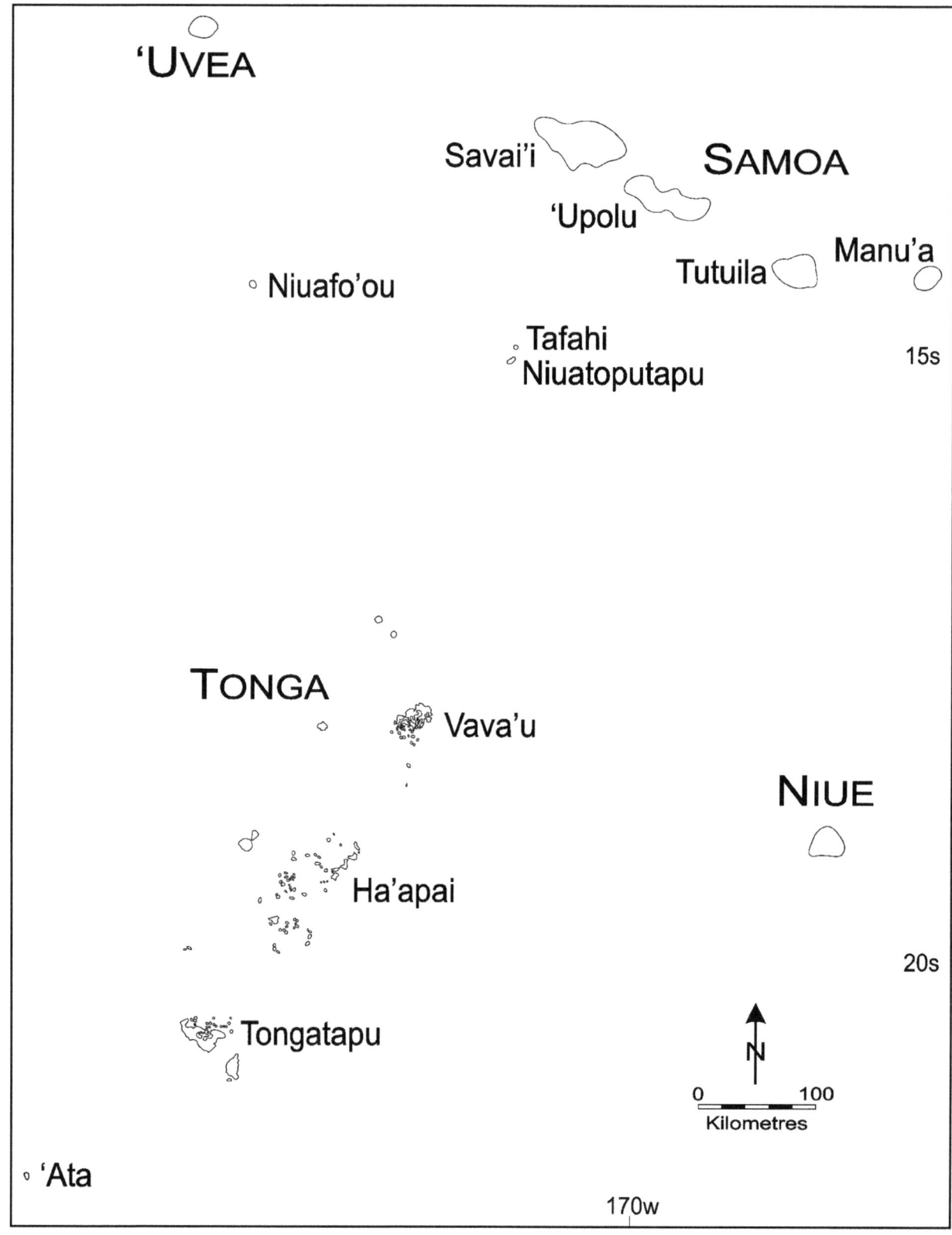

Figure 1. Map illustrating location of Vava'u relative to other islands along the Tongan/Samoan travel corridor.

at ceramic period sites where potential appeared to be present for larger scale excavation. Excavations were conducted in 2004 and 2005 at four sites, each having Lapita and Polynesian Plainware phase occupation strata. In the following paper, I present results of the survey and consequential interpretations for early settlement processes and patterns in Tongan prehistory. The excavation results provide a settlement chronology and inform interpretation but are not reported upon in any degree of detail. These data only now are being analysed. The findings of the Vava'u project are important beyond the understanding of Tongan settlement progression. They document and reflect upon the processes of Lapita expansion as it moved northward into Niuatoputapu and Samoa, with important implications for population distributions in the initial half millennium of the Polynesian Plainware phase in west Polynesia.

Previous Research and Strategising a Survey Approach

In 1920/1921, William McKern (1929) of the Bayard Dominick Expedition to Tonga reported 15 archaeological sites in Vava'u, most being earthen mounds or platforms. None of these included ceramic sherds, nor did McKern document "kitchen middens" as were present on Tongatapu. Janet Davidson, then of the Auckland Institute and Museum, undertook the first expansive archaeological survey of Vava'u almost a half century later in 1969. This was predicated on the "dearth of knowledge" of this "large and fertile area" (Davidson 1971:29), especially in light of work previously carried out on Tongatapu (Groube 1971; Poulsen 1987). Davidson (1971:29) established three goals for the project - 1) to identify the major categories of field monuments in Vava'u; 2) to investigate the occurrence of the "distinctive pottery characteristic of Tongatapu"; and 3) to assess the potential for excavation and settlement pattern survey. Her coverage included both the main island of 'Uta Vava'u as well as other principal islands in the group. With respect to Davidson's second goal focusing upon ceramic period sites, the results were tentative. Ceramics were found "in most of the areas searched" but the vast majority consisted of "weathered plain body sherds .... sufficient only to indicate that at some time in the past pottery was in use somewhere in the general vicinity" (Davidson 1971:37-38). Davidson nevertheless concluded that a next step "must be the excavation of various sorts of site in Vava'u" and that several "pottery-bearing sites offer good prospects for the investigation of earlier periods" (Davidson 1971:37-38).

From 1990 to the present, I have carried out a study of Lapita colonisation and its transformation into the Polynesian Plainware phase in southern and central Tonga. This has involved survey and excavations throughout the Ha'apai islands (1990-1992, 1995-1997) as well as on Tongatapu (1998-1999). This project provides an abundance of new data, and it has refined understanding of Lapita/Plainware settlement chronology, settlement pattern, subsistence economy, anthropogenic impacts on island landscapes and other issues (Burley 1998; Burley et al. 1995, 1999, 2001). Occasional visits to and limited survey in Vava'u for comparative purpose found little beyond Davidson's observations of widely dispersed weathered sherds (Burley 1996). Vava'u, at least from the observations of Davidson and myself, had far fewer ceramic period sites than on Tongatapu or the islands of Ha'apai, and this implied a more restricted occupation and population size during the Lapita and Polynesian Plainware phases. Alternatively, it might be argued that ceramic sites in Vava'u are deeply buried or destroyed as a consequence of regional geomorphological processes. This is proposed for Samoa (Clark 1996; Green 2002) where earlier ceramic sites similarly are limited. Resolution of this problem was considered critical for the longer-term study of first Tongan settlement and its aftermath throughout the archipelago.

The importance of coastal geomorphological processes and sea levels in Tonga was recognised early on during archaeological survey in Ha'apai. Geologist William Dickinson was invited to address these issues, and his findings became essential for site discovery as well as interpretation of site location on island landscapes (Dickinson et al. 1994, 1999). Relative sea level in Tonga at the time of first Lapita occupation was as much as 2 m higher than present, resulting from a mid-Holocene hydro-isostatic highstand throughout the central South Pacific region. Sea levels then fell over the next millennium, ultimately stabilising during the late Polynesian Plainware phase. The impact of declining sea levels for shoreline progradation in Tonga, however, is regionally varied. The Tongan archipelago is cross cut by transverse geological faults that define a series of discrete structural blocks. Each block is independent, subsiding or emerging at different rates, and this serves to amplify or negate the effects of sea level fall for island shorelines. For example, the Lapita-age palaeoshoreline in the Hahake block of northern Ha'apai is elevated and far inland of the present shore; that in the Nomuka block further to the south is now submerged as a result of subsidence. Extension of Dickinson's palaeoshoreline surveys to Vava'u in the 1990s led to a hypothesis that the Vava'u block subsides at a rate equivalent to sea level decline since mid-Holocene times (Dickinson et al. 1999:695). Lapita-age shorelines in Vava'u, then, are consistent with or close to modern shorelines throughout the group today. This hypothesis was proven robust in 2003 through the discovery of Lapita and Polynesian Plainware sites in contemporary back-beach settings on multiple islands in the group (Dickinson and Burley 2007).

Dickinson's hypothesis on the concurrence of Lapita-age and contemporary shorelines was central to the development of the 2003 Vava'u survey strategy. Island coastlines could be quickly reconnoitered by boat with high potential areas identified for further examination. A combination of three factors determined areas to have high potential. First there had to be ease of access to the beach for Lapita sailing canoes. Second, an adjacent reef flat for subsistence foraging was considered important. And third, a back-beach sand flat or coastal strip had to be sufficiently large and protected to accommodate settlement. Not surprisingly this combination of features on a majority of islands is coincident with a present day village. Shorelines on 'Uta Vava'u predominantly are cliffed, steeply sloped or otherwise inaccessible to watercraft. Survey here focused first along lower-lying coastal margins regardless of access, and then in upland villages. On both 'Uta Vava'u and other islands, survey methods incorporated examination of subsurface exposures for ceramics or midden-related deposits, auger testing where subsurface exposures were limited, and in a smaller number of cases controlled test excavations in shell midden deposits where ceramics were not present on the surface. Recently ploughed or planted gardens outside of villages occasionally were examined to extend survey coverage and, where possible, back beaches on exposed windward coasts also were surveyed. Finally, village residents were interviewed for site knowledge, particularly for the location of *kolo motua* (old villages).

Survey Results

The Vava'u survey examined 24 islands in 2003, including 'Uta Vava'u and Late, with varying degrees of coverage (Table 1). Of these islands, 11 are without contemporary villages. In a few cases where an island was considered to have a high potential for early settlement, but where a site was not located (Ovaka, Euakafa), re-examination was carried out in subsequent field seasons. In the case of Fua'amotu in far southern Vava'u, vegetation of the coastal fringe and back beach was impenetrable, and survey was abandoned. The volcanic island of Late is approximately 60 km distant from western Vava'u with shore access made difficult by the absence of a protective fringing reef. Survey here was limited to but a few hours of time, the principal goal being to collect samples of andesitic basalt beach cobbles for source identification.

Notwithstanding cases such as Fua'amotu and Late, overall survey coverage was comprehensive, and all major islands of the Vava'u group have been inspected. It is conceivable that deeply buried sites have been missed, and that numerous scatters of surface ceramics have gone unrecorded in inland areas, especially on 'Uta Vava'u. I believe, nevertheless, that the survey results reasonably represent both settlement distribution and population for Lapita and Polynesian Plainware phases in Vava'u. Survey results (Table 1)(Figures 2 and

Table 1. Islands upon which archaeological survey in Vava'u was conducted and the results. Plainware midden refers to sites with in situ buried deposits. The table does not include the high volcanic island of Late.

	Island Size	Present Villages	Lapita Site	Plainware midden	Plainware scatters
North					
'Uta Vava'u	89 km²	17	0	2	3
Southeast					
Koloa	2 km²	2	0	1	1
Faioa	< 1 km²	0	0	0	0
'Umuna	< 1 km²	0	0	1	0
Kenutu	< 1 km²	0	0	0	1
Okoa	< 1 km²	1	0	0	1
'Olo'ua	< 1 km²	1	0	0	1
Mafana	< 1 km²	0	1	0	0
Ofu	1.2 km²	1	1	1	1
Southcentral					
Pangaimotu	8.8 km²	1	1	2	4
Tapana	< 1 km²	0	0	1	0
Fua'amotu	< 1 km²	0	0	0	0
'Utungake	< 1 km²	2	0	0	2
Kapa	6 km²	3	2	3	2
Taunga	< 1 km²	1	0	1	1
Euakafa	1 km²	0	0	0	0
'Euaiki	< 1 km²	0	0	0	0
Southwest					
Lape	< 1 km²	1	0	0	0
Avalau	< 1 km²	0	0	0	0
Nuapapu	2.7 km²	2	0	0	1
Vaka'eitu	1 km²	0	0	0	1
Ovaka	1.3 km²	1	0	0	0
Hunga	5 km²	1	0	0	1
Total		34	5	12	20

3) include the discovery of five settlement locales with decorated Lapita ceramics and 12 sites with buried Polynesian Plainware occupations. Of the latter, four overlay the previously noted Lapita phase components. Twenty ceramic scatters associated with the Polynesian Plainware phase were also documented. All Lapita phase sites were test excavated to establish integrity, depth, stratigraphy and excavation potential. Four of these were excavated more fully in 2004 and 2005, each including an overlying Polynesian Plainware phase component (Table 2). Three Polynesian Plainware sites also were tested in 2003.

Lapita Phase Settlement in Vava'u

Prior to the 2003 survey, the only documented Lapita ceramics from Vava'u were two surface finds from the village of 'Otea on Kapa Island by Davidson (1971:38; pers. comm.). Survey, auger testing and test excavations located five sites with buried Lapita components on Mafana, Ofu, Pangaimotu (Vuna site)

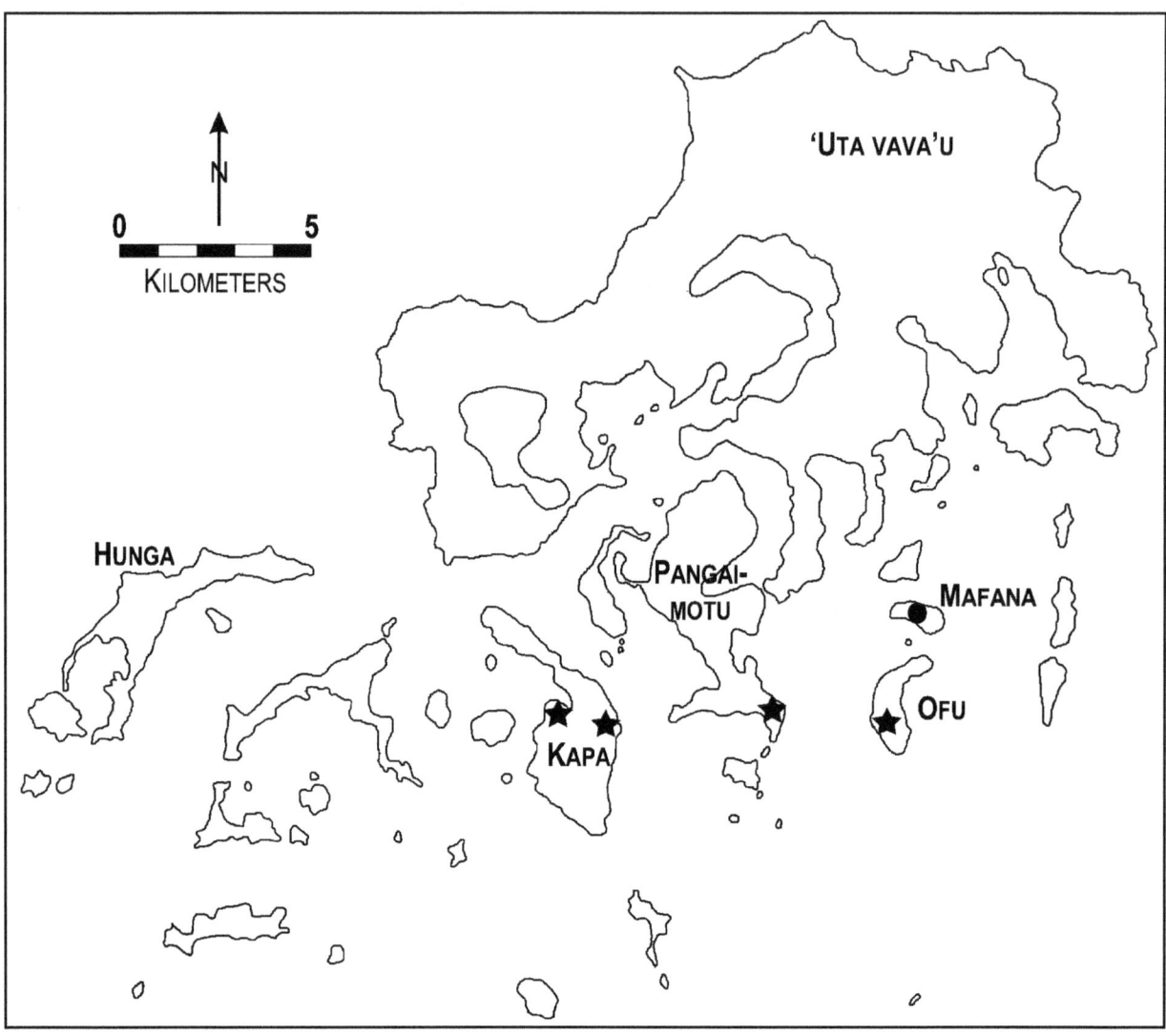

Figure 2. Map of Lapita site locations in Vava'u. Stars represent excavated sites.

and Kapa ('Otea and Falevai sites) islands. With the exception of Mafana, these sites are characteristically positioned on back beach sand flats or dunes, they face or are close to a collecting reef, and they have easy access for sailing canoes. They also include long-term continuity of occupation with substantial Polynesian Plainware phase components overlying the Lapita settlement. Mafana is unique in that it has no Plainware component and it is less than 400 m² in overall size. It is back from the shore of a very small bay with decorated Lapita sherds scattered through a clay loam agricultural soil rather than a back beach sand. Given its close proximity to the Ofu site, Mafana most likely is a special-use locale or a short-lived outlier of that settlement. The only other notable variation in the five Lapita sites occurs at Falevai on Kapa Island. Here first settlement occurred at the end of the Lapita period in

Table 2. Summary information for Lapita/Polynesian Plainware phase site excavations in Vava'u, 2004-2005.

	Ofu	**Vuna**	**Otea**	**Falevai**
Island	Ofu	Pangaimotu	Kapa	Kapa
Depth	1.0 m	1.6 m	2.5 m	2.0 m
Size	1500 m²	1500 m²	800 m²	600 m²
Excavation	22 m²	26 m²	16 m²	13 m²
C14 dates	2	3	3	3
Total ceramics	13118	23143	18414	10195
Decorated	702	743	557	61
Non ceramic	189	290	155	70
Year	2005	2004	2004	2004

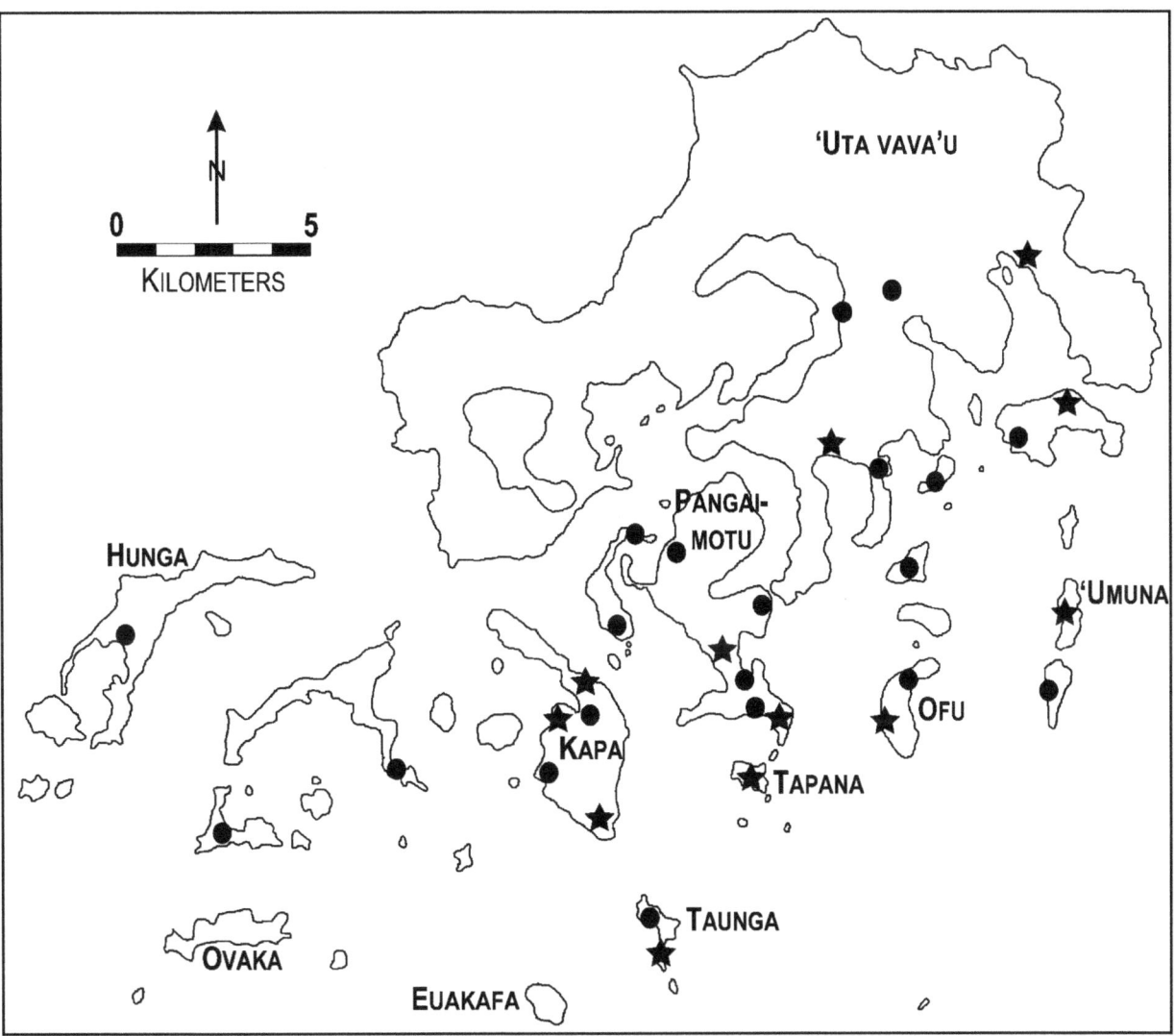

Figure 3. Map of Polynesian Plainware phase sites in Vava'u. Stars represent sites with *in situ* buried deposits while dots are surface scatters.

Vava'u, and only a very small assemblage of decorated Lapita ceramics occurs in the site's lowest level (Connaughton, this volume)

From 2004/2005 excavations at the Ofu, Vuna, 'Otea and Falevai sites, 11 AMS radiocarbon dates were acquired and these provide a coherent chronology for the initial Lapita occupation of Vava'u as well as its transition to the Polynesian Plainware phase (Burley and Connaughton in press) (Table 3). The earliest radiocarbon date comes from Ofu and documents first landfall by 2800 cal BP or slightly earlier. Circumstantial support for Ofu as a first settlement also is present through an abundant presence of indigenous birds and turtle in the Lapita deposit, and in preliminary impressions of the decorated ceramic assemblage. Significantly, however, Lapita strata radiocarbon dates from each of the four sites substantially overlap at 2-σ and it seems certain that all were simultaneously occupied sometime between 2800 and 2750 BP. Also significant, and as described by Connaughton (this volume), radiocarbon dates from Falevai indicate the disappearance of decorated Lapita pottery and the beginning of the Polynesian Plainware phase within a century of first Lapita presence in Vava'u.

The occurrence of but five Lapita sites in Vava'u with only three (Vuna, Ofu and 'Otea) having substance is informative. First, it supports a hypothesis that the Lapita population of Vava'u was small during the initial settlement phase of Tonga. Second, the location of the three sites and their contexts illustrate a settlement pattern that is identical to that in Ha'apai (Burley *et al.* 1999). That is, settlement locales were

Table 3. Radiocarbon dates for Lapita/Polynesian Plainware site excavations in Vava'u, 2004-2005. Calibrations were undertaken using the CALIB 5.1 program (Stuiver and Reimer 2005) and the southern hemisphere calibration curve SHCal04 (McCormac et al. 2004).

Site	CAMS Ref	Date BP	Cal 1σ BP	d 13C	Phase
Ofu	119699	2626 ± 35	2755-2545 BP	-25.9	Lapita
Ofu	119700	2765 ± 35	2854-2769 BP	-26.9	Lapita
Otea	119697	1615 ± 35	1516-1407 BP	-28.8	Plainware
Otea	119698	2505 ± 30	2693-2363 BP	-24.0	Lapita
Otea	119701	2705 ± 35	2790-2740 BP	-28.9	Lapita
Vuna	111659	2650 ± 35	2762-2621 BP	-24.6	Lapita
Vuna	111661	2480 ± 30	2668-2358 BP	-25.5	Lapita
Vuna	111662	2715 ± 35	2837-2744 BP	-25.8	Lapita
Falevai	119694	2500 ± 35	2685-2362 BP	-27.9	Plainware
Falevai	119695	2645 ± 35	2760-2620 BP	-28.2	Plainware
Falevai	119696	2685 ± 35	2779-2733 BP	-27.9	Lapita

chosen on each of Ofu, Pangaimotu and Kapa islands for their access to open water, their position relative to a foraging reef, and for the presence of a back beach setting in which to establish a hamlet. And third, Lapita settlement was concentrated in the south of Vava'u in immediate proximity to a direct sailing corridor back to a homeland in Ha'apai or Tongatapu.

As is characteristic of the Lapita phase in other areas of Tonga, the archaeological record in Vava'u illustrates foraging to have both been productive and a substantive component of subsistence activities. Roy (1997:170) has noted that "low nutrient levels or other water quality factors" have led to low biogenic productivity in western Vava'u as compared to the east. This helps to explain the absence of Lapita sites on western islands, not the least including Ovaka, an island with optimal settlement potential that was unsuccessfully surveyed on a number of occasions. I suggest elsewhere that Lapita agricultural activity in Tonga may have been limited to "a low-energy swidden-type cultivation system" and it was secondary to foraging in relative importance for settlement location (Burley 1998:355). Lapita sites in Vava'u potentially contradict this characterisation. All five incorporate a settlement feature that speaks, at least circumstantially, to early horticultural practice as part of the colonizing process. Each is immediately adjacent or to the front of a small inland swale where *Colocasia* and/or *Cyrtosperma* taro could be grown with reasonable success (Kirch 1997:211).

Polynesian Plainware Phase Occupation in Vava'u

The Polynesian Plainware phase of central and southern Tonga occurs between c. 2600 and 1550 BP. It is marked by the complete loss of decorated Lapita ceramics, by a reduction in diversity of ceramic vessel types, by an expansion of population and settlement to inland and offshore locations, and by a transition in economy where agricultural intensification occurs, and where agricultural production becomes the centre of subsistence activities (Burley 1998:350-365). I have estimated that even a small population of between 500 and 600 individuals at the end of the Lapita phase in Tonga would lead to full land capacity in the interval 2150 to 1750 BP based on an exponential growth rate of 0.005 - 0.008 (Burley in press). The archaeological records of Tongatapu and Ha'apai clearly support this projection with widespread and dense distributions of Plainware sites in even marginal areas. In some cases the spatial extent of the Polynesian Plainware site indicates substantial growth over time to form a village-sized complex. As Groube (1971:291) described, pottery became so abundant along the shore of Fanga'Uta Lagoon on Tongatapu that Tongans today consider it part of the soil itself. He also noted:

> Rubbish dumps, wells, latrines, agricultural activities, house-building, earth-oven construction and the myriad destructive acts of everyday living are constantly stirring the deposits and shattering the fragments of pottery into ever smaller pieces. It is impossible in these areas today to dig a ditch or earth oven, fill in a hole or build a house platform without uncovering potsherds.

The results of the 2003 archaeological survey identify Vava'u as a significant exception to this description. Polynesian Plainware sites in Vava'u are only marginally more abundant than those of the Lapita period unless one counts scatters of surface sherds. And most of the latter include no more than a handful of specimens which, as Davidson concluded, serves only to say that pottery was used somewhere in the vicinity.

Polynesian Plainware ceramic sites in Vava'u again are concentrated in the southeast and south central islands following the pattern established in Lapita times, particularly on the islands of Pangaimotu and Kapa. This includes not only continuity of occupation at earlier Lapita sites, but expanded numbers of settlements on these larger islands. More ephemeral hamlets also appear on the smaller islands of Koloa, 'Umuna, Tapana and Taunga as well as on 'Uta Vava'u in two locales. Reduced biogenic productivity in western Vava'u, arguably, continued to be a factor for settlement distribution. Preliminary observation of ceramic rim forms suggests most of the ephemeral hamlets on small islands, as well as surface scatters, are associated with the last half of the Polynesian Plainware phase from c. 1950 BP onward. If this is true, then the limited population present in the Lapita period continued to be small throughout the first half of the Polynesian Plainware phase. A substantial rise in population densities on Tongatapu and Ha'apai, and the possibilities for in-migration from both, may have fueled population expansion in Vava'u at or near the end of the Plainware period.

Excavation of Polynesian Plainware sites was limited to strata superimposed over Lapita levels at Ofu, Vuna, 'Otea and Falevai. Each, however, includes a Polynesian Plainware occupation extending through a full extent of the phase. Analyses of these assemblages, once complete, provide detailed information on stylistic and other change in ceramics and non-ceramic artifacts. Importantly, all excavated Polynesian Plainware phase occupations incorporate flakes of volcanic glass. Similar flakes in assemblages from Ha'apai are geochemically sourced to Tafahi, an island immediately north of Niuatoputapu (Sheppard pers. comm.). Tafahi origins are expected for the Vava'u materials indicating inter-island voyaging northward if not formalised exchange (Kirch 1988). Collection of andesitic-basalt beach cobbles from the volcanic outlier of Late provides secure samples for geochemical characterisation. Unexpectedly, Late basalt was found distinguishable from other Tongan basalts on the basis of colour, ranging from a darker blue/black with greenish hue to a lighter gray-green. A Late basalt adze was excavated from an upper Polynesian Plainware level at 'Otea, and several other specimens were recovered from Falevai. Settlement of the high volcanic island of Late, then, can be hypothesised no later than the Plainware phase.

Matters Arising

Without detailed analysis of the excavated assemblages, including fauna, a definitive interpretation of the Lapita and Polynesian Plainware phase occupation in Vava'u is not feasible at this stage. At the same time, knowledge of site distributions, contexts, and radiocarbon dates provide new and significant insight into the processes of settlement. They also raise questions with significant implications for Tongan prehistory specifically, and settlement in West Polynesia in general. As a conclusion to this paper, these insights, and the matters arising are briefly examined.

Radiocarbon dates for first Lapita settlement in Vava'u suggest an initial occupation on the island of Ofu by c. 2800 BP but with expansion to Pangaimotu and Kapa islands shortly thereafter. In relative comparison to radiocarbon dates from Tongatapu and Ha'apai, Vava'u dates are not appreciably later. Rather, the calibrated

2-σ range for Lapita dates throughout Tonga sufficiently overlaps to make them indistinguishable. Ceramic types of Western Lapita aspect at the site of Nukuleka on Tongatapu, combined with slightly earlier radiocarbon dates, indicate the southern island was colonized first (Burley and Dickinson 2001; Burley and Connaughton in press). Northern exploration and expansion into Ha'apai, Vava'u, Niuatoputapu, Samoa and possibly Uvea and Futuna would have taken place within a half century time span, no doubt facilitated by seasonal southeast tradewinds and a natural sailing corridor on a southwest to northeast axis.

None of the Vava'u Lapita sites exceed 1500 m^2 in areal extent, indicating small hamlet-sized communities. The exclusive location of these sites on southeast and south central coral limestone islands is argued to be a consequence of reduced biogenic productivity in the western islands. While this is not surprising given the importance of reef foraging to Lapita settlement pattern on Tongatapu and Ha'apai, the fact that it continued to influence site distribution through at least the first half of the Polynesian Plainware phase does seem noteworthy. That some degree of horticulture was practiced from the Lapita phase onward also is evident. The presence of a small inland swale at all Lapita sites suggests this terrain feature was being sought out for wet taro production. Unfortunately the data at hand do not provide insight into external relations and the position of Vava'u within the Eastern Lapita province. The sites on Ofu, Pangaimotu and Kapa islands are positioned at the southern entry to Vava'u, and in close proximity to open water and the sailing corridor back to Ha'apai and Tongatapu. This hints at Vava'u being a frontier periphery, a characterisation supported by the limited population size that is assumed to be present.

Radiocarbon dates from the Falevai site on Kapa Island illustrate an immediate loss of decorated ceramics shortly after Lapita expansion into Vava'u. Estimated to fall in the interval 2750-2700 BP (Burley and Connaughton in press), this is approximately 100 to 150 years earlier than is projected for Ha'apai and Tongatapu (Burley 1998). Why this would be the case is difficult to determine with any degree of certainty. Speculatively, geographic isolation and the effective number of potters are factors likely to be involved. Both Clark (1993) and Kirch (1993) associate Polynesian Plainware ceramics with early radiocarbon dates and the earliest settlement phase in Samoa. The Vava'u pattern, then, may not be in isolation, and possibly indicative of a trend found in northward expansion to Samoa. Intermediate between Vava'u and Samoa is Niuatoputapu where a single early Eastern Lapita site occurs. Unfortunately "*precise* beginning and end dates" for the period of dentate stamped ceramics cannot "be fixed give the nature of the ^{14}C corpus" (Kirch 1988:241, italics in original). For Uvea, Sand (1996) documents a Lapita presence at the site of 'Utuleve almost identical in age and site features to those on Vava'u. He (1996:108) further opines that the limited presence of Lapita sites on Uvea suggests "the production of dentate-stamped Lapita pottery was limited to a few generations". The only potential conflict with claims for an early northern transition to the Polynesian Plainware phase occurs on Futuna. Eastern Lapita dentate stamped ceramics occur there in a somewhat later context, one potentially dating to the interval 2650-2350 BP (Sand 1990:130-131).

Survey results in Vava'u are striking for the lack of success in finding abundant and extensive occupation of the islands during both Lapita and Polynesian Plainware times. Davidson's survey in 1969 clearly forecast this result. This failure is not the consequence of destructive geomorphological processes or sea level change. Rather, with island emergence in tandem with sea level fall, Lapita-age paleoshorelines remain consistent with those present today. Admittedly additional ceramic period sites will be discovered in future years and added to the Vava'u inventory. Expansive surveys by Davidson and the one reported here, nevertheless, securely document a distribution pattern at odds with settlement and demographic processes in Ha'apai and on Tongatapu. In Vava'u, a small founding population in Lapita times did not grow substantially for the next several hundred years while populations on Tongatapu and Ha'apai were significantly on the rise. On the shores of Fanga'Uta Lagoon, for example, the founding site of Nukuleka expanded to no less than 17 other settlements during the Lapita phase alone, providing a settlement aggregation potentially larger than that of the Polynesian Plainware phase in Vava'u over a several hundred year time span.

The Lapita/Polynesian Plainware settlement of Vava'u, or lack thereof, finds intriguing parallels in Samoa. It has potential importance, therefore, for explaining or reflecting upon the Samoan case. In Samoa there is but a single site with decorated Lapita ceramics reported on 'Upolu, and only a very small number of other sites predating 2250 BP. Green (2002:131) explains this distribution as a result of geological processes that have destroyed, deeply buried, capped or submerged the early settlement landscape. Among these processes are coastal subsidence on 'Upolu and Savai'i, active volcanism on Savai'i, colluvial infilling of valley floors on Tutuila, and progradation of the coastal plain on Ofu in the Manu'a group. These processes and their potential impact on the Samoan archaeological record cannot be denied. At the same time one cannot ignore the failure of archaeologists to find such sites on coastal landforms that have not been affected. This is especially so in American Samoa where cultural resource management programs have required intensive survey, test excavations and excavation projects over the past two decades. The lack of early ceramic sites in American Samoa, and concerns for a claim of early Polynesian Plainware occupation at A'oa on Tutuila, lead Addison (pers. comm.) to a similar conclusion. Indeed, he now believes the absence of early ceramic sites in Samoa speaks not only to a highly restricted pre-2250 BP population but possibly even abandonment after initial Lapita exploration. That Samoa was not totally abandoned in the early Polynesian Plainware phase is documented at the site of To'aga on Ofu island in American Samoa (Kirch and Hunt 1993). Similarly, earlier Plainware phase occupations are present on Niuatoputapu (Kirch 1988) and Uvea (Sand 1996). How dense a population these sites represent during the initial half of the Polynesian Plainware phase cannot be determined however. A hypothesis that Vava'u and islands further to the north including Samoa were part of a low population density frontier remains plausible for the period up to c. 2250 BP.

Acknowledgements

Field work in Vava'u was funded through a research grant from the Social Sciences and Humanities Research Council of Canada. I gratefully acknowledge this support. I also thank the Government of Tonga for assistance and support for the project, especially that given by the late 'Akauola, Governor of Vava'u. Finally I thank Andrew Barton of Simon Fraser University for assistance in preparation of the figures.

References

Burley, D. V. 1996. Archaeological Survey of Euakafa and Taunga Islands Vava'u and the Legend of Talafaiva. Unpublished report prepared for Honourable 'Akauola. On file with author, Simon Fraser University, Burnaby.

Burley, D. V. 1998. Tongan archaeology and the Tongan past: 2850-150 BP. *Journal of World Prehistory* 12:337-392.

Burley, D. V. in press Archaeological demography and population growth in the Kingdom of Tonga - 950 BC to the historic era. In P. V. Kirch and J. Rallu (eds.), *Long Term Demographic History in the Pacific Islands*. Honolulu: University of Hawaii Press.

Burley, D. V. and S. Connaughton in press. First Lapita settlement and its chronology in Vava'u, Kingdom of Tonga. *Radiocarbon* 49(1).

Burley, D. V. and W. R. Dickinson 2001. Origin and significance of a founding settlement in Oceania. *PNAS* 98:11829-11831.

Burley, D. V., E. Nelson and R. Shutler Jr. 1995. Rethinking Lapita chronology in Ha'apai. *Archaeology in Oceania* 30:132-134.

Burley, D. V., E. Nelson and R. Shutler Jr. 1999. A radiocarbon chronology for the Eastern Lapita frontier in Tonga. *Archaeology in Oceania* 34:59-72.

Burley, D. V., W. R. Dickinson, A. Barton and R. Shutler Jr. 2001. Lapita on the periphery: New data on old problems in the Kingdom of Tonga. *Archaeology in Oceania* 36:89-104.

Clark J. 1993. Radiocarbon dates from American Samoa. *Radiocarbon* 35:323-330.

Clark J. 1996. Samoan prehistory in review. In J.M. Davidson, G. Irwin, B.F. Leach, A. Pawley and D. Brown (eds), *Oceanic Culture History: Essays in Honour of Roger Green*, pp. 445-460. Dunedin: New Zealand Archaeological Association Special Publication.

Crane, W. 1992. *The Environment of Tonga A Geography Resource*. Lower Hutt: Wendy Crane Books.

Davidson, J. 1971. Preliminary report on archaeological survey in the Vava'u Group Tonga. In R. Fraser (ed.), *Cook Bicentenary Expedition in the Southwest Pacific*, pp. 29-40. Wellington: Royal Society of New Zealand Bulletin 8.

Dickinson, W. R. and D. V. Burley 2007. Geoarchaeology of Tonga: geotectonic and geomorphic controls. *Geoarchaeology* 22:229-259.

Dickinson, W. R., D. V. Burley and R. Shutler Jr. 1994. Impact of hydro-isostatic Holocene sea-level change on the geologic context of islands archaeological sites, northern Ha'apai group, Kingdom of Tonga. *Geoarchaeology* 9:85-111.

Dickinson, W. R., D. V. Burley and R. Shutler Jr. 1999. Holocene paleoshoreline record in Tonga: Geomorphic features and archaeological implications. *Journal of Coastal Research* 15:682-700.

Green, R. C. 2002. A retrospective review of settlement pattern studies in Samoa. In T. Ladefoged and M. Graves (eds), *Pacific Landscapes Archaeological Approaches*, pp. 125-152. Los Osos, California: The Easter Island Foundation.

Groube, L. 1971. Tonga, Lapita pottery and Polynesian origins. *Journal of the Polynesian Society* 80:278-316.

Kirch, P. V. 1988 *Niuatoputapu: The Prehistory of a Polynesian Chiefdom*. Seattle: The Thomas Burke Memorial Washington State Museum Monograph No.5.

Kirch, P. V. 1993 Radiocarbon chronology of the To'aga site. In P.V. and T. L. Hunt (eds), *The To'aga Site, Three Millennia of Polynesian Occupation in the Manu'a Islands, American* Samoa, pp. 85-92. Berkeley: University of California Archaeological Research Facility, Contribution No. 51.

Kirch, P. V. 1997 *The Lapita People: Ancestors of the Oceanic World*. Oxford: Blackwell.

Kirch, P. V. and R.C. Green 2001. *Hawaiiki, Ancestral Polynesia: An Essay in Historical Anthropology*. Cambridge: Cambridge University Press.

Kirch, P. V. and T. L. Hunt (eds) 1993. *The To'aga Site, Three Millennia of Polynesian Occupation in the Manu'a Islands American Samoa*. Berkeley: University of California Archaeological Research Facility, Contribution No. 51.

McKern, W. C. 1929. *The Archaeology of Tonga*. Honolulu: B. P. Bishop Museum, Bulletin 60.

Poulsen, J. 1987. *Early Tongan Prehistory: The Lapita Period on Tongatapu and its Relationships*. Canberra: Department of Prehistory, The Australian National University. Terra Australis 12.

Roy, P.S. 1997. The morphology and surface geology of the islands of Tongatapu and Vava'u, Kingdom of Tonga. In A. Sherwood (compiler), *Coastal and Environmental Geoscience Studies of the Southwest Pacific Islands*, pp. 153-173. SOPAC Technical Bulletin 9.

Sand, C. 1990. The ceramic chronology of Futuna and Alofi: An overview. In M. Spriggs (ed.), *Lapita Design, Form and Composition*, pp.123-133. Canberra: Department of Prehistory, The Australian National University. Occasional Papers in Prehistory 19.

Sand, C. 1996. Archaeological research on Uvea Island, Western Polynesia. *New Zealand Journal of Archaeology* 18: 91-123.

Stuiver, M. and P.J. Reimer 2005. Radiocarbon calibration program CALIB rev. 5.1 < http://calib.qub.ac.uk/calib >.

12

Can We Dig It? Archaeology of Ancestral Polynesian Society in Tonga: A First Look from Falevai

Sean P. Connaughton

Department of Archaeology
Simon Fraser University
8888 University Drive
Burnaby, British Columbia
V5A 3R5 Canada
spconnau@sfu.ca

Introduction

Polynesian culture has long captivated the attention of both academic researchers and the wider public. A primary interest for archaeologists has been the explanation and understanding of the development of Polynesian cultures, which it has been proposed, have their roots in an ancestral homeland situated in western Polynesia and more specifically Tonga and Samoa (Burley 1998; Groube 1971; Kirch 1984, 1997; Kirch and Green 2001). However, an ongoing debate in Pacific anthropology is whether archaeologists can convincingly identify and explain the historical trajectory of an Ancestral Polynesian Society (APS) (Kirch and Green 2001; Smith 2002). Kirch and Green (2001) argue that Western Polynesian culture developed from a founding Eastern Lapita base and succeeding Ancestral Polynesian Society. The most visible cultural marker distinguishing these ancestral Polynesians is plain earthenware pottery, which characterises archaeological assemblages for a millennium following the Lapita phase. Smith (2002) on the other hand, has asserted that the archaeological evidence does not support the concept of a specifically proto-Polynesian ancestral society in Western Polynesia during the ceramic phase.

Critical to understanding ancestral Polynesian development is the sequence of ceramic transition from the colonising Eastern Lapita phase to the subsequent Polynesian Plainware phase. I contend that this archaeological transition and succeeding development of Ancestral Polynesian Society in the Polynesian Plainware phase reflects internal social and economic change, with limited influence from groups outside of Tonga. This paper outlines recent arguments for a Polynesian Homeland being evident in Tonga and Samoa as well as presenting an overview of fieldwork undertaken in 2005 at the Lapita/Polynesian Plainware site

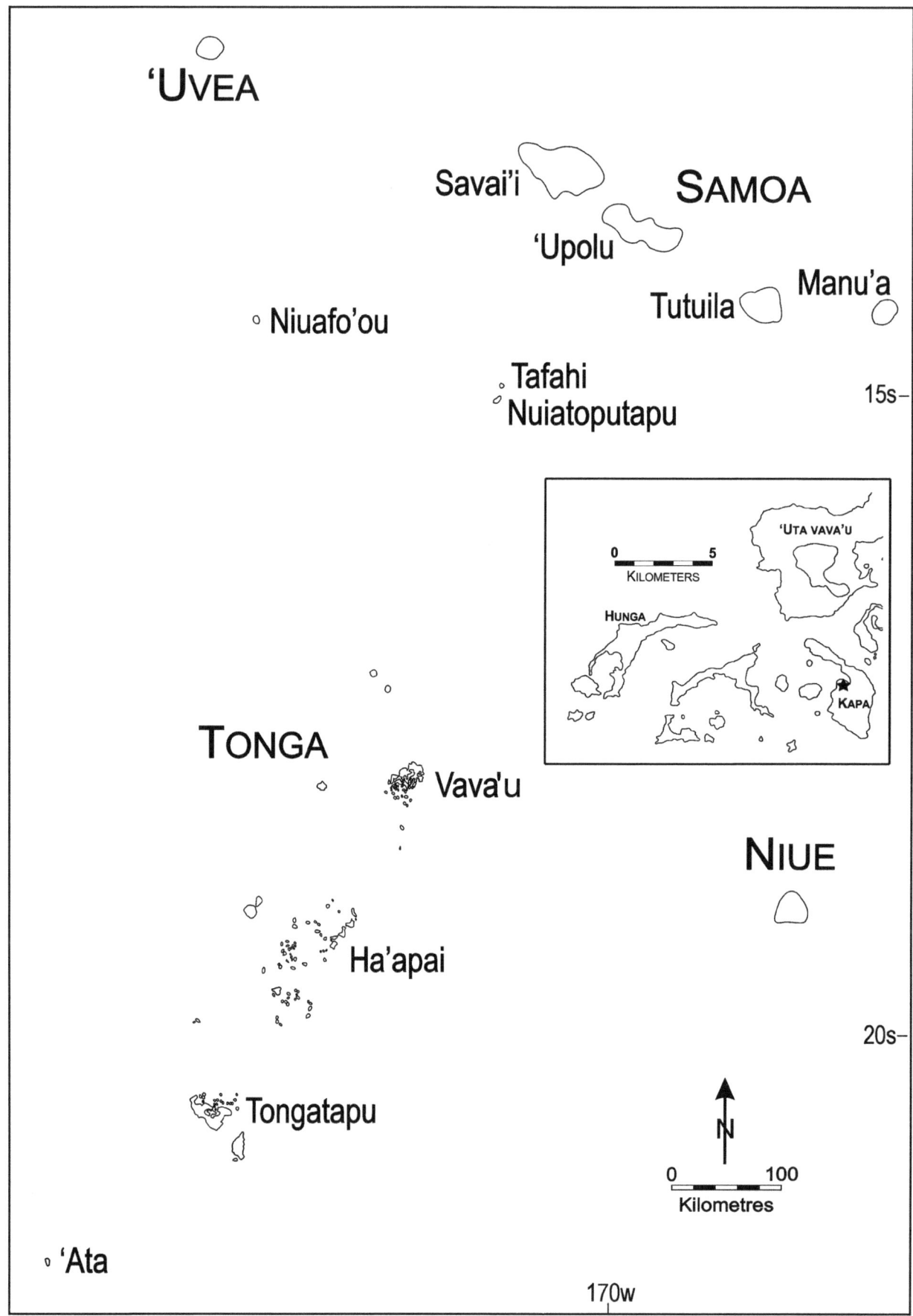

Figure 1. Tonga, Samoa, 'Uvea and Niue. Inset shows Kapa Island, Vava'u.

of Falevai in the Vava'u group, Kingdom of Tonga. The data from the latter are not yet fully analysed, but do point towards new insights into regional considerations of the Polynesian Plainware phase.

Background

The Kingdom of Tonga comprises over 160 islands on the western flank of the Polynesian triangle with Fiji to the west and Samoa to the northeast (Figure 1). Three main island groups, Tongatapu, Ha'apai, and Vava'u, make up the archipelago; volcanic islands and sea mounts form the Tofua Volcanic Arc to the west. Most inhabited islands are coral limestone formations lying on the eastern non-volcanic chain sitting atop the submerged Tonga Ridge.

Tonga has a lengthy culture history, beginning with colonisation by Austronesian-speaking Lapita peoples approximately 2850 BP (Figure 2). The Lapita phase is defined by the distinctive dentate-stamped decorated earthenware pottery, which has a distribution range from the Bismarck Archipelago to West Polynesia (Kirch 1997). In Tonga, most decorated pottery has been defined and labeled Eastern Lapita and is characterised by markedly simplified Lapita motifs when compared to Lapita motifs in Fiji and further west (Burley *et al.* 2002; Kirch 1997). However, Western Lapita motifs have been identified in Tonga during the initial settlement period (Burley and Dickinson 2001).

During the Polynesian Plainware phase, social transformation and cultural adaptation including aspects such as settlement dispersal, population growth and development of dryland agriculture, presumably contributed to the emergence of an Ancestral Polynesian Society that developed over the course of the next 1000 years. This ancestral culture was the template for later Polynesian societies who eventually explored and ultimately colonised all of the islands of the Polynesian triangle (Burley 1998:337; Kirch 1997; Kirch 2000). This paper focuses on the small but significant slice of time, the transition from the Eastern Lapita phase to the subsequent Polynesian Plainware phase as represented at Falevai.

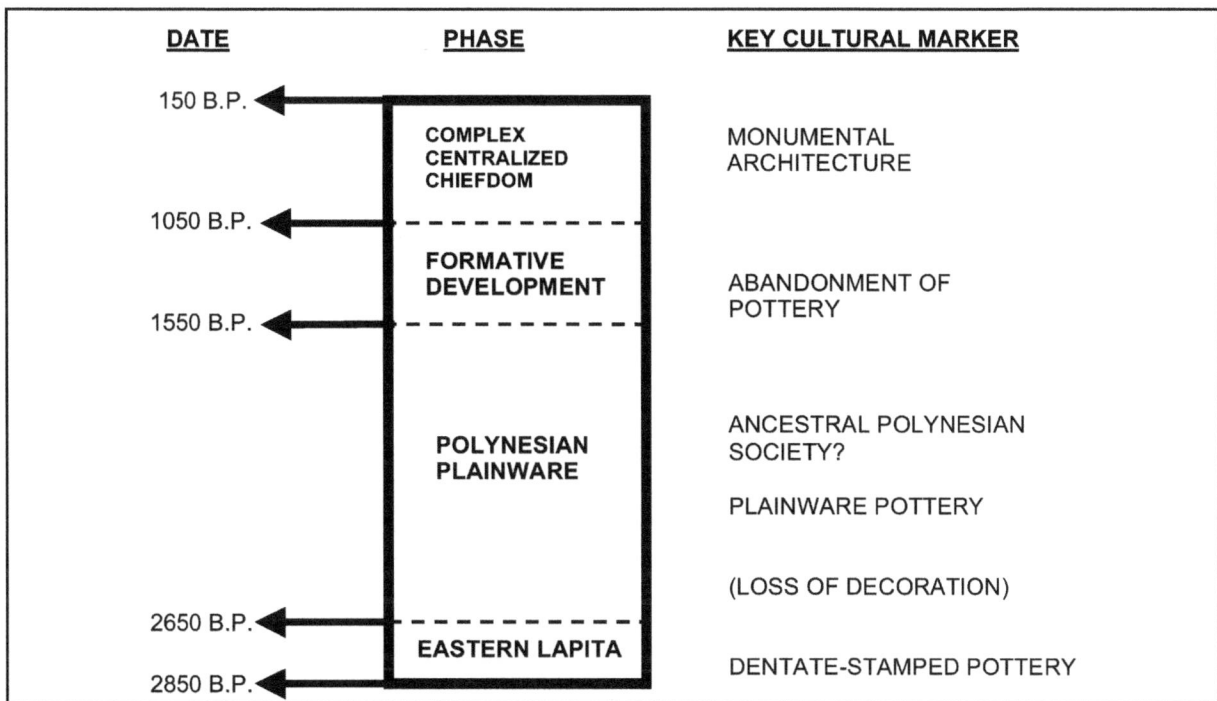

Figure 2. Culture history of Tonga (after Burley 1998).

"Ancestral Polynesian Society"?

Following the lead of earlier anthropologists (Flannery and Marcus 1983; Taylor 1948; Sapir 1916), Kirch and Green (2001) employ archaeological, ethnographic, biological and linguistic data to reconstruct aspects of Ancestral Polynesian Society. They outline in detail the arguments and evidence found in the archaeological record in West Polynesia that support the concept of an Ancestral Polynesian Society that developed from Lapita ancestry (Kirch and Green 2001). They argue that it is largely through *in situ* development and transformation, involving factors such as population growth, settlement dispersal and changing subsistence practices which contribute to the emergence of an Ancestral Polynesian Society. They outline a range of distinctive material culture including plainware pottery, shell adzes, fishhooks, beads, rings, and basalt adzes which is seen as being associated with Ancestral Polynesian Society (Kirch and Green 2001:163-200). At the same time they highlight a much wider range of material objects used in traditional Polynesian society which were made of wood, bamboo, bark, fiber, leaves, cordage and feathers and have not survived. With this taphonomic aspect in mind they emphasise that archaeology does not, or is it ever likely to tell us everything there is to know (Kirch and Green 2001:164-165). They also note that archaeological research into sites associated with Ancestral Polynesian Society are generally characterised by limited test excavations rather than extensive horizontal investigations. They emphasise the need for undertaking large areal excavations of these sites if we are to move beyond our current understanding (Kirch and Green 2001:83).

Contrary to the claims of Kirch and Green, Smith asserts that the early archaeological record is insufficient to claim an Ancestral Polynesian homeland in Western Polynesia stating that "there is no necessary chronological relationship between the early archaeology of the region and the origins of the socio-cultural characteristics that have been used to identify a society as Polynesian" (Smith 2002:195). While Smith (2002:188) acknowledges the viability of the model of the development of Ancestral Polynesian Society from an ancestral Lapita base, her contention is that the archaeological data in support of such a model is not visible. Furthermore, she claims that the ceramic sequence transition from decorated pottery to completely undecorated pottery in the Polynesian Plainware phase reflects a continuum of pottery technology with no social or economic implications. The assertion that Ancestral Polynesian Society developed in the early stages of colonisation and is manifest during the Plainware Phase is unsupported in Smith's view.

Smith's (2002) focus was on an assessment of separate artefact classes (i.e., ceramics, adzes, and fishhooks) rather than the cultural package as a whole. There are certainly gaps in the archaeological record, as emphasised by Kirch and Green (2001:83, 165) and Smith did not have access to non-analysed plainware vessel data sets, but to claim that the archaeological record is unable to adequately assess change over time ignores a millennium's worth of locally manufactured pottery in West Polynesia. A more detailed ceramic chronology is certainly required for a full understanding of the Polynesian Plainware phase and the possible emergence and development of Ancestral Polynesian Society and as Smith (2002:146) proposed a site with a late Lapita or a transitional Polynesian Plainware assemblage is a necessary starting point. Falevai in the Vava'u Group of Tonga provides this starting point for documenting change during the transition and up until the end of the Polynesian Plainware phase when pottery was abandoned.

The Importance of Polynesian Plainware Pottery Studies

My investigation of the plainware component of Lapita assemblages and subsequent plainware assemblages, in corroboration with economic and population data, will eventually provide further insights into the emergence of an Ancestral Polynesian Society in Tonga. Our current inability to fully understand or explain the anthropological significance of the transition from Lapita decorated ware to Polynesian Plainware is in large part due to a complete lack of focus in the study of plainware ceramics. Generally identified as utilitarian ware, plainware is often considered mundane in comparison to decorated Lapita vessels. As a consequence, plainware has been neglected in archaeological studies in the Pacific as a whole (Burley 1998; Kirch 2000). Decorated pottery sherds rarely make up more than 4-5 % of a Lapita vessel assemblage in Tonga (Burley *et al.* 2002), yet they have customarily been the major focus of archaeological inquiry (Kirch 2000:102). With the exception of Niuatoputapu, we know relatively little about the Plainware phase and its ceramic sequence through Tongan prehistory (Burley 1998; Kirch 1988).

Polynesian Plainware: The ceramics of Ancestral Polynesian Society

Investigations conducted by Burley (1998), Dye (1996), Green (1972, 1986), Groube (1971), Kirch (1988), Poulsen (1987), and Spennemann (1989) provide the current basis for classifying Polynesian Plainware pottery. Such vessels represent a continuing tradition of pottery production from the founding Eastern Lapita phase. Polynesian Plainware is characterised by a limited range of vessel form and decoration is virtually absent (Burley 1998; Dye 1996; Kirch 1988).

Plain pottery is considered a utilitarian ware (Burley 1998:361; Kirch and Green 2001:168), and was most likely used for storage, serving and possibly cooking (Spennemann 1989). Three vessel forms are reported to have been retained in Tonga; (1) subglobular jars with a slightly restricted orifice and narrowing below the rim; (2) simple cups; and (3) bowls (Burley 1998:361). Dye's (1996) analysis of Plainware variation on Tongatapu and Lifuka demonstrated an increasing shift from vessel forms with an everted rim orientation to a more vertical orientation. In conjunction, there was a steady decline over time in bowl frequencies while subglobular pots increased in frequency.

At the same time, when Fijian Plainware from the Sigatoka Sand Dune site in Viti Levu is compared with Tongan Plainware, the Fijian Plainware assemblages diversify in terms of form, decoration and manufacturing while the Tongan Plainware remains relatively homogeneous before disappearing altogether (Burley 2005). Tongan Plainware invokes a pan-Tongan flavor across the archipelago, potentially resulting from the combined effects of isolation from outside influence and the development of a stronger shared local identity. Ultimately, the production of Tongan Plainware and pottery altogether ceases around 1550 BP while Fijian Plainware continues to be made through to 1450 BP when it is replaced by the Navatu phase style in western Fiji approximately (Burley 2005).

Associated Developments during the Polynesian Plainware Phase

The transition from a Lapita occupation to Polynesian Plainware phase is demarcated predominantly by the loss of decorated ceramics, mainly dentate-stamping, in conjunction with the loss of certain vessel forms (e.g., collared jars). Lip notching, rim thickening and changes in wall thickness might also occur (Kirch and Green 2001). Nevertheless, it is not just the ceramics that are changing, other significant changes are apparent in settlement and subsistence patterns, site distribution, and population growth during the Plainware phase in Tonga (Burley 1998; Burley in press; Spennemann 1989). Evaluating these avenues of inquiry provide a more holistic framework from which to interpret the archaeological record and better understand how ancestral Polynesian culture developed through time.

It is argued that during the Polynesian Plainware phase, populations continue to grow and settlements stretch beyond the shoreline to inhabit the interior of larger islands throughout Tonga as well as offshore islands and outliers. The widespread distribution of ceramics, suggests an expansive if not full use of the landscape by the end of the Plainware phase (Burley in press; Spennemann 1989). Recent work in the Vava'u Group by Burley (Burley this volume) certainly demonstrates this trend. Earlier Lapita sites were not being abandoned as continuous occupation does occur on most of these sites. In some cases, there is evidence suggesting there has been an expansion of site size from small hamlets to larger village size complexes (Burley in press). However, the limited number of Lapita sites reported from Vava'u, in comparison to Tongatapu and Ha'apai, suggests a more limited number of people traveling northward (Burley this volume).

With growing populations inhabiting most of the islands in the Tongan Archipelago by the onset of the Polynesian Plainware phase, dry land agriculture intensifies across the Tongan landscape with less reliance on natural resources (Burley 1998:362-363). Spennemann (1989) documented and recovered copious quantities of pottery across the interior of Tongatapu which points to settlement expansion into the interior along with an associated increase in intensive dry-land agriculture. Foraging on the reef continues, but the dominant role it once played in initial Lapita settlement now seems to be diminished. During initial Lapita settlement, indigenous fauna, particularly iguanas and birds, became extirpated and in some cases extinct (Steadman *et al.* 2002a:3677; Steadman *et al.* 2002b) and shellfish and turtle were also heavily exploited (Spennemann 1989). Comparative analysis of faunal assemblages from both Lapita and Plainware sites will further enhance our understanding of changing subsistence practice.

These shifts in human behavior have implications for the emergence of an Ancestral Polynesian Society, whereby an increase in human populations and developmental adaptations within the Tongan environment convey a changing mode of life. The ceramic transition is critical, not just for demarcating some arbitrary boundary for culture history purposes, but for the underlying social changes it reflects (Burley 1998).

Falevai

The site of Falevai is situated on the southwest leeward shore of Kapa Island located in the Vava'u Group (Figure 1 inset). The site shares its name with the nearby village of Falevai, but occurs on land known as *vakataumai*, which refers to the ease at which one can bring a canoe ashore. Falevai is situated approximately 50 m from the sea and sits atop a prehistoric back beach dune that was capped with coral gravel infill.

An initial 1 x 1 m test unit was excavated by Burley in 2003 to assess ceramic period occupation and stratigraphy. Based on ceramics recovered from the test unit, Falevai was identified primarily as a Polynesian Plainware phase site with a relatively shallow Eastern Lapita phase component in the lowest levels. No charcoal samples were obtained for radiocarbon dating from this test unit. A small number of decorated sherds (n = 9) were recovered from the bottom levels of the test unit that reached a depth of 2.2 m. Given the shallow Lapita occupation level and ensuing metre or so of Polynesian Plainware ceramics, Falevai was seen as an ideal site to potentially document first settlement by Lapita people and the subsequent transformations to the end of the Polynesian Plainware phase.

In the summer of 2005, I excavated a 3 x 4 m block unit at Falevai to document first settlement and determine the time frame in which decorated Lapita pottery disappears from the archaeological record. A further aim was the establishment of a detailed ceramic chronology that equated with Ancestral Polynesian Society. The Falevai data set could then be compared with three other ceramic sites from across the Tongan Archipelago to control for change across space and time (Figure 3).

Falevai was excavated contiguously in block units comprising eleven 1 x 1 m square units to control for stratigraphic breaks and feature exposures. Each unit was excavated by trowel and shovel in arbitrary levels of 10 cm and dry sieved through both 6.4 mm and 3.2 mm mesh sieves. Due to time constraints and previous site knowledge supplied by Burley, the first 90 cm was expediently removed and not screened with the exception of Unit 2, which was excavated in the above fashion as a control unit. The control unit confirmed initial interpretations that the upper 50 cm of the deposit was aceramic and that it largely contained fill deposit with little in the way of material culture. A 50 x 50 cm shell column sample was removed in 10 cm intervals and dry sieved through both 6.4 mm and 3.2 mm mesh sieves. We also collected all pottery from this same shell column which was left unwashed for future residue analysis.

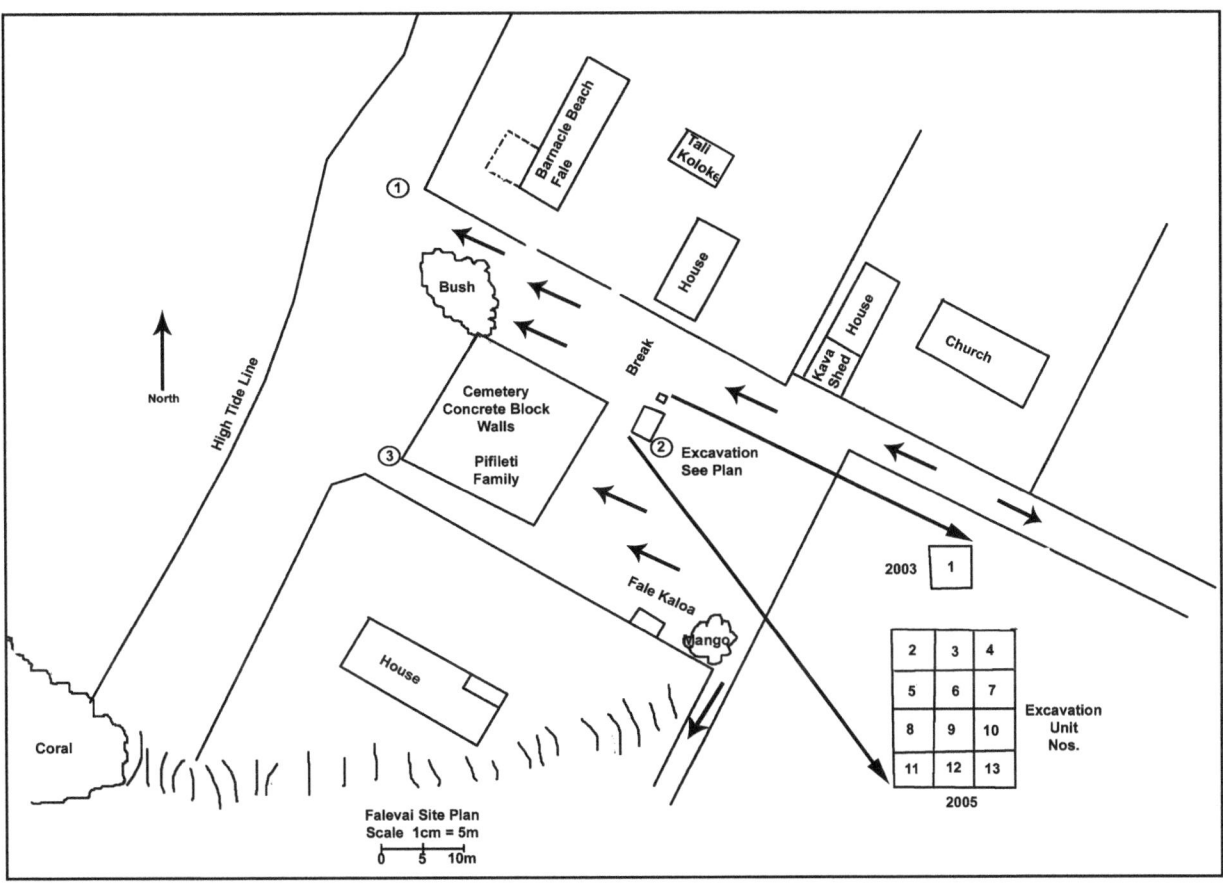

Figure 3. Falevai site plan and excavations.

Stratigraphy

The stratigraphy at Falevai is relatively homogenous overall, yet four distinct strata have been identified (Figure 4). Strata have been labelled from I-IV from the uppermost sod layer to the lower sterile deposit (Table 1). Pit features, *umu* features and post-holes were noted in profile and plan view. Unit 2 displayed a pit feature intruding into the lowest levels of Stratum IV containing Stratum III matrix originating from the Polynesian Plainware occupation levels. This feature appears to have been responsible for disturbing the context of the lower levels in Unit 2 and thus displacing dentate-stamped Lapita sherds (n = 4) into the upper levels of the later Polynesian Plainware phase.

With the exception of Unit 2, the overall stratigraphy within Stratum III and IV at Falevai seemed to be relatively undisturbed providing good context for evaluating ceramic change through time. From my preliminary analysis thus far, I have noticed that the condition in which pottery is recovered from the lowest level compared with the upper-most levels reveal patterns of decreasing sherd size due to degradation, weathering and human impact on the landscape. While Stratum IV to the mid levels of Stratum III yield an abundance of well-preserved pottery, the very upper levels of Stratum III show a decrease in sherd frequency and size. Stratum II contains pottery sherds intermixed with some historic artifacts and coral gravel infill, but they are highly degraded and crumb-sherd in size. My impression is that the very upper levels of Stratum III and particularly Stratum II, represent the aceramic period when pottery production was abandoned in Tonga. Although I do not have a representative date for this period at Falevai, at the site of Otea also on Kapa Island, Polynesian Plainware phase ceramics are capped and separated from aceramic strata by a very compact shell layer. This cap has been dated at 1615 ± 35 BP and establishes the date of loss of ceramics at the end of the Plainware phase (Burley and Connaughton in press).

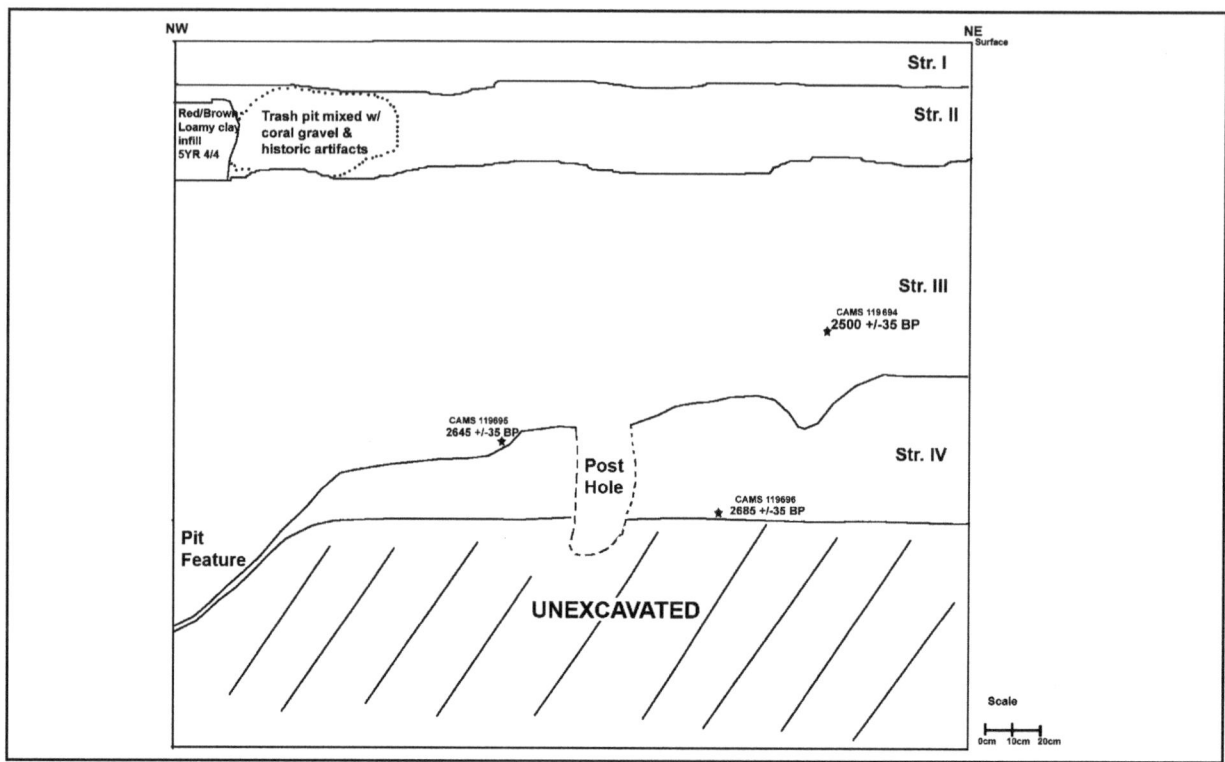

Figure 4. Falevai north wall profile.

Table 1. Stratigraphy description of Falevai.

Stratum	Max. Depth cm BS	Munsell Color	Description
I	18	5YR 3/1	Very dark gray topsoil with roots and very small traces of shell and historic artefacts.
II	52	7.5YR 3/2	Dark brown, loamy soil with coral gravel infill creating a flat surface prehistorically. Some historic artefacts are intermixed such as glass, nails and ceramics but is mainly isolated in trash pit seen in profile; some pottery but highly degraded and very small.
III	218	7.5YR 4/2	Dark brown/brown loamy/clay soil mixed with coral, shellfish (broken and whole), rocks and pumice. Fauna is relatively low in frequency and comprised mainly of fish. Pottery is recovered in high volume, particularly Plainware with rims and potstand fragments. This stratum is quite homogenous and appears to be a solid representation of plainware occupation.
IV	220	2.5Y 7/4	Pale yellow sand with coral and pumice; some shellfish and very small amounts of pottery were recovered from the top of this stratum, otherwise, culturally sterile.

Falevai Plainware Pottery

It is premature to present an in-depth detailed analysis of the plainware pottery at Falevai during the Plainware phase for this paper. However, I can provide insights and patterns that have emerged from my preliminary investigation in an attempt to characterise the ceramic assemblage. A sherd level of analysis was undertaken for the purpose of this paper focusing primarily on vessels forms.

A total of 10,155 sherds were recorded from Falevai with 552 representing plain rim sherds and another 42 decorated rim sherds (Table 2). Decorated rim sherds account for 7 % of the total rim assemblage. Only jars were identified as having been decorated, no bowls displayed any decoration. Decoration on rim sherds is largely restricted to the to the lip with occasional instances on the neck. Of these decorated sherds, dentate-

Table 2. Sherd inventory from Falevai.

	Dec. Rim	Dec. Neck	Dec. Shoulder	Dec. Body	Plain Rim	Plain Neck	Plain Shoulder	Plain Body	Total
Falevai 12 m² area	42	6	1	12	552	81	20	9441	10155

stamping is represented by ten sherds and is found predominantly in the lower levels of the unit, corresponding with the initial Lapita phase. A small number (n = 4) of dentate-stamp sherds do occur in the upper Polynesian Plainware phase but this is most likely due to disturbance caused by *umu* construction, post-hole insertions and pit features. In comparison, finger-notch impressed and incised sherds accounted for 33 and 7 sherds respectively and correlate within the transitional horizon from Lapita into the Polynesian Plainware phase. It is interesting to note the frequency of finger impressed decorated sherds relative to dentate-stamped sherds for it suggests that dentate-stamped decoration was on the decline and was abandoned soon after initial occupation. Meanwhile, decorated finger-notch impression sherds presumably continued into the early Polynesian Plainware phase, along with the production of fully plainware vessels, before being abandoned.

A limiting factor in the analysis of Plainware sherds is the almost total lack of complete reconstructable vessel forms due to the small size of sherds. Typically, rim sherds account for no more than 5-10 % of the complete rim of a vessel. This is the norm in Pacific sites, yet the most precise information about vessel forms is usually ascertained from rim sherds. Rim sherd analysis provides data on rim orientation, rim diameter, lip form and lip thickness. I will briefly describe different vessel forms that characterise the ceramic assemblage at the present time.

Jars dominate the assemblage at Falevai, with a variety of forms of jars having been identified (Figure 5). The most conspicuous attribute of a jar is its neck. The first type, described by Burley (1998:361) and others (Groube 1971; Kirch 1988; Poulsen 1987), is a relatively thin-walled, subglobular jar with restricted orifice and slightly to strongly inverted rim orientation. Rim diameters range from 10-44 cm. The second type of jar resembles a "fishbowl" like form, with relatively thin walls and restricted orifice but the degree of rim orientation appears more strongly inverted than the first type of jar described. Rim diameters range from 10-28 cm. Short-neck jars make up the third form and are constituted by a neck less than 3 cm in length from the lip. They appear to have a subglobular form with restricted orifice and slightly inverted rims. Rim diameters range from 10-26 cm. The fourth type is collared jars. A collar usually begins at the point of maximum diameter, or at a slight restriction close to it, and the orifice is not significantly reduced relative to the body (Rice 1987). Rim diameters range from 16-26 cm. Plain collared jars appear to be retained into the early Polynesian Plainware phase but soon drop out of the record altogether. The other three jar forms are found throughout the Plainware phase. Overall, inverted rims account for 82 % of total vessel rim orientation amongst plainware jars that tend to be slightly to strongly inverted. Quantifying the degree of invertedness has yet to be undertaken at this time. Simple bowl vessel forms represent 3 % of the total plain rim assemblage. Most had a slightly everted to straight rim orientation. Only fourteen rim sherds were identified as bowls. Rim diameters for bowls range from 14-26 cm.

There is no evidence that Plainware vessels were used for cooking. The occurrence of soot would provide solid evidence that a pot was used directly over a fire. Soot is usually most prevalent at the shoulder and maximum diameter of a vessel, rather than at the base (Hally 1983:8). Recording instances of soot deposition and their placement on the vessel allow for inferences as to how the pot was positioned relative to the fire. No such evidence was found within the Falevai assemblage. Furthermore, evidence for spalling, due to leaching and cracking while being heated, as well as pedestalled temper, due to the stirring or scraping motion of utensils against the walls of the pot (Rice 1987), was also not observed. Moreover, the high frequency of non-

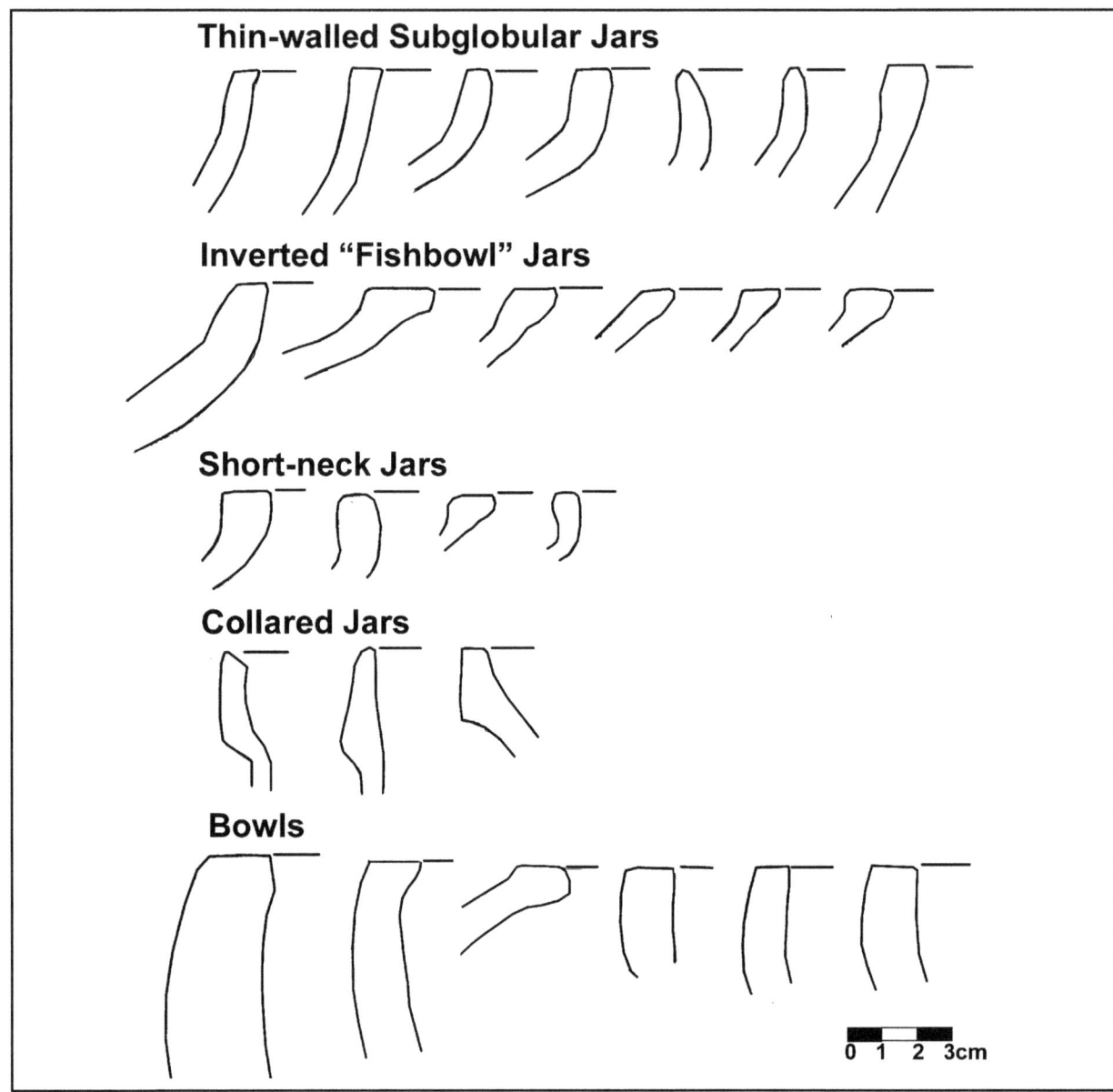

Figure 5. Vessel form types from Falevai.

cooking jar vessel forms (n = 172) and the limited amount of bowls represented (n = 14), suggests that these vessels were used primarily for storage. What was exactly being stored has yet to be established and is a topic that may be examined in future research.

Ultimately, my Ph.D. research will provide a comprehensive ceramic analysis from Falevai, as well as a selection of other Plainware phase sites excavated by Burley since 1990. Included are Tongoleleka, Ha'ateiho, and Holopeka. It is too early to discern the detailed nuances of plainware pottery present in Tonga during the Plainware phase for this paper. Nevertheless, my initial impression from Falevai is that whilst the loss of decoration was relatively rapid after initial colonization, a range of plainware pots retaining certain distinctive vessel and rim forms continued at first before a shift to decreasing diversity and variation over time. Manufacturing techniques such as paddling and wiping appear common amongst recovered plainware sherds. Within the plainware levels, pot-stand fragments (n = 6) of various shapes and sizes were recovered along with the addition of unfamiliar forms and thicker pieces of pottery. Again, further analysis is needed to assess vessel form variation and use through time.

Non-ceramic data

Non-ceramic artifacts have been sorted and counted but not analysed in any detail (Table 3). Shell valuables dominated by shell bracelet/ring fragments are present throughout Lapita and Plainware occupations. Octopus lure parts are represented by cut Cypraea tops and in two cases, the top of the Cypraea has been shaved down very cleanly. A variety of tools made of pumice and coral are present but andesitic-basalt tools occur most frequently. A total of eight basalt adze fragments were recovered along with two whole adzes; one from both the Plainware (Type Va) and Lapita (Type IIIb) levels (Green and Davidson 1969). Based on color (Burley this volume), it is likely that the two whole adzes are from Late, a volcanic outlier to the south and west of Vava'u. However, all the basalt artifacts have yet to be sourced using x-ray fluorescence techniques (Weisler 1998). Obsidian flakes were recovered from the upper Plainware levels and again need to be geochemically sourced. Interestingly, obsidian was not recovered from the initial Lapita occupation levels or within the early Polynesian Plainware occupation levels. This absence is intriguing, for if basalt is being procured from local sources and exchanged predominantly within Tonga, as well as the local production of pottery, then this might suggest relatively isolated societies during the Lapita and early plainware periods. The appearance of obsidian in a very late ceramic context potentially suggests new interaction, albeit still Tongan, especially if the obsidian is sourced to Tafahi. If that is the case, this would imply the integration of a Tongan polity along the axis of the archipelago facilitating internal development with no significant outside cultural intrusions.

Table 3. Non-Ceramic Artefact Count.

Artefact Type	
Shell bracelet/ring fragment	15
Shell adze/chisel fragment	1
Shell scrapers	5
Shell net weights	1
Shell long unit fragment	1
Cut pearl shell	1
Shell plaque	1
Triton trumpet shell fragment	1
Octopus lure parts	7
Stone adze (whole)	2
Stone adze fragments	8
Grinding/Pounding stone	3
Beach stone (grooved)	1
Stone ring (pot stand) fragment	1
Misc. stone	2
Obsidian flake	4
Pumice abrader	4
Coral abrader fragment	3
Modified sea-urchin spine	1
TOTAL	**62**

Radiocarbon Samples

Three wood charcoal samples from Falevai (Table 4) were radiocarbon dated (see Burley and Connaughton in press). None were identified to species. The samples occurred as small concentrations of flecks or chunks within sealed stratigraphic contexts. All dates are AMS measurements. Samples were submitted to the Center for Accelerator Mass Spectronomy (CAMS), the Lawrence Livermore National Laboratory, Davis, California. Calibrations were carried out using CALIB 5.1 radiocarbon calibration program (Stuiver and Reimer 2005). The Southern Hemisphere calibration curve, SHCa104, was applied (McCormac et al. 2004). Falevai presents a unique case within Tonga as it appears to have been settled during the Lapita/Polynesian Plainware transition where dentate-decorated Lapita ceramics were beginning to disappear. The radiocarbon dates of 2685 ± 35 BP (CAMS 119696) and 2645 ± 35 BP (CAMS 119695) provide a benchmark for the loss of decorated ceramics at Falevai and the continuation of plainware pottery manufacture. Interestingly, this is approximately 100 years earlier than occurs in Ha'apai and Tongatapu (Burley this volume). A detailed analysis of the plainware assemblage from both the Lapita and the Polynesian Plainware occupation strata will further aid our understanding of

Table 4. Radiocarbon Dates from Falevai (after Burley and Connaughton, in press).

Falevai	Date	Unit	Level	Stratum	Description
CAMS 119694	2500 ± 35 δ13C -27.9	4	11	III	Charcoal, 105 cm below surface, associated with the Polynesian Plainware occupation level. 2686-2362 cal BP (1σ), 2704-2356 cal BP (2σ), median probability 2503 cal BP.
CAMS 119695	2645 ± 35 δ13C -28.2	9	15	III	Charcoal, 145 cm below surface, associated with the Polynesian Plainware occupation level. 2759-2620 cal BP (1σ), 2778-2501 cal BP (2σ), median probability 2729 cal BP.
CAMS 119696	2685 ± 35 δ13C -27.9	10	18	IV	Charcoal, 180 cm below surface, associated with the Lapita occupation level. 2777-2735 cal BP (1σ), 2844-2622 cal BP (2σ), median probability 2755 cal BP.

the archaeological record to help tease out such particulars. Nonetheless, at 2 σ, this time period substantially overlaps with Lapita dates from other sites in Vava'u (see Burley and Connaughton in press), indicating that the disappearance of decorated ceramics may have been a rapid event shortly after initial Lapita settlement.

The third date from Falevai, 2500 ± 35 BP (CAMS 119694), is affected by the calibration curve flattening for the interval 2530-2420 BP resulting in multiple calibration curve intercepts and substantially widening the calibrated age range (Burley and Connaughton in press). This is a major problem with dating of post-Lapita sites generally and specifically later Polynesian Plainware occupations. These plateaus have not helped archaeologists to accurately map the transition from Lapita to Plainware, especially when attempting to characterise later plainware ceramic assemblages up until the abandonment of pottery. With respect to the two earlier dates, this third date suggests a later event based on the fully plainware assemblage associated with these strata from Falevai. Exactly how much later is impossible to tie down given the affects of the calibration curve flattening. This does not mean that the late part of the ceramic sequence is missing. As mentioned above, due to the paucity of recovered sherds in the very upper levels of Stratum III and Stratum II as a whole, these levels potentially demarcate the aceramic period when pottery production was abandoned in Tonga.

Conclusion

How early specifically Polynesian societies adapted and developed within their island environments is of considerable interest in Oceanic studies. This paper provides an initial overview from Falevai, which can now be situated in the wider debate regarding the emergence of Ancestral Polynesian Society during the Lapita/Polynesian Plainware transition in Tonga. Radiocarbon dates have been provided and discussed in conjunction with the stratigraphy encountered at Falevai in order to establish the context in which this site was occupied. Initial ceramic vessel forms are described but further analysis is currently being conducted.

Smith (2002:135) has argued that the transition from decorated Lapita to fully Polynesian Plainware vessels does not signal significant social change nor do plainware ceramics provide a satisfactory correlate for the appearance of a distinctly different society in West Polynesia. Furthermore, Smith (2002:180) has asserted that Polynesian Plainware assemblages show little, if any, change through time. However, considering the Polynesian Plainware phase encompasses a millennium or so of pottery production, it seems highly unlikely that plainware vessel forms do not change across time and space to some degree in Tonga. This is certainly the impression gleaned from the preliminary analysis of the Falevai ceramic remains as outlined here.

My research once complete is aimed at providing a more in-depth and detailed study of the complete plainware ceramic assemblage from the beginning of the Polynesian Plainware phase to the point at which pottery production ceases altogether. Additionally, I plan to profile the vessel forms that were being utilised at the end of the sequence in Tonga and compare them with other pottery traditions in West Polynesia just before the abandonment of pottery production. This will provide a better assessment of cultural similarities and differences through time amongst island societies.

If Polynesian culture did develop in Western Polynesia following initial Lapita settlement then the evidence for such social and economic change has a good chance of being identified in the archaeological record. More detailed investigation of targeted sites of this period is clearly a priority as noted by both Kirch and Green (2001:83) and Smith (2002). By closely examining the plainware ceramic sequence that is claimed to be associated with Ancestral Polynesian Society, we can further evaluate the strength of the argument for internal development predicated upon isolation from outside pottery making communities. However, as outlined earlier, pottery is but a single avenue of inquiry and other aspects of cultural and social change such as settlement and subsistence patterns, site distribution, and population growth must have had significant influence in the emergence and development of an Ancestral Polynesian Society. It is only with the compilation and assessment of such relevant data that we will be able to construct a more holistic and robust view of proto-Polynesian culture in Tonga.

Acknowledgements

Fieldwork was made possible by Dr. David V. Burley through a research grant from the Social Sciences and Humanities Research Council of Canada. I gratefully acknowledge his support as well as commenting on my initial draft of this paper. Gratitude is given to the Government of Tonga for assistance and support, in particular, the late 'Akauola, Governor of Vava'u. A giant *malo aupito* goes to the people of Falevai, whose generosity, support and interest in my project allowed me to enjoy every single moment under the sun with them. Particularly, I thank my field crew: Peau Halaingano, Peni Latu, Amelani Subuya, Sione Niu, Tomasi To'oa, Tonga Kemo e 'atu, Taukave Hakalo, Viliami Leakona, Ofa Blake and Solo Mone Hala e 'ioa. I also thank Dr. George Nicholas for editing an earlier draft, Jessi Witt for her preparation of the figures and comments on an earlier draft of this paper and David Burley and Christophe Sand for further critical comment.

References

Burley, D.V. 1998. Archaeology and the Tongan past; 2850-150 BP. *Journal of World Prehistory* 12:337-392.

Burley D.V. 2005. Mid-Sequence Archaeology at the Sigatoka Sand Dunes with Interpretive Implications for Fijian and Oceanic Culture History. *Asian Perspectives* 44(2):320-348.

Burley D.V. in press. Archaeological Demography and Population Growth in the Kingdom of Tonga-950 BC to the Historic Era. In P.V. Kirch and J. Rallu (eds), *Long Term Demographic Evolution in Oceania*. Honolulu: University of Hawaii Press.

Burley, D.V. and S.P. Connaughton in press. First Lapita settlement and its chronology in Vava'u, Kingdom of Tonga. *Radiocarbon* 49(1).

Burley, D.V. and W.R. Dickinson 2001. Origin and Significance of a Founding Settlement in Polynesia. *PNAS* 98 (20):11829-11831.

Burley, D. V., A. Storey and J. Witt 2002. On the Definition and Implications of Eastern Lapita Ceramics in Tonga. In S. Bedford, C. Sand, and D.V. Burley (eds), *Fifty Years in the Field. Essays in Honour and Celebration of Richard Shutler, Jr's Archaeological Career*, pp. 213-227. Auckland: New Zealand Archaeological Association Monograph 25.

Dye, T. S. 1996. Early eastern Lapita to Polynesian plainware at Tongatapu and Lifuka: An exploratory data analysis. In J. Davidson, F. Leach, A. Pawley, and D. Brown (eds), *Oceanic Culture History: Essays in Honour of Roger Green*, pp. 461-473. Dunedin: New Zealand Journal of Archaeology Special Publication.

Flannery, K. V. and J. Marcus (eds) 1983. *The Cloud People: Divergent Evolution of the Zapotec and Mixtec Civilizations*. New York: Academic Press.

Green, R. C. 1972. Revision of the Tongan sequence. *Journal of the Polynesian Society* 81:79-86.

Green, R. C. 1986. Some basic components of the Ancestral Polynesian settlement system: Building blocks for more complex Polynesian societies. In P.V. Kirch (ed.), *Island Societies: Archaeological Approaches to Evolution and Transformation*, Cambridge: Cambridge University Press.

Green, R. C. and J. M. Davidson (eds) 1969. *Archaeology in Western Samoa*, vol. 1. Auckland: Auckland Institute and Museum, Bulletin 6.

Groube, L. 1971. Tonga, Lapita pottery and Polynesian origins. *Journal of the Polynesian Society* 80:278-316.

Hally, D. J. 1983. Use Alteration of Pottery Surfaces: An Important Source of Evidence for the Identification of Vessel Function. *North American Archaeologist* 4:3-26.

Kirch, P. V. 1984. *Evolution of the Polynesian Chiefdoms*. Cambridge: Cambridge University Press.

Kirch, P. V. 1988. *Niuatoputapu: The Prehistory of a Polynesian Chiefdom*. Seattle: Thomas Burke Memorial Washington State Museum, Monograph No. 5.

Kirch, P. V. 1997. *The Lapita peoples: ancestors of the Oceanic world*. Blackwell: Cambridge, Mass.

Kirch P. V. 2000. *On the Road of the Winds: An Archaeological History of the Pacific Islands before European Contact*. Berkeley: University of California Press.

Kirch, P.V. and R.C. Green 2001. *Hawaiki, Ancestral Polynesia: An Essay in Historical Anthropology*. Cambridge: Cambridge University Press.

McCormac, F.G., H.G. Hogg, P.G. Blackwell, C.E. Buck, T.F.G. Higham and P. J. Reimer 2004. SHCal04 Southern Hemisphere calibration, 0-11.0 cal kyr BP. *Radiocarbon* 46(3):1087-1092.

Poulsen, J. 1987. *Early Tongan Prehistory: the Lapita period on Tongatapu and its Relationships*. Canberra: Department of Prehistory, Australian National University. Terra Australis 12.

Rice, P. M. 1987. *Pottery Analysis: A Source Book*. Chicago: University of Chicago Press.

Sapir, E. 1916. *Time Perspective in Aboriginal American Culture: A Study in Method*. Ottawa: Government Printing Bureau. Department of Mines, Geological Survey Memoir 90 Anthropological Series 13.

Smith, A. 2002. *An archaeology of West Polynesian Prehistory*. Canberra: Pandanus Books. Terra Australis 18.

Spennemann, D.H.R. 1989. *'Ata 'a Tonga mo 'Ata 'o Tonga: Early and Later Prehistory of the Tonga Islands*. Unpublished PhD thesis, Australian National University.

Steadman, D.W., G.K. Pregill and D.V. Burley 2002a. Rapid prehistoric extinction of iguanas and birds in Polynesia. *PNAS* 99(6):3673-3677.

Steadman, D.W., A. Plourde and D. V. Burley 2002b. Prehistoric Butchery and Consumption of Birds in the Kingdom Of Tonga, South Pacific. *Journal of Archaeological Science* 29:571-584.

Stuiver, M. and P.J. Reimer 2005. Radiocarbon calibration program CALIB rev. 5.1. < http://calib.qub.ac.uk/calib >.

Taylor, W. W. 1948. *A Study of Archaeology*. Menasha, WI: American Anthropological Association Memoir 69.

Weisler, M. 1998. Hard evidence for prehistoric interaction in Oceania. *Current Anthropology* 39:529-532.

13

The implements of Lapita ceramic stamped ornamentation

Wal Ambrose

Department of Archaeology and Natural History,
Research School of Pacific and Asian Studies,
The Australian National University,
Canberra ACT 0200, Australia
wra410@coombs.anu.edu.au

Introduction

Observers of early Lapita ceramic technology generally concede that the elaborately ornamented vessels were low-fired and made with un-standardised raw materials (Clough 1992:189; Intoh 1982:169), often including calcareous sand tempering from the prevalent use of beach sands in accord with the coastal setting of sites in the Bismarck Archipelago (Dickinson 2006:113). Both Clough and Intoh see the wide variation in pottery fabric and firing temperature as evidence of technological experimentation by potters faced with unfamiliar raw materials. Although the clay body was un-standardized in the sense that it used locally found raw materials, in contrast the decorated pottery is often self or red-slipped, producing a fine textured surface ideally suited to detailed decorative treatment, and differs from what Sand (1999a:146) refers to as an 'everyday ceramic' that was also produced within the same settlement region. The relative brevity of the notable Lapita ceramic tradition, once it spread beyond the Bismarck Archipelago (Anderson 2001), has been affirmed by Bedford's (2006:190) summary of developments in Vanuatu in the context of a wider presence in Remote Oceania of other short-lived Lapita ceramics. The localised production in widely dispersed settlements could provide an impetus for divergence from the superficially unified design. The transition from fastidious Lapita ornamentation on a wide range of vessel forms to more prosaic less varied pottery containers fashioned for different purposes signals the reduced importance of the emblematic appearance borne by the prepared pottery surface. The secularisation or re-working of founder emblems is part of the human colonising experience, but what seems less likely is the quick abandonment of a useful technology that was a feature of the art form's production, even while ceramics continued to be made. The loss of a technology that had a singular ability to produce such distinctive abstract and formal-figurative references may be a deliberate rejection of both the message and its linked medium as suggested by Siorat (1990).

Lapita pottery as decorated artefact

The implements fashioned for Lapita vessel ornamentation have not been found, nor were they carried forward to ornament later wares, but that they were especially fashioned for the purpose cannot be doubted. The loss of this art form technique is curious. Perhaps the labour-intensive stylistic emulation requiring special tools became too burdensome to descendent settlers with their increasing local social priorities. But as the technique was not similarly employed in decorating later wares it is more likely that it was as an inseparable part of the design's redundant message. Two to three centuries of strictly maintained decorative treatment within the Bismarck Archipelago passed before a century long eastward movement as far as Samoa occurred. There is evidence that the further the Lapita settlement was from the Bismarck Archipelago the faster became the transition to a plain ware (Kirch 2000:102), with the simultaneous loss of the stamping technology. Whatever the compulsion or allure that drove this dramatic eastward migration there remain the interesting questions of why the pottery was so elaborately ornamented, what social information it bore apart from being a cultural mnemonic, and what implements were used to produce it. The sudden appearance of the finely ornamented Lapita wares with its 'fullest flowering' (Best 2002:96) in the Bismarck Archipelago appears to be without an archaeologically visible antecedent (Bellwood 1997:234), either in expression as a developed art style, in the dentate stamping technique, or in the use of a non-standardised ceramic body as a base for the designs. A possible explanation for this would envisage a fusion of intrusive Austronesian and indigenous Papuan cultures as noted by Kirch (2000:93) following Green's (1991) Triple I model of Intrusion/ Innovation/ Integration. This would imply that a formal decorative system has been transferred from a pre-existing medium and applied to different materials using an innovative stamping technique. However, none of Green's distinctions (2000:374) for determining intrusive versus indigenous elements can explain the elaborate dentate stamped designs that appear fully developed on the first pottery in the Bismarck Archipelago. The model does not identify the inventors of the stamp technology or the origin of the designs apart from drawing an analogy with tattooing implements found at Lapita sites (Kirch 2000:105).

An alternative view consistent with Green's Triple I model focuses on the primary connection of both Lapita design and stamping technology that was originally confined within the Bismarck Archipelago. The attenuation of both these features away from the influence of a 'Bismarck Homeland' raises the question of Papuan input into the Lapita design elements and structural principles as are found in two-dimensional designs on arrow foreshafts from northern New Guinea (Craig 2005:505). Craig's thesis could help to explain the loss of a design repertoire as it moved away from the influence of a borrowed Papuan decorative art fashion in the Lapita 'homeland' area. This still leaves the sophisticated dentate stamping technology as an innovation confined to the Bismarck Archipelago.

Spriggs (1997:106) questions the appropriateness of 'Integration' in the Triple I model within the Bismarck Archipelago as a putative Lapita homeland by claiming that '*A local component is not denied but it may be relatively insignificant.*' This view can be compared with that of Best (2002:50) that '*The invention of the roulette stamp is likely to have had significant and far-reaching effects on Lapita society… While the decoration itself is seen as part of a wider system, itself a response to some other social force, the (apparently) sudden appearance of these striking designs can only have had a reinforcing and intensifying effect on the society*'. Whether or not the roulette wheel (see Figure 1) was reinvented, Best's claim for the importance of the designs and their florescence in tandem with the introduction of pottery is a serious observation. On the other hand such a strong claim for the use and importance of roulette stamps has lead Spriggs (2002:53) to extend this proposition to explain the lack of the Lapita design system in any developed form further west in Island Southeast Asia. Best (2002:46) cites several authors whose views were simply at the level of cursorily deciding whether or not a roulette was used, but having elevated the discussion to include wider social ramifications it is timely to examine this view by closer observation of the dentate stamped designs on Lapita pottery.

Dentate stamping

Apart from reasserting that Lapita pottery dentate stamping is an invention devised in the Bismarck Archipelago, this paper avoids further speculations surrounding the discussion of the 'why and whence' of the elaborate ornamentation and considers the more prosaic and accessible question of 'how'. Green's (1990:33) admonition against defining Lapita solely on the basis of the technology of dentate stamping has merit, but it should not exclude attention to the basic technology behind the ceramic's distinctive appearance. It appears that early in the ceramic's introduction its low-fired quality was accompanied by a prepared fine-textured surface produced to bear sophisticated dentate designs. There has been little detailed investigation of the dentate stamp as an artefact, but it could provide insights into the relative effort invested in producing the pottery as a measure of its social value. For example Siorat's approach in examining the irreducible elements of the art has led to a better understanding of the aesthetic basis of the design rules leading to the more integrated system proposed by Chiu and Sand (2005). As a well-developed complex design system that arose suddenly in the Bismarck Archipelago, and that suffered a decline as it extended eastwards, it clearly warrants analysis in its own right, as is normal with any other art/artefact analysis. This is the approach adopted in the detailed study by Best (2002) who has given the subject an important investigation at several levels, from the iconic clout the designs may have given to the colonising Lapita peoples, to the details of the pottery stamping tools used in the vessel's production.

Best has published a simulation using roulettes of a face image found on a Lapita ceramic (Best 2002:48), but the simulation fails to acknowledge that a wider range of stamp impressions was produced with a defined tool kit, such as that described by Siorat (1990). For example Siorat refers to the parabolic forms of the curved stamps, among others, a view confirmed by identifying the family of geometric curves commonly observed on sherds at the Malekolon site on Ambitle Island (Ambrose 1999). Best's study also makes a claim for the greater efficiency in time and effort in using a roulette stamp. If true this would be an important conclusion because it reduces the level of skill and devotion to detail that would otherwise be needed to produce the designs using repeated single stamps. It would therefore have an implication for the priority the society gave to the production of the elaborate designs. The suggested labour saving device of a roulette-applied design would devalue the importance of the pottery as an individual item compared with its slower production by more laborious use of single stamps.

The stamp materials

Some naturally occurring materials have been considered but rejected as ready-made stamps suited to produce the Lapita design corpus (Siorat 1990:60), such as the impressed ventral margin crenellation of various bivalve shellfish, occasionally recognized both in Lapita and later wares. Hollow sectioned bird bone could be used to make circular impressions while incised designs could be made with a multitude of pointed tools. The distinctive dentate stamping technology was a quite different matter requiring specially manufactured implements. Parallel examples are the multi-pronged bone tools found at Lapita sites that are matched by ethnographic examples of tattooing needles in bone (Poulsen 1987:207). Tattooing is a widespread human practice pre-dating any Lapita designs in the Bismarck Archipelago. The art of tattooing may be analogous to similar treatment of a prepared smooth pottery surface (Kirch 1997:131; 2000:105), but further understanding of any relationship between the implements for tattooing on skin and the tools for dentate stamping on pottery remains in the realm of conjecture. The dentate stamp impressions investigated in the Malekolon Lapita collection do not support a view that the same tools were used for tattooing purposes (Siorat 1990:60). This is clearly seen in the silicone moulds of the stamped designs in Figure 2, and for Lapita sherds from New Caledonia (Sand 1997:25), showing that the stamps had stumpy points or flat edges quite unsuited for penetrating skin, compared with the edge of bone tattooing implements that are straight and sharp (Poulsen 1987, Vol 2:185).

A novel claim for a fingernail sharpened to a saw-tooth edge as a dentate stamp has been suggested along with the use of a serrated end-rounded spatula to be used in a semi-roulette fashion (Basek 1993). The postulated use of these items to create the appearance of dentate stamped designs on Lapita wares has been eclipsed by Best's claim (2002:47) that a roulette was used in order to delineate not only design boundaries but most or all of the main designs. In order to test this most strongly claimed proposition a detailed inspection was made of sherds from the Malekolon site on Ambitle Island.

The Malekolon Lapita Collection

Although the Malekolon (EAQ) Ambitle site is disturbed, probably by flooding associated with a volcanic event around 2300 years ago, it contains Lapita style sherds from two excavated collections, the first accepted as an associated Far Western Lapita group that includes Eloaue and Talasea (Anson 1986:163),

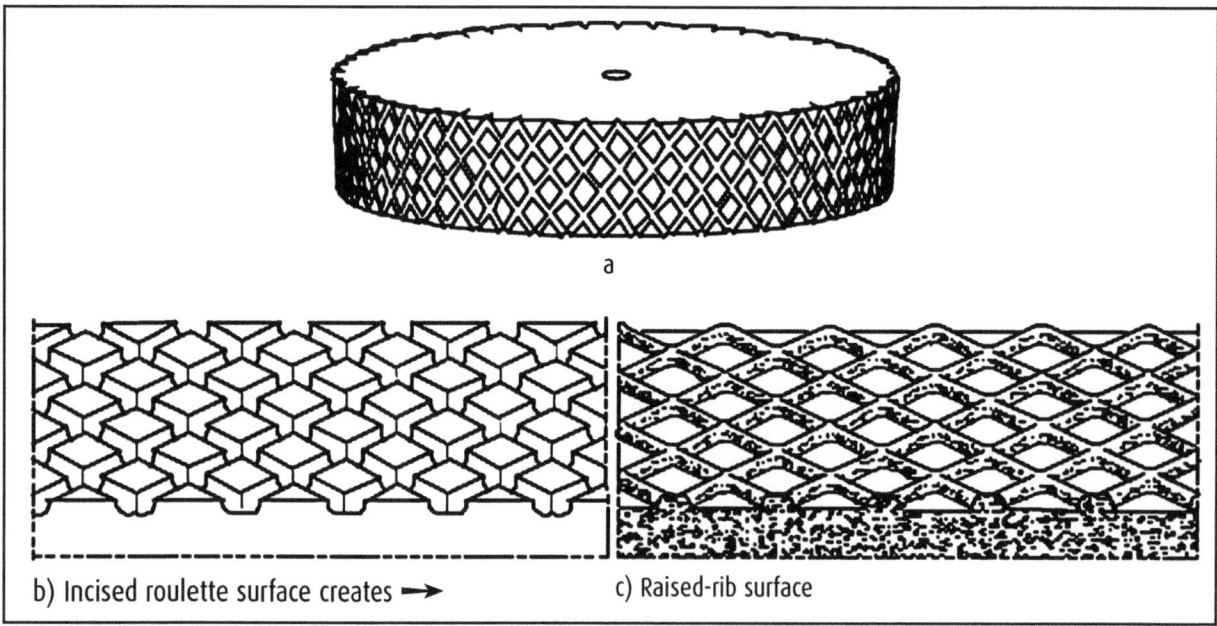

Figure 1. Hypothetical diagonally hatched incised roulette surface (a), and the implied grid form of ridges produced when applied to soft clay (b). None of the inspected sherds in the Malekolon collection has evidence of the raised ribs shown in (c) that a roulette would produce.

The implements of Lapita ceramic stamped ornamentation

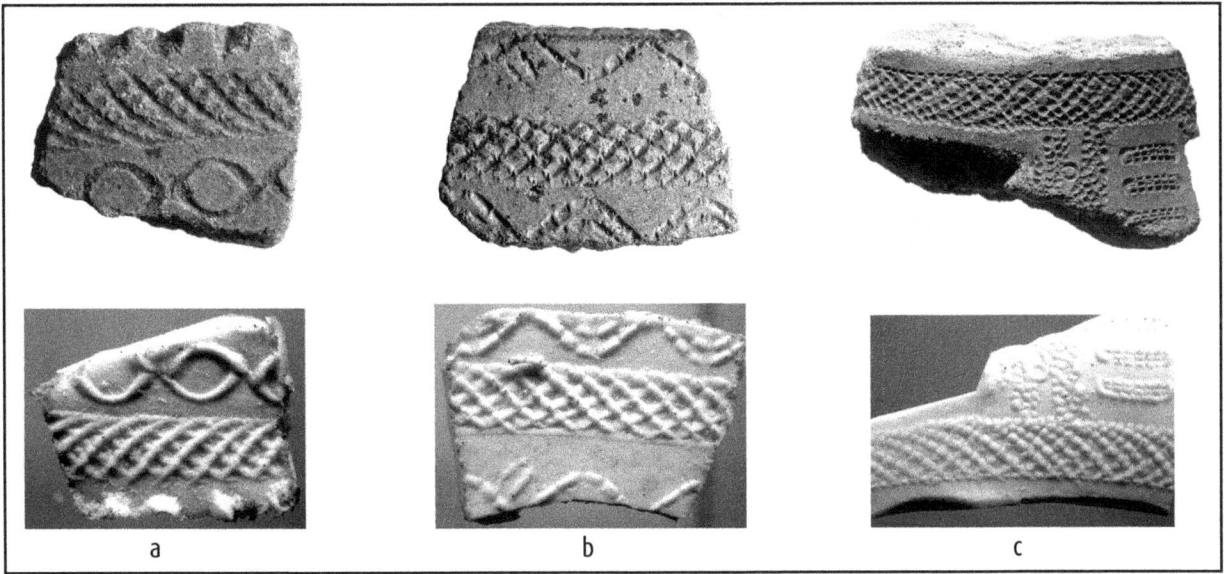

Figure 2. The top row of sherds show imprinted compound zone markers. The bottom row shows silicone moulds of these sherds. The mould surface clearly demonstrates repeating overlapping curved elements that form the wide ribbon units in the pottery. Sherd (a) is imprinted with plain curved stamps; sherd (b) has weakly developed dentate impressions; sherd (c) has more developed dentate stamp impressions, but all three share the same repeating technique. Each repeating stamp is sited on a previously drafted guideline. The sherd widths are (a) 22 mm, (b) 34 mm, (c) 48 mm.

and the second ascribed to Middle Western Lapita (Summerhayes 2000:173). The Malekolon Lapita pottery therefore possesses a range of design characteristics found at many other sites. This paper reports the result of a macroscopic examination of all decorated sherds in the first Anson-studied Malekolon collection. Sand (1997:25) shows the same evidence with silicone casts of single stamp impressions from New Caledonian Lapita sherds. An examination of the hypothetical impressions produced by roulette, compared with the impressions actually found in the sherd collection helped to clarify the matter. The study failed to produce evidence of roulette use.

Roulette and other impressions

Consider the photograph by Best (2002:47, plate 2) of the surface of two roulette stamps produced by incising crossed diagonal lines as in Figure 1a to produce a wide parallel edge with raised quadrilateral tiles as illustrated in Figure 1b. Roulettes of this design would produce a grid pattern of tiled depressions separated by raised ribs in a soft material, as shown by the surface effect and cross section produced diagrammatically in Figure 1c. This result is not found in any of the examined Lapita dentate stamp sherds from the Malekolon collection contradicting the claim for roulette use, particularly as it refers to wide bands appearing as design zone boundaries in the overall vessel ornamentation.

The repetitious curved impressions and their geometric similarities have not been adequately considered in Best's presentation of the case for the use of roulettes. The wide-band zone boundaries that appear on the Malekolon sherds are all formed from a series of multiple curved or straight elements in plain and dentate form. An individual stamp can often be recognised in a band by its identical curvature and, where they occur, by the number of tines and slight unevenness in their spacing. In setting the design field layout a single guideline on the clay can sometimes be still observed. The draft line served to assist regular stamp alignment while providing a margin for the terminal ends of both the plain and dentate curved stamps in a carefully

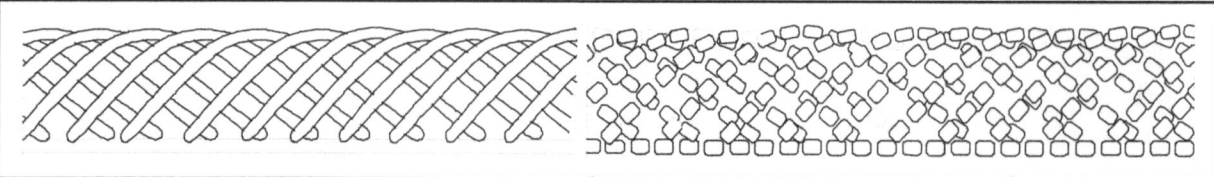

Figure 3. Unlike the raised rib band that would accompany the use of a continuous cross-hatched roulette, the evidence from the Malekolon collection is that a band was formed by repeated use of a single curved stamp as shown diagrammatically. The band can consist of repeated plain or dentate curves to produce the desired effect. Guidelines are found for the hanging arms of the repeating stamps that would otherwise leave a ragged edge, whereas the curve apices form their own continuous frieze margin.

controlled manner to produce the required zone boundary strips. This can be seen in the sherds and the silicone casts of these illustrated in Figure 2 where the overprinted trailing limb of each stamp impression is preserved to produce a wide band that could act as a design zone boundary. Figure 3 indicates diagrammatically how the basic curved elements that make up the graphic zone boundaries are created with repeated single stamps. There is clear evidence for the direction of stamping with multiple line zone markers when one trailing end of each curved stamp impression is overprinted.

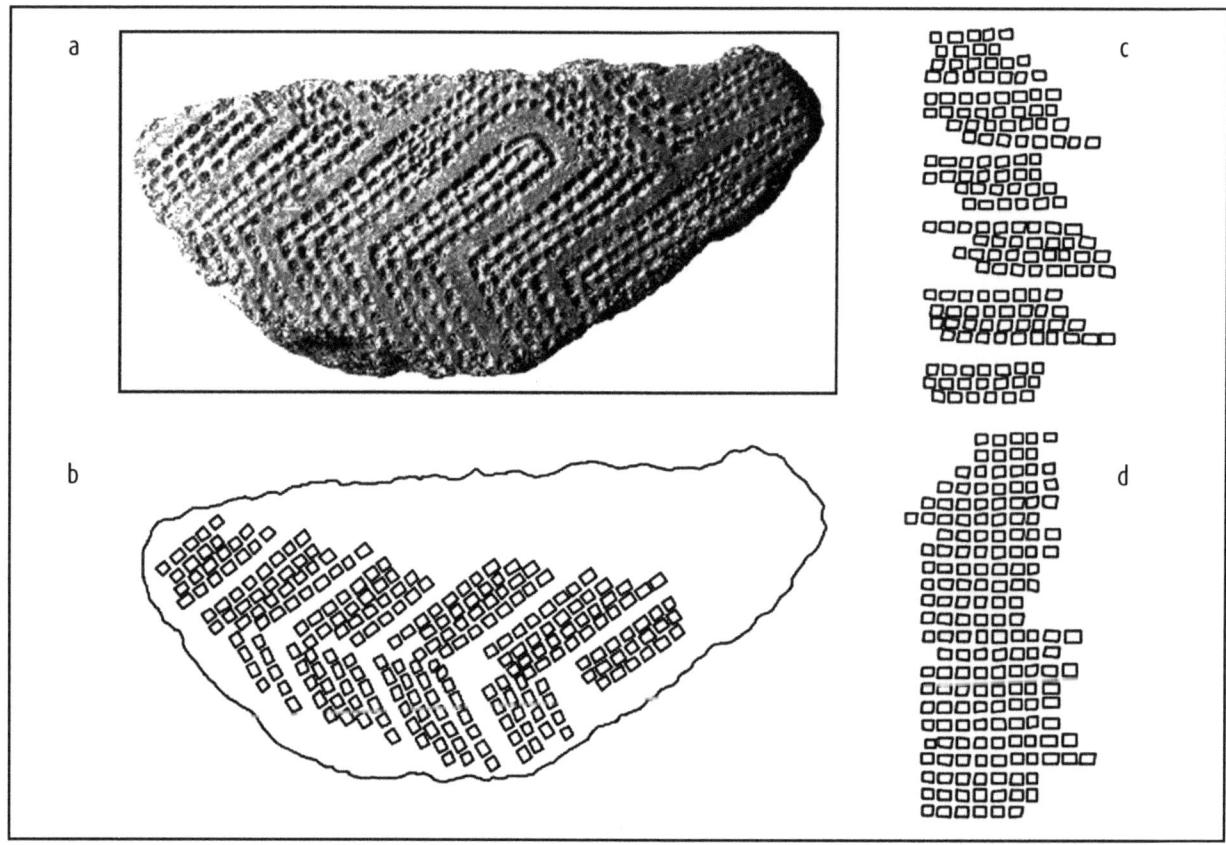

Figure 4. The sherd shown at (a) has the complex interlocking labyrinth design found as a design field on Lapita pottery from the Bismarck Archipelago to New Caledonia. A central zone has been abstracted as rectangular tine imprints shown in (b). The topmost course is realigned into a horizontal series at (c) where the semi-parallel stamp lines show the irregular nature of each four-line band. When the individual lines of (c) are re-aligned as in (d) it appears that a single stamp tool could produce all the features of the topmost stamp course. Another feature of the design appears to be that the stamped impressions are adjusted by crowding some lines in order to satisfy the complementary design requirements of the un-stamped areas. Overlapping stamp impressions have not been included in the diagram. The sherd width is 44 mm.

Straight dentate stamps are equally important in producing Lapita designs. The Lapita labyrinth design shown with extraordinary complexity on the well-preserved vessels excavated in New Caledonia (Sand 1999b:41-3) is a good example. Detailed inspection again provides no evidence that roulettes were used for any of the sherds in the Malekolon collection. As with the New Caledonian examples the complex interlocking angular labyrinth on the Malekolon sherd (Figure 4) would be particularly difficult to apply as a repeating two-dimensional geometric design to a three-dimensional curved surface area. The pottery surface preparation and draft outline would require careful execution to ensure that the complete design was applied with the symmetry expected in early Lapita pottery ornamentation. Three stamps appear to be employed on this single sherd, one straight with at least eleven tines, one curved with up to twenty tines, and another short, curved and plain. Overlapping areas can be seen where both the straight and curved stamps meet. The design that needed to be accommodated on the pottery surface is not simply produced by the stamped areas but also in the design of the blank zone between. In cases where it is possible to see the blank design it is clear that the dentate areas are sometimes crowded to allow the alternate blank areas to be seen in correct form. Figure 4 illustrates this feature when the dentate stamp area is slightly overprinted to produce a narrower zone of multiple lines. The illustrated sherd in Figure 5 (a) has sets of parallel dentate lines in the composition of the image. The two abstracted tine line sets in (b) are enlarged in (c) and (d) to clearly demonstrate that each line is offset, no doubt to fit the design requirement at the edge intersections of the lozenge-shaped central figure. The importance of

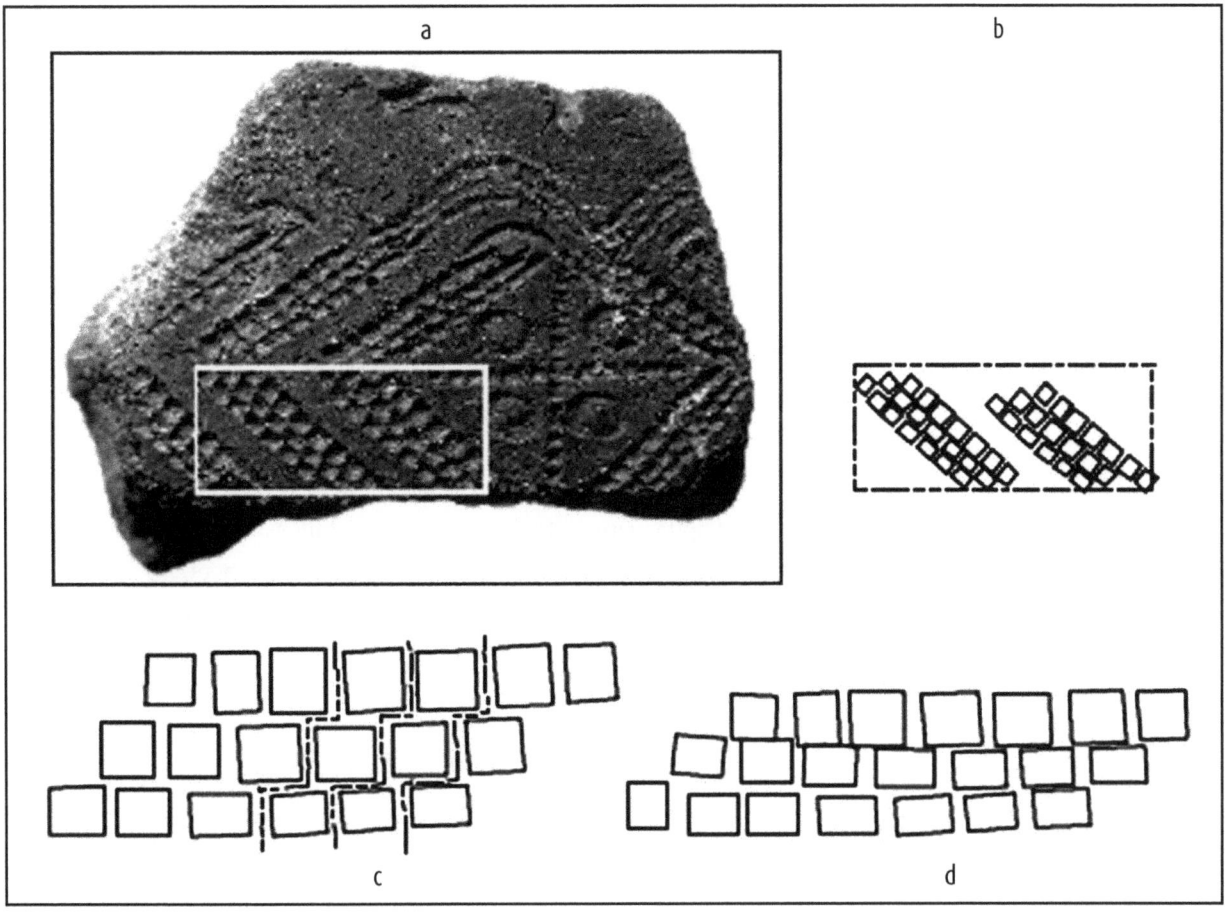

Figure 5. The offsets in individual stamp imprints show that multiple dentate lines were used to produce the composite image in (a). The extracted segments shown in (b) are enlarged in c and d. The offsets indicated by the dashed lines in (c) show that individual linear imprints are used to produce a wide frame for the enclosed design. In (d) there are lateral distortions that squeezed the repeated lines together, to produce a narrower design frame but allowing for equal width of the parallel plain zones. The sherd width is 30mm while the top dentate course in (c) is 7.5 mm.

maintaining the width of the intervening non-dentate design has been observed by crowding the triple-line strip as seen in (d). Other sherds, not illustrated here, show that the negative image can take precedence by reducing the number of individual stamp lines in a multiple stamp band, from say four to three.

Conclusion

I have argued elsewhere that the material used to produce the stamping tools was readily available in the form of turtle shell, particularly from the hawksbill turtle *Eretmochelys imbricata* (Ambrose 1997, 1999). Turtle scute can be easily bent into a range of curves when it is heated to around 90°C. Even so, in the case of the Malekolon collection there is a narrow range of curves closely matching the parabolic geometry of conic sections. Given the flexibility and relative plasticity of scute when heated, it is clear that the range of curves applied to the pottery has been limited to the simplest bent forms. Both the meticulous way in which the designs were applied, and the formal complexity of some of the design fields are evidence of strict design rules. Other possible linear marks made with stamping tools apart from the straight and single bent curves appear to be absent. Although there was close adherence by the potters to very constrained rules of design, within those limits they were able to achieve a remarkable visual complexity. A roulette was not used to assist quick application of the various designs emphasising the laborious task of producing such a wide corpus of work, often on large pottery vessels using only repeated single stamps. The imprinting of detailed patterns on clay vessels that needed to be kept semi-plastic for an extended period while the work was done, and with often complex symmetry underlines the skill of the designers. This implies that an important social investment was made in the production of this ornamented pottery beyond any value that a utilitarian ware may have had.

References

Anderson, A. 2001. Mobility models of Lapita migration. In G.R. Clark, A.J. Anderson and T. Vunidilo (eds), *The archaeology of Lapita dispersal in Oceania*, pp.15-23. Canberra: Pandanus Books, Australian National University. Terra Australis 17.

Ambrose, W. R. 1997. Contradictions in Lapita pottery, a composite clone. *Antiquity* 71(273):525-538.

Ambrose, W. R. 1999. Curves, tines, scutes and Lapita ware. In J-C. Galipaud and I. Lilley (eds), *Le Pacifique de 5000 à 2000 avant le present*, pp. 119-126. Paris: Institut de Recherche pour le Développement.

Anson, D. 1986. Lapita pottery of the Bismarck Archipelago and its affinities. *Archaeology in Oceania* 21:157-65.

Bedford, S. 2006. *Pieces of the Vanuatu Puzzle, Archaeology of the North, South and Centre*. Canberra : Pandanus Books, Australian National University. Terra Australis 23.

Basek, M. 1993. *A Lapita edge*. BA (Hons) thesis. University of Sydney.

Bellwood, P. 1997. *Prehistory of the Indo-Malaysian Archipelago*. Honolulu: University of Hawai'i Press.

Best, S. 2002. *Lapita: A view from the East*. Auckland: New Zealand Archaeological Association Monograph 24.

Chiu, S. and C. Sand 2005. Recording of the Lapita motifs: proposal for a complete recording method. *Archaeology in New Zealand*, 48(2):133-150.

Clough, R. 1992. Firing temperatures and the analysis of Oceanic ceramics: a study of Lapita ceramics from Reef/Santa Cruz, Solomon Islands. In J-C. Galipaud (ed), *Poterie Lapita et Peuplement*, pp 177-192. Nouméa: ORSTOM.

Craig, B. 2005. What can material culture studies tell us about the past in New Guinea? In A. Pawley, R. Attenborough, J. Golson and R. Hide (eds), *Papuan Pasts, cultural, linguistic and biological histories of Papua-speaking peoples*, pp. 493-513. Canberra: Research School of Pacific and Asian Studies, Australian National University. Pacific Linguistics 572.

Dickinson, W.R. 2006. *Temper sands in prehistoric Oceanian pottery*. Special Paper 406, Boulder Colorado: The Geological Society of America.

Green, R. 1990. Lapita design analysis: the Mead system and its use; a potted history. In M. Spriggs (ed), *Lapita Design, Form and Composition*, pp. 33-52. Canberra: Dept of Prehistory, Australian National University. Occasional Papers in Prehistory 19.

Green, R. 1991. The Lapita Cultural Complex: Current Evidence and Proposed Models. *Bulletin of the Indo-Pacific Prehistory Association* 11(2):295-305.

Green, R. 2000. Lapita and the cultural model for intrusion, integration and innovation. In A. Anderson and T. Murray (eds), *Australian Archaeologist; Collected papers in honour of Jim Allen*, pp 372-392. Canberra: Centre for Archaeological Research Australian National University, and Department of Archaeology, Latrobe University. Coombs Academic Publishing, Australian National University.

Intoh, M. 1982. *The physical analysis of Pacific pottery*. MA thesis. University of Otago.

Kirch, P.V. 1997. *The Lapita Peoples: Ancestors of the Oceanic World*. Oxford: Blackwell.

Kirch, P.V. 2000. *On the Road of the Winds, An Archaeological History of the Pacific Islands before European Contact*. Berkeley: University of California Press.

Poulsen, Y. 1987. *Early Tongan Prehistory*. Canberra: Dept of Prehistory, Australian National University. Terra Australis 12.

Sand, C. 1997. *Lapita Collection de poteries du site de Foué*. Nouméa: Les Cahiers de l'archaéologie en Nouvelle-Calédonie, Volume 7.

Sand, C. 1999a. Lapita and non-Lapita ware during New Caledonia's first millennium of Austronesian settlement. In J-C. Galipaud and I. Lilley (eds), *Le Pacifique de 5000 à 2000 avant le present*, pp.139-159. Paris: Institut de Recherche pour le Développement.

Sand, C. 1999b. Exhibition catalogue, *Archaéology des Origines le Lapita Calédonian*, New Caledonia, Service des Musées et du Patrimoine de Nouvelle Calédonie.

Siorat, J.P. 1990. A technological analysis of Lapita pottery decoration. In M. Spriggs (ed.), *Lapita Design, Form and Composition*, pp. 59-82. Canberra: Dept of Prehistory, Australian National University. Occasional Papers in Prehistory 19.

Spriggs, M. 1997. What is Southeast Asian about Lapita? In T. Akazawa and E.J.E. Szathmary (eds), *Prehistoric Mongoloid dispersals*, pp. 324-348. Oxford: Oxford University Press.

Spriggs, M. 2002. They've grown accustomed to your face. In S. Bedford, C. Sand and D. Burley (eds), *Fifty years in the field. Essays in honour and celebration of Richard Shutler Jr's archaeological career*, pp. 51-57. Auckland: New Zealand Archaeological Association Monograph 25.

Summerhayes, G. 2000. Recent archaeological investigations in the Bismarck Archipelago, Anir-New Ireland Province, Papua New Guinea. *Bulletin of the Indo-Prehistory Association* 19:167-174.

14

The excavation, conservation and reconstruction of Lapita burial pots from the Teouma site, Efate, Central Vanuatu

Stuart Bedford[1], Matthew Spriggs[2], Ralph Regenvanu[3], Colin Macgregor[4], Takaronga Kuautonga[3] and Michael Sietz[4]

[1] Department of Archaeology and Natural History
Research School of Pacific and Asian Studies
The Australian National University
Canberra, Australia
stuart.bedford@anu.edu.au

[2] School of Archaeology and Anthropology
College of Arts and Social Sciences
The Australian National University
Canberra, Australia
matthew.spriggs@anu.edu.au

[3] Vanuatu Cultural Centre
P.O. Box 184, Port Vila, Vanuatu
ralph.regenvanu@vanuatuculture.org

[4] Australian Museum
Sydney, NSW 2010, Australia
colin.macgregor@austmus.gov.au

Introduction

The recovery of complete Lapita pots is an extreme rarity. Of the over two hundred sites so far identified across the Lapita spectrum and particularly those sites associated with the earlier phase of the pottery sequence, discoveries have to date largely been restricted to the eponymous site of Lapita in New Caledonia (Coote and Sand 1999; Sand 1996, 1999, 2000; Sand *et al.* 1998). At that site, within a pit feature, two whole pots had been buried on top of and beneath large sherds of other pots. Their excavation and conservation ultimately led to detailed reconstruction of eleven pots, providing a major impetus to the characterisation of the New Caledonian Lapita ceramic repertoire. Up to three further complete carinated vessels from the same site have been more recently discovered and are still undergoing conservation treatment (Sand pers. comm.). A whole collection of reconstructable late Lapita vessels have also been recovered from the Sigatoka sand dunes over many decades (Birks 1973; Burley and Dickinson 2004). In January 2004 the Teouma Lapita site was discovered on the southeast coast of Efate, Vanuatu (Bedford *et al.* 2004; 2006). Three field seasons at the site have enabled the identification of an extensive Lapita cemetery with almost 50 burials. Associated with some of these burials were a number of fragmented but complete decorated Lapita pots, including four carinated vessels and a flat-

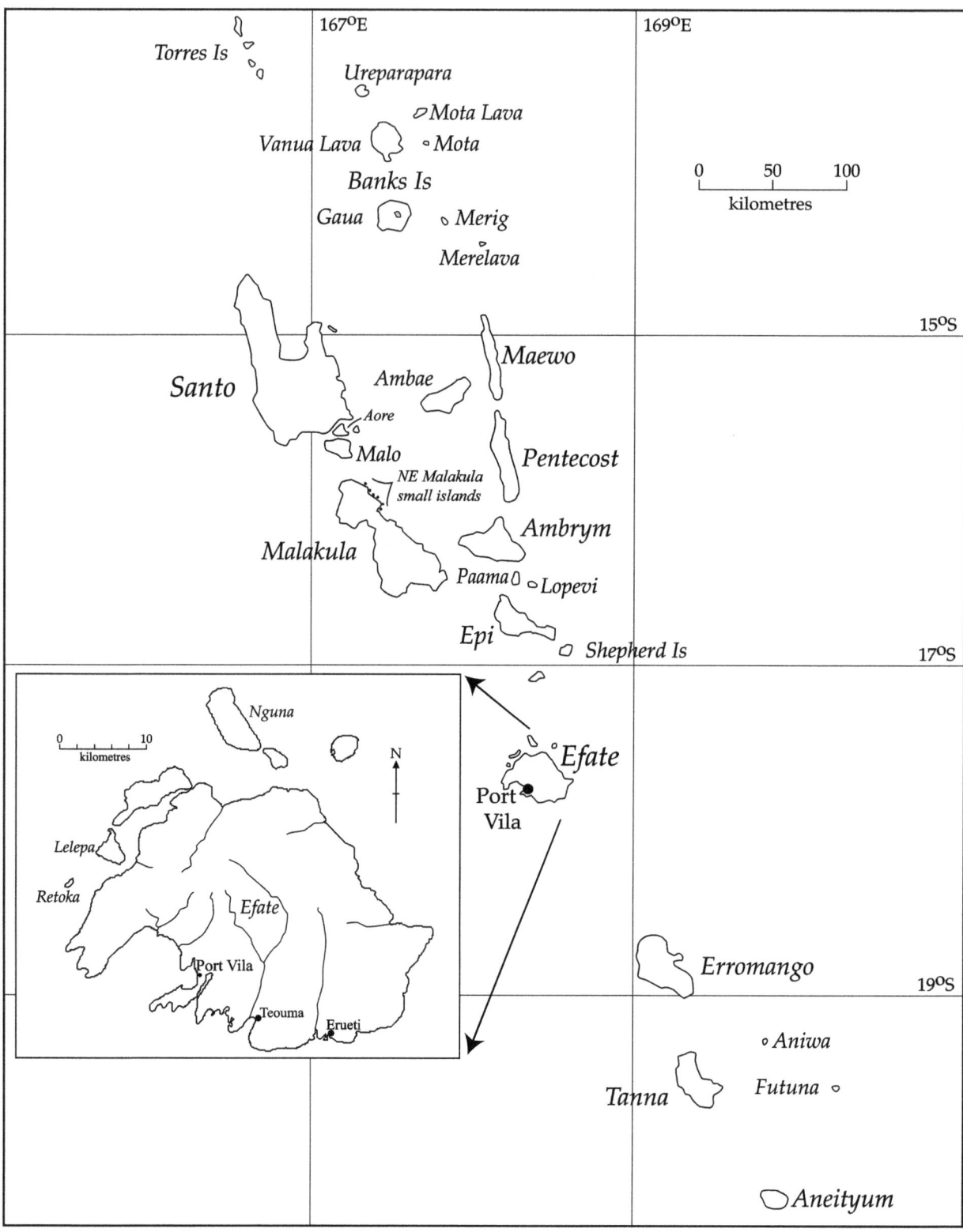

Figure 1. Teouma, Efate, Vanuatu.

bottomed dish. A complete undecorated pot stand has also been recovered. Following their excavation, they were conserved and reconstructed at the Australian Museum. This discovery provides a rare opportunity to profile these decorated pots that were linked to mortuary practice.

Excavation and recovery

The Teouma Lapita site is located 800 m from the sea, on the edge of an upraised former beach terrace and reef some eight metres above current sea level, on the north eastern side of Teouma Bay, southeast Efate (Figure 1). The site sits on top of a former rolled-coral upper beach and uplifted karstic reef terrace. Just prior to the arrival of colonising communities on Efate a thick layer of tephra was deposited across the uplifted terrace. When people did arrive, the site would have been located on a low promontory bounded by the sea on its western side and the small stream on its northeast side. The largely unweathered orange/yellow tephra that had been deposited prior to human arrival created a level surface across the craggy uplifted reef. The primary use of the area was as a cemetery where burials were placed in shallow graves dug into the tephra in gaps in the uplifted reef and the former upper beach area. Subsequent to the site being used as a cemetery, some 50 cm of midden was deposited across the site as a result of habitation activities, which in turn was later sealed by further tephra deposits (Bedford *et al.* 2004; 2006).

Figure 2. Excavation of the Teouma cemetery, 2005. Upturned Pot 3 is in the centre and Pot 2 with skull is on the right (the flat-bottomed dish has been removed). Excavators are Frédérique Valentin and Jacques Bolé. Fidel Yoringmal is the illustrator.

There is evidence across much of the cemetery that decorated Lapita pots were intimately connected with mortuary practice at the site. However, as is the case with the burials themselves, there is no standard or regular pattern that is apparent with the placement or use of the pots associated with the burials. Many of the pots had been disturbed during the use of the site for burial and in many cases concentrations of sherds of a single pot were found across one or two square metres. There were several instances of pot bases containing assorted human bone being recorded *in situ* and associated upper parts of the pot being scattered nearby (Bedford and Spriggs 2007). This suggested that these particular pots had been buried only up to the carination and/or subsequent activity had disturbed the upper decorated section.

Three of the complete pots discussed here (Pot 2 and 3 and the flat-bottomed dish) were concentrated amongst a cluster of burials interred within the tephra matrix in a solution hole in the former reef (Figure 2). Grave cuts and or other cut features contemporary with activity at the cemetery were extremely difficult to identify as they were being cut into and filled with the same undifferentiated tephra. There was little evidence for weathering or other deposits in the area where the pots were recovered. The pots appear to have been buried after being placed near burials as they are surrounded and sealed by the undifferentiated tephra. This concentration of burials and pots was also somewhat protected by a combination of depth of tephra and the surrounding remnant uplifted reef. This was dramatically emphasised when teeth marks from a mechanical excavator were found carved into a section of the adjacent remnant reef some 100 mm above the flat-bottomed dish.

Figure 3. Flat-bottomed dish being removed piece by piece. Excavator is Andrew Hoffman. Note both the top of the skull (centre of the dish) and the rim of Pot 2 can also be seen (bottom right of dish).

Although the chronology and other specifics of mortuary practice at the site including pottery associations will be discussed in detail in a subsequent publication, some general context relating to the complete pots is provided here. Sherds from Pot 1 were simply surface collected by workmen following mechanical earthmoving and quarrying at the site. Pot 2, a carinated vessel, contained a complete skull that sat on top of a broken *Conus* sp. ring. The flat-bottomed dish had been turned upside down and placed directly on top of Pot 2, acting as a lid (Figure 3). Most of Pot 2 is very thin walled, generally only 5 mm thick except for the carination area where it is some 15 mm thick. The pot had primarily broken at the carination and collapsed in onto the skull. The nature of this breakage indicates that once the skull had been placed in the pot it was not infilled with soil prior to the placement of the flat-bottomed dish. A lack of extra support that would have been supplied by a fill, combined with the added weight of the dish and subsequent infill, encouraged collapse (Figure 4). Pot 3, another carinated vessel, situated adjacent to Pot 2 and the dish, was found inverted and sitting on its rim. Some collapse had also occurred in the carination area but generally the pot had retained much of its original structural form, indicating that the pot must have been fully buried after placement (Figure 5).

Pot 4 was recovered during excavations in 2006. Another carinated vessel, it had been buried in the upper beach deposits adjacent to a number of burials. Later activity on the site, in the form of a large posthole associated with the later midden layer, had partly damaged the pot. Structural failure had occurred in the carination area, with the lower part of the neck shifting inwards while the upper part of the pot collapsed outward (Figure 6). This suggests that the upper part of the pot may not have been buried immediately after

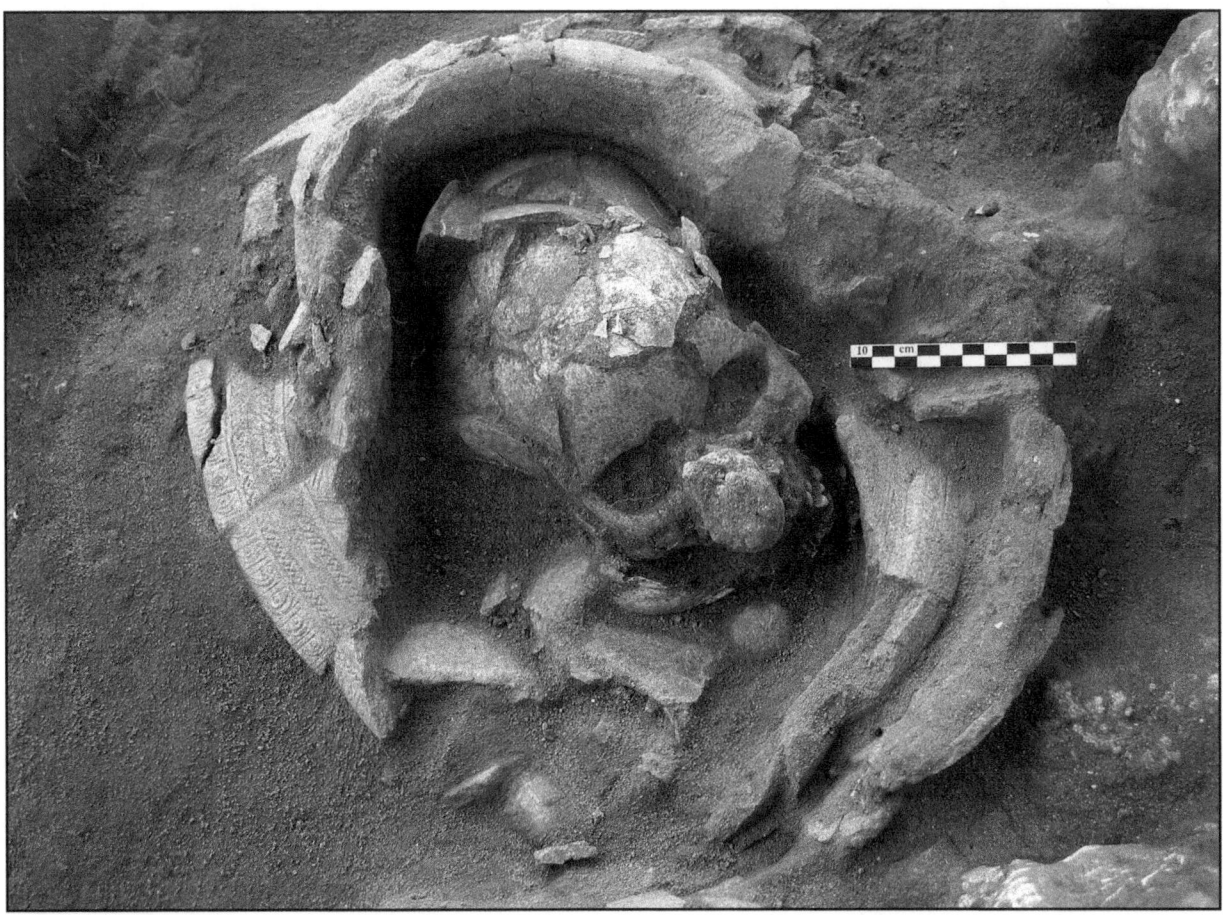

Figure 4. Pot 2 which had broken at the carination and collapsed inward.

Figure 5. Pot 3 in the foreground with globular base and part of the carination exposed. In the centre is Pot 2 (much of which has been removed) with the skull exposed.

its deposition. A concentration of very small Cypraea sp. shells was found in the base of the pot. The plain pot stand was also found in 2006, lying on its side adjacent to several burials. It seems likely to have been associated with mortuary activities but found somewhat removed from its original context. It was largely intact apart from a section near the rim. Following an on-site assessment by Colin Mcgregor and Takaronga

Kuautonga it was decided that due to its robust and intact nature, its conservation and reconstruction could be carried out in Port Vila.

On-site recording of the pots was undertaken with both a photographic record and illustrations. The excavated vessels were lifted and bagged on site after the layout of fragments was accurately drawn onto plans. These plans and photos were essential in facilitating the later reconstruction process.

Description of pots

The well-preserved pottery remains from the Teouma cemetery and midden dumping deposits will ultimately provide a detailed profile of Lapita vessel forms and decorative motifs which up until now has been completely lacking from Central Vanuatu. It will also provide a robust data set with which to make wider comparisons with more complete collections (Bedford and Spriggs in prep). In this paper we focus only on the five most complete pots and pot stand that were clearly in association with mortuary practice and have been discussed above. As noted five of these vessels were excavated *in situ* (Pots 2-4, flat-bottomed dish and pot stand) and another collected from bulldozed deposits (Pot 1). Description of design motifs and zone markers follows that of Donovan (1973) where applicable.

Figure 6. Pot 4 showing neck and rim splayed outward. Excavator is Colin Macgregor.

Pot No. 1 Carinated vessel with flat base

Dimensions: full height: 215 mm, carination to the base: 90mm, diameter: 310 mm, thickness: 5-10 mm (Figure 7).

It is this pot that lay at the centre of a whole series of serendipitous coincidences that led to the discovery of the site. A single large dentate-stamped sherd from this pot was the key to finding the site (Bedford *et al.* 2004) but the subsequent recovery of a dozen other sherds from the same vessel, ultimately some 75 % of the whole vessel which enabled a full reconstruction of the pot, were equally opportune and unexpected. Prior to earthworks at the site this pot was almost certainly complete although fragmented as indicated by weathered breaks on most sherds. This contrasted with several fresh breaks inflicted during the earthmoving activities. There was no stratigraphic context for this pot apart from the fact that it was retrieved from the Lapita deposits during quarrying. At the start of excavations in 2004 further sherds of this vessel were donated by Madame Monvoisin, the leaseholder of the land on which the site is located, who had retrieved them along with a number of other sherds, from a workshop situated on the farm.

Reconstruction of the pot began at the start of 2006 and at the same time further sherds, which had been collected while the site was being bulldozed, were donated from nearby Eratap village. News also came back from Sydney that suggested the base of the pot was flat rather than rounded. A search through a selection of unusual plain sherds that could not earlier be assigned to any vessel form revealed sections of the base. This distinctive vessel form is a first for Vanuatu and there do not appear to be any further examples at Teouma. One example only of this form of flat-bottomed carinated vessel has been identified in New Caledonia (Christophe Sand pers. comm.) suggesting that it is vary rare generally, although in the case of some sites this may be partly due to poor sherd preservation and an inability to securely define vessel form.

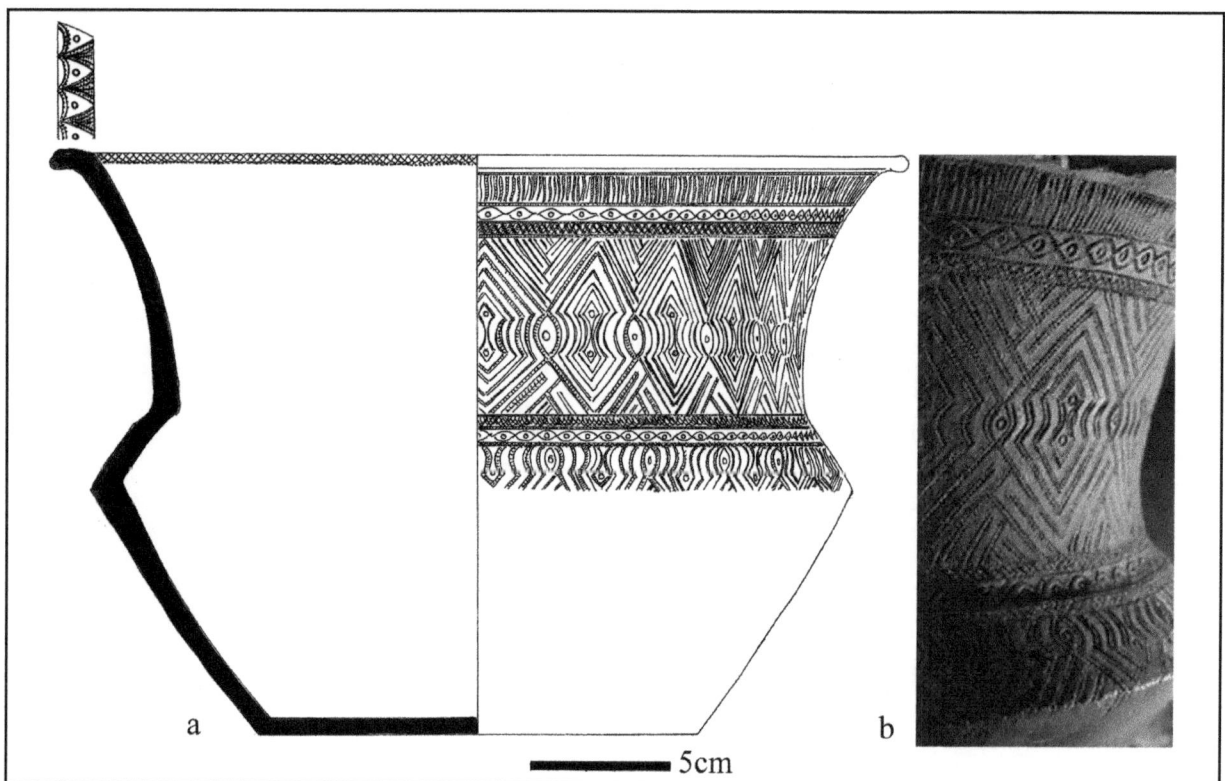

Figure 7. a. Pot 1 form and decoration and b. photograph of full motif.

The pot itself is very robust and finely decorated with a strongly flaring rim that is wider in circumference than the carination area. The neck region of the pot where the bulk of the decoration is situated is 65 mm in width. From the top of the pot downwards the dentate design is as follows. The interior rim is decorated with a restricted zone marker (RZ 3) and on the wide flat rim with M19.14. The design on the neck of the pot is bounded by a transverse zone marker, M28.3 and below that M5.6. The central band or frieze is a variant of M13(2).5 (bounded by a restricted zone marker [RZ 3]) with M5.6 repeated below that. The lowest band of decoration (separated from M5.6 by a further restricted zone marker [RZ 3]), situated on the upper part of the carination proper is a variant of M14(2).7.

Illustration of these pots was commenced in 2005 prior to their reconstruction and when they were returned to the Vanuatu Cultural Centre in 2006 the drawings were rechecked. Generally minimum modification was required but the hazards of speculation or assumption when dealing with fragmentary collections was highlighted when the flat base of Pot 1 was revealed. It had already been incorrectly published as having a curved base (Bedford et al. 2006: Fig.7).

Pot No. 2 Carinated vessel

Dimensions: full height: 245 mm, carination to base: 137 mm, diameter: 324 mm, thickness: 5-15 mm (Figure 8).

Some ninety per cent of this carinated vessel was preserved but it was one of the more fragmented, comprising almost 200 separate sherds. As outlined, this may have been due to the combined factors of poor vessel robusticity, position and the added weight of the flat-bottomed dish as a lid. Decoration on the inner rim of this vessel comprise a restricted zone marker (RZ 4) and on the wide flat rim M19.14, in this instance in mirror image to that seen on Pot 1. A restricted zone marker (RZ 4) runs around the circumference of the upper part of the rim and below this, the central frieze is made up of a variant of M13. Below that there are two restricted zone markers (RZ 4) one above the other. Below these, on the upper part of the carination proper is a variant of M59. The neck is more curved and restricted in its width (59mm) than the other carinated vessels at the site. The dentate-stamping tends to be coarsely applied and the central frieze design is expanded (Figure 9).

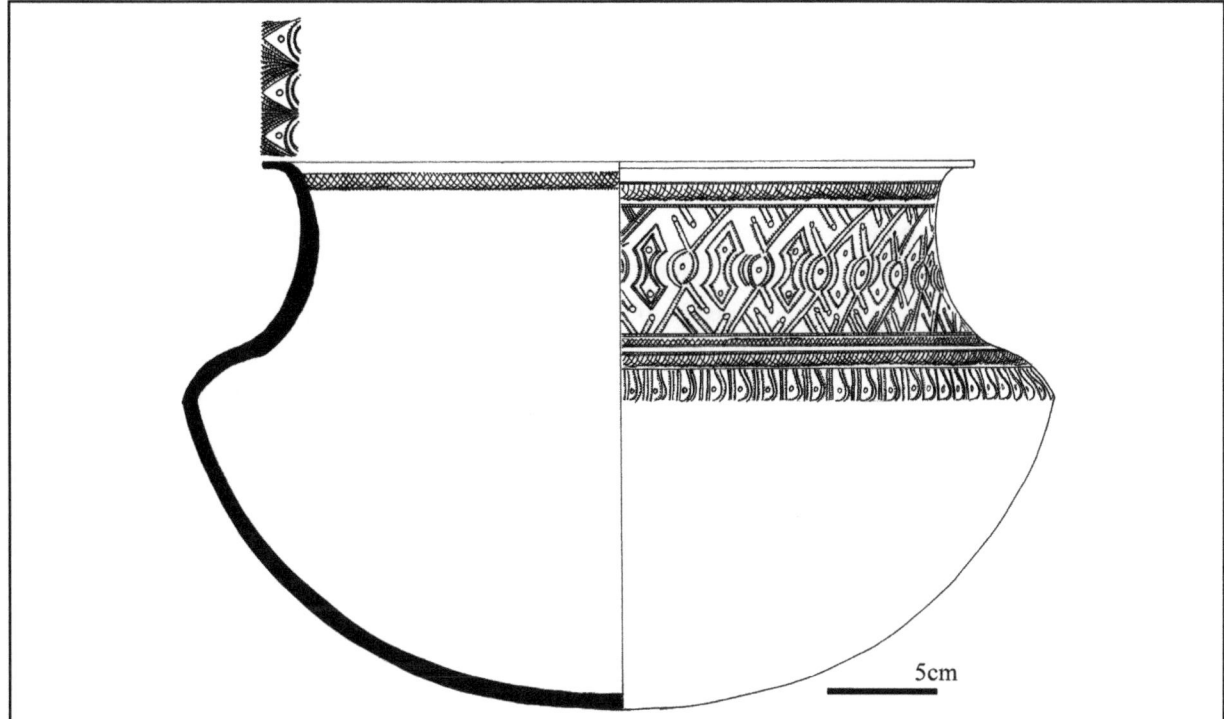

Figure 8. Pot 2 form and decoration.

Figure 9. Close up of Pot 2 decoration.

Pot No. 3 Carinated vessel

Dimensions: full height: 400mm, carination to base: 210mm, diameter: 450mm, thickness 5-8 mm (Figure 10).

This is one of the two largest recovered pots, coming close in overall size to the largest carinated vessels found in New Caledonia (Clark this volume; Sand *et al.* 1998). There is no decoration on the inner rim. The lip is decorated with M77.4. The uppermost decoration below the lip is a zone marker followed by a restricted zone marker (RZ 4). The primary decoration on the neck (95 mm wide) of the vessel, the central frieze, is a distinctive geometrical motif that has elements of both M100 and M27 and is bounded by zone markers. Below this a further restricted zone marker (RZ 4) completing the decoration of the neck. On the upper part of the carination is M1.6 in mirror image bounded on the lower side by a further zone marker (RZ 4). Motif M19.7 completes the lower part of the design just on the edge of the upper part of the carination. The dentate on this vessel tends to be less fine and the central frieze design, as in the case of Pot 2, is expanded or exploded rather than being compactly formatted.

Pot No. 4 Carinated vessel

Dimensions: full height: c. 340 mm, carination to base:115mm, diameter: 550 mm, thickness: 5-10 mm (Figure 11).

This fourth carinated vessel excavated in 2006 has also recently been conserved and reconstructed by the Australian Museum. While detailed measurements were taken on a series of large sherds prior to it being sent to Sydney, the final reconstruction has provided greatly enhanced accuracy. It is, along with Pot 3, one of the two largest carinated vessels recovered from the site. There is no decoration on the inner rim. Decoration from the top down commences on the wide flat lip with M14(2).4. Just below the lip, the upper most decoration is a restricted zone marker (RZ 4) followed by a dentate version of M6.1. The primary decoration on the neck of the vessel, the central frieze, is a labyrinth design similar to M73 but without any additional motifs. The width of the central band design is 125mm. It is bordered by restricted zone markers (RZ 4). Below that is M5.6 separated from the motif decorating the upper part of the carination by a repeat of RZ 4. The lowest motif, which is not listed in Donovan but might be seen as a variant of M14(2).10, comprises what can be simply described as a series of interlocking concentric carinated vessel forms (labelled by Sand as interlocking triangles [Sand 1999:57]) interrupted by two sets (on opposite sides of the pot) of three vertical nubbins or lugs. In between the lugs are singular versions of the concentric carinated vessel form.

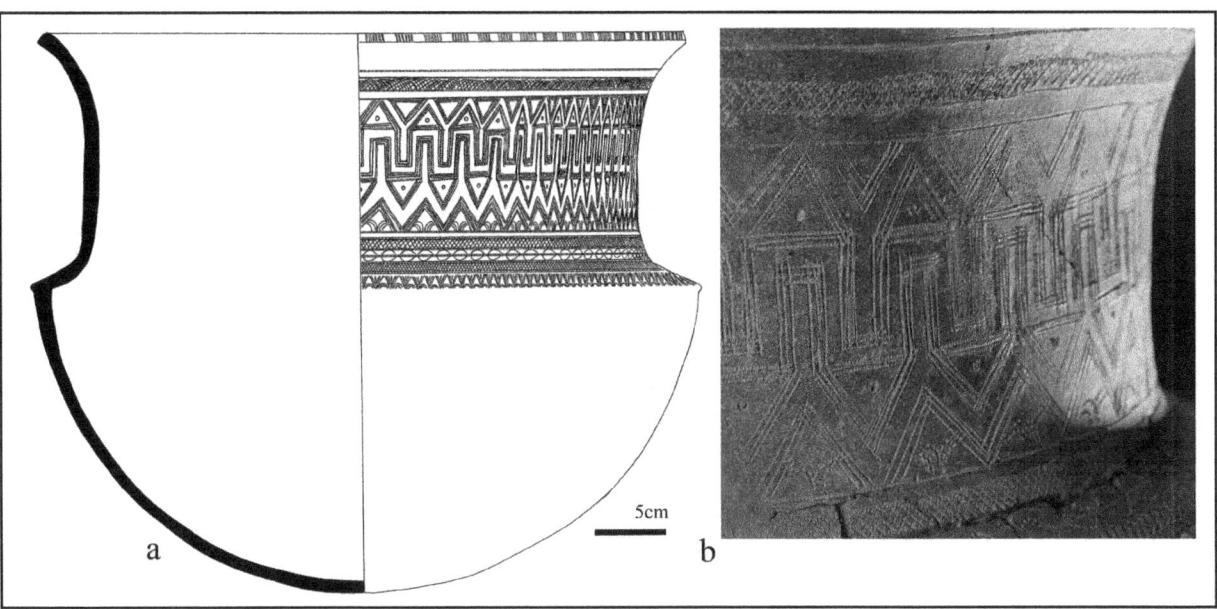

Figure 10. a. Pot 3 form and decoration and b. photograph of central frieze.

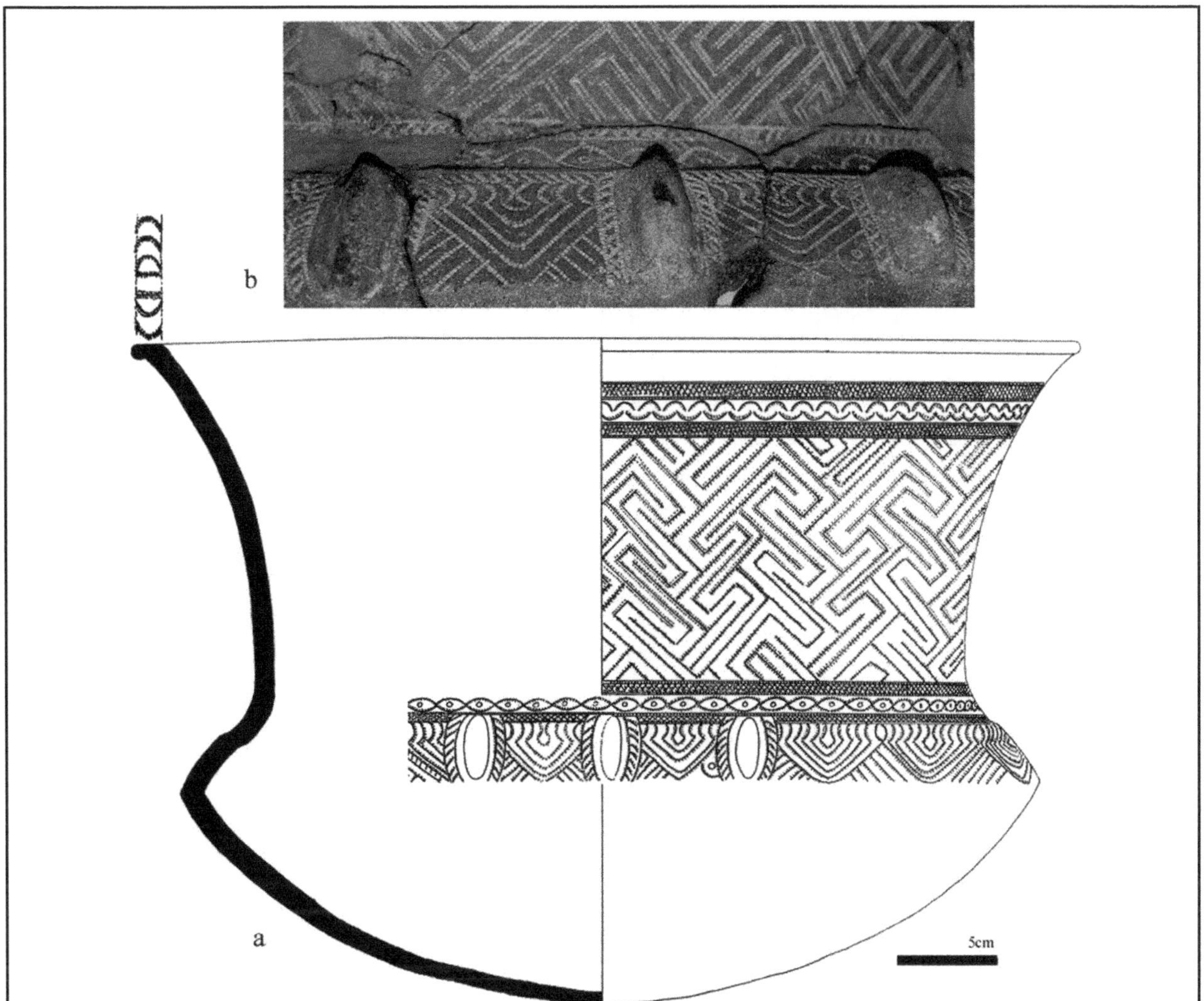

Figure 11. a. Pot 4 form and decoration and b. closeup of lugs or nubbins.

In the field it was difficult to determine whether the base was flat or curved due to its crushed nature. Once reconstructed, however, it could be firmly established that the vessel in fact has a very shallow base (115 mm from carination to base). This is a particularly distinctive feature of this vessel which has the effect of further emphasising the central frieze.

Flat-bottomed dish

Dimensions: height: 70 mm, diameter: 360 mm, thickness 9-12 mm thick (Figures 12, 13).

The flat-bottomed dish is a relatively robust vessel with generally thicker walls and base. A total of 12 sherds were recovered which comprised 95 % of the vessel. The dish has a circular groove (9.5 mm in diameter) in the centre of its base, a strong indication that it was originally made to sit on top of a cylinder stand. Several of these stands have been identified amongst the recovered materials. This is further emphasised with the strongly flaring nature of the rim, where without elevation, the full design is to some extent obscured. The only decoration on the interior rim is a restricted zone marker (RZ 3). The lip is decorated with a variant of Motif 19 combining a row of impressed circles (nearest the interior) and a curved version of M19.1. Restricted zone markers (RZ 3) run the full circumference of the dish just below the lip and also just above the base. Just below the upper restricted zone marker M19 is found encircling the dish, although interrupted at various points where an inverted face motif is found. The decoration of the dish is dominated by a double face motif that is replicated around the full circumference of the dish, the joining point of which is facilitated by an extra 'nose' infilled with impressed circles (Figure 13).

Double face motifs have been noted further west and in New Caledonia (Chiu 2005; Sand 1996; Spriggs 1990:93, 1993, 2002) but are always set within a single design, one above the other. The alternating double face motif found on the Teouma dish is thus far unique, although its uniqueness may be simply related to the fragmentary nature of most Lapita sherd collections (see Chiu this volume). The alternating double face motif might be seen as an adaptation of the other double face motifs where the triangular face with a semi-circular cap is often a central feature. This motif is also found singularly (Chiu 2005:28; Sand 1999:54) although again the fragmentary nature of collections often makes assessment of this difficult. The inverted triangular face is combined with the 'long nose' or 'elongated face' motif (Sand 1999:55), a motif that has again been recorded across much of the Lapita distribution (Chiu 2005; Spriggs 1990, 1993). Given restrictions of space on the vessel, the triangular face has been flipped and placed adjacent to the elongated face motif. In many respects the motif is very similar structurally to the elongated face motifs with 'earplugs'. The 'earplugs' in this case, however, have been replaced with inverted triangular faces. The dentate-stamping on this dish is fine and the motif is tightly structured.

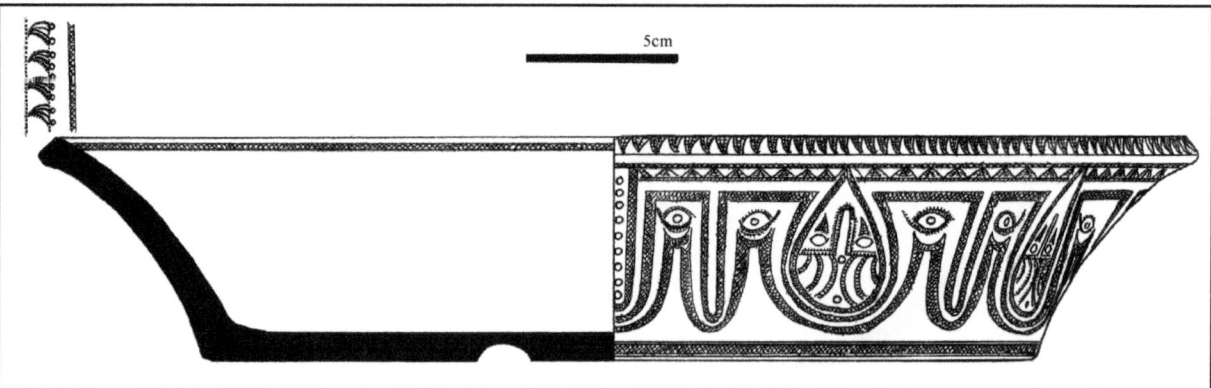

Figure 12. Flat-bottomed dish form and decoration.

Figure 13. Joining point of double face motif on flat-bottomed dish.

Plain pot stand

Dimensions: Height: 90 mm, diameter top: 140 mm, diameter base: 190 mm (Figure 14).

We have tentatively labelled this almost complete vessel as a pot stand. It was found lying on its side, half buried in the upper most Lapita-associated occupation levels of the site. A number of burials were subsequently recorded in the near vicinity. Its hourglass form and wide rim and basal diameters indicate that it could have been used to support either flat or circular bottomed vessels. It is largely tubular apart from a solid section in the centre of the stand. There is no decoration evident on any part of the pot stand. It thus far appears to be a unique form although, as is so often the case, it would be very difficult to confidently assign small sherds to such a form.

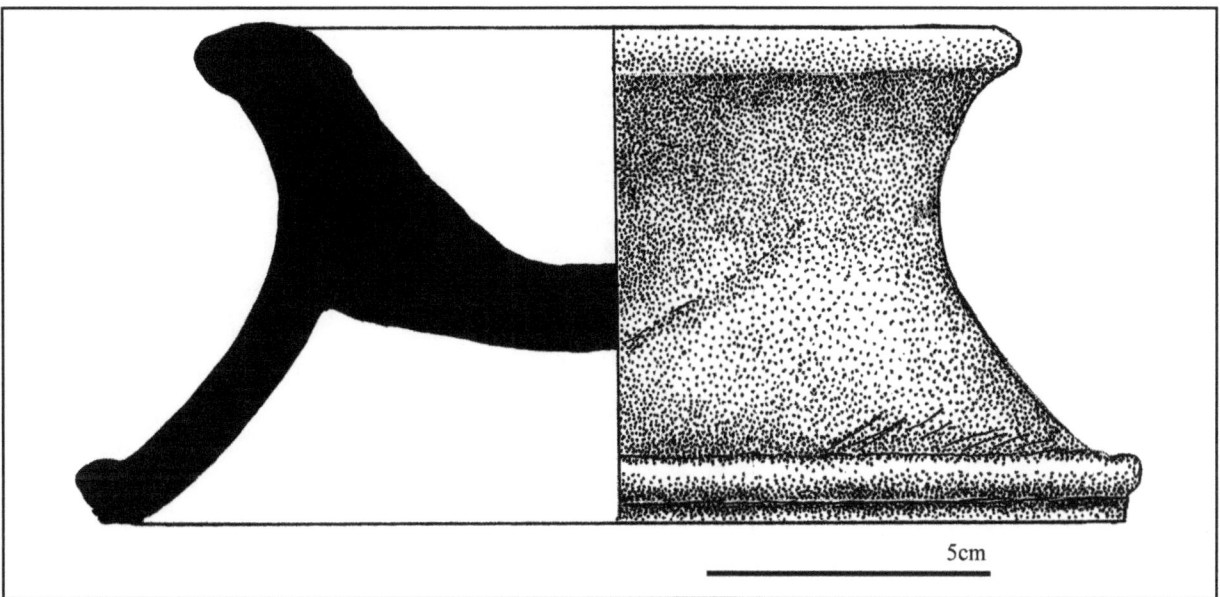

Figure 14. Plain pot stand form.

Conservation and reconstruction

Five pots have been conserved and reconstructed at the Australian Museum in Sydney by the Collection Integrity Unit (Macgregor and Sietz 2006) and four have already been returned to the Vanuatu Cultural Centre. The pots each displayed different styles of form and decoration and the condition of the material varied. The reconstruction of each pot, therefore, presented different challenges. The overall techniques and materials applied, however, were the same for each pot. It is crucial that on-site lifting techniques of such pots are carefully considered and block lifting should only be chosen if there is a clear benefit to be had by supporting the pot as one piece with soil infill, until it reaches the lab. In the case of the Teouma pots the fragments needed to be dismantled anyway in order to clean edges and re-assemble the sherds. The procedure that was followed and deemed to be the most suitable in this case involved the careful mapping, lifting, bagging and packing of individual sherds.

Sherds that were surface collected during the initial reconnaissance to find the site in 2004 appeared robust and well preserved despite having been exposed during quarrying some four months previously. This suggested that soluble salts were not a major problem at Teouma as they had been at WKO013A Lapita (Coote and Sand 1999; Sand *et al.* 1998). If large amounts of soluble salts have accumulated in the fabric of the sherds, serious physical damage can occur post-excavation due to the recrystallisation of the salts following periods of high humidity (Cronyn 1990). The stability of the Teouma ceramics was further confirmed over the following twelve months as the surface collected and excavated sherds from the first season of fieldwork showed no sign of physical change. To verify this observation sherds from the complete vessels were tested for the presence of soluble salts. Fragments of the flat dish were soaked for two days in water and the conductivity of the bath was measured. The results were 9.5μS in the distilled water and 60μS after soaking the sherds. This moderate increase in conductivity indicates that there was not a significant amount of soluble salt in the fabric of the pots.

All sherds were initially dry brushed. This was the preferred method for cleaning the sherds as the fabric of some of the pots (Pots 2 and 3) would have been prone to disintegration if washed in water. Harder

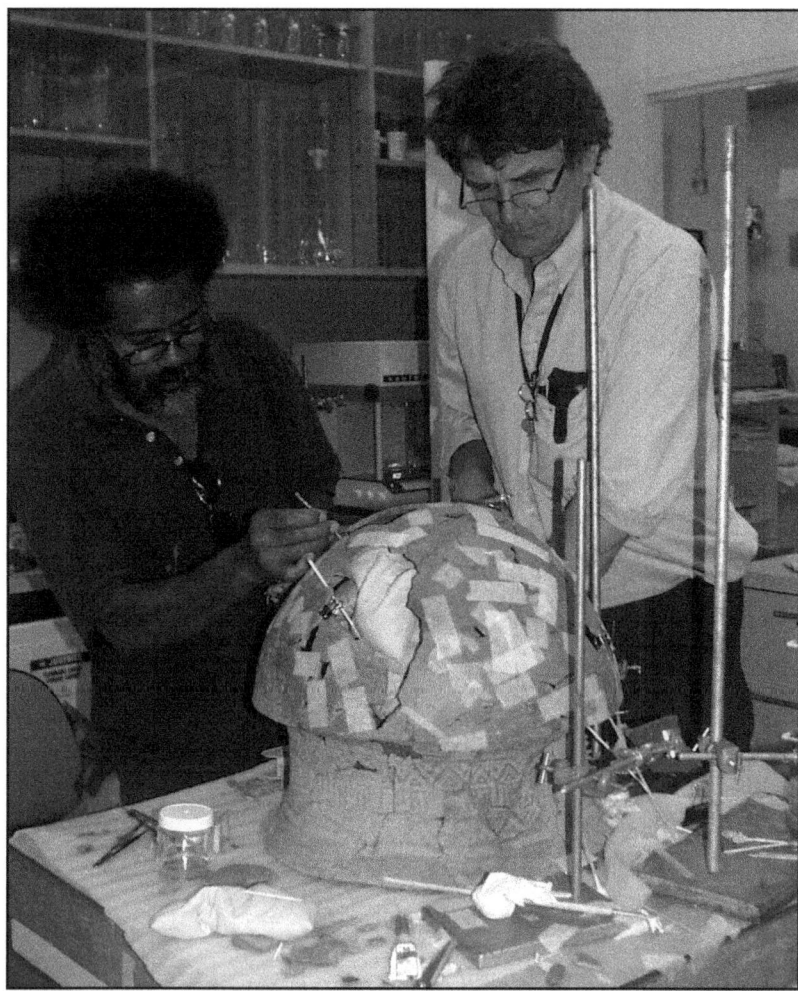

Figure 15. Takaronga Kuautonga and Colin Macgregor reconstructing Pot 3. Note small sand bag and structural supports.

accretions were removed from the edges using scalpels where necessary. In general, there was a conscious effort to avoid over-cleaning of the internal and external surfaces to avoid impeding future analysis by removing trace residues that may be present. Prior to assembly the edges were consolidated by applying a thin solution of Paraloid B72 acrylic resin in acetone to the edges (Koob 1986). The concentration of the solution was varied between 5-10 % depending on the porosity of the pot. The solution was applied with either a fine brush or a pipette. This localised consolidation strengthens the edges and prevents the adhesive migrating into the fabric during reconstruction. The condition of the pots did not warrant complete consolidation of the fabric by total immersion in solution. Total consolidation by immersion is sometimes necessary with pottery, due to its extremely friable nature caused by crushinga or salt damage.

The sherds were joined using a premixed Paraloid B72 adhesive, applied directly onto the broken edges or by injection into the gaps of the assembled edges. Surgical paper adhesive bandage tape was used to preassemble sections to ensure a good fit and also to secure the sherds in position whilst the adhesive hardened. In order to provide adequate strength in areas where the edges had eroded resulting in very narrow points of contact, a thickened paste of adhesive was applied consisting of a mixture of Paraloid B72 (30 %) in acetone and glass micro-balloons. This increased the contact area with the two surfaces considerably.

All three carinated pots were assembled upside down beginning with the decorated rim and neck sections. For Pots 2, 3 and 4, a wall of sand bags and PE-foam sheets was used to support the round bottom from inside (Figure 15). The carinated vessels also required areas of loss to be gap-filled with pigmented plaster. This was generally applied where required to provide enough strength for long-term stability. No decorations were imitated with the infillings. To protect the surface, areas along gaps are covered with liquid latex during the infilling process. The liquid plaster is supported from one side by a mould of plasticine or a thin sheet of PE-foam covered with foil. The final retouching of the colour to blend with the overall look of the pot was carried out using acrylic paints and added dry pigments.

Discussion and Conclusion

The discovery of well-preserved archaeological sites often injects a sudden burst of increased knowledge to areas of research that are more commonly assessed and profiled through the steady incremental accumulation of data. In the case of Lapita, and more specifically the characterisation of the distinctive decorated pots, a number of sites fall into this former category, namely the Arawes, Mussau, Reef-Santa Cruz, Site 13 at Lapita and Sigatoka. While Teouma can now be added to this list, the remains at the site also highlight the complexity found with even a well preserved archaeological record and the inherent difficulties in interpreting and explaining human behaviour and activity.

The cemetery at Teouma furnishes insights into the mortuary practices of the earliest Lapita settlers of Remote Oceania which appear to have been a multi-faceted and on-going process (Bedford et al. 2006). Certain aspects of the mortuary practices at Teouma, including the use of pots in burial ceremony have close parallels with mortuary practices in Island Southeast Asia, including Taiwan, during earlier and contemporary periods (Bellwood 1997). As long hypothesised, decorated pots clearly had a significant role in Lapita ceremonial activity (Kirch 1997), but as demonstrated in the case of the Teouma burials, there are both patterns and peculiarities in their use and function. All of the excavated reconstructed vessels, and almost certainly the carinated vessel retrieved during earthmoving, were associated with mortuary activity. There is no standard positioning or use of the pots. Pots were placed in upturned positions, others upright with assorted human bone deposited within them and in one case of clear secondary or even opportunistic use, a flat-bottomed dish was used as a lid. Carinated vessels dominate in the reconstructed sample as they do with the collection of less complete excavated sherds across the cemetery, but they vary greatly in size and in some aspects of their shape (Figure 16). The complete pots are all

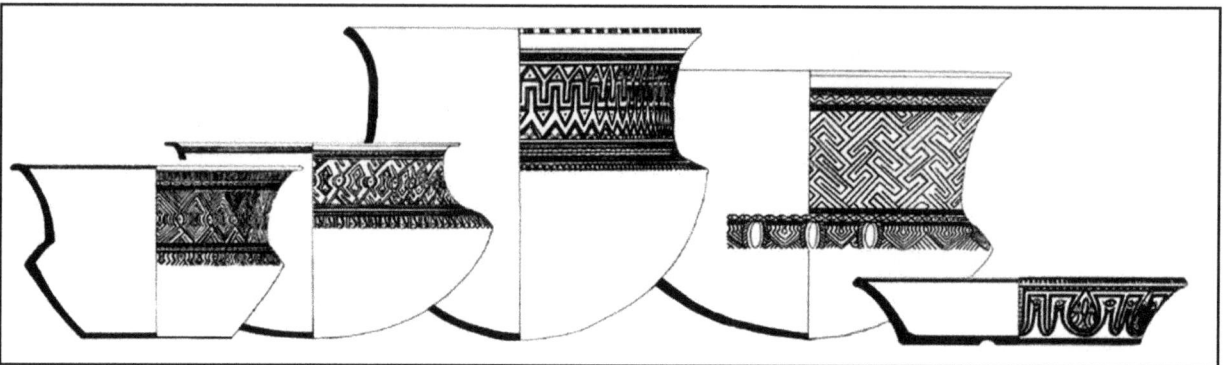

Figure 16. Broad relative size comparisons of the complete vessels. From left to right, Pot 1, 2, 3, 4 and flat dish.

decorated, although with a range of both fine and coarse dentate decoration, one with a face motif and the others with geometric designs. These features from Teouma underscore conclusions reached by other researchers in relation to gauging chronological variation in Lapita ceramics: that is that vessel form, decorative finesse, and design structure and content are not always a definitive marker of chronological divergence (Chiu 2005:27, this volume; Sand *et al.* 1998:41).

For a long time Lapita in Vanuatu has been somewhat of a confused picture, with only limited reporting being restricted to the mixed deposits from Malo (Hedrick 1971, nd; Hedrick and Shutler 1969) and the very limited numbers of sherds from Erueti on Efate (Garanger 1972: Fig. 9) and Erromango (Bedford 2006a:102). The recent discovery, however, of the well preserved sites of Makue on Aore (Galipaud 2001; Galipaud and Swete-Kelly this volume; Galipaud and Vienne 2005), sites on the small islands (Vao, Atchin, Wala and Uripiv) off the northeast coast of Malakula (Bedford 2003, 2006b) and Teouma are set to dramatically change the situation, particularly in terms of providing a robust profile of the Lapita ceramics of Vanuatu which is essential for inter-regional comparisons. As perhaps we should expect, none of the complete vessels from Teouma have direct parallels with any of the whole pots from New Caledonia, although many elements of the full designs are indeed present. Virtually all the motifs present on the Teouma pots can be found in the assemblages from the Reefs-Santa Cruz Group but this again might be expected as it is far easier to find direct parallels amongst single motifs from a large collection of fragmented sherds from several sites than a limited range of whole pots. What the growing corpus of complete design motifs is certainly highlighting, however, is the extensive range of motif permutations and combinations that were produced by Lapita potters. One of the more distinctive decorative features found on the complete pots from Teouma is the sets of applied vertical lugs or bars seen on Pot 4 (a feature that has also been found on Vao). This is a decorative feature not found thus far in sites further west or in New Caledonia but is found in modified form in both Fiji and Tonga (Davidson *et al.* 1990:Fig. 15; Poulsen 1987 Vol 2:145), hinting at potential Vanuatu origins or links.

Not all decorated Lapita pots were associated with burials but rather with a whole range of ceremonial activities (Clark and Murray 2006:114). The difficulty for archaeologists, however, is being able to identify these in the often very mixed and disturbed deposits that comprise most Lapita sites. The discovery of sites such as Teouma provides us with a rare opportunity to investigate Lapita mortuary ritual and establish a detailed profile of the associated pottery (cf. Clark and Wright in press). These data can then potentially be used to glean greater information and definition from the myriad of other excavated materials from Lapita sites which have not been so well preserved.

Acknowledgments

The Teouma Archaeological Project is a joint initiative of the Vanuatu National Museum and The Australian National University (ANU), directed by Professor Matthew Spriggs and Dr Stuart Bedford of the ANU and Mr Ralph Regenvanu, Director of the Vanuatu Cultural Centre until December 2006. Funding of the project in 2004 and 2005 was provided by the Pacific Biological Foundation, The Royal Society of New Zealand (Marsden Fastart) and the Department of Archaeology and Natural History and School of Archaeology and Anthropology at the ANU. Excavations in 2006 were funded primarily through a National Geographic Society Scientific Research Grant with additional funding from the Australian Research Council (DP0556874). The drawing skills of Fidel Yoringmal were invaluable both in recording the pots on site and the illustration of the complete pots figured here. Thanks must also be extended to our collaborators in the field, Jacques Bolé, Hallie Buckley, Nancy Tayles, Willy Damelip, Stuart Hawkins, Andrew Hoffman and Frédérique Valentin. The support of the leaseholder Robert Monvoisin and family is acknowledged, as is the support and assistance of the traditional landowners of Eratap Village. Staff of the Vanuatu Cultural Centre were enthusiastic and supportive throughout. Conservation and reconstruction of the pots was primarily funded by the Australian Museum with additional funding from the International Council of Museums and AusAID which facilitated the participation of Takaronga Kuautonga, curator at the National Museum of Vanuatu. Photographs labelled Figures 7b, 9 and 10b were taken by Stephen Alvarez and permission for their reproduction was granted by the Picture Editor, National Geographic Magazine. Christophe Sand and Geoff Clark read earlier drafts of the paper and provided productive criticism.

References

Bedford, S. 2003. The timing and nature of Lapita colonisation in Vanuatu: the haze begins to clear. In C. Sand (ed.), *Pacific Archaeology: assessments and prospects*, pp. 147-158. Noumea: Les Cahiers de l'archéologie en Nouvelle-Calédonie 15.

Bedford, S. 2006a. *Pieces of the Vanuatu Puzzle: Archaeology of the North, South and Centre*. Canberra: Pandanus Press, Australian National University. Terra Australis 23.

Bedford, S. 2006b. The Pacific's earliest painted pottery: an added layer of intrigue to the Lapita debate and beyond. *Antiquity* 80:544-557.

Bedford, S., A. Hoffman, M. Kaltal, R. Regenvanu and R. Shing 2004. Dentate-stamped Lapita reappears on Efate, Central Vanuatu: a four decade-long drought is broken. *Archaeology in New Zealand* 47(1):39-49.

Bedford, S., M. Spriggs and R. Regenvanu 2006. The Teouma Lapita site and the early human settlement of the Pacific Islands. *Antiquity* 80:812-828.

Bedford, S. and M. Spriggs 2007. Birds on the rim: a unique Lapita carinated vessel in its wider context. *Archaeology in Oceania* 42:12-21.

Bedford, S. and M. Spriggs in prep. Lapita vessel form and decoration in Central Vanuatu: characterisation and comparison.

Bellwood, P. 1997. *Prehistory of the Indo-Malaysian Archipelago*. Honolulu: University of Hawaii Press.

Birks, L. 1973. *Archaeological Excavations at Sigatoka Dune Site, Fiji*. Suva: Bulletin of the Fiji Museum, No. 1.

Burley, D. and W. Dickinson 2004. Late Lapita occupation and its ceramic assemblage at the Sigatoka Sand Dune site, Fiji and their place in Oceanic prehistory. *Archaeology in Oceania* 39:12-25.

Chiu, S. 2005. Meanings of a Lapita Face: Materialized Social Memory in Ancient House Societies. *Taiwan Journal of Anthropology* 3:1-47.

Coote, K. and C. Sand 1999. The conservation of Lapita pottery: ignore it at your peril. In J-C. Galipaud and I. Lilley (eds), *The Western Pacific from 5000 to 2000 BP. Colonisation and transformations,* pp. 333-343. Paris: IRD Éditions.

Clark, G. and T. Murray 2006. Decay characteristics of the eastern Lapita design system. *Archaeology in Oceania* 41:107-117.

Clark, G. and D. Wright in press. Reading Pacific Pots. In A. Anderson (ed.), Title TBA. Dunedin: University of Otago Press.

Cronyn, J. 1990 *The elements of archaeological conservation.* London: Routledge.

Davidson, J., E. Hinds, S. Holdaway and F. Leach 1990. The Lapita site of Natanuku, Fiji. *New Zealand Journal of Archaeology* 12:121-155.

Donovan, L. J. 1973. Inventory of Design Elements and Motifs in Lapita Reef-Santa Cruz Island Pottery. Unpublished appendices to MA research essay, University of Auckland.

Hedrick, J. 1971. Lapita Style Pottery from Malo Island. *Journal of the Polynesian Society* 80 (1):5-19.

Hedrick, J. nd. Archaeological Investigations of Malo Prehistory. Lapita Settlement Strategy in the Northern New Hebrides. Manuscript draft of PhD dissertation, University of Pennsylvania.

Hedrick, J. and M. E. Shutler 1969. Report on "Lapita Style" Pottery From Malo Island, Northern New Hebrides. *Journal of the Polynesian Society* 78 (2):262-65.

Kirch, P.V. 1997. *The Lapita Peoples. Ancestors of the Oceanic World.* Oxford: Blackwell.

Koob, S. 1986. The Use of Paraloid B72 as an adhesive: its application for archaeological ceramics. *Studies in Conservation* 31:7-13.

Macgregor, C. and M. Sietz 2006. The Conservation of Four Lapita Pots from the Teouma Excavations, Vanuatu. Unpublished report, Australian Museum.

Galipaud, J-C. 2001. Survey of Prehistoric Sites in Aore. Preliminary assessment. Unpublished report to Vanuatu Cultural Centre.

Galipaud, J-C. and B. Vienne. 2005. Chronologie du peuplement et réseaux d'échanges dans le nord du Vanuatu. Mission Santo 2005. Rapport préliminaire. Nouméa: IRD.

Garanger, J. 1972. *Archéologie des Nouvelles-Hébrides: contribution à la connaissance des îles du centre.* Publications de la Société des Océanistes, No.30. Paris: ORSTOM.

Poulsen, J. 1987. *Early Tongan Prehistory.* 2 Vols. Canberra: Department of Prehistory, Australian National University. Terra Australis 12.

Sand, C. 1996. *Intervention d'urgence sur le site WKO013A de lapita octobre 1995.* Noumea: Départment Archéologie du Service des Musées et du Patrimoine de Nouvelle-Calédonie .

Sand, C. 1999. *Lapita. The pottery collection from the site at Foué, New Caledonia.* Noumea: Les cahiers de l'archéologie en Nouvelle-Calédonie, Volume 7.

Sand, C. 2000. The specificities of the "Southern Lapita Province": the New Caledonian case. *Archaeology in Oceania* 35(1):20-33.

Sand, C., K. Coote, J. Bole and A. Ouetcho 1998. A pottery pit at locality WKO013A, Lapita (New Caledonia). *Archaeology in Oceania* 33:37-43.

Spriggs, M. 1990. The Changing face of Lapita: the transformation of a design. In M.T. Spriggs (ed.), *Lapita design, form and composition: proceedings of the Lapita design workshop, Canberra, Australia, December 1988,* pp.83-122. Canberra: Department of Prehistory, Australian National University. Occasional Papers in Prehistory 18.

Spriggs, M. 1993. How Much of the Lapita Design System Represents the Human Face? In P. Dark and R. Rose (eds), *Artistic Heritage in a Changing Pacific,* pp.7-14. Bathurst: Crawford House Press

Spriggs, M. 2002. They've grown accustomed to your face. In Bedford, S., C. Sand and D. Burley (eds), *Fifty Years in the Field: Essays in Honour and Celebration of Richard Shutler Jrs Archaeological Career,* pp.51-58. Auckland: New Zealand Archaeological Association Monograph 25.

15

Detailed analysis of Lapita Face Motifs: Case Studies from Reef/Santa Cruz Lapita Sites and New Caledonia Lapita Site 13A

Scarlett Chiu

Center for Archaeological Studies
Research Center for Humanities and Social Sciences
Academia Sinica
#128, Section 2, Academia Road
Nankung, Taipei, 11529, Taiwan
chius@gate.sinica.edu.tw

Introduction

The complex, often elaborate and very distinctive dentate-stamped Lapita designs were first identified at a site on Watom Island, in the northern coastal islands of Papua New Guinea, almost 100 years ago (Meyer 1909, 1910). It was not recognised until much later that this particular way of decorating pots was associated with a cultural complex that occurred throughout the Southwest Pacific (Golson 1961, 1971). Encompassing such a large region (Figure 1), from Island New Guinea across to Samoa, both temporal and spatial variation in terms of decorative style was to be expected. Lapita pottery was mostly manufactured by a uniform method of slab-building, strengthened with paddles and anvils, smoothed and decorated with various techniques, then fired at low temperatures (Bellwood 1978:258; Golson 1971; Green 1974; Green 1991; Hunt 1988). Chemical and petrographic studies from a number of Lapita sites indicate that there was no strict control over raw materials used to produce these pots and there is a lack of restricted correlation between tempers and motifs ([Arawes] Summerhayes 2000a:234; [Reber-Rakival] Anson 2000; [Site 13A] Chiu 2003a). With the exception of Mussau Island, (Kirch 1988a; Kirch 1991; Kirch et al. 1991), most Lapita pottery has been identified as having been locally made, and exchanged only among nearby local communities (Dickinson et al. 1996; Galipaud 1990; Summerhayes 2000a).

Regional "communication boundaries" have been proposed and the area encompassing the Lapita Cultural Complex has been divided into a number of regions based on stylistic analyses of motif and vessel forms (Green and Kirch 1997:30). These include Western and Eastern Lapita (Anson 1983; Green 1978), Western Fijian and Lau-West Polynesian (Best 1984; Geraghty 1996), Southern and Northern West Polynesian (Kirch

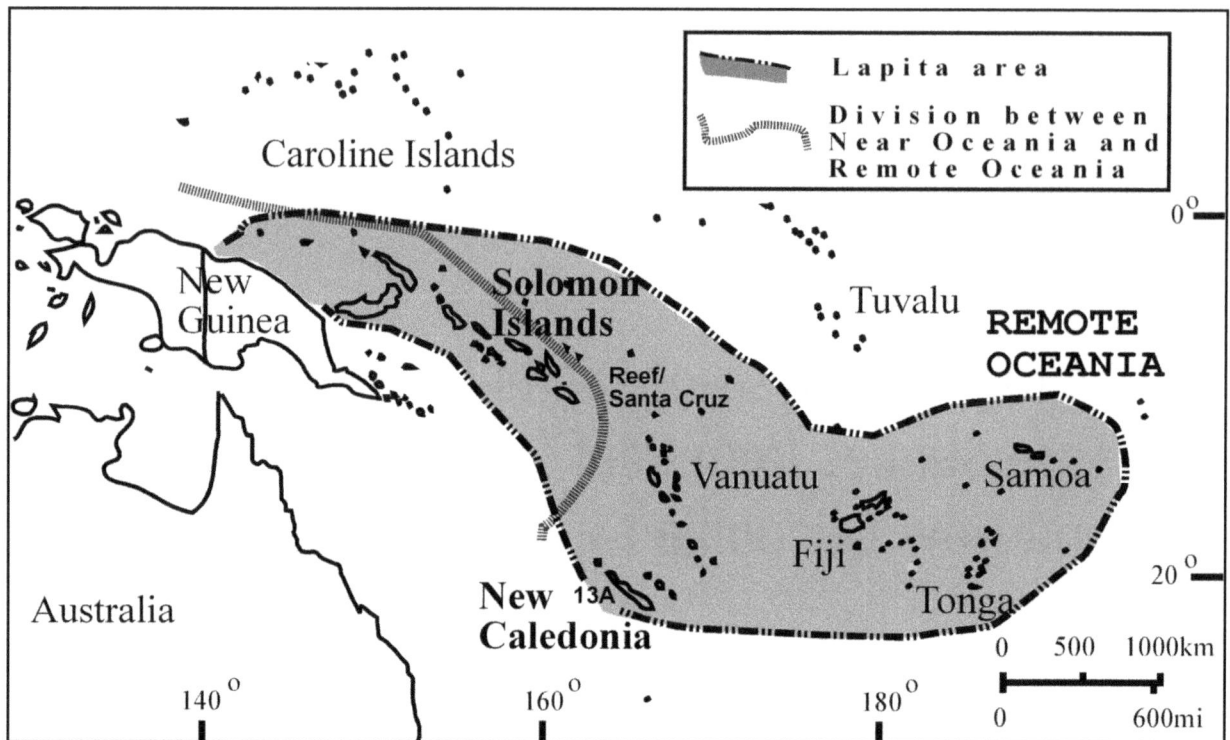

Figure 1. Distribution of the Lapita cultural complex.

1988b), and New Caledonia and Vanuatu Lapita (Anson 1983; Green 1978). It has been suggested that variations observed in pottery decorative style and technique can be interpreted "as the differentiation, both linguistically and culturally, of more localised ethnic identities", and they reflect "the declining frequency of exchanges across these boundaries" through time (Green and Kirch 1997:30). The Lapita pottery repertoire generally changed from complex and naturalistic depictions on elaborate vessel forms in the earliest and most westerly-located Lapita sites in the Bismarck Archipelago, to more simplified and geometric designs on simple vessel forms in the eastern Fiji-Tonga-Samoa region. This contention of progressive stylistic variation across the Lapita spectrum has dominated much of our understanding and interpretations of the nature of Lapita pottery.

Combined with the migration model, this trend has further been interpreted as an effort to maintain lifelines, or strong connections with the homeland community by daughter colonies. The maintenance of exchange systems has been argued as representing an effort in "maintaining community viability, particularly through such critical problems as acquiring suitable marriage partners, in a previously unoccupied, occasionally hazardous and still sparsely-populated region at some distance from 'home'"(Kirch 1988a). Once Lapita peoples moved out of their homeland regions, the incentive to invest time and energy in producing a range of vessel forms with complex motifs in an effort to maintain their identity with their homeland was short-lived, particularly after successful new colonies had been established. As exchange networks began to break down, and less and less effort was made in maintaining links to the homeland, the decorative pottery style too began to significantly change and ultimately in some regions the pottery-making tradition itself disappeared altogether.

This paper aims to challenge the validity of the previously assumed trends of motif transformation through a detailed re-analysis of Lapita face motifs found at Nenumbo-Reefs (SE-RF-2), Gnamanie-Reefs (SE-RF-6), and Nanggu-Santa Cruz (SE-SZ-8) of the eastern Solomon Islands, and those identified from Site 13A (WKO013A), Koné, New Caledonia. It attempts to establish a model for constructing possible motif transformation rules, in order to provide a more complex interpretation of these face designs and their possible meanings within the ancient Lapita tradition.

Lapita face motifs

One of the more distinctive motifs found on Lapita pottery are the human face motifs. Produced with a combination of an introduced dentate-stamped technique and locally innovated design motifs, these face motifs represent a new way of presenting social identities in this region more than 3000 years ago. There are at least two kinds of human representation. The first category contains the three-dimensional face motifs, usually found as moulded ceramic heads (Best 1981:11; Frimigacci 1981; Sand 1996:122, Fig. 162; Summerhayes 1998; Torrence and White 2001:135), but also represented by a carved bone figurine from Talepakemalai site (ECA) (Kirch 1997: frontispiece). Ceramic heads from Babase and Boduna are "decorated in the manner of tattoos" on the cheeks (Torrence and White 2001:138) and are similar in appearance to the second dominant form of presentation, the two-dimensional faces dentate-stamped on pottery surfaces (e.g., Green 1979:23, Figs. 1-3, 1-4 middle right; Kirch 1997:135, Pl. 5.5, 137, Fig.5.5; Sand 1999:53-55; Spriggs 1990:83-84).

Different types of face motifs were employed to decorate different forms of vessel. In the Far Western Lapita Province, the double-face motifs from ceramic assemblages are usually found on vessel forms "best suited for display or serving, not for storage or cooking," such as "cylinder stands" and "open bowls supported by pedestal feet or rings" (Kirch 1997:139-140). A similar practice may also be found in central Vanuatu Lapita sites (Bedford 2007; Bedford *et al.* 2006). Later in the archaeological sequence of the Far West, single-face motifs appear on flat-bottomed dishes with flaring sides (Kirch 1997:139-140), and possibly on lids as well (Spriggs 2002:53). No face motif has ever been found on smaller bowls or on globular carinated pots in the Far West. A similar pattern was found in the Arawe Islands (Summerhayes 2000a). This restriction was relaxed in the Southern Lapita Province, where the majority of face motifs occurred on carinated pots, although they were still applied to flat-bottom dishes and dishes supported by pedestal feet or rings (Sand 2000, 2001:Fig. 7).

What is in a Lapita face?

Many attempts have been made to comprehend the social characteristics inherent in these Lapita face motifs (Best 2002; Chiu 2005; Ishimura 2002; Kirch 1997; Newton 1988; Noury 2005; Sand 1999:53-55, 2000; Spriggs 1990, 1993, 2002). Spriggs recognised two trends of transformation in the face designs within the Lapita decorative inventories based on the then available chronological information of various sites. As "the designs would follow a progression from complex to simple over time", so can there be seen "a parallel progression from more naturalistic to more abstract designs" during a period of "at least 1000 years scope" (Spriggs 1993:9). He further suggested that "a considerable proportion of the entire Lapita design corpus" should be viewed as transformed face designs (Spriggs 1993:13). Based on information available at the time, Spriggs classified the face motifs according to temporal and spatial aspects, thus he demonstrated not only that Lapita faces have chronological values, but they also signal rapid social transformation, presumably due to local innovations, after initial settlement. A "logical sequence" was proposed, with "double-face" motifs occurring in the early part of the sequence (before about 2800 BP), "single-face" motifs generally appearing in later contexts, and they were ultimately transformed into simplified geometric forms (Spriggs 1993:13–14).

Assuming this progress of complex to simple is irrevocable in nature, Ishimura identified fourteen types of faces and arranged them in a family-tree structure that indicated the "irreversible" evolution of these motifs (Ishimura 2002:79). He further argued that these face motifs were typical of each Lapita region, indicating that each motif represented a particular transformational stage in the wider process. Unfortunately, factors such as the occupational span or the duration of production of these face motifs at each site, and *in situ* variation and alteration of these "typical" faces were ignored in his analysis.

In situ variation and the possible use of both complex and Simplified face motifs during the same time period can be inferred from Fijian assemblages. Although Best states that "examples of quite complex anthropomorphic designs are not uncommon in Eastern Lapita…These occur in the lowest levels of the sites, and the process of stylisation can be shown to have taken place" (Best 2002:43), he admits that during the short occupation of the Naigani site, it is evident that both elaborate and highly simplified anthropomorphic designs were employed simultaneously (Best 2002:44). The same phenomenon has been recognised at Makekur (FOH) in the Arawe Islands (Phelan 1997:139; cited from Best 2002:44), at Teouma in Central Vanuatu (Bedford 2007), at the "pot-burial pit" and other parts of Site 13A in New Caledonia (Chiu 2005; Sand 2000:26), and at the Nenumbo site on the Reef Islands.

Thus the proposed "sequence of increasing abstraction of the face design over time" (Spriggs 2002:52-3) should be reassessed, as the coexistence of both elaborate naturalistic and very abstract face motifs at single sites contradicts this assertion. Both Best and Spriggs tend to question the precision of the radiocarbon dates of some of the sites listed above (Spriggs 2002:53), but at the same time insisting that such a process of simplification over time is unquestionable (Best 2002:44). This paper proposes an alternative working hypothesis for examining and trying to explain why the "logical sequence" is likely to be much more complex than currently assumed. It argues that a simple, uniform trend did not exist in prehistory, as social factors need also be taken into account when one investigates the meanings that these Lapita faces might have contained some three thousand years ago. The complexity of these colonising societies has to be taken into account. They

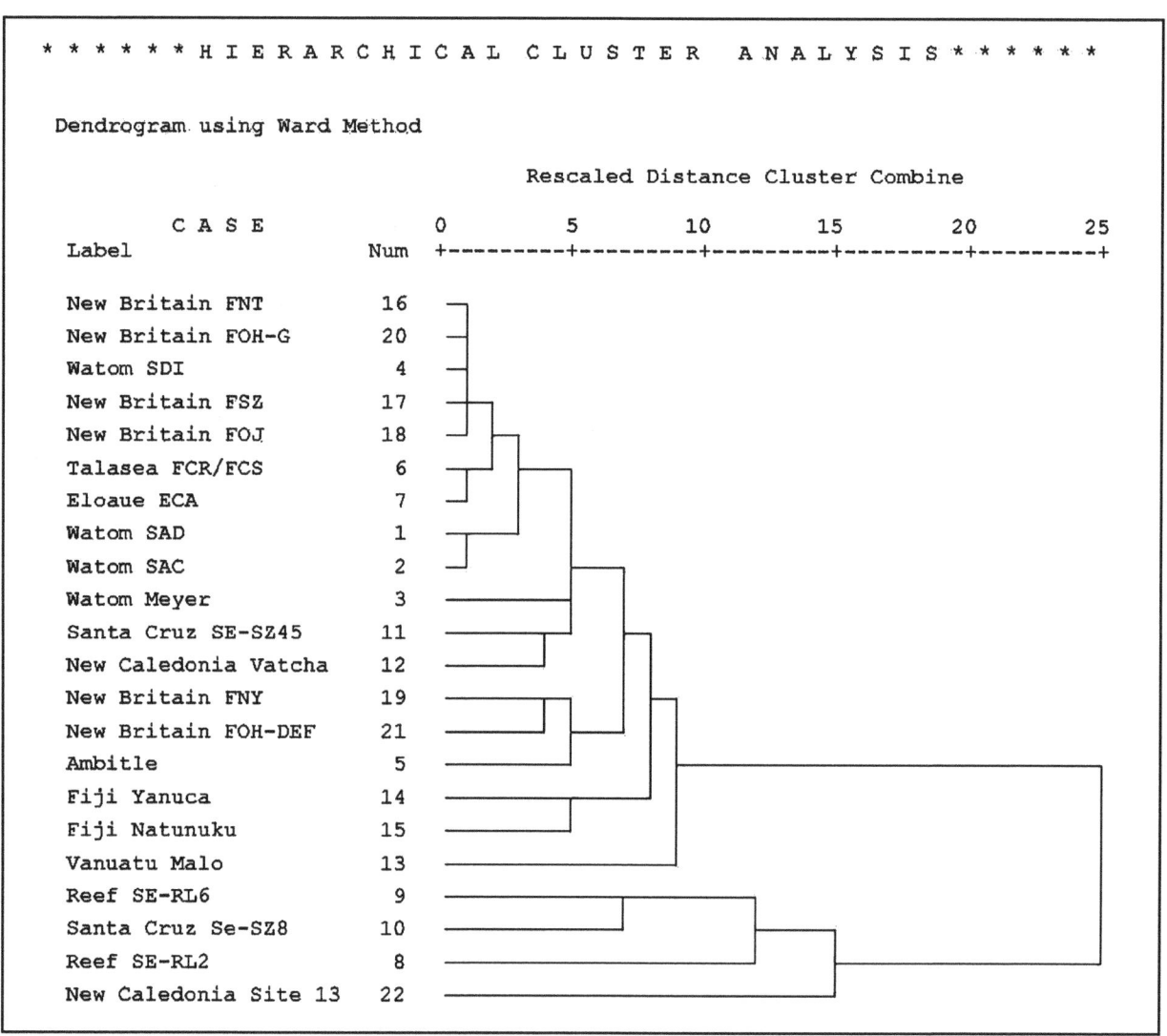

Figure 2. Dendrogram showing the grouping of sites based on motif similarity using Ward's method (after Chiu 2003b:229, Table 6-1).

Table 1. Number of face motifs identified at 4 Lapita sites with Chi-square test result.

			type					Total
			T	AI	L	HD	S	
site	SZ8	Count	1	0	8	4	2	15
		Expected Count	1.1	.0	2.4	1.7	9.8	15.0
		% within site	6.7%	.0%	53.3%	26.7%	13.3%	100.0%
	RF6	Count	3	0	0	2	0	5
		Expected Count	.4	.0	.8	.6	3.3	5.0
		% within site	60.0%	.0%	.0%	40.0%	.0%	100.0%
	RF2	Count	12	0	43	25	2	82
		Expected Count	6.0	.2	13.3	9.1	53.3	82.0
		% within site	14.6%	.0%	52.4%	30.5%	2.4%	100.0%
	13A	Count	11	1	9	10	236	267
		Expected Count	19.5	.7	43.4	29.7	173.7	267.0
		% within site	4.1%	.4%	3.4%	3.7%	88.4%	100.0%
Total		Count	27	1	60	41	240	369
		Expected Count	27.0	1.0	60.0	41.0	240.0	369.0
		% within site	7.3%	.3%	16.3%	11.1%	65.0%	100.0%

Chi-Square Tests

	Value	df	Asymp. Sig. (2-sided)
Pearson Chi-Square	264.842[a]	12	.000
Likelihood Ratio	274.623	12	.000
Linear-by-Linear Association	94.657	1	.000
N of Valid Cases	369		

a. 11 cells (55.0%) have expected count less than 5. The minimum expected count is .01.

Symmetric Measures

		Value	Approx. Sig.
Nominal by Nominal	Contingency Coefficient	.646	.000
N of Valid Cases		369	

a. Not assuming the null hypothesis.
b. Using the asymptotic standard error assuming the null hypothesis.

may well have been organised along the lines of "house-based" social groups, where various social hierarchies were likely to have existed both within and outside a "house" amongst the local community itself, and often supplemented with external exchange partners, which may all have contributed to the complexity of motifs that we have seen on the Lapita pots.

In my previous study of the Site 13A Lapita pottery assemblages, where 117 face motif sherds were identified, it was demonstrated that the social forces of both differentiation and unification were at play. Potters created, modified and altered several face motif forms, adding certain "operators" ("friezes" or complex "zone markers") to the same motif designs to highlight social differences (Chiu 2005). In this study I hope to demonstrate that the same social forces are at play in the Reef/Santa Cruz Lapita and Site 13A assemblages which have previously been shown to share the highest degree of similarity in terms of motif inventories among all island groups (Chiu 2003b; see Figure 2). The study tackles the issue of diversity observed between Lapita face motifs excavated from four Lapita sites (Table 1), with the aim of determining whether Lapita potters and consumers preferred using this particular materialised symbol to signify their group identity, to differentiate and to unify certain groups in various conditions. It also tests whether we may, as long-distant outside observers, use the identification of subtle changes in motif construction patterns, as a means to help us infer the underlying social, economic, spiritual, and political forces that moulded the pots into being.

Face motifs from Site 13A came from one unit excavated in 1992, four units in 1994, and the 56 units in 1996, plus surface collections of both the 1995 and 1996 field seasons. Sherds excavated and documented by Gifford and Shutler (1956), and the Phoebe A. Hearst Museum of Anthropology at UC Berkeley collection, hand-drawn by Peter White and his students in 1976, were also included in this study. During a visit to the University of Auckland in 2005, I was able to examine all the Reef/Santa Cruz decorated sherds that had been excavated in 1976 along with some of the larger sherds collected during the 1971 field season. The face motifs included in this study include those motifs identified by myself in 2005, plus those published by Donovan (1973), Parker (1981) and Spriggs (1990) in previous studies. Motifs without a clear indication of being part of a face, i.e., with a noticeable "eye-to-nose" structure intact, or could not be determined as being part of the complex headdress, were not included in the study.

Face motifs identified

In our paper, "Recording of the Lapita motifs: Proposal for a complete recording method" (Chiu and Sand 2005), Christophe Sand and I have suggested that concentrating on the use of space, instead of dissecting face motifs into various design elements in complex motifs, may be a profitable method for the analysis of the design motifs. We argue that while the design elements may be interchangeable from case to case, the underlying construction rules for each of these complex motifs might have remained the same. I have followed this concept in establishing the classification of face motifs recorded for this study. Examples for each subcategory of face motif types are shown in Figures 3-8. Developed out of the major categories established by Spriggs (1990), I have classified the face motifs into five general categories. There are two categories of Triangular face motifs (Triangular face [T]; Alternating inverse [AI]) (Figures 3-5), two categories of single face motifs (Long-nose [L]; Simplified [S]) (Figures 6, 7) and a headdress motif (HD) (Figure 8). Within each category of face motif, there are several sub-categories identified according to changes in certain design units within the whole structure. At this stage, the classification system is still under construction, and rules governing the classification of face motifs are still under investigation.

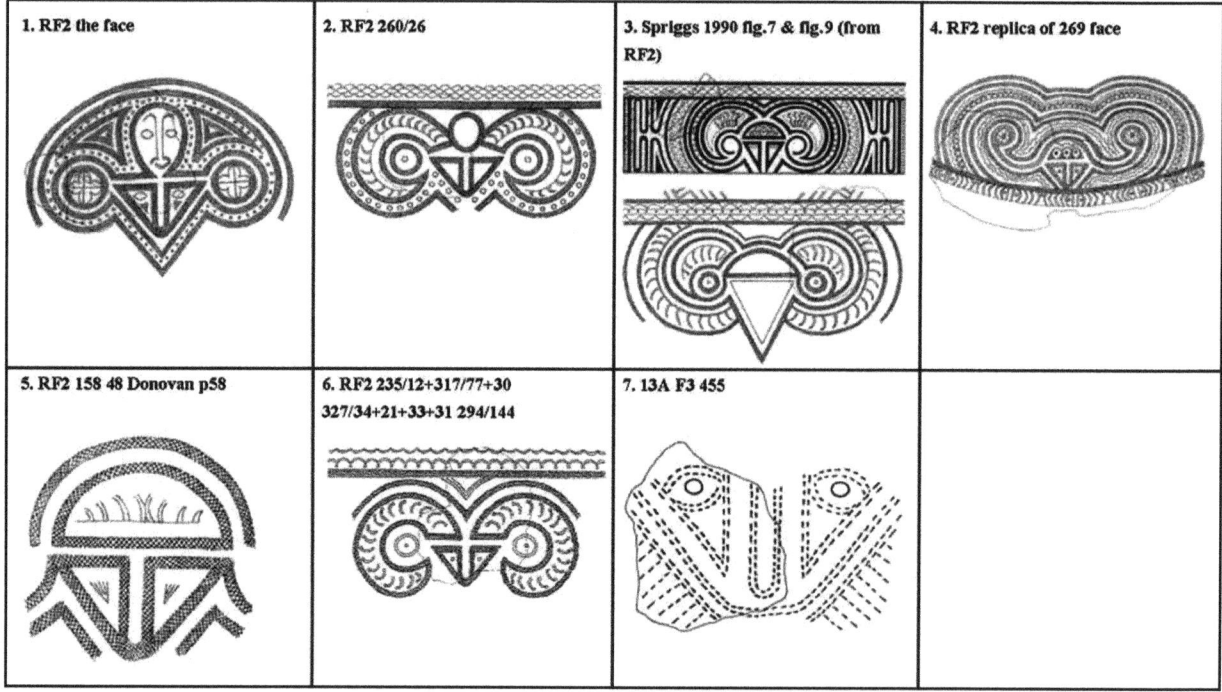

Figure 3. Triangular (T) face motif sub-categories identified.

Triangular face motifs (T)

The Triangular face motifs (T) parallel those labeled by Spriggs as "double face" motifs. Face motifs of this category always have the lower triangular face part present in the design, while the upper, more naturalistic face motif may be replaced by various other designs (Figure 3). Among the Reef/Santa Cruz sites, the Triangular face motifs were highly elaborated. Therefore in an effort to distinguish them according to the possible construction rules, I have classified these face motifs according to several parts of the motif: 1) the appearance of the naturalistic face on the top of the triangular face; 2) the presence/absence of a semi-circle on the top of the triangular face; 3) the position of "pendants" in the entire motif layout, i.e., whether it is located above the triangular face or on the sides of it; 4) the shape of lines encircling the "pendants" on the sides of the triangular face; 5) the design elements used to fill in these horn-like or fern-shoot-like spaces; 6) the friezes attached either above or under the face motif; 7) the shape of the eye inside the Triangular face motif; and lastly, 8) the presence/absence of division motifs in between face motifs.

Based on these rules, I have identified 7 sub-types of triangular faces (see Figure 3). Table 2 shows the presence/absence data of each Triangular face motif sub-type identified from sites studied. The first one is the original "double face" (Figure 3.1), where a naturalistic human face appears on top of a triangular face, with rounded "pendant" designs appear right next to the Triangular face motif. There are two faces in this first sub-type recognized so far: one is from SE-RF-2, the other from SE-SZ-8.

The faces in the second group may be seen as transformation of the first, as the upper human face is being replaced by just an empty circle (Figure 3.2), retaining only the outline of a human face. It is rather hard to tell from the fragmented sherds whether the "pendant" designs are placed right next to the Triangular face motif at this moment, but it is very likely the structure of the entire motif did not change too radically at this moment.

The third sub-category of Triangular face motifs has a semi-circle filled with elaborated designs, replacing the upper naturalistic human face motif (Figure 3.3). There are horn-like structures encircling a round space on the sides of the Triangular face motif. The round circles are usually filled with different "pendant" designs. In some cases, eyes within the triangular face were replaced with triangle "pendants", while the basic structure of the face motif remained the same.

The fourth sub-category of Triangular face motifs (Figure 3.4) comes also with a semi-circle on the top of the triangular face, with the use of an upraising fern-shoot-like design to push the "pendant" designs farther away from the face itself.

In the fifth sub-category of Triangular face motifs, while the semi-circle is still intact, the eye inside the triangular face is replaced by pendant-like symbols (Figure 3.5). Face motifs belong to this category have been separated out from the rest Triangular face motifs due to its special treatment of the eye inside the triangular space. A similar motif has been found on Vao Island in Vanuatu (Chiu 2005:28, Fig. 11).

The sixth sub-category shows a triangular face in which the semi-circle part of the face disappeared totally from the design, while the horn-like structure encircling a round space on the sides of the Triangular face motif remained the same (Figure 3.6). There are at least 3 different alloforms within this particular sub-category (Figure 4), each containing subtle differences in the design elements employed to generate the overall structure of the face motif.

Table 2. Presence/absence data of Triangular face motif sub-categories at 4 sites and Spriggs 1990 data.

Triangular	T1	T2	T3	T4	T5	T6	T7
Spriggs 1990	fig. 2	fig. 4	fig. 7 & 9	fig. 5 & 6	fig. 10	fig. 12	
SZ8	P						
RF6	P						
RF2	P	P	P	P	P	P	
13A			P			P	P

Figure 4. Examples showing the subtle modification of face motif elements from T6 (Figure 3).

The seventh sub-category comes from fragmented sherds collected at Site 13A, each showing the outline of a triangular shape, with the eyes now decorated with pendants directly underneath (Figure 3.7). Based on the similar treatment around the eyes of the Triangular face motif, it seems that this group of face motifs may be closely related to the original Triangular face motif.

Alternating inversed face motif (AI)

The second set of triangular faces which I have labeled "alternating inverted double face" motifs (AI), have only just been recognised recently from Teouma in Vanuatu (Bedford *et al* 2006:819, Fig. 5), and from Site 13A 1995 surface collection (Figure 5). The upside down Triangular face motif, the most characteristic feature of this motif category, may be viewed as part of the earplug design that fills the space between Long-nose face motifs, and such a particular arrangement of two different face motifs in vertically opposite positions is quite intriguing, and deserves more detailed comparison among various ethnographic cases if one wishes to understand its possible meanings.

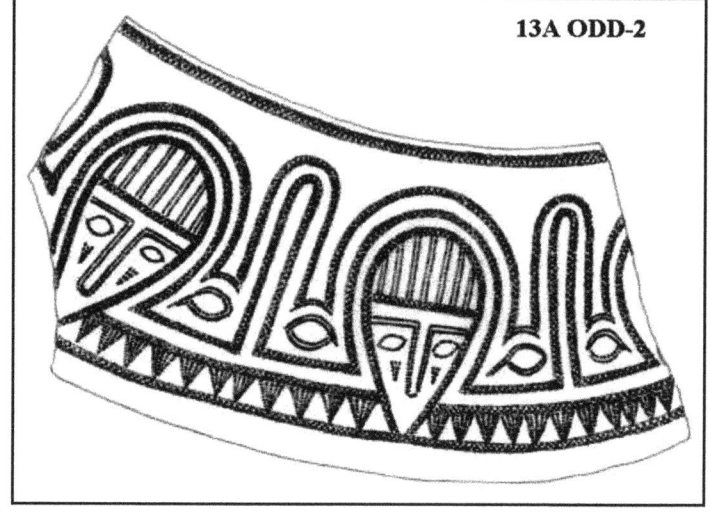

Figure 5. Alternating inversed (AI) face motif sub-category.

Long-nose face motifs (L)

Two categories of single face motifs have been developed from Spriggs' original "single face motif" category. The first is the Long-nose with earplugs (L) that still contains the more complex structure of a face (Figure 6 and Table 3); and secondly, the Simplified face motif (S), where earplugs disappeared from the design and geometric eye designs replaced the more naturalistic Long-nose design (Figure 7). The Long-nose face category motifs from the Reef/Santa Cruz clearly shared the same design structure as the triangular ones found at the same sites. Others share the same design structure with the New Caledonian Long-nose face motifs, with only slight differences in terms of design elements that have been used to fill up the "pendants" (Figure 6). Division of the Long-nose face motifs into subcategories was based on the following rules: 1) the position of "pendants" in the motif layout; 2) the shape of the "pendants" on the sides of the Long-nose face; 3) the design elements used to fill in the "pendants" and spaces around the face itself; 4) the friezes attached either above or under the face motif; 5) the shape of the eye; and lastly, 6) the presence/absence of division motifs in between face motifs. Based on these rules, 5 different subcategories of Long-nose face motifs have been identified. Table 3 shows the presence/absence data of each Long-nose face motif sub-type identified from sites studied.

From the examples shown in Figure 6, it is clear that while some rare Long-nose face motifs are separated by headdress and "pendants" as also seen with the Triangular face motif category (subcategory L1 and L2 [Figures 6.1 and 6.2]), most motifs have two faces sharing a single "pendant" (sub-category L3 [Figure 6.3]).

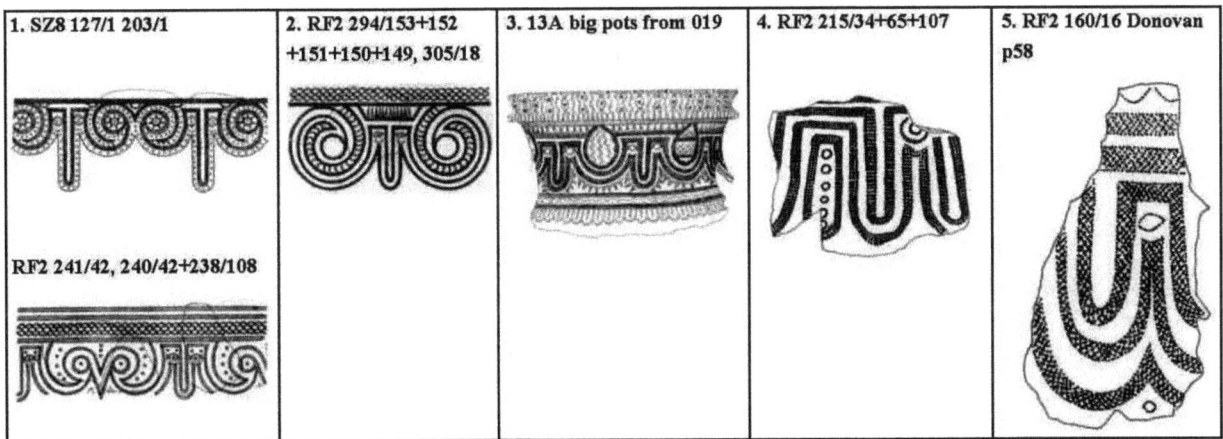

Figure 6. Long-nose (L) face motif sub-categories identified.

Table 3. Presence/absence data of Long-nose face motif sub-categories at 4 sites and Spriggs 1990 data.

Long-nose	L1	L2	L3	L4	L5
Spriggs 1990	fig. 18	fig. 19	fig. 23 & 24	fig. 26	
SZ8	P				
RF6					
RF2	P	P	P	P	P
13A			P		

Simplified face motifs (S)

Classification of the Simplified face motifs is primarily based on 1) the friezes attached either above or under the face motif, and 2) the shape of the eye. The general construction rule for this type of face motif, as Spriggs has pointed out, is the loss of "pendants", the replacement of the original naturalistic eyes with all sorts of symbols, and the ultimate loss of eyes from the design. There are 25 sub-categories of this type of face motif that have been identified to date (see Figure 7). S1 to S11 (Figure 7.1-7.11) presumably represent different face motifs, while S12 to S21 (Figure 7.12-7.21) represent instances of altered or merged face motifs. S22 to S25 (Figure 7.22-7.25) are rare

Figure 7. Simplified (S) face motif sub-categories identified.

types that may represent another method of simplifying complex motifs in this category. Some of them are more popular than others, such as the "X-shaped" or ")(-shaped" ones. Site 13A has a large number of Simplified face motifs. In contrast, there are only two clear cases of Simplified face motifs identified from SE-RF-2. One of which (S9) was recovered from the upper black layer of the site, the other (S23, reconstructed from three pieces) was found inside an oven pit used at the later period at this site, indicating that both were either a later innovation by local potters, or an introduction from other places. Table 4 shows the presence/absence data of each Simplified face sub-type identified from sites studied.

Table 4. Presence/absence data of Simplified face motif sub-categories at 4 sites and Spriggs 1990 data.

Simplified	S1	S2	S3	S4	S5	S6	S7	S8	S9	S10	S11	S12	S13	S14	S15	S16	S17	S18	S19	S20	S21	S22	S23	S24	S25
Spriggs 1990																							fig.28	fig.27	
SZ8																						P			
RF6																									
RF2									P														P		
13A	P	P	P	P	P	P	P	P		P	P	P	P	P	P	P	P	P	P	P	P			P	P

Anomalous Simplified face motifs

Rare variants of the Simplified face motif (Figure 7.22-7.25) deserve further attention. The first one (S22) from SE-SZ-8 appears to be a direct transformation from the Long-nose face motif. The eyes of the face have been enlarged into circles, with no indication of a "pendant" on the sides of the face. Another rare motif (S23) comes from SE-RF-2, with the Long-nose clearly laid out in the design, but the eyes are enclosed by triangular spaces. The set grammar of constructing a face is being challenged here, as half of the motif retains the usual form, while other elements of it have been altered (Figure 7.23). The third case (S24) is from Site 13A, where the nose is still present, but the eyes have totally disappeared, and the pendants are emphasised. The last case (S25) is a sherd with an intriguing design. On the left part of the motif, it seems to carry part of the design commonly seen in the Long-nose face (see Figure 6.2). However, on the right and center of the motif there are two simplified "X-shape" eye motifs (Figure 7.25). What is usually a recognisable Long-nose face is now being replaced with a geometric face design, the most dominant type of Simplified face motifs found at Site 13A. This particular motif shows signs of transforming from the more complex Long-nose face directly to a simplified one, while retaining the headdress/pendant part of the original. This further strengthens the argument for the analysis of these face motifs and their simplification using structural rules, not simply the designs used in the image. This particular replacement of the oval eye motif with the x-shape simplified eye motif within a formal structure demonstrates both the importance of retaining the major structural forms of the motif, and the significance that these interchangeable eye motifs might have had in Lapita culture.

Headdress motifs (HD)

In this presentation, a fifth category, the Headdress motif (HD), is also included, for motifs of this category are usually associated with the Triangular face motifs, but sometimes with the Long-nose motifs as well. Without clear indication of a face layout, I have at this stage just listed them as a separate category that may well ultimately be part of the face motifs. There are 9 different headdress motifs identified from the assemblages (Figure 8). Some can easily be associated with Triangular face motifs, while others are from Long-nose face motifs. In Figure 8 I have listed all the different forms of headdress motifs that lack clear indication of whether they belong to a Triangular or Long-nose face motif. Table 5 shows the presence/absence data of each headdress motif sub-type identified from the sites studied.

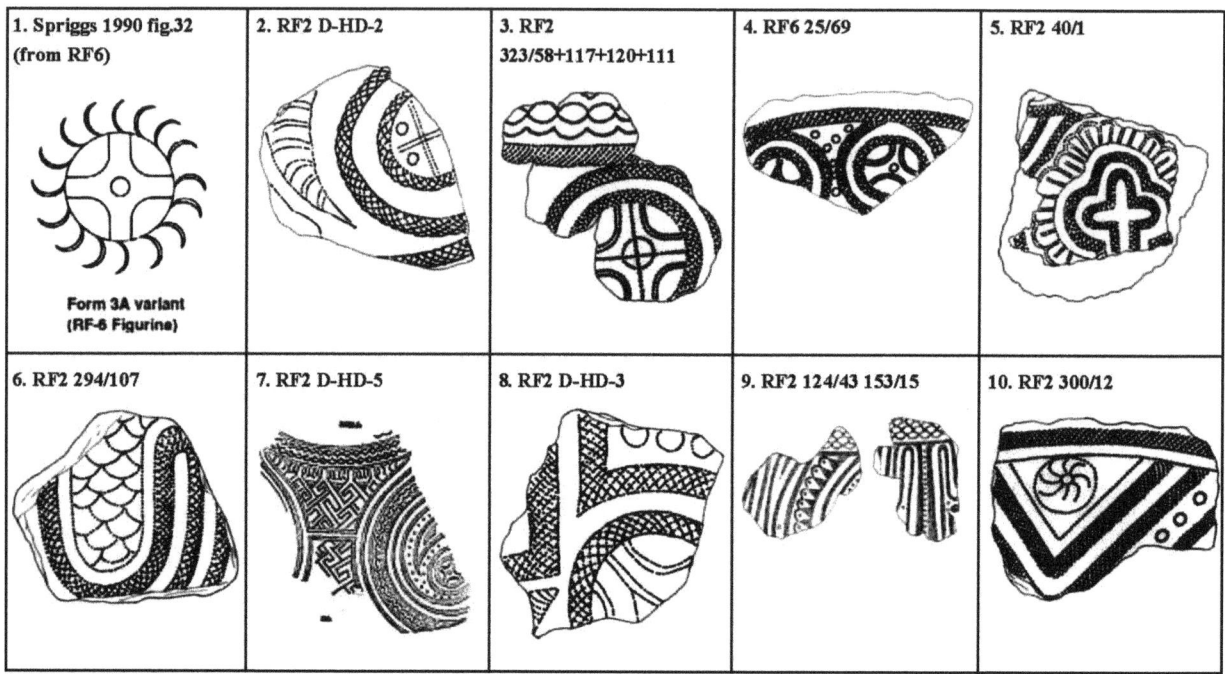

Figure 8. Headdress (HD) motif sub-categories identified.

Table 5. Presence/absence data of Headdress motif sub-categories at 4 sites and Spriggs 1990 data.

Headdress	HD1	HD2	HD3	HD4	HD5	HD6	HD7	HD8	HD9
Spriggs 1990	fig. 32		fig. 21				fig. 8	fig. 11	fig. 7
SZ8									
RF6	P			P					
RF2		P	P		P	P	P	P	P
13A									

Face motifs in summary

A total number of 15 face and "headdress" motifs were identified from SE-SZ-8, 5 from SE-RF-6, 82 from SE-RF-2, and 267 from Site 13A. The raw number of face motifs identified from each site is listed in Table 1, and it is clear that these sites contain different types of face motifs. The percentage of face types found at each site are as follows; Triangular face motifs make up 14.6 % at SE-RF-2, 60 % at SE-RF-6, 6.7 % at SE-SZ-8 and 4.1 % at Site 13A. As Headdress motifs are usually associated with the Triangular face motifs, we can combine the number of triangular and headdress motifs and arrive at figures of 45.1 % for SE-RF-2, 33.4 % for SE-SZ-8, and 100 % for SE-RF-6. In striking contrast, at Site 13A, only 7.8 % of face motifs belong to the combined Triangular and Headdress motifs. The Long-nose face motif category shows the same tendency. At SE-RF-2, 52.4 % of the face motifs belong to this category, and at SE-SZ-8, 53.3 %. While at Site 13A, only 3.4 % of the face motifs are from this category. The tendency of employing more complex Triangular and Headdress motifs and the Long-nose face motifs in the Solomons is apparent.

In terms of Simplified face motifs, only 2.4 % at SE-RF-2 and 13.3 % of SZ-8 face motifs belong to the simplified category, while at SE-RF-6, there is none so far reported. In contrast, at Site 13A, 88.4 % of face motifs found are simplified ones. Due to the fact that there are only 5 face motifs found at RF-6, and all of them belong to the most complex Triangular face motifs, it is hard to tell at this stage whether it may also show a similar pattern of preferring the Long-nose face motifs as the other two Reef/Santa Cruz sites.

Another design element that separates the Reef/Santa Cruz sites from Site13A is the extensive use of small impressed round circles. Most of the face motifs, including the triangular ones found in the Reef/Santa Cruz contain these circles in the design, yet at Site 13A, while they are found in various motif designs, they are rarely used in face motifs. Designs infilling the "pendants" on the sides of the face motif, as seen in the Triangular face motifs, also vary dramatically from one to the other.

In order to determine whether the differences observed are statistically significant or not, I use the chi-square tests for homogeneity to see if these face motifs come from the same cultural population. It is assumed that if the face motifs are from the same distribution, the proportions of each category from each site should be about the same [1]. The result suggests that the proportion of 5 face motif types does show significant difference among them, thus they show quite different patterns in terms of preferred face motif types. This test suggests that there is a sharp difference in terms of variation of face types between the Reef/Santa Cruz and New Caledonia, and this observation cannot be explained solely by the difference of sample size alone.

In summary, in the Reef/Santa Cruz assemblages, there appears to be a preference for Long-nose type face motifs both at SE-SZ-8 and SE-RF-2, while at Site 13A, 88 % of the face motifs are the more geometric, simplified forms. The extremely low number of Simplified face motifs and the emphasis on elaborated Triangular face motifs found at SE-RF-2 forms a sharp contrast with what has been found at 13A. This statistically meaningful difference in terms of preferred face motifs at each site must be assessed in terms of cultural selection of signifiers rather than simply explaining it as merely a result of different sampling strategies.

Face motif construction rules

Different rules were employed and options available in governing the change of face motifs. In the case of the Triangular face motif category, everything but the outline of the triangular face could be modified: the naturalistic face and the semi-circle above it, the location of the "pendants", the shape of the horn-like structure that encircles the "pendants", the shape of the eye inside the triangular face outline, and the shape of the entire headdress. Modification of the Long-nose face motifs, is seen with the location of "pendants", the shape of the entire design, the shape of the eye, and the number of faces sharing a single "pendant". In the Simplified face motif category, only the friezes and the shape of the eyes could be changed.

Thus it is clear that what was not changed was the basic face outline, whether it be the Triangular, Long-nose, or the Simplified forms. In most cases, the basic outline remained the same while modification and alteration occurred on various parts of the full design. Therefore it may be argued that, whether or not the face motifs were transformed through time and space, the ideas of how to express social identity or difference were shared by potters who produced these seemingly very different face motifs. The rules governing the production of the face motifs were very restricted in most cases.

I will now use materials at hand to further discuss whether a sequence of motif transformation may be found within a site, within an island group, and within the Lapita Cultural Complex. Site SE-RF-2 serves as the example of what face motifs were employed during a short occupation period, while at 13A we may be looking at a 200 to 400 year time span. Will we find the transformation from complex to Simplified face motifs as time progressed at both sites? The general pattern of spatial distribution of face motifs for both sites will also be discussed.

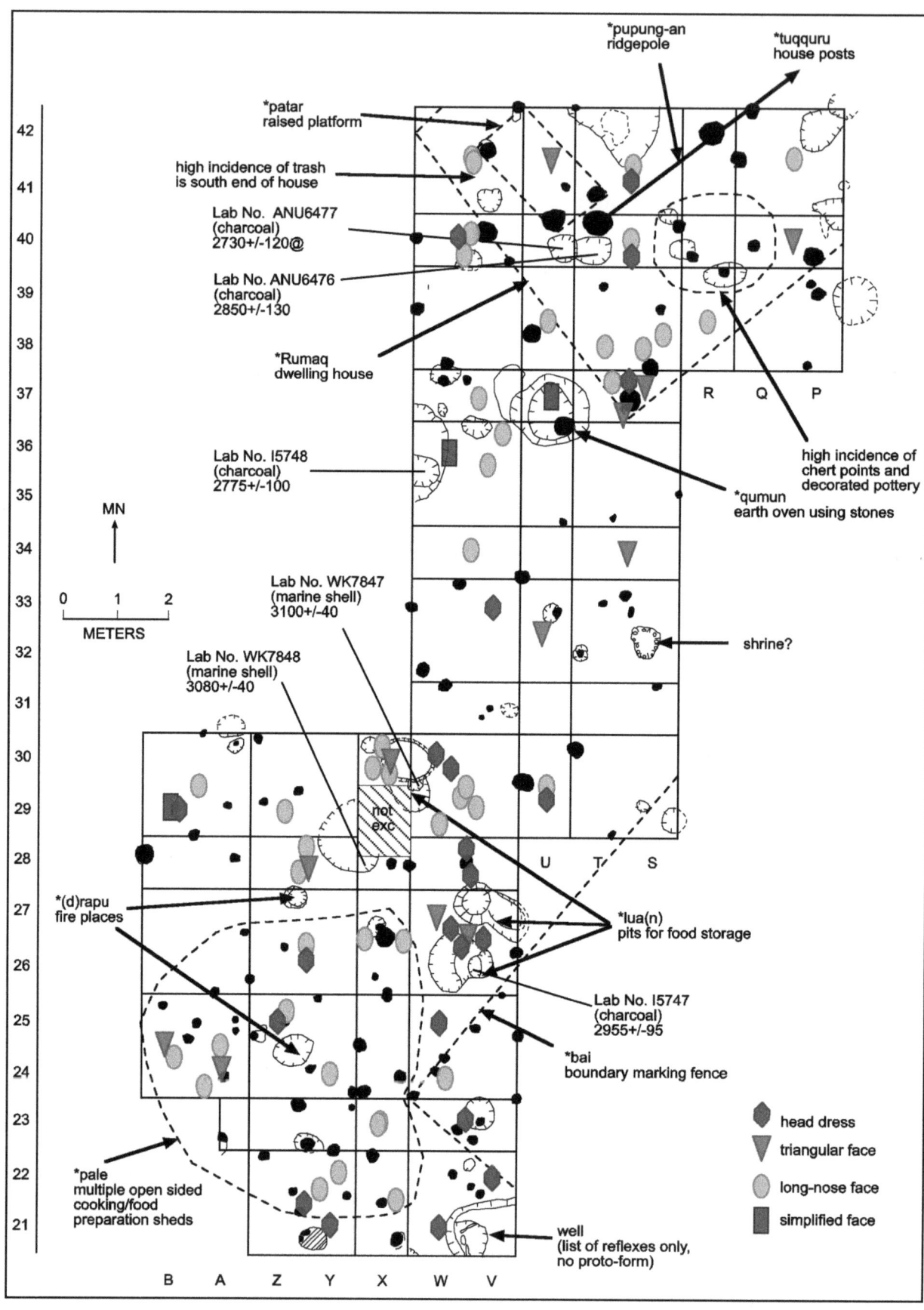

Figure 9. Spatial distribution of 4 face motif types at SE-RF-2.

Face motifs employed within a single site

Spatial and temporal distribution of face motifs at Nenumbo-Reefs (SE-RF-2), Solomon Islands

Six out of the 7 sub-categories of Triangular and all 5 sub-categories of Long-nose face motifs are found in SE-RF-2. Seven out of 9 Headdress motif sub-categories are found there as well, while only 2 Simplified face motifs were identified. Preference for the more complex face motifs is clearly demonstrated. In general, Triangular type face motifs from SE-RF-2 show signs of replacement and alteration of several parts of the entire design, a process very similar to what was identified from the Simplified face motifs collected from Site 13A of New Caledonia (Chiu 2005).

Figure 9 shows the spatial distribution of 4 types of face motifs (T, L, S and HD) at SE-RF-2, with features and activity areas identified by Green and Pawley (1999). From the spatial distribution of different types of motifs at this site, it can be argued that most pots bearing face motifs are clustered either in the area of the main house structure in the north, or the southern kitchen area in the south. The area between the main structure and the cooking area contains fewer materials, however, all of the so far identified Simplified face motifs were also found in this part of the site. No clear pattern can be generated at this stage in distinguishing varying use of the face motifs from different parts of the site. As vessel forms are still being reconstructed, it is difficult to say whether vessels carrying face motifs were used solely for food consumption or presentation at SE-RF-2. With the recent evidence from Vanuatu of face motif vessels being used as burial urns (Bedford and Spriggs 2007), the task of identifying possible multi-functions of a given vessel form clearly deserves further attention.

There is no sharp difference in the distribution of face motifs between the upper black, weathered tephra layer and the lower sandy charcoal-stained grey layer. This is probably due to the fact that both layers are seen as belonging to the same cultural period that lasted for about 50-100 years (Jones et al. 2007). We can therefore assume that all the face motifs found were utilised during a short period of time, suggesting a high degree of social desire for differentiation.

An example of motif differentiation may be seen in Figure 4. All three Triangular face motifs illustrated are from SE-RF-2, but by adding or removing a particular design element from the total layout, we may be seeing evidence of an expression of social differentiation within the social group, where all had the right to use the same basic image. It might be argued that while the basic pattern of such a face is an expression of group identity, the subtle alteration of certain elements may represent sub-groups within a group or community. The interchangeable elements may have been used to maintain social hierarchy within such a group.

Spatial and temporal distribution of face motifs at Lapita (Site 13A), New Caledonia

Most face motifs were located in the earlier eastern part of Site 13A (Figure 10). It also seems highly likely that face motifs found in the western part of the site (Zone 3-6) are associated with post-depositional disturbance (Figure 11). As in the case of SE-RF-2, all types of face motifs were present throughout the mostly undisturbed eastern part of Site 13A, indicating that both elaborate and simplified anthropomorphic designs were employed simultaneously. However, it is clear that at Site 13A the most frequently occurring motif was the Simplified face motifs. Twenty-three out of the 25 sub-categories of Simplified face motifs were found there. Variation in the Simplified face motif category is generated by altering various elements and the shapes of the eye, or by merging different eye shapes to form a new image (Figures 7.12-7.21). Though rare in the face motif assemblage, these merging face motifs illustrate the integration of two individual motifs into a

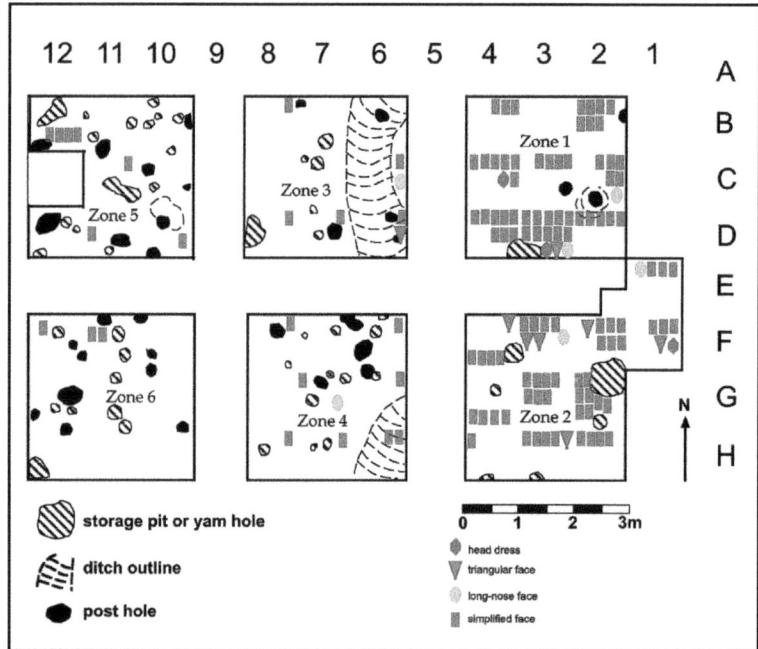

Figure 10. Spatial distribution of 4 face motif types at Site 13A.

new one. This might indicate that materialised symbols representing both the desire for social differentiation and integration are evident here (Chiu 2005). In contrast to SE-RF-2, only three forms of Triangular Face and one form of Long-nose face motif with a different infill pattern of the "pendants" occurred at Site 13A. This indicates yet again the tendency for a sharing of the same general face design while at the same time there is the signaling of subtle differences.

Forces of social integration can be inferred from face motifs that combine different eye forms. The integrating symbols may also indicate the successful acquirement of the right to use face motifs inherited from two different house-based groups through marriage, adoption, or even conquest. New Caledonian sherds have been found in the Loyalty Islands (Galipaud 1990, Sand 1995), and Vanuatu (Dickinson 1971; Spriggs and Wickler 1989), a pattern that indicates some degree of local or even long-distance exchange along with the specialisation of pottery production (Dickinson et al. 1996). The integration of face motifs may represent the achievement of a local community leader or leaders enhancing their collaborative resources and thereby potentially gaining some advantage in relationships with other communities.

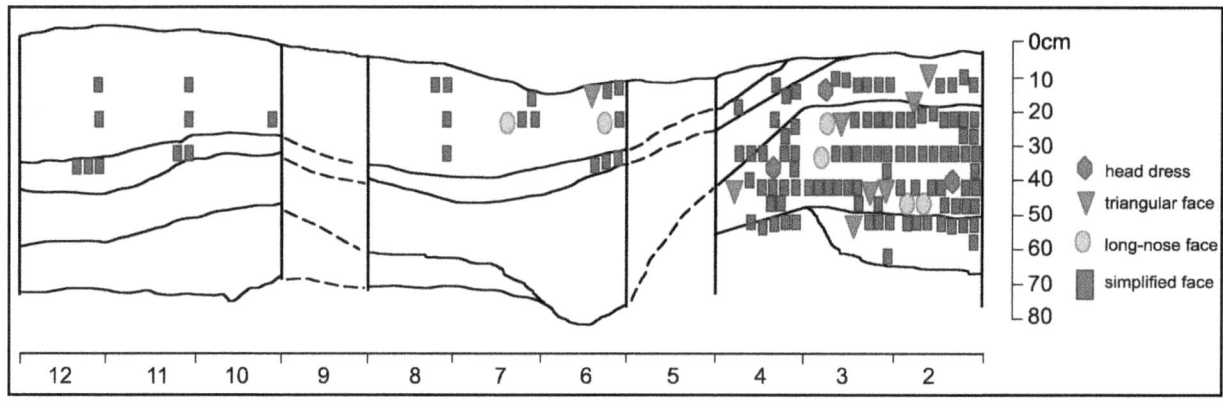

Figure 11. Temporal distribution of 4 face motif types at Site 13A.

Comparison of face motifs between SE-RF-2 and Site 13A

It has been argued that settlement at site SE-RF-2 began at around 3100 BP and was occupied for a limited period of some 50 years or so (Green 2006:35, Green and Pawley 1999:77, Jones *et al.* 2007). Site 13A on the other hand, while initially settled at around 3100 to 3000 BP was occupied for a period of several hundred years, to around 2800-2750 BP (Sand 1998). The differences, therefore, observed both in style and selective use of particular face motifs cannot be explained simply by the passage of time, or by diffusion of motifs from the Reef/Santa Cruz Islands to New Caledonia. As demonstrated, all three kinds of face motifs, the Triangular (assumed to occur very early in the sequence), the Long-nose face, and the Simplified face, previously assumed to be late in the sequence, are all found at these two sites. While settlement duration may contribute to the variation seen at Site 13A, the same interpretation is not valid in the case of Reef/Santa Cruz sites. As SE-RF-2 was only occupied for about 50-100 years, around 1 to 4 generations, the range of face motifs found at the site cannot be explained as a result of a lengthy period of evolution from complex, anthropomorphic designs to simplified, geometric face motifs.

From the chi-square test conducted, it has been shown that there is a significant difference between SE-RF-2 and Site 13A in terms of what types of face motifs were utilised. If we examine the presence and absence data of what motifs are shared by both Reef/Santa Cruz and New Caledonia (Chiu 2003b:229, Table 6-1), the sharp contrast in face motifs is even more striking. These two island groups share a high number of Lapita motifs, a similarity so high that it separates them out from Lapita sites from other island groups. What then could be the possible explanation for the sharp difference observed in the face motif category, which comprises only a small part of the overall Lapita motif inventory? What were the underlying social forces that created and maintained the tradition of producing these face motifs across widespread island groups? What were the functions of these motifs in a society that was constantly expanding into new territory? Was the preference of face motifs employed at these two sites a result of differing identities, or of other yet to be established reasons?

Symbols at work

Thus, stylistic behavior, like other forms of symbolic behavior, may be seen as part of a motivated social strategy. From this perspective, style is more than a way of doing, a set of rules, a simple choice among culturally constrained alternatives, or a means of communicating social identity. It is a set of rules to be manipulated, and a set of choices to be made, in the negotiation of social identity. The question then becomes: What are the motives and strategies of the actors? (Bowser 2000:242)

What were the causes of the differences observed so far? The transformational trend proposed by Green and others may well have been a factor, as a shift from the more naturalistic, complex motif inventories found in early Lapita sites to the more simplified, abstract motifs of the later period have been inferred from many cases. But as Summerhayes has demonstrated, "time" alone is unlikely to have been the sole factor behind this shift, as spatial separation also contributed to the local innovation of new motif inventories (Summerhayes 2000b). However, while factors of time and space may serve as a starting point, they are not sufficient on their own in explaining both the variation and continuity observed in assemblages across the Lapita spectrum. In certain cases Lapita designs remained largely unchanged, in others the basic overall structure was retained (as in the case of certain face motifs) while a range of design elements were altered and there are examples of motifs having been combined and others newly created.

In previous studies I have tried to demonstrate that in the case of face motifs we can see the ongoing construction of both social identity and hierarchy of the Lapita peoples (Chiu 2003b, Chiu 2005). It has been suggested that face motifs were acting like "signs of history" (Parmentier 1987) that linked the present to the past, and that generally Lapita motifs were quite limited in terms of construction rules. The face motifs were employed to signal to outsiders the status and power a house-based group had in its local community, its inherited rights to economic resources, and its intention to manipulate and produce history as new face motifs and histories associated with certain images were being created. Various alloforms of a given face motif may have served as a means of demonstrating hierarchy within house-based groups themselves and in the wider community. If a house-based group became influential in its community, it may then have acquired the rights to generate new motifs through the integration of existing motifs, or created new and distinctive motifs in an effort to distinguish themselves from others. Thus, there are at least two forces at work here, one expressing differentiation within a social group, be it household, clan, or local community, and the other expressing integration, a means of signifying the economic and political strength of a local leader (Chiu 2005). Those who owned these "inalienable possessions" (Weiner 1992) would have had to successfully defend their rights of reproducing such signaling symbols not only within the local community, but also amongst their neighbours, as the images represented the status and identity of these groups. Motif construction rules were shared by Lapita peoples from the Bismarcks to Fiji-Tonga-Samoa over many generations. The limited use of face motifs thus suggests that the owners of motifs wielded strong social control over long distances, and over time.

As Lapita pottery was generally produced *in situ*, it can be argued that the technical knowledge required to produce pottery was an aspect that was shared by Lapita potters. Shared structural rules for producing face motifs can also be demonstrated. A Triangular face motif (T2) found at Vatcha in New Caledonia (Sand 1996: Fig.52) shares the structural rules of a Triangular face motif from SE-RF-2 (Figure 3.1) including the rarely used (in New Caledonia) small circles as decorative elements. In another case a sherd from SE-RF-6 with a Triangular face motif shares the exact motif layout as another sherd excavated from Vao Island, northern Vanuatu (Bedford 2003; Chiu 2005). The exact arrangement of design elements, with differences only in the number of lines impressed, the same size of the motif and vessel wall thickness, suggests that reproduction of this image was governed by restricted rules and use (Chiu 2005). They are the single examples of this face motif form amongst the entire motif inventory at both sites. The rarity of these two motifs from two different island groups suggests that not only was there a social desire to continue the reproduction of this particular motif, but that there was also a heavy social charge associated with these motifs that restricted its use. The newly identified and rare "Alternating inverted double face" motif (AI) from Teouma and Site 13A (Figure 5) further strengthens this argument, with its distinctive layout being retained at the two sites and only the infill inside the semi-circle above the inverted face motif showing any variation.

The use of highly similar construction rules is also evident in other categories of face motifs. All the Long-nose motifs and the Alternating inversed face motif found at Site 13A share the same design structure of Long-nose face motifs from the Solomons and other Lapita sites. In the context of a down-the-line exchange system that Green (1982; Summerhayes 2000b) has proposed, Lapita potters of the Reef/Santa Cruz would have kept in some contact with others in the region. If this was the case then the preference for using Simplified face motifs at Site 13A was not the result of being unaware of the existence of more complex motifs, but rather a conscious selection of a particular group of face motifs, in an effort to express particular group identity. In the same context, the preference for Triangular and Long-nose face motifs at SE-RF-2 and SE-SZ-8 was also due to cultural preference rather than a lack of knowledge of the Simplified face motifs.

Another hypothesis that demands our further attention is the possibility that these observed rather limited motif inventories are actually resulting from the fact that there were only limited number of professional artisans available at any given point in time. If Lapita pottery was produced mainly by a small group of skillful potters who traveled from village to village, producing pots locally in exchange for both marine and territorial resources such as food staples and stone quarries (Diamond 2005:349), then it may also explain the high degree of similarity of motif construction rules. In such a scenario, motifs would have been owned by migrating and traveling potters and not by land-owning house-based groups. These motifs could be seen as the "trade markers" of those who produced them. In a sense, this is close to what Terrell has proposed when arguing that Lapita pottery was just a "tradeware" (Terrell 1989).

What is lacking in such an argument is any assessment of the underlying ideology that would have contributed to such high motif similarity amongst island groups across such a vast region. As Lemonnier and others have argued, whether a new technical element is accepted or rejected by a society depends on how the society classifies the newly introduced elements into its own existing symbolic system, rather than simply on aspects such as physical usefulness (Lemonnier 1993). If these motifs were reproduced by a small group of traveling potters who inherited such images, the decision as to whether such motifs were acceptable or valued was still in the hands of the local consumers. If we were to accept such a hypothesis, one has to identify the underlying social forces that encouraged Lapita peoples from different island groups, and different time spans, to use highly similar motifs in the decoration of pottery vessels. In other words, what made these motifs acceptable and meaningful to Lapita peoples?

I have previously stressed the importance of viewing these face motifs as symbols representing social identity of house-based groups within the Lapita Cultural Complex, and how the inherited rights of such images, linked ancestors, houses, territorial rights and other privileges to a given house (Chiu 2005). As the Lapita Cultural Complex was itself likely to have been a mixture of ethnic groups (albeit dominated by Austronesian-speaking populations), involving multi-dimensional scales of migration and integration, I suggest that particular motifs were employed not only to claim inherited rights, but they may also have served as unifying symbols for ethnic groups within an exchange network. As time passed these motifs might have further contributed to these different ethnic groups ultimately sharing similar cultural ideologies and values. As suggested by Linnekin and Poyer (1990:8), "in Oceanic societies identity is continually demonstrated, a matter of behavior and performance", identities are constructed out of *practice*. By adopting the existing symbols at work (both material and linguistic), newcomers would have been able to participate in the established Lapita social framework, mark their worth in the network, and eventually gain influential status in a community that may well have been spread across different island groups. These people, along with their descendants, may have enjoyed the freedom of maintaining multiple identities, by conducting required "behavioral attributes - such as residence, language, dress and participation in exchanges" in acquiring a certain identity (Linnekin and Poyer 1990:9).

In the context of an exchange network face motifs may have served in establishing social hierarchy among exchange partners, confirming and maintaining social relationships that may have lasted for generations among multiple ethnic/linguistic groups, a relationship termed "inherited friendship" by Terrell and Welsch (1997; Welsch and Terrell 1998). While participants were not descendants of a common ancestor, or from the same house-based groups, they still actively participated in a symbolic system that may have facilitated the expression of their identities when traveling to other communities. Specific motifs may have served as an authentic item for identifying one's exchange partners aboard, ensuring a safe and trustworthy environment. The preferred Triangular and Long-nose face motifs in the Solomons, in contrast to the Simplified face motifs at Site 13A, may have symbolised differentiation within a given community, but at the same time could also have acted as representative symbols of that community in relations with outsiders.

The transformation from complex to simple motifs did not generally occur because of a decreasing need to maintain links with an increasingly distant homeland; in contrast, they demonstrate a continuity of social identity that was shared among these colonisers. The image of a motif may have differed, but the message it contained remained the same. An example of this can be seen through the observations of Mead who noted that, "Yanuca potters have added a decorative dimension to these (boundary/zone) markers... In some cases, too, zone markers comprise the *only* decoration on a pot" (Mead 1975:21, emphasis added). Simplified motifs that had been used to decorate more complex central band motifs gradually gained their own rights of display after having a long history of association with high status symbols. Once geometric and simplified versions of the original motifs had gained the same social recognition and status, they too became powerful symbols in their right. Thus by the time Lapita people had moved into New Caledonia and the Eastern Lapita region, some of these simplified motifs had begun to replace the more complex central bands. In terms of face motifs, the simplified ones had gained equal status with high status complex face motifs and were produced to symbolise or characterise local identities. Evidence of continuing high status being associated with different symbols might be seen in the case of Simplified face motif S25 (Figure 7.25) that includes the more complex headdress decoration usually associated with complex Long-nose face motifs.

Whether pottery was produced by members of a local house or by professional potters traveling among islands does not affect the argument that the rights to reproduce such motifs were highly charged with social meaning. What was produced was what had been desired. The fact that most Lapita pottery was locally produced indicates that there was no production centre that supplied communities near and far with similar products. The social control over what motifs could be reproduced was strongly controlled by local consumers, and the symbols at work were selected by local communities that shared the general ideology of the entire cultural complex.

Conclusion

Social hierarchy, constructed and based on the inequality of age, sex, wealth, or fame among members of a given group, is expected to be found in any type of society. I have argued that the Simplified face motifs found contemporaneously with highly elaborate ones at the Reef/Santa Cruz and Site 13A Lapita sites should not be interpreted merely as a late introduction or sharing of motifs among Western and Eastern Lapita peoples. Instead, they may be witness to the conscious selection of certain types of face motif through which Lapita people at Site 13A expressed their own identity, while at the same time being well aware of other types of face motifs in fashion in other island groups. The social desire amongst communities for segregating "us" from "them" can be seen at both SE-RF-2 and Site 13A.

In conclusion, it has been demonstrated that there is a significant difference in terms of what type of face motifs were present at the Reef/Santa Cruz and Site 13A Lapita sites. The differences observed are not the result of sample size effect, and instead suggest that they demonstrate people's social preferences. As Simplified face motifs appeared contemporaneously with more elaborate ones at the same Lapita sites, the previously suggested "logical sequence" of abstraction over time is not applicable in these two cases. The range of face motifs found at the two sites, Triangular, Long-nose, and Simplified have been illustrated. It is proposed that using alloforms of certain face motifs, members of house-based groups differentiated membership and levels of access to inherited rights between themselves. Social groups may have expanded the range of motifs to encompass and integrate other social groups into their own symbolic systems, irrespective of ethnic background, in order to establish social relationships that may have lasted for generations. This entire process was ongoing as Lapita peoples expanded further into the Pacific. By using these highly regarded symbols, with firm control over image innovation and reproduction, Lapita peoples were generating social hierarchy across their social and economic networks, while at the same time transforming themselves and the symbolic system.

Acknowledgements

I would like to express my deep gratitude to Professor Roger Green who not only generously granted me the access to his Solomon collections, but also the full rights to use his illustrations, unpublished papers and notes in my papers and has provided invaluable insights in my study of Lapita motifs in general. A DVD containing all the images of the Lapita potsherds from the Solomon sites studied and other unpublished data, notes, and papers are currently being collated. I would also like to thank Dr. Christophe Sand for his support over the years. Thanks also go to Dr. Stuart Bedford for showing me Teouma and Vao Lapita potsherds that led to the recognition of highly similar pieces from Site 13A and SE-RF-6. His thorough editing of this paper is also greatly appreciated. I thank also Ms. Yijing Shen and Mrs. Jui-Feng Chen for helping out on tables and illustrations of this paper, and to Dr. Glenn Summerhayes, Dr. Jennifer Kohn, and Ms. Aggie Lu for proof-reading the paper. This study was funded by the National Science Council (NSC-93-2412-H-001-037) and the Research Center of Humanities and Social Sciences, Academia Sinica, Taiwan, Republic of China.

Note

1. The null hypothesis states that 5 largest types of face motifs are distributed with same proportion at four different sites (see Table 2). The chi-squared test states that the set significance level is reached when degree of freedom is 12 (Asymptotic significance is 0.000, less than the set value of 0.05). There are 55 % of cases have expected counts less than 5, and the minimum expected count is less than 1. The chi-squared test value in this case is likely to be higher than real, causing a higher chance of rejecting the null hypothesis when it is actually true. This is known as the "Type I error" which means "a significant relationship or difference is being claimed when none really exists" (Shennan 1988:52). One way to avoid the "Type I error" is to set the level of significance at a more conservative level, in this case 0.01. When ($\infty = \nu$, $0.01 = \alpha$), the tabulated t-distribution value is set at 2.576 in a 2-sided t-distribution table (Shennan 1988:Table C). It is clear that at significance level is still reached when degree of freedom is 12. As contingency coefficient that measures degree of association between the variables is at 0.639, a high degree of association is indicated in this case.

References

Anson, D. 1983. Lapita pottery of the Bismarck archipelago and its affinities. PhD thesis, University of Sydney.

Anson, D. 2000. Reber-Rakival dentate-stamped motifs: Documentation and comparative implications. *New Zealand Journal of Archaeology* 20 (1998):119-135.

Bedford, S. 2003. The timing and nature of Lapita colonisation in Vanuatu: the haze begins to clear. In C. Sand (ed.), *Pacific Archaeology: assessments and prospects: Proceedings of the International Conference for the 50th anniversary of the first Lapita excavation*, pp.147-158. Nouméa: Les Cahiers de l'archéologie en Nouvelle-Calédonie 15.

Bedford, S. 2007. Crucial first steps into Remote Oceania: Lapita in the Vanuatu archipelago. In S. Chiu and C. Sand (eds), *From Southeast Asia to the Pacific. Archaeological Perspectives on the Austronesian Expansion and the Lapita Cultural Complex*, pp. 157-185. Taipei: Academia Sinica.

Bedford, S. and M. Spriggs 2007. Birds on the rim: a Unique Lapita carinated vessel in its wider context. *Archaeology in Oceania* 42:12-21.

Bedford, S., M. Spriggs and R. Regenvanu 2006. The Teouma Lapita site and the early human settlement of the Pacific Islands. *Antiquity* 80:812-828.

Bellwood, P. 1978. *Man's Conquest of the Pacific.* Auckland: Collins.

Best, S. 1981. Excavations at Site VL21/5 Naigani Island, Fiji, a preliminary report. Unpublished typescript, Department of Anthropology, University of Auckland.

Best, S. 1984. Lakeba: the prehistory of a Fijian Island. PhD thesis, University of Auckland.

Best, S. 2002. *Lapita: A View From The East.* Auckland: New Zealand Archaeological Association Monograph 24.

Bowser, B.J. 2000. From Pottery to Politics: An Ethnoarchaeological Study of Political Factionalism, Ethnicity, and Domestic Pottery Style in the Ecuadorian Amazon. *Journal of Archaeological Method and Theory* 7:219-248.

Chiu, S. 2003a. Social and economic meanings of Lapita pottery: a New Caledonian case. In C. Sand (ed.), *Pacific Archaeology: assessments and prospects: Proceedings of the International Conference for the 50th anniversary of the first Lapita excavation*, pp. 159-182. Nouméa: Les Cahiers de l'archéologie en Nouvelle-Calédonie 15.

Chiu, S. 2003b. The Socio-economic Functions of Lapita Ceramic Production and Exchange: A Case Study from Site WKO013A, Koné, New Caledonia. PhD thesis, University of California.

Chiu, S. 2005. Meanings of a Lapita face: materialized social memory in ancient house societies. *Taiwan Journal of Anthropology* 3:1-47.

Chiu, S. and C. Sand 2005. Recording of the Lapita motifs: Proposal for a complete recording method. *Archaeology in New Zealand* 48:133-150.

Diamond, J.M. 2005. *Guns, Germs and Steel: The Fates of Human Societies*. London: Vintage.

Dickinson, W.R. 1971. Temper sands in Lapita-style potsherds on Malo. *Journal of the Polynesian Society* 80:244-246.

Dickinson, W.R., R. Shutler Jr., R. Shortland, D.V. Burley and T.S. Dye 1996. Sand tempers in indigenous Lapita and Lapitoid Polynesian Plainware and imported protohistoric Fijian pottery of Ha'apai (Tonga) and the question of Lapita tradeware. *Archaeology in Oceania* 31:87-98.

Donovan, L.J. 1973. A study of the decorative system of the Lapita potters in Reefs and Santa Cruz Islands. MA Research essay, University of Auckland.

Frimigacci, D. 1981. *Fouilles de sauvetage en Nouvelle-Calédonie 1981*. Nouméa: ORSTOM.

Galipaud, J-C. 1990. The physico-chemical analysis of ancient pottery from New Caledonia. In M. Spriggs (ed.), *Lapita Design, Form and Composition*, pp. 134-142. Canberra: Department of Prehistory, Australian National University. Occasional Papers in Prehistory 19.

Geraghty, P. 1996. Pottery in Fiji: A preliminary survey of locations and terminology. In J. Davidson, G.J. Irwin, B.F. Leach, A.K. Pawley and D. Brown (eds), *Oceanic Culture History: Essays in Honour of Roger Green*, pp. 421-431. Dunedin: New Journal of Archaeology Special Publication.

Gifford, E.W. and R. J. Shutler Jr. 1956. *Archaeological Excavations in New Caledonia*. Anthropological Records 18 (1). Berkeley and Los Angeles: University of California Press.

Golson, J. 1961. Report on New Zealand, Western Polynesia, New Caledonia and Fiji. *Asian Perspectives* 5(2):166-180.

Golson, J. 1971. Lapita ware and its transformations. In R.C. Green and M. Kelly (eds), *Studies in Oceanic Culture History*, pp. 67-76. Honolulu: Bernice P. Bishop Museum, Department of Anthropology.

Green, R.C. 1974. Sites with Lapita pottery: Importing and voyaging. *Mankind* 9:253-259.

Green, R.C. 1976. Lapita Sites in the Santa Cruz Group. In R.C. Green and M.M. Cresswell (eds), *Southeast Solomon Islands Cultural History: A Preliminary Survey*, pp. 245-265. Wellington: The Royal Society of New Zealand Bulletin 11.

Green, R.C. 1978. *New Sites with Lapita Pottery and Their Implications for Understanding the Settlement of the Western Pacific*. Auckland: Working Papers in Anthropology, Archaeology, Linguistics, and Maori Studies, University of Auckland.

Green, R.C. 1979. Early Lapita art from Polynesia and Island Melanesia: continuities in ceramic, barkcloth and tattoo decoration. In S.M. Mead (ed.), *Exploring the visual art of Oceania: Australia, Melanesia, Micronesia, and Polynesia*, pp.13-31. Honolulu: University of Hawaii Press.

Green, R.C. 1982. Models for the Lapita cultural complex: an evaluation of some current proposals. *New Zealand Journal of Archaeology* 4:7-20.

Green, R.C. 1991. The Lapita Cultural Complex: current evidence and proposed models. In P. Bellwood (ed.), *Indo-Pacific Prehistory 1990: Proceedings of the 14th Congress of the Indo-Pacific prehistory Association*, pp. 295-305. Canberra: Indo-Pacific Prehistory Association.

Green, R.C. 2006. An evaluation of adequacy for motif analyses of decorated ceramic collections from three Reef/Santa Cruz Lapita sites in the Outer Eastern Islands of the Solomons. Unpublished document.

Green, R.C. and P.V. Kirch 1997. Lapita exchange systems and their Polynesian transformations: Seeking explanatory models. In M.I. Weisler (ed.), *Prehistoric Long-Distance Interaction in Oceania: An Interdisciplinary Approach*, pp.19-37. Auckland: New Zealand Archaeological Association Monograph 21.

Green, R.C. and A.K. Pawley 1999. Early Oceanic architectural forms and settlement patterns: Linguistic, archaeological and ethnological perspectives. In M. Spriggs and R. Blench (eds), *Archaeology and Language III: Artefacts, languages and texts*, pp.31-89. New York: Routledge.

Hunt, T.L. 1988. Lapita ceramic technological and composition studies: A critical review. In P.V. Kirch and T.L. Hunt (eds), *Archaeology of the Lapita Cultural Complex: A Critical Review*, pp. 49-60. Seattle: The Thomas Burke Memorial Washington State Museum Research Report No.5.

Ishimura, T. 2002. In the Wake of Lapita: Transformation of Lapita Designs and Gradual Dispersal of the Lapita Peoples. *People and Culture in Oceania* 18:77-97.

Jones, M., F. Petchey, R.C. Green, P.J. Sheppard and M. Phelan 2007. The Marine ΔR for Nenumbo: a case study in calculating reservoir offsets from paired sample data. *Radiocarbon* 41(1).

Kirch, P.V. 1988a. Long-distance exchange and island colonization: The Lapita case. *Norwegian Archaeological Review* 21:103-117.

Kirch, P.V. 1988b. *Niuatoputapu: The Prehistory of a Polynesian Chiefdom*. Seattle: The Thomas Burke Memorial Washington State Museum Monograph No.5.

Kirch, P.V. 1991. Prehistoric exchange in Western Melanesia. *Annual Review of Anthropology* 20:141-165.

Kirch, P.V. 1997. *The Lapita Peoples: Ancestors of the Oceanic World*. Oxford: Blackwell.

Kirch, P.V., T.L. Hunt, M.I. Weisler, V. Butler and M.S. Allen 1991. Mussau Islands prehistory: results of the 1985-86 excavations. In J. Allen and C. Gosden (eds), *Report of the Lapita Homeland Project*, pp.144-163. Canberra: Department of Prehistory, Australian National University. Occasional Papers in Prehistory 20.

Lemonnier, P. 1993. Introduction. In P. Lemonnier (ed.), *Technological Choice: Transformation in material cultures since the Neolithic*, pp.1-35. London and New York: Routledge.

Linnekin, J. and L. Poyer 1990. Introduction. In J. Linnekin and L. Poyer (eds), *Cultural Identity and Ethnicity in the Pacific*, pp.1-16. Honolulu: University of Hawaii Press.

Mead, S.M. 1975. The decorative system of the Lapita potters of Sigatoka, Fiji. In S.M. Mead, L. Birks, H. Birks and E. Shaw (eds), *The Lapita pottery style of Fiji and its associations*, pp.19-43. Wellington: The Polynesian Society.

Meyer, O. 1909. Funde prähistorischer Töpferei und Steinmesser auf Vuatom, Bismarck Archipel. *Anthropos* 4:215-252.

Meyer, O. 1910. Funde von Menschen- und Tierknochen, von prähistorischer Töpferei und Steinwerkzeugen auf Vuatom, Bismarck Archipel. *Anthropos* 5:1160-1161.

Newton, D. 1988. Reflection in bronze. Lapita and Dong-Son art in the Western Pacific. In J.P. Barbier and D. Newton (eds), *Islands and Ancestors: Indigenous Styles of Southeast Asia*, pp.10-23. Oxford: Prestel.

Noury, A. 2005. *Le Reflet de l'ame Lapita*. Versailles: Privately published.

Parker, M. 1981. Vessel forms of the Reef Island SE-RF-2 site and their relationships to vessel forms in other western Lapita sites of the Reef/Santa Cruz and Island Melanesian area. MA thesis, University of Auckland.

Parmentier, R.J. 1987. *The Sacred Remains: Myth, History, and Polity in Belau*. Chicago and London: The University of Chicago Press.

Phelan, M. 1997. Scratching the Surface. The Lapita Pottery of Mekekur, Papua New Guinea. Unpublished MA thesis, La Trobe University.

Sand, C. 1995. *Contribution à la reconstitution de la préhistoire des îles Loyauté. Premiers résultats des fouilles archéologiques de 1994-1995, Lifou, Maré, Ouvéa*. Nouméa: Les Cahiers de l'Archéologie en Nouvelle-Calédonie Volume 5.

Sand, C. 1996. *Le Début du Peuplement Austronésien de la Nouvelle-Calédonie. Données Archéologiques Recéntes*. Nouméa: Les Cahiers de l'Archéologie en Nouvelle-Calédonie Volume 6.

Sand, C. 1998. Archaeological Report on Localities WKO013A and WkO013B at the site of Lapita (Koné, New Caledonia). *Journal of the Polynesian Society* 107:7-33.

Sand, C. 1999. *Lapita. The pottery collection from the site at Foué, New Caledonia*. Nouméa: Les Cahiers de l'Archéologie en Nouvelle-Calédonie Volume 7.

Sand, C. 2000. The specificities of the "Southern Lapita Province": the New Caledonian case. *Archaeology in Oceania* 35:20-33.

Sand, C. 2001. Evolutions in the Lapita Cultural Complex: A view from the Southern Lapita Province. *Archaeology in Oceania* 36:65-76.

Shennan, S. 1988. *Quantifying Archaeology*. San Diego: Academic Press.

Spriggs, M.J.T. 1990. The Changing Face of Lapita: transformation of a Design. In M. Spriggs (ed.), *Lapita Design, Form and Composition: Proceedings of the Lapita Design Workshop*, pp. 83-122. Canberra: Department of Prehistory, Australian National University. Occasional Papers in Prehistory 19.

Spriggs, M.J.T. 1993. How much of the Lapita design system represents the human face? In P.J.C. Dark and R.G. Rose (eds), *Artistic Heritage in a Changing Pacific*, pp.7-14. Honolulu: University of Hawaii Press.

Spriggs, M.J.T. 2002. They've Grown Accustomed to Your Face. In S. Bedford, C. Sand, and D. Burley (eds), *Fifty Years in the Field. Essays in Honour and Celebration of Richard Shutler Jr's Archaeological Career*, pp. 51-57. Auckland: New Zealand Archaeological Association Monograph 25.

Spriggs, M.J.T. and S. Wickler 1989. Archaeological Research on Erromango: Recent Data on Southern Melanesian Prehistory. *Bulletin of the Indo-Pacific Prehistory Association* 9:68-91.

Summerhayes, G.R. 1998. The Face of Lapita. *Archaeology in Oceania* 33:100.

Summerhayes, G.R. 2000a. *Lapita Interaction*. Canberra: Department of Archaeology and Natural History, Centre for Archaeological Research, Australian National University. Terra Australis 15.

Summerhayes, G.R. 2000b. Far Western, Western and Eastern Lapita - A re-evaluation. *Asian Perspectives* 39:167-174.

Terrell, J.E. 1989. What Lapita is and what Lapita isn't. *Antiquity* 63:623-626.

Terrell, J.E. and R.L. Welsch 1997. Lapita and the temporal geography of prehistory. *Antiquity* 71:548-572.

Torrence, R. and J.P. White 2001. Tattooed faces from Boduna Island, Papua New Guinea. In G.R. Clark, A.J. Anderson and T. Vunidilo (eds), *The Archaeology of Lapita dispersal in Oceania: Papers from the Fourth Lapita Conference*, pp.135-140. Canberra: Pandanus Books.

Weiner, A.B. 1992. *Inalienable Possessions: The Paradox of Keeping-While-Giving*. Berkeley: University of California Press.

Welsch, R.L. and J.E. Terrell 1998. Material Culture, social fields, and social boundaries on the Sepik coast of New Guinea. In M.T. Stark (ed.), *The Archaeology of Social Boundaries*, pp. 50-77. Washington, DC: Smithsonian Institution Press.

16

Looking at the big motifs: a typology of the central band decorations of the Lapita ceramic tradition of New Caledonia (Southern Melanesia) and preliminary regional comparisons

Christophe Sand

Department of Archaeology of New Caledonia
Nouméa
New Caledonia
christophe.sand@gouv.nc

Introduction

For decades, the study of Lapita pottery has been limited by the often small size of the ceramic remains that archaeologists recovered in their test-pit excavations. Although the very first Lapita sherds published at the turn of the twentieth century by Father Meyer comprised some half pots (Meyer 1909, 1910; Green 2000), successive generations of researchers were mostly unlucky in their search for well-preserved Lapita remains. Consequently, up until the last few decades, most studies that focused on Lapita designs and the related ceramic forms on which the decorations were applied, were largely constructed on often very fragmented sherds. The progressive discovery of well preserved sites (Green 1976; Kirch 1987) has, amongst other things, allowed us to start to get a better understanding of the main categories of motifs that form the Lapita design system. Starting in the late 1970s Green was able to convincingly show a marked difference between the dentate-stamped motifs produced in the Melanesian crescent and the Fiji/West Polynesian region (Green 1978, 1979). Subsequent to Green's initial Western and Eastern Lapita styles a number of discrete Lapita Provinces have now been defined (Anson 1983; Kirch 1997; Summerhayes 2000). Amongst these, New Caledonia has been argued as forming a Southern Province, with a whole series of local specificities developing after first settlement (Sand 2000).

Although it is acknowledged that non-ceramic data greatly contributes to our knowledge of the Lapita Cultural Complex (Green 2003), it must be said that our working models still largely rest on the study of the intricately decorated Lapita pots. Not surprisingly, different types of analysis of the dentate-stamped and incised motifs have been adopted over the years. Moving away from the recording system proposed by Mead (Mead *et al.* 1975) and from the seriation tables compiled by Anson (1983), Siorat was amongst the first to propose an analysis of the Lapita designs based on the study of the decorative method and the tools employed to produce the dentate-stamped patterns (1990). This approach, applied to the Lapita collection of site WBR001 of Nessadiou in New Caledonia (Siorat 1992), enabled him to propose a typology of friezes as well as central decorative bands, much in common with what Donovan (1973) had obtained for the Reef/Santa Cruz material. Over the last decade, this type of analysis has been expanded by our local Department of Archaeology for the other Lapita collections excavated in New Caledonia, showing its benefits in identifying the main decorative patterns that compose the Southern Lapita "repertoire" (Sand 2006). This paper presents a general review of the studies underway on this topic. The first part will discuss the new information that has been gained through a detailed analysis of the decorative technique employed to stamp the dentate motifs. This methodological approach will introduce a proposed typology for the Lapita motifs of New Caledonia (Figure 1), before a preliminary regional comparison of presence/absence of the main motifs in the different Lapita Provinces is presented.

Stamping the clay: methods and rules

Since their first discovery, the intricacy of the decorated Lapita sherds have led to multiple interpretations on the technique used to obtain these regular patterns. Needles and a type of roulette were proposed by the first observers (see Best 2002:46 for a review), although by the 1960s, the use of a comb with an alignment of teeth was firmly established (Poulsen 1967). The identification of a comb, traditionally used for Pacific tattooing, rapidly led to a series of parallels between the motifs printed on the clay and the art

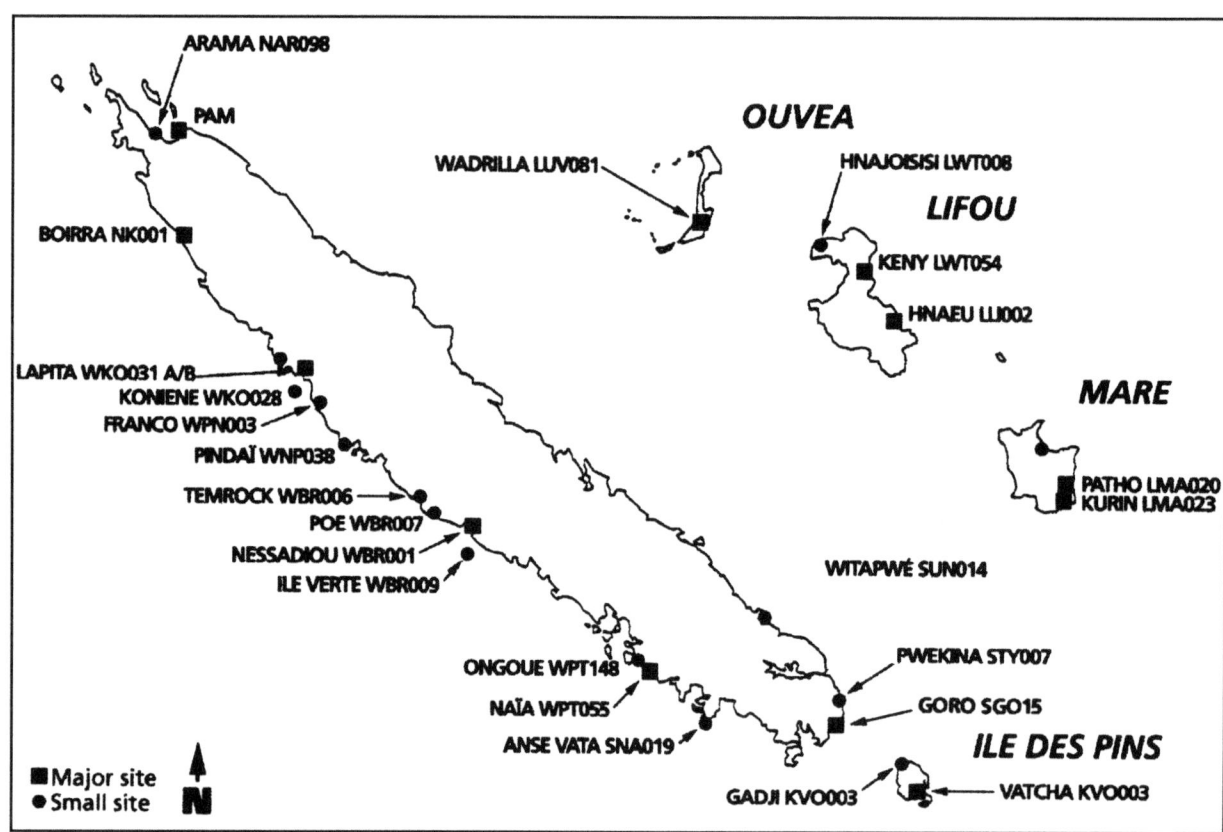

Figure 1. Map of New Caledonia, with the main Lapita sites discovered to date across the archipelago.

of tattooing. Siorat (1990) has identified the existence of two main forms of tools to achieve the dentate-stamping, along with a rounded tube for full stamps. Although challenged for a period by Basek, who advocated that "dentate Lapita pottery decoration (...) do not (...) need to use a series of toothed stamps with straight and curved teeth rows to impress straight and curved lines" (Basek 1993:63), the proposal has proven its validity though more recent studies (cf. Ambrose 1999, this volume; Sand 2006). Detailed study and profiling of the imprints from different potsherd collections has provided a fairly good knowledge of the two main tool-types used in the Southern Lapita Province. The first type of tool is straight, with the use of combs of at least two different sizes: one is short, with 7 to 12 teeth on average and the other is long, with between 20 and 30 teeth. The second form of tool is curved, composed of 10 to 18 teeth in general. On some pots the use of two sizes of curved combs can be identified (Figure 2).

Figure 2. Dentate-stamped patterns around a face-motif, demonstrating the use of different sized straight and curved toothed tools.

In New Caledonia, very few sherds have dot impressions of around 0.5 mm, a size that characterises the Early Lapita pots of the Bismarck Archipelago (Anson 1983; Summerhayes 2000). Elongated impressed dots of Eastern Lapita type (Burley *et al*. 2002), measuring 2-3 mm long and up to 1-1.5 mm wide, are also extremely rare in New Caledonia. Most dots can be grouped in the size 1 mm to 1.5 mm, with a square or elongated shape. Close-up observations of the imprints of curved tools have identified "both trapezoidal and rectangular spaced intervals" (Ambrose 1997:527) between the teeth, thus showing in the Southern Province the same pattern of possible bent turtle scute as for the site of Ambitle in Northern Melanesia (Ambrose 1999). The identification of this specific bended tool across the Lapita area might tell us something about the process of development of the dentate-stamped Lapita technique in Near Oceania and/or further west, as this tool on turtle scute is not directly usable as a tattooing chisel. Significantly, the dentate-stamped sherds of pre-Lapita chronology in Island Southeast Asia (cf. Tsang 2007: Fig. 2) have mostly straight dotted lines, compatible with known tattooing tools. The absence of curved stamps on these pots may indicate that the transfer of the tattooing methods to clay was not straight forward as often advocated (Kirch 1997:142-143), but included an adaptation and innovation process, with the creation of the curved, bended comb (Sand 2006). The outcome of this is that probably, part of the Lapita patterns were not used as tattoo designs but were developed during this innovation process, seemingly as part of the development of new traditions linked to the first Austronesian expansion into the region.

The different tools were each used for specific purposes during the decoration process. The long straight comb appears mainly identifiable in the lines dividing different bands of the decoration, as well as in some large straight motifs like the labyrinth. Aside from its use in complex motifs, the short straight comb is mainly used in successive alignments of vertical imprints or in different types of triangular patterns in the friezes. The curved tool can be used to form individual imprints in successive rows, but also partly superimposed imprints, allowing to obtain dense alignments forming some of the dividing bands that Mead had termed "zone markers" (Mead 1975). The macroscopic observation of these specific imprints on numerous Lapita sherds

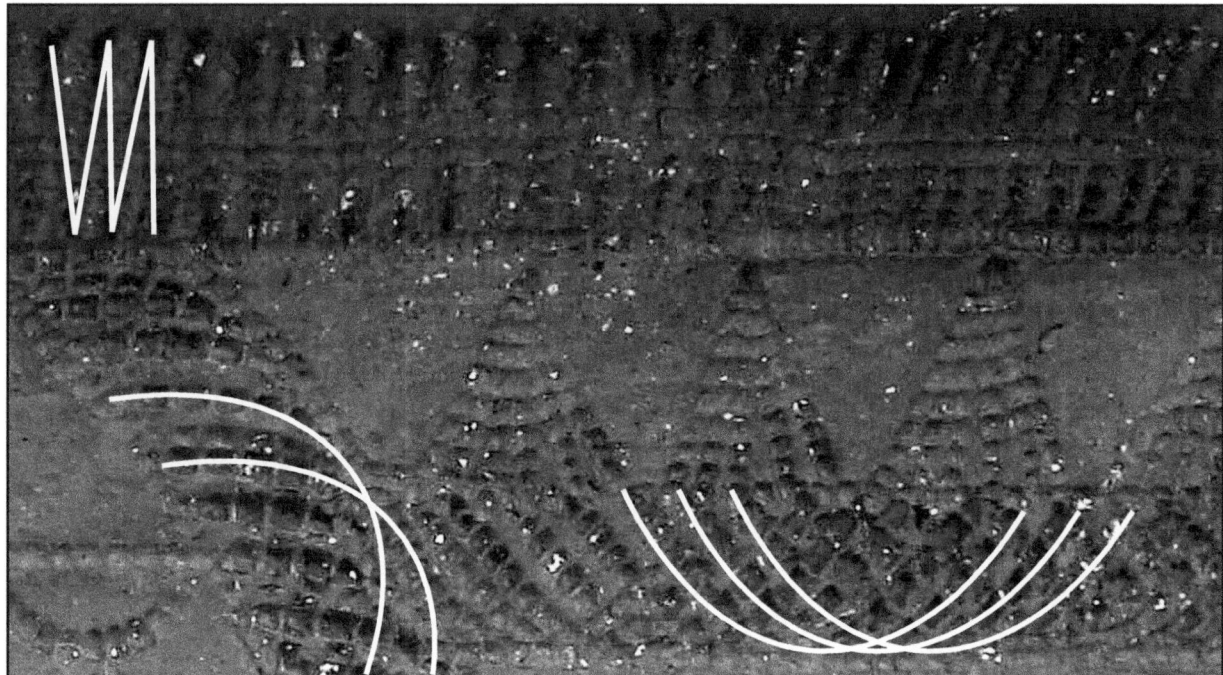

Figure 3. Close-up view of Figure 2, highlighting the imprints of a straight and a curved tool to create two types of "zone marker".

(Figure 3), leads to the rejection of the proposal made by Best with reference to material from New Caledonia (Best 2002:47), of the use of a "roulette" to obtain the densely imprinted "zone markers" characterising Lapita patterns in Island Melanesia (Best 2002:46-50). Without any doubt, all these alignments have been achieved simply with a curved (or small straight) comb, the superimposition of the successive curved imprints that partly cover the preceding print being clearly visible under a microscope (cf. Sand 2006, Fig. 3.42-3.43) (see also Ambrose this volume).

Typology of dentate-stamped motifs for New Caledonia

The study of the actual tools that were used to produce the Lapita patterns as a preliminary stage in the construction of a typology of motifs, has proven essential in understanding the rules governing the decoration. As already identified by Siorat nearly two decades ago (1990), the principle of decoration for the Southern Lapita Province has been systematically constructed around a two-part structure: a central motif horizontally encircling the pot and always surrounded by a series of horizontal friezes over and under the central motif. No example of two successive central bands has been identified in New Caledonia, contrary to some Bismarck Archipelago and Reef/Santa Cruz sites for example (Green 1976: Fig. 77; Summerhayes 2000: Fig. 5.17 and 5.18). Sometimes, three-dimensional adding, mainly in the form of vertical clay bands and nubbins, allowed the division of these successive horizontal alignments into different blocs (Figure 4). On the carinated pots, which form the principal ceramic form identified for Southern Lapita, the decoration is restricted mainly to the upper part of the vessel, with one to three friezes present under the carination of some of the pots of small size. On most of the flat bottom dishes, the decoration is limited to the visible outer part of the dish, but it can be continued on the flat bottom for those dishes that appear to have had a pedestal. Variation is also identifiable on the rims, with decoration sometimes placed on the upper part of the inner side of the vessel.

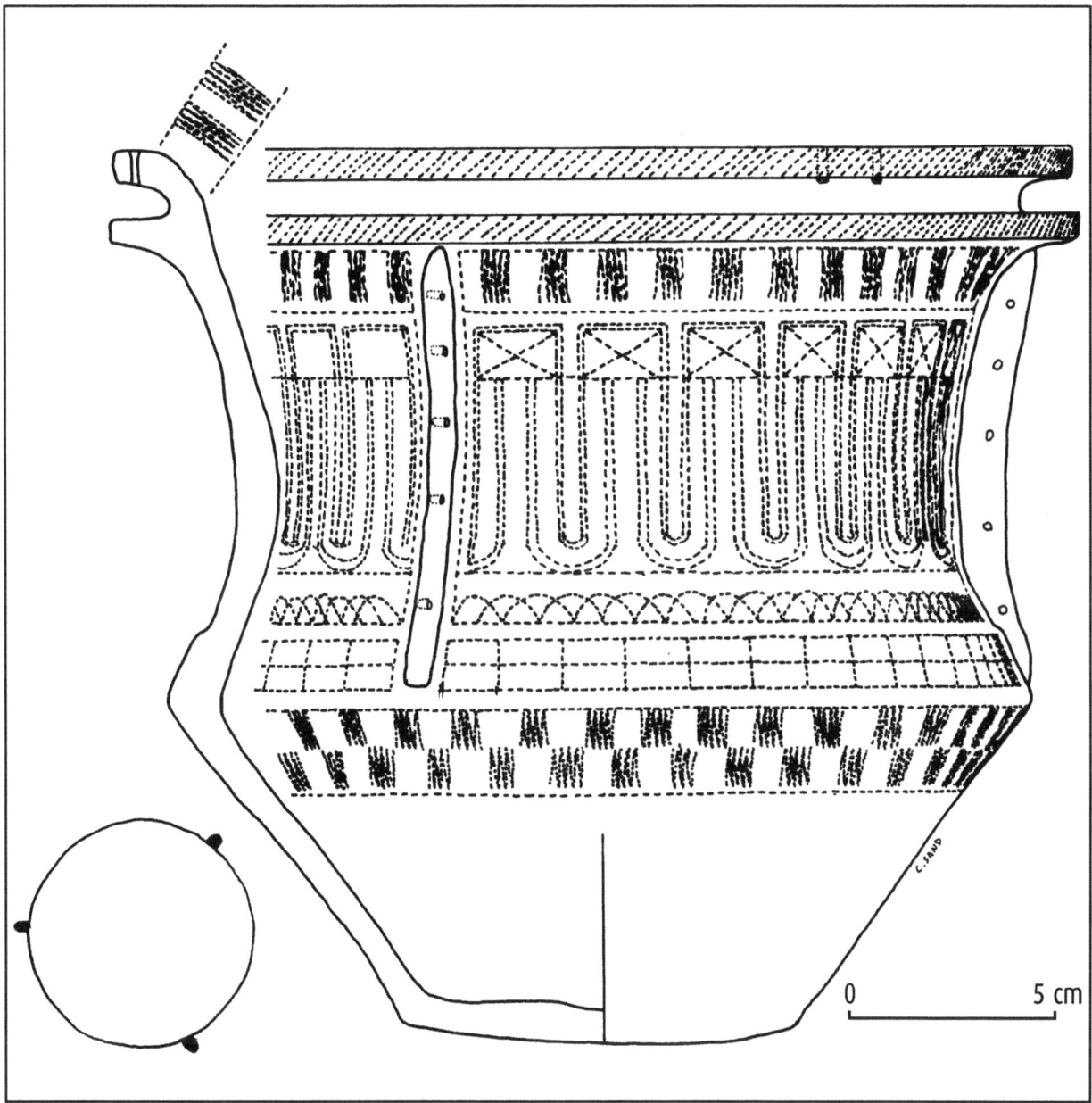

Figure 4. Carinated pot with vertical clay-bands separating the central band and the friezes in three parts (site LPO023, Kurin).

The significant number of excavations conducted on Lapita sites in New Caledonia over the last 50 years and the good preservation of some sites, makes it one of the archipelagos of the Western Pacific where the largest amount of large sherds as well as nearly complete or complete pots has been discovered to date (Sand 1999; Sand *et al.* 1998) (Figure 5). This unique situation has allowed us to gain a fairly complete view of the main motifs that were stamped and/or incised on the Lapita pots in the Southern Lapita Province. Although no detailed presentation is proposed in the context of the present paper, it must though be emphasised that the typology of dentate-stamped friezes can be subdivided into three main categories: the motifs made with only the straight tool, those made with only the curved tool, and the friezes combining two or three tools, with the adding of the round imprint. As had been highlighted in Anson's tables (1983) as well as in the figures published by Donovan (1973) and Siorat (1990), a fairly large amount of designs combining the possibilities offered by the three tools was developed on the Lapita pots (Sand 2006: Figs. 3.102-3.104).

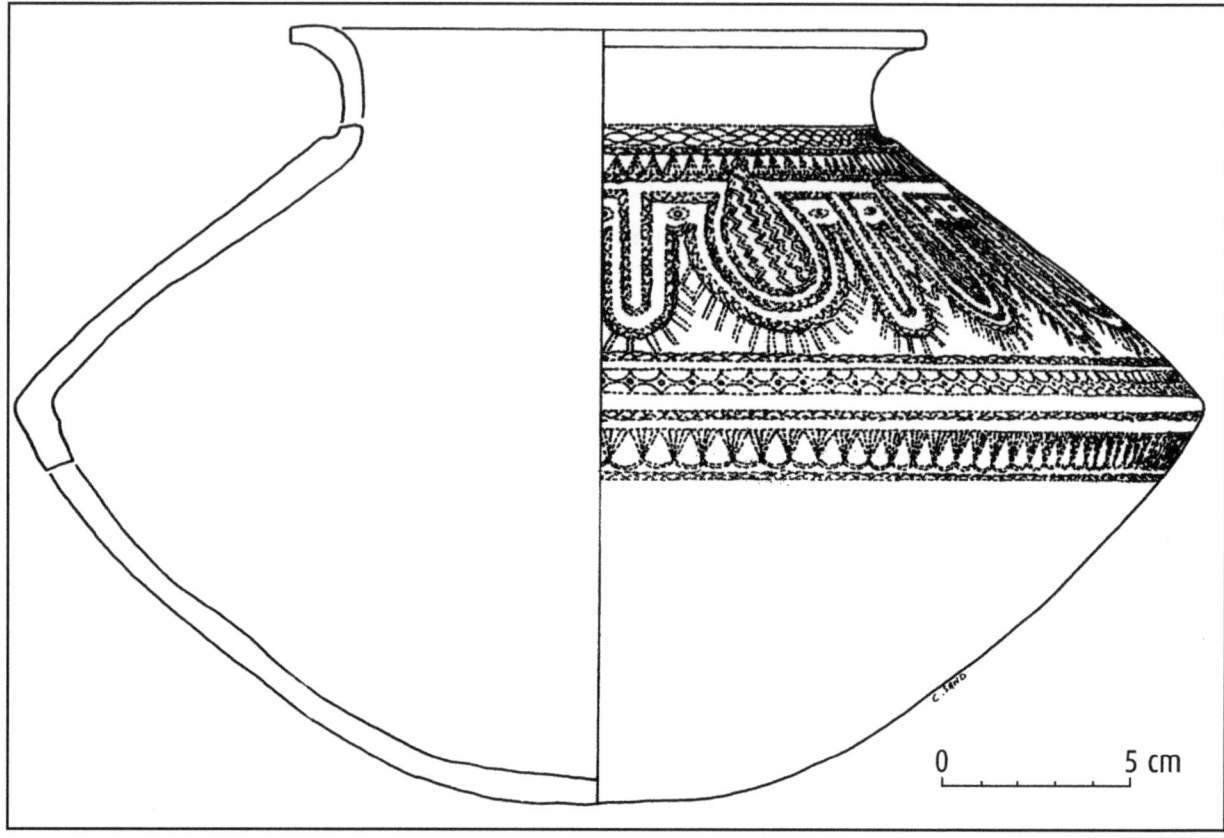

Figure 5. Example of a nearly complete carinated pot profile bearing a "long nose" anthropomorphic motif with "earplugs" (site WKO013A, Lapita).

Surprisingly, for the central band that forms the main decoration of the pots, only 9 categories of dentate-stamped geometric patterns (divided into 6 main types and 3 sets of uncommon types), 4 categories of dentate-stamped anthropomorphic patterns and one principal category of incised pattern have been identified to date in New Caledonia amongst tens of thousands of decorated sherds. This section of the paper proposes to detail each category in turn, specifying the principal inner variations[1].

a. The geometric motifs

i. The "labyrinth" category (Anson's codes 426-430)

The "labyrinth" category (Figure 6) is probably the most complex graphic pattern applied on Lapita pots. It is characterised by a succession of interlocking rectangles succeeding each other and placed each time at a near right angle to one another. Structurally, this pattern can be compared to mat weaving, defined through one to three parallel lines for each rectangle. The complexity of the design and the need to follow a standard rule of construction, does not allow for major variations. The main variation identified relates to the direction of the pattern, which can in some cases be reversed from the direction observed on most pots. The number of successive vertical rectangles is evidently dependent on the overall size of the central band, the larger pots having two interlocking rows. The only areas where specific patterns can be applied are the lower and upper triangles that are not filled by the main design, along the borders of the central band. When they were not left plain, a whole series of motifs have been used to fill-in these triangles, ranking from possible zoomorphs to interlocking triangles or squares (cf. Sand 2006, fig. 3.64).

Figure 6. Examples of "labyrinths".

ii. The "undulated" category (no Anson equivalent, Donovan's motif 86)

This category (Figure 7) is constructed around a standard basis: a series of successive X imprints, whose points are connected horizontally by two curved imprints with their central part turned downwards. Often a third curved imprint is placed in-between, unconnected to the central part of the X. Usually, only one row of the undulated motif is present, but on some larger pots have been identified two successive rows (Figure 8), and even a specific pattern with interlocking successions of curved imprints. While the lower part of the central band of this category shows diverse sets of design, the upper part appears to

Figure 7. Examples of "undulated" motifs.

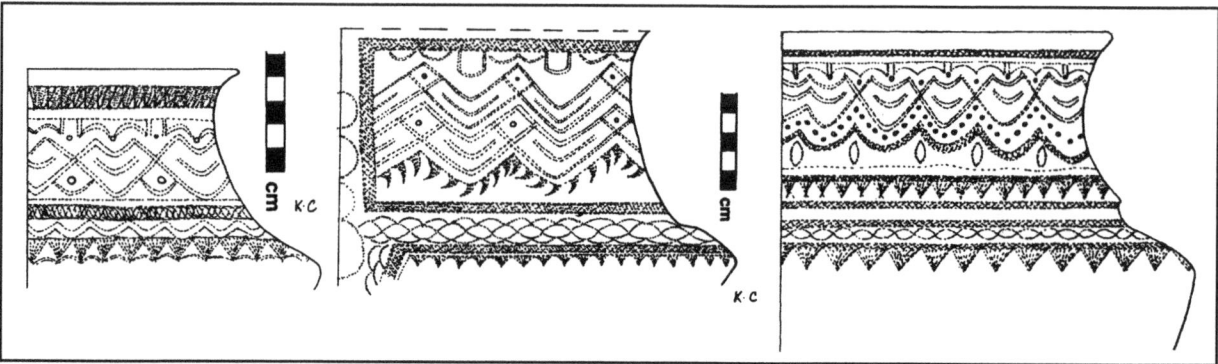

Figure 8. Partly complete pots bearing classic "undulated" motifs (site WKO013A, Lapita).

have had a fairly standard decoration. This consists of two vertical imprints placed over the centre of the curved imprints composing the main motif, each connected to the next vertical imprint by two curved imprints in horizontal succession, with their central part usualy turned upwards.

iii. The "interlocking triangles" category (Anson's codes 129-132/146-148)

This category (Figure 9) is characterised by a succession of mostly double-lined V-shaped triangles placed one inside the other, leading necessarily to a progressive reduction of the size of the triangles. The lower parts of the triangles are either rounded, pointed, or rest on the horizontal line forming the lower border of the central band. The upper parts of each V-shaped triangle are topped face-to-face by a curved imprint placed vertically, with the front part towards the centre of the pattern. On some large central bands, a reversed series of interlocking triangles, with the point towards the top, has been added to the main pattern, starting on-top of the curved imprints. A few odd motifs probably representing a deviation of this category have been identified in the New Caledonian collections.

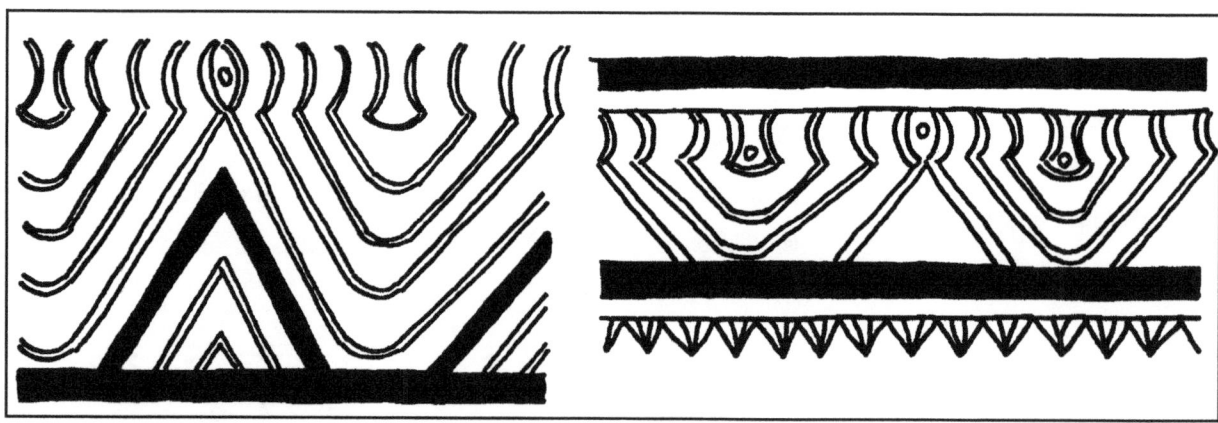

Figure 9. Examples of "interlocking triangles".

iv. The "rectangles" category (Anson's codes 278-289/370/422-424)

The geometric pattern represented by the rectangle, allowing the formation of one to five horizontal bands and as many vertical divisions as permitted by the size of the pot, is one of the most simple graphic structures of the Lapita design tradition. At the same time, the rectangular motif has allowed for the development of a large variety of different infill, making this category the most diverse of the typology identified to date in New Caledonia (Figure 10). These rank from the simplest types, open boxes left empty, to the insertion of simple horizontal, vertical or diagonal bars often put in reverse sense from one box to the next, providing a clear difference. On some pots, the vertical and horizontal divisions of the rectangles have disappeared, leaving only a diamond-shaped pattern. Rectangles can be divided into triangles, one being left plain while the other is filled, or each triangle being filled with a specific pattern. The most complex graphic structure is obtained through the division of each rectangle into four triangles, with specific infill. The full diversity of this category certainly remains to be completed.

Figure 10. Variety of "rectangular" motifs.

v. The "joined triangles" category (Anson's codes 187-195)

This category is defined by a succession of joining triangles in one row, one out of two being reversed (Figure 11). This motif appears to be present exclusively on small pots and the category might be seen as only a derivation from the rectangular motif, adapted to the small size of some vessels.

Figure 11. Examples of "joined triangles".

vi. The "simple zigzags" category (Anson's codes 267-269)

This is the simplest dentate-stamped decoration identified in the New Caledonian collections. It consists of successive imprints of a straight or curved tool in a balanced movement, creating a loose pattern of zigzags. On large pots bearing this motif (Figure 12), the zigzags were placed vertically, mainly on the upper body and horizontally above the carination. Although this motif was present from the very start of the Lapita period, it developed mainly in the Loyalty Islands over the following two centuries, the toothed comb being finally replaced by a tool without teeth.

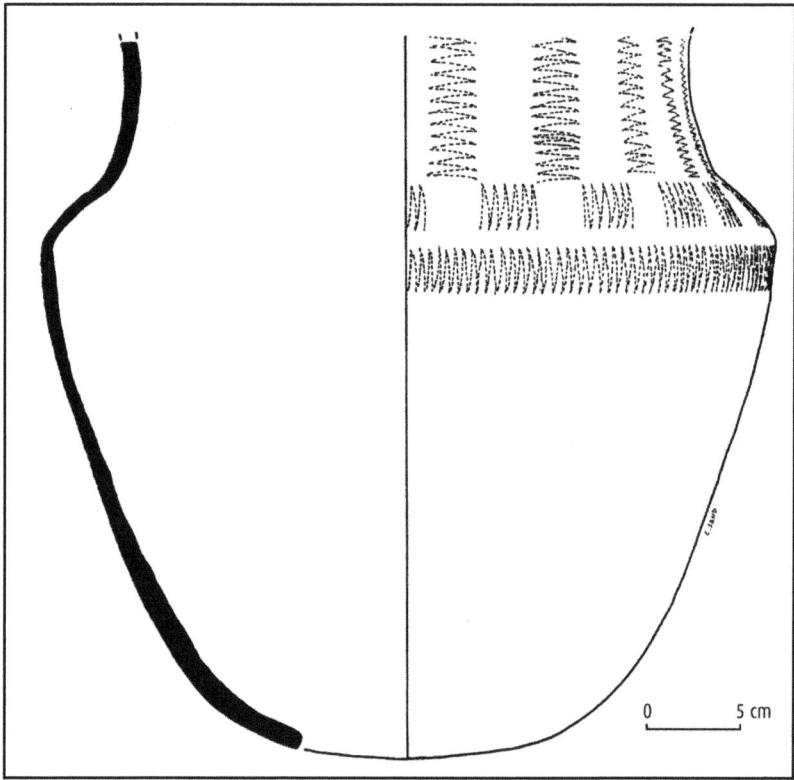

Figure 12. Large oval-shaped pot with "simple zigzag" patterns (site WKO013B, Lapita).

vii. The "vertical zigzags" category (Anson's codes 270-275)

This category in defined by small straight imprints placed in opposite angles, forming successive vertical zigzag patterns. Very few sherds bearing this motif have been discovered in New Caledonia (Figure 13).

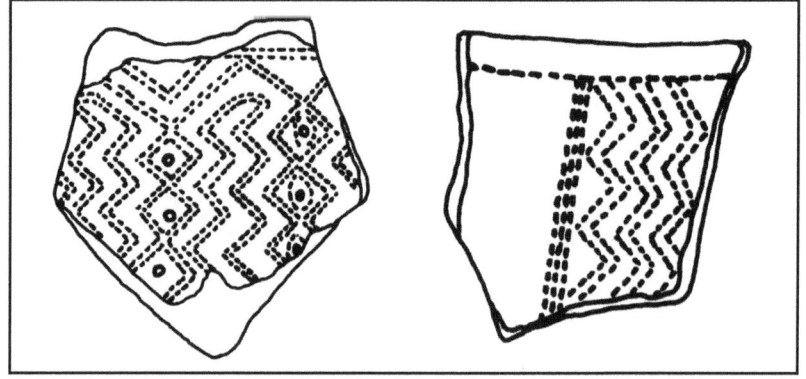

Figure 13. Examples of the "vertical zigzag" motif.

viii. The "wave" category (no Anson equivalent)

A few sherds have shown the existence of a simple wavy curved motif that appears to be developed in one single direction on some pots but in opposite directions on some flat bottom dishes (Figure 14). This category appears at present to be unique to New Caledonia.

Figure 14. A "wave" motif on a flat-bottom Lapita dish (Site KVO003, St Maurice - Vatcha).

ix. Other rare motifs

Surprisingly few sherds do not fit in the main categories defined above. The first case is composed of motifs present on small sherds, for which the identification of the overall design is difficult. This is especially the case for the partial designs probably part of complex face motifs (see below). The second case is formed of motifs that are mainly used as patterns of friezes, but multiplied in different rows to fill-in a central band. Regional comparisons show that this tradition was developed also in the other Lapita Provinces. Finally, some motifs, known in other Lapita Provinces, appear almost absent from the Southern Province, having been identified on only one or a few sherds. This is the case for example of a large pot bearing a specific V-shaped motif (Sand *et al.* 1998, Fig. 4b) identified mainly in Fiji (Anson's codes 224-227). Another case is the well-known complex motif with a flower pattern (Figure 15) (see Spriggs 1990, Fig. 27), that bears

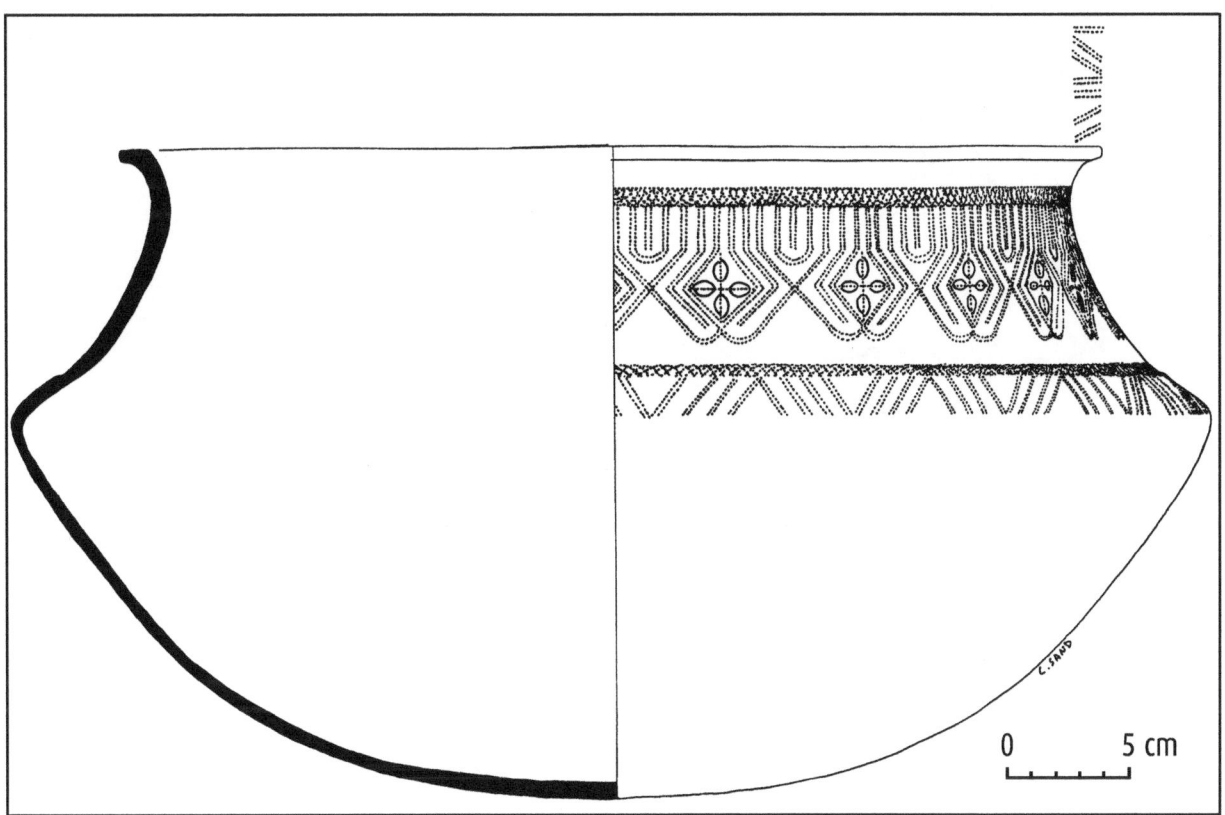

Figure 15. Large dentate-stamped Lapita vessel bearing a unique pattern with a flower-motif (site WBR001, Nessadiou).

resemblances with partial motifs of the Bismarck Archipelago. On the contrary, some widespread design patterns appear nearly totally absent from the Southern Lapita design system. This is for example the case of the "house-like" motif (Anson's code 503), identified on only three small sherds for the entire New Caledonian corpus. Although future studies will have to incorporate these rare designs into a general motif classification, it does not appear useful at this stage to create a specific category for each of these patterns.

b. The anthropomorphic motifs

i. The "double-faced" category

The double face motif is defined by a stylised representation of a human body, with an oval head, a triangular body and extensions figuring the arms. The body is highlighted by a triangular anthropomorphic figure, the whole motif being enclosed in a round-shaped envelope. The double-faced motif has been clearly identified to date on only one sherd found in Isle of Pines (Figure 16). Other less well preserved sherds bearing rounded patterns and triangular faces that fit this category have been identified in various other sites of the Archipelago.

Figure 16. Computer reconstruction of the double-face sherd discovered on site KVO003 of St Maurice - Vatcha (Isle of Pines).

ii. The "simple triangular-faced" category

A different category is composed of anthropomorphic representations of one single triangular face (Figure 17). The designs surrounding the face are often complex, probably a sign that this category was developed in parallel to the double-faced motif and not simply as its simplification. On a number of the well-preserved examples, the head is covered by a sort of hat, sometimes topped by what appears to be

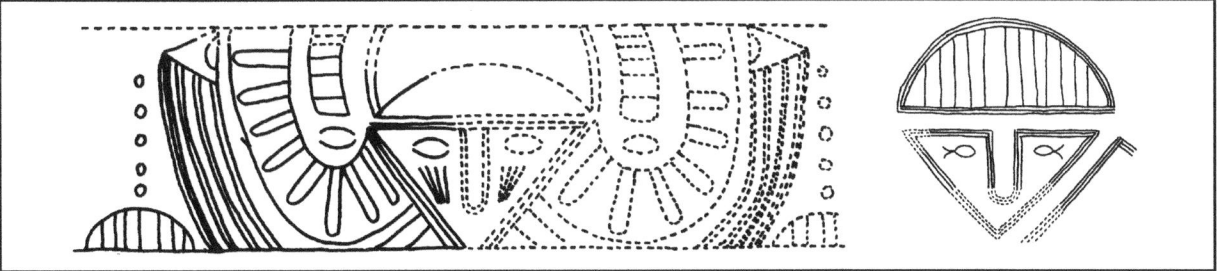

Figure 17. Examples of "triangular face" motifs.

an ornament of plumes or leaves. The design of the eyes and nose are fairly standard, the main differences of treatment being restricted to the decoration of the cheeks and what appears to be eyelashes. No mouth is present. A more stylised use of the triangular face has been identified on some sherds, with a partial superimposition of two triangles, leading to the sharing of the same eye by two faces (Figure 18). One unique example of a more naturalistic face has been discovered at the site of Lapita, probably printed on a large flat-bottom dish (Sand 1999:44).

Figure 18. Examples of stylised "triangular face" motifs.

iii. The "long-nose anthropomorphic with earplugs" category
This other classic Lapita face motif is characterized by an anthropomorphic face (see Terrell and Schechter 2007 for an alternative hypothesis) with a long nose, two clearly marked eyes, no mouth, separated from the next face by a rounded or oval motif defined as an "earplug" by Spriggs (1990) or an "emblem" by Kirch (1997:136). This category is present on all the main Lapita sites of New Caledonia, on flat-bottom dishes as well as on carinated jars (Figure 19). It has not been possible to show in the Southern Province

Figure 19. Examples of "long-nose" faces.

Figure 20. Large carinated vessel with two different motifs defining the "earplugs" (site WK0013A, Lapita).

the existence of two successive "earplugs" separating faces (cf. Spriggs 1990: Fig. 18). On one well preserved carinated pot of the site of Lapita, the inner motifs of the "earplugs" are repeated each two faces (Figure 20).

iv. The "stylised long-nose" category (Anson's codes 344-352)

As for the triangular face category, the New Caledonian collections have revealed a *simplification* of the main long-nose motif, by removing the "earplugs" and creating a succession of eye-nose-eye-nose. This simpler pattern has allowed a diversification of the treatment of the face motif, defined by one to three lines, different forms of nose as well as eye treatments (Figure 21). In some extreme examples, the eye

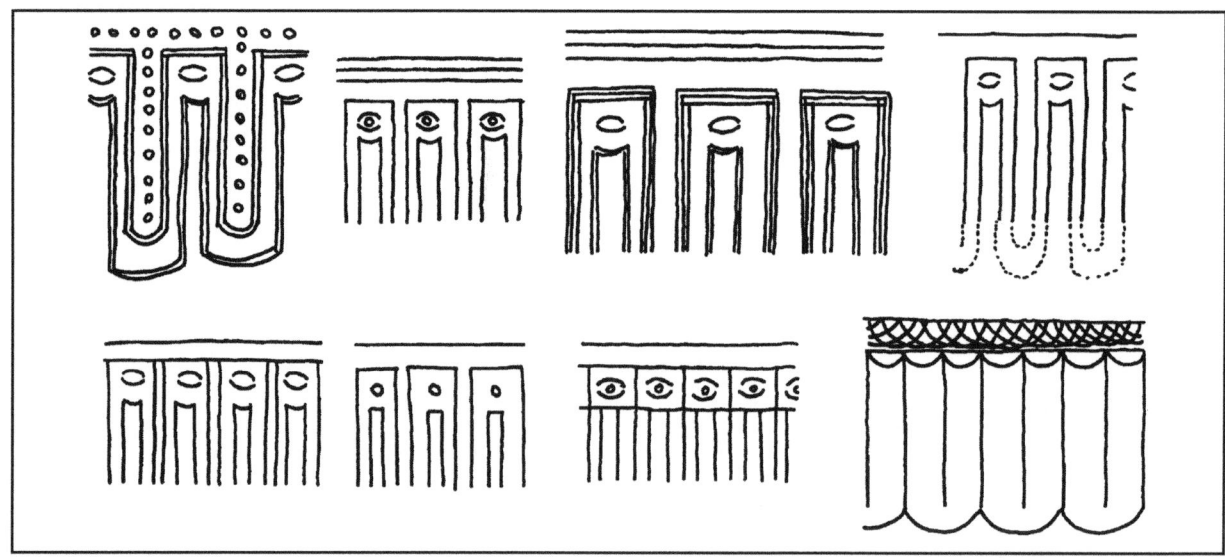

Figure 21. Diversity of the "stylised long nose" category still bearing a naturalistic representation of the eye.

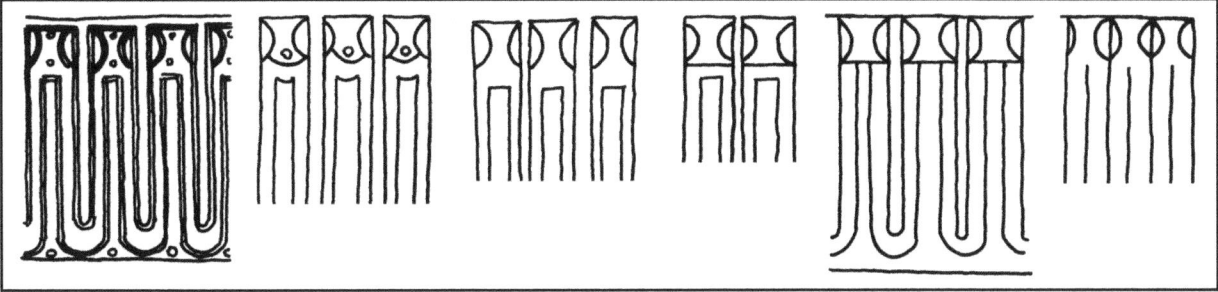

Figure 22. Diversity of the "stylised long nose" category with curved motifs replacing the eye.

becomes illustrated by only a rounded circle or a curved imprint. In other cases, the eye is replaced by curved imprints placed in various directions (Figure 22), successions of crosses, or the space is left empty (Figure 23). These changes witnessed by the stylised long-nose face have led to the regular inclusion of a rectangle to define the upper part of the motif and multiple ways to illustrate the "nose".

Figure 23. Diversity of the "stylised long nose" category with squares and X motifs.

c. The incised motifs

Although incised sherds represent about a fifth of the decorated items in the overall collections of the Lapita sites in New Caledonia, only one main incised type of central band design and two other rare categories have been identified to date.

i. The "triangles in a row" category (no Anson equivalent)

The main category consists of a succession of triangles (Figure 24 a-b), with one point placed in the centre of the band and the two extremes touching the horizontal incised lines marking the upper and lower end of the band. The two lines joining these points are straight or curved inwards, while the line joining the high and low points of the triangle is straight or curved towards the outside, a new triangle being positioned in the centre of this crescent. The inner part of each triangle is filled with parallel curved lines, as is the space between the triangles and the upper and lower limits of the central band. Although on most large sherds, the succession of triangles appears to be in only one direction, some more complete pots are decorated with triangles that are mirror-faced in one part of the central band (Figure 24 c).

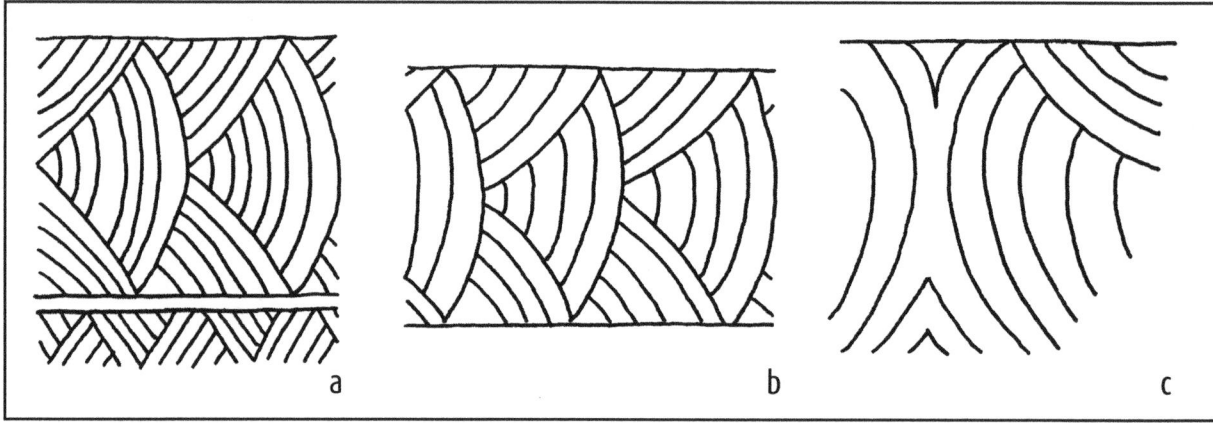

Figure 24. Examples of incised "triangles in a row" category.

ii. The "joined triangles" category (Anson's codes 433-434)

One rare motif is characterised by a succession of joined curved triangles forming a horizontal band, one in two being reversed (Figure 25). The infill of each triangle is made with parallel curved incisions, whose directions are reversed from one triangle to the other, in order to highlight the overall pattern.

iii. The "diamond-shaped" category (Anson's code 230)

A rare incised motif is made of simple opposed diagonal lines, creating diamond-shaped patterns, limited by the horizontal incisions that define the limits of the central band.

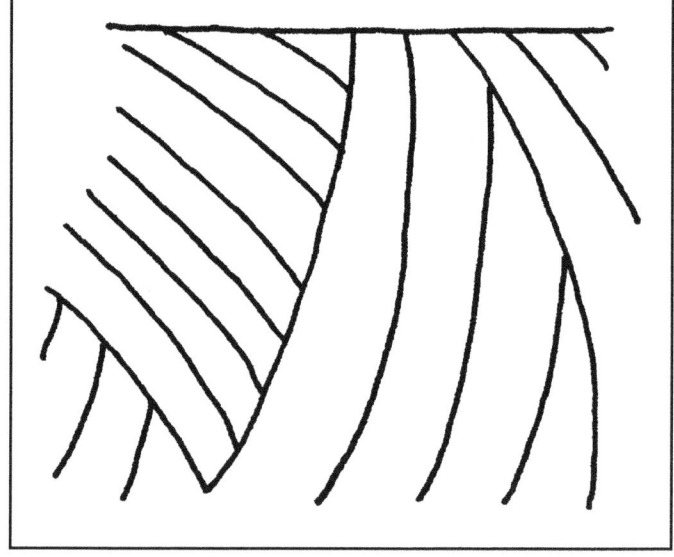

Figure 25. Example of incised "joined triangles" category.

Southern Lapita central band motifs in regional perspective

As noted in the introduction of this paper, it has since long been identified that major regional variations were present amongst the main dentate-stamped motifs produced in the different Provinces of the Lapita area (cf. Kirch 1997). The study of the Cultural Complex has led over the last decades to progressive refinements in the overall understanding of the subtle differences developed between the main archipelagos, starting with the division of the Lapita region into a Western and an Eastern Province by Green in the 1970s (1979), then a definition of a Far Western Province by Anson (1983) and a Southern Province by Kirch (1997; Sand 2000), before the probable future definition of a Central Province in the years to come (Sand 2001) (Figure 26). The comparisons have shown a series of local trends, and already 25 years ago, Anson could for example identify a specific development of stylised Lapita faces in the New Caledonian collections (Anson 1983, codes 344-352; see Chiu 2003 and this volume for an update). Studies focusing on the tools as a starting point for the analysis of the Lapita repertoire, can today broaden our understanding of the Lapita design corpus and its production, by identifying different elements that might have influenced regional variation. For example, it is probably not mere coincidence if the finest dentate imprints are found on pots produced in regions where obsidian was readily available through short (Bismarcks) or long-distance (Reef/Santa Cruz, Northern Vanuatu) trade (Galipaud and Swete-Kelly this volume; Sheppard 1993; Summerhayes 2003), while the coarsest and largest tooth imprints are found in Western Polynesia, where small sharp flakes are rare in Lapita sites (Kirch 1988; Poulsen 1987; Sand 1993). Observations on the overall structuring of the decorations highlights differences between Provinces that have already been shown through other methods of analysis, with a more complex set of rules in the Bismarck archipelago than in Remote Oceania (Figure 27), like the presence of the two successive central bands around pots. Examples could be multiplied, all underlining regional variability as well as chronological changes in each Province, that need to be taken into consideration when we deal with the Lapita ceramic repertoire.

The presentation in this paper of a structured typology of the motifs identified on the central bands of the Lapita pots produced in the Southern Province, provides an illustration of these differences through an approach focusing on the main categories of designs instead of the multiple variations between sherds and individual sites (Anson 1983; Chiu 2003; Summerhayes 2000; Wickler 2001). This is by necessity a preliminary

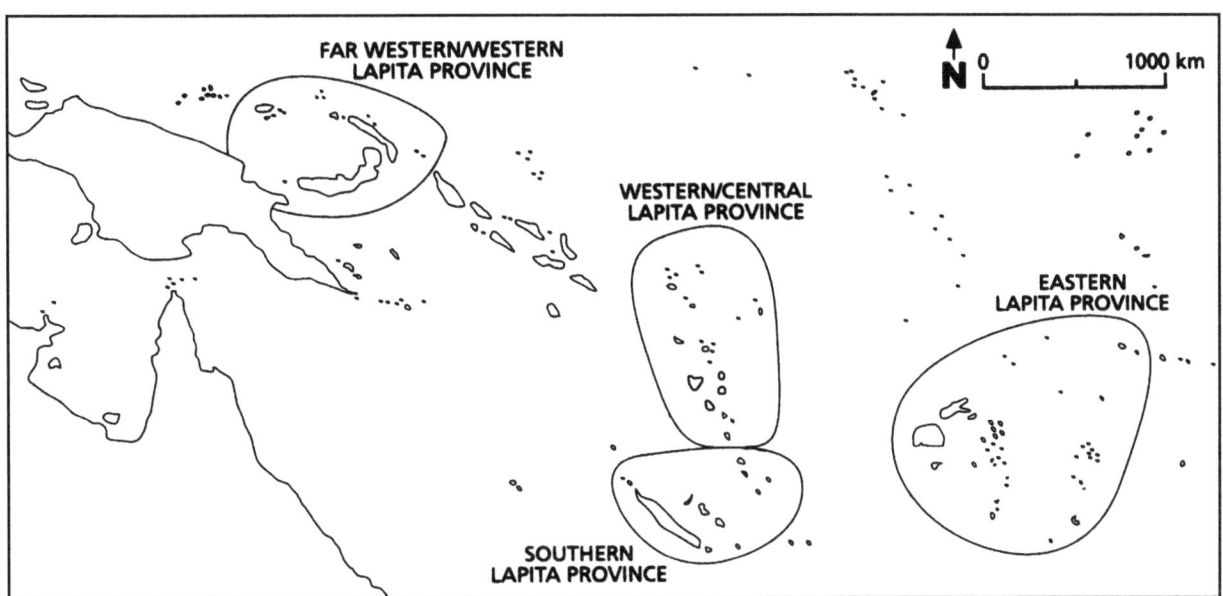

Figure 26. Location of the different Lapita Provinces defined to date.

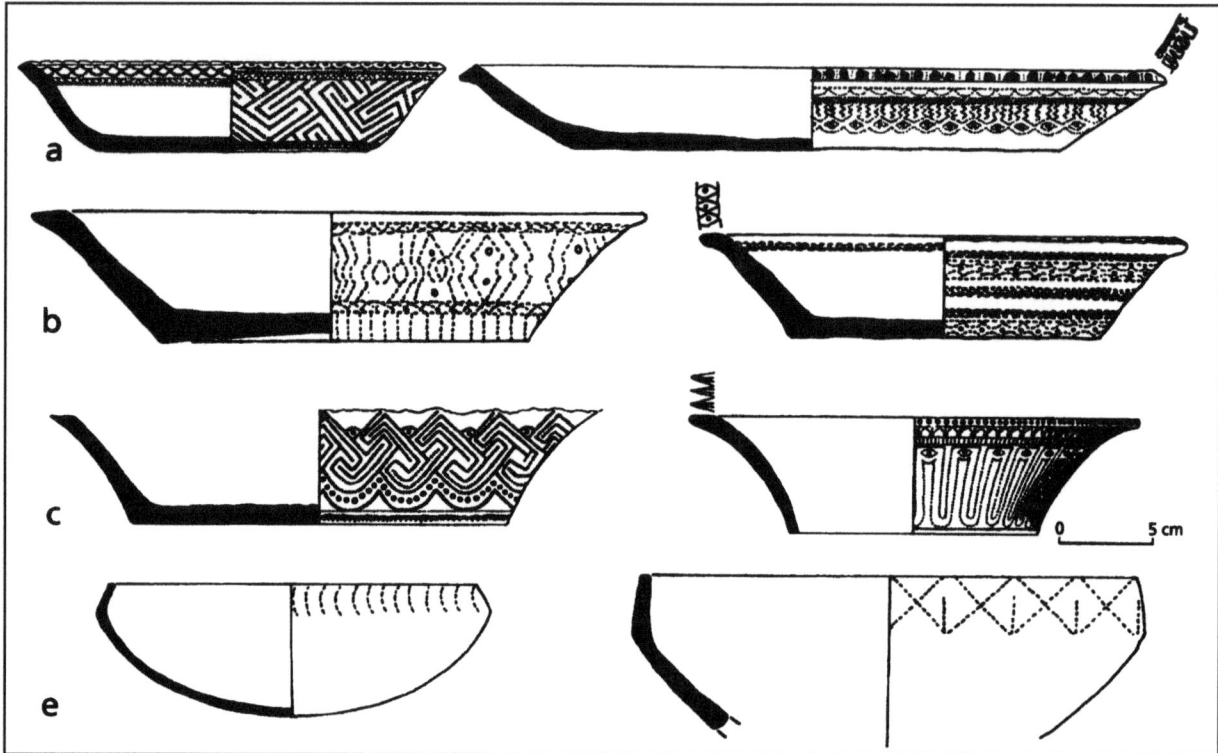

Figure 27. Diversity of flat bottom dishes and bowl-shaped vessels between the different regions of the Lapita area. (a) Bismarck Archipelago; (b) Reef/Santa Cruz; (c) New Caledonia; (d) Tonga.

attempt not taking into account the chronological changes of the motifs over time, this data being mostly unavailable, as numerous Lapita sites in Island Melanesia are awaiting full publication. The summary comparisons proposed for this paper draw on multiple publications of material, in final monographs or grey literature, as well as personal recording of collections[2]. For the scope of the exercise, it has been decided to limit the study of the categories identified in New Caledonia, to their presence/absence in major sites of each Province, focussing on the sites whose material is the most accessible in published form. Two categories have been removed: the "wavy motif" and the "unique motifs", that appear for most to be unique to New Caledonia at this stage. For the final table, the West New Britain area is represented by the sites of the Arawes (Phelan 1997; Summerhayes 2000), East New Britain by the sites of Watom and Duke of York (Anson 1983; Green and Anson 2000; White pers. comm. 2002), with the sites of Ambitle-Kamgot (Ambrose pers. comm. 2003; Summerhayes pers. comm. 2005) illustrating the data for the east of the Bismarcks. The different Lapita sites of the Reef/Santa Cruz (RF-2, SZ-8 and RL-6) have been grouped in one column (Donovan 1973; Green pers. comm. 2004), as have the sites of Vanuatu (Malo and Tcouma) (Hedrick nd; Green pers. comm. 2004; Bedford pers. comm. 2005). For this archipelago, the table is certainly incomplete, a large amount of as yet unpublished data having been collected over the last years in northern as well as central Vanuatu (Bedford 2007; Galipaud and Swete-Kelly this volume). The Lapita sites of Western Fiji (Natunuku, Yanuca, Naigani) (Mead et al. 1975; Kay 1984) have been grouped in one column, separate from the sites of Eastern Fiji and West Polynesia (Best 1984; Poulsen 1987). There has been no attempt to create new categories, or to identify specific motifs in each site.

The final table (Table 1) shows a composite set of results. Depending on each site, there appears to be a strong variability in the categories of motifs present/absent. The clinal West to East diversity of the overall Lapita motifs is nevertheless clearly visible, the sites in the Bismarck Archipelago on one side and Eastern Fiji/West Polynesia on the other side having the least shared categories with New Caledonia (Figure 28). This is especially the case for Watom, which often appears in the comparative graphs as closely related to the Southern

Table 1. Presence/absence in major Lapita sites/regions, of the motif categories identified for the Southern Lapita Province.

	West New Britain	East New Britain	Anir Islands	Reef/Santa Cruz	Vanuatu	New Caledonia	West Fiji	East Fiji/West Polynesia
labyrinths		X	?	X	X	X	P	?
undulated motifs			P	X		X	P	
interlocking triangles		X		X	X	X	X	X
rectangular motifs			X	X	X	X		X
joined triangles		X	X	X		X	?	
simple zig-zag					X	X	X	
vertical zig-zag	X	X	X		X	P	X	
double-face motif		X		X	?	X		
triangular face motif	P	P		X	?	X		
long-nose face		X	X	X	X	X	P	
stylised long nose face				X	X	X		
incised triangles in a row	X	X	X	X	X	X	X	X
incised joined triangles	X					X	X	X
incised diamond-shaped triangles	X		X	X	X	X	X	

Lapita Province sites (Anson 1983, Fig. LXVI). Western Fiji shares a significant number of categories with New Caledonia, although on detailed observation, most of these correspond to only a few sherds discovered in first settlement contexts. The main affinities remain clearly with the Reef/Santa Cruz and Vanuatu, even if the comparative study between the different collections has shown the existence, in these two archipelagos, of a series of patterns that do not appear in Southern Lapita. As specified in the typology part, one of the main motifs nearly totally absent of the New Caledonian collection, numbering three specimens amongst tens of thousands of decorated sherds, is the "house" motif (Anson's codes 245-249/301-305/311-314/353-361/503), present in all the other Provinces (Anson 2000:127 for Watom; Donovan 1973:128 for the Reef/Santa Cruz; Bedford et al. 2006 for Teouma; Kay 1984:84 for Naigani). Less surprising is the absence of pot-stands with deep grooves or cut-outs, as well as the bowl-shaped vessels with a thickened rim and complex stylized faces restricted to the upper part of the pottery, that make up a significant amount of the early Lapita productions from the Bismarck Archipelago (Summerhayes 2000, Figs. 5.3b and 5.6a) to at least Aore in northern Vanuatu (Galipaud pers. comm. 2006). This Far Western production is also characterised by a series of specific motifs that have never been identified in New Caledonia, like the seed-like motif (Anson's codes 111/120), the alignment of small squares with a rounded imprint in the centre (Anson's codes 489-490), and the vertical imprint of multiple successive curved lines. Aside from the region-wide category of incised triangles in a row, the comparative study has highlighted the existence of a number of other rare incised motifs, without showing at this stage clear sub-regional groupings. The most important information gathered from this comparison of multiple collections through a rigid typology canvas has been to show that, with the removal of specific stylised face-motifs from the Bismarck Archipelago and unique Eastern Lapita patterns, there does not appear to be a significant number of other major motif categories in the Lapita repertoire.

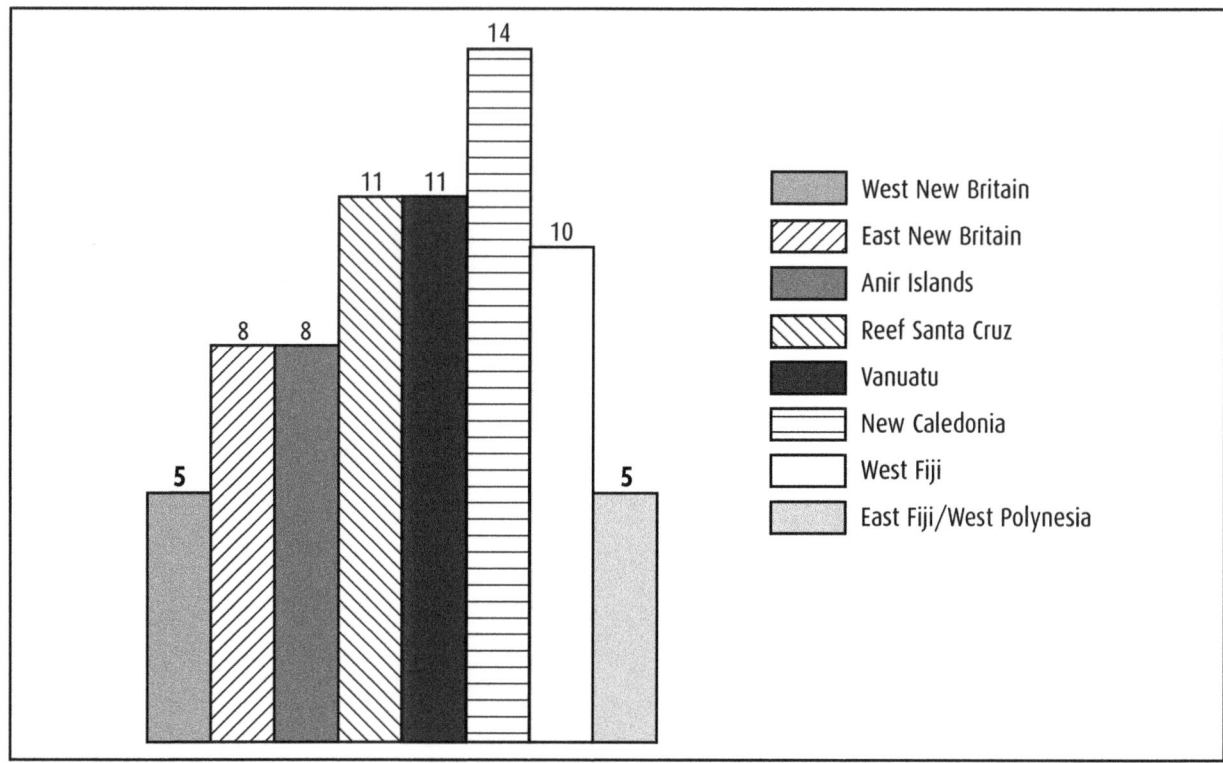

Figure 28. Graph showing the motif categories shared amongst the different sites/regions with the Southern Lapita Province.

Conclusion

The construction of a typology for the central band of Lapita pots discovered in New Caledonia has allowed the identification of a definitive restricted range of main motifs. Although variations are present in all categories identified, the overall small number of distinct motifs in the collections is testimony that Lapita potters did not print freely-inspired patterns on the clay surface of their carinated pots, flat bottom dishes, pedestal stands and lids. This conclusion highlights once again the specific nature of the dentate-stamped Lapita decoration, which must have carried a type of meaning or message needing to be replicated from generation to generation during the Austronesian settlement process of Near and Remote Oceania. After a first phase of analysis which has favoured mainly time-distance decay to explain the observable changes in the dentate-stamped motif repertoire during the Oceanic settlement from West to East (Green 1978; Ishimura 2002), new analytical paths have recently appeared, with for example the proposal of two different Lapita groups spreading across the Western Pacific (Noury 2005) or the possible existence of various Lapita groups in the Bismarck Archipelago, which did not all expand into Remote Oceania and all at the same time (Sand 2007). To test these new hypotheses, we need to complete the large database that has been built over the last decades mainly on the friezes (Donovan 1973), to progressively incorporate a more structured typology of the different categorises of central band motifs created during the Lapita period. This has been the task achieved for New Caledonia (Sand 2006), Tonga (Burley et al. 2002), and Fiji to a certain extent (Clark and Murray 2006). A regional effort of this kind will certainly lead, aside from the definition of the main categories, to the identification of minor motifs that may tell us far more about site-to-site connections than the classic labyrinth or long-nose designs that make up most of our studies. Hidden "emblems" (Kirch 1997:136), postulated by some to be "house-society symbols" (Chiu 2005) or "group" symbols (Noury 2005), these unique patterns isolated amongst thousands of potsherds, await to be identified in their own right as links between far-distant regions, from Island Southeast Asia to Remote Oceania. Their social significance may be a reminder of the inappropriateness of building our archaeological models on simple scenarios. There is evidently in these dentate-stamped and incised Lapita potsherds much more information awaiting our scrutiny. It is vital information that will further emphasise the over-simplistic nature of the one-way directional arrows of Lapita spread out of the West towards New Caledonia and Fiji/West Polynesia, that still highlight most of our maps of the Austronesian spread out into Remote Oceania.

Notes

1. The detail on the origin of each sherd illustrated in the motif categories can be found in Sand 1996: 156.
2. I have had the opportunity to study first-hand a series of Lapita collections encompassing the whole region, thanks to the kindness of the excavators and/or custodians of these remains scattered in a number of institutions across the planet: material from the Arawes (Canberra and Melbourne), Ambitle (Canberra), Watom (Bale and Paris), Reef/Santa Cruz (Auckland), Teouma (Port Vila), Lapita (Berkeley), Natunuku and Yanuca (Suva), Tonga (Auckland, Vancouver).

References

Anson, D. 1983. Lapita Pottery of the Bismarck Archipelago and its Affinities. Unpublished PhD thesis, University of Sydney.

Anson, D. 2000. Reber-Rakival Dentate-Stamped Motifs: Documentation and Comparative Implications. *Journal of New Zealand Archaeology* 20(1998):95-118.

Ambrose, W.R. 1997. Contradictions in Lapita pottery, a composite clone. *Antiquity* 71 (273): 525-538.

Ambrose, W.R. 1999. Curves, tines, scutes and Lapita ware. In J-C. Galipaud and I. Lilley (eds), *The Western Pacific, 5000 to 2000 BP: Colonisations and transformations*, pp. 119-126. Paris: IRD Publications.

Basek, M. 1993. A Lapita edge. Unpublished BA, University of Sydney.

Bedford, S. 2007. Crucial first steps into Remote Oceania: Lapita in the Vanuatu Archipelago. In S. Chiu and C. Sand (eds), *From Southeast Asia to the Pacific. Archaeological perspectives on the Austronesian Expansion and the Lapita Cultural Complex*, pp. 157-185. Taipei: Centre for Archaeological Studies.

Bedford, S., M. Spriggs and R. Regenvanu 2006. The Teouma Lapita site and the early human settlement of the Pacific Islands. *Antiquity* 80:812-828.

Best, S. 1984. Lakeba: the prehistory of a Fijian Island. Unpublished PhD thesis, University of Auckland.

Best, S. 2002. *Lapita: a view from the East*. Auckland: New Zealand Archaeological Association Monograph 24.

Burley, D., A. Storey and J. Witt 2002. On the Definition and Implications of Eastern Lapita Ceramics in Tonga. In S. Bedford, C. Sand and D. Burley (eds), *Fifty years in the field. Essays in honour and celebration of Richard Shutler Jr's archaeological career*, pp. 213-226. Auckland: New Zealand Archaeological Association Monograph 25.

Chiu, S. 2003. The Socio-economic Functions of Lapita Ceramic Production and Exchange: A case study from site WKO013A, Koné, New Caledonia. Unpublished PhD thesis, University of California, Berkeley.

Chiu, S. 2005. Meanings of a Lapita Face: Materialized Memory in Ancient House Societies. *Taiwan Journal of Anthropology* 3(1):1-47.

Clark, G. and T. Murray, 2006. Decay characteristics of the eastern Lapita design system. *Archaeology in Oceania* 41:107-117.

Donovan, L.J. 1973. A study of the Decorative System of the Lapita Potters of the Reefs and Santa Cruz Islands. Unpublished MA, University of Auckland.

Green, R.C. 1976. Lapita sites in the Santa Cruz Group. In R.C. Green and M.M. Cresswell (eds), *Southeast Solomon Islands Cultural History: A Preliminary Survey*, pp. 245-265. Wellington: Royal Society of New Zealand Bulletin 11.

Green, R.C. 1978. *New Sites with Lapita Pottery and their Implications for an Understanding of the Settlement of the Western Pacific*. Working Papers in Anthropology, Archaeology, Linguistics and Maori Studies 51. Auckland: Department of Anthropology, University of Auckland.

Green, R.C. 1979. Lapita. In J.D. Jennings (ed.), *The Prehistory of Polynesia*, pp. 27-60. Cambridge: Harvard University Press.

Green, R.C. 2000. An Introduction to Investigations on Watom Island, Papua New Guinea. *New Zealand Journal of Archaeology* 20 (1998):5-27.

Green, R.C. 2003. The Lapita horizon and traditions – Signature for one set of Oceanic migrations. In C. Sand (ed.), *Pacific Archaeology: assessments and prospects. Proceedings of the International Conference for the 50th anniversary of the first Lapita excavation. Koné-Nouméa 2002*, pp. 95-120. Nouméa: Les Cahiers de l'Archéologie en Nouvelle-Calédonie 15.

Green, R.C. and D. Anson 2000. Excavations at Kainapirina (SAC) Watom Island, Papua New Guinea. *New Zealand Journal of Archaeology* 20 (1998):29-94.

Hedrick, J. nd. Archaeological investigations in Malo Island. Lapita settlement strategy in the northern New Hebrides. PhD draft Manuscript, University of Pennsylvania.

Ishimura, T. 2002. In the Wake of Lapita: Transformation of Lapita Designs and Gradual Dispersal of the Lapita Peoples. *People and Culture in Oceania* 18:77-97.

Kay, R. 1984. Analysis of archaeological material from Naigani. Unpublished MA, University of Auckland

Kirch P.V. 1987. Lapita and Oceanic Cultural Origins: Excavations in the Mussau Islands, Bismarck Archipelago. *Journal of Field Archaeology* 14:164-180.

Kirch, P.V. 1988. *Niuatoputapu. The Prehistory of a Polynesian Chiefdom*. Seattle: Burke Memorial Washington State Museum Monograph 5.

Kirch, P.V. 1997. *The Lapita Peoples*. Oxford: Blackwell.

Mead, S.M. 1975. The decorative system of the Lapita potters of Sigatoka, Fiji. In S.M. Mead, L. Birks, H. Birks and E. Shaw (eds), *The Lapita Pottery Style of Fiji and Its Associations*, pp. 19-43. Wellington: Polynesian Society Memoir 38.

Mead, S.M., L. Birks, H. Birks and E. Shaw 1975. *The Lapita Pottery Style of Fiji and Its Associations*. Wellington: Polynesian Society Memoir 38.

Meyer, P.O. 1909. Funde prähistorischer Töpferei und Steinmesser auf Vatom, Bismarck-Archipel. *Anthropos* IV:1093-1095.

Meyer, P.O. 1910. Funde von Menschen- und Tierknochen, von prähistorischer Töpferei und Steinwerkzeugen auf Vatom, Bismarck-Archipel. *Anthropos* V:1160-1161.

Noury, A. 2005. *Le reflet de l'âme Lapita. Essai d'interprétation des décors des poteries Lapita. En Mélanésie et en Polynésie Occidentale entre 3300 et 2700 avant le présent*. Versailles: Privately published.

Phelan, M. 1997. Scratching the Surface: the Lapita pottery of Makekur, Papua New Guinea. Unpublished BA, La Trobe University, Melbourne.

Poulsen, J. 1967. A Contribution to the Prehistory of the Tongan Islands. Unpublished PhD thesis, Department of Prehistory, Australian National University.

Poulsen, J. 1987. *Early Tongan Prehistory* (2 vols). Canberra: Department of Prehistory, Australian National University. Terra Australis 12.

Sand, C. 1993. Données archéologiques et géomorphologiques du site ancien d'Asipani, Futuna (Polynésie occidentale). *Journal de la Société des Océanistes* 96(2):117-144.

Sand, C. 1996. *Le début du peuplement austronésien de la Nouvelle-Calédonie. Données archéologiques récentes*. Nouméa : Les Cahiers de l'Archéologie en Nouvelle-Calédonie 6.

Sand, C. 1999. *Archéologie des Origines: le Lapita calédonien/Archaeology of the Origins: New Caledonia's Lapita*. Nouméa: Les Cahiers de l'Archéologie en Nouvelle-Calédonie 10.

Sand, C. 2000. The specificities of the "Southern Lapita Province": the New Caledonian case. *Archaeology in Oceania* 35:20-33.

Sand, C. 2001. Evolutions in the Lapita Cultural Complex: a view from the Southern Lapita Province. *Archaeology in Oceania* 36:65-76.

Sand, C. 2006. Le Lapita Calédonien. Archéologie d'un premier peuplement insulaire océanien. Unpublished "Habilitation à diriger les recherches", EHESS Paris.

Sand, C. 2007. « Strings of pearls » and Provinces : modeling the divergent ceramic chronologies of the western Pacific during the Lapita period. Paper presented at the "Lapita antecedents and successors" Conference, Honiara, Solomon Islands, July 2007.

Sand, C., K. Coote, J. Bole and A. Ouetcho 1998. A pottery pit on locality WKO013A, Lapita (New Caledonia). *Archaeology in Oceania* 33:38-44.

Sheppard, P.J. 1993. Lapita lithics: Trade/exchange and technology. A view from the Reefs/Santa Cruz. *Archaeology in Oceania* 28:121-137.

Siorat, J.P. 1990. A technological analysis of Lapita pottery decoration. In M. Spriggs (ed.), *Lapita Design, Form and Composition*, pp. 59-82. Canberra: Department of Prehistory, Australian National University. Occasional Papers in Prehistory 19.

Siorat, J.P. 1992. Analyse test sur les décors des bandeaux principaux de la poterie Lapita du site WBR001 de Nouvelle-Calédonie. In J-C. Galipaud (ed.), *Poterie Lapita et Peuplement*, pp. 193-206. Nouméa: ORSTOM.

Spriggs, M. 1990. The changing face of Lapita: transformation of a design. In M. Spriggs (ed.), *Lapita Design Form and Composition*, pp. 83-122. Canberra: Department of Prehistory, Australian National University. Occasional Papers in Prehistory 19.

Summerhayes, G. 2000. *Lapita Interaction*. Canberra: Department of Archaeology and Natural History and the Centre for Archaeological Research, Australian National University. Terra Australis 15.

Summerhayes, G. 2003. Modelling differences between Lapita obsidian and pottery distribution patterns in the Bismarck Archipelago, Papua New Guinea. In C. Sand (ed.), *Pacific Archaeology: assessments and prospects. Proceedings of the International Conference for the 50th anniversary of the first Lapita excavation. Koné-Nouméa 2002*, pp. 135-145. Nouméa: Les Cahiers de l'Archéologie en Nouvelle-Calédonie 15.

Terrell, J. and E. Schechter 2007. Deciphering the Lapita Code: the Aitape Ceramic Sequence and Late Survival of the 'Lapita Face'. *Cambridge Archaeological Journal* 17(1): 59-85.

Tsang, C.H. 2007. Recent Archaeological discoveries in Taiwan and Northern Luzon. Implications for Austronesian expansion. In S. Chiu and C. Sand (eds), *From Southeast Asia to the Pacific. Archaeological perspectives on the Austronesian Expansion and the Lapita Cultural Complex*, pp. 47-74. Taipei: Centre for Archaeological Studies.

Wickler, S. 2001. *The Prehistory of Buka: A Stepping Stone Island in the Northern Solomons*. Canberra: Department of Archaeology and Natural History and the Centre for Archaeological Research, Australian National University. Terra Australis 16.

17

Specialisation, standardisation and Lapita ceramics

Geoffrey Clark

Department of Archaeology and Natural History,
Research School of Pacific and Asian Studies,
The Australian National University,
Canberra ACT 0200, Australia.
geoffrey.clark@anu.edu.au

Introduction

In anthropological theory, craft specialisation is a defining feature of complex societies, and is viewed as a key factor in the development of the political economy (Costin and Hagstrum 1995; Longacre 1999). Specialisation is the investment of labour and capital in the production of a particular good or service beyond what is required for domestic consumption, with surpluses providing the capital required for economic exchanges (Benco 1988). Craft specialisation is closely linked to the standardisation of material culture because the production of goods in large quantities is facilitated when artisans reduce the amount of artefact variability (Costin and Hagstrum 1995; Rice 1981). For ceramics, the standardisation hypothesis holds that a high-degree of similarity in vessel characteristics (physical and stylistic) reflects specialised production, such as from a workshop, while heterogeneity indicates dispersed household production (Benco 1988). Among Pacific cultures, communities which specialised in manufacturing and trading pottery developed in late prehistory, and they have been documented, particularly, in coastal New Guinea (Allen *et al*. 1997; Irwin 1985; Vanderwal 1973).

Craft specialisation has also been advanced as a potential explanation for the similarity of Lapita culture ceramics dated to 3300-2600 cal. BP, a proportion of which includes vessels marked with distinctive dentate-stamped designs, among other types of decoration (Bedford 2006; Summerhayes 2001). For instance, some Lapita communities might have specialized in making and exporting pots (Chiu 2003; Green 1982; Hunt 1988:57), using a uniform and potentially specialised production technology (Bellwood 1978:258; Golson 1971), with the possibility that Lapita pottery was made by women and used by men in maritime trade networks (Marshall 1985).

Recent compositional study of Lapita ceramics does not support, however, the idea of standardised pottery production and bulk transport over long distances (Chiu 2003; Summerhayes 2000; but see Hunt 1989), although a few pots certainly accompanied migrants between archipelagos (Burley and Dickinson 2001). Rather, as Summerhayes (2001:57, 60) recognized in his analysis of pottery from the Bismarck Archipelago, a fundamental divide exists within early Lapita ceramics between 'specialised' highly decorated vessels and utilitarian 'standardised' wares.

The presence of both specialised, and standardised sets of ceramics within Lapita assemblages is an exception to the standardisation hypothesis. It is an exception also found in complex societies, when specialists produce goods for elites. Such items may be extremely heterogeneous in their size, decoration and materials, as elite patrons sponsor the production of goods whose value in the political economy stems from their uniqueness. There is little evidence, as yet, that Lapita groups were highly stratified with a strict division between craft specialists, that in the case of ceramics might be recognised by limited variation in the raw materials used to construct pots.

As specialised ceramic *production* is not demonstrated, we must posit a specialized *function* for highly decorated Lapita ceramics, and interrogate the politically and socially symbolic dimensions of the pottery (e.g. Best 2002; Chiu 2005; Kirch 1997; Spriggs 1990; Summerhayes 2000). These aspects should be most apparent in vessels that signify a high labour cost relative to utilitarian wares, identifiable from their size, complexity and quantity of formal decoration. Establishing the size of Lapita vessels is important as the amount of social information displayed on a ceramic container relates both to the size of the design field, which is a function of vessel size, and also of design density (the number of decorative elements in a defined area).

In this paper, I examine how 'specialised' and 'standardised' Lapita ceramics might be distinguished, and explore the hypothesis that highly decorated 'specialised' Lapita vessels were used in public contexts and were actively signalling or messaging Lapita groups. If that is the case, we would expect such vessels to have increased social visibility, and to be larger than utilitarian/domestic ceramics, and to also carry substantially greater amounts of decoration than domestic wares.

Comparing Lapita Vessels

Estimating the amount of variability in decorated versus utilitarian components of a Lapita assemblage is made difficult by the degree of container fragmentation, and the constraints on reconstructing accurately the physical dimensions of ceramics from sherds (e.g. DeBoer 1980; Plog 1985). Finds of complete or substantially complete prehistoric ceramic vessels have been reported from several parts of the Pacific, including Lapita contexts, and these vessels provide a more reliable indication of vessel size and the amount of decoration than do reconstructions derived from small sherds. However, a focus on the decorated component of Lapita assemblages, termed 'dentate-centric' by Summerhayes (2001:54), has dominated research, and as a result there is little detailed information about the utilitarian pottery used by Lapita groups that can be used to compare 'specialised' decorated vessels with 'standardised' utilitarian wares within a single assemblage. As a result it is not currently feasible to undertake an intra-assemblage analysis with published information to directly examine the idea that decorated Lapita ceramics were larger than utilitarian pots.

The idea might be tested, at least in a preliminary fashion, at the inter-assemblage level because of different rates of change in the decorated ceramic component compared with utilitarian pottery. According to Summerhayes (2001), the specialised dentate-stamped vessels changed rapidly during the early Lapita era in the Bismarck Archipelago, while the utilitarian pottery displayed little change, suggesting continuity in domestic function. Although Lapita pottery clearly has distinct regional expressions, which underwent specific transformations in particular archipelagos and islands (Burley *et al.* 2002; Chiu 2003; Sand 2001), there is a general trend over time for the simplification of vessel forms and a reduction in the amount of decoration, especially dentate-stamping. These changes have been interpreted as signalling the transition to a predominantly utilitarian/domestic set of ceramics and the elimination of specialised pottery vessels (Kirch 1990; Summerhayes 2000). By contrasting a set of specialised 'early' Lapita vessels from one location with predominantly utilitarian vessels from a 'late' Lapita site at another, we can begin to examine how 'specialised' Lapita ceramics were differentiated by their size and amount of decoration from domestic-utilitarian ceramics.

In New Caledonia an early Lapita ceramic assemblage of reconstructable vessels dated to ca. 3000 cal. BP was found in a pit discovered eroding from the WKO013A site (Sand *et al.* 1998). In the pit were two carinated high-necked jars which had had their bases broken before burial (Sand 1999:34). Around and over the two pots, base and rim sections from another 17 vessels had been layered, including remains of a vessel with a flat base. The context, size and number of vessels buried in the pit strongly indicates the vessels had a non-utilitarian function (Sand 1999). The dimensions of ten decorated carinated jars from the WKO013A site were derived from the published vessel profiles and vessel measurements (Sand 1999, 2001; Sand *et al.* 1998).

A late-Lapita assemblage of pots and bowls dating to 2600 cal. BP has been excavated from the Sigatoka Sand Dunes in Fiji (Birks 1973; Burley and Dickinson 2004). The pot assemblage probably represents utilitarian cooking pots as these vessels have a relatively low frequency of red slip and burnishing in the exterior, and a high frequency of carbon deposits, suggesting they were used to cook food (Birks 1973:21). In the typology of Birks (1973), expanded-rim vessels were included in three types of 'cooking pot' (Type 1A, 1B and 1C), which were differentiated from each other by minor variation in the neck and body. Birks (1973:24) noted that the vessel typology was subjective and his three types overlapped. To maintain consistency in vessel type, only pots with distinctive expanded rims (also known as 'collar rims'), with an ovoid-to-sub-globular body, illustrated in Birks (1973) were used in the analysis ($n=35$). In the sample 46 % of the expanded rim pots had a carbonised residue on the interior vessel surface, suggesting they were used to cook food.

For this study ceramic profiles were scanned and digitally enlarged to the vessel dimensions (e.g. maximum body width and vessel height) reported in Birks (1973), or in the case of the New Caledonian carinated jars, vessel profiles were scaled using a single measurement or associated scale units – a process which is likely to involve a larger amount of error than resizing vessels which have multiple measurements. Image distortion was minimized by removing the illustrations from the publication binding before scanning. Vessel profiles were traced and resized with Adobe Illustrator 9.0. The percentage of a vessel carrying decoration was calculated by measuring the profile area covered with tool designs, and comparing the value to the total vessel area (profile error estimate ± 2-4 cm^2). Design density was measured on the vessel scans by placing a 10 cm^2 square divided into 1 cm^2 units on the design field, and counting the number of squares with tool-made decoration.

Size variation in Lapita vessels

The analysis of ceramic size from digital profiles and outlines from the only two assemblages, with an adequate number of reconstructed vessels and of an appropriate antiquity, was made to investigate three questions about the proposed division of Lapita assemblages into a specialised set of ceramics and a standardised group of utilitarian vessels:

1. Are carinated vessels from New Caledonia larger than the utilitarian, expanded-rim pots from Fiji, indicative of a specialised vessel used in public contexts?

2. Is the amount of decoration on New Caledonian vessels significantly greater than that of late Lapita pots from Fiji, consistent with their having a signalling or messaging role in Lapita society?

3. Does the size variability of pots with expanded rims from Fiji indicate a standardised 'utilitarian' assemblage?

1. Specialized vessels: size comparison

The scaled vessel profile of 10 carinated vessels from New Caledonia and 35 expanded-rim pots from Fiji is shown in Figure 1. Both sets of vessels exhibit substantial size variation, but it is clear that the carinated vessels from New Caledonia are generally larger than those from Sigatoka in Fiji. The size variation in the carinated jar sample suggests three distinct size classes (small, medium, large), although this may be an artefact of the small sample. Two carinated jars are missing sections from the neck and rim, but based on body width, both are in the 'large' size range.

Except for one expanded-rim vessel (Birks Vessel No.82), all of the utilitarian cooking pots from Sigatoka have smaller dimensions than the 'medium' and 'large' jars from New Caledonia, and are approximately equal to, or slightly larger than, the two smallest carinated vessels. The carinated jars have a lip diameter that is 73-88 % of maximum body width, and a vessel height ranging from 65-86 % of maximum body width. The latter variability indicates a difference between carinated jars that have a body that is deeper than the height of the carination, and those with a body height that is similar to the carination height. Regardless of carinated jar size, there is a strong linear correlation between vessel height and maximum body width ($r^2=0.96$), which is likely to indicate either vessel production by a small group of potters, or manufacture of a vessel type with defined proportions.

The large size and stylised shape of the carinated jar demonstrates considerable artisan skill and a high labour investment that is consistent with their having a specialised function and high social visibility.

If carinated jars also had active role in public contexts, then the amount and density of decoration placed on them should be significantly greater than the decoration found on ceramics made for domestic cooking and storage.

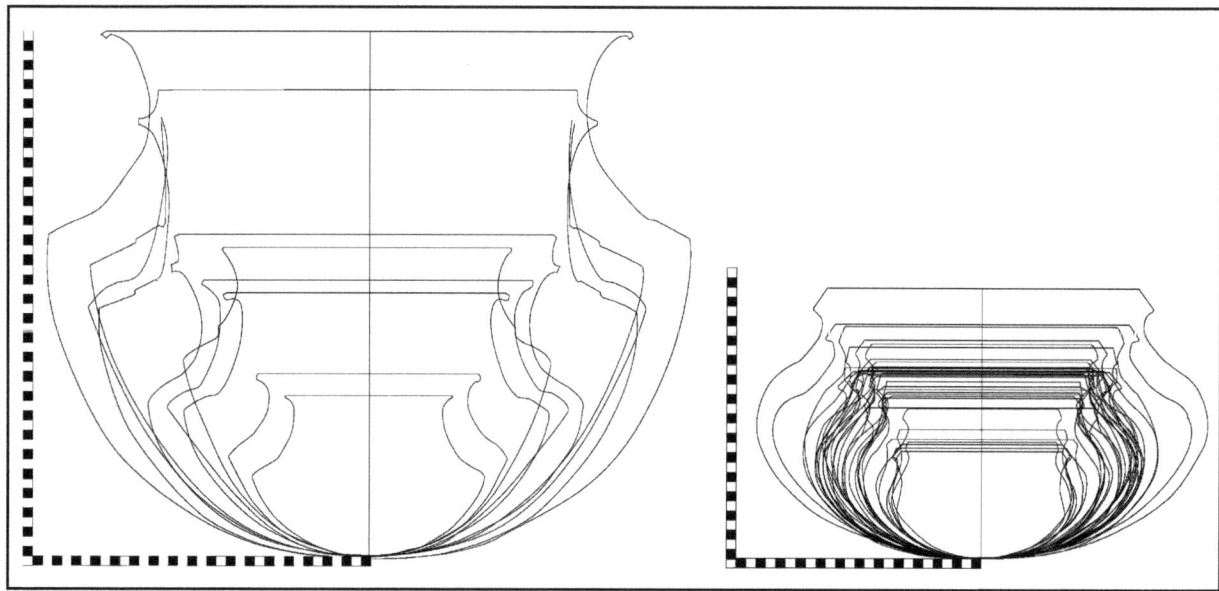

Fig. 1. Scaled vessel profiles of 10 carinated jars from New Caledonia and 35 expanded-rim pots from Sigatoka. The Sigatoka vessels scanned from Birks (1973) were numbers: 4, 6, 10, 21, 26, 29, 37, 40, 48, 50, 61, 66, 67, 68, 69, 71, 72, 79, 82, 86, 88, 89, 90, 94, 95, 99, 101, 103, 111, 112, 113, 117, 121, 122, 141. Note that two of the carinated jars from New Caledonia are missing sections of the upper rim. Scale bars in cm.

2. Specialized vessels: decoration comparison

The carinated jars were all dentate-stamped, except for one vessel that was incised (Sand et al. 1998), while the Sigatoka pots were tool impressed (nail, shell, other tool, $n=21$), incised ($n=6$), excised ($n=1$) and dentate-stamped ($n=1$)).

The design area of the New Caledonian jars measured on vessel profiles varied from ca. 1000 cm² for the largest jars and ca. 140-210 cm² for the smallest jars. By comparison, six of the 35 late-Lapita pots from Sigatoka were plain (17 %), and the remainder had a decorated area ranging from ca. 18 to 80 cm², substantially less than any of the carinated jars.

Similarly, the density of decoration measured by the number of 1 cm² squares with tool decoration in a grid of 100 cm² was high for the carinated jars, with a design area of ca. 80-100 cm², compared with ca. 7-30 cm² for the expanded rim vessels from Fiji.

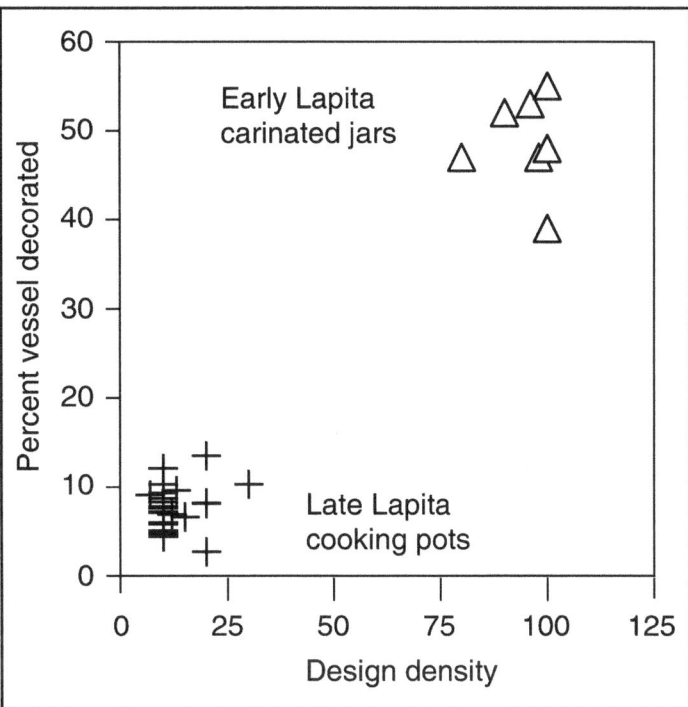

Fig. 2. Design density (number of 1 cm² squares with decoration in a 10 cm by 10 cm grid) plotted against percent of vessel decorated (size of the design field measured on vessel profiles). Triangles = New Caledonia carinated jars. Crosses = Sigatoka expanded rim pots.

The proportion of vessel decoration also differentiates the carinated jars, which had 39-56 % of the vessel surface carrying decoration, while the decoration percentage on the Sigatoka pots ranged from 0 to 14 %. Figure 2 shows the unambiguous separation between the two assemblages achieved by plotting design density against vessel decoration percentage.

A much greater amount of decoration on the New Caledonian vessels is consistent with a messaging/signalling purpose, with the social information conveyed by the designs amplified by the large size of the vessels.

3. Standardization and utilitarian ceramics

The specialised function of the early Lapita carinated jars from New Caledonia was suggested by their deliberate interment, and is also supported by the above analysis of vessel size and decoration. The contrast between specialised and standardised sets of vessels should also be demonstrated by the reduced size variability of utilitarian vessels as a result of economic constraints imposed by the domestic environment. A commonly used statistic to measure size variation is the coefficient of variation (CV), which is the standard deviation of a sample multiplied by 100, divided by the sample mean. The resulting figure expresses the percentage variance around the sample mean. For the 35 expanded rim pots from Sigatoka, the CVs for three measurements (vessel height, maximum body width and external orifice diameter) ranged from 18 % to 23 %, while the same measurements from the eight New Caledonian carinated jars gave CVs of 33-41 % (Table 1), bearing in mind that some of the CVs include an unknown error margin as they are based on measurements derived from scaled vessel profiles.

The lower CVs of the Sigatoka pots show an assemblage which overall has a reasonably high amount of size variability, even though the CVs are much less than those of the New Caledonia carinated jars. This might be due to the inclusion of vessels that were made by potting communities separated by a century

Table 1. Measurement variation in reconstructed ceramics from New Caledonia (Early Lapita carinated jars from Site WK0013A), Fiji (Late Lapita utilitarian pots from Level 1, Sigatoka), and Island New Guinea (20th century, Mailu Island). All measurements in cm. CV = coefficient of variation (percent variance around the mean).

Fiji: Sigatoka			
Expanded rim pots (n=35)	MEAN	STDEV	CV
Max. body width (cm)	29	7	23
Vessel height (cm)	18	4	21
Ext. orifice (cm)	22	4	18
New Caledonia: WK0013A			
Carinated jars (n=8)	MEAN	STDEV	CV
Max. body width (cm)	42	14	33
Vessel height (cm)	32	13	41
Ext. orifice (cm)	34	12	35
Island New Guinea: Mailu			
Utilitarian vessels (n=59)	MEAN	STDEV	CV
Vessel height (cm)	21	3	12
Orifice (cm)	31	4	12
Rim height (cm)	6	1	13

or more, and the production of different-sized pots reflecting functional variation and/or social divisions (Blackman et al. 1993).

The emic categories employed by prehistoric potters is likely to increase the amount of variation in an archaeological sample, making the identification of standardisation difficult. However, if utilitarian containers were primarily manufactured for a domestic purpose, and container size was under the deliberate control of a potter, then a vessel size analysis might be used to identify similar-sized pots that also had a similar function, or groups of vessels that potters might have recognized as being suitable for a particular task.

A K-means cluster analysis was performed on 35 late-Lapita pots from Sigatoka using three measurements (Max. width, Vessel height, Ext. orifice) using SPSS. The K-means algorithm separated the data into a number of spherical clusters by determining a cluster centre and comparing vessel measurements to a cluster in an iterative process (Hintze 1997). The cluster analysis identified three size groupings, with a group of small pots (*n*=7) and a group of the largest pots (*n*=2), surrounding a middle group containing the majority of vessels. Excluding the smallest and the largest pots, CVs for the middle group of 26 vessels varied between 9 % and 12 %. These values compare well with a sample of 59 utilitarian containers made by the pottery producing community on Mailu in island New Guinea recorded by Irwin (1985), which have CVs of 12-13 % (Table 1).

Discussion and Conclusion

The analysis of Lapita ceramics often focuses on the comparison of dentate-stamped and incised designs, but vessel size is also an important indicator of a specialised function. The size of a ceramic container constrains the dimensions of the decorative 'canvas', with large vessels able to exhibit more decoration than small vessels. When the size of a ceramic vessel is enlarged to accommodate and expose greater amounts of decoration, potters have to invest more time on manufacture and embellishment, compared with utilitarian containers. Large vessels also tend to be harder to produce than small vessels, due to the difficulty of controlling thermic variation in a large clay object under open firing conditions (Clough 1992:182; Gosselain 1992).

The presence of large handmade ceramics indicates a high labour input and specialised vessel function. Despite this correlation, ceramicists have not been able to explore systematically size variability in Lapita assemblages due to the degree of fragmentation in excavated collections, with the result that the division of early Lapita vessels into 'standardised-decorated' and 'specialised-utilitarian' sets has received little empirical testing. In this study vessel reconstructions were scanned and resized allowing a novel comparison of early Lapita and late Lapita container profiles, and the calculation of decoration area and design density. The size and decoration measures distinguished the specialised jars in the early Lapita site on New Caledonia from the more standardised, utilitarian pots of late Lapita age from Fiji, and although some measurement error from resizing is expected, the significant differences found between specialised and standardised ceramics appears robust. Results suggest that the specialised function of decorated Lapita wares was expressed in larger overall vessel size, and greater size variability within a vessel type, although an intra-assemblage analysis of decorated versus utilitarian containers from an early Lapita assemblage is required to confirm the hypothesis.

The specialized ceramics of Lapita culture were likely to have had a range of purposes, including in burial ritual, as demonstrated by the association of Lapita vessels with human remains in Vanuatu (Bedford et al. 2006, this volume). However, dentate-stamped and other decorated vessels are often found at sites with remains otherwise indicative of domestic habitation. Chiu (2005) has suggested that some dentate-stamped designs were clan markings and new designs were generated by inter-clan marriages (see also Washburn 1999), which implies that dentate-stamped designs were employed in formal inter-group events.

This idea might be further examined for the carinated jars found in a pit at the WKO013A site. The vessels are all highly decorated, although the dentate-stamped decoration applied to the largest jars appears to be more open and less dense compared with smaller jars (an observation that might be tested using a smaller grid to measure design density). When the size of the 10 carinated jars is taken into account there is a design division between the largest-sized jars and the smaller jars. Three of the four largest vessels were decorated with the 'interlocking check' design (Sand et al. 1998:37), with one representing a simplified form of the design with a vertical 'eye'. Three of the 'smaller' carinated jars have a design featuring an enveloped crescent (Figure 3).

Temper analysis for each vessel is not yet available, so the possibility that vessels with similar designs were made from similar temper sands and clays, indicating the presence of two social groups, remains to be tested (Sand pers. comm. found that different dentate-tools were used to decorate jars with the interlocking check design). In a wider study of ceramic tempers, Chiu (2003: 176) found there was no evidence for exotic temper at the WKO013A site, and the Lapita potters probably collected temper sands from "right beside their houses or workshops to a distance of 8-15 km." The distance is similar to that recorded for ethnographic potting communities, where most travelled a distance of 10 km or less to obtain temper materials (Arnold 1985:49; Rice 1987). This implies that dentate-stamped vessels were usually made with local materials and produced primarily for local communities.

The New Caledonian jars exhibit significant size variability, and overall they are larger than utilitarian containers. The production of over-sized material-culture has received little attention in material culture studies, although it is a relatively common phenomenon. In New Zealand, for instance, some burial ornaments at the early Wairau Bar site were much larger than those made in tropical East Polynesia (Duff 1956), and Leach (1993) notes the presence of very large stone adzes in Polynesia. Malinowski (in Sheppard 1996:103) and others have noted that the size of an object is an attribute useful for conveying social information. Large ceremonial adzes in the Trobriand islands, for instance, were commissioned by chiefs who supported craft specialists with gifts of surplus food: 'Both producer and consumer like to make or acquire an article which is strikingly big, or strikingly well finished, or of a strikingly fine material, even though in the process

Fig. 3. Similar dentate-stamped designs found on New Caledonia carinated jars from the pottery pit at the WKO013A site. Left: 'Interlocking check' design variants on three of the largest reconstructed vessels. Right: 'Enclosed crescent pattern on three smaller carinated jars (see Sand *et al.* (1998) and Sand (1999) for vessel decoration).

the article were to become unwieldy, breakable, and good for nothing but display... they might still be placed in specially beautiful handles and carried by a man of rank during a ceremony'. Unlike large ornaments and adzes that most likely signalled the high status of individuals (cf. Blanton *et al.* 1996), the enhanced visibility of dentate-stamped jars points to their use in collective events, as does the volume of the carinated jars. The average volume of the utilitarian Sigatoka pots, calculated with the algorithm of Senior and Birnie (1995), was ca. 8 litres, while the largest carinated jars from the WKO013A site had volumes ca. 8-13 times larger. What was placed in the carinated jars might be discoverable by an analysis of residues, but the large vessel volumes suggest the contents were being utilised by larger groups than the family units, which are presumed to have produced the utilitarian late-Lapita pots at Sigatoka.

Vessel designs include at least two sets (interlocking check and enclosed crescent), as well as 'eye' and 'face' motifs, and further study of vessel temper and tool markings may link vessels with particular potters or 'clan' groups (i.e. Chiu 2005). Societies with poorly developed hierarchical divisions are characterised by Wason (1994: 119) as having designs made up of the repetition of simple elements arranged symmetrically (see also Washburn 1999), the inclusion of empty or irrelevant space, and the delineation of figures without enclosures. These traits apply in general to the decoration on the carinated jars, and the termination of two of the largest carinated jars (and perhaps all of the vessels found in the pit) by punching a hole in the base of the vessel (Sand et al. 1998:37) also attests to purposeful destruction, rather than the accumulation of 'wealth' objects.

The specific meaning of the designs is, of course, uncertain, although they likely represent a belief system that was integral to group identity during Lapita expansion, and in abstract and figurative form was used to mark specialised Lapita vessels. Among colonising populations entering new environments, like those of Remote Oceania, where the impetus to social fragmentation was essentially unconstrained by the relative abundance of land and wild food resources, symbols, events and performances emphasising social cohesion would have been particularly important (i.e. at key events such as marriage, death, group feasting). Applied to specialised Lapita ceramics, such a view is somewhat similar to signaling theory (see also Summerhayes and Allen this volume), where the 'cost' of manufacturing, using and removing non-utilitarian vessels by relatively small colonising populations was repaid by their role in maintaining the connectivity between social groups that was crucial to the long-term biological survival of colonists (Moore 2001). Costly signaling along with other theories of profligate production and consumption (e.g. Bliege Bird and Smith 2005), might also help to explain technical deficiencies in the manufacture of Lapita vessels (Ambrose 1997), and why colonisation deposits of different ages in Remote Oceania, such as those of those of Lapita culture and Archaic East Polynesian culture in New Zealand, often appear far richer in material culture and faunal remains than those of later occupation phases.

References

Allen, J., S.G. Holdaway and R. Fullagar 1997. Identifying specialisation, production and exchange in the archaeological record: The case of shell bead manufacture on Motupore Island, Papua. *Archaeology in Oceania* 32: 13-38.

Ambrose, W.R. 1997. Contradictions in Lapita pottery, a composite clone. *Antiquity* 71: 525-538.

Arnold, D.E. 1985. *Ceramic theory and cultural process*. Cambridge: Cambridge University Press.

Bedford, S. 2006. The Pacific's earliest painted pottery: an added layer of intrigue to the Lapita debate and beyond. *Antiquity* 80: 554-557.

Bedford, S., M. Spriggs and R. Regenvanu. 2006. The Teouma Lapita site and the early human settlement of the Pacific Islands. *Antiquity* 80:812-828.

Bellwood, P. 1978. *Man's conquest of the Pacific*. Auckland: Collins.

Benco, N.L. 1988. Morphological standardization: An approach to the study of craft specialization. In C.C. Kolb and M. Kirkpatrick (eds), *A pot for all reasons: Ceramic ecology revisited*, pp. 57-72. Philadelphia: Temple University.

Best, S. 2002. *Lapita: A view from the east*. Auckland: New Zealand Archaeological Association Monograph 24.

Birks, L. 1973. *Archaeological Excavations at Sigatoka dune site, Fiji*. Suva: Bulletin of the Fiji Museum No.1.

Blackman, M.J., G.J. Stein and P.B. Vandiver 1993. The standardization hypothesis and ceramic mass production: Technological, compositional, and metric indexes of craft specialization at Tell Leilan, Syria. *American Antiquity* 58:60-80.

Blanton, R.E., G.M. Feinman, S.A. Kowalewski and P.N. Peregrine 1996. A dual-process theory for the evolution of Mesoamerican civilization. *Current Anthropology* 37: 1-14.

Bliege Bird, R. and E.A. Smith 2005. Signaling theory, strategic interaction, and symbolic capital. *Current Anthropology* 46: 221-248.

Burley, D.V. and W.R. Dickinson 2001. Origin and significance of a founding settlement in Polynesia. *Proceedings of the National Academy of Sciences of the USA* 98: 11829-11831.

Burley, D.V., A. Storey and J. Witt 2002. On the definition and implications of eastern Lapita ceramics in Tonga. In S. Bedford, C. Sand and D. Burley (eds), *Fifty years in the field. Essays in honour and celebration of Richard Shutler Jr's archaeological career*, pp. 213-225. New Zealand Archaeological Association Monograph 25.

Burley, D.V. and W.R. Dickinson 2004. Late Lapita occupation and its ceramic assemblage at the Sigatoka Sand Dune site, Fiji, and their place in Oceanic prehistory. *Archaeology in Oceania* 39:12-25.

Chiu, S. 2003. Social and economic meanings of Lapita pottery: a New Caledonian case. In C. Sand (ed.), *Pacific Archaeology: Assessments and Prospects*, pp. 159-182. Nouméa: Les cahiers de l'archéologie en Nouvelle-Calédonie 15.

Chiu, S. 2005. Meanings of a Lapita face: Materialized social memory in ancient house societies. *Taiwan Journal of Anthropology* 3: 1-47.

Clough. R. 1992. Firing temperatures and the analysis of Oceanic ceramics: a study of Lapita ceramics from Reef/Santa Cruz, Solomon Islands. In J-C. Galipaud (ed.), *Poterie Lapita et Peuplement*, pp. 177-192. Nouméa: ORSTOM.

Costin, C.L. and M.B. Hagstrum 1995. Standardization, labor investment, skill, and the organization of ceramic production in late Prehispanic Highland Peru. *American Antiquity* 60: 619-639.

DeBoer, W.R. 1980. Vessel shape from rim sherds: an experiment of the effect of the individual illustrator. *Journal of Field Archaeology* 7:131-135.

Duff, R. 1956. *The Moa-hunter period of Maori culture*. Wellington: New Zealand Government Printer.

Golson, J. 1971. Lapita ware and its transformations. In: R.C. Green and M. Kelly (eds.), *Studies in Oceanic Culture History*, Vol. 2, pp. 67-76. Hawaii: Pacific Anthropological Records No. 12.

Gosselain, O.P. 1992. Bonfire of the enquiries. Pottery firing temperatures in archaeology: what for? *Journal of Archaeological Science* 19: 243-259.

Green, R.C. 1982. Models of the Lapita cultural complex: an evaluation of some proposals. *New Zealand Journal of Archaeology* 4: 7-20.

Hintze, J.L. 1997. NCSS 97. *Statistical system for Windows*. Salt Lake City: Number cruncher statistical systems.

Hunt, T.L. 1988. Lapita ceramic technological and composition studies: A critical review. In P.V. Kirch and T.L. Hunt (eds), *Archaeology of the Lapita cultural complex: A critical review*, pp. 49-60. Seattle: Thomas Burke Memorial Washington State Museum Research Report No. 5.

Hunt, T.L. 1989. *Lapita ceramic exchange in the Mussau Islands, Papua New Guinea*. Unpublished PhD thesis, University of Washington.

Irwin, G. 1985. *The emergence of Mailu: as a central place in coastal Papuan prehistory*. Department of Prehistory, Australian National University. Terra Australis 10.

Kirch, P.V. 1990. Specialization and exchange in the Lapita complex of Oceania. *Asian Perspectives* 29:117-133.

Kirch, P.V. 1997. *The Lapita Peoples. Ancestors of the Oceanic World*. Blackwell: Oxford.

Leach, H. 1993. The role of major quarries in Polynesian prehistory. In M.W. Graves and R.C. Green (eds), *The evolution and organisation of prehistoric society in Polynesia*, pp. 33-42. Auckland: New Zealand Archaeological Association Monograph 19.

Longacre, W.A. 1999. Standardisation and specialisation: What's the link? In J.M. Skibo and G.M. Feinman (eds), *Pottery and people. A Dynamic interaction*, pp. 44-58. Salt Lake City: University of Utah Press.

Marshall, Y. 1985. Who made the Lapita pots? A case study in gender archaeology. *Journal of the Polynesian Society* 94:205-233.

Moore, J.H. 2001. Evaluating five models of human colonization. *American Anthropologist* 103:395-408.

Plog, S. 1985. Estimating vessel orifice diameters: measurement methods and measurement error. In B.A. Nelson (ed.), *Decoding prehistoric ceramics*, pp. 243-253. Carbondale and Edwardsville: Southern Illinois University Press.

Rice, P.M. 1981. Evolution of specialized pottery production: A trial model. *Current Anthropology* 22:219-240.

Rice, P.M. 1987. *Pottery Analysis. A sourcebook*. Chicago: The University of Chicago Press.

Sand, S., K. Coote, J. Bole, and A. Ouetcho 1998. A pottery pit at locality WKO013A, Lapita (New Caledonia). *Archaeology in Oceania* 33:37-43.

Sand, C. 1999. Archaeology of the Origins: New Caledonia's Lapita. *Les cahiers de l'archéologie en Nouvelle-Calédonie* Volume 10.

Sand, C. 2001. Evolutions in the Lapita cultural complex: a view from the Southern Lapita province. *Archaeology in Oceania* 36:65-76.

Senior, L.M. and D.P. Birnie 1995. Accurately estimating vessel volume from profile illustrations. *American Antiquity* 60:319-334.

Sheppard, P.J. 1996. Hard rock: Archaeological implications of chert sourcing in Near and Remote Oceania. In J. Davidson, G. Irwin, B.F. Leach, A. Pawley and D. Brown (eds), *Oceanic Culture History: Essays in honour of Roger Green*, pp. 99-115. New Zealand Journal of Archaeology Special Publication, New Zealand.

Spriggs, M. 1990. The changing face of Lapita: Transformation of a design. In M. Spriggs (ed.), *Lapita design, form and composition. Proceedings of the Lapita Design Workshop, Canberra, Australia – December 1988*, pp. 83-122. Canberra: Department of Prehistory, Australian National University. Occasional Papers in Prehistory No. 19.

Summerhayes, G. 2000. What's in a pot? In A. Anderson and T. Murray (eds), *Australian Archaeologist. Collected papers in honour of Jim Allen*, pp. 291-307. Canberra: Coombs Academic Publishing, Australian National University.

Summerhayes, G. R. 2001. Lapita in the far west: recent developments. *Archaeology in Oceania* 36: 53-63.

Vanderwal, R.L. 1973. Prehistoric studies in central coastal Papua. Unpublished PhD thesis, Australian National University.

Washburn, D. 1999. Perceptual anthropology: The cultural salience of Symmetry. *American Anthropologist* 101: 547-562.

Wason, P.K. 1994. *The archaeology of rank*. Cambridge: Cambridge University Press.

www.ingramcontent.com/pod-product-compliance
Lightning Source LLC
Chambersburg PA
CBHW061546010526
44114CB00027B/2946